WOMEN'S PERIODICALS IN THE UNITED STATES

Recent Titles in
Historical Guides to the World's Periodicals and Newspapers

This series provides historically focused narrative and analytical profiles of periodicals and newspapers with accompanying bibliographical data.

American Humor Magazines and Comic Periodicals
David E. E. Sloane, editor

Index to City and Regional Magazines of the United States
Sam G. Riley and Gary W. Selnow, compilers

International Music Journals
Linda M. Fidler and Richard S. James, editors

American Mass-Market Magazines
Alan Nourie and Barbara Nourie, editors

Military Periodicals: United States and Selected International Journals and Newspapers
Michael E. Unsworth

Regional Interest Magazines of the United States
Sam G. Riley and Gary W. Selnow, editors

Business Journals of the United States
William Fisher, editor

Corporate Magazines of the United States
Sam G. Riley, editor

American Literary Magazines: The Twentieth Century
Edward E. Chielens, editor

Consumer Magazines of the British Isles
Sam G. Riley, editor

Trade, Industrial, and Professional Periodicals of the United States
Kathleen L. Endres, editor

Popular Religious Magazines of the United States
Mark P. Fackler and Charles H. Lippy, editors

WOMEN'S PERIODICALS IN THE UNITED STATES

CONSUMER MAGAZINES

Edited by

Kathleen L. Endres and Therese L. Lueck

Historical Guides to the World's Periodicals and Newspapers

Greenwood Press
Westport, Connecticut • London

Library of Congress Cataloging-in-Publication Data

Women's periodicals in the United States : consumer magazines / edited
   by Kathleen L. Endres and Therese L. Lueck.
       p.   cm.—(Historical guides to the world's periodicals and
   newspapers, ISSN 0742–5538)
     Includes bibliographical references and index.
     ISBN 0–313–28631–0 (alk. paper)
       1. Women's periodicals, American—History.   I. Endres, Kathleen L.
   II. Lueck, Therese L.   III. Series.
   PN4879.W6   1995
   081'.082—dc20   94–46930

British Library Cataloguing in Publication Data is available.

Library of Congress Catalog Card Number: 94–46930
ISBN: 0–313–28631–0
ISSN: 0742–5538

First published in 1995

Greenwood Press, 88 Post Road West, Westport, CT 06881
An imprint of Greenwood Publishing Group, Inc.

Printed in the United States of America

The paper used in this book complies with the
Permanent Paper Standard issued by the National
Information Standards Organization (Z39.48–1984).

10 9 8 7 6 5 4 3 2 1

Contents

Preface

Consumer women's magazines have mirrored the changing roles, responsibilities, duties, and interests of America's females ever since the early days of the Republic. Literally thousands of magazines have served the reading interests of generations of women in the United States. Chronicling all these magazines in a single volume is an impossible task. Therefore, hard decisions had to be made about the content and direction of this book.

An argument could be made to include only the women's magazines that are currently published. But this ignores the rich, long history of women's magazines in the United States and their many contributions to the country's social, literary, and artistic history. Instead, the editors attempted to capture a hint of the rich history of women's magazines by providing profiles of some of the most profitable—and most provocative—periodicals that have long since died. These ranged from the relatively short-lived *Gentleman and Lady's Town and Country Magazine* to a number of magazines launched during the Jacksonian period that helped foster American literature. The profiles of periodicals of the Gilded Age chronicle the role these magazines played in supporting American literature and art.

This volume attempts to reach beyond New York City publishing to offer the geographic variety of women's magazines. Although the Northeast and especially New York City dominated in nineteenth-century and early twentieth-century publishing, many magazines in the South, Midwest, and West offered many important perspectives. Accordingly, this volume provides profiles of magazines—both historical and contemporary—from across the country.

The largest number of the magazine profiles are currently published. These periodicals reflect the variety in the field—from covering such traditional "women's" subjects as child care and home decorating to more contemporary concerns such as health and fitness, from highlighting the ethnic and racial diversity in the country to catering to the reading interests of all ages. Some might argue that a few of the titles included are not traditionally defined as women's magazines. The editors concede this. However, this does not mean that these titles should not be included. Each magazine profiled has at least 70 percent readership being women. Thus, the traditional definitions of "women's magazines" might actually be too limited for the realities of the 1990s American woman and her reading interests.

Given this variety and the long history of women's magazines in the United States, the final selection was difficult to make. Editors compiled a list of approximately 500 publications that was whittled down to 200 and, finally, to about 75. The final selections were based on the magazine's editorial excellence, historical significance, and position within its niche. The magazines selected represented the mass circulation monthlies (the "Seven Sisters" and the "Big Six") to periodicals that only had circulations in the hundreds (several periodicals that fall within the historical classification with limited—but influential—readerships).

The individuals who agreed to do entries often faced monumental obstacles. While many of the publications profiled in this book were among the most profitable in the nation, have long histories, and have made contributions to American life and letters, they often have not been retained by libraries. Contributors were often troubled by the lack of full runs of these magazines and problems finding even limited years of the periodical. Similarly, few archives have retained the letters and manuscripts of these editors or business records of the periodicals that have ceased publication. Too few editors and/or publishers have committed their experiences to books. Thus, contributors were sometimes at a disadvantage as they prepared these histories. Nonetheless, these contributors had the wherewithal to follow up on leads to locate as many extant issues as possible, interview former editors, and find long-hidden sources.

These contributors, then, should be thanked for all their work in the preparation of this volume. Other individuals also played an important part in the preparation of this work. The staffs of many libraries should be thanked for their cooperation with the researchers; Cleveland Public Library, New York Public Library, Middle Tennessee State University Library, American Antiquarian Society, Ohio Wesleyan University Archives, Cincinnati Historical Society, University of Western Ontario Library, University of Michigan Library (Ann Arbor), Tennessee State Library and Archives, and Library of Congress immediately come to mind, but many librarians at other locations also helped researchers as they prepared their entries.

In addition, I thank Linda Miller and Luberta Rookard for their assistance during the preparation of this book. Both my coeditor and I thank our families for their patience during the preparation of this work.

This volume offers much technical information that needs to be explained. Circulation is an important part of a periodical's story, but the numbers reflect only a moment in time. Accordingly, the circulation information in the appendix provides a specific date as well as a source of that information. ABC stands for Audit Bureau of Circulations; BPA, for the Business Publications Audit of Circulations Inc. These are auditing groups that monitor the circulations of members. A number of publications profiled are not members or were not in existence when the ABC and BPA were formed. Several abbreviations are used for these publications. For the historical magazines, APS stands for the American Periodical Series; Mott, for Frank Luther Mott's *History of American Magazines*; Ayer, for *Ayer Directory Newspapers, Magazines and Trade Publications* (as well as the other versions of that title); self-reported, for the periodical itself offering the information. For contemporary magazines, Gale, for *Gale Directory of Publications and Broadcast Media*; SRDS, for Standard Rate and Data Service's *Consumer Magazine and Agri-Media Rates and Data*; Ownership Statement, for the publication's statement of circulation. Demographic information is extensive in some of the entries in this volume and authors use abbreviations in their citations. SMRB stands for Simmons Market Research Bureau and MRI for Mediamark Research Inc. The asterisks that appear throughout this volume denote the magazines profiled elsewhere in the book.

As in other books in this Greenwood Press series, magazine titles are arranged alphabetically. Each entry offers a historical essay that covers the publication's founding, editorial development, business information, and content. The Information Sources section in each entry offers a *selected* bibliography, index sources (where available), and selected location sources. The Publication History section provides the magazine title and the various title changes, volume and issue data, publishers and places of publication, editors and circulation figures.

It is this editor's hope that this volume will represent a useful *beginning point* in the examination of consumer women's magazines in the United States.

Kathleen L. Endres

Introduction

The consumer magazines aimed at women are as diverse as the audience itself. Magazines are aimed at the young (*Barbie*,* *Seventeen*,* *YM*,* and *'Teen**) and at the not-so-young (*Lear's** and *Workbasket**). The "Seven Sisters" (*Ladies' Home Journal*,* *Redbook*,* *Better Homes and Gardens*,* *Good Housekeeping*,* *McCall's*,* *Family Circle*,* and *Woman's Day**) serve audiences in the millions; their "cousins," more specialized magazines, appeal to the specific interests and hobbies of a smaller number of readers (*Self** and *Art & Antiques**). Magazines aim to serve the needs of ethnic and racial minorities (*Essence*,* *Black Elegance*,* *Ser Padres*,* and *Vanidades Continental**). Others deal with women's lifestyle changes (*Working Woman**), interest in sports and fitness (*Women's Sports & Fitness*,* *Golf for Women*,* and *WB Magazine**), and curiosity about sex (*Playgirl**).

A large number of magazines continue to deal with the "traditional" interests, duties, and responsibilities of women, albeit from a 1990s perspective. Home/decorating books (*House Beautiful** and *House & Garden**) often compete with art books as they present the "best" homes in the United States and the world. Fashion magazines never seem to go "out of style," although they have changed. Some appeal to the young (*Mademoiselle** and *Glamour**), some to the slightly older (*Harper's Bazaar*,* *Vogue*,* and *Elle**) and some to the mature (*Mirabella**). Cooking magazines (*Gourmet*,* *Bon Appetit*,* and *Cooking Light**) appeal to those with epicurean tastes. Parenting publications (*Parents** and *American Baby**) advise grandmothers, mothers, mothers-to-be—and a certain number of fathers as well—on the fine art of child rearing. Indeed, consumer women's magazines have a variety that mirrors the changing roles, responsibilities, duties, and interests of today's American female.

From a historical perspective, consumer women's magazines offer an interesting perspective on the life and times of American women. At the same time, the magazines played a role in the development of American art and literature.

The seeds of the genre of consumer women's magazines were planted in the early days of the republic. Then, *Gentleman and Lady's Town and Country Magazine** offered enlightened perspectives on marriage and education. Unfortunately, this magazine suffered from the same afflictions as the other periodicals of the time. *Gentleman and Lady's Town and Country Magazine* lasted only eight issues; its life span was only slightly briefer than that of the other magazines of the day.

The Jacksonian period nurtured the growth of women's periodicals. At this time some women's magazines achieved a national following while others were pleased with their regional and/or specialized following. Yet, most shared certain characteristics—a commitment to literature, a love of art, and an editorial message that has been subsequently labeled the "Cult of True Womanhood."

Barbara Welter, a twentieth-century historian, coined the phrase.[1] At the heart of the "Cult of True Womanhood" rested four attributes: piety, purity, submissiveness, and domesticity, virtues upon which antebellum women were judged. These same virtues represented a common thread woven into the departments, advice columns, editorials, and short stories reprinted in many of the women's magazines of the day. Welter specifically cited *Godey's,** The Ladies' Companion,** and *The Ladies' Repository** as evidence in her essay, although she could have easily included *Peterson's** as well. One notable exception was *The National Magazine; or, Lady's Emporium,** edited and owned by Mary Barney, a short-lived and much more progressive—by nineteenth-century standards—magazine with regard to its vision of women in society. Barney's magazine, however, survived only about a year, while the magazines that subscribed to the "Cult of True Womanhood" endured generations. The circulation of Barney's magazine is unknown; the magazines of the other group together reached close to a million. *Godey's* and *Peterson's* were the largest of that group. With circulations in excess of 200,000, these two were among the largest circulating magazines in the nation at the time.

Not only did *Godey's* and *Peterson's* help define the standards of behavior for women at the time, but they also helped to develop a distinctly American literature, introducing many young women writers to a reading public and helping support better-known male and female writers of the day. Ralph Waldo Emerson, Nathaniel Hawthorne, Henry Wadsworth Longfellow, and Edgar Allan Poe all published in *Godey's.* Sarah Josepha Hale, editor of *Godey's,* and Ann S. Stephens and Charles J. Peterson, editors of *Peterson's,* seemed committed to supporting the idea of women writers. The magazines published the work of a number of promising women writers, including Harriet Beecher Stowe, Eliza Leslie, Caroline M. S. Kirkland, and Hannah F. Gould. The *Magnolia; or, Southern Apalachian** represented the southern counterpart, committed to furthering the literature of that region, even if written by women. At a time when their literary work was dismissed as the output of a "d———d mob of scribbling women,"[2] female writers found women's magazines important publishing outlets.

The women's magazines also represented important outlets for artists and engravers. *Godey's* and *Peterson's* offered fashion prints that still remain popular collectors' items. However, the real outlets for artists and engravers in the women's magazines were smaller books. Especially important was the Methodist-Episcopal *Ladies' Repository* with its lovely, original steel engravings of the highest quality. The printing techniques of the day, as well as the expense of such engravings, did not allow a large number of illustrations in each issue. Nonetheless, the art reproduced in the *Ladies' Repository* hinted at a potential that would be realized in the next generation of women's magazines—after the Civil War.

During the Civil War, the women's magazines had special roles to play. They had to sustain morale, even in the darkest days of the war. That job, of course, was more difficult for the Confederate publications. The *Magnolia: A Southern Home Journal,* * one of the few women's magazines published in the South during the war, not only had to sustain the morale of Confederate women but also had to deal with the same paper and printing shortages and militia demands on employees that other southern newspapers and magazines faced. Nonetheless, the *Magnolia* endured and helped foster a wartime southern literature.

The far more numerous women's magazines of the North—firmly established and financially secure by the time of the Civil War—offered the Union perspective in the news departments, advice columns, editorials, and fiction. The *Ladies' Repository*—both Methodist–Episcopal and Universalist—offered a more "radical"[3] approach. In contrast, *Godey's* and *Peterson's*, more strongly tied to the "Cult of True Womanhood," took a more conservative role and were less pronounced in their Union support.[4]

After the war, one generation of women's magazines died, and another was born. Many of the magazines of this new generation grew out of the fashion industry. Pattern companies saw magazines as a way to promote their fashion offerings and launched a number of popular monthlies in the post–Civil War period. Although these magazines (*McCall's,* * *Pictorial Review,* * and *Delineator**) retained their fashion base, they quickly expanded their editorial content to include short stories, nonfiction, and advice.

Another set of magazines in this "new generation" had no formal ties to the fashion industry. Although fashion always had a place in these magazines, these monthlies were lifestyle-based—but a lifestyle in keeping with the traditional roles and responsibilities of women. Thus, these new magazines (*Ladies' Home Journal, Woman's Home Companion,* * and *Good Housekeeping*) carried a range of advice columns on cooking, child care, and housekeeping.

All these magazines lasted into the twentieth century. Several (*Pictorial Review* and the *Delineator*) were victims of the depression, as they were unable to sustain their advertising base in the competitive market. The *Woman's Home Companion* lasted into the 1950s. *McCall's, Ladies' Home Journal*, and *Good Housekeeping* continue today as part of a family of magazines known as the "Seven Sisters."

In the late nineteenth and early twentieth centuries, the "Big Six" (*Ladies'*

Home Journal, Woman's Home Companion, Delineator, Pictorial Review, Good Housekeeping, and *McCall's*) defined women's magazines, although many smaller, less widely circulated publications thrived on the periphery (*Southern Woman's Magazine**). The "Big Six" could be considered "service" periodicals in the 1990s publishing sense. These magazines were guides to carrying out the traditional duties and responsibilities of women through departments on cooking, sewing, child care, and fancywork. This is not to say, however, that they all followed an identical editorial path. The *Pictorial Review*, for example, endorsed woman suffrage; the other five of the "Big Six" avoided the issue, even as they were reporting social ills during the muckraking period and urging readers to correct these problems—but not by voting.[5]

While there was some diversity in editorial stances on social issues and variety in the investigative reporting during the muckraking period and later, the "Big Six" did share certain characteristics. Like the generation of women's magazines before them, these mass circulation monthlies were committed to promoting American art and literature. Indeed, these magazines represented a large, lucrative market for artists and writers. These magazines—with circulations reaching into the millions—had large budgets to pay artists and writers.

With each issue having a different front cover, these magazines consumed a large amount of original art. Many were done by some of the better-known artists of the day, such as Bessie Pease Gutmann, Howard Chandler Christy, and Harrison Fisher. Some of these covers were so popular that they were reissued (without the magazine's nameplate) and sold individually.

Fiction was a mainstay of these magazines. The best-known American novelists serialized their work in these magazines, for example, P. G. Wodehouse, Zona Gale, Edna Ferber, Hamlin Garland, Kathleen Norris, and Irving S. Cobb. Others, like A. A. Milne and F. Scott Fitzgerald, offered short stories and essays. Some of the best-known, highly acclaimed works of American writers first appeared in the women's magazines of the day. For example, Edna Ferber's Pulitzer Prize-winning *So Big* first appeared in the *Woman's Home Companion.*

The twentieth century brought enormous growth to women's magazines as a genre. The rest of the "Seven Sisters" (the current name of the largest-circulating women's magazines) were born: *Redbook* in 1903, *Better Homes and Gardens* in 1922, *Family Circle* in 1932, and *Woman's Day* in 1937. Yet, the story of women's magazines, particularly in the first half of the twentieth century, cannot be told solely by the largest-circulating magazines. There was enormous diversity within the women's magazine family. A heretofore unserved branch of the family—the less affluent women—discovered the appeal of the true-life, true-love *True Story.** The enormous success of *True Story* spawned a whole new type of magazine, the "confessional," which, for a time, enjoyed great success. Few remain today. The most successful remains the first, *True Story.*

Not even the Great Depression could stop publishers from introducing periodicals, one of which went on to become one of the most successful publications of the 1990s. In 1934, Wells Drorbaugh introduced *So You're Going to Be Married*, which soon became *The Bride's Magazine*, then simply *Bride's*, and finally *Bride's and Your New Home*. In 1991 that magazine claimed the title of the largest consumer magazine ever published and a place in the *Guinness Book of World Records*.

Other magazines launched during the depression never achieved records but still enjoyed large enough profits to survive into the 1990s. The *Workbasket* today still provides craft patterns and guides to almost 800,000 readers. *WB* (for the "woman who bowls") now claims the title of the oldest continuously published women's sports magazine.

Almost half of the periodicals profiled in this book were launched after World War II. This does not necessarily show the editors' interest in newer magazines; instead, it merely reflects marketplace realities. The women's magazine niche grew, changed, and diversified after the war. Two events coalesced to explain this development. First were industrywide trends. After the war, Americans wanted new, more specialized publications. This affected the whole magazine industry as many large, mass-circulating periodicals died. Even the women's magazine genre itself was not immune. The *Woman's Home Companion*, a long-publishing, mass circulation monthly, was a casualty of this trend. But this trend fit nicely with the changing roles of women in America, the second event affecting the women's magazine niche. The postwar period found women in a multiplicity of roles, a variety of interests (both within and outside the home), and a myriad of values and goals. More women were working; divorce was increasing; women were assuming more responsibilities and finding new interests. The launches after the war (and especially after 1965, when the women's movement was rejuvenated, and more women were entering the labor force) illustrated that American women wanted to read more than the "Seven Sisters." The new magazines were highly specialized. Few had an editorial mission specifically appealing to the "liberated woman." *Ms.** was one of the notable exceptions.[6] A number of magazines clearly had feminist underpinnings, including *Women's Sports & Fitness*. Others were tied to the traditional concerns, values, and interests of women, including *Virtue,** *Today's Christian Woman,** and *Quilt World.** A few took the traditional responsibilities of women and shifted them to late twentieth-century concerns; *Cooking Light* merged cooking with new interests in health for a profitable venture. Many new launches capitalized on women's growing interest in health, sports, and fitness: *Health,** *Weight Watchers,** *Golf for Women*, and, of course, *Women's Sports & Fitness*. The "home" remained a central reading interest for many women in America. Although one stalwart "home/decorating" publication died in the 1990s (*House & Garden*), many survived in the highly competitive market. Many of the survivors shared a more specialized focus, either by geographic region (*Southern Living** and *Southern Accents**) or by subject matter (*Metropolitan Home** and *Art & Antiques*).

Today, women's magazines reflect a diversity not only in subject matter but also of ownership. A large number of companies are involved in the publishing of women's magazines. These range from the smaller publishing houses, including Good Family Magazines, the publisher of *Virtue*, to relatively recent arrivals in the American publishing field, including Hachette Filipacchi Magazines, publisher of *Elle* and *Metropolitan Home*. While many different publishers are involved in the women's magazine field, two, in particular, remain highly important in this industry because of their holdings: Condé Nast and Hearst Magazines. Hearst Magazines, the publisher of *Good Housekeeping, Cosmopolitan,* Harper's Bazaar, House Beautiful, Victoria,** and many others not profiled in this work, owns many of the most widely circulated and some of the oldest women's magazines still publishing in the United States.

Condé Nast has always had, as its base, women's magazines. The three that formed its original corporate base back in the early twentieth century were *Vogue, Vanity Fair*, and the now defunct *House & Garden*. Since then, however, through launch and acquisition, Condé Nast has accumulated a family of publications, many of which are aimed at the upscale female reader: *Bride's & Your New Home, Glamour, Gourmet, Bon Appetit, Mademoiselle, Self*, and a number of others not included in this volume.

This concentration of ownership of some of the largest magazines in the hands of a few publishing companies is consistent with trends across the magazine industry in the United States. Indeed, this point needs to be emphasized. While women's magazines are often pulled out for separate consideration in volumes such as this one, this is a distinct branch of American journalism that needs to be integrated into historical accounts. Women's magazines suffered from the same financial constraints as others of the same time, as the entry on the *Gentleman and Lady's Town and Country Magazine* points out. They had a role to play in the literary and artistic development of the nation, as the entries on *Godey's, Peterson's, Magnolia* (both versions), *Ladies' Companion, Woman's Home Companion, Southern Woman's Magazine*, and others point out. They shared muckraking commitments, as entries on *Ladies' Home Journal, Pictorial Review*, and others emphasize. They have always been an integral part of American journalism. Unfortunately, too often, they remain overlooked.

Notes

1. Barbara Welter, "The Cult of True Womanhood: 1820–1860," in Thomas R. Frazier (ed.), *The Underside of American History: Other Readings* (New York: Harcourt Brace Jovanovich, 1973), pp. 211–220.

2. Nathaniel Hawthorne is credited with that remark. Caroline Ticknor, *Hawthorne and His Publishers* (Boston: Houghton Mifflin, 1913), pp. 141–143.

3. As defined in the historical sense as being committed to the immediate emancipation of slaves, a vigorous pursuit of the war, and an extended reconstruction once peace was achieved. See, for example, Eric Foner, *Free Soil, Free Labor, Free Men: The Ideology of the Republican Party before the Civil War* (New York: Oxford University Press, 1970).

4. Kathleen L. Endres, "The Women's Press in the Civil War: A Portrait of Patriotism, Propaganda, and Prodding," *Civil War History* 30:1 (March 1984), pp. 31–53.

5. Kathleen L. Endres, "Women and the 'Larger Household': An Examination of Muckraking in Women's Magazines," a paper presented to the Association for Education in Journalism and Mass Communication convention, Atlanta, August 1994.

6. The periodicals of the women's liberation movement and its organizations will be discussed in a forthcoming volume from Greenwood. In general, however, these failed to be commercial successes.

Kathleen L. Endres

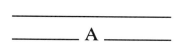

AMERICAN BABY

A diaper service—not the stork—delivered the first issue of *American Baby* in 1938. The magazine was originated by the American Diaper Service as a gift to new customers—"tucked into the diaper bundle—the clean one, we assure you."[1] When the diaper service realized that printing a magazine was a full-time job, the printer, Eli Levine, bought the publication to ensure regular work for his press.[2]

When disposable diapers hit the market in the 1970s, *American Baby* was mailed directly to new and expectant mothers.[3] In the 1970s, spin-offs of the magazine focusing on birth and aspects of childhood were created; and in the 1980s, *American Baby* television shows began.[4] The magazine has become one of the most technologically sophisticated periodicals of the 1990s.

Over the years, the name and look of the magazine have changed. A 1992 makeover brought bright colors and a nameplate that emphasized the word "baby."[5] Subtitles have signaled the magazine's shift from mothers to parents, from *The National Monthly Magazine for Mothers and Babies* and *The Monthly Magazine for Mothers of Infants* in the 1940s and *The Mother-to-Be and New Mother* in the early 1970s to *Expectant and New Parents* in March 1974. The shifts in the subtitle indicate the magazine's keeping abreast of the times, or, as one male reader in the 1970s wrote:

> Though yours is a fine magazine, I have one suggestion to make for future editions. It is time that the American father, as well as the American mother, is represented in all discussions of parenthood. Your ads, parent references, and apparently your whole magazine's tone is almost exclusively feminine.[6]

To remedy this, *American Baby* offered a new feature "written by, about and for fathers" the next month. In March, "parenthood" made it to the masthead and was directly addressed by the editor:

> The idea that child rearing is "for women only" is as outdated as knickers and the men have been the first to tell us. . . .
>
> From now on, in the pages of *American Baby* as well as on its cover, the stress will be on parenthood, not just motherhood.[7]

Despite this 1970s recognition of parenting, "that there are two people caring for this infant, not one,"[8] and despite the subtitle change it maintained, by the 1980s, the magazine had reinstated a primarily female, home-centered focus. After living the social changes of the 1980s, Judith Nolte, the same editor who had stressed parenthood over a focus on motherhood, had, by 1987, recanted her 1970s philosophy:

> It seems to me that women are still destined to be the primary parent in most families today, and it's a bit insincere to preach to men about involvement and equality. . . .
>
> Change, when and if it occurs, will be slow and silent and subtle, and women will have to make it happen. . . . And when it comes, will we be prepared to back away and give up the leading role?[9]

Today, *American Baby*'s readership is primarily female, or, more precisely, a 26-year-old white woman with a household income of $34,200, with 43 percent of the women planning to have more children.[10] Despite a tighter focus on the mother, the magazine has not hesitated to broaden its definition of "family" as the times have shown the American family changing:

> Is the family an endangered species? If you define a family the way most of us did in past decades—a working dad and a stay-at-home mom, married to each other, and their children—the answer is yes. . . . But if you expand the definition of a family to encompass the multitude of living arrangements spawned by many social changes, the answer would be less certain and much more complicated. . . . In the next ten years, experts believe, American family life will only get more varied, more complex, and more stressful.[11]

American Baby reaches its audience primarily through medical offices and maternity stores. Subscription cards are available at these and other places expectant and new mothers frequent. These coupons, also found in the magazine itself, offer a free six-month initial subscription; subscriptions can then be continued as paid. Longtime editor Nolte explained that advertising drives the subscription policy: "They want to reach new people all the time."[12] *American Baby* readers are women in their childbearing years. She characterized *American Baby*'s market as a "market created by time" in that the audience is ever-changing, yet always interested in primarily the same subject matter.[13]

Because this audience has a relatively quick turnover, not only themes but entire stories can be rerun. The primary focus has remained on infant care, from baby fashions, such as seasonably appropriate ways to dress baby for activities, to nutrition, such as breastfeeding and baby food, from socialization to problems of infants and young children. A secondary focus has been the care of the mother—how to eat and exercise during pregnancy, the birthing experience, losing weight after the baby is born, fashions, and health.[14]

The magazine has explored myths and revisited controversies, such as methods of birthing, breastfeeding, mothers working outside the home, and day care. Even baby foods have not been without controversy; the magazine advocated commercial baby foods in a special issue on nutrition (February 1974) and was countered by a reader knowledgeable in homemade baby foods in a later issue.[15] The magazine has not forgotten where babies come from, with frequent articles on sex, particularly during and after pregnancy. Kept central to this focus on baby and family has been family planning. The magazine has not ignored abortion or contraceptives, including the Pill, quipping that "one a day keeps the obstetrician away."[16] Also, the magazine has covered the work of pediatrician/author Dr. Benjamin Spock and of children's book author Dr. Seuss; it has focused on feminism, fetal surgery, and cesareans. The magazine is primarily written by freelance writers, and readers often offer their own personal parenting experiences.

Over the years, babies have cooed and crawled across the covers (ironically, often bare in spite of the diaper-clad launch). Babies, cover to cover, have always been happy. On the July 1941 cover, the baby was photographed in the bath, its hair smoothed up into the popular shampoo spike. The March 1943 cover baby sat atop the parental bed waving an American flag. On the 1942 cover, a bonneted (yet bared-bun) baby advocated buying war bonds. The 1980s and 1990s covers showed much of the diversity of the market, with bare-bottomed babies of different ethnicities.

Like a baby in a dry diaper, *American Baby* has emerged smiling from several changes. While initially it was distributed free by selected diaper services, the advent of disposable diapers forced a different distribution method. Free subscription cards became available in obstetricians' offices. Circulation topped the 1 million mark in the early 1970s, as the magazine absorbed the magazine *Mothers-to-Be*. The magazine grew from about 60 pages to about 80 pages in the late 1970s.

In the 1980s, Cahners Publishing Co., one of the largest specialized business publishers in the nation, entered the consumer market by buying American Baby Inc., the owner of *American Baby*.[17] Cahners was interested in owning a consumer magazine that could be managed in much the same way as a trade publication. *American Baby*'s profile fit the company's needs; the vertical publication fit nicely into the publishing company's already existing distribution methods.[18] Instead of risking the launch of a new magazine, Cahners picked up the already successful *American Baby*[19] in September 1986 with the intention of maintaining it and its sister publications—*Childbirth Educator*, *Childbirth '86*, and *First Year of Life*—with separate circulation, advertising, and editorial staffs.[20]

The strategy Cahners used was to "acquire the leading publication in certain kinds of fields where the advertising . . . is, in some cases, as important as the editorial."[21] Expectant parents and parents of newborns fit into that category. Contrasted with editorial-driven publications that keep readers' interest by changing the subject matter, *American Baby* has readers that come for its very specific subject matter—and then move on. Advertisers hope to establish brand loyalty in that short period of time. Advertising has ranged from laundry soaps to soap operas—most featuring enchanting babies. Sometimes an article advocates a product or industry that advertises in the magazine, from Disneyland to car seats to, of course, diapers.

Since Cahners acquired the magazine, *American Baby* has increased the number of spin-offs. Wanting to follow its audience's interests into child rearing, *American Baby* launched *Healthy Kids* magazine in 1989 in conjunction with the American Academy of Pediatrics, which approves all articles as well as advertising.[22] This advertiser-driven publication comes out six times a year. Its success led to its split into *Healthy Kids Birth–3* and *Healthy Kids 4–10*. The company uses computer databases to cross-market spin-offs such as the annuals, *Childbirth*, and *The First Year of Life*, as well as its single-sponsor publications *Grandparents Today* (Fisher-Price) and *First Time Parents* (Playskool).[23] The editorial product does not change much in these types of spin-offs, but the standing editorial content maintains its vitality because the audience changes. Therefore, such advertiser-driven products must be able to track their readership and their potential audience. Cahners has capitalized on the *American Baby* market, characterized as "easily segmented and hungry for information," by creating "one of the most advanced database marketing operations around."[24] Perhaps most notable is the company's ability, with *American Baby* itself, to produce "as many as 200 different versions of the magazine each month"[25] targeted to different segments of its readership. Managing editor Anne Winthrop characterized the process as "editorially supported and advertiser driven" in that the editorial is independent from the advertising, but versions of the same issue may vary in size depending on their advertising inclusions.[26]

Winthrop said that the staff was "very happy with the direction" of the magazine and that no changes are planned for *American Baby* in the near future.[27]

With the birthrate expected to drop only slightly and the magazine's already sophisticated marketing and advertising strategies in place, *American Baby* is "toddling" along toward a healthy future.

Notes

1. "American Baby," May 1988, p. 9.
2. Ibid.
3. Ibid.
4. By the mid-1990s, the regular shows were "American Baby TV Show" and "Healthy Kids TV Show."
5. In what was perhaps an unintentional shift in the January issue, the subtitle read, *For Expectant and New Mothers*, all in caps; by February, "parents" had been reinstated.
6. Stan Smith, "Letters to the Editor: A Father Speaks Out," January 1974, p. 10.
7. Judith Nolte, "Dear Reader," March 1974, p. 6.
8. Ibid.
9. Judith Nolte, "Dear Reader," June 1987, p. 10.
10. Media Kit, 1994.
11. Carol Turkington, "Families in the '90s," January 1990, p. 55.
12. Judith Nolte interview, August 30, 1994.
13. Ibid.
14. However, some issues are consistently covered from a conservative industry perspective; for instance, the potential harm pesticides pose was minimized in both March 1989 and May 1993, although the threat of cat feces was discussed.
15. Roxi Smith, "In Defense of Home-Made Baby Foods," letter, May 1974, p. 8.
16. "The Pill," May 1988, p. 119. In this special 50th-anniversary issue, 50 ideas that changed the American baby are highlighted.
17. Cara S. Trager, "Special Report: Publishers Mix Business, Pleasure Reading," *Advertising Age*, November 10, 1986, p. S24.
18. Ibid.
19. Thomas J. Tyrer, "Crossing Over," *Advertising Age*, May 24, 1989, p. 60.
20. Trager, "Special Report: Publishers Mix Business, Pleasure Reading," p. S24.
21. Judith Princz, publisher of *American Baby*, quoted in Tyrer, "Crossing Over," p. 60. Ellipses are *Advertising Age*'s.
22. Nolte interview.
23. Ibid.
24. Karen Berman, "Three Database Power-Users," *Folio*, March 1, 1993, p. 52.
25. Ibid.
26. Anne Winthrop interview, August 5, 1994.
27. Ibid.

Information Sources

BIBLIOGRAPHY:

Berman, Karen. "Database Marketing: A New Secret Weapon." *Folio*, March 1, 1993, pp. 50–52, 122.

———."Three Database Power-Users." *Folio*, March 1, 1993, p. 52.

Freeman, Laurie, and Scott Hume. "Sears Finds Soft Spot for Its Baby Store." *Advertising Age*, November 17, 1986, p. 12.

Trager, Cara S. "Special Report: Publishers Mix Business, Pleasure Reading." *Advertising Age*, November 10, 1986, p. S24.

Tyrer, Thomas J. "Crossing Over." *Advertising Age*, May 24, 1989, pp. 58, 60–62+.

INDEX SOURCES: Abstrax; Cumulative Index to Nursing and Allied Health Literature;
    Consumer Health & Nutrition Index; Health Index; Magazine Index.
LOCATION SOURCES: Library of Congress; Cleveland Public Library; Kent State Uni-
    versity, and other libraries.

Publication History

MAGAZINE TITLE AND TITLE CHANGES: *American Baby* (sometimes with an initial
    "The") (1938–1966); *American Baby Magazine* (1967–1970); *Mothers-to-Be/*
    American Baby (1971–1972); *American Baby* (1973–present).
VOLUME AND ISSUE DATA: Vols. 1– (May 1938–present). Monthly.
PUBLISHER AND PLACE OF PUBLICATION: American Diaper Service (1938–1940);
    American Baby Inc. (1940–1986); Cahners Publishing Co. (September 1986–
    present). New York.
EDITORS: (early editors unknown) Beulah France (1943–1963); Joyce Chase (1964);
    Rochelle Rifkin (1965); Margaret Markham (1966); Martha Bluming (1967);
    Karen Palmer (1968); Myrna Libman (April 1968–November 1969); Judith Nolte
    (December 1969–present).
CIRCULATION: BPA, 1993: 1,318,232; plus 17,770 nonpaid.

Therese L. Lueck

AMERICAN HEALTH

The history of *American Health* is the story of a magazine that exploded like a
meteor into the public consciousness, rising to spectacular heights in its early
years. It is the story of a magazine that almost crashed from the weight of its
own success, only to be scooped up and saved by the financial and managerial
expertise of the Reader's Digest Association. It is the story of serving readers,
then nearly abandoning them for the almighty advertising dollar, and then serving them once again.

Founded in 1982, *American Health: Fitness of Body and Mind* was the brain-
child of Owen Lipstein, the former general manager of *Science '81*, and T
George Harris, who revived and edited *Psychology Today* from 1968 through
1976. Compelling research that showed the link between mind and body and a
profound shift in what Harris calls the individual's "locus of control" inspired
Harris and Lipstein to create a magazine that would help people manage their
health rather than rely on other people to do it for them.[1] *American Health*, says
Harris, provided a venue for him to explore not just the mind, as he did at
Psychology Today, but the relationship between physiology and psychology.

The emphasis on holistic health strategies emerged in the magazine's first
issues, which included a balance of stories on such subjects as preventing disease, promoting a healthy sex life, exercise, yoga, nutrition, and alternative medicine. Departments also covered the gamut: "Doctors/Patients" focused on
developing give-and-take relationships, "Cash & Care" focused on money and
health care, and "Health Style" focused on health-related lifestyle issues. Also

included were departments on technology, fitness, stress, nutrition, dental care, and medical advances. Virtually all departments were composed of news and research-oriented short articles written in a lively, conversational manner. The magazine, says Judith Groch, who joined the magazine's staff in 1983 and now is its executive editor, was not "anti-doctor, but it was about working with your doctor as a partner in staying healthy."[2]

During *American Health*'s first year, its editorial content and ads seemed largely to appeal to both men and women. Early on, ads promoted many natural products for hair and skin, as well as natural, healthful foods. Ads for vitamins and cold medicines, exercise clothes and equipment, beer, air treatment systems, and dental care products also were featured.

This mix of stories and ads apparently worked: at the end of its first year, *American Health* had nearly a half-million readers and was carrying 180 pages of advertisements. But the magazine's success at commingling ads aimed at both men and women was not to last. By mid-1983, food ads began to predominate, and in the July/August 1983 issue, an ad for Tampax appeared. A year later, the magazine was running more ads for feminine products, including panty hose, cosmetics, women's birth control, and sanitary napkins and tampons; the food and medicine ads featured women models.

The desire of advertisers to reach women put increasing pressure on Harris—pressure that Harris says he had to resist from the beginning—to create a complementary editorial product. It's not that Harris objected to attracting more women readers; he just wanted any changes made in editorial content to stay true to the magazine's mission. "I wanted to make sure that we never sank into that sort of patronizing women's service magazine approach of saying 'sit down girlies and we'll tell you what to do.' "[3]

Equally important to Harris was maintaining an editorial focus on both men and women, especially since women are the primary health educators as well as consumers. According to Harris, "something like 70 percent of women make the health decisions regarding their families."[4]

Instead of just caving in and creating a women's service magazine, Harris says he tried to turn advertising pressure into new editorial strengths. In the July/August 1983 issue, the magazine introduced a new department—"Skin, Scent & Hair"—with a distinctly feminine edge. During the next year, the magazine began featuring more articles geared to women, including cover stories on "What's Your Natural Weight?" (May 1983) and "Exciting New Fruits and Vegetables You Can Buy Now" (July/August 1984). In November 1984, the magazine added a fashion department and included a feature on women's sensible shoes. It also began using more women models to illustrate its stories and its covers.

Despite the shift, Harris insisted on maintaining the emphasis on the connection between mind and body, even in stories about fashion and beauty. In early 1985, he added two new departments that were biased more to readers than advertisers: "The Brain Report," which later became "Mind/Body News," and

"The Family Report." He also launched a series of Gallup surveys that explored Americans' attitudes and behaviors regarding health and fitness.

Even as pressure to attract advertising mounted, the quality of *American Health*'s editorial product flourished. In 1985, the effort paid off in a big way— the magazine received the National Magazine Award for General Excellence in the circulation category of 400,000 to 1 million, the most prestigious honor given to consumer magazines. The judges called *American Health* "a lively and credible blend of news and service journalism. Excellent science-based reporting and authoritative medical health features are presented in an innovative format that commands attention and invites readership."[5]

The National Magazine Award marked a high point for *American Health*. During the same year, it shot to the top of *Adweek*'s "10 Hottest Magazines," and it had a circulation of 850,000, all of which seemed to confirm *American Health*'s status as the premier health and fitness magazine.[6] Its status gave the magazine momentum to build on its success.

During the next five years, *American Health*'s efforts to report on a wide variety of health and fitness subjects grew more ambitious. The magazine regularly offered special reports in which related articles were packaged to provide comprehensive coverage of specific subjects, including killer diseases, exercise, beauty, drug abuse, medical miracles, eating habits, pleasure, love, work, aging and, in January/February 1989, "The American Male in Transition." These sections occasionally were accompanied by Gallup polls. *American Health*'s success with its editorial product also spawned several ancillary products, including books, audiotapes and videotapes, a fitness bulletin, and participation in a public television series.

But as the magazine matured, it also began to drift away from readers in the interest of attracting advertising, says executive editor Groch. The magazine introduced several new departments that, while they could be justified as part of the magazine's editorial mission, gave advertisers opportunities to promote allied products. These included "The Family Pet"; "Body Style," a fashion department; and "Know Your Sport," which offered tips for playing and buying the clothes for one particular sport. Besides being a boon to advertising, these departments also were designed to make *American Health* look even more like a women's magazine, especially "Body Style" and "Know Your Sport," which took on the appearance of fashion layouts.

American Health's phenomenal success came, in part, because it entered the market at just the right time, on the cusp of the health and fitness movement, when there was little competition to impede its progress. But the magazine's success also was bound to entice rivals: from 1985 to 1990, a number of magazines were launched that vied directly for readers and advertisers, including *Hippocrates* (now *Health*) and *Cooking Light** in 1986, *Shape* in 1987, and *Fitness* and *Longevity* in 1988. These books wrestled not only with each other for advertising revenues but against virtually every other women's magazine. To make matters worse, *American Health* was expensive to produce because of the imperative to report, edit, fact-check, and copyedit articles with almost scientific thoroughness.[7]

These forces, along with what Groch and Harris call financial mismanagement, brought the magazine to the brink of ruin. *American Health*'s credibility was damaged in 1989, when Lipstein failed to tell media buyers that issues had been mailed late to subscribers or not mailed at all. In January 1990, Lipstein sold the publication to the Reader's Digest Association after a drawn-out process that brought the selling price down from $40 million to $29.1 million.[8] Lipstein and Harris resigned after the magazine's eighth-anniversary issue in March 1990, leaving Sheila Wyle to continue as publisher and Joel Gurin as editor. A year later Wyle was replaced by Susan Baron, and Carey Winfrey, the former editor of *Memories* and *Cuisine*, took the position as the new editor in chief.

Winfrey made his debut as editor in the March 1991 issue in a big way. The magazine was redesigned to make it more readable and accessible. Some departments were recast with new names: for example, ''Medical News,'' ''The Fitness Report,'' ''The Nutrition Report,'' and ''The Tooth Report'' became ''Medicine,'' ''Fitness,'' ''Nutrition,'' and ''Dental Care.'' New departments also were added, including ''Ask *American Health*,'' ''Close Encounters'' (a column written by *New York Times* sports columnist Robert Lipsyte), ''Moments'' (literary and historical excerpts related to health and fitness), ''Second Opinion'' (which covers a controversial topic such as company policies on protecting fetuses), and ''Medicine Chest'' (a last-page department that features a photo of the inside of a celebrity's medicine chest).

These changes gave the magazine a new look, but, in fact, they did not signal a change in *American Health*'s mission. From the time Winfrey took the helm, the magazine has continued to offer thoroughly researched, practical, and accessible articles on medical and health issues. Since 1991, articles on such topics as medical con artists, food controversies, pain, yoga, dieting, fitness and workouts, cancer and heart disease, and ways to save on medical bills have appeared on the magazine's pages.

In Winfrey's first column as editor of *American Health*, he confessed to a lack of expertise in the health field but said that doing his job well depended more on marrying ''reliance on a staff vastly more knowledgeable about health matters than I am, to the idea of a chief editor functioning largely as a surrogate for the reader.''[9] So, if anything, the changes Winfrey made reflected an effort to reconnect with readers, about 75 percent of whom are women.

American Health keeps in touch with readers through surveys and even phone calls from staff members. In response, the magazine has added several new departments: ''Pulsepoints,'' a collection of medically related news briefs; ''How It Works,'' which each month explains how a specific part of the body works; ''Environment,'' featuring health-related environmental stories; and ''Quiz,'' which allows readers to rate their own levels of fitness, stress, reasons for smoking, and the like. Groch said the magazine is also much more tightly edited than it used to be. ''Our readers like charts, graphs; they are less fond of the literary columns because they can get that somewhere else. We have a theory that if you read a health magazine for three years, you get to learn so much about health that you don't need to read about it anymore. So it's a constant challenge to keep our readers interested—and to attract new readers.''[10]

The need to pull in new readers accounts for one of the most visible changes in the magazine: its covers are now designed with newsstand buyers in mind. With sell lines like ''30 Days to a Slimmer You,'' ''Sleeping Together: Make It Better, Better, Better,'' ''Bad Seeds: Is Violence in Your Genes?'' and ''Flesh Eating Bacteria,'' *American Health*'s covers now read with all the subtlety of a supermarket tabloid. The fact that the magazine's content clearly is *not* sensational does not seem to matter: the strategy is working. *American Health* also was redesigned in November 1993 in an effort to shake what Groch called ''its downtown, somewhat dark'' design.[11] Kay Spear Gibson, formerly the art director at *Mademoiselle*,* came on board to create a magazine full of bright graphics, bold type, and primary colors.

''*American Health* today is not edited and designed to win awards,'' Groch said. ''It is edited and designed to win readers by helping them stay fit and healthy and become intelligent participants in their own medical care. This makes the magazine much more appealing to the people who keep *American Health* in business—readers and advertisers.''[12]

Notes

1. T George Harris interview, August 26, 1994.
2. Judith Groch interview, August 29, 1994.
3. Harris interview.
4. Ibid.
5. Owen Lipstein, ''Publisher's Page,'' July/August 1985, p. 8.
6. Karrie Jacobs, ''T George Harris: Making His Enthusiasm for American Health Infectious,'' *Adweek*, January 27, 1986, pp. 12–13.
7. Groch interview.
8. Scott Donaton, '' 'Am. Health' Finds Relief in New Owner,'' *Advertising Age*, April 27, 1992, p. 51.
9. Carey Winfrey, ''True Confessions,'' March 1991, p. 3.
10. Groch interview.
11. Ibid.
12. Ibid.

Information Sources

BIBLIOGRAPHY:
Donaton, Scott. '' 'Am. Health' Finds Relief in New Owner.'' *Advertising Age*, April 27, 1991, p. 51.
Jacobs, Karrie. ''T George Harris: Making His Enthusiasm for American Health Infectious.'' *Adweek*, January 27, 1986, pp. 12–13.
INDEX SOURCES: Consumer Health & Nutrition Index; Cumulative Index to Nursing and Allied Health Literature; Health Index; Physical Education Index. Also avail-

able on microform and through the British Library Document Supply Centre, Faxon Research Services, the UnCover Company.

LOCATION SOURCES: Library of Congress and other libraries.

Publication History

MAGAZINE TITLE AND TITLE CHANGES: *American Health: Fitness of Body and Mind.*

VOLUME AND ISSUE DATA: Vols. 1– (March 1982–present). Bimonthly until 1984; thereafter monthly, except February and August.

PUBLISHER AND PLACE OF PUBLICATION: American Health Partners (1982–1990); RD Publications Inc., a subsidiary of the Reader's Digest Association Inc. (1990–present). New York.

EDITORS: T George Harris, editor in chief (1982–1990); Joel Gurin, editor (1982–1990), editor in chief (1990–1991); Carey Winfrey, editor (1991–present).

CIRCULATION: ABC, 1993: 820,087 (paid; 756,199 subscriptions, 63,888 single-copy sales).

Carol E. Holstead

ART & ANTIQUES

Art & Antiques premiered with its July/August 1980 issue under the title *American Art & Antiques*. Susan Meyer, the magazine's first editorial director (who acted as editor until the second issue), stated that the magazine's special mission was to

> reflect changing attitudes toward the American past . . . to be authoritative without being stuffy . . . practical without being commercial . . . beautiful to behold and pleasant to read . . . concerned with what was and is valued, eliminating the 100-year definition of ''antique'' when necessary.[1]

In an editorial in the second issue, Meyer explained why Billboard Publications created *American Art & Antiques*:

> The idea for a new magazine was conceived by a group of professional publishers who recognized the absence of a quality publication dealing with the subject of American fine and decorative arts in a lively and practical way.[2]

Originally a specialized trade magazine aimed at the aspiring art and/or antique collector, *Art & Antiques* also hoped to appeal to older, more serious collectors through specialized features. The premier issue contained articles on specific types of collectibles and matters of interest to new and experienced collectors alike. Articles included ''Early Rocking Chairs,'' ''Folk Art in New Mexico,'' ''Art Pottery,'' ''Displaying Textiles,'' and ''Battling IRS'' (an article about a collector's allowable income tax deductions). The 142-page bimonthly journal had several full-page ads for antique stores and galleries and what was, for the time, a hefty three-dollar cover price.

The second issue added Mary Jean Madigan as editor. An editorial introduced Madigan as a scholar, lecturer, book reviewer, writer on Americana, and former curator of the Hudson River Museum. That issue also expanded subject areas to include both American fine art and the decorative arts.[3] With the January/February 1980 issue the name changed to *Art & Antiques: The American Magazine for Connoisseurs & Collectors*, though the magazine's editorial thrust remained unchanged. As the magazine developed, Meyer slowly faded from the picture. In the March/April 1981 issue she was listed as editorial consultant; by the July/August 1981 issue she had disappeared from the staff box.

By 1981, the pictures and articles of *Art & Antiques* had begun to appeal to furniture designers and decorators in a variety of industries. The magazine became required reading for many college-level interior design History of Furniture classes and for theatrical scene designers. In this period *Art & Antiques* featured large, color photo spreads, and advertisements dominated, taking up over half its pages. Regular departments included book reviews, listings of upcoming shows, "Marketplace" (features and prices on specific collectibles), and classified and business-card-size ads.

In the September/October 1983 issue, just after *Art & Antiques* celebrated its fourth anniversary, Mary Jean Madigan's editorial hinted at deep trouble:

> What *would* we say if this were to be the last hop up on the soapbox? We'd say "thank you," first of all, to the readers who've given us a hearty vote of confidence by resubscribing year after year. Then we'd bow to our advertisers. . . . And then we'd mention, one by one, the fine staff members whose full-throttle dedication has brought *Art & Antiques* to the threshold of its sixth year of publication.[4]

That proved to be the final issue of *Art & Antiques* under Billboard's control. As Madigan wrote her farewell, Wick Allison was in the process of acquiring the magazine, which was on the verge of closing.[5] The magazine was not reissued until March 1984, when it reappeared under Allison's control without its earlier subtitle, format, or staff. The main title, *Arts & Antiques*, and the subscription list were the only parts of the magazine to survive.

Allison—a Texas entrepreneur who had previously published *Texas Homes* and *D* and who was credited with turning around *Sport*—relied on creative financing to raise the capital to revitalize *Art & Antiques*. After buying the magazine from Billboard at a "fire sale" price, Allison approached Mutual Benefit Products, a subsidiary of Mutual Benefit Life Insurance Co., in search of capital to finance the magazine's expansion. Mutual Benefit Products created a number of limited partnerships in the magazine that provided investors with a three-year tax shelter (accomplished through rapid depreciation of the subscription list) and a predicted (though apparently never realized) annual after-tax return of 20 percent. Twenty-two limited partnerships were sold for $66,000 each, providing Allison with the capital to finance a new marketing campaign in an effort to boost circulation.[6]

With these newfound funds, Allison held a debut party for 500 at the Guggenheim Museum[7] to show off the remade magazine. The March 1984 "premier issue" increased the size of Art & Antiques to a 9" × 12" coffee-table format, doubled the number of pages, added a lacquered cover on 60-pound stock, and upped the cover price to six dollars. Volume numbers were dropped, and the magazine was issued monthly except for a summer issue, which was substituted for the June, July, and August issues.

The new editorial staff was headed by Allison as publisher (who later took the title of editor as well) and Alexandra Anderson as editor in chief. They augmented the magazine's mission with a new focus on creating a high-circulation, consumer-oriented magazine for upwardly mobile professionals.[8] Allison saw Art & Antiques as a "magazine for the affluent, upper-end part of the market . . . grounded in a subject—in this case the visual and decorative arts."[9]

Even before bringing out his first issue, Allison arranged a direct mail offer to the 1.4 million holders of Neiman Marcus charge cards as part of his efforts to build circulation. The mailing referred to Art & Antiques as a magazine for a "generally cultured audience" and offered subscriptions at the bargain rate of $36 for ten issues.[10] Allison claimed the campaign brought in 70,000 new subscribers, although Ayer's Directory listed only 55,170 total circulation for the next year.[11]

Allison's marketing campaign dramatically changed the profile of the magazine's target audience. Previously, Art & Antiques had competed with specialized trade titles such as Art in America, Art News, and Antiques. While it continued to compete with those magazines for readers, Allison's efforts to broaden the magazine and market it to a predominantly upper-class female audience (Neiman Marcus cardholders) brought Art & Antiques into competition with magazines such as Connoisseur, Vanity Fair,* House & Garden,* Town & Country, and The New Yorker.[12]

In the September 1984 issue, editor in chief Alexandra Anderson offered a new mission statement for the magazine:

> There is one thing that will not change at the new Art & Antiques: a firm conviction that the human spirit most clearly expresses itself through works created by the human eye and hand. At a time when cultural values seem to have been trivialized, shaken, and very nearly dislodged, we stand with our readers in reaffirming the belief—call it a joyful wager—that quality remains the test of art, and that art remains essential to any life lived deeply and with pleasure.[13]

With its advent as an upscale consumer magazine, different types of articles began to appear that were only peripherally connected to the world of collectors and collecting. For example, one article, titled "High Tea for Two," speculated that some of John Singer Sargent's portraits might have been modeled on characters from Henry James's novels.[14] Though this article was about art, namely, Sargent's portraits, it had little to do with collecting that art or even collecting copies of James's books.

Allison experimented with different formats and features as he further focused on his desired audience. One such experiment was a series of reflective essays on art appreciation and similar issues, printed as an insert on heavy stock, which appeared from March through September 1984.

Despite the infusion of money, the magazine continued to experience both economic and editorial difficulties. In 1984, Isolde Motley became executive editor, though Allison continued to write the editorials. In May 1986, Jeffery Schaire became executive editor. Schaire stayed with the magazine for the next six years, providing much-needed stability, and the magazine began slowly moving toward profitability.

Art & Antiques began to attract display ads for women's jewelry, hard liquor, and makeup in early 1986, reflecting its changing readership demographics. To judge by the advertising, the magazine was at least partially successful in attracting a broader audience, especially women. But Allison continued to experiment with the cover price and size as he struggled to make the magazine profitable. In late 1986, the size of *Art & Antiques* was reduced from the coffee-table format to a standard 9" × 11" format, and the cover price dropped to $4.75 with the summer 1988 issue.

Although Allison continued to be listed as editor in chief, Schaire began signing the "Notes from the Editor" column with the summer 1987 issue, though the staff box listed him as executive editor. Schaire was listed as editor in the December 1987 issue, in which Allison acknowledged that Schaire had effectively been the editor since the previous summer.[15]

With Schaire at the helm, *Art & Antiques* turned a profit in 1988 for the first time since Allison's takeover.[16] However, difficulties with the publishers soon put an end to the magazine's stability. The November 1989 issue showed the first hints of the troubles to come. In that issue, Mutual Benefit Life Insurance Inc. shared the title of publisher with Allison Publications. In March 1990, the magazine's cover changed format, the cover price was dropped for the second time (to a modest $2.95, the lowest it has ever been), and Michael Pashby was listed as publisher. In August 1990, Allison was forced to leave the magazine entirely, after it lost around $2 million in the previous year. Allison then sold some of his partnership rights to Mutual Benefit for an undisclosed amount.

After Allison's departure, Mutual Benefit abandoned its efforts to boost circulation through low cover prices. Alison Bliss Selover, the estranged wife of Mutual Benefit Life Insurance Co.'s president, was made publisher. The cover price was increased to $3.95 with the January 1991 issue. But the difficulties of *Art & Antiques* were quickly overshadowed by a larger crisis at Mutual Benefit Life. New Jersey placed the insurance company under state control in July 1991 because of concerns over its financial stability.[17] Wick Allison filed a lawsuit against Mutual Benefit Life Insurance and the 22 limited partners the next month, claiming that Alison Bliss Selover was responsible for a 28 percent decline in advertising and had ruined the magazine, broken promises made to him, and "thrown the publishing venture into a tailspin."[18]

Mutual Benefit Life Insurance Co. was dropped from the staff box with the summer 1991 issue and replaced by Art & Antiques Associates L.P. (Limited Partners). Following an aborted effort by Martin Davis to buy control of the magazine, Trans World Publishing Co. purchased *Art & Antiques* from Mutual Benefit Life in February 1992. Trans World's other titles include the trade magazine competitor of *Art & Antiques*, *Antiques Monthly*.[19] By 1992, *Art & Antiques* was a money-losing monthly magazine with a circulation of 153,000. Trans World kept the magazine's 28 staff members but dropped Selover as publisher. The company soon announced plans to revive a Japanese edition of the magazine, which had appeared as a trial issue in October 1991.[20]

Trans World held to Schaire's vision of the magazine as a consumer magazine, focused on decorating with antiques. The magazine also produces a theme issue, subtitled *Decorating with Art & Antiques*, every September.[21] The first of those issues, brought out under Trans World's control, contained a sad note from the magazine's new editor, Robert Kenner:

As I write this note, our entire staff is still reeling from the shock of Jeff's announcement that he has tested HIV positive. As he moves on to concentrate on his life . . . I step forward to continue his mission.[22]

But while Trans World maintained the magazine's editorial thrust, it continued to make changes in the format and staff of *Art & Antiques*. The October 1992 issue was thinner, at 96 pages, and pricier ($4.95), with a new masthead and page design. Kenner served as editor for less than a year. The May 1993 staff box shows Kenner replaced by managing editor Scott Gutterman. While Gutterman remains managing editor, Mark Mayfield became editor with the September 1993 issue.

Although circulation dropped in 1993 (to 150,012), *Art & Antiques* increased its advertising ratio, and is now half advertisements and half editorial copy. While most readers may be women, Trans World does not see *Art & Antiques* as a women's magazine.[23] Despite Trans World's changes, *Art & Antiques* is essentially the same magazine that Wick Allison and Jeffery Schaire created in the late 1980s. The magazine features large photo spreads and full-page ads for fine art galleries and auction houses such as Christie's, Kennedy Galleries, and Alexander Milliken. A visual feast of color and splendor, this consumer magazine has adapted to the decline of conspicuous consumption by focusing on the investment potential of art and antique collectibles.

Notes

1. Susan Meyer, "Editorial," July/August 1978, p. 6.
2. Susan Meyer, "Editorial," September/October 1978, p. 7.
3. Ibid.
4. Mary Jean Madigan, "This Slippery Soapbox," September/October 1983, p. 10.
5. Udayan Gupta, "A Magazine Thrives on Red Ink," *Venture*, December 1984, p. 146.
6. Ibid.
7. Kevin Pritchett, "Mutual Benefit Life Faces Lawsuit over Job for Former Officer's Ex-Wife," *Wall Street Journal*, September 27, 1991, sec. B, p. 4e.
8. Susan Roy, "Mastering Seat-of-the-Pants Publishing," *Advertising Age*, March 26, 1984, p. M10.
9. Ibid.
10. Stuart J. Elliot, "Art Book, Neiman Seek Subscribers," *Advertising Age*, February 25, 1985, p. 39; Roy, "Mastering Seat-of-the-Pants Publishing," pp. M10–12.
11. "Art & Antiques Emerges as Upscale Consumer Book," *Marketing & Media Decisions*, April 1984, p. 40, *The IMS 1985 Ayer's Directory of Publications*, 118th ed. (Fort Washington, Pa.: IMS Press, 1984), p. 668.
12. "Art & Antiques," p. 40; Roy, "Mastering Seat-of-the-Pants Publishing," p. M10.
13. Alexandra Anderson, "From the Editor," September 1984, p. 9.
14. Louis Auchincloss, "High Tea for Two," September 1984, pp. 64–71.
15. Wick Allison, "Curiosity and Passion," December 1987, p. 20.
16. Tony Silber, "*Art & Antiques* Sold Amidst Legal Wrangle," *Folio*, November 1991, p. 40.
17. Ibid.
18. Pritchett, "Mutual Benefit Life Faces Lawsuit," p. 4e.
19. "Noted . . . ." *Wall Street Journal*, December 3, 1991, p. B7. For the Davis effort, see Silber, "*Art & Antiques* Sold," p. 40.
20. Silber, "*Art & Antiques* Sold," p. 40.
21. Robin Domenizoni interview, August 22, 1993.
22. Robert Kenner, "Facing the Future," September 1992, p. 12.
23. Domenizoni interview.

Information Sources

BIBLIOGRAPHY:

"*Art & Antiques* Emerges as Upscale Consumer Book." *Marketing & Media Decisions*, April 1984, p. 40.

Elliot, Stuart J. "Art Book, Neiman Seek Subscribers." *Advertising Age*, February 25, 1985, p. 39.

Gupta, Udayan. "A Magazine Thrives on Red Ink." *Venture*, December 1984, p. 146.

The IMS 1985 Ayer's Directory of Publications, 118th ed. Fort Washington, Pa.: IMS Press, 1984.

Pritchett, Kevin. "Mutual Benefit Life Faces Lawsuit over Job for Former Officer's Ex-Wife." *Wall Street Journal*, September 27, 1991, sec. B, p. 4e.

Roy, Susan. "Mastering Seat-of-the-Pants Publishing." *Advertising Age*, March 26, 1984, p. M10.

ART & ANTIQUES

17

Silber, Tony. "*Art & Antiques* Sold Amidst Legal Wrangle." *Folio*, November 1991, p. 40.

INDEX SOURCES: American History and Life; Art and Archaeology Technical Abstracts; Historical Abstracts; Art Index; Popular Magazine Review.

LOCATION SOURCES: Library of Congress and other libraries.

Publication History

MAGAZINE TITLE AND TITLE CHANGES: *American Art and Antiques* (July/August 1978–December 1979); *Art & Antiques: The American Magazine for Connoisseurs & Collectors* (January/February 1980–September/October 1983); *Art & Antiques* (March 1983–present).

VOLUME AND ISSUE DATA: Vols. 1– (July/August 1978–present). Bimonthly (1978 to 1983); monthly, except June/July/August (summer) combined issue (1984–present).

PUBLISHER AND PLACE OF PUBLICATION: Billboard Publications (1978–1983); Art & Antiques Associates L.P. (1984–1989); Allison Publications in partnership with Mutual Benefit Life Insurance Co. (1989–1991); Art & Antiques Associates L.P. and Mutual Benefit Life Insurance Co. (1991); Art & Antiques Associates L.P. (1991–1992); Trans World Publishing Co. (1992–present). New York.

EDITORS: Susan Meyer (1978); Mary Jean Madigan (1978–1983); Alexandra Anderson (1984); Wick Allison (1984–1987); Jeffery Schaire (1987–1989); Wick Allison with Jeffery Schaire (1989–1991); Jeffery Schaire (1991–1992); Robert Kenner (1992–1993); Scott Gutterman (1993); Mark Mayfield (1993–present).

CIRCULATION: ABC, 1993: 150,012 (paid, primarily subscriptions).

Lisa Beinhoff

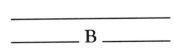

B

BARBIE

"*Barbie* is one of our most popular children's magazines," a Toledo librarian said, explaining why it was difficult to find the periodical on the shelf and intact. "It's commercial but the girls really like it." That commercial base distressed Bill Katz and Linda Sternberg Katz, writing in *Magazines for Libraries*. They characterized *Barbie* as "gimmicky and highly commercialized." They explained:

> There are many advertisements, some so subtle that they appear to be supplementing text. Readers will have to look closely to determine whether photographs complement an article or promote a product.[1]

That may be why the authors of this well-respected reference work do not recommend *Barbie* for acquisition by libraries.

Barbie magazine—not to be confused with *Barbie Bazaar*, the periodical aimed at adult "Barbie" collectors—is published by Welsh Publishing Group, a company that specializes in children's magazines. Most of the magazines Welsh publishes are linked to television characters or popular toys. Besides *Barbie*, the company also publishes *Garfield*, *Teenage Mutant Ninja Turtles*, *Mickey Mouse*, *Bugs Bunny Presents Looney Tunes*, *Superman & Batman*, and *Simpsons Illustrated* magazines. The original Welsh children's publication, *Muppet Magazine*, has since died.[2] Thus, *Barbie* is the oldest of the company's family of children's magazines, although not the largest in terms of circulation.

Donald Welsh, majority owner of Welsh Publishing Group and publisher of *Barbie*, got involved in children's magazine publishing just as the niche began to grow. In 1982, when *Muppet Magazine* began, and 1983, when *Barbie* was started, new publishers were beginning to see the enormous potential in the youth market. As a result, many new "youth" publications were launched in the 1980s; many were aimed at a large, affluent group: children 13 and younger, many from dual-income families. In 1991, these children spent—or influenced the spending of—more than $170 billion.[3]

Barbie's core audience is female, ages 5 to 12 years. They come from affluent homes with an average household income far in excess of the national average.[4] *Barbie* is a magazine that mothers and daughters share.[5] In 1993, *Barbie* reported that the majority of the parents read the magazine with their daughters.[6]

Barbie magazine is a licensed franchise of the Mattel Corp. As such, the magazine's logotype is the familiar design used on all "Barbie" products. Mattel previews every issue, and *Barbie* editor Andrea Posner goes over ideas with Mattel. Meryl Friedman, vice president of marketing for Mattel, acts as creative consultant for the magazine.

Barbie magazine seems to be the ideal periodical for children brought up with "Sesame Street" and Saturday morning cartoons. The magazine, now published bimonthly, is loaded with action-filled, four-color photographs and drawings. Unlike more traditional publications, such as *Highlights for Children*, editorial copy is kept to a minimum. Most departments and features are linked to the doll "Barbie." Departments include "Barbie and You" (new products available for "Barbie") and "Best of Barbie" (new products carrying the official "Barbie" logo—and an 800 number for ordering). "Barbie" herself writes a letter to readers in each issue. Readers respond in "Dear Barbie," fan letters written to the editor, and "We're into Barbie!" letters that are always accompanied by four-color photographs. If those photos are indicative of the readership, the audience is drawn from a number of ethnic and racial backgrounds. All girls pose with a range of "Barbies" and/or a variety of "Barbie" ancillary products.[7]

One of the consistent features of *Barbie* magazine has been "The Barbie Photodrama," in which "Barbie," with an assortment of her friends, tells a story in photos, comic-book style. "Barbie," "Ken," "Skipper," "Stacie," and the other friends pose in a series of photos with quote balloons telling what each character is "saying." The centerspread is a poster of "Barbie" and her friends based upon the "panorama" of that issue. Over the years, the "panorama" has shown "Barbie in New York" as a model; "The Glamour Gourmet" ("Barbie" on television demonstrating cooking); "Moonbeams and Moon Dreams" ("Barbie" on the moon); and "Rappin' & Rockin' Together" ("Barbie" and her pals as a rapping rock group).[8]

Other departments are more lifestyle-based. The column "What's Up!" highlights new videos, books, music, computer games, clothes, and television. Each brief summary is accompanied by a photograph or a drawing. The photos, drawings, and type are never limited to the typical three-column magazine format. Pictures are placed on diagonals. The layout is always action-filled.[9]

That layout often makes it difficult to differentiate editorial material from advertising. The word "advertisement" appears above all ads offering "Barbie" products. (Mattel is a major advertiser in the magazine.) However, other advertising is not accompanied by a label. Those advertisements are for movies, cereals, candy, clothes, and video games and represent some of the largest manufacturers of children's products, including Disney, Sega, Nickelodeon, Huffy and Rollerblade. Nestle, Hershey, Quaker Oats, Procter & Gamble, and Borden also advertise.[10]

"Lifestyle" features are an important part of *Barbie*'s editorial package. The magazine approaches this in a number of different ways. Some issues include interviews with "famous" preteens. Mary Kate and Ashley Olsen, television actresses and recording stars, and Georgina Armstrong, star of the movie *Black Beauty*, were subjects of "The Barbie Interview."[11]

The magazine also highlights ordinary girls with special qualities. For example, in its tenth-anniversary issue,[12] *Barbie* featured ten talented girls. In another issue,[13] the magazine spotlighted youthful dancers in New York City. Of course, there are puzzles to solve, recipes to follow, crafts to make, fashions to see, and vacations to share. All this makes *Barbie* a lifestyle magazine for the preteen. Jacob Hill, advertising director for Welsh Publishing Group, characterized *Barbie* as a "*Seventeen* magazine for 8-year-old girls."[14]

Approximately 600,000 girls read *Barbie* every other month.[15] That translates to more than 15 percent of all American girls between the ages of 5 and 12.[16] This magazine is very much a lifestyle periodical that transmits values and goals to an impressionable, young audience. The continued success of this magazine illustrates that both the girls and their parents are pleased with the editorial content of this periodical.

Notes

1. Bill Katz and Linda Sternberg Katz, *Magazines for Libraries* (New Providence, N.J.: R. R. Bowker, 1992), pp. 242–243.

2. "Market & Media: Cypress Capital Buys 49% of Common Stock of Welsh Publishing," *Wall Street Journal*, July 22, 1993, p. B3; Liz Horton, "The Simpsons Turn to Print," *Folio*, May 1, 1991, pp. 57–58; Jacob Hill interview, July 14, 1994.

3. Deirdre Carmody, "Children's Magazines Look to Future," *New York Times*, November 23, 1992, p. D6.

4. *Barbie* cites the average household income for subscribers at $47,000, 51 percent higher than the national average. "Research Highlights," *Barbie* Media Kit.

5. Recent research has emphasized the continued popularity of "Barbie" as a toy. See, for example, Jacquelyn Mitchard, "Much Ado about Barbie," *Parenting*, April 1994, p. 87; Sydney Ladensohn Stern, "A Design for Fantasy: The Evolution of 'Barbie,'" *Education Week*, June 13, 1990, p. 32; Bella English, "Of Mothers, Daughters and Barbie Dolls," *Boston Globe*, December 17, 1992, p. 1; "Barbie Magazine Fast Facts," *Barbie* Media Kit.

6. In its Media Kit material, *Barbie* reports that 84 percent of parents read or look

through their child's magazine, and 56 percent read the magazine with their children. "Research Highlights," *Barbie* Media Kit.

7. See, for example, March/April 1994, p. 36, and September/October 1993, p. 64.

8. Spring 1985, Fall 1985, Fall 1986, and Fall 1992, all reprinted in the tenth-anniversary issue, September/October 1993, pp. 57–58, 60.

9. See, for example, January/February 1994, pp. 6–7, and May/June 1994, pp. 6–7.

10. "Partial Advertiser List," *Barbie* Media Kit.

11. In each of these stories, "Barbie" is pictured conducting the interview. "Sister Act," January/February 1994, pp. 22–23; "Galloping Georgina!" May/June 1994, p. 12.

12. "Presenting the 10 Outstanding Girls of America!" September/October 1993, pp. 34–43, 45, 47.

13. "Spotlight on You Tip-Top Tappers," May/June 1994, pp. 27–29.

14. Hill interview.

15. This is the circulation on which advertising rates are based. "Barbie Magazine Fast Facts," *Barbie* Media Kit.

16. "Research Highlights."

Information Sources

BIBLIOGRAPHY:

Carmody, Deirdre. "Children's Magazines Look to Future." *New York Times*, November 23, 1992, p. D6.

Cleaver, Joanne Y. "Rise of the Dual Income Makes Kids a Hot Target." *Advertising Age*, November 10, 1986, p. S4.

English, Bella. "Of Mothers, Daughters and Barbie Dolls." Boston *Globe*, December 17, 1992, p. A1.

Horton, Liz. "The Simpsons Turn to Print." *Folio*, May 1, 1991, pp. 57–58.

Katz, Bill, and Linda Sternberg Katz. *Magazines for Libraries*. New Providence, N.J.: R. R. Bowker, 1992.

List, S. K. "The Right Place to Find Children." *American Demographics*, February 1992, pp. 44–47.

Loer, Stephanie. "A New Leaf in Magazines for Children." *Publishers Weekly*, February 24, 1992, pp. 20–21.

"Magazine Deal Aims at Youth." *New York Times*, November 20, 1993, p. A46.

"Marketing & Media: Cypress Capital Buys 49% of Common Stock of Welsh Publishing." *Wall Street Journal*, July 22, 1993, p. B3.

Richardson, Selma K. *Magazines for Children: A Guide for Parents, Teachers and Librarians*, 2d ed. Chicago: American Library Association, 1991.

INDEX SOURCES: None.

LOCATION SOURCES: Various community libraries.

Publication History

MAGAZINE TITLE AND TITLE CHANGES: *Barbie*.

VOLUME AND ISSUE DATA: Vols. 1– (Winter 1984 [with 1983 copyright]–present). Quarterly (1983–1991); five times (1992?); bimonthly (1993–present).

PUBLISHER AND PLACE OF PUBLICATION: Telepictures Publications Inc. (1983–1987?); Welsh Publishing Group (1987?–present). New York.

EDITORS: Karen Harrison; Evan Levine; Brett Mirsky; Andrea Posner (1994–present).
CIRCULATION: Ownership Statement, 1994: 592,182 (average number of copies issued
    1993, paid, primarily through subscriptions).

Kathleen L. Endres

BETTER HOMES AND GARDENS

Few magazines have affected American homes and domestic life as greatly as
Better Homes and Gardens. Two generations of cooks have grabbed the familiar
red-and-white checkerboard *Better Homes and Gardens Cookbook* for directions
for the evening meal. Millions of husbands and wives have followed plans for
inexpensive, easy-to-do home improvement projects offered in the magazine.
Countless gardens have been planted and carefully tended with the advice of
the "plain dirt" gardener. *Better Homes* founder E. T. Meredith would be proud,
although not surprised. He always knew that the American reading public
needed a "first-class journal for the average family."[1] Yet, it took some time
before Meredith could convert his dream of a magazine for the American home
into a reality.

Meredith used his *Successful Farming*, one of the largest farm periodicals of
the day,[2] to launch a trial balloon for the home magazine he hoped to start. In
June 1913, *Successful Farming* carried an ad soliciting gardening ideas and
announcing "a bright, clean, inspiring, helpful and attractive monthly magazine
. . . for all who have gardens or raise fruits."[3] It took another nine years before
that magazine became a reality. World War I and Meredith's tenure as secretary
of agriculture in President Woodrow Wilson's administration intervened.

Meredith returned to Des Moines in 1922 and quickly started work on his
new magazine, *Fruit, Garden and Home.* Meredith hoped for a June 1922 debut,
but that proved to be unrealistic; after all, Meredith had not yet even hired an
editor for the new publication. He had to rely on staffers of *Successful Farming*
for much of the planning and production of the first issue, which came out in
July 1922. That issue, as well as the subsequent month's edition, was sent free
to readers.

Meredith found his editor in Chesla Sherlock, only 27 when he started. Meredith and Sherlock initially got along well and crafted a magazine that would
capture the imagination of millions of readers.

From the beginning, the two worked against established principles of success in
magazine publishing. *Fruit, Garden and Home* refused to carry fiction, fashion, or
sex, the three components that assured success for many of the mass circulation
magazines of the day. But such would not be in keeping with what Meredith and
Sherlock both saw as the audience for the magazine. As Meredith wrote:

> We are appealing particularly to the men and women who are interested
> in their yards, gardens and interiors of their homes, but our suggestions

are going to be along modest lines and within the reach of families with incomes from three thousand and twenty-five thousand dollars, rather than to make a *Country Life* or *House Beautiful*.[4]

The magazine has always been true to those words.

In the 1920s, the magazine was a cozy, homey guide appealing to "ordinary folks," with stories and projects designed to improve their domestic life. Stories ranged from how to plant peonies to furnishing a young person's home, from the enormously popular "Homes of Famous Americans" to meal planning.[5] Both Meredith and Sherlock exchanged pleasantries with readers in columns, and readers responded similarly, relating home experiences and helpful hints in a column entitled "Among Ourselves."

Although this editorial formula would eventually assure success, the earliest years of *Fruit, Garden and Home* were not financially successful. Advertisers did not rush to the new magazine. However, readers, prompted by both the small cost (only 35¢ a year) as well as the editorial material, flocked to the magazine. By 1923, the magazine had a circulation of 300,000.[6] Nonetheless, the magazine still lost money. *Successful Farming* underwrote the new magazine until 1927, when *Fruit, Garden and Home*, by then named *Better Homes and Gardens*, finally showed a profit.[7]

The magazine's name had always been a problem. *Fruit, Garden and Home* seemed to confuse advertisers. Just what kind of magazine was this? It was not clear from the name. After much discussion about a variety of alternatives,[8] *Better Homes and Gardens* was selected, and the name debuted with the August 1924 issue. As Meredith explained to readers, the new name better expressed "the real purpose behind the publication." "*Better Homes and Gardens* will continue to serve the homemakers in cities, towns and suburbs in a practical, useful way."[9] A growing number of readers liked what they saw.

Although the subscription price went up (to 60¢ a year),[10] circulation grew: 500,000 in 1924,[11] 700,000 in 1925,[12] 900,000 in 1927,[13] and more than 1 million in 1928.[14] Meredith moved to assure his readers of the credibility of the growing number of advertisers in the magazine. In 1925, the magazine announced an "advertising guarantee," one that still exists today. As the editor explained to readers, if any advertiser failed "to live up to his bargain with you, *Better Homes and Gardens* will either secure redress for you from him or stand any loss incurred itself."[15] It was not an unusual promise for the day. A number of mass circulation periodicals aimed at women, including *Good Housekeeping*,* offered that assurance.

Although the magazine was growing in circulation, in amount of advertising, and in size, problems were brewing behind the scenes. The warm relationship between Meredith and Sherlock had cooled. Increasingly, the two were disagreeing. In 1927, the editor resigned to become associate editor of *Ladies' Home Journal*.*[16] Meredith began his search for a new editor.

While Meredith searched, two women, Lou Richardson and Genevieve A. Cal-

lahan, assumed the responsibility for the magazine. They, apparently, did not hold
the title of editor; not until the 1990s did a woman hold the title of editor. When a
woman was suggested for Sherlock's position in 1927, Fred Bohen, Meredith's
son-in-law, responded, "We didn't wish to consider a woman as editor."[17] E. T.
Meredith also did not want anyone with an eastern, urban background; he urged
Bohen to "keep in mind all the time that we do not want anyone who has lived in
New York, Philadelphia, or some eastern section all his life."[18]

Elmer T. Peterson, a midwestern newspaper editor, was the choice. Peterson
shared Meredith's view of the home as the foundation of American life.
Throughout his ten years as editor, Peterson emphasized this repeatedly in uplifting editorials. He also brought to the magazine a strong news sense that would
be increasingly important in the days of the deepest depression. He also introduced many of the innovations for which *Better Homes and Gardens* has been
credited.

Peterson led the magazine—and instituted most of those innovations—without the guidance of Meredith. E. T. Meredith, who considered himself not only
the publisher but the managing editor of the magazine,[19] died less than a year
after Peterson took over as editor.[20]

The changes were instituted quickly. In 1930, the enormously successful *Better Homes and Gardens Cookbook* was offered readers as a subscription-renewal
premium. It was also offered for sale; the 100,000th copy of the book was
delivered to First Lady Mrs. Herbert Hoover in the White House in 1931.[21]

The magazine introduced the "Bildcost Home Plan" in 1932, designed to
increase the likelihood of home ownership for young couples.[22] That same rationale was behind an editorial published in the May 1929 issue of the magazine
that was credited with instigating lasting changes to the building industry and
home finance policies.

In 1929, problems in the home mortgage field were already arising; some
resulted from problems with construction, and others were based on a lack of
uniform mortgage standards. In his editorial, Peterson argued for a national
association to develop a new, rigid code of building standards. He also urged a
uniform, long-term amortization to relieve the pressure of debt.[23] This plan was
eventually adopted by a national organization of home financial interests[24] and
was similar to the National Housing Act enacted in 1934.[25] In addition, the
magazine offered practical advice to readers on the verge of losing their homes
in foreclosures.[26]

Like its readers, *Better Homes and Gardens* was facing its own problems
during the depression. Advertising was down substantially. In 1932 and 1933,
the magazine was especially thin. It seemed to try everything to improve its
advertising picture and even sponsored a contest for the best letter that showed
"How I (or my family) Have Benefited by Reading Advertisements in *Better
Homes & Gardens*." Things improved after the passage of the National Housing
Act, which supported remodeling projects in addition to home mortgages. In
1937, the editor was finally able to report that the magazine's April issue had

broken all records. The magazine had its largest number of subscriptions (unlike many magazines, it suffered no major circulation declines during the 1930s), pages, and advertisements.[27]

Just as the magazine was breaking records, its editor left. Frank W. McDonough, a longtime *Better Homes and Gardens* man, took over and soon brought his own style of change and innovation to the book. The magazine soon "grew," to a larger 9½" × 12½" size, and there were more four-color and bleed photographs.[28] The magazine was not only bigger in size, but also larger in circulation. By 1938, the magazine could boast of a circulation of more than 1.75 million.[29] That figure kept increasing until World War II, when paper restrictions curbed the magazine's growth.[30]

During the war, *Better Homes and Gardens* was the patriotic magazine for the home front. Readers were urged to buy bonds, conserve, eliminate "nervous pleasures," plant "victory" gardens, and, in some cases, work for defense industries.[31]

The war, with its paper shortages, represented only a brief respite in the continuous growth of *Better Homes and Gardens*. When the veterans returned from war, the country experienced a building spree. *Better Homes and Gardens* was there to report on new developments in construction, home design, and gardens. J. E. Ratner, former managing editor, tookover for McDonough in 1950. Two years later, Hugh Curtis was appointed editor. With him was Bert Dieter as art director; he was editor of the magazine throughout much of the 1960s.

The 1950s were grand times for *Better Homes and Gardens*. Its circulation reached into the millions: 3.5 million in 1952, 3.7 million in 1953, and 4.25 million in 1956. It was a time for innovation editorially and architecturally. The magazine introduced the concept of the "family room" in the 1950s, and builders soon reported huge demands for the addition. Popular television and radio stars Fibber McGee and Molly offered a guide to curing "cluttered closets." The magazine was forever announcing larger and larger home improvement contests.[32]

The magazine was also adjusting to the 1950s by expanding its editorial mix. Concern about national security brought the feature "Scramble Two . . . Bogey at 40,000." Increased rates of cancer triggered the story "New Hope in the War against Cancer." The first passenger jet flight across the country meant that poet Carl Sandburg recorded it all for the magazine's readers.[33]

The 1950s also brought experiments in layout and production. In May 1955, the magazine tested cover effectiveness by offering two versions: one with an appetizing dessert, the other of the inside of a porch; the art director was trying to determine which would sell better, but results of the tests were never released. In addition, by the end of the decade, the magazine was published in two editions.

The 1960s were strange times for the magazine. While the nation was torn apart by the social unrest of the civil rights, antiwar, and women's rights movements, *Better Homes and Gardens* was a peaceful haven of traditional values and concerns. Seven million subscribers[34] looked to the magazine for projects in the kitchen, in the garden, and in the workshop in these tumultuous times.

In July 1963, the magazine introduced one of its most successful features ever, "100 Ideas under $100." Proposed by David Jordan, who later became the editor of *Better Homes*, the idea was originally "10 Ideas under $10." Too modest by project standards of *Better Homes and Gardens*, the idea quickly expanded to the one that has spelled so much success for the magazine over the decades that followed.[35] This feature runs in the July issue, often the top newsstand seller of the year.[36] In the 1960s also, the magazine introduced the first of its "special interest publications."

In the 1970s, under editors James A. Riggs and James Autry, the magazine came to terms with some of the issues that were deeply troubling the American family. Features began dealing with children being arrested, teens on drugs, and problems in the schools.[37] Perhaps the most challenging was "How to Help Your Son Face the Draft." In a straightforward, nonjudgmental account, the author offered alternatives from how to enlist and what to expect, to how to evade the draft (including not registering and going to Canada). Above all, the author reminded the readers that "you and your son should respect each other's views, and talk over the decision calmly."[38]

Controversial topics did not reduce the magazine's popularity with readers. In November 1973, the magazine reported 7,777,777 subscribers; in July 1978, that figure was 8 million. It remained an advertising success story. The magazine was crammed with four-color ads. Nonetheless, the magazine was facing some economic problems. Beginning with the January 1977 issue, the magazine was reformatted to the smaller, standard size of 8" × 11" from its oversize 9½" × 12½" because of financial considerations. Postage was on the increase, and the new size reduced the amount of paper needed. The editor promised that there would be "no change in our basic home and family editorial outlook."[39] There was, however, a difference in price; the magazine went from 75¢ per issue to 95¢ in 1978—still inexpensive by contemporary standards.

The late 1970s brought another innovation, for which *Better Homes and Gardens* is still known. The magazine began surveying its readers on the pressing problems of the day—the often repeated "What's Happening to the American Family," "How Is Working Affecting American Families?" and "Today's Parents: How Well Are They Doing?"[40] These surveys of hundreds of thousands of readers may serve as important guides to changing attitudes in America for future historians.

In the 1980s, also, the magazine began experimenting with different ways to deliver information: television, computers, and interactive cable systems. Unlike many other mass circulation periodicals that have only belatedly gotten involved in new technology, *Better Homes and Gardens* has long experimented with its potential. In 1983, "The Better Homes and Gardens Idea Notebook" premiered on USA cable television. The magazine offered "Cook's Underground" on CompuServe, a recipe exchange that included a nutritional and cost analysis that was seldom available in the magazine. *Better Homes and Gardens* was also part of the Qube interactive cable experiment in Columbus, Ohio.[41] More recently, *Better Homes and Gardens* is an innovator in the video market; the magazine capitalizes on its practical how-to approach in these videos.[42]

Gordon Greer followed Autry as editor. He continued most of Autry's innovations. Greer spent only about four years in that position, and then David Jordan took over, staying nine years as editor. He balanced the surveys with a deep concern for social and environmental concerns. A new department, "Our Environment," highlighted that issue. Features dealt with teaching children about acquired immunodeficiency syndrome (AIDS), helping homeless families, and gender bias in schools.[43] The magazine formed its own foundation to help homeless families; Jordan headed the foundation.

Jordan continued to head that foundation after he bid adieu to *Better Homes and Gardens* readers in 1993 and began his new assignment of starting new magazines for Meredith. He was replaced by the magazine's first woman editor, Jean LemMon, the former editor of *Country Home*, another Meredith property. This represented a "coming home" for LemMon, who started her career with *Better Homes and Gardens*.[44]

LemMon took over at an exciting time in the history of the magazine, which not only is the flagship for the prosperous Meredith Corporation but also gives its name to a whole range of products from garden centers, to a real estate chain, to books, and videos.[45] *Better Homes and Gardens* also continues to be a launching pad for Meredith magazines, including, most recently, *Traditional Home* and *Metropolitan Home*. In addition, the name *Better Homes and Gardens* continues to be associated with a range of special-interest publications.[46]

Few magazines have ever achieved such success. However, the real estate, the garden centers, the videos, and the books are only by-products. The heart of this merchandising empire is a magazine about to enter the twenty-first century with the same traditional values on which it was founded: "to help families live a better life by giving them ideas, information and inspiration."

E. T. Meredith probably would be comfortable with today's *Better Homes and Gardens*. The magazine still follows his dictate of "no fiction, no fashion, no piffle, no passion."[47] It is an editorial approach that still seems to work.

Notes

1. E. T. Meredith to "My dear sir" letter, April 12, 1922, Meredith Papers, University of Iowa as quoted in Carol Reuss, "*Better Homes and Gardens*: Consistent Concern Key to Long Life," *Journalism Quarterly* 51:2 (Summer 1974), p. 292.

2. Meredith launched *Successful Farming* in 1902. The magazine is still published, although the circulation of *Better Homes and Gardens* has long since dwarfed that of *Successful Farming*.

3. "Cash Prizes for Letters about Gardening," *Successful Farming*, June 1913, p. 45, as quoted in Carol Reuss, "*Better Homes and Gardens* and Its Editors: An Historical Study from the Magazine's Founding to 1970" (Diss., University of Iowa, 1971), p. 15.

4. E. T. Meredith to L. B. Jones, August 12, 1922, Meredith Collection, University of Iowa, as quoted in Reuss, "*Better Homes and Gardens* and Its Editors," p. 23.

5. "Plant Peonies in Your Gardens," "Furnishing the Young Folks' Room," "Homes of Famous Americans," and "How to Plan Your Meals," September 1923, pp. 5–6, 12–13, 15, 20.

6. September 1923, p. 3.

7. Meredith noted that in January 1923, the investment in the new magazine was $133,800 and that *Successful Farming* was supporting the new magazine. E. T. Meredith to J. C. Billingslea, January 23, 1923, E. T. Meredith Collection, Reuss, "*Better Homes and Gardens* and Its Editors," p. 39. Reuss also reported that *Successful Farming* underwrote *Fruit, Garden and Home*'s 1923 loss of $180,000 and 1924 loss of $130,000. See Reuss, p. 40.

8. See Reuss, "*Better Homes and Gardens* and Its Editors," pp. 40–41.

9. August 1924, p. 3.

10. January 1925, p. 3.

11. "A Chat with the Publisher," December 1924, p. 3.

12. "Across the Editor's Desk," September 1925, p. 70.

13. May 1927, front cover.

14. January 1928, front cover.

15. Chesla Sherlock, "Across the Editor's Desk," May 1925, p. 70.

16. Sherlock committed suicide in 1938. Gordon Greer, "Editor at Large," July 1982, p. 5.

17. Fred Bohen to R. F. Rogers, June 23, 1927, Meredith Collection, University of Iowa, as quoted in Reuss, "*Better Homes and Gardens* and Its Editors," p. 52.

18. Meredith to Bohen and Lawrence W. Lane, May 13, 1927, Meredith Papers, University of Iowa, as quoted in Reuss, "*Better Homes and Gardens* and Its Editors," p. 52.

19. January 1928, p. 3.

20. "Edwin T. Meredith," August 1928, p. 5.

21. "Across the Editor's Desk," March 1932, p. 94, and Reuss, "*Better Homes and Gardens* and Its Editors," p. 61.

22. "Announcing—*Better Homes and Gardens*' Bildcost Home Plan," January 1932, pp. 10–11.

23. "For Better Home Financing," May 1929, p. 7.

24. "Across the Editor's Desk," August 1934, p. 74.

25. James A. Moffett, administrator of the Federal Housing Administration, asked Peterson to explain the act to *Better Homes and Gardens* readers. See Elmer Peterson, "What the New Housing Act Will Do for You," September 1934, p. 7, and "The Home," p. 4.

26. "Across the Editor's Desk," October 1933, p. 4.

27. "All Records Broken," April 1927, p. 4.

28. Reuss, "*Better Homes and Gardens* and Its Editors," p. 77.

29. Ibid.

30. Ibid. By January 1941, circulation reached 2.2 million. By the end of the year, that figure reached 2.4 million. January 1941, p. 4, and November 1941, p. 4.

BETTER HOMES AND GARDENS

31. Advertisement, April 1942, p. 4; "Our Job on the Home Front," May 1942, p. 10; "More Heat from Less Fuel," September 1942, pp. 36–37; Gladys Denny Shultz, "Who's Going to Take Care of Me, Mother, If You Take a War-Plant Job," May 1943, pp. 9, 61.

32. "Anniversary Almanac: Celebrating Seven Decades of Family Living," July 1987, p. 18; "To the Rescue of Cluttered Closets," August 1954, p. 56; "$25,000.00 Home Improvement Contest for 1956," April 1956, p. 6.

33. November 1954, p. 66; July 1954, p. 23; April 1959, pp. 56–57.

34. January 1968.

35. David Jordan, "Editor at Large," March 1985, p. 13.

36. Reuss, "*Better Homes and Gardens* and Its Editors," p. 134.

37. "Your Child under Arrest?" May 1970, p. 20; "Youngsters and Drugs: Making Sense of What's Happening," October 1970, pp. 34–36; "Schools: What Are Your Legal Rights?" March 1978, pp. 14, 16, 18, 20.

38. November 1970, p. 30.

39. "A Few Words about Our New Size," January 1977, p. 6.

40. May 1978, p. 23; February 1982, p. 19; January 1983, p. 24; October 1986, p. 36.

41. Gordon Greer, "BH&G on the Air," January 1983, p. 4. More recently, the magazine was involved in a syndicated home repair show for Worldvision Enterprises. See Wayne Walley, "Home-Improvement TV Fight Builds," *Advertising Age*, June 5, 1989, p. 37. In 1993, *Advertising Age* reported that Meredith, the corporate parent of *Better Homes and Gardens*, was exploring the development of a cable television network based on its magazines. The proposed network would emphasize home and family topics. Two magazines in particular would figure into this package: *Better Homes and Gardens* and *Ladies' Home Journal*. Scott Donaton, "Meredith Eyes Cable," *Advertising Age*, October 18, 1993, p. 52.

42. Tom Cunneff, "Video: Better Homes and Gardens—Refinishing Furniture," *People Weekly*, November 7, 1988, pp. 28–29. Dan Bencivenga, "Better Homes Launches Videos with Aggressive Campaign," *Target Marketing*, March 1988, pp. 23–24.

43. "Talking to Your Children about AIDS," February 1992, p. 62; "Helping Homeless Families," May 1992, p. 78; "Gender Bias: Is Your Daughter's School Prepping Her for Failure?" April 1993, p. 40.

44. David Jordan, "A Fond Farewell and a New Beginning," July 1993, p. 12.

45. See Meredith Corp., 1993 Annual Report.

46. Some special-interest publications have circulations in the hundreds of thousands. For example, 500,000 of the *Holiday Appetizers* special publication were printed and available for sale in 1993.

47. David Jordan, "Happy Birthday to Us," July 1987, p. 10.

Information Sources

BIBLIOGRAPHY:

Bencivenga, Dan. "Better Homes Launches Videos with Aggressive Campaign." *Target Marketing*, March 1988, pp. 23–24.

Cunneff, Tom. "Video Better Homes and Gardens—Refinishing Furniture." *People Weekly*, November 7, 1988, pp. 28–29.

Donaton, Scott. "Meredith Eyes Cable." *Advertising Age*, October 18, 1993, p. 52.

Edwin T. Meredith: A Memorial Volume. Des Moines, Iowa: Meredith, 1931.

Mott, Frank L. *A History of American Magazines*, vol. 5. Cambridge: Belknap Press of
    Harvard University Press, 1968.
Peterson, Theodore. *Magazines in the Twentieth Century*. Urbana: University of Illinois
    Press, 1964.
Reuss, Carol. "*Better Homes and Gardens* and Its Editors: An Historical Study from the
    Magazine's Founding to 1970." Diss., University of Iowa, 1971.
————. "*Better Homes and Gardens*: Consistent Concern Key to Long Life." *Journal-
    ism Quarterly* 51:2 (Summer 1974), pp. 292–296.
Walley, Wayne. "Home-Improvement TV Fights Build."*Advertising Age*, June 5, 1989,
    p. 37.
INDEX SOURCES: Cumulative Index to Nursing and Allied Health Literature; Health
    Index; Index to How to Do It Information; Junior High Magazine Abstracts;
    MELSA Messenger; Popular Magazine Review; Readers' Guide to Periodical
    Literature; Text on Microfilm.
LOCATION SOURCES: Library of Congress and many university and community li-
    braries.

Publication History

MAGAZINE TITLE AND TITLE CHANGES: *Fruit, Garden and Home* (1922–1924);
    Better Homes and Gardens (with and without ampersand) (1924–present).
VOLUME AND ISSUE DATA: Vols. 1– (July 1922–present). Monthly.
PUBLISHER AND PLACE OF PUBLICATION: E. T. Meredith (1922–1928); Meredith
    Publishing (1928–present). Des Moines, Iowa.
EDITORS: Chesla Sherlock (1922–1927); Elmer T. Peterson (1927–1937); Frank W.
    McDonough (1938–1950); J. E. Ratner (1950–1952); Hugh Curtis (1952–1960);
    Bert Dieter (1960–1967); James A. Riggs (1967–1970); James Autry (1970–
    1979); Gordon Greer (1979–1983); David Jordan (1984–1993); Jean LemMon
    (1993–present).
CIRCULATION: ABC, 1992: 8,002,585 (paid, primarily subscriptions).

Kathleen L. Endres

BLACK ELEGANCE

Black Elegance debuted in 1986, ready to challenge *Essence** magazine, the
long-dominant magazine in the African American women's publication niche.
Both are lifestyle magazines that offer a similar editorial fare: health, beauty,
fashion, and relationships. Nonetheless, *Black Elegance*'s former editor, Sharyn
Skeeter, insists that her product is different from *Essence.*

Skeeter emphasizes that *Black Elegance*'s audience is different, targeting the
career-oriented woman (age 25 to 44) who does not have much time to spend
reading magazines. "What *Black Elegance* does is have more pictures and photos than *Essence* because women [we serve] don't have time to sit down and
read a magazine. We have shorter and more concise articles and hope pictures
can tell the story."[1]

Not only is this an editorial strategy, but it also figures in the marketing of the magazine. The pictures of *Black Elegance* help sell the magazine on the newsstand and help differentiate it from *Essence*, the better-known and larger magazine.

Black Elegance's success, in large part, is due to Sharyn Skeeter. She was not the magazine's first editor, who was Dottie Watkins and who stayed with the magazine only about a year. Nor is Skeeter the current editor; former associate editor Sonia Alleyne replaced Skeeter in early 1994 because of "mutually agreeable situations."[2]

Yet, during her seven years with the magazine, Skeeter defined *Black Elegance*. She was a natural to do so, as she knew the competition well, having worked for *Essence* for four years. (Previously, she had been with *Mademoiselle*.*) She helped develop the graphic approach that has brought *Black Elegance* success, even though facing the formidable competition of *Essence*.

The presence of *Essence* never really daunted either Skeeter or *Black Elegance*'s publisher/founders Robert Tate and William Trammel. Tate and Trammel founded Starlog Telecommunications as a subsidiary of the Starlog Group specifically to launch *Black Elegance*.[3] After a shaky start as a beauty and fashion magazine, *Black Elegance* (under Skeeter) repositioned. Starting in 1989, it added lifestyles to its editorial mix.[4] Since then, the magazine has offered a blend of fashion, beauty, and lifestyles, often by reporting on celebrities. Many features spotlight celebrities modeling fashions, along with brief biographical sketches.

Black Elegance does not ignore men. The magazine carries a regular department highlighting male celebrities, entitled "Men in Fashion." Another department, "Man Talk," keeps readers up-to-date on what men are talking about. This issue-oriented section of the magazine gives the African American male a forum to present viewpoints on topics of interest to women.

The magazine, however, is not primarily the voice of men talking to women. The largest number of features deal with topics of importance to women, are without a male point of view, and are not male-written. The magazine carries such departments as "Health Beat," "Beauty Quest," and "Your Money's Worth."

Features often showcase the black presence in fashion. The magazine typically features emerging African American designers as well as Africa-influenced clothing. In a number of issues, *Black Elegance* has featured color photographs of clothing made from the highly colorful Kente-patterned material.

Such photographs most commonly show tall, slim women. However, the magazine is sensitive to the needs "of the spectrum of women" and notes that it caters to "petite, full-figured, average, tall and even pregnant women."[5] In one issue, an article explained figure-flattering swimwear for the larger woman.

Other features cater to the more affluent readers of *Black Elegance*. Travel articles often highlight exotic—and expensive—locations, such as luxurious vacations in the Caribbean.

Skeeter's editorials tended to deal with topics important to her readers, such as lifestyle, beauty, and health. In her commentary, Skeeter, a former instructor of black literature, often has a literary edge, and she often blends in African American poetry into her discussion. In the April 1994 issue of *Black Elegance*, for example, she speaks on the inherent ability of African American women to strengthen and renew others. Reflecting on the poem, "I Am a Black Woman," Skeeter suggests that black women put more emphasis on renewing themselves.

Black Elegance defines itself as a magazine for the "upscale woman."[6] Some advertisers clearly cater to that market. Two of the magazine's principal advertisers are Adriana Furs and McQuay Furs. The largest amount of advertising sells cosmetics. Many ads feature Africentric appeals. For example, "African Pride" by Shark Products offers a line of hairdressings made of herbs and natural ingredients. *Black Elegance* has more of an Africentric advertising stance than does *Essence*. The advertising in *Essence* features more white models; few white models are pictured in *Black Elegance*.

Skeeter insists that the African American woman's market is large enough to support more than one magazine. She notes that *Vogue,** *Elle,** and others compete within the same niche. Why not several African American magazines? "*Black Elegance* and *Essence* do not negate each other because we [African American women] are a very diverse people."[7]

Notes

1. Sharyn Skeeter interview, September 17, 1993.
2. Robert Tate interview, March 16, 1994.
3. Ibid.
4. Skeeter interview.
5. Media kit.
6. Ibid.
7. Skeeter interview.

Information Sources

BIBLIOGRAPHY:

Calvacca, Lorraine. "Black History Promotion Gets Results." *Folio: The Magazine for Magazine Management*. May 15, 1993, p. 18.
Carmody, Deirdre. "Black Magazines See Sales in Unity." *New York Times*, May 4, 1992, p. D9.
Haenlin, Joy L. "She's Being All That She Can Be." *Stamford Advocate*. May 22, 1987.
Posey, Lisa. "Black Elegance Celebrates 1st Year." *Los Angeles Sentinel*. October 22, 1987, p. C5.
Wynter, Leon E. "Business & Race: Joint Effort Lifts Black Magazines." *Wall Street Journal*, March 24, 1992, p. B1.

INDEX SOURCES: None.
LOCATION SOURCES: Library of Congress and other libraries.

Publication History

MAGAZINE TITLE AND TITLE CHANGES: *Black Elegance*.
VOLUME AND ISSUE DATA: Vols. 1– (June 1986–present). Monthly.

PUBLISHER AND PLACE OF PUBLICATION: Starlog Telecommmunications, Inc. New York.
EDITORS: Dottie Watkins (1986–1987); Sharyn Skeeter (1987–1994); Sonia Alleyne (1994–present).
CIRCULATION: SRDS: 1993: 315,107 (primarily single-copy sales).

Kimetris N. Baltrip

BON APPETIT

It is a long way between liquor store throwaway and number one in the epicurean magazine market. Nevertheless, that was the distance that *Bon Appetit* traveled. How the magazine went from a give-away promotional product to a slick monthly with a circulation in excess of a million and advertising revenue in the millions of dollars is a hard story to tell because its earliest history is murky.

The magazine was launched in 1956 as a bimonthly; its first issue was probably dated November/December of that year.[1] American Colortype of Chicago was the publisher.[2] After that, the magazine went through a succession of owners and moved from place to place with each sale. Between 1956 and 1970, *Bon Appetit* at one time or another called Chicago, San Francisco, Wichita (Kansas), and Kansas City (Missouri) home. The circulation during those years ranged between 190,000 and 250,000, with the readership at the lower end of that scale in the late 1960s.[3]

Things appeared to be turning around when Pillsbury purchased the magazine in 1970 and began a building process. During the five years that Pillsbury owned the magazine, the editorial product apparently improved.[4] By the time Pillsbury sold the magazine (in 1975), *Bon Appetit* was a chatty, small, down-to-earth bimonthly that covered food, wine, and some travel, all from a fairly provincial point of view. For example, the magazine covered the "Treasures of China," an exhibition at the Nelson Gallery in *Bon Appetit*'s hometown of Kansas City, with the following description:

> China is on the other side of the globe. Its ways and language are at times difficult to interpret even for the expert. But the time has come to reevaluate stereotypes which cloud China in a romantic image of mystery, or which treat its people, as so many units in an economic equation.[5]

Shortly after that piece appeared, the magazine was sold again, this time to Knapp Communications. According to newspaper stories at the time, Knapp paid $85,000 for the bimonthly and quickly announced plans to refocus the new property. First, Cleon "Bud" Knapp, owner of Knapp Communications, announced plans to shift from the bulk of the magazines being distributed via liquor retailers and convert "liquor-store freebie-getters into subscribers."[6] Second, he disclosed intentions to convert *Bon Appetit* to a monthly. Third, he announced that the editorial content of the magazine would change. As he explained, *Bon Appetit* under Knapp would be a magazine of good eating and drinking for a relatively affluent audience over 30 years of age. "Our editorial will be less esoteric than *Gourmet** and a little more creative than the tuna-fish-casserole type."[7]

Those plans were quickly put into place. By December 1975, the magazine was a monthly. Frank Jones stayed on briefly as editor but left once the magazine was moved to Los Angeles, where Knapp Communications's corporate headquarters was located. Taking Jones's place was Paige Rense, Knapp's top editor, who had transformed *Architectural Digest* from a small, specialized business publication to the top home magazine for the affluent. She soon worked her magic on *Bon Appetit.*

Rense transformed *Bon Appetit* into a how-to magazine for the upscale cook who lived a full life and was too busy to shop all around town for the obscure ingredients often featured in *Gourmet* magazine's recipes. Or, as Rense explained, "I think that food is love . . . and I think we should make love easy."[8] She made food not only easy in *Bon Appetit* but also graphically appealing and fun.

Rense transferred many of the techniques that had worked so well in *Architectural Digest* to the new acquisition. In *Architectural Digest,* readers loved to see the homes of celebrities. Rense soon had celebrities cooking for readers and sharing their favorite recipes. Comedian Phyllis Diller, singer Dionne Warwick, acting couple Natalie Wood and Robert Wagner, and actor Ed Asner were just a few of the celebrities who welcomed *Bon Appetit* into their kitchens.[9]

At *Architectural Digest,* Rense had discovered the importance of a strong graphics package with striking photographs. She transformed *Bon Appetit* into a delight to the senses. The tantalizing four-color photographs of food enticed the reader to experiment with the recipes.

Those experiments usually resulted in easy-to-make, economical, healthy foods. Early on, *Bon Appetit* under Rense's leadership recognized that women were busy and did not have much time to cook. Soon the magazine began offering the still popular columns "Too Busy to Cook" and "All about Quick Microwave Cooking!" Convenience, however, did not necessarily have to be expensive. Many of the features emphasized the economical aspect of the recipes: "Affordable Veal: How to Buy, How to Cook—Sensational Recipes!" "Dinner for Eight for under $40," and "Superstar Hamburgers."[10] Easy-to-cook, economical dinners also could be healthy. *Bon Appetit* emphasized low calorie dinners early, offering a range of recipes designed to help readers lose weight: "Diet Secrets from the Experts," "Food Writer's Diet," and "Fabulous Diet Recipes."[11] Those lessons were not lost on the two editors who followed Rense: Marilou Vaughan and William J. Garry. Under these editors, the magazine highlighted convenient, economical, and healthy foods. That type of coverage helped differentiate *Bon Appetit* from *Gourmet,* its principal competition.[12]

The features in *Bon Appetit* were often written in a casual, first-person style, often blending humor into the recipe stories. As Jan Weimer wrote about tossing pizza,

> Whenever I try to pitch a baseball, it drops on my toe. The one time I sailed a Frisbee, it nearly decapitated my brother's mother in law. I have never been able to hurl a ring toss or even throw a bone to my dog.[13]

The magazine also changed in advertising content. Under Pillsbury, the bimonthly *Bon Appetit* was short on advertising. Under Knapp with its established network of advertising reps who also represented the eminently successful *Architectural Digest*, the amount of advertising (particularly for upscale products) substantially improved quickly. Just three months after the acquisition, Knapp reported that the number of advertising pages was up 45 percent.[14] But that was just the beginning. *Bon Appetit* was aimed at an audience with a higher than average income, as opposed to *Gourmet*'s high-end demographics. That meant that *Bon Appetit* drew not only advertisers for fine wines, expensive liquor, good food, and expensive cars (many of whom were already advertising in *Architectural Digest*) but also advertisers for the less expensive, less exotic food products like Bacon Bits, Uncle Ben's rice, and mayonnaise.

The amount of advertising increased substantially as *Bon Appetit*'s circulation grew. By 1979, *Bon Appetit* had overtaken *Gourmet* in circulation.[15] In the 1980s and after, *Bon Appetit* had a circulation in excess of 1 million. Although by this time *Bon Appetit* was nationally known and financially successful, the magazine never stopped evolving.

In 1986, under William J. Garry, *Bon Appetit*'s front cover was redesigned. No longer would the four-color photo of tantalizing food be bound by borders; it would bleed. It seemed that the front cover could not hold the food, that it spilled off the page. The next year, the inside of the magazine was redesigned to make it easier to read and follow. That same design increased the "editorial well" from 44 to 50 percent of each issue.[16] That additional editorial space was needed because the magazine was venturing into new areas. Travel and entertainment had always had a place in *Bon Appetit*; however, in the late 1980s, the magazine increased substantially its coverage of those topics. *Bon Appetit* traveled to Paris for the great hotel restaurants and Baden, Germany, for its "culinary paradises."[17] Soon the magazine offered "Special Collector's" editions. In 1990, it was the best of Italy, followed by Paris in 1991 and Spain in 1993.

In 1991, the redesign continued. *Bon Appetit* converted to a "brighter," heavier, and better-quality paper stock to enhance the reproduction quality of the photographs. The cover stock was improved as well. Photographs leaped out at the reader; the four-color reproduction had improved substantially. But the changes were more than graphic. Stories became self-contained. There were no more jumps to the back of the magazine and the clutter of ads. New columns were added, and others were expanded, including "Cooking Healthy" and

"Diet Watch."[18] *Bon Appetit* looked more and more upscale, not only in its graphics but in its editorial content. The travel pieces, the new "Collecting the Best" column, and the entertainment stories suggested a shift to a slightly more affluent readership. Those changes, however, were not accompanied by a reduction in the number of readers. Since the late 1980s, *Bon Appetit*'s circulation has hovered around the 1.3 million mark.

In the late 1980s, *Bon Appetit*, like many of the other magazines in its niche, moved to further diversify its advertising base. Publisher George Dippy reported that while food remained *Bon Appetit*'s largest advertising category, automotive showed the largest growth, followed by travel and home furnishings.[19] Dippy and his sales representatives were successful in diversifying and enlarging *Bon Appetit*'s advertising base. In the 1990s, 200-page issues were not unknown.

In 1993, *Bon Appetit* was number one in its niche—and up for sale. After five months on the market, Knapp Communications was sold to Condé Nast. Details of the sale were never released, although insiders reported that Condé Nast paid $175 million in a largely cash deal, effectively outbidding K-III Communications, Cahners, Hearst, and Gruner + Jahr for the property.[20] In the sale, Condé Nast acquired both *Bon Appetit* and *Architectural Digest*. Bernard Leser, president of Condé Nast, said, "They [*Bon Appetit* and *Architectural Digest*] are two great magazines and they will fit beautifully with the ones we have."[21] The sale meant that Condé Nast owned the two largest magazines in the epicurean market: *Gourmet* and *Bon Appetit*. Industry insiders were soon speculating that the sale would benefit the two longtime competitors since the corporate advertising sales staff could sell the titles as a package with other Condé Nast magazines.[22]

So far, Condé Nast has not changed its new property much. *Bon Appetit* has a new publisher, J. Kevin Madden, but William J. Garry remains editor. *Bon Appetit* continues to be published in Los Angeles, although most Condé Nast magazines come out of editorial offices in New York. *Bon Appetit* is not expected to be moved soon, if at all, since the provisions of the sale commit Condé Nast to the rental of the Los Angeles offices.

In spite of the increased competition within the epicurean niche, *Bon Appetit*—with a successful editorial formula, graphic excellence, and now the corporate sales network of Condé Nast behind it—should be able to retain its number one position in the epicurean magazine niche.

Notes

1. Library records indicate that *Bon Appetit*'s first issue was November/December 1956. However, that information is followed by a question mark, indicating there is some doubt as to this information.

2. Irene Hansen provides the most complete information about *Bon Appetit*'s first years in her essay "Bon Appetit," in Alan Nourie and Barbara Nourie (eds.), *American Mass-Market Magazines* (Westport, Conn.: Greenwood Press, 1990), pp. 41–46.

3. Circulation in 1962 was 200,000, according to a publisher's report; 205,465 in

1964; 197,375 in 1966; and 191,001 in 1967. *N. W. Ayer & Son's Directory Newspapers and Periodicals* (Philadelphia: N. W. Ayer & Son), 1962, p. 122; 1964, p. 408; 1966, p. 590; 1967, p. 593.

4. This cannot be gauged precisely because issues prior to 1975 are difficult to locate.

5. Marc Wilson, "The Treasures of China," April/May 1975, p. 5.

6. "Architecture and Bon Appetit," *New York Times*, April 4, 1975, p. 51.

7. Ibid.

8. N. R. Kleinfield, "A Growing Appetite for Food Magazines," *New York Times*, July 1, 1980, p. B10.

9. Barbara Wilkins, "Phyllis Diller Cooks," June 1977, pp. 37–41; Joanne O'Donnell, "Dionne Warwick Glamorous Staging for Down-to-Earth Dinners!" February 1977, pp. 46–50; Barbara Wilkins, "Family Recipes for a Russian Dinner," October 1977, pp. 52–56; Barbara Wilkins, "Ed Asner out of the Newsroom, into the Kitchen," November 1977, pp. 56–59.

10. Rita Leinwand, June 1977, pp. 42–47; Richard Nelson, January 1982, p. 64; June 1979, pp. 58–62, 64.

11. Ruth Spear, January 1979, pp. 29–31; Lynne Kasper, January 1982, pp. 40–44, 46–48, 50, 93; Jane Helsel Joseph, January 1984, pp. 42–46, 50, 52.

12. Bill Katz and Linda Sternberg Katz emphasize that *Bon Appetit* is "more health conscious than Gourmet." *Magazines for Libraries* (New Providence, N.J.: R. R. Bowker, 1992), p. 526; Kleinfield, "A Growing Appetite for Food Magazines," p. B10.

13. Jan Weimer, "Best Pizza Ever!" March 1982, p. 74.

14. "Bon Appetit to Be Monthly," *New York Times*, September 16, 1975, p. 63.

15. In 1979, *Ayer* reported *Bon Appetit* had a circulation of 894,171, compared with *Gourmet*'s 665,122. *Ayer Directory Newspapers, Magazines and Trade Publications* (Philadelphia: Ayer Press, 1979), pp. 154, 603.

16. Amy Alson, "Recipes for Growth," *Marketing & Media Decisions*, November 1988, p. 49.

17. "The Grand Hotel Restaurants of Paris," March 1987, pp. 106–110; John Dornberg, "Baden—Germany's Culinary Paradise," June 1987, p. 116.

18. William J. Garry, "The Best Recipe," March 1991, p. 14.

19. Alson, "Recipes for Growth," p. 49.

20. Deirdre Carmody, "Food and Design Magazines Are Bought by Condé Nast," *New York Times*, March 3, 1993, pp. D1, 17.

21. Ibid.

22. Scott Donaton, "Condé Nast Paying Premium for Knapp," *Advertising Age*, March 8, 1993, pp. 1, 44.

Information Sources

BIBLIOGRAPHY:

Adelson, Andrea. "Knapp Communications Is for Sale." *New York Times,* November 24, 1992, p. D17.

Alson, Amy. "Recipes for Growth." *Marketing & Media Decisions,* November 1988, pp. 48–50.

"Bon Appetit." *New York Times*, April 4, 1975, p. 51.

"Bon Appetit to Be Monthly." *New York Times*, September 16, 1975, p. 63.

Carmody, Deirdre. "Food and Design Magazines Are Bought by Condé Nast." *New York Times*, March 3, 1993, pp. D1, D17.

Donaton, Scott. "Condé Nast Paying Premium for Knapp." *Advertising Age*, March 8, 1993, pp. 1, 44.

Green, Michelle. "Tipping the Scales." *Washington Journalism Review*, May 1983, p. 38.

Hansen, Irene. "Bon Appetit." In Alan Nourie and Barbara Nourie (eds.), *American Mass-Market Magazines*. Westport, Conn.: Greenwood Press, 1990, pp. 41–46.

Katz, Bill, and Linda Sternberg Katz. *Magazines for Libraries*. New Providence, N.J.: R. R. Bowker, 1992.

Kleinfield, N. R. "A Growing Appetite for Food Magazines." *New York Times*, July 1, 1980, p. B10.

Powell, Joanne. "Paige Rense, Editor in Chief of *Architectural Digest, Bon Appetit* & *GEO*." *Washington Journalism Review*, May 1983, pp. 36–41.

INDEX SOURCES: Access; Canadian Magazine Index; Popular Magazine Review.

LOCATION SOURCES: Library of Congress and many other libraries.

Publication History

MAGAZINE TITLE AND TITLE CHANGES: *Bon Appetit.*

VOLUME AND ISSUE DATA: Vols. 1–(November/December 1956–present). Bimonthly (1956–1975); monthly (1975–present).

PUBLISHER AND PLACE OF PUBLICATION: American Colortype Co. (1956–1959); Home Publications Inc. (1959–1961); Beverage News Inc. (1962–1964); Billett Publishing Co. (1964); Financial Publications (1964–1970); Bon Appetit Division of Pillsbury (1970–1975); Knapp Communications (1975–1993); Condé Nast (1993–present). Chicago (1956–1959); San Francisco (1959–1961); San Francisco and Wichita, Kans. (1962–1964); Wichita, Kans. (1964); Kansas City, Mo. (1964–1975); Kansas City, Mo. and Los Angeles (1975–present).

EDITORS: James A. Shanahan (1956–1961); Alan Shearer (1961–1962); Charles Walters (1962–1963); Betty Paige (1963–1964); W. C. Carreras (1964); Floyd Sageser (1964–1965); M. Frank Jones (1965–1976); Paige Rense (1976–1983); Marilou Vaughan (1983–1985); William J. Garry (1985–present).

CIRCULATION: ABC, 1993: 1,294,945 (paid, primarily subscriptions).

Kathleen L. Endres

BRIDE'S & YOUR NEW HOME

Not many magazines can claim a place in the *Guinness Book of World Records,* but *Bride's & Your New Home* has found its way into the record book not once but twice. Each time, *Bride's* set records for the largest magazine ever published. The February/March 1990 issue reached 1,030 pages. The next year's February/ March issue was even larger, thereby achieving yet another record. Those records were made possible by American wedding traditions; no matter what the economic climate, couples get married, and they (or their parents) spend a good deal of money in the process. That fact has not been lost on America's advertisers. Huge amounts of advertising explain *Bride's* colossal size.[1] However,

Bride's continuing popularity with readers hinges on its ability to reflect changing customs and expectations about marriage and weddings.

The magazine was launched in 1934, after Wells Drorbaugh, advertising manager for *House & Garden*,* read a story in *Fortune* that observed that, even in bad economic times, couples still got married and purchased all kinds of products. Drorbaugh made a notation of that on the back of an envelope, and that started the planning for a magazine for brides. The problem, however, was distribution. Drorbaugh solved that with a limited launch and sending his new magazine, then called *So You're Going to Be Married*, to women whose engagements were listed in society pages. The magazine was initially distributed only in New York, New Jersey, and Connecticut. A few years later, the quarterly went national and soon had a different name, *The Bride's Magazine*.[2] That initial distribution method greatly affected the magazine and its development. From its beginning, the magazine was aimed at an upscale female audience, the type of woman whose betrothal would be announced in the society pages of newspapers. Today, *Bride's* continues to draw a relatively affluent, well-educated female readership.[3]

From its first issue in the autumn of 1934, the magazine was devoted to weddings, honeymoons, and marriage—all from a relatively affluent, traditional perspective. In the first issue, for example, "stylish furs were considered a trousseau necessity."[4] The bride was advised to consult her husband on household furnishings because "a man's judgment is better than a girl's."[5]

Agnes Foster Wright, the first editor in chief, explained the new periodical's editorial mission:

Most girls who get married hope and sincerely believe that this man they choose will be their husband for life. The wedding ceremony to them is more than a social function. We sincerely hope this magazine will be inviting and charming and gladden hearts already gladdened by that lovely thing called Love.[6]

This approach, apparently, struck a responsive chord. In both its limited and national launch, the magazine did well. By 1942, the magazine had a circulation of 140,000. However, the magazine still retained its "controlled"—free—distribution method.[7]

World War II illustrated how the magazine could change with the times. Although the targeted audience remained affluent young women, the magazine began incorporating war themes into its editorial material. Women were advised on how to give an elegant wedding and still maintain their patriotism:

Wear for a formal church or home wedding a gown that combines traditional bridal beauty with of-the-moment wartime streamlining—a gown that is lovely despite its planned-for-conservation, clean-cut silhouette, despite its patriotically shorter train that does not exceed two yards.[8]

The magazine also offered guidelines on how to arrange a wedding during a furlough, but it never forgot the new bride at home. The magazine even provided advice on handling domestic help.[9] The magazine also prepared wives for their postwar households when products would become more plentiful. Advertising followed suit. Home-related products from appliances to wallcoverings were advertised, as were cars, an acknowledgment, perhaps, of the wife's input into decisions on such products.[10]

After the war, the magazine continued to grow. After a brief circulation decline after the war (*Ayer's* reported a circulation of 100,000 in 1947), the magazine's circulation quickly increased to 151,033 in 1949 and 186,265 in 1950. Although *Ayer's* continued to report the circulation as controlled, the magazine was shifting to a paid circulation. In 1949, the magazine began to be sold on the newsstands. (Newsstand sales still represent the largest portion of the magazine's circulation.) The shift toward a paid circulation was complete by 1954, when 121,816 of the circulation was paid, and only 25,966 was sent out free. By 1956, *Bride's* ABC–audited circulation was completely paid (152,671).[11]

At the same time, *Bride's* was facing its first real competition. In 1949, as *Bride's* began its shift to a paid circulation, another bridal magazine premiered. *Modern Bride* was launched by Ziff-Davis Publishing Co. as a paid-circulation, nationally distributed quarterly. By the 1950s, the new magazine represented a real threat to *Bride's*. By 1956, the two magazines had virtually identical circulations.[12]

Whether because of this competitive situation or for some other reason, Wells Drorbaugh, still the principal stockholder of the magazine, sold his publishing company, Brides House Inc., to Condé Nast in 1959. Drorbaugh was no stranger to Condé Nast. He had been advertising director of *House & Garden*, one of Condé Nast's original publications, and had *Bride's* magazine printed at Condé Nast Press since 1950. At the time of purchase, no price was disclosed. However, under the terms of the sale, Drorbaugh remained chief executive officer of Brides House Inc. and became a director of Condé Nast.[13]

That sale brought the financial support of Condé Nast to *Bride's*. However, it did not assure that *Bride's* would retain its dominance in the field. Indeed, in the later 1970s and early 1980s, *Modern Bride* was the larger publication in terms of circulation. However, by 1982, *Bride's* had regained its dominance in the bridal publishing niche.

After Condé Nast acquired *Bride's*, no major changes on the editorial side occurred. Longtime editor Helen E. Murphy remained. The editorial thrust remained much the same. The magazine continued to offer its editorial mix of stories and advice on how to achieve the perfect wedding, how to make a husband happy, and how to have a happy home.[14] Changes, however, were occurring on the business side. The magazine was growing enormously in circulation. By 1966, the magazine reached a circulation of 251,758 (compared with *Modern Bride*'s 190,908). Responding to *Modern Bride*'s new bimonthly frequency cycle, *Bride's* shifted to the same frequency and even, briefly in the late 1960s and early 1970s, came out eight times a year. However, by 1974, the magazine fell back to the bimonthly cycle that it maintains today.

Editorially, the magazine seemed to have difficulty keeping up with the tumultuous social changes of the 1960s. In the early 1960s, women were urged to continue many of the behaviors associated with traditional marriages. Women were urged to adjust to the husband's shortcomings. "If you snore, roll over. If your husband snores, ignore it," advised one writer in 1964.[15] However, after Barbara Tober took over as editor in chief, the magazine began to come to terms with many of the challenges facing women in the 1960s and began carrying stories on the sexual revolution and birth control advertising.[16]

The continued social complexities of the 1970s forced *Bride's* to shift from its more "traditional coverage" of bridal fashions and home furnishings to stories about relationships, alternative weddings, and wedding fashions for both bride and groom.[17] However, that approach did little to ease *Bride's* position competitively with *Modern Bride*, which became the leader in terms of circulation.

The balance shifted back to *Bride's* in the early 1980s. The so-called me decade brought a return to "style" and "sophistication" in weddings, which became more expensive and required new products and services. Advertisers rushed to *Bride's* with their expensive lines of wedding gowns, cosmetics, jewelry, crystal, china, silver, and cigarettes. The magazine became more pertinent to 1980s realities. Stories dealt with prenuptial agreements, commuting marriages, and remarriage.[18] While the majority of the editorial content continued to focus on the first-time bride in her 20s, the magazine began carrying a separate section entitled "Marrying Later and Marrying Again."

The magazine in the 1990s, still under editor Barbara Tober, remains successful; in 1990, it was the largest consumer magazine published in the country.[19] In spite of that enormous success, Condé Nast decided to experiment with the editorial formula of *Bride's* and changed the magazine's name. Effective with the December 1991/January 1992 issue, the phrase "& Your New Home" was added to the familiar *Bride's* logotype. Condé Nast called it a natural transition. The news release announcing the change explained, "The strategic change targets an area of growing interest to newlywed couples—the establishment of their new homes—and offers more of the information they seek during the period between engagement and first anniversary." Editor Tober called it a "logical evolution."[20] Publisher Elliot Marion called it an appropriate move "as we enter the '90s, an era that foresees an even greater emphasis on the home." Scott Donaton of *Advertising Age* saw it as a reaction to the growing competition in the bridal market, an appraisal that publisher Marion denied. Nonetheless, Donaton explained that the move should allow the magazine to sell more subscriptions, even as single-copy newsstand sales were suffering industrywide. It would also make the magazine more attractive to home-oriented advertisers.[21]

Although the redesign, which brought separate covers and tables of contents to each of the three major sections—"For the Wedding," "Honeymoon, Travel," and "Home/Marriage"—has been in place for some time, the extent of the increase of home-oriented advertising has been modest, as has the number of subscriptions sold. *Bride's* continues to rely primarily on single-copy newsstand sales and an advertising base centered around the wedding/honeymoon market. The magazine remains the largest publication in the increasingly crowded bridal niche. It remains to be seen if the magazine can retain its dominance. *Modern Bride,* now owned by Cahners Publishing Co., ranks as the fourth largest consumer magazine in the nation (*Bride's* is number one); and in 1992, the Cahners property boasted a circulation larger than *Bride's*. But the bridal niche is no longer a two-magazine market. Globe Communications's *Bridal Guide* and Pace Communications's *Elegant Bride*, as well as many smaller, often geographically specialized periodicals, are complicating the picture. Publishers have discovered what Wells Drorbaugh found during the depression: couples marry even in the worst economic times, and this audience represents a lucrative market for advertisers.

Notes

1. In the late 1980s and early 1990s, almost every issue of *Bride's* exceeded 500 pages.

2. The exact date when the magazine went national is unclear. Theodore Peterson says it was five years after the launch, but *Bride's* magazine notes this occurred in 1936. Theodore Peterson, *Magazines in the Twentieth Century* (Urbana: University of Illinois Press, 1964), pp. 262–263; "In Our Honor," August/September 1984, p. 84; Barbara Tober, *The Bride: A Celebration* (Stamford, Conn.: Longmeadow Press, 1992), p. 160.

3. The magazine estimates that its "dual-career couple" makes $48,600, about 30 percent more than the average U.S. household. See "The Bride's Dual-Career Couple," based on 1993 MRI Primary Reader Study, Media Kit.

4. "Then & Now," August/September 1994, p. 58.

5. "Their Pink House," Autumn 1934, as reprinted in "Then & Now," p. 58.

6. As reprinted in "Then & Now," p. 58.

7. *N. W. Ayer & Son's Directory Newspapers and Periodicals* (Philadelphia: N. W. Ayer & Son, 1942), p. 648.

8. "Army Bride," Autumn 1943, as reprinted in "Then & Now," p. 58.

9. "How to Get Along with Your Maid," Summer 1944, as reprinted in "Then & Now," p. 58.

10. "60 Years of Authority," promotional brochure, 1994, p. 2.

11. "In Our Honor," p. 84; *N. W. Ayer & Son's Directory Newspapers and Periodicals* (Philadelphia: N. W. Ayer & Son, 1947), p. 646; 1949, p. 662; 1950, p. 658; 1954, p. 672; 1956, p. 689.

12. *N. W. Ayer & Son's Directory Newspapers and Periodicals* (Philadelphia: N. W. Ayer & Son, 1956), pp. 689, 715.

13. "Publication Sale," *New York Times,* January 5, 1959, p. 46; "Directors Exchanged," *New York Times*, January 22, 1959, p. 51.

14. "60 Years of Authority," p. 3.

15. An Elementary Course in Bediquette," Winter 1964, as reprinted in "Then & Now," p. 58.

16. "60 Years of Authority," p. 4.

17. "Focus on Brides," Fall 1994, Media Kit, p. 2.

18. "Prenuptial Agreements," February/March 1988, p. 384; Kathy Millins, "Long Distance Love," February/March 1989, p. 236; Diane Galusha, "When Mothers Marry," February/March 1989, p. 48.

19. *Modern Bride* was ranked number four. Matthew Schifrin, "The Newlywed Game," *Forbes*, September 2, 1991, p. 85.

20. "Bride's Magazine Is Renamed Bride's & Your New Home," news release, undated.

21. Scott Donaton, "Altar-ations Ahead," *Advertising Age*, September 30, 1991, p. 43.

Information Sources

BIBLIOGRAPHY:

"Directors Exchanged." *New York Times*, January 22, 1959, p. 51.

Donaton, Scott. "Altar-ations Ahead." *Advertising Age*, September 30, 1991, p. 43.

Peterson, Theodore. *Magazines in the Twentieth Century.* Urbana: University of Illinois Press, 1964.

"Publication Sale." *New York Times.* January 5, 1959, p. 46.

Schifrin, Matthew. "The Newlywed Game." *Forbes*, September 2, 1991, pp. 85–86.

Tober, Barbara. *The Bride: A Celebration.* Stamford, CT: Longmeadow Press, 1992.

INDEX SOURCES: Popular Magazine Review.

LOCATION SOURCES: New York Public Library; Library of Congress; and other (primarily community) libraries.

Publication History

MAGAZINE TITLE AND TITLE CHANGES: *So You're Going to Be Married* (1934–1938?); *The Bride's Magazine* (1939?–1964); *Bride's* (1964–1991); *Bride's & Your New Home* (1991–present).

VOLUME AND ISSUE DATA: Vols. 1–(Autumn 1934–present). Quarterly (1934–64); bimonthly (1964–1968?); eight times a year (1969?–1973?); bimonthly (1974?–present).

PUBLISHER AND PLACE OF PUBLICATION: Bride's House Inc. (1934–1959); Condé Nast (1959–present). New York.

EDITORS: (incomplete) Agnes Foster Wright; Marian E. Murtfeldt; Helen E. Murphy; Mallen De Santis; Barbara Marco; Barbara Donovan; Robert M. Thorsen; Barbara D. Tober.

CIRCULATION: ABC, 1992: 305,010 (paid, primarily single-copy sales).

Kathleen L. Endres

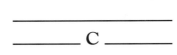

COOKING LIGHT

Cooking Light is more than just a magazine. It is a way of life, and that is precisely what the magazine's founders intended when they launched *Cooking Light: The Magazine of Food and Fitness* in March 1987. They wanted to give readers a "recipe for living," whose key ingredients were sound nutrition and exercise. Most important, they wanted the recipe to taste good. If people had to choke down a healthy lifestyle, the founders surmised, they would not stick with it for very long.[1]

Cooking Light was the offspring of *Southern Living,** a nationally circulated lifestyle magazine with a regional flavor. Both magazines are owned by Southern Progress Corporation of Birmingham, Alabama, which also publishes *Progressive Farmer*, as well as several other titles. In the early 1980s, *Southern Living* featured a column called "Cooking Light," which generated such a positive reader response that the magazine hired its first registered dietitian to develop the kind of low-calorie, nutritious recipes that readers were demanding.

As the popularity of the column grew, Oxmoor House, Southern Progress Corporation's book publishing company, saw the potential for expanding the feature into a cookbook. Katherine Eakin, food editor at Oxmoor House, was assigned to coordinate the project with Susan McIntosh, who was then a *Southern Living* registered dietitian and food editor. The single-title *Cooking Light Cookbook* came out to rave reviews in 1983. It was chosen runner-up for cookbook excellence in the 1984 Taste Maker Awards.

Given the success of this single title, Oxmoor House began making plans for a new annual cookbook. Early in the development stage, the company recognized that to sustain reader interest, an annual "light" cookbook would have to offer more than just nutritious recipes; it would have to offer a way of life. "The Food & Fitness Connection," together with healthy, nutritionally analyzed recipes, became the foundation for the annual *Cooking Light Cookbook*. Under Eakin's editorship, the first edition was successfully direct-marketed in 1986.

Readers loved the annual cookbook. The combination of good-tasting, good-for-you recipes and health and fitness information resonated demand for more of the same, and Southern Progress listened. In early 1986, a prototype magazine was successfully tested on the newsstand. In the summer of 1986, the company put together a team of people from existing staffs at Southern Progress to flesh out a concept for a new magazine to be called *Cooking Light*. Eakin, along with Jean Liles, Martha Johnston, and John Floyd, made up the editorial staff, and Don Logan, then president of Southern Progress, filled the publisher's seat.[2] In January 1987, Eakin was named editor of the magazine. In March 1987, the first bimonthly issue of *Cooking Light* premiered on newsstands and was sent to about 250,000 subscribers who had responded to a direct mail promotion.[3]

In the first issue of *Cooking Light*, readers received much of what they still receive today: dozens of satisfying, nutritious recipes presented in a clean format with enticing photos, along with a generous dose of health and fitness information. In one of her monthly columns, Eakin noted, "Our goal was to publish a magazine filled with accurate, useful information to help our readers achieve a healthier lifestyle."[4] The first issue taught readers how to season with herbs, create light, luscious desserts, and stir-fry. It offered recipes on everything from pizza, to pork, salads, and cookies. The magazine also had one main article on exercise.

From the beginning, departments have played a central role in the content of *Cooking Light*. The first issue included nine departments and a recipe index. Short pieces on health and fitness were incorporated into "Heartbeat"; short takes on food topics were presented in "Food for Thought." "Taking Aim" offered one person's story about setting a fitness goal and sticking with it, and "Downfall" offered one person's humorous struggle with a food habit. Readers also could learn how to cook "For Two" and get tips on technique in "What's Cooking." The issue also included a question-and-answer department called "Ask Us" and a department on the latest food and health-related books.[5]

The magazine's style was, and still is, direct and conversational. It presented information in a no-nonsense way; most of the articles and departments were relatively short. Food articles wasted little time getting to the recipes, which are the heart of the magazine. Since the start of *Cooking Light*, the magazine's recipes have been created and tested by a staff of professional home economists in 8 of the company's 24 test kitchens. All recipes that appear in the magazine meet dietary guidelines established by *Cooking Light*.

When the magazine was started, its home economists primarily relied on experience and the nutrient content of commercially available light foods to develop the magazine's guidelines. Initially, the magazine set rather strict fat and calorie standards for its recipes. In 1990, the magazine revised its standards to bring them in line with current recommended daily allowance (RDA) guidelines and to allow for more calories and a greater pecentage of fat in some foods, such as desserts. Still, most of the magazine's recipes derive 30 percent or fewer of their calories from fat. The magazine does not publish its standards but does provide a nutritional breakdown on each of its recipes. In every issue, the magazine also prints the recommended daily intake of fat, calories, and nutrients for women aged 23 to 50. Using these daily guidelines for reference, *Cooking Light* readers then can create menus that meet their daily nutritional needs.[6]

After the first year of publication, *Cooking Light* gained a solid foothold with its advertisers and its audience. The average size stood at 96 pages, and the magazine generated more than a half-million readers.[7] At this point Southern Progress president Don Logan decided it was time to hire a publisher. The job went to Jeffrey Ward, a 12-year veteran of Time Warner Inc.'s *People Weekly*. (Time Warner is the parent company of Southern Progress.) Ward says his experience at *People* gave him a solid background in packaged goods, which was just what *Cooking Light* needed to build on its advertising base.[8] Ward continues to serve as publisher today.

Early issues of the magazine derived much of their advertising from food companies, but they also included ads for related nonfood products such as kitchen appliances, fitness books, and equipment and diet programs like Weight Watchers. But as the magazine has matured, the balance of advertising has tilted away from food toward nonfood products, which now account for more than half of the magazine's advertising. "We are now carrying more automotive ads, more ads for household products, and we are working hard on the apparel category, and health and beauty," Ward says.[9] The shift in advertising may, in part, account for the growth in average size of each issue to about 150 pages.

But while the nature of *Cooking Light* advertising has changed, its editorial content has remained basically the same, one of the clearest indicators, Ward says, of the strength of the magazine's concept.[10] The magazine still runs most of its original departments. Over the years it has added several departments, most with an emphasis on food. In 1989, it created a department called "Kids' Fitness," which featured practical tips on getting children to exercise.

At the core of the *Cooking Light* editorial philosophy is the desire to get readers involved with the magazine. "Make It Light" solicits recipes from readers and then adapts them to *Cooking Light* nutritional standards; "Reader Recipes" features readers' favorite light recipes. The magazine also added a "Letters" department in the September 1993 issue to enhance reader involvement even more.[11]

Efforts to draw readers into the *Cooking Light* life clearly have paid off. A spring 1993 Mediamark Research Inc. study showed that *Cooking Light* ranked number one in reader involvement when compared with 24 other women's, health, epicurean, and beauty-fashion magazines. The study revealed that *Cooking Light* readers spent more time reading the magazine and used its recipes and ads more often than they did with any of the other magazines analyzed, which included *Bon Appetit,** *Gourmet,** *Food & Wine, Prevention,** *American Health,** and *Weight Watchers.**[12]

Ward considers the other epicurean magazines as the primary competition for *Cooking Light.* But among these other magazines, *Cooking Light* stands alone as the only publication geared toward a healthy lifestyle. At first glance, *Eating Well* appears to aspire to the same goal, but that magazine's focus is narrower and more intellectually oriented than that of *Cooking Light,* says Eakin. Ward describes the other epicurean magazines as "fantasy publications" that people read more for entertainment than for practical application. "This gives us an enormous opportunity to be the only hands-on book in the business," Ward says.[13]

The desire of the *Cooking Light* editorial team to make the magazine a practical and enticing tool for readers accounts, in large part, for its first major redesign in 1990. The January/February 1990 issue greeted readers with a bold new logo, a more detailed and compartmentalized table of contents, livelier typefaces throughout the magazine, and more photos and illustrations. The redesign dovetailed changes made to the magazine's format in 1989. Then, all fitness departments and articles were grouped at the front of the magazine; food departments and short articles about food were moved to the back of the book. The magazine's main articles remained sandwiched in the middle of the book. While the order of the food departments was not standardized, the move to group departments made it easier for readers to find stories of interest to them. After the redesign, *Cooking Light* also began using subtitles on all of its departments, which provided readers with another point of entry into the magazine's editorial content.

Providing readers with quick access to information is a central goal at *Cooking Light* and one the magazine has continued to refine. In the July/August 1993 issue, *Cooking Light* expanded its table of contents to two full pages so readers could get a more detailed description of the magazine's content. Then in May 1994, the magazine was redesigned once again, this time under the direction of a new editor, Doug Crichton, who replaced Eakin in December 1993.

The new design encompassed both cosmetic changes as well as the development of some new departments and a repackaging of older departments. The front-of-the-book section of short, health-related news items called "Heartbeat" is now called the "Well-Body Almanac." It features some new subdepartments and is written by professional writers instead of doctors to make the tone less didactic and more conversational. A collection of new departments called "Second Helpings" was added, which includes such subdepartments as "Quick Cuisine," "Globetrotters," and "Main Attractions." The magazine's format was cleaned up, and its look now is more slick, graphic, and colorful. The new design, Crichton says, does not reflect a change in philosophy, just a shift in the way the philosophy is expressed. "We're just trying to make the writing style more fun, and the magazine more clean and accessible."[14]

The effort at *Cooking Light* to create a publication that keeps pace with readers' interests has fueled growth of the magazine's circulation. The September 1994 Audit Bureau of Circulations report confirmed that *Cooking Light* had an average paid circulation of 1.2 million readers, more than four times the number of readers the magazine had at its outset. Ninety percent of the magazine's circulation comes from subscriptions; the rest is in single-copy sales.[15] Ward says that plans are under way to expand newsstand marketing of *Cooking Light*, particularly at supermarkets, to increase single-copy sales even more. "We're finding that newsstand sales are a great way to promote subscriptions. Many of our readers start out by picking up *Cooking Light* on the newsstand."[16]

In addition to beefing up newsstand marketing, Southern Progress also plans to enhance the visibility of *Cooking Light* by increasing the number of issues published each year. Currently, the magazine comes out seven times a year— six regular bimonthly issues plus a holiday issue published in December. In 1994, an eighth issue was added. Ward predicts the magazine will be publishing ten issues a year by 1996.[17]

The popularity of *Cooking Light* magazine and the considerable expertise generated by the magazine's staff have spurred the creation of numerous ancillary products. Since the magazine's inception, Southern Progress has continued to publish the annual *Cooking Light Cookbook*, complete with fitness and nutrition information. The company now also offers several specialty cookbooks, including *The Low-Fat Way to Cook*, a cookbook for diabetics, and *The Healthy Heart Cookbook*. In addition, readers can subscribe to "binder continuities," which allow them to collect recipe cards in three-ring-binder cookbooks, and order a videotape on holiday entertaining. *Cooking Light* also is beginning to branch into special interest publications. In 1994, it published its first two, *Desserts without Guilt* and *Kathy Smith's in Shape for Summer.*[18]

The success of *Cooking Light* magazine can be measured in numerous ways, like its ever-expanding number of readers and advertisers and the growth of its ancillary products. But perhaps the most meaningful indicator is the profound impact the magazine has had on the people who read it. Before *Cooking Light* came along, Eakin says, "you had people who exercised long and hard, and people who dieted strenuously, but not a lot of people who combined diet and exercise." *Cooking Light* supplies its readers with the knowledge they need to do both, and it emphasizes moderation, not fanaticism, and moderation is the most practical means to a healthy end, says Eakin. "We've taken a positive approach to what people can do, the small changes people can make to improve their lives."[19]

Notes

1. Katherine Eakin interview, editor of *Cooking Light*, July 22, 1993.
2. Ibid.
3. Allen Vaughan interview, director of database marketing for Southern Progress Corp., August 2, 1993.
4. K. Eakin, "About Us," February/March 1988, p. 4.

5. Contents, March/April 1987, p. 3.
6. Mary Creel interview, food editor of *Cooking Light*, October 6, 1993.
7. Jeffrey Ward interview, publisher of *Cooking Light*, July 22, 1993.
8. Ward interview.
9. Ibid.
10. Ibid.
11. Eakin interview.
12. "When It Comes to Page Exposure, *Cooking Light* Outshines the Competition," Cooking Light Media Kit, 1993.
13. Ward and Eakin interviews.
14. Doug Crichton interview, editor of *Cooking Light*, June 15, 1994.
15. Magazine Publisher's Statement, *Cooking Light* (for six months ending December 31, 1992).
16. Ward interview.
17. Ibid.
18. Ibid.
19. Eakin interview.

Information Sources

BIBLIOGRAPHY:
Kissling, Mark (ed.). *1993 Writer's Market*. Cincinnati: Writer's Digest Books.
1993 Consumer Magazine and Agri-Media Rates and Data. Wilmette, Ill.: Standard Rate and Data Service, June 1992.
INDEX SOURCES: None.
LOCATION SOURCES: Library of Congress and other libraries.

Publication History

MAGAZINE TITLE AND TITLE CHANGES: *Cooking Light: The Magazine of Food and Fitness*.
VOLUME AND ISSUE DATA: Vols. 1–(March/April 1987–present). Bimonthly plus one holiday issue (1987–1993); eight times a year (1994–present).
PUBLISHER AND PLACE OF PUBLICATION: Southern Progress Corp. (1987–present). Birmingham, Ala.
EDITORS: Katherine M. Eakin (1987–1993); Doug Crichton (1993–present).
CIRCULATION: ABC, 1992: 1,025,555 (paid; 903,753 subscriptions, 121,758 single-copy sales).

Carol E. Holstead

COSMOPOLITAN

For most of its life, *Cosmopolitan* was a rather staid, family-oriented magazine—a sharp contrast to the brash, sexy remake launched in 1965. The original magazine of 1886 was described by one historian as a "clergyman's child . . . conservative and domestic."[1] The publisher promised

a first-class family magazine . . . with articles on fashions, on household
decoration, on cooking, and the care and management of children, etc.;
also a department . . . for the younger members of the family.[2]

But the bulk of the magazine was devoted to translations of European literature,
travel sketches, and full-page reproductions of recent paintings. Although the
publishers claimed a monthly circulation of 25,000 copies by the second year,
Cosmopolitan had difficulty securing the advertising needed to make the magazine pay, even after cutting subscription rates in half (to two dollars, or 20¢ a
copy, low for the time) and expanding from 64 to 80 pages in an effort to boost
circulation.

Cosmopolitan went through two changes of ownership in 1888, as successive
publishers failed. It was briefly published by Joseph Newton Hallock, publisher
of *Christian at Work*, who introduced serialized fiction and book reviews to the
magazine. By the end of the year, circulation was down to 20,000 copies, and
the magazine was on the verge of closing. In 1889, Hallock sold *Cosmopolitan*
to John Brisben Walker, who served as its editor and publisher for the next 16
years, before selling the magazine to William Randolph Hearst for an estimated
$400,000. The Hearst Corporation has owned the magazine ever since.

Under Walker's management, *Cosmopolitan* expanded its circulation to
400,000. In an effort to strengthen *Cosmopolitan*'s literary prestige, Walker
briefly engaged novelist William Dean Howells as coeditor in 1892, but the two
quickly clashed. By the end of 1892, *Cosmopolitan* was one of the country's
leading illustrated magazines, featuring 144 pages of poems, short stories, travelogues, and essays on public affairs, industry, and literature. It was illustrated
with halftones and woodcuts throughout the magazine and continued to publish
art reproductions at the back of the magazine. Walker built circulation through
relentless promotion and increased subscription rates to $3 and advertising rates
from $60 to $200 a page.[3]

Cosmopolitan reached profitability in 1892, competing with other moderate-
circulation, quality magazines until Walker slashed the cover price to 12.5¢ in
July 1893. Two years later *Cosmopolitan* joined *McClure's* and *Munsey's* at
10¢, after experimenting with a 15¢ price. Although *McClure's* appeared on
newsstands first, Walker claimed he had originated the idea of the low-priced
magazine but had been betrayed by a printer who leaked his plans:

> *The Cosmopolitan* inaugurated the low-priced magazine . . . demonstrating
> to the world that a magazine of the highest quality could be made at this
> low figure. . . . It marked a step in the world's progress only second in
> importance to the public-school system. . . .
>
> To-day in even the humblest home you find at least one magazine. . . .
> In the leisure hour, when, worn out with the day's work, the woman or
> man seeks a comfortable chair, the almost invariable companion is the
> magazine.

Magazine fiction soothed the tired mind, while educational articles taught the duties of life and informed readers of the latest scientific discoveries.

> Calculate for a moment the instruction conveyed by the million magazines sent each month into the homes of America. . . . Every member of the household is rested, refreshed or advanced by one thing or another which these books of pleasure and instruction carry into the home circle.[4]

Walker's *Cosmopolitan* embodied these ideals. The November 1895 issue, for example, carried articles on the German empire, developments in mass transit, criminology, science, and letters, together with an article by New York City Board of Police Commissioners president Theodore Roosevelt on his efforts to reform the New York City police and extensive fiction, poetry, and eight pages of "Examples of Recent Art." The title page bore the magazine's motto: "From every man according to his ability; to every one according to his need."[5] Under Walker's editorship, *Cosmopolitan* was an educational and reform magazine, though hardly a crusading one. The magazine took its educational mission quite literally at times, as in its effort to establish a correspondence school, Cosmopolitan University.

As a reformer, Walker was greatly concerned with growing inequality. He admired the national corporations and trusts that were then emerging for their productive capacities and ran admiring profiles on captains of industry. But he feared the enormous power being concentrated in their hands and hoped it would be used to assure a more just division of social wealth.[6]

With Hearst's unannounced takeover of the magazine, the content quickly shifted to a more sensational focus on celebrities, muckraking, and fiction—not necessarily in that order. Hearst's editors boasted of circulation gains and increased editorial quality in a new column, "Magazine Shop-Talk." "The readers of the new Cosmopolitan are finding this earth a very pleasant planet" because of its humorous features and fiction:

> Then too we are going to print articles about social and economic affairs such as a people, stirred to revolt by existing conditions, will eagerly peruse and think over and talk about.[7]

While such articles were a relatively small part of the editorial mix, *Cosmopolitan*'s "Treason in the Senate" led President Theodore Roosevelt to coin the term "muckraking" in 1906. David Graham Phillips's vitriolic, thinly documented series drew new readers but also helped discredit muckraking. Roosevelt said the articles included "so much more falsehood than truth that they give no accurate guide for those who are really anxious to war against corruption," while fellow muckraker Mark Sullivan said Phillips "substituted tawdry literary epithets" for facts. But these and other muckraking articles, such as Edwin

Markham's carefully documented attack on child labor, drew public attention, built circulation, and, in some cases, led to corrective legislation.[8]

Such articles ran side by side with romantic fiction, travelogues, human interest stories, and a series of articles defending Christian Science.[9] While it aimed for a broad audience, the Hearst organization explicitly targeted the magazine to women readers:

> Some idea of what we have been preparing to interest our feminine readers will be gained by looking over this magazine. . . . We are well aware of the fact that a purely man's magazine is not what is wanted in this day and generation, and if the women are not interested in what we have been printing and are now getting up for them, then we have studied feminine tastes in vain. . . . As for the men—well, we don't think they need to complain.[10]

Cosmopolitan was Hearst's first venture into consumer magazine publishing, and Hearst went through a rapid succession of editors while building circulation from the 450,000 copies reached in 1906 to the 1 million mark finally attained in 1914. *Cosmopolitan* abandoned muckraking in 1912, instead focusing on the mix of short stories and serialized novels that dominated the magazine's pages for the next 50 years; *Cosmopolitan* continued to carry nonfiction (largely devoted to film and stage celebrities but also serious topics) and poetry as well. Fiction took the place of muckraking in building circulation, and the magazine contracted for the total output of its chief contributors in order to maintain a steady stream of work by a dozen or so tested favorites. While the fiction often seems formulaic and tame by modern standards, Frank Luther Mott said that "the dominant subject in every number from 1912 until 1918 was sex—sex in society, sex in adventure, sex in mystery."[11]

Cosmopolitan was prosperous when Ray Long took over as editor in 1918. Long had edited *Red Book** for seven years before Hearst lured him to *Cosmopolitan* with a generous salary. Long abandoned the formula of relying on a few writers, instead presenting a variety of fictional offerings. Public affairs had largely been transferred to *Hearst's International*, the former *World To-day*, which Hearst bought in 1911 and later transformed into an entertainment magazine. The two magazines were consolidated in 1925 under the title of *Hearst's International and Cosmopolitan*, although *Cosmopolitan* was typographically dominant. The merger added 300,000 copies to *Cosmopolitan*'s circulation, and the first merged issue's cover boasted: "More novels, more stories, more features than any magazine in the world." Each number carried three or four serials, as many as a dozen short stories, and a half dozen short features. When Long resigned in 1931, after running afoul of Hearst for taking too much credit for the magazine's success, *Cosmopolitan* had a circulation of 1.7 million copies and was billing some $4 million a year in advertising.[12]

Harry Payne Burton, editor for the next 11 years, gradually shifted the editorial formula toward publishing a short novel, a novelette, a half-dozen short stories, and several nonfiction pieces in each issue. Some of this material was notable, including serialized novels by Sinclair Lewis and nonfiction articles by George Bernard Shaw and Albert Einstein and an article by president-elect Franklin Roosevelt. In the 1940s, *Cosmopolitan* moved to what it called a four-book magazine, including a novelette, several short stories, several nonfiction articles and short features, a "book-length novel," and a digest of current nonfiction books in 200 pages or more of editorial. The emphasis on fiction gradually declined in the 1950s (although remaining prominent), supplemented by picture essays and articles on fashion, popular psychology, travel, movies, and health.

Cosmopolitan responded to increasing costs and competition from television for advertising dollars by cutting its circulation in half between 1953 and 1955. Hearst slashed its promotional budget, stopped sending renewal notices to subscribers, and concentrated on newsstand distribution. In 1953, *Cosmopolitan* lost money on a circulation of nearly 2 million copies; by 1955, it was profitable with about a million. By the 1960s, *Cosmopolitan*'s circulation was almost entirely single-copy sales (today 76 percent of circulation is in single-copy sales), but the format had grown stale, and sales and advertising were both languishing.[13]

Cosmopolitan was reborn in July 1965, when Helen Gurley Brown became its first woman editor. The transformation was so complete that *Cosmopolitan* dedicated its November 1985 issue to a celebration of its twentieth anniversary, while largely ignoring its centenary the next year.[14] Brown was an advertising copywriter with no magazine experience when her 1962 *Sex and the Single Girl* became a best-seller. Brown's book was based on the premise that women should work hard to change themselves to interest men, a philosophy she later applied to *Cosmopolitan*. In 1964, Brown floated a prospectus for a magazine to be called *Femme*. When she was unable to find a backer, her publisher referred the idea to Hearst, which was already considering reorienting *Cosmopolitan* from housewives to younger career women. Hearst promptly offered Brown the editorship. Circulation began climbing almost immediately (from 740,000 when she took the reins to more than 2 million today), and she has edited the magazine ever since with an eye toward "working women—single girls or married girls who 'think single'—between the ages of eighteen and thirty-four and eager to get the most out of work or play."[15]

The new *Cosmopolitan*—and the image of the "Cosmopolitan girl" it promoted—has been controversial ever since. Where, in the 1950s, *Cosmopolitan* featured articles on helping husbands get ahead in their jobs,[16] it now addressed women as (career, social, sexual) actors in their own right. *Cosmopolitan* adopted racier cover photographs, titillating cutlines, an annual horoscope supplement, and material such as an April 1972 centerfold featuring a nude Burt Reynolds.[17] *People* magazine characterized its audience as "anxious, ambitious, man-hunting single women."[18]

Feminists have criticized *Cosmopolitan* and its many imitators for negative images that can erode women's self-esteem and criticized editor Brown for attaching little importance to issues of power raised by rape, incest, and sexual harassment. A "sexual profile" of *Cosmopolitan* readers published in the magazine, for example, relegated rape and incest statistics (24 percent of respondents reported having been victims of incest) to the final paragraph of a brief section titled "Pressures to Have Sex." Brown refuses to publish articles on sexual harassment, instead recalling a "dandy game" from her days as a secretary where male coworkers chased secretaries through the halls and forcibly removed their underpants.[19] There has been some pressure to change. *Cosmopolitan*'s advertising agency recently announced that the magazine would no longer call its readers "girls," instead describing itself as "the largest selling young women's magazine in the world." But "as long as I'm editor," Brown quickly responded, "there is always going to be a Cosmo girl, because I believe we can be *both* girls inside, and women. We can rise to different occasions."[20] Elsewhere, Brown described *Cosmopolitan* as "a feminist magazine. . . . A COSMO woman likes being a sex object as long as she is also the object of respect and appreciated for other attributes. . . . At our core we are still girlish and feminine."[21]

But for now the basic elements of the *Cosmopolitan* format remain in place. Every issue begins with a cover girl, invariably photographed by Francesco Scavullo. "We try to select the prettiest women in the world," Brown says, looking for "lots of hair, cleavage . . . and bare skin." Surrounding the photo are blurbs written by Brown's husband that promise readers sex, hope, and/or opportunities for self-improvement.[22] Inside are 200–350 pages featuring advertisements, short fiction, and a jumbled array of short articles on health, fashion, money, entertainment, relationships, and sex. More than half the magazine's pages are devoted to advertisements. Brown acknowledges that sex plays a considerable part in the magazine's appeal. "Our big challenge now is that everybody's sexy. . . . Whatever it is, the subject has been covered, from orgasm to incest. I used to have it all to myself. . . . We have to work very hard to be a step ahead of the pack."[23] The format is copied in 28 other editions published in 12 languages and distributed throughout the world, prompting the magazine to declare *Cosmopolitan* "a universal language." *Cosmopolitan* spun off the short-lived *Cosmo Living* in the 1980s and, in 1992, the annual *Cosmopolitan Life After College*. Hearst also distributes exercise videos, sportswear, paperback books (with Hearst's Avon subsidiary), and pop music compilations under the Cosmopolitan name.[24]

But *Cosmopolitan* admits that the world—or at least its readers—has changed somewhat from the days when Brown took the reins back in 1965. Its publisher, Seth Hoyt, describes the magazine as "a big sister . . . a support system" that helps its readers cope with personal and professional challenges. *Cosmopolitan* has long described its target audience as women 18–34, and most readers fit the description. The magazine is the top-selling magazine in college bookstores but also reaches many older women reentering the job and dating marketplace after a divorce. Most readers (by a narrow margin) are single, and nearly three-fourths hold jobs. In 1992, *Cosmopolitan* led its competitors in total advertising pages (with 1,995.5) and in categories such as cosmetics, automotive, cigarettes, alcoholic beverages, and food products. But despite the upscale tone of many articles and advertisements, the typical reader is a young working woman, employed in low-paid clerical or service work.[25]

The 1965 changeover made a staid, conservative magazine mired in the 1950s sexy and sassy. Readers responded by buying it in droves, and *Cosmopolitan* came to stand for a new era in women's roles. But today the magazine is once again mired in the past, unable to address the issues of the day and unwilling to tamper with the formula that brought such success.

Notes

1. Algernon Tassin, *The Magazine in America* (New York: Dodd, Mead, 1916), p. 358.

2. Quoted from vol. 1, no. 1 by Frank Luther Mott, *History of American Magazines, 1885–1905* (Cambridge: Harvard University Press, 1957), p. 480.

3. Mott, *History of American Magazines, 1885–1905*, p. 484.

4. John Brisben Walker, "The Modern Magazine as an Educator," June 1905, unnumbered prefatory page.

5. This motto replaced the original publisher's motto, "The world is my country and all mankind are my countrymen." It was removed in 1905 when Hearst bought the magazine. Theodore Peterson, *Magazines in the Twentieth Century* (Urbana: University of Illinois Press, 1964), p. 213.

6. John Brisben Walker, "The World's Greatest Revolution," April 1901, pp. 677–680. Walker hoped that the monopolists would use their enormous power for social good. For articles addressing these issues, see, for example, the "Captains of Industry" series beginning May 1902; Richard Ely, "Public Control of Private Corporations," February 1901, pp. 430–433.

7. December 1905, unnumbered page.

8. Walter Brasch, *Forerunners of Revolution: Muckrakers and the American Social Conscience* (Lanham, Md.: University Press of America, 1990), pp. 96–98, 113.

9. Under Walker's control *Cosmopolitan* published an article by Mark Twain (October 1899) attacking Christian Science. Hearst's editors ran articles on the religion by church members in February, March, and May 1907, the last of which explicitly replied to Twain's earlier attack.

10. "Magazine Shop-Talk," April 1906, pp. 734–735.

11. Mott, *History of American Magazines, 1885–1905*, p. 497.

12. Ibid., p. 502.

13. Ibid., pp. 503–505; Peterson, *Magazines*, p. 215; Audit Bureau of Circulations Publisher's Statement for six months ending December 31, 1992, in Media Kit, 1993.

14. Stuart Elliott, " 'Cosmo' Celebrates 'That Girl's' 20th," *Advertising Age*, July 22, 1985, pp. 3, 57.

15. "Helen Gurley Brown," *Current Biography* (New York: McGraw-Hill, 1969), p. 58.

16. Special Section: "How to Live with Success," February 1958.

17. The centerfold was reprinted in the magazine's November 1985 "Giant Birthday Issue," celebrating Brown's 20th year as editor.

18. Quoted in Elliott, " 'Cosmo' Celebrates 'That Girl's' 20th," p. 57.

19. For a discussion of the *Cosmopolitan* "sexual profile" and the magazine's handling of sexual roles more generally, see Kathryn McMahon, "The *Cosmopolitan* Ideology and the Management of Desire," *Journal of Sex Research*, August 1990, pp. 381–396, esp. pp. 390–392. See Shari Roan, "Negative Images?" *Los Angeles Times*, August 18, 1992, pp. E1, E4, for a report of a study finding that 20-year-old (on average) women who read magazines such as *Cosmopolitan* say the magazines make them feel insecure, ugly and less confident. Brown discusses sexual harassment and the "dandy game" "Scuttle" in "At Work, Sexual Electricity Sparks Creativity," *Wall Street Journal*, October 29, 1991, p. A22. For critical responses see Nancy McCarthy and others, "Sex and the Single 'Scuttler': Yucck," *Wall Street Journal*, November 6, 1991, p. A19; Roger Simon, "Odd Ideas from the Original Cosmo Girl," *Los Angeles Times*, November 3, 1991, p. E11.

20. Stuart Elliott, " 'That Cosmopolitan Girl' Won't Be a Girl Anymore," *New York Times*, January 4, 1993, p. D13; Liz Smith, "Bountiful Time for a Baby," *Los Angeles Times*, January 6, 1993, p. F2.

21. Helen Gurley Brown, "Step into My Parlor," in Media Kit, 1993.

22. Helen Gurley Brown and David Brown, "Creators Keep 'Cosmo' Cookin'," *Advertising Age*, October 24, 1988, pp. S36, 38.

23. Elliott, " 'Cosmo' Celebrates 'That Girl's' 20th," p. 57.

24. The British edition (the oldest, launched in 1972) is owned by Hearst's National Magazine Company; five editions are joint ventures between Hearst and local publishers; the remainder are published under licensing agreements. "International Franchise Fact Sheet" and "The Publisher's Turn," Media Kit, 1993.

25. 1993 Media Kit, citing 1992 SMRB and MRI data; McMahon, "The *Cosmopolitan* Ideology and the Management of Desire," pp. 382–383; Elliott, " 'That Cosmopolitan Girl' Won't Be a Girl Anymore." The MRI data indicate that 16.4 percent of *Cosmopolitan* readers are men (SMRB puts it at 10.9 percent); those readers are excluded from all subsequent tables in the media kit. The median wage for women readers is $17,739 (SMRB) or $18,587 (MRI), but some 57 percent of readers earn less than $15,000.

Information Sources

BIBLIOGRAPHY:

Brown, Helen Gurley. *Sex and the Single Girl*. Chicago: Bernard Geis, 1962.

———, and David Brown. "Creators Keep 'Cosmo' Cookin'." *Advertising Age*, October 24, 1988, pp. S36, S38.

Elliott, Stuart. " 'That Cosmopolitan Girl' Won't Be a Girl Anymore." *New York Times*, January 4, 1993, p. D13.

McMahon, Kathryn. "The *Cosmopolitan* Ideology and the Management of Desire." *Journal of Sex Research*, August 1990, pp. 381–396.

Mott, Frank Luther. *A History of American Magazines, 1885–1905* Cambridge: Harvard University Press, 1957.

Peterson, Theodore. *Magazines in the Twentieth Century*. Urbana: University of Illinois Press, 1964.

Roan, Shari. ''Negative Images? Twentysomethings Say Women's Magazines Can Erode Self-Esteem.'' *Los Angeles Times*, August 18, 1992, pp. E1, 4.

Tassin, Algernon. *The Magazine in America*. New York: Dodd, Mead, 1916.

Thomas, Erwin K., ''John Brisben Walker.'' In Sam G. Riley (ed.), *Dictionary of Literary Biography 79*. Detroit: Gale Research, 1989, pp. 298–301.

INDEX SOURCES: Poole's Index; Readers' Guide to Periodical Literature; Magazine Index.

LOCATION SOURCES: Library of Congress and other libraries.

Publication History

MAGAZINE TITLE AND TITLE CHANGES: *Cosmopolitan Magazine* (March 1886–1925); *Hearst's International Combined with Cosmopolitan* (1925–1952); *Cosmopolitan* (1952–present).

VOLUME AND ISSUE DATA: Vols. 1– (March 1886–present). Monthly (March 1886–present, except June–July 1888, March 1908).

PUBLISHER AND PLACE OF PUBLICATION: Schlicht & Field (1886–1887); Schlicht & Field Company (1887–1888); Joseph N. Hallock (1888–1889); John Brisben Walker (1889–1905); International Magazine Company (1905–1936); Hearst Magazines (1937–1951); Hearst Corporation (1952–present). Rochester, N.Y. (1886–1887); New York (1888–1894); Irvington-on-the-Hudson, N.Y. (1895–1905); New York (1905–present).

EDITORS: Frank P. Smith (1886–1888); E. D. Walker (1888); John Brisben Walker (1889–1905) (with William Dean Howells, 1890 and Arthur Sherburne Hardy, 1893–1895); Bailey Millard (1905–1907); S. S. Chamberlain (1907–1908); C. P. Narcross (1908–1913); Sewell Haggard (1914); Edgar Grant Sisson (1914–1917); Douglas Z. Doty (1917–1918); Ray Long (1918–1931); Harry Payne Burton (1931–1942); Frances Whiting (1942–1945); Arthur Gordon (1946–1948); Herbert R. Mayes (1948–1951); John J. O'Connell (1951–1959); Robert Atherton (1959–1965); Helen Gurley Brown (1965–present).

CIRCULATION: ABC, 1993: 2,705,224 (paid, primarily single-copy sales).

Jon Bekken and Lisa Beinhoff

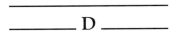

THE DELINEATOR

The Delineator was a magazine of "American Fashion"[1] for the world and one of the "Big Six" women's magazines during the fin de siècle period. *The Delineator* was also known for its political commentary, serialized novels, short stories, and housekeeping articles. It was published from 1873 until it merged with the *Pictorial Review** in 1937. According to the last editor before the merger, Oscar Graeve, it was the second oldest women's magazine in the United States at the time of its death.[2]

At the suggestion of his wife, Ebenezer Butterick founded the Butterick Pattern Company in 1863. A year later, Butterick issued a forerunner of *The Delineator*, *The Ladies Quarterly Review of Broadway Fashion*,[3] to sell patterns, but it proved to be inadequate for the demand. In 1868, Butterick began the *Metropolitan Monthly* to keep up with the increasing call for paper patterns and fashion news. However, the demand kept growing. In 1873, Butterick merged the *Lady's Quarterly* and the *Metropolitan Monthly* to begin *The Delineator*.[4] Between 1873 and the early 1890s, Jonas Warren Wilder, a partner in the Butterick Company, and R. S. O'Loughlin handled the editing. In 1887, O'Loughlin was joined by Charles Dwyer, and the two men jointly edited *The Delineator* for approximately seven years.[5] During that time, the contents of the magazine focused on visual representations of the Butterick designs and paper patterns.

In 1894, when Charles Dwyer became sole editor, the magazine expanded its content to include editorials; and in 1897, *The Delineator* published its first fiction. By 1899, Ebenezer Butterick had withdrawn from publishing the magazine; and in 1902, the Butterick Company reorganized so that Butterick Patterns focused strictly on paper patterns, and the Butterick Publishing Company concentrated on periodicals.[6] According to historian Theodore Peterson, "The Butterick Publishing Company, which issued thirty-two periodicals, ranked as one of the largest magazine publishers in the United States." During this period,

The Delineator, with its editorial changes, flourished. In 1876, Butterick claimed *The Delineator*'s circulation was 30,000; by 1900, circulation had risen to 480,000.[7]

By 1912, the Butterick Publishing Company was publishing *The Delineator* in an English edition for the United States, England, and Canada and in three foreign language editions: *Le Miroir des Modes* (French), *Moden Revue* (German), and *El Espejo de la Moda* (Spanish).[8] Also by 1912, the company maintained publishing offices in New York, Chicago, San Francisco, Atlanta, Boston, and St. Louis, as well as foreign offices in Paris, London, Toronto, and Winnipeg. *The Delineator*, in its middle and late years, from 1902 until the mid–1930s, truly was a magazine of American fashion for the world.

One usually thinks only of clothing and accoutrements as "fashion." A 1920 advertisement for *The Delineator* pitched, "She needs it [the magazine], to keep posted as to the trend of the new fashions."[9] However, *The Delineator* defined "fashion" in a broad sense. "Fashion," within its framework, was not only clothing but home decorating and housekeeping, women's issues, health, and the arts as well. In each of these areas, *The Delineator* presented a distinctly American viewpoint to the rest of the world.

As a publication of fashion, *The Delineator* focused on home sewing for the middle-class American woman. It featured clothing for women, girls, children, and, occasionally, men. The styles were of a practical nature with a streamlined silhouette not necessarily featured in the Parisian designs. These were garments women could easily afford and wear; they were not frocks professional dress-makers would make for the leisure class. Writer Helen Woodward has noted that the paper patterns

> have had an incalculable influence in pushing forward equality among women. The patterns naturally made their clothes more alike, greatly de-creas[ing] the sharp difference between the clothes of women of different social circles. Paper patterns also gave them more leisure and that in-creased their power.[10]

In the early years of *The Delineator*, the fashions were shown in black-and-white lithographs. By the early years of the twentieth century, the black-and-white pictures were joined by full-color plates. Keyed to each garment was a Butterick pattern number and information about fabric and notions needed to make it. In 1920, Butterick introduced and prominently featured "The Deltor" pattern guide for laying out the pattern on the fabric using the least amount of material. In full-page advertisements, *The Delineator* emphasized the cost savings "The Deltor" guide achieved.[11]

Besides fashion plates and patterns, *The Delineator* also featured articles discussing the making and wearing of clothing. In the December 1912 issue, Eleanor Chalmers's article, "Good Taste in Modern Mourning," addressed the current style of mourning clothes, how to wear them, who should wear them, and when to wear them."[12] At this time, Chalmers also wrote a regular column, "Dressmaking Made Easy," which gave written instructions and line drawings to show how tucks, pleats, revers, and other special elements of clothing were made.[13] Another article by Chalmers, in the November 1921 issue, was titled, "America, A Nation of Dressmakers."[14]

The Delineator also featured photographs and line drawings on embroidery and needlework to "finish" garments and to decorate items for the home. The magazine keyed pattern numbers for Butterick transfer patterns, which could be purchased in a dry goods store. The designs were transferred to fabric and then worked to create a unique, personalized garment, pillow slip, tablecloth and napkin set, or doilies. Some issues included articles and pictures of crocheting or tatting, but the emphasis was on paper patterns and transfers produced by Butterick.

The fashion advertisements in *The Delineator* were for items such as undergarments, dress shields, hosiery, shoes, shirtwaist belts, and hairpieces. An August 1922 advertisement for Keds casual shoes featured styles for women, men, and children and emphasized the benefits of wearing Keds after months of wearing stiff, formal shoes.[15] Most of the advertisements were small and in black and white. Others, such as the Keds ad, were half-page and two-color. Other than the Butterick pattern plates, few fashion ads were in full color during the first 30 years of this century.

The Delineator also defined "fashion" as home decorating and even building. By 1912, the shift from the cluttered Victorian style was creating a cleaner, sparse look in decorating. Articles and full-color plates in *The Delineator* defined modern style for the home. Window treatments, such as drapes and curtains, furniture arrangement, painting and wallpapering, furniture, and appliances were all covered. In an October 1922 editorial, Mrs. William Brown Maloney stated:

> No year passes without beholding a change for the better in implements, machinery, working conditions, in every division or department of American Industry—save one.
>
> And that exception is the average American Home—the factory in which twenty million women toil everyday of the year, Sundays and holidays included, and eighteen million of them without an assistant or helper.[16]

With this statement, Mrs. Maloney and *The Delineator* introduced the "Better Homes Campaign" for the 1920s. In a series of articles and pictures, the publication featured modern decor for every room of the house, including the basement. This campaign also included ways to prevent fires and train children to observe safety rules around the home and plans for modern, efficient houses. Women were urged to remove clutter and dangerous accumulations of junk, use wasted space for unique storage areas, and decorate the home in practical fashion. The style was a clean line with well-defined shape. Lace curtains were shown combined with tailored drapes for window coverings; stylish, yet comfortable furniture was arranged to lead the eye around the room to a central focal point (usually a fireplace and mantel, a large window, or a large piece of furniture such as a sofa).

Following its own advice, *The Delineator* also introduced new house plans, which it called modern, practical, and efficient.[17] The first plan, in the March 1923 issue, was for a four-room, two-story house with kitchen, two bedrooms, and a large living room. Designed by Donn Barber, the drawings for this house, which included an exterior view of the house and floor plans, showed a modern, comfortable home with practical living areas. Accompanying the first house plan was an article by the architect that discussed house building traps for the homeowner to avoid.[18]

The Delineator also ran articles on floor coverings and home decorating tips. In the autumn issues, the decorating articles focused on seasonal decorations for Halloween, Thanksgiving, and Christmas. In late winter and early spring, the articles focused on Valentine's Day and Easter. In the December 1922 issue, articles focused on decorating interior and exterior doorways for Christmas[19] and the ''new'' custom of a community Christmas tree.[20]

Decor advertisements run in *The Delineator* corresponded to the light and airiness of the modern home. Kirsch curtain rods were regularly advertised, and, beginning in the 1920s, so were linoleum floor coverings by Blabon, Congoleum, and Armstrong. The linoleum ads were four-color plates showing the product's use in different rooms of the house. One of the major selling points was the efficiency of keeping the floor clean. Another decor product advertised was the phonograph. Both R.C.A. Victor and Brunswick ran full-page, color ads highlighting the phonograph as a piece of furniture that was essential for modern decorating. In 1922, Kroehler Furniture advertised its davenport bed in both color and black-and-white ads.

If a woman was to have a modern home, then she had to keep it clean and well provisioned. *The Delineator* covered cleaning and housekeeping in several ways. Regular features included ''Helpful Hints'' and ''Dollar Savers.'' One hint was how to ''dryclean'' [*sic*] clothes at home using soap and gasoline.[21] A 1922 article focused on how to clean the house efficiently by keeping cleaning agents and tools on each floor or in a carrying case with handles. Photographs showed ''how to'' clean different parts of the house—wall, floors, furniture—while drawings showed ''how to'' keep your cleaners and equipment.[22] An article by Harold Cary, ''Rest as You Work,'' discussed ways in which time-motion studies by Frank and Lillian Gilbreth and others, originally done for factories, could be applied to housekeeping.[23]

Cleaning and housekeeping advertisements were usually black-and-white line drawings with testimonial copy, though by the 1920s, color plates of products were being published in *The Delineator*. Cleaning products included Fels-Naptha bar laundry soap and Bon Ami and Old Dutch cleansers. Appliance ads included the New Perfection Oil Range ("cooks as fast as gas") and the Na-panee Dutch Kitchenet, which used time-motion studies to demonstrate how the stove saved "housewives from exhaustion."[24]

The Delineator also discussed canning foods, preparing meals, and home gar-dening. Other articles focused on unusual cooking such as an article in the September 1921 issue, "Cooking with the Gipsies [*sic*]."[25] In the article, the author discussed how to build an open fire and how to cook over it and gave several recipes, all gleaned from English gypsies.

"Women's issues" were also defined and covered by *The Delineator*. The definition of "issues" varied as the political climate and the magazine's editors changed. Early twentieth-century issues focused on women's rights and suc-cesses, while later editions redefined "issues" in terms of love, womanliness, and care of children. In 1911 and 1912, a multipart series on "laws concerning women" by editor William Hard focused on the legal rights of mothers and wives. *The Delineator* and Hard proposed a "Declaration of Principles," which would grant women property and child custody rights to correct the archaic primogeniture laws that existed in most states.[26] Other articles prior to World War I supported women's suffrage[27] and explored the terrible working condi-tions of women factory workers[28] and the Chinese practice of "feet-binding."[29]

During the Progressive Era *The Delineator* was edited by novelist Theodore Dreiser and William Hard. Both of these editors were muckrakers who supported progressive programs such as cleaning up slums, legal regulation of industries, especially food processing, and women's rights. Under their guidance, *The De-lineator* sponsored a "Child Rescue Campaign," which placed 21,000 children in adoptive homes out west.[30] Other projects of *The Delineator* were raising money for a gram of radium for Marie Curie, relief work during and after World War I, and better health care and education for American children.

Success stories about, for, and by women were also featured in *The Deline-ator*. "Women Who Have Won" was a series of articles focusing women's attentions on what they could accomplish outside the home. Other articles cov-ered Adeline Gehrig, a fencing champion, and Elsie K. Lempke, an Aladin Homes factory manager.[31] Mrs. Samuel B. Sneath, director of the Interstate Trust and Banking Company of New Orleans, wrote "Left Alone with Money," which showed women how to establish and keep their businesses financially sound.[32]

World War I and the Red Scare of 1919–1922 seem to have affected the progressive tone of *The Delineator*. Articles focused women's attention away from rights and financial independence to fighting Communism and a redefini-tion of feminine. A change of editorship did occur during these years, Honoré Willsie Morrow editing the magazine from 1917 to 1921 and Mrs. William Brown Maloney from 1921 to 1926, but the content shift does not appear linked to this change. *The Delineator* kept its aim to have "the best" writers, features, and literature, and the style of the publication did not change. The overall po-litical climate changed during these years for women and the United States, and this appeared to have a major effect on the subjects covered and how they were covered by the magazine.

Prior to the mid-1920s, major political figures did not write articles on political subjects. However, by 1923, in the middle of Brown's tenure as editor, Vice President Calvin Coolidge wrote a three-part series on Communism that pointed out what must be cleansed, who must be cleansed, and how the cleansing process must be carried out.[33] Brown introduced this series by stating it was "a call to America."[34] Other series, such as the pure foods campaign, may have had political implications, but this was the first overtly ideological series *The Delineator* published.

The Better Homes Campaign also went through an ideological shift. Initially focusing on improving the design and care of the house for greater efficiency, it was now highlighted by a Better Homes in America Week. Brown stated that "[ap]propriately enough, it begins on Mother's Day and ends on Peace Day—for the making of a better home is a mother's duty and peace is her due in the home of her making."[35]

Three other articles from the mid- to the late 1920s also suggested a redefinition of the word "feminine." Alice Duer Miller's series, "Are Women Wives?" looked at the many duties of married women and addressed the needs of the "neglected husband."[36] Erma Hollen contributed "Keeping Him Interested,"[37] while another article asked the question, "Love—Luxury or Necessity?" and stated that the reader should not "make the mistake of the emancipated woman who thinks she can get along without romance."[38] Corresponding to these articles were contributions about the male perspective on the home by Secretary of Commerce Herbert Hoover.[39]

Along with this shift in "women's issues," *The Delineator* began to increase and emphasize its coverage of health, motherhood, and children. In 1912 and 1913, the magazine featured columns on the "Home Kindergarten," for mothers.[40] It also published children's features such as "scissors pictures" and paper dolls and sponsored the Jennie Wren Clubs for girls and the Boys' Knights Clubs for boys.[41] These were activities *for* children. However, by the 1920s, the clubs and kindergarten features were gone, and only paper dolls remained for girls to "do." *The Delineator* focused its attention on "how" children were being raised (they should be raised scientifically) and research on child development, and the four *Delineator* Baby Clubs served the "Expectant Mothers," "Mothers of Infants," "Mothers of 2–6 Year-Olds," and "Mothers of School-age Children." Columns on child psychology by New York City school principal Angelo Patri appeared along with series such as a three-part report on the Iowa Child Welfare Research[42] and the "Happy Child Campaign."[43] As *The Delineator* stated in August 1922, the U.S. Census Bureau reported that "1,141,939 babies died in the U.S. in ten years; more than fourteen babies for every soldier killed in the World War."[44] This was the justification for the focus shifting from things for children to things mother must do. Articles in the series were overseen by Dr. L. Emmett Holt of the Child Health Organization, and all were written by male experts who brought a scientific viewpoint to child raising. Other articles, though not in the "Happy Child" series, were written by experts such as educators John Dewey and Arnold Gesell.

Between 1894 and 1926, *The Delineator* not only featured fashion, home-making, and child care but also brought plays, theater, opera, literature, and poetry into the lives of its readership. Regular articles in the magazine published plays that women's clubs could produce, synopses of popular operas, and reports of women's literary clubs. The publication also conducted writing contests for aspiring writers, such as Earl Derr Biggers, who in 1912 won a $300 prize and had his short story, "Lilacs and Cobblestones," published.[45] This was approximately a year before he left the *Boston Traveler* and his novel, *Seven Keys to Bald Pate*, was made into a Broadway hit by stage director George M. Cohan. Other major writers who contributed to *The Delineator* were Lady Gregory of Ireland's Abbey Theatre, Lucy Maude Montgomery, the creator of the *Anne of Green Gables* books, and Edith Wharton, Pulitzer Prize-winning author for her novel *The Age of Innocence*. Each issue of *The Delineator* had short stories, poetry, and an installment of a serialized novel. Often, these stories and novels were illustrated by major artists such as N. C. Wyeth and James Montgomery Flagg.

Also during this time frame, *The Delineator* followed a text-dominant layout style. Advertisements were limited and placed in the margins of the pages. After 1920, though, the publication included more photographs and other visuals, which lightened its overall style. This change did not seem to affect *The Delineator*'s emphasis on fashion, for the black-and-white and color plates kept to a consistent number. More advertising was also included after 1920 and went to half- and full-page size. It also went to more testimonial copy than before. Princess Yedigarov of Russia and Mrs. Fritz Kreisler endorsed Lux soap while Eleanor Roosevelt endorsed Simmons beds, springs, and mattresses, and Eddie Cantor promoted Fleischmann's yeast as a laxative.

A major content shift began in 1928, when Oscar Graeve became editor, and lasted until 1935. In 1928, another Butterick fashion magazine, *The Designer*, was merged with *The Delineator*,[46] and the publication went back to its roots as a fashion magazine and limited the amount of copy. It also focused on more upscale fashion, primarily from the designer houses in Paris. This change was gradual at first, between 1928 and 1935, but with greater competition from the ready-made clothing market and other fashion magazines, Graeve had to speed up the shift.

"From the Editor's Point of View," which had been the major editorial voice, gave way to "The Living Delineator." Cover art went from a romantic style to an abstract one, with major illustrators such as Dynevor Rhys, Helen Dryden, and Rose O'Neill contributing cover illustrations that emphasized style over "the home." The beautiful full-color fashion plates were replaced by black-and-white photographs that suggested more silhouette than the style and cut of garments.

During this period of change, *The Delineator*'s circulation was 2 million (up from 1 million in 1920). As the economy grew worse in the early 1930s, Graeve chose to move the magazine into a special niche. In April 1935, *The Delineator* "decided to abandon the mad struggle for the largest circulation claims and limit its circulation to women who really wanted it."[47] It also became a "different" women's magazine, "keyed to the modern scene, the modern woman and her staccato mood."[48] Features were limited to no more than three installments, and short stories and articles were no more than a page long.

Even with these changes, *The Delineator* struggled in 1936 and early 1937. Advertising agencies continued to cut budgets, and less revenue came into the Butterick Publication Company. By 1937, the readership of *The Delineator* was at 1,487,118, down almost a half-million.[49] Then, in April 1937, "[w]ith almost no warning, *Delineator* ceased publication. . . . It was merged the next month with William Randolph Hearst's *Pictorial Review*, in which its identity was completely lost."[50]

The demise of *The Delineator* ended an era of great gains by women during which publications for females were major leveling forces and voices for change. Despite the setbacks during the post–World War I backlash period, *The Delineator* and others cautiously argued for women's rights and the improvement of their homes, work opportunities, and families. *The Delineator*, with its fashion plates, advertisements, health, homemaking, and literature, answered many needs of homebound and professional women during its years of publication. It brought the world to women and, by doing so, helped fashion that world.

Notes

1. William Hard, "From the Editor's Point of View," January 1913, p. 2.
2. Oscar Graeve, "Speaking of *Delineator*," *The Quill*, January 1937, p. 10.
3. Ibid.
4. Mabel Potter Daggett, "When *The Delineator* Was Young," November 1910, pp. 365–366, 419.
5. Ibid.
6. Theodore Peterson, *Magazines in the Twentieth Century* (Urbana: University of Illinois Press, 1956), p. 153.
7. Ibid.
8. Honoré Willsie Morrow (ed.), "From the Editor's Point of View," January 1913, p. 2.
9. "Give 'HER' a Year's Subscription to *THE DELINEATOR*," December 1920, p. 20.
10. Helen Woodward, *The Lady Persuaders* (New York: Ivan Obonlensky, 1960), p. 62.
11. "The Deltor," August 1921, pp. 40–41.
12. Eleanor Chalmers, "Good Taste in Modern Mourning," December 1921, pp. 452–453.
13. Eleanor Chalmers, "Dressmaking Made Easy," March 1912, p. 210.
14. Eleanor Chalmers, "America, A Nation of Dressmakers," November 1921, p. 21.

15. Keds Advertisement, August 1922, p. 40.

16. Mrs. William Brown Maloney, "From the Editor's Point of View," October 1922, p. 1.

17. "*Delineator* Houseplan Number One," March 1923, p. 15.

18. Donn Barber, "Pitfalls for the Home Builder," March 1923, p. 14.

19. "Decorating Doorways for Christmas," December 1922, p. 12.

20. Hetty L. Sorden, "Trees of Light," December 1922, p. 16.

21. "Helpful Hints for the Home," April 1912, p. 351.

22. Mary W. Leonard, "Watch Your Steps in Housecleaning," August 1922, p. 8.

23. Harold Cary, "Rest as You Work," April 1923, p. 13.

24. "Napanee Dutch Kitchenet Advertisement," November 1921, p. 68.

25. Louise Rice, "Cooking with the Gipsies," September 1921, p. 26.

26. William Hard, "With All My Worldly Goods I Thee Endow," July 1911 through May 1912.

27. Senator William E. Borah, "Why I'm for Suffrage for Women," August 1910, p. 85.

28. "Women Toilers," May 1912, pp. 376–377.

29. Edward Alsworth Ross, "Unbinding the Women of China," April 1912, p. 283.

30. Graeve, "Speaking of *Delineator*," p. 3.

31. "Women Who Have Won," February 1923, p. 20.

32. "Left Alone with Money," February 1923, pp. 12, 105.

33. Calvin Coolidge, "Enemies of the Republic," June–August 1921.

34. Mrs. William Brown Maloney, "Enemies of the Republic," August 1921, p. 10.

35. Mrs. William Brown Maloney, "From the Editor's Point of View," June 1924, p. 2.

36. Alice Duer Miller, "Are Women Wives?" April 1926, pp. 11, 80.

37. Erma Hollen, "Keeping Him Interested," November 1925, p. 10.

38. Katherine Anthony, "Love—Luxury or Necessity?" November 1921, pp. 7, 79.

39. Herbert Hoover, "What Men Should Know about Homes," April 1925, p. 11.

40. William Hard, "From the Editor's Point of View," January 1912, p. 2.

41. "Boys Knights Page," February 1912, p. 147.

42. Bird T. Baldwin and Anne O'Hagan, "Iowa Child Welfare Research," September through November 1921.

43. Mrs. William Brown Maloney, "From the Editor's Point of View," August 1922, p. 2.

44. Ibid.

45. Earl Derr Biggers, "Lilacs and Cobblestones," March 1912, p. 5.

46. Peterson, *Magazines in the Twentieth Century*, p. 153.

47. Graeve, "Speaking of *Delineator*," p. 10.

48. Ibid.

49. "Ladies Line Up," *Time*, February 15, 1937, p. 50.

50. Peterson, *Magazines in the Twentieth Century*, p. 154.

Information Sources

BIBLIOGRAPHY:

Graeve, Oscar. "Speaking of *Delineator*." *The Quill*, January 1937, p. 10.

"Ladies Line Up." *Time*, February 15, 1937, p. 50.

Peterson, Theodore. *Magazines in the Twentieth Century*. Urbana: University of Illinois Press, 1956.

Woodward, Helen. *The Lady Persuaders*. New York: Ivan Obonlensky, 1960.

INDEX SOURCES: The Readers' Guide to Periodical Literature; The Union List of Serials; American Periodical Series Index.

LOCATION SOURCES: Akron Public Library; Cincinnati Public Library; Cleveland Public Library; Kent State University Library; Oberlin College Library; and other libraries.

Publication History

MAGAZINE TITLE AND TITLE CHANGES: *Ladies Quarterly Review of Broadway Fashions* (1863–1873) and *The Metropolitan Monthly* (1868–1873) combined to form *The Delineator* (1873–1937).

(*Designer* merged with *The Delineator* [1928]; *The Delineator* merged with *The Pictorial Review* [1937–1939].)

VOLUME AND ISSUE DATA: Vols. 1–123 (July 1873–April 1937). Monthly.

PUBLISHER AND PLACE OF PUBLICATION: Butterick Pattern Company (1873–1899); Butterick Publishing Company (1899–1937). New York.

EDITORS: Jonas Warren Wilder (1873–18?); R. S. O'Loughlin (1887–1894); Charles Dwyer (1894–1906); Theodore Dreiser (1907–1910); William Hard (1910–1913); George Bair Baker, managing editor (1913–1917); Honoré Willsie Morrow (1917–1921); Mrs. William Brown Maloney (1921–1926); Mary Day Winn, managing editor (1926–1927); Oscar Graeve (1928–1937).

CIRCULATION: (claimed by *The Delineator*) 1895: 500,000; (Peterson, *Magazines in the Twentieth Century*, pp. 153–154) 1920: more than 1 million and 1929–1935: more than 2 million.

Lynn O'Neal Heberling

DEMOREST'S MONTHLY MAGAZINE

William Jennings Demorest established a monthly magazine in September 1864 to secure his influence in the publishing field beyond fashion—and to sell dress patterns. Demorest and his wife, Ellen Louise Curtis (Nell), who had developed a dress pattern made of tissue paper, had marketed the product successfully through a quarterly fashion publication beginning in 1860. Yet, Demorest, a vocal reformer who also was interested in publishing, wanted to try his hand in the area of general publishing.

Actually, Demorest came to publishing late in his career. Born in 1822, he owned a dry goods store in New York before he was forced to declare bankruptcy in the early 1850s. His fortunes revived, however, when he began mass-producing and marketing the paper patterns that could be used to make fashionable clothing. Nell, who was William's second wife, took naturally to fashion ideas—she had studied dressmaking, millinery, and fashion before establishing a millinery shop in Saratoga, New York.

After their marriage, Nell gave up her business. Together they developed the patterns and marketed them, initially from their home in Philadelphia. When customers responded enthusiastically to the new product, the Demorests moved north to New York to be in the center of America's fashion capital. From there, in 1860, Demorest published the quarterly *Mme. Demorest's Mirror of Fashions*, which featured engravings, some of them hand-colored, of Paris fashions for children and women. Even the name of the publication, which sold for 10¢, hinted that the clothing featured within was the height of style. The quarterly provided a sample pattern as a premium and, with detailed illustrations, effectively advertised the dress patterns.

The Demorests employed consultants in Europe to anticipate trends in fashion that could be quickly reproduced in New York. Nell's sister, Kate Curtis, helped tailor the French styles to American needs. Thus, readers of *Demorest's* were treated to the cutting edge of fashion. With tactics such as this, the quarterly flourished even during the height of the Civil War and managed a respectable circulation of about 60,000.[1] During the war, *Demorest's* did not circulate in the South, where there simply was no fabric for fine clothing. In fact, the quarterly promoted fashion and generally ignored the details of the conflict, except to feature many types of mourning clothes on the fashion pages.[2]

Despite the success of the quarterly, Demorest believed he needed a monthly publication and also sought a national platform for his reform ideas. He bought the weekly *New York Illustrated News*, which was one of the first newspapers to feature pictures, in January 1864 and merged that a few months later with the quarterly *Mirror of Fashions*. The resulting monthly magazine featured fashions, advice, sheet music, and fiction aimed especially at women.

Demorest's Illustrated Monthly and Mme. Demorest's Mirror of Fashions appeared in September 1864.[3] Its success was immediate; in its earliest days, circulation stood at 100,000.[4] In addition to the promise of a dress pattern, readers could select one of several premiums if they subscribed for three dollars a year. Subscribers initially received one dollar's worth of patterns or an 18" × 24" engraving of General George Washington. Readers also were encouraged to solicit other subscribers—anyone who signed up 35 subscribers could, for example, earn a new sewing machine.[5]

The Demorests moved to East Fourteenth Street in New York before the war's end and opened an emporium on Broadway for women to preview the latest fashions; there and at a manufacturing shop, the couple employed more than 200 women to sell, cut, fit, and design the patterns. In fact, employment for women—and later, Prohibition—was a favorite reform advocated within the magazine. The Demorests also expanded into other products—they marketed corsets, sewing machines, sewing aids, and fashion accessories.

The first issue of the 24-page *Demorest's Illustrated Monthly* featured a colored engraving of children's fashionable clothing and a layout of women in cloaks and also featured poetry, sheet music, and several serial fiction works. Advice on the "Parlor, Kitchen and Nursery" was furnished by the popular journalist Jane Cunningham Croly, who wrote under the pen name "Jennie

June.'' Domestic advice included methods for canning fruit and pickling pears and peaches. The last two pages of the first issue featured illustrated advertisements for blemish cream, jewelry, a fountain pen, hair dye, and a clothes wringer. Self-promoting ads included pattern-cutting advice from the Demorests, and Jennie June's new book, *Talks on Women's Topics*.

From the inaugural issue, William and Nell Demorest were joined by Croly as editors. Sometimes described as an editor or assistant editor, in reality Croly wrote much of the editorial content in the publication. The magazine's name changed in 1866 to *Demorest's Monthly Magazine and Mme. Demorest's Mirror of Fashions* and in January 1879 to *Demorest's Family Magazine*. For many years, though, the editorial content on the magazine remained stable, and, by 1870, *Demorest's* touted itself as the "model parlor magazine of America." Serious advice and essays mixed with fashion features, cooking tips, recipes, fiction, and sheet music from mostly melodramatic and forgettable songs ("What Will I Do When My Mother Is Dead?" for example).[6] The editors tapped well-respected authors, including Edgar Allan Poe, Margaret Sangster, Louisa May Alcott, Robert Louis Stevenson, Theodore Dreiser, and Alice Cary, for essays, poetry, and fiction. An illustrated version of Poe's most famous poem, "The Raven," for example, appeared in the May 1870 edition.[7] *Demorest's* instituted a "Ladies Club" section in which readers wrote letters and sought advice—a forerunner of the advice and lovelorn columns that still are popular today. Readers also received etiquette advice and tips on European travel—information clearly in keeping with the needs of the magazine's middle-class readers.

The magazine, indeed, was intended to appeal to the sensibilities of the middle and upper classes. These women constituted the first generation of women who were seeking some sort of fulfillment and influence beyond their homes—Nell Demorest and Jennie Croly helped them find their way. Both William and Nell Demorest always were interested in progressive reforms, and Croly was a journalist whose vision of a wider sphere for women evolved within the pages of *Demorest's*. From the first volume of the magazine, Croly wrote a "Talks with Women" column that sometimes considered the mundane problems facing a housewife—food, marriage, the art of conversation—but also wrestled with some of the explosive issues confronting women—education, employment, and their proper sphere. *Demorest's* advocated kindergartens for young children, a progressive idea at the time, and argued that enforced idleness caused most of the female complaints of nerves and illness.[8]

Within the pages of the magazine, Croly promoted her idea for a Woman's Parliament to be held in New York City to consider woman's role in society and the important reforms that needed her attention. "Can we not assert our womanhood by being all that we can that is noblest and best in women? Can we not prove our queenship by giving (the prerogative of royalty) ourselves— name, influence, strength, effort—to the work of aiding and elevating women, and, through women, men, society and the world at large?'' she asked her readers.[9]

Croly and Nell Demorest used the magazine to urge a wider sphere for women: they urged colleges to open their doors to women, they encouraged women to seek employment, and they applauded the success of women in the professions of medicine and law.

In fact, Croly urged in the 1860s that women be allowed to work. She said the desire for employment exceeded any aspirations by women for suffrage. "The right that women most want in this country is the right to work, without feeling that it is a degradation or that by doing so, they lose caste, and forfeit position in society."[10] This argument emphatically presented the dichotomy that Croly and Nell Demorest wrestled with throughout their lives and on the pages of their magazine—they wanted a wider sphere for women, but they wanted to maintain their social status as women of society.

Nell Demorest and Croly believed a way to resolve this dilemma was through association with other women in clubs. In fact, clubs afforded middle-class women a socially acceptable opportunity to socialize with other similar women and to expand their sphere of influence beyond their homes. These semitraditional women found safety in numbers and respectability despite their more public profiles.

Croly and the Demorests publicized the evolution of the women's club movement on the pages of *Demorest's*. Croly, herself one of the founders of the women's club movement, organized a group of women, including Nell Demorest, at her home in March 1868. Activities of this early club, which came to be known as Sorosis, were chronicled in *Demorest's* and provided a prototype for other women's clubs that were springing up throughout the United States. Readers were urged to form study clubs and to read literature rather than the romantic novels that were in vogue. The public accomplishments of women were applauded monthly in a column, "What Women Are Doing," which appeared in the 1880s.

The two women concerned themselves with progressive ideas and reform issues, but their interests in other areas of the magazine differed. While Nell Demorest ensured that her magazine reflected the very latest in fashion, Croly promoted dress reform in her columns. While these two interests often were compatible, they did at times collide. The Demorests lifted skirts to make them less dangerous and tailored clothes to make them more comfortable. They also marketed a "health corset," which they asserted would help American women from becoming stooped and prematurely aged. Croly, however, decried equipment such as this in her column.[11]

While Nell Demorest and Croly concerned themselves with the plight and sphere of women, William Demorest used the pages of the magazine as a platform to promote his favorite reform—Prohibition. After he turned control of the magazine over to his sons in 1885, he intensified his campaign against alcohol and increasingly used the magazine to publicize his beliefs. In a column in

January 1892, for example, he described alcohol as "an atrocious public nuisance, and monster of vice and misery."[12] The magazine reported on the Women's Christian Temperance Union and highlighted such propaganda poetry as "Three Famous Old Roads to Ruin" (beer, rum, and wine).

In addition to editorial advice and guidance, the intricate illustrations and engravings of *Demorest's* helped assure its popularity with the reading public. In September 1870, the magazine began including a series of popular illustrations that were designed to be clipped and hung in the home.[13] Later, the magazine printed a monthly feature of portraits of famous people, which were meant to be clipped and pasted into a collector's album.

By 1874, *Demorest's* magazine generally ran about 40 pages, with approximately 4 pages of advertisements in the back of the book. The "Mirror of Fashion" inset in the magazine featured 6 pages of fashion copy and illustration. The advertising rates were 75¢ per line for ordinary pages; many of the ads promoted Demorest's patterns and related sewing products.

Having met success with a monthly magazine, the Demorests sought to extend their influence even further. They published *Demorest's Young America*, a juvenile magazine, beginning in 1866 but then incorporated a "Young America" supplement into the monthly in 1875. That magazine never turned a profit because, they said, children of the day were too sophisticated: "They imbibe a taste for the horrible, the exaggerated, and marvelous, which is catered to by unscrupulous persons, and which makes all else seem insipid and namby-pamby to them."[14] They also published occasional fashion specials, such as the quarterly *Demorest's Journal of Fashions*, which cost 10¢ and a semiannual offering, *What to Wear and How to Make It*, which was popular for many years.

While Demorest was a savvy businessman who sought patents for many of his inventions and products, including a sewing machine, hoop skirts, and cosmetics, he never patented the tissue paper patterns. In 1863, Ebenezer Butterick marketed his patterns and patented them. Like Demorest before him, Butterick looked to publishing to promote his product. In 1872, the Butterick pattern company issued *The Delineator.** For a time, the field was broad enough for the rival companies, but by the 1880s, the competition intensified. In 1880, *Demorest's* circulation stood at 50,000, compared with 85,000 for *The Delineator*.[15] *Demorest's* circulation climbed modestly over the next decade to about 58,666 while *The Delineator* circulation soared to an estimated 300,000.[16] *Peterson's Magazine** responded to the increasingly crowded field of women's publications in 1878 by including a folded pattern in each issue as a supplement. This continued into the 1890s and must have put pressure on *Demorest's*.[17] *Godey's Lady's Book,** the grande dame of women's magazines, had lost circulation ground to *Peterson's* during the Civil War but continued to be a formidable competitor throughout the 1880s.[18] *Demorest's* also felt competition from *Harper's Bazar,** which premiered in 1867 under the editorship of Mary L. Booth. Like *Demorest's*, *Harper's Bazar* combined an emphasis on fashion with quality fiction.

In the 1880s, 18 fashion magazines originated from New York and Philadelphia, and competition also was keen from such popular publications as *Frank Leslie's Popular Monthly*.[19] William Demorest announced, in 1882, that *Demorest's* would widen its editorial content beyond women's concerns into "human interests and industrial activities."[20] The Ladies Club section of letters and advice was curtailed, and the writings of some women correspondents were eliminated.

Demorest turned control of the magazine over to his sons, Henry and William, in 1885. Under them, *Demorest's* strayed further from its fashion roots and took on an even more literary tone. Croly was so unsettled by the new leadership that she looked around for alternative work.[21] In March 1887, Croly bought a half-interest in the then-failing *Godey's Lady's Book* and turned her editorial attention to that publication.

Demorest's phased out the colored plates and, in January 1892, introduced photography to its pages with a 14-photograph essay on "Burma and the Burmese," in a travelogue similar to those published in *National Geographic*. The magazine by this time published issues between 60 and 70 pages in length. *Demorest's* maintained the format of photographs, essays, and some fashion, but certainly less than readers had been accustomed to under the guidance of the elder Demorests and Croly. Typical of the article about Burma, the brothers concentrated more on news of the world and international features.[22]

After they passed on editing duties to the next generation, the Demorests also sold the pattern business to a company that continued to use the "Mme. Demorest" name. Demorest, however, was enraged when one of the fashion sheets included a liquor advertisement, and he obtained an injunction against the firm.[23]

William Demorest died in 1895, and Nell died three years later. Also in 1898, the Arkell Publishing Co., owners of the magazine *Judge*, bought *Demorest's Family Magazine*.[24] The magazine, however, folded abruptly with the December 1899 issue, although its circulation had climbed to a respectable 120,000.[25] It also contained about 19 pages of ads in its final Christmas number. *Demorest's* (and *Godey's Lady's Book*, which ceased publication in 1898) faded from the publishing scene, supplanted in popularity by a new generation of magazines, such as the still popular *Ladies' Home Journal** and *Good Housekeeping*.*[26]

Notes

1. Ishbel Ross, *Crusades and Crinolines: The Life and Times of Ellen Curtis Demorest and William Jennings Demorest* (New York: Harper and Row, 1963), p. 23.

2. Ibid., p. 30.

3. In his *History of American Magazines, 1865–1885* (Cambridge: Harvard University Press, 1938), Frank Luther Mott stated that *Demorest's* was first published as a monthly magazine in January 1865. This assertion, however, is wrong. The September 1864 issue was published as Vol. 1, No. 1 and can be found in the collection at the New York Public Library.

4. Ross, *Crusades and Crinolines*, p. 47. While the 100,000 figure seems high, especially in light of the lower circulation numbers in later years, it could perhaps be

explained by the fact that two publications with established circulations were merged to create the new magazine.

5. September 1864, p. 20.

6. "What Will I Do When My Mother Is Dead?" February 1870, unnumbered page in front of magazine.

7. Ross, *Crusades and Crinolines*, p. 82.

8. Jennie June, "Talks with Women: Work," April 1866, p. 89.

9. Jennie June, "What Can I Do?" January 1870, p. 25.

10. Jennie June, "Talks with Women: Woman's Rights," August 1866, p. 204.

11. Ross, *Crusades and Crinolines*, p. 117.

12. W. Jennings Demorest, "An Atrocious Public Nuisance, and Monster of Vice and Misery," January 1892, p. 191.

13. Ross, *Crusades and Crinolines*, p. 82.

14. Ibid., p. 147.

15. Circulation figures found in *Ayer & Son's American Newspaper Annual* (Philadelphia: N. W. Ayer & Son, 1880).

16. Circulation figures from *Ayer & Son's American Newspaper Annual* (Philadelphia: N. W. Ayer & Son, 1890).

17. Mott, *History of American Magazines*, vol. 2 (Cambridge, Mass.: Belknap Press, 1957), p. 309.

18. Michael Emery and Edwin Emery, *The Press and America: An Interpretative History of Mass Media*, 6th ed. (Englewood Cliffs, N.J.: Prentice-Hall, 1988), p. 169.

19. Ross, *Crusaders and Crinolines*, p. 220.

20. Ibid., p. 198.

21. J. C. Croly, New York, to Aubertine Woodward Moore, ALS, December 26, 1886, Moore Collection, State Historical Society of Wisconsin.

22. Ross, *Crusades and Crinolines*, p. 237.

23. Ibid., p. 231.

24. Frank L. Mott, *History of American Magazines, 1865–1885*, vol. 3 (Cambridge, Mass.: Belknap, 1957), p. 328.

25. Circulation figures from *Ayer & Son's Newspaper Annual* (Philadelphia: N. W. Ayer & Son, 1899).

26. Ross, *Crusades and Crinolines*, p. 275.

Information Sources

BIBLIOGRAPHY:
Aubertine Woodward Moore Collection, State Historical Society of Wisconsin.
Ayer & Son's American Newspaper Annual. Philadelphia: N. W. Ayer & Son, 1880.
Mott, Frank L. *History of American Magazines, 1865–1885*, vol. 3. Cambridge, Mass.: Belknap, 1957.
Ross, Ishbel. *Crusades and Crinolines: The Life and Times of Ellen Curtis Demorest and William Jennings Demorest*. New York: Harper and Row, 1963.
INDEX SOURCES: None.
LOCATION SOURCES: New York Public Library and other sources.

Publication History

MAGAZINE TITLE AND TITLE CHANGES: *Mme. Demorest's Mirror of Fashions* (quarterly forerunner of magazine, 1860–1864); *Demorest's Illustrated Monthly and Mme. Demorest's Mirror of Fashions* (1864–1866); *Demorest's Monthly Magazine and Mme. Demorest's Mirror of Fashions* (1866–1879); *Demorest's Family Magazine* (1879–1899).

VOLUME AND ISSUE DATA: Vols. 1–36 (September 1864–December 1899).

PUBLISHER AND PLACE OF PUBLICATION: William Jennings Demorest (1865–1885); Henry and William Demorest (1885–1897); Arkell Publishing Co. (1898–1899). New York.

EDITORS: William Jennings Demorest, Ellen Demorest, Jane Cunningham Croly (1864–1885); William C. Demorest and Henry C. Demorest (1885–1897).

CIRCULATION: Ayer's, 1899: 120,000.

Agnes Hooper Gottlieb

ELLE

America's fashion magazine arena was dominated by two names, *Vogue** and *Harper's Bazaar,** until France's *Elle* entered the spotlight in 1985. In France, *Elle* is considered the grande dame of the fashion publishing world.[1] It has been published there since 1945 by Hachette. In America, *Elle* (first half of 1993 circulation of 887,852, up 1.9 percent from 1992) quickly took the number two circulation position away from *Harper's* (1993 circulation of 715,680, down 2.3 percent from 1992), and it is thriving, even in the shadow of *Vogue* (whose circulation for the first half of 1993 was 1,204,058, down 8.3 percent from 1992).[2]

In terms of advertising market share, *Elle* ranked number three in the first quarter of 1993 with 20.6 percent, following *Vogue*'s 39.8 percent and *Harper's* 25.6 percent.[3] But only during the 1992–1993 seasons did *Harper's* regain the position of being the second-ranked fashion magazine in the United States in terms of market share, and this only after a dramatic revamping of itself, *Elle*-style. In fact, the *New York Times* called the new version of *Harper's* "younger and hipper and honing in on *Elle*'s territory."[4] But during the last six months of 1993, *Elle*'s average monthly sales were up by "2.7 percent year-on-year to 220,615," which puts its average circulation at 900,000 plus.[5] This is the highest circulation *Elle* has seen since the publication peaked in 1989 at 826,000 when "60 percent of *Elle*'s circulation came from newsstand sales which are significantly more profitable than costly subscription sales."[6] Clearly, *Harper's* will not keep the number two position without a fight, and *Elle* has a history of surprising its challengers with its style, revenues, and circulation figures.

Elle first blasted onto the American fashion scene in 1984, when France's Hachette joined with the United States' *The New Yorker* to publish a highly successful pilot issue. *Elle* was well received, but *The New Yorker* was bought out by Newhouse and lost interest in the new magazine. Hachette was left in the United States without a partner, and the French corporation's method of expansion into new countries was through joint publication agreements. Fortunately, Rupert Murdoch's News Corporation stepped into the void left by *The New Yorker*. Murdoch and Hachette signed a 50/50 publishing agreement. In November 1985, the first regular monthly issue of *Elle* was published. It sold 75 percent of its newsstand copies. Most magazines, according to *Fortune*, on the average sell 40–50 percent.[7] *Elle* was already doing better than average, and it looked as if it might actually be a successful challenger to *Vogue*, the undisputed queen of America's fashion magazines.

In the past, one other French fashion magazine—*L'Officiel*—had sought out America's fickle fashion world. It failed miserably because it did not change to capitalize on the American market. It remained too French. It also made the fatal mistake of challenging *Vogue* in its niche by focusing on older women who favored high fashion.[8] *Elle* entered the market and found the consumers *Vogue* was neglecting—the younger American woman who knows what she wants but wants it packaged in a new way. The *Dallas Morning News* described *Elle* as a "very slick, handsome, upscale fashion/essay/celebrity/life skills magazine for young women."[9] In 1986, when *Elle* first began its amazing rise to the forefront of the fashion magazine industry, then-publisher Marybeth Russell described its niche as one of style.[10] The *New York Times* described *Elle*'s entry and subsequent challenge to *Vogue*'s dominance as sending "ripples of excitement through the fashion world with its vivaciousness, its stylish European sensibility and its clear appeal to young women, who had come to think of *Vogue* as a magazine for their mothers."[11] When *Elle*'s readers are compared with *Harper's* and *Vogue*'s, the "MRI numbers, a measurement of the demographics of a magazine's readership, consistently show *Elle* in the enviable position of having the youngest and most affluent readers."[12]

Elle was frightening the competition in more ways than just finding a large, responsive readership. *Elle* was innovative. It presented the 1980s readers with clothing choices, and its covers featured what the *Los Angeles Times* called "unpredictable beauties of various ethnic extractions" that showed "beyond doubt that a face need not look Caucasian to have newsstand appeal."[13] The magazine did not continue its featured articles in the back ad pages (a fact advertisers liked). *Elle*'s style has influenced magazine newcomer *Mirabella** as well as the old-timers—*Vogue* and *Harper's*. Indeed, as previously mentioned, *Harper's* has been so influenced and challenged that it was forced to overhaul its entire magazine. Even now *Elle* continues to spawn fashion clones.

In 1988, Murdoch sold his interest in U.S. *Elle* and British *Elle* to Hachette for, reportedly, more then $150 million. Diamandis Communications Inc. took over operation of the U.S. edition for its parent corporation Hachette.[14] Industry sources told *Advertising Age* that Murdoch sold because people at News Corporation thought *Elle* had peaked as a magazine.[15] Whoever those people were, they were wrong.

From 1985 to 1989, *Elle*'s popularity skyrocketed. *Advertising Age* cited

Elle's U.S. edition as "one of the fastest-growing consumer magazines ever until its growth rate cooled off in 1985."[16] During the last six months of 1990, circulation rose to 836,556, but the newsstand figures decreased by 23.9 percent.[17] By 1993, *Elle* was on its fifth publisher (Diane Wichard Silberstein) since it began, *Harper's* had slipped past and regained the number two ranking by selling 499.19 ad pages to *Elle*'s 387.98 in the first quarter, and *Elle*'s editors were acknowledging that sales were off and that something needed to be done.[18] What was wrong? Perhaps part of the problem lay in the magazine's mismanagement of human resources. According to *Inside Media*, "*Elle* is not a place you go to if you're concerned about retirement plans."[19] It further reported that "eight top editors, among them Rona Berg, Marian McEnvoy, Karen Anderegg and Joyce Caruso, have departed."[20] Other critics thought the magazine was losing its edge and was filled with fluff articles.

Elle's solution was to hire Amy Gross (who was a key part of journalistically structuring Murdoch's *Mirabella*) to be its editorial director and enhance the content of the features contained within the publication. At *Mirabella*, Gross "assigned stories on Sandra Day O'Connor and a harrowing photo essay on an anorexic woman."[21] As for the magazine's fashion pages, Hachette Filipacchi president David J. Pecker told the *New York Times* that readers did not want these pages changed; they loved them as they were.[22] In the May 1994 issue, *Elle* scooped both magazines and newspapers with an exclusive, candid interview with First Lady Hillary Rodham Clinton, who spoke about the Whitewater fiasco and its effect on her and her family. Quotes from the interview were repeated in newspapers and magazines nationwide. Obviously, Gross is hard at work, and *Elle* is on its way back to the ultimate goal of dethroning and replacing *Vogue* as the queen of the fashion industry.

Notes

1. Lisa Gubernick, "Ideas, Not Instruction," *Forbes*, May 5, 1986, p. 140.

2. Scott Donaton, "Recession Keeps Circulation Idling for Magazines," *Advertising Age*, August 23, 1993, p. 20.

3. Iris Cohen Selinger, "*Elle* Tells: As It Approaches Its Eighth Birthday, *Elle* Is No Longer the Flavor of the Month for Fashion Advertisers. But a New Crew Hopes to Restore It to Preeminence," *Inside Media*, May 26, 1993, p. 48+.

4. Geraldine Fabrikant, "Hachette Set to Give Elle a Makeover," *New York Times*, August 17, 1992, p. 1D.

5. "Quick Tales," *Evening Standard*, February 23, 1994, p. 47.

6. Fabrikant, "Hachette Set to Give Elle a Makeover," p. 1D.

7. Gubernick, "Ideas, Not Instruction," p. 140.

8. Ibid.

9. Ann Melvin, "Messages about AIDS Drowned Out," *Dallas Morning News*, April 16, 1994, p. 31A.

10. Eileen B. Brill, "Fashion Newcomers to Divide, Conquer," *Advertising Age*, November 10, 1986, p. S26.

11. Deirdre Carmody, "A New Elle Publisher Is Named," *New York Times*, December 9, 1992, p. 5D.

12. Selinger, "Elle Tells," p. 48.

13. Paddy Calistro, "Looks: An Era of Extremes; The Overriding Constant in Style in the 80s Was Change—Lots of It," *Los Angeles Times*, December 24, 1989, Magazine Sec., p. 32.

14. Scott Donaton, "Changing Fashions: New Publishers Try to Shape-up Magazines," *Advertising Age*, April 29, 1991, p. 49.

15. Patrick Reilly, "Diamandis Fashions a Place for U.S. 'Elle,' " *Advertising Age*, September 26, 1988, p. 87.

16. Ibid.

17. Donaton, "Changing Fashions," p. 49.

18. Selinger, "Elle Tells," p. 48

19. Ibid.

20. Ibid.

21. Ibid.

22. Ibid.

Information Sources

BIBLIOGRAPHY:

Brill, Eileen B. "Fashion Newcomers to Divide, Conquer." *Advertising Age*, November 10, 1986, p. S26.

Calistro, Paddy. "Looks: An Era of Extremes; The Overriding Constant in Style in the 80s Was Change—Lots of It." *Los Angeles Times*, December 24, 1989, Magazine Sec., p. 32.

Carmody, Deirdre. "A New Elle Publisher Is Named." *New York Times*, December 9, 1992, p. 5D.

Donaton, Scott. "Changing Fashions: New Publishers Try to Shape-up Magazines." *Advertising Age*, April 29, 1991, p. 49.

———."Recession Keeps Circulation Idling for Magazines." *Advertising Age*, August 23, 1993, p. 20.

Fabrikant, Geraldine. "Hachette Set to Give Elle a Makeover." *New York Times*, August 17, 1992, p. 1D.

Gubernick, Lisa. "Ideas, Not Instruction." *Forbes*, May 5, 1986, pp. 138–140.

Melvin, Ann. "Messages about AIDS Drowned Out." *Dallas Morning News*, April 16, 1994, p. 31A.

"Quick Tales." *Evening Standard*, February 23, 1994, p. 47.

Reilly, Patrick. "Diamandis Fashions a Place for U.S. 'Elle.' " *Advertising Age*, September 26, 1988, p. 87.

INDEX SOURCES: Lexis/Nexis; The Serials Directory.

LOCATION SOURCES: Library of Congress, Middle Tennessee State University Todd Library, and other libraries.

Publication History

MAGAZINE TITLE AND TITLE CHANGES: *Elle.*

VOLUME AND ISSUE DATA: Vols. 1–(November 1985–present). Monthly.

PUBLISHER AND PLACE OF PUBLICATION: Hachette Filipacchi Magazines, Inc. New York.

EDITORS: Amy Gross, editorial editor (1993–present).
CIRCULATION: ABC, 1993: 924,429 (paid, primarily subscriptions).

Jennifer L. Bailey

ESSENCE

The debut issue of *Essence*, a lifestyle magazine directed at upscale African American women, appeared on newsstands in May 1970. From the start, it struck a resounding chord with its sophisticated target audience, a group long ignored by traditional women's magazines. Here, at last, was a magazine that celebrated the beauty, the intelligence, and the talent of black women. Here was a magazine that spoke—sister-to-sister—about the joys and trials of being black and female in America. Here was a magazine that reflected their spirit, applauded their triumphs, and related to them in a manner that no other publication—including the venerable black magazines—had ever attempted.

No wonder, then, that black women—from the very first issue—embraced *Essence* like manna from Heaven. Throughout the 1970s and early 1980s, as opportunities for blacks increased, and the black middle class grew at an unprecedented rate, the ranks of faithful *Essence* readers swelled, too. Today, *Essence* indisputably is the preeminent lifestyle magazine for African American women, enjoying a circulation of close to 1 million and a readership of more than 5 million.[1] Though its *Cosmo**-style amatory indulgences (''Am I the Last Virgin?'') and its occasionally thick overlay of trendy spiritualism (particularly editor in chief Susan Taylor's monthly column) have led to criticism and some competition, there is no disputing *Essence*'s extraordinary penetration of the market.

This market is attractive, though underestimated. *Essence*, according to Simmons Market Research Bureau, reaches 50 percent of all black women who earn $50,000 or more. It is the highest-ranking African American publication in household incomes of $60,000 or more. Nearly 38 percent of the readers are college graduates.[2]

Like *Ms.*,* which came into being in the same era, *Essence* is as much a movement as a magazine. Launched at a critical juncture in history—a time when feminists and black nationalists were reshaping the American dialogue on race and gender—*Essence* came to be an important forum for issues related to the role of black women in society. Though fashion and fitness, the editorial staples of traditional women's magazines, figure prominently in the *Essence* editorial mix, the legions of 18-to-49-year-old women who dutifully turn to the magazine each month look there for everything from career advice to news affecting African Americans throughout the diaspora. Moreover, *Essence* provides them with uplifting role models and inspirational success stories. In fact, few other magazines have played such a major role in chronicling the political and social development of African American women in the last quarter of the twentieth century.

As one of the nation's most prominent minority-owned business ventures, *Essence* also is held aloft as a model of African American entrepreneurship. The magazine is the centerpiece of a privately held multimedia company, Essence Communications, Inc., which also has a licensing division and produces mail order catalogs and syndicated television programs. The company had total revenues in the neighborhood of $43 million in 1992.[3]

It has not, however, been an altogether easy climb for *Essence* cofounders Edward T. Lewis and Clarence O. Smith, who are chief executive officer and president of Essence Communications, respectively. While the niche and the need for the magazine were clear from the outset, it has been an uphill battle convincing investors and potential advertisers of the viability of the black market. To this day, many media buyers remain loath to recognize any distinctions among the major African American magazines.

As *Essence*'s midwest advertising sales director Jocelyn B. Brown noted: "Too many people who control advertising dollars view the Black media as one entity. They see no difference between *Ebony* [a general interest magazine], *Black Enterprise* [a publication aimed at black businesspersons] and *Essence*. So we constantly have to educate them about the variety in Black media."[4]

Similarly, the sales representatives at *Essence* and its brethren in the black media have had to educate prospective advertisers about the most effective ways to appeal to black consumers. Initially, many advertisers balked at the magazine's insistence that black models be used in advertisements, though years of organized lobbying for this concession have helped break down the resistance.[5]

Still, it was difficult convincing some of the country's largest cosmetic companies that *Essence* was a sound advertising vehicle for their products. Even with research showing the relative affluence of the *Essence* readership (the average household income is $37,000[6]) and with studies indicating that African American women buy more cosmetics and other such products than practically any other consumer group, the magazine for years was snubbed by cosmetic industry giants like Revlon and Estée Lauder. In fact, not until the early 1990s did major fragrance and cosmetics companies begin taking pages in *Essence*.[7] The breakthrough was significant. But then, *Essence*'s history is replete with breakthroughs, each of them significant for the magazine and for black women.

But *Essence* was not born out of feminist conviction. Rather, it was the child of opportunity and capitalist ambition. The magazine had its genesis in a 1968 meeting in New York sponsored by Shearson-Hammill (now Shearson Lehman Brothers) to determine how to attract more young African Americans into business. It was not altruism that prompted the meeting, but the spate of riots that followed the assassinations of the Reverend Martin Luther King, Jr., and Senator Robert Kennedy. The Nixon administration's response to the unrest was to advance the notion that stimulating black capitalism would quiet the storm in

America's cities. Many influential people in the business community bought the concept, and thus the Shearson-sponsored meeting came into being.[8]

Among the ideas for new businesses tossed around during that meeting was a fashion magazine for black women. It was suggested—though no one quite remembers by whom—that black women were yearning for a magazine they could call their own. One of the people attending that meeting was a Harvard-educated young black man from the South Bronx named Edward Lewis, who then was working as a loan officer at First National City Bank (now Citibank). Though he knew nothing about fashion or the magazine industry, Lewis recognized a good business opportunity when he saw one, and this idea about starting a black fashion magazine struck him as a winning proposition. He established a partnership with Clarence Smith, another product of the South Bronx who then was working as an insurance salesman with Investors Planning Corp., and two other young black businessmen, Jonathan Blount and Cecil Hollingsworth. Together, they blithely set out to raise money for the new magazine.[9]

They had no idea how difficult the task would be. "[I]t was not easy then—nor is it easy now," Lewis wrote in the magazine's 20th-anniversary issue. "We were undercapitalized, forced to operate with little money because investors resisted the concept of a magazine for African-American women. We were exploited by vendors because we lacked experience. We made mistakes. We argued. And yet we never lost faith in our vision to build an institution of which you could be proud."[10]

Their business plan called for working capital in the neighborhood of $1 million. Despite a yearlong effort by several minority venture capital firms, they were still able to raise only $130,000 from six investors: Chase Manhattan Bank, Citibank, CBS, Newsweek, Time, Inc. and Young & Rubicam. Ultimately, those investors—and new ones, including Equitable Life Assurance Society of the U.S. and Bancap, Inc.—anted up about $1.87 million, mostly in loans, and *Essence* was on its way.[11]

Lewis was installed as the magazine's publisher—a post he still holds today—and the partners recruited Gordon Parks, the noted black photographer and writer, as editorial director.

Originally, the magazine was to be called *Sapphire*. It is telling that the four male founders thought the name would be taken as a compliment, a reference to the precious jewel. But *Essence*'s first editor, Ruth Ross, argued that the title most assuredly would conjure up images of the head-rolling, loud-talking character on the old ''Amos 'n Andy'' television program, a stereotype black women continue to find offensive. Fortunately, Ross prevailed, but it still took several years and a couple of editors for *Essence* to develop the look and the voice its loyal readers now find so comforting.[12]

In the early years, the focus was clearly on fashion and beauty, and that was enough to please the audience, given the novelty of the *Essence* approach. Before the ''exotic'' look of black models was in vogue, *Essence* established that it would expand the American beauty standard to include *all* black women, not just the caramel-colored, thin-lipped "white girls in blackface" who were the preeminent black models of the day. *Essence* paraded black women of all shapes, sizes, complexions, and hair textures. The first issue set the tone. It featured a regal black woman with a large Afro hairstyle.

The creative force who is credited with advancing *Essence* beyond its limited and limiting concentration on fashion was Marcia Ann Gillespie. Two editors had come and gone before Gillespie took the editorial reins in 1971 at age 26. She realized that black women could get fashion forecasts from other publications, so she steered the magazine in the direction of more lifestyle and service-oriented features.

The Gillespie-inspired editorial formula remains largely in place at *Essence* today. The stories tend to be short (1,000 words is a lengthy *Essence* feature), with provocative titles ("Why Are All the Good Guys Gay?"). They are written in a breezy, conversational manner that captures the spirit of sisterhood. There is a heavy reliance on celebrity profiles, updates, and new personality features. Though in the early days *Essence* covers featured a variety of black models, in recent years the cover strategy has shifted. Today's covers generally feature a high-profile black woman—though several men have graced the cover also—coiffed, coutured, and airbrushed to perfection.

There is plenty of service and advice in *Essence*, too, ranging from tips on love ("Marrying an African: Can You Go Home Again?"), to recipes ("Cooking the Muslim Way"), but the slant is decidedly Afrocentric.

The changes Gillespie instituted helped *Essence* take giant leaps forward. Under her leadership, the magazine achieved its first break-even issue in March 1973. In the six years that followed, circulation quadrupled.[13]

While Gillespie tinkered editorially, there was turmoil on the business side of the magazine during its bumpy first decade. In the mid-1970s, the four founders locked horns over the direction of the business and the magazine. The result was a financially draining takeover battle that pitted Lewis and Smith against Blount and Hollingsworth. Though Lewis and Smith emerged the victors (they control 51 percent of Essence Communications, Inc.), the fight left the company cash-strapped for several years.[14]

Still, Gillespie pressed on. She helped usher *Essence* into its present position as the country's principal outlet for the fiction and poetry of black women writers. Nikki Giovanni, Ntozake Shange, Toni Morrison, Gloria Naylor, Alice Walker, Terry McMillan—indeed, all of the towering contemporary black women of letters—have had work featured in *Essence*, often well before they became literary stars. In the same vein, *Essence* has been an important showcase for black women journalists and essayists, featuring Jill Nelson, Paula Giddings, Bebe Moore Campbell, and Audrey Edwards.

By the time Gillespie left *Essence* in 1980, the magazine had become an institution. Circulation was nearing the 650,000 mark—up from 162,000 when she took over—and the magazine was profitable, with advertising revenue in the $4 million range.[15]

The remaining partners tapped Susan L. Taylor to succeed Gillespie as editor in chief. A former actress and makeup artist, Taylor came to the magazine in 1971 as beauty editor. She was appointed editor in chief ten years later, and during her reign she has expanded *Essence*'s coverage in two critical areas—international reporting and men.

On the international front, Taylor, whose parents hail from Jamaica, has included in the magazine's area of concentration news about women in Africa and the Caribbean, specifically highlighting achievements in art, music, and literature but also offering a good deal of coverage about social, economic, and political developments. *Essence* probably has devoted more space to exposing the brutality of the widespread African practice of female circumcision than any other magazine.

On the subject of black men, Taylor has been particularly successful in broadening *Essence*'s scope and readership. While the magazine always talked *about* men—how to get a man, how to get rid of a man, how to get along without a man—Taylor is credited with shifting the focus to *include* men, making the magazine a forum for discussion of black male-female relationships in which men were invited to participate.

In 1981, Taylor launched the November men's issue, now an annual attraction devoted to the status, lifestyles, and desires of black men in America. In 1983, she instituted the "Say, Brother" column (now simply called "Brothers"), which offers men a chance each month to speak to the sisters about their innermost feelings. "Understanding what is in the hearts and minds of our men is important to empowering the Black community," Taylor says. "*Essence* encourages Black men to express their deepest longings and feelings as well as their many frustrations, which are often-times ignored."[16]

That philosophy may help account for the fact that 27 percent of the *Essence* readership is male, a relatively high percentage for a women's magazine.[17]

Taylor brought something else to the table when she took over *Essence*—star quality. With her flawless mahogany complexion and her long cornrows, plaited away from her face and streaming down past her shoulders (she was a pioneer of this now-popular braided hairstyle), she cut a dramatically beautiful figure and quickly became the symbol of the *Essence* woman. She was the host and executive producer of the *Essence* talk show, a nationally syndicated television magazine that enjoyed a moderately successful four-season run in the mid-1980s. That platform not only heightened her profile but cemented her bond with readers. Just as Helen Gurley Brown is the *Cosmo* girl, and Gloria Steinem is the embodiment of *Ms.*, Susan Taylor, to many readers, became the personification of *Essence*. While few of the magazine's readers would recognize the names—let alone the faces—of Edward Lewis and Clarence Smith, the men who founded and have ultimate control of the magazine, practically everyone who reads *Essence* is familiar with Taylor. Even the company logo, the silhouetted profile of a black woman with a flowing cornrow hairstyle, bears a striking resemblance to her.[18]

Moreover, as a single mother juggling the demands of her career with the rearing of her now-adult daughter, Shana Nequai, Taylor has been an inspiration to the thousands of *Essence* readers who face similar challenges. Her monthly column, "In the Spirit," is designed to help others tap into the source of her strength, Taylor says. "I try to encourage my sisters to develop their spiritual consciousness, to push back any boundaries—real or perceived—and not limit their power to fully love and embrace themselves."[19]

Some critics, however, charge that the column—and the magazine—are too full of hollow platitudes and facile solutions to the complex problems facing black America. In the wake of such charges, *Essence* has faced its share of challenges, most recently from *S'azz*, a glossy fashion book that flared up and flamed out in 1990. No one has been able to unseat *Essence* from its commanding position as *the* black women's magazine.[20]

It is a testament to the success of Lewis and Smith that the fiercely competitive publishing magnate John H. Johnson, the founder of *Ebony*, the oldest and most successful black magazine in the world, sought and acquired a 20 percent stake in Essence Communications in the mid-1980s rather than launch a competing magazine. To Johnson, a man hailed in the black community for his sound business instincts, it was clear that the company's fortunes were on the rise.[21]

Essence continues to face challenges. Advertising pages dropped almost 12 percent during the crippling recession that ushered in the 1990s. While the big cosmetics manufacturers are at long last discovering the potency of the African American market, they still indiscriminately buy pages in black media with their "special markets" dollars. The advertising in *Essence* is dominated by alcohol and cigarettes, the biggest buyers of black media. Naturally, the magazine gets healthy advertising support from African American hair care manufacturers. It also features a good deal of "image ads" from companies that either are recruiting blacks or hope to demonstrate their liberal goodwill and support of African American institutions and causes.

With circulation still inching upward and a postrecession uptick in ad pages, *Essence* currently sits in a healthy position. It has demonstrated remarkable resilience through the years—fending off challenges from without and within—and managed to build a loyal sisterhood of readers who remain grateful to see themselves fully reflected in the pages of a magazine.

Notes

1. 1994 Media Kit.
2. Simmons Market Research Bureau, Inc., 1992, Study of Media and Markets.
3. Bernard E. Anderson and Alfred A. Edmond, "The B.E. 100s: Top Industrial and Service Businesses for 1993," *Black Enterprise*, June 1993, pp. 85–204.
4. Jocelyn B. Brown interview; Chicago, October 13, 1993.
5. Ibid.
6. Mediamark Research, Inc., Magazine Total Audiences Report, Spring 1992.

7. James Brady, "The 'Essence' of Smith & Lewis," *Advertising Age*, January 13, 1992, p. 24.

8. Ibid.

9. Marjorie McManus, "The Essence Magazine Success Story," *Folio*, December 1976, p. 28.

10. Edward Lewis, "In Celebration of Our Twentieth Anniversary," May 1990, p. 20.

11. Terri Agins and Udayan Gupta, "Black Women Enjoy Vogue, but Essence Is a Magazine for Them," *Wall Street Journal*, December 11, 1986, p. 1.

12. Lewis, "In Celebration of Our Twentieth Anniversary," p. 20.

13. McManus, "The Essence Magazine Success Story," p. 28.

14. Shawn Kennedy, "In Essence, A Celebration of Black Women," *New York Times*, May 7, 1990, sec. 2, p. 2.

15. Ibid.

16. Susan Taylor quote from the 1994 Media Kit.

17. Magazine Total Audiences Report.

18. Media Kit.

19. Ibid.

20. Kennedy, "In Essence, A Celebration of Black Women," p. 2.

21. Agins and Gupta, "Black Women Enjoy Vogue, but Essence Is a Magazine for Them," p. 1.

Information Sources

BIBLIOGRAPHY:

Agins, Terri, and Udayan Gupta. "Black Women Enjoy Vogue, but Essence Is a Magazine for Them: It Also Is a Small Business That Is Turning a Dollar after 16 Difficult Years." *Wall Street Journal*, December 11, 1986, sec. 1, p. 1.

Anderson, Bernard E., and Alfred A. Edmond, "The B.E. 100s: Top Industrial and Service Businesses for 1993." *Black Enterprise*, June 1993, pp. 85–204.

Brady, James. "The 'Essence' of Smith & Lewis." *Advertising Age*. January 13, 1992, p. 24.

Kennedy, Shawn. "In Essence, A Celebration of Black Women." *New York Times*, May 7, 1990, sec. 2, p. 2.

McManus, Marjorie. "The Essence Magazine Success Story." *Folio*, December 1976, pp. 28–29.

INDEX SOURCES: Book Review Index; Child Book Review Index; Current Literature in Family Planning; Health Index; Index to Periodical Articles by and about Negroes (Index to Black Periodicals); Magazine Index; Media Review Digest; Popular Magazine Review; Readers' Guide to Periodical Literature; Text on Microfilm.

LOCATION SOURCES: Library of Congress; New York Public Library; and other libraries.

Publication History

MAGAZINE TITLE AND TITLE CHANGES: *Essence*.

VOLUME AND ISSUE DATA: Vols. 1– (May 1970–present). Monthly.

PUBLISHER AND PLACE OF PUBLICATION: Essence Communications (1970–present). New York.

EDITORS: Ruth Ross (1970); Ida Lewis (1970–1971); Marcia Ann Gillespie (1971–1980); Susan L. Taylor (1981–present).
CIRCULATION: ABC, 1992: 900,350 (primarily subscriptions).

Charles Whitaker

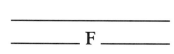

_____ F _____

FAMILY CIRCLE

Family Circle, a home service magazine with a circulation of more than 5 million in 1993, began its life in 1932 as a promotional giveaway, handed out in food store chains. Harry Evans, a managing editor of *Life* magazine, conceived the idea for the publication and produced it, with the financial help of Charles E. Merrill. Evans sold the magazine to retailers such as Piggly Wiggly, Sanitary Grocery Co. (later Safeway), and Reeves Stores, who gave it away to customers. The publication benefited the supermarkets as well as the stores' customers; its contents, emphasizing food, child care, fashion, and beauty, encouraged readers to buy products. The first issues also contained fiction, jokes, and articles about movies and radio. From its inception *Family Circle* carried some advertising.[1]

The title remained free until 1946, when a five-cent price was added, and the publication switched from weekly to monthly publication. Three years later, *Family Circle*'s distribution expanded considerably when the Kroger chain began carrying the magazine.[2] Shopping, homemaking, decorating, home equipment, fashion, and child-rearing tips, as well as a feature directed at teens called "Teen Scene," formed the nucleus of *Family Circle*'s content through the early 1950s.[3] By 1951, *Family Circle* was distributed in 8,500 stores, including Kroger, Safeway, and 12 other chains. The next year, *Family Circle* guaranteed 3.5 million in circulation, second only to *Woman's Day** among the food store magazines.[4]

Founder Evans, who had initially edited the magazine, had been replaced in 1936 with Robert Endicott, who oversaw the practical homemaking content appearing in *Family Circle* from 1936 through 1954. Robert Jones then took over, leaving a position at *Better Homes and Gardens** to do so. Both editors directed the material in the magazine at cost- and time-conscious housewives.

The 1950s proved a time of great competition among supermarket magazines. Pioneers *Family Circle* and *Woman's Day* had been joined in 1939 by *Every-*

woman. Then, in the 1950s, numerous other grocery store titles appeared. But the market failed to sustain so many publications, and most died. In 1958, *Everywoman* joined *Family Circle*, giving the merged *Everywoman's Family Circle* (with the first word printed in small letters) a circulation of 5 million, with distribution in 12,500 grocery stores.[5]

During those years the circulation achieved by *Family Circle* (as well as that of competitor *Woman's Day*) came almost completely from single-copy issues, sold primarily at supermarkets. This distribution system fueled circulation growth, and by 1962, *Family Circle* was selling more copies than the longtime women's magazine leader *Ladies' Home Journal*.*

This successful distribution system and the high single-copy sales interested Cowles Magazines and Broadcasting, publishers of *Look*; and in 1962, the company bought *Family Circle*. Under Cowles the ''Everywoman'' in the title (taken on with the 1958 merger) was eliminated. But the content of the magazine continued to consist of well-tested recipes, decorating ideas, fashion, and beauty advice, with a few nonfiction features and little fiction, all sold at a relatively low price. Despite his interest in the distribution system of *Family Circle*, Gardner Cowles remained mystified by the appeal of the journal. He remarked, ''I can't get it out of my head that 7-million women every month voluntarily pick this Family Circle up and buy it.''[6] But a good market existed for the economical home-oriented information in the magazine, and by 1963, 7 million readers were purchasing the title.

Arthur Hettich took over as editor of *Family Circle* in 1965, a position he held for 20 years. Gay Bryant held the editorial spot briefly, then Hettich resumed the job until 1988. Under Hettich, service and do-ability were the magazine's watchwords. Food, crafts, decorating, and fashion formed its backbone. Gradually, health and money management issues were added.[7] Advertisers continued to move into the magazine, making it a profitable property.

In 1971, when Cowles Co.'s major publication, *Look*, was suspended, the company sold *Family Circle* to the New York Times Co. Throughout the 1970s, *Family Circle* jockeyed with rival *Woman's Day* for the top spot in women's magazine circulation, with each of them boasting circulations of more than 8 million for most of that decade. Both continued their use of single-copy sales, a tactic other magazine publishers envied in the face of rising postal costs and the expense of fulfilling subscriptions. *Family Circle* increased frequency of publication, finally stopping at 17 times a year in 1979 (every three weeks). An emphasis on service features, plentiful do-it-yourself projects, and a series on changing lifestyles were some of the reasons for the magazine's popularity.[8] Advertisers liked the publication as well. As advertising increased, editorial content in the magazine dropped from 51.2 percent of the magazine in 1970 to 44.2 percent in 1980.[9]

During the 1970s, *Family Circle*'s name became associated with tennis, as the magazine began sponsoring a national women's tennis tournament. The magazine also sponsored an award recognizing excellence in nutrition education.[10]

By the 1980s, the top circulation spot in the women's magazine race had shifted to "shelter" journal *Better Homes and Gardens**; *Family Circle* continued to hold this second slot. Newsstand sales of all magazines had been hurt in those same years. In the middle of the 1980s, *Family Circle*, which had grown to greatness on single-copy sales, began pushing subscriptions, a tactic competitor *Woman's Day* was forced to imitate several years later. The magazine consciously began publishing more articles on children in the 1980s to attract younger readers (the 28-to-34-year-olds).[11] Advertising for most women's journals had declined in the late 1970s and early 1980s; *Family Circle*'s advertising dropped 32 percent between 1978 and 1988.[12]

Circulation stood at about 5.75 million in 1987. The price of the journal remained low at 99¢. Each issue carried about 60 percent advertising. Advertisers could opt for regional or subregional editions.[13] But as circulation continued to decline, and competition for ad revenues heightened, *Family Circle* got a new publisher. Charles Townsend joined the publication in December 1986. Townsend made several changes to boost the magazine. He joined his distribution operation with Time Inc.'s, increasing by more than ten times the number of field representatives checking supermarket racks to ensure that *Family Circle* had good placement.[14]

Townsend also hired a new editor, Jacqueline Leo. Leo, cofounder and editor of *Child* magazine, came to *Family Circle* in 1988. She retained the basic *Family Circle* service mix. However, to differentiate the magazine from its competitors (such as *Woman's Day*, which readers complained was similar), Leo began running investigative pieces on issues of interest to women. Health topics and environmental issues received consistent attention, added to the ubiquitous recipes, crafts, and diet features. A striking example of Leo's new approach came with the magazine's exposé of toxic waste in an Arkansas town, a piece that won a National Magazine Award. Other articles discussed transportation of hazardous chemicals and abuses of child labor among teenagers.[15] The magazine excerpted an important piece about cluster disease that originally appeared in the *New Yorker*; *Family Circle* editors had author Paul Bodeur condense the 30,000-word story into 2,500 for their readers.[16]

Health articles have abounded in *Family Circle* (as in other women's magazines) in recent years, generating great reader response. Leo also tried to include more information on African American women, making the magazine for middle-class black, as well as white, women.[17] The magazine now, as always, publishes little or no fiction.

A regular feature appearing for a number of years has been "Women Who Make a Difference," highlighting individuals performing socially useful activities. Examples include a woman who founded a home for runaway children, a dancer who ran classes for disabled children, and two ex-actresses who established a residential treatment center for abused children.

Despite the shifts in emphasis, Leo did not change the cluttered, information-packed cover that had long characterized the title. Usefulness and practicality remained the magazine's watchwords. Leo tied the investigative journalism articles neatly together with the magazine's overall mission by claiming that her publication was "the magazine of family advocacy."[18] While recognizing the changing lifestyles of women and the notion that increasing numbers of women worked outside the home, *Family Circle* still focused editorially on the woman who either was a full-time homemaker or identified homemaking as her most important job. The bow to women holding jobs outside the home came primarily in increased articles and ideas for saving time (in addition to the ubiquitous features on saving money).

The magazine published special-topic issues since 1961 on subjects such as food, exercise, and health. In 1975, these were coordinated as the Great Ideas Program, special-topic issues that appeared regularly. In 1990, these were replaced with *Family Circle Now*, special subject issues appearing bimonthly, focused on the younger, time-conscious portion of the magazine's audience. This strategy allowed the general-interest, large-circulation *Family Circle* to attract smaller segments of readers.[19]

During these years, competition for single-copy sales intensified. One blow came from Bauer Publishing's 1989 debut of *First for Women,** an inexpensive, highly promoted, supermarket-distributed publication. (Previously, Bauer had brought out *Woman's World*, which sold all of its copies on the newsstand; the publication appeared first regionally in 1981, then went national in 1984).[20] This hurt *Family Circle*, which still, in 1991, sold over half its copies on newsstands.

Despite its problems, in 1991, *Family Circle* netted $36.8 million, and in 1993, *Family Circle* ranked 13th of all magazines in advertising revenues.[21] By this time the publication had British, Japanese, and Australian editions.

In March 1994, Leo moved up to the position of senior vice president and editorial director of the Women's Magazine Group. Veteran staffer and deputy editor Susan Kelliher Ungaro took over.

In June 1994, Gruner + Jahr USA Publishing (part of the publishing division of German media conglomerate Bertelsmann) made a deal to buy the Women's Magazine Division of the New York Times Co., including *Family Circle* (other titles included *McCall's** and *Child*), at the end of July.[22] The company reputedly paid $350 million for the group. Few changes were planned for *Family Circle*, at least in the near future; Gruner + Jahr International Publishing President Axel Ganz stated that "Family Circle has a clear position in the market."[23] Ganz, however, announced plans to focus on a slightly younger market than *Family Circle*'s current readers in their early 40s.

Notes

1. Sharon Tabachnick, "Family Circle," in Alan Nourie and Barbara Nourie (eds.), *American Mass-Market Magazines* (Westport, Conn.: Greenwood Press, 1990), p. 119; Stuart J. Emmrich, " 'Family Circle' Marks 50th," *Advertising Age*, September 6, 1982, p. 10; "Graduates of Life," *Time*, October 3, 1932, p. 19.

2. Theodore Peterson, *Magazines in the Twentieth Century* (Urbana: University of Illinois Press, 1964), p. 283.

3. Erwin V. Johanningmeier, "Family Circle's Portrayal of the Post-World-War II Teenager: The Way We Were," paper presented at the annual History of Education Society meeting, Kansas City, Mo., October 1991.

4. "Food-Store Magazines Hit the Big Time," *Business Week*, February 9, 1952, pp. 108, 110.

5. *Everywoman's Family Circle* advertisement in *New York Times*, March 6, 1958, p. 44.

6. Quoted in Tabachnick, "Family Circle," pp. 122, 123.

7. John Peter, "Women's Magazines—A Survey of the Field," *Folio*, April 1977, pp. 75–76.

8. Babette Ashby, "Family Circle Is Looking for New Talent, but . . . ," *The Writer*, November 1978, p. 21.

9. Maureen McFadden, "Sibling Rivalry: How the Seven Sisters Are Making It through the '80s," *Magazine Age,* January 1982, p. 51.

10. Tabachnick, "Family Circle," p. 121.

11. Gay Bryant, "Writing for *Family Circle*," *The Writer*, August 1985, p. 22.

12. Nancy Yoshihura, "Women's Magazine Dilemma," *Los Angeles Times*, December 23, 1979, sec., 4 pp. 1, 5; Cecilia Lentini, "Balancing Act in Women's Magazines," *Advertising Age*, October 19, 1981, pp. S62, 640.

13. Tabachnick, "Family Circle," p. 121.

14. Eric Schmuckler, "Sob for the Sisters," *Forbes*, April 4, 1988, p. 113.

15. Ben A. Franklin, "Family Circle Gets Tough," *Washington Journalism Review*, November 1990, pp. 48–52; Diane Hales, "Cluster Diseases: Is Your Family at Risk?" April 24, 1990, pp. 55–61; Thomas Clavin, "Poisoned Cargo: How the Nation's Railroads Put Millions at Risk," February 1, 1994, pp. 100–103; John Masterton, "Profit Profile: *Family Circle*," *MagazineWeek*, February 24, 1992, p. 36.

16. Clavin, "Poisoned Cargo."

17. Jackie Leo interview, April 13, 1990.

18. Masterton, "Profit Profile," p. 36.

19. Liz Horton, "Two Consumer Giants Take a 'Special Interest' in Niche Publishing," *Folio*, March 1990, pp. 49, 51; Tabachnick, "Family Circle," pp. 120–121.

20. Ira Teinowitz, " 'First' Shock Wave," *Advertising Age*, August 21, 1989, pp. 1, 66.

21. Masterton, "Profit Profile."

22. Geraldine Fabrikant, "Gruner to Buy Times Women's Magazines," *New York Times*, June 17, 1994, pp. D1, D15.

23. Keith J. Kelly, "Gruner & Jahr Thinks Younger," *Advertising Age*, June 27, 1994, p. 4.

Information Sources

BIBLIOGRAPHY:

Franklin, Ben A. "Family Circle Gets Tough." *Washington Journalism Review*, November 1990, pp. 48–52.

Masterton, John. "Profit Profile. Family Circle." *MagazineWeek* February 24, 1992, p. 36.

Peterson, Theodore. *Magazines in the Twentieth Century.* Urbana: University of Illinois Press, 1964.

Tabachnick, Sharon. "Family Circle," in Alan Nourie and Barbara Nourie (eds.), *American Mass-Market Magazines.* Westport, Conn.: Greenwood Press, 1990, pp. 119–126.

INDEX SOURCES: Access; Consumers Index; Current Literature in Family Planning, Index to How to Do It Information, MELSA Messenger.

LOCATION SOURCES: Cleveland Public Library and other (primarily community) libraries.

Publication History

MAGAZINE TITLE AND TITLE CHANGES: *The Family Circle* (1932–1958); *Everywoman's Family Circle* (1958–1962); *Family Circle* (1963–present).

VOLUME AND ISSUE DATA: Vols. 1–(September 9, 1932–present). Weekly (1932–1946); monthly (1946–1976); 13 times a year (1977); 14 times a year (1978); 17 times a year (1979–present).

PUBLISHER AND PLACE OF PUBLICATION: Evans Publishing Company (1932–May 1958); Family Circle, Inc. (June 1958–1994); Gruner + Jahr (1994–present). New York.

EDITORS: Harry Evans (1932–1936); Robert Endicott (1936–1954); Robert Jones (1955–1965); Arthur Hettich (1965–1985); Gay Bryant (1985–1986); Arthur Hettich (1986–1988); Jacqueline Leo (1988–1994); Susan Kelliher Ungaro (1994–present).

CIRCULATION: ABC, 1993: 5,071,968 (paid, majority single-copy sales).

Mary Ellen Zuckerman

FIRST FOR WOMEN

With an unusual introductory distribution, *First for Women* hit the newsstands in February 1989. West German-based Heinrich Bauer flooded supermarkets and convenience stores with 8 million copies selling at the introductory price of 25¢, which retailers were able to keep. The price was raised to one dollar per copy for the next issue of the monthly magazine.

As a newsstand-only publication, *First* went head-to-head with *Woman's Day* and *Family Circle,* though it was designed as a direct rival to the entire "Seven Sisters" group, which also included *Better Homes and Gardens,* *Redbook,* and *McCall's.*[1] Circulation of the "Seven Sisters" had dropped from 46 million in the 1970s to 38 million in the 1980s.

First for Women was launched eight years after Bauer broke into the U.S. market with *Woman's World,* a weekly tabloid also sold primarily at supermarkets. In an aggressive distribution move, Bauer secured top rack positions at stores by paying a onetime promotion incentive of $27 per checkout and quarterly payments of $9 per checkout.

Bauer reportedly spent $15 million in television advertising for the national rollout of *First*; a 90-day blitz of television ads began the day before the magazine appeared at newsstands. The launch formula, unusual in the United States, also included almost a complete dependence on revenue from single-copy sales. To discourage subscriptions, Bauer set that price at $2 an issue, double the newsstand price.

First's initial policy also called for limiting advertising to one-third of the pages; other women's service magazines were carrying at least half their pages as ads.

First proved typical of other women's magazine fare. The cover of the first issue featured a young model, suggesting that the magazine sought young readers. Articles focused on things to make, recipes, fashion, and a birth control update. Dennis Neeld, an Englishman who had earlier plied his trade with *The National Enquirer,* served as *First*'s first editor.

Initially, *First*'s ad rate base was 2 million; that doubled to 4 million in six months. *First*'s strong start appeared to have a jolting effect on the veteran supermarket magazines. *Woman's Day* dropped 21 percent from December 1989 through August of the next year, and *Family Circle* saw a double-digit decline after raising its cover price. Analysts felt it was too early to determine whether *First*'s entrance into the service magazine competition was the primary factor affecting the rival titles or whether long-term changes were in the offing in the women's magazine sector.

Within the next year, *First*'s shock-wave start began to unreel as credibility with advertisers plummeted.[2]

A 1990 ad marketing tactic called for giving volume discounts based on total advertising placed by the agency, rather than by the client. The strategy drew criticism from media buyers, particularly those at small firms. The rate base fell 25 percent to 3 million in April 1990 and was down to 2.5 million by March 1991.

By its third anniversary in 1992, *First*'s rate base was down to 1.5 million, and a new ad sales program was met with criticism. The program guaranteed circulation numbers to advertisers committing to at least three issues. If the guarantees were not met, the ads would be repeated until the guarantee level was met.

First for Women became an example of how transferring foreign publishing ideas to the United States can prove difficult. Bauer experienced success with *Woman's World*, a tabloid with little advertising. That publication, however, is advice-packed and entertaining in nature. *First for Women* mirrored *Woman's Day* and *Family Circle* as a magazine designed to help a woman with a home and family.

Although Bauer never revealed a monetary figure, publishing executives surmised that by May 1991, two years after its launch, *First* had lost $60 million or more. To counter the slide, *First* began courting advertisers. From 472 ad pages in 1991, the magazine recorded 557 pages in 1992 and 612 in 1993. The last figure represents a 42 percent increase over 1990 numbers.

Editorial content continued to target an audience of young homemakers. By 1992, the median age of *First* readers was 39; for all the others in the "Seven Sisters" group, the median age was 43.

As of 1993, *First* was publishing 17 issues a year under the editorship of Jane Traulsen. Circulation, all single-copy sales, was close to 1.3 million, down from 1.45 million the previous year and more than 2 million in 1991. The highest percentage of sales for a geographical area was in Minnesota, Iowa, Missouri, the Dakotas, Nebraska, and Kansas, where sales totaled more than 18 percent of the overall circulation.[3]

Each issue included a short story, puzzle, horoscope, shopping directory, and advice column, as well as feature stories and pieces on beauty, consumer issues, work, relationships, kids, health/fitness, food, and garden topics. The stories, many penned by freelancers, were concise and rather informal in style. Color photos accompanied most articles. *First* has not emerged as a threat to the established women's service magazines but, rather, is a publication with a special niche as a single-copy entity with a younger reading audience.

Advertising policies have changed dramatically at *First* since its 1989 launch. The first issue had no ads until page 23; the editions in 1994 featured double-truck ads on pages 2 and 3 for products like Marlboro cigarettes. The original plan to make large profits almost exclusively from circulation has not materialized as it did with *Women's World*. But *First*, with a 1994 cover price of $1.59, continues to occupy premier space at the supermarket checkout line and, like its first issue, often features young models on the cover.

Notes

1. Geraldine Fabrikant, "Bauer Starts 2d Magazine for Women," *New York Times,* February 16, 1989, sec. 4, p. 21.

2. Liz Horton, "New Ad Marketing Tactic: Agency Discounts," *Folio,* February 1990, p. 15.

3. Magazine Publisher's Statement (Schaumburg, Ill.: Audit Bureau of Circulations, June 1993).

Information Sources

BIBLIOGRAPHY:

DeNitto, Emily. "Two Women's Magazines Try Cents-Off Couponing in Stores." *Supermarket News,* June 11, 1990, p. 8.

Donaton, Scott. " 'First' Faltering in Ad Page Sales." *Advertising Age,* February 12, 1990, p. 20.

———. " 'First' Retrenches." *Advertising Age,* November 25, 1991, p. 10.

Fabrikant, Geraldine. "Bauer Starts 2d Magazine for Women." *New York Times,* February 16, 1989, sec. 4, p. 21.

———. "Many Readers, Few Ads for Bauer." *New York Times,* May 22, 1991, p. D1.

Feldman, Curtis. "Bang the Drum Loudly." *Marketing & Media Decisions,* November 1988, p. 22.

Horton, Liz. "New Ad Marketing Tactic: Agency Discounts." *Folio*, February 1990, p. 15.

Hovey, Brian "Coming to America." *Folio*, May 1990, pp. 49–51.

Mandese, Joe. "First Sign of Relief." *Advertising Age,* April 27, 1992, p. 40.

Masterson, John. "Can Bauer Regroup after Setbacks?" *Folio*, July 1990, p. 17.

Melloan, George. "A German Publisher Courts American Women." *Wall Street Journal,* March 21, 1989, p. 23.

Reilly, Patrick. " 'First' Readies Unusual Debut." *Advertising Age,"* January 23, 1989, p. 32.

Teinowitz, Ira. " 'First' Shock Wave." *Advertising Age,* August 21, 1989, p. 1.

INDEX SOURCES: Business Index; Infotrac; Trade and Industrial Index; DIALOG.

LOCATION SOURCES: Local libraries and the magazine consultancy.

Publication History

MAGAZINE TITLE AND TITLE CHANGES: *First for Women* (1989–present).

VOLUME AND ISSUE DATA: Vols. 1–(February 1989–present). Seventeen a year.

PUBLISHER AND PLACE OF PUBLICATION: Heinrich Bauer Publishing (1989–present). Englewood Cliffs, New Jersey.

EDITORS: Dennis Neeld (1989–1990); Jackie Highe (1990–1991); Dennis Neeld (1991–1992); Jane Traulsen (1992–1994); Dena Vane (1994–present).

CIRCULATION: ABC, 1993: 1,269,735 (paid, single-copy sales).

Tina Lesher

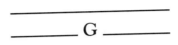

GENTLEMAN AND LADY'S TOWN AND COUNTRY MAGAZINE

In 1784, when the first magazine to include women as an important part of its target audience was established, the United States was not even a year old. America and its magazines were still in their infancy, just beginning to sit up and crawl. Indeed, *The Gentleman and Lady's Town and Country Magazine; or, Repository of Instruction and Entertainment* (long titles were the norm) was one of only two magazines being published at the time.

The years prior to the American Revolution had seen only a handful of magazines established in the colonies. Designed to emulate their British counterparts, colonial magazines labored under a myriad of problems. Between 1741, when Benjamin Franklin and Andrew Bradford issued the first magazines within three days of each other, and 1794, when magazines were given postal mailing privileges, only 45 magazines were published.[1] Half of those were established in an eight-year period from 1786 to 1794; there were never more than 3 American magazines available at any one time.[2] The average life of a magazine was only 18 months, and 60 percent of the periodicals that started between 1741 and 1794 did not survive the first year.[3] *The Gentleman and Lady's Town and Country Magazine* published only eight issues, from May 1784 through December 1784.[4] So it is not surprising that Noah Webster, who tried to publish several magazines before turning to his dictionary, said in 1788: "The expectation of failure is connected with the very name of a magazine."[5]

The United States in May 1784 had been recognized as a nation for just nine months. The 13 states were governed under the weak, loosely constructed Articles of Confederation. The territories of this new United States extended north to Canada, west to the Mississippi River, and south to Florida. But for all practical purposes, magazine readership was centered in a narrow strip from Boston to Baltimore.

One of the major problems facing all magazines in the new republic was distribution. Roads were few in the eighteenth century, and the stagecoach averaged only two miles an hour. The journey from Boston to New York, a distance of 208 miles, took a stagecoach eight to ten days.[6]

The mail system was primitive, and post roads were aligned along a north-south axis near the seaboard through the late 1780s.[7] Post offices were few, numbering only 75 and scattered over a thousand miles of roads as late as 1789.[8] The colonies had enjoyed a postal system since Queen Anne's Act of 1710, but no specific provisions had been made for carrying periodicals in the mails.[9] Each postmaster had considerable discretion over what could and could not be sent through the mails. Magazines were bulkier than newspapers or letters and were often rejected. When they were allowed to use the mails, periodicals had to pay considerably more than newspapers for the same service. Postage was paid by the subscriber in addition to the magazine's subscription cost.[10]

The Gentleman and Lady's Town and Country Magazine avoided high postal costs by being locally distributed in Boston and surrounding communities. The yearly subscription rate for the 48-page magazine was 12 shillings (the equivalent of about two dollars a year). Publishers Job Weeden and William Barrett expected payment in "lawful money," a result of the confused state of the currency following the American Revolution.[11] This price meant that purchasing the magazine was prohibitive for the average New England family of 1784, as two shillings a day were high wages for ordinary labor.[12] Clearly, the publication was aimed at a specific social and economic group with some discretionary income—the gentlemen and ladies of the area, who were quite distinct from farmers and shopkeepers.

Literacy in colonial and post-Revolutionary New England was the highest in America, a result of its Puritan heritage, which so valued male literacy that a system of public education was required by law in the seventeenth century. It is estimated that 90 percent of all men were literate in Suffolk (Boston is its seat) and Middlesex counties in Massachusetts by 1790.[13] As for women, those who lived in Boston were likely to have a 60 percent literacy rate by 1787, versus 45 percent for women living in rural areas.[14] So it is reasonable that *The Gentleman and Lady's Town and Country Magazine* had "only one major editorial policy in mind: definitely to appeal to feminine readers. For the first time in American magazine history this policy governed the title of a periodical."[15]

Subscriptions were the primary source of revenue for publishers like Weeden and Barrett since advertising was scanty following the Revolution. Periodically, books, money changing (involving the "old continental and new emission state money"), and classes in reading, writing, and arithmetic were advertised in *The Gentleman and Lady's Town and Country Magazine*. No issue contained more than four ads, the largest taking about two-thirds of the 5¾" × 8¾" page. All ads were run on the front or back covers (the inside front and back cover pages were always blank) and consisted entirely of type.

Interestingly, the lone advertisement to appear within the editorial pages of the magazine was for a wife. Erudite in tone, the clearly labeled advertisement is obviously a forerunner of today's classified singles ads. Wrote C. N. after complaining of two women he rejected, one who was "much inclined to gadding about" and the other who insisted "every thing must be settled her way":

> I want no extra beauty, let her be only affable and tender, a prudent, discreet lady, with such perfections as are necessary for my circumstances, who will give up luxuries and propagate love: Such a lady, possessed of a mind equal to this, will do a great favor to her humble servant, by giving him notice in your next monthly production.[16]

The ad was answered by Julia of Boston in the June 1784 issue, with C. N. replying in July under the heading "Julia Answered." These last two ads were clever and informative. Julia, who said she had the qualifications preferred, closed with rhymed couplets, while C. N. soberly described himself: "I am of a middle stature, and fair complexion, well proportioned—so much for outward shew, and as to other qualifications I make bold to say there will be no occasion of divorcement on account of any inability in the marriage rites."[17] Readers can only assume the two met, as no further advertising correspondence appeared.

The third largest city at this time, Boston had justifiable aspirations as a center of culture and education. (Harvard, founded in 1636, was the oldest American college, and the first public library was established in the city in 1653.) Boston was the home of the only two magazines being published in 1784. *Boston Magazine*, started in 1783, was distributed by competitors of printers Weeden and Barrett.[18]

The rival *Boston Magazine* "was masculine in its major appeal—although some women wrote for it and undoubtedly found in it many articles and poems congenial to them. Job Weedon [*sic*] and William Barrett were astute in soliciting the special regard of women."[19] In their respectful announcement to the public of their new editorial venture, Weeden and Barrett wrote: "The Ladies in particular, are requested to patronize this Work, by adding the elegant polish of the Female Pencil, where purity of sentiment, and impassioned Fancy, are happily blended together." This request was not intended to discourage male readers or writers, as the "Learned and Ingenious" were asked to submit "valuable Correspondence" with the promise that "all pieces of Merit will be carefully noticed, and those which are refused, neither blasted by indelicate Censure, or solemn Criticism."[20]

The Gentleman and Lady's Town and Country Magazine "followed a form sanctified by English usage, for however capable the editors felt of dispensing with British guidance in government, they showed no inclination to discard it in literature."[21] Though imitative of the *Lady's Magazine* of London, this Boston offering retained a distinctly New England tone, making sure that all material was geared toward the interests of its local readers, male and female. *The Gentleman and Lady's Town and Country Magazine* showed a shrewd understanding of the new republic's woman and how her status was undergoing subtle changes in the years following the American Revolution.

As often happens during wartime, women were expected to keep the economic fabric of society spinning. So it was not surprising that the American Revolution found women working at traditionally male occupations as butchers, silversmiths, gunsmiths, jail keepers, and upholsterers. Consequently, "in the years after the war American women grew increasingly willing to challenge the conventional wisdom about feminine faults. Whereas in the 1760s and early 1770s criticism of women's 'natural' tendencies and failings had for the most part gone unanswered, during and after the Revolution women were less inclined to allow such remarks to pass without comment."[22] Women of the post-Revolutionary period were more willing to express themselves on paper and to share their thoughts with others.

Although the Revolution had brought women into public life, their legal status had not changed since the seventeenth century. American women had more freedom and esteem than their European and British counterparts, but their place in society still was determined through the men in their family or the men they married. "In other words, they participated in the hierarchy as daughters and wives, not as individuals."[23] Their place was at home, caring for brothers and sisters or husbands and children. So despite the "self-evident truths" of the Declaration of Independence, American society was not egalitarian. Women could not vote, and most were denied higher education. Married women were subservient to their husbands, legally still under Blackstone's dictum that "the husband and wife are one and that is the husband. . . . Her right to hold property was narrowly restricted; she had no right to make a will, enter into contract, or sue in court without her husband's consent."[24]

A letter to the publishers in the July 1784 issue of *The Gentleman and Lady's Town and Country Magazine* showed just how legally precarious women's positions were. Listed in the table of contents under the title "Curious Queries with Regard to Bigamy" (p. 116), A. B. justifiably wailed: "I am one of those unhappy young women whom fortune favoured with a husband; but not long after the conjugal rites were ended, he, void to all humanity, left me and went and married a second wife." A. B. asked whether she "can by the law marry afterwards, during his life? Or if it is a felony in the wife then, was it not a felony in the husband first?" Although she requested an answer to her queries "from any of your kind correspondents," no responses were found in subsequent issues.

During the 1780s, numerous authors proclaimed the importance of America's female citizens: "If women adhered to high standards of behavior, they would cause men to adopt similar standards."[25] "Republican theorists, concerned about the future of the nation, invested new meaning in the traditional cliché that women were the source of virtue in a society. . . . In short, in the wake of the war both men and women in America began to rethink the hitherto unchallenged negative characterizations of woman's nature and role."[26] The key to this focus was the responsibility a republican mother had for children, who "should be taught rationally and carefully, preferably by example, and it was the mother's role to do so successfully."[27] This meant that women had to be educated and of equal marital status so their children would be instilled with the proper republican values, and their husbands would be supported politically at home as well as in the workaday world. This was a significant change from previous attitudes, but traditional views toward marriage and female education did not disappear overnight.

The Gentleman and Lady's Town and Country Magazine reflected the changes that were occurring in the status of women in the new nation. Side by side with articles calling for "mutuality and reciprocity in matrimony [were] . . . essays advocating female subordination and male dominance in marital relationships, evidently without recognizing or ascribing significance to the inherent contradiction."[28] Such extremes could be seen in two articles appearing within months of each other in The Gentleman and Lady's Town and Country Magazine. In the May 1784 issue, advice on the best ways of getting and keeping a husband could be found on page 28. Written by an unidentified author, "Rules and Maxims for Promoting Matrimonial Happiness" offered an interesting mixture of useful and unrealistic tips: (1) "Avoid, both before and after marriage, all thoughts of managing your husband"; (2) "Never endeavour to deceive or impose on his understanding; nor give him uneasiness, (as some do very foolishly) to try his temper"; (3) "Resolve, every morning, to be good natured and chearful that day"; (4) "Dispute not with him, be the occasion what it will; but much rather deny yourself the trivial satisfaction of having your own will, or gaining the better of an argument, than to risque a quarrel"; and (5) "Read frequently with due attention, the Matrimonial service; and take care, in doing so, not to overlook the word Obey."

The opposite note was struck a few months later when an anonymous writer asked, "Wherein does the happiness of the married state consist?" The answer: "In a mutual affection, a similarity of tempers, a reciprocal endeavour to please, and an invariable aim to each other's comfort (under the blessing of Heaven) must constitute the very essence of connubial bliss."[29]

Finally, men were given marital advice. B. W. commented, "It has often been wondered at that so many people are unhappy in matrimony." The fault, he argued, dwelt with the man, who must learn "to contribute to the happiness of the more delicate sex." Possibly the first time men were admonished and told to contribute to "matrimonial felicity," the husband was advised that "he must divest himself of each unruly passion, his ambition should be to please the woman he has chosen for his friend; he must, in every thing, promote her ease; he must share with her his every joy, and with a delicate tenderness, let her partake also of his griefs."[30]

If matrimonial equality was one of the new republican ideals to be found in this magazine, education for women was the other. In October 1784 appeared a rousing essay about the importance of female education by early feminist

Judith Sargent Murray, writing under the pen name of Constantia. Murray, who has been identified as ''the chief theorist of republican womanhood,'' wrote her first essay for *The Gentleman and Lady's Town and Country Magazine* when she was 33 years old.[31] She was one of the most original and thoughtful writers to appear during the eight-month run of the magazine.

In her ponderously titled ''Desultory Thoughts upon the Utility of Encouraging a Degree of Self-Complacency, Especially in Female Bosoms,'' Murray stressed that an ideal education should ''teach young minds to aspire.'' In describing her plan for the education of girls, Murray wrote ''that every thing in the compass of mortality'' would be placed within their grasp. A young woman who always had been addressed ''as a rational being'' was unlikely to marry the first man who flattered her. This was an important concept for the times because women who lacked a strong and positive sense of identity too often rushed into an inappropriate marriage to establish their social status. Murray concluded, ''I would early impress under proper regulations, a reverence of self; I would endeavour to rear to worth, and a consciousness thereof.''[32]

Murray's use of the pseudonym Constantia is one of the few instances where writers of this period have been identified by historians. Bylines with initials or double entendre Greco-Roman names like Philanthropos and Rusticus were the rule for men and women rather than the exception in early American periodicals like *The Gentleman and Lady's Town and Country Magazine*. Some women used names such as Lucia, Frances, and Emilia, which may or may not have been their given names. There were no professional writers at the time, as writing for money was frowned upon as unbecoming to ladies and unsporting for gentlemen.[33] Consequently, there is a wheedling, almost obsequious tone on the part of publishers when requesting original material from contributors. In the December 1784 issue, space on the cover page was devoted to the following request: ''The Publisher of The Gentleman & Lady's Magazine, would esteem it a particular favour of his Correspondents, who are so kind as to honour him with their lucubrations, to forward their favours earlier in the month, as he shall thereby be enabled to prosecute his part with punctuality.''

Only two other writers were fully identified in the pages of the magazine. Maria Frankly wrote to the publishers asking if she could ''swear the peace or a rape'' against her new husband. She explained that she agreed to marry ''upon one single article which was, that we would always have separate beds.'' But after the wedding when she went to her own bedroom, Mr. Frankly followed her, forced open the door, and ''violated my bed, in despite of all the opposition and outcries I made, and not one of the barbarous servants, though there were several females in the house, came to my assistance or relief.'' Admitting that her father laughed at her and that her aunt was not sympathetic, Maria Frankly wanted advice. The publishers responded: ''This Lady's case, though it may appear at present very lamentable to her, will no doubt, in a short time wear a more favourable aspect.''[34]

What made this letter noteworthy was its tone of dismay and hysteria over "the savage creature" and "husbands, a race of vicious animals." More than one letter in *The Gentleman and Lady's Town and Country Magazine* discussed serious concerns—suicide, debauchery, evil, and madness—but in a rational, cool voice. Other letters brought up issues that were spiritual (hope) and practical (bringing up youth). These letters to the publishers (taking anywhere from a half to a full page, with their own titles, and scattered throughout the magazine) seemed to suggest a need for an eighteenth-century Ann Landers to soothe away concerns. Yet the Maria Frankly letter was the only one to receive a response from the editors. Many of these letters were of special interest to women, offering advice that had both sense and sensibility. However, since these letters also were read by men, new relationship possibilities were established between the sexes as both enlarged their spheres of intellectual topics and issues.

The other writer to have full identification was the late Heman Harris of Wrentham, Massachusetts, whose poems were submitted by his heirs. Five of Harris's poems were published, showing his hand at such varying styles as blank verse, rhymed stanzas, and a dirge. Harris's "The Thunder Storm," "in heroic couplets describing the approach, deluge, and retreat of a storm of rain, is one of the earlier American poems treating a moving force of nature with elaborate panoramic detail, and is suggestive of the slowness with which mid-eighteenth century English nature poetry was imitated in some details in the Colonies."[35]

At most magazines during this period, original poetry seemed to come to the editorial desk more readily than editorial prose.[36] A six-to-eight-page section devoted to poetry appeared in every issue of *The Gentleman and Lady's Town and Country Magazine*. Many writers offered brief, sentimental love poems (generally addressed "to a lady") and other light verse, but some efforts were more ambitious. An imitation of Hamlet's most quoted soliloquy by Alexis, titled "The Batchelor's Deliberation" (November 1784, pp. 310–311), managed to be both instructional and entertaining, which was the stated intent of the magazine. Eulogistic poems to fallen officers at Bunker Hill and other Revolutionary battles were popular, as were odes based on Horace or translations of his work. Imitations of Pope, Dryden, and the Graveyard school also found a place in the magazine. Rounding out the poetry section were enigmas, rebuses, and riddles, which likely gave readers hours of amusement; the best answers appeared in later issues. "In summary, it may be said of the contributors of poetry that, though they lacked the powers which make for great individual work, they were somewhat schooled and of good intellect; and though they borrowed tools, patterns, and materials from English writers, they wrote with commendable skill."[37]

In studying the content of each issue, what is most impressive is its eclectic material. After all, "the word *magazine* meant miscellany to most eighteenth century readers, and . . . the magazines maintained that tradition."[38] There were several pieces with exotic Eastern locales, like "Unbounded Tyranny Punished," about an Oriental potentate's lust for a virtuous wife, who chooses suicide to escape his power (May 1784, pp. 9–12). Such stories were the nearest thing to fiction to be found. At this time, fiction was "disapproved of on grounds that it was dishonest or a type of false witness to life, and sentimental fiction was particularly frowned on by some who thought it encouraged an indulgence in the feelings at the expense of rational attention to moral principles."[39] However, "moral tales" like "The Discontented Man" (October 1784, pp. 253–256 and November 1784, pp. 281–284), which chronicled Zohar's search for happiness along the banks of the Euphrates and neighboring lands, were acceptable because they ended in the realization of one's self-sufficiency.

Not all moral tales took place in the Orient, and those with a contemporary setting, like "History of Auretta" (May 1784, pp. 17–20 and June 1784, pp. 54–57), were prefaced with long introductions on the foible being illustrated and protestations that the story "is founded in fact." "History of Auretta; or, the Fatal Effects of Impatience" was the best of its type in this magazine—a rapidly moving, sentimental story of enduring love with an ending that had a decidedly American twist to the tragedy befalling a woman who loves one man but whose father demands that she marry another. Each issue featured at least three and sometimes as many as five such tales. Also filling every magazine were essays on such topics as friendship and flattery, moderation, impudence, and rules of conversation, many of them in the style of Joseph Addison and Richard Steele, though it was more than 50 years since their deaths. Excerpts and "epitomes" from popular books, scientific articles about the properties of heat and fire or the solar system, and travel articles to the South Seas were included, often serialized over two or three issues.

In general, magazine editors had problems obtaining original material. Weeden and Barrett were no exception, stating that they "doubt not in a short time to adorn their monthly Productions entirely with original Composition, and if they are indebted to Europe for any Literary pieces, they will be selected from the most approved Authors."[40] Unfortunately, reprinted British material—supposedly included to "oblige a correspondent"—remained a significant percentage, sometimes as much as one-third, of the editorial. It was not surprising that many early magazines reprinted material from British periodicals since there were no copyright laws to prevent outright pirating of material.[41]

Concluding every issue of *The Gentleman and Lady's Town and Country Magazine* was the "Monthly Intelligencer," with current foreign and domestic news, the text of congressional proclamations and state legislative documents, and lists of marriages, births, baptisms, and deaths in Boston and neighboring towns. Averaging six pages, these notes painted a picture of an informed readership who wanted to know what was happening on the political scene far (London, Paris, Dublin, Rome) and near (Philadelphia, New York, Providence).

Certainly, the magazine's editorial copy offered readers diverse, thoughtful, and entertaining reading, as promised. The pages were densely packed with Caslon Old Style typeface—the same used in the Declaration of Independence and very popular with printers through 1800.[42] Reading the magazine 200 years later proves difficult at times for several reasons. First, the "long s," where the letter "s" has been modified to resemble a lowercase "f" when standing for the sibilant "s" sound, was standard in old-style types. Second, the type size was a minuscule seven points. Third, capricious capitalization and punctuation are another hindrance. Finally, the quality of printing was not consistent, the result of the magazine being printed from hand-set type and hand-operated wooden presses that had seen better days. The rag paper was rough but obviously durable since it has survived to this date, though yellowed and crumbling at the edges. Covers, added before the table of contents page when there were advertisements, were of a flimsier, pale blue paper stock.

Graphic design was nonexistent, with no type embellishments and limited type variation of size or family. A one-point rule was all that separated the end of one article and the start of the next. There were no consistency in placement of bylines or headlines and no coherent article flow, as pieces ended arbitrarily (not logically, at an exciting, cliff-hanging moment) when serialized. In short, *The Gentleman and Lady's Town and Country Magazine*, with its narrow two columns of type per page, was gray and visually boring. Few magazines of the period included illustrations to break up pages of type, since woodcuts and copper plate engravings were expensive and time-consuming to produce. In the first issue the publishers apologized for the lack of a "frontspiece and other plates," saying these could not be obtained. The one engraving to appear in the publication illustrated "The Precipitate Love," a moral tale extracted from an English publication; the elegantly detailed copper plate was titled "The Parting of M. Harrison & Miss Osgood" (October 1784, p. 226).

The Gentleman and Lady's Town and Country Magazine abruptly ended with the eighth issue, December 1784. This was despite a jubilant third issue when the magazine was enlarged from 40 to 48 octavo pages. Weeden and Barrett wrote then that they "most gratefully acknowledge the kind reception which their 1st and 2d Numbers met with, from an indulgent liberality of sentiment" and said they were "confident of that success, which modesty may be assured of, without presumption."[43] On the August 1784 cover, they had bragged about the addition of an "Elegant Type, vastly preferable for beauty and size, to the type hitherto made use of" (though this reader could see no improvement). They also announced they had moved to a larger and more central location. Businessmen were assured of "the extensive circulation of the magazine" and offered advertising space on the covers.

As to the exact circulation of *The Gentleman and Lady's Town and Country Magazine*, figures were not published. During the eighteenth century, "only occasionally did subscription lists attain one thousand to sixteen hundred names, and probably the average list did not extend beyond five hundred."[44] Assuming a 500 circulation for this magazine, its impact would be far greater than the actual number of copies printed. Magazines were read with care by a number of individuals, passed along from mother to daughter, father to son, neighbor to neighbor. Although based in Boston, *The Gentleman and Lady's Town and Country Magazine* reached at least as far north as New Hampshire, southwest into Connecticut, and south into Rhode Island, based on the locales indicated by writers.

Just six months after its start-up, one of the ongoing problems of early magazine publishers was addressed—the delinquent subscriber. Throughout the eighteenth century, publishers trustingly sent magazines on credit; and readers, more frequently than not, avoided paying the requested costs. Stated boldly on the October 1784 cover of *The Gentleman and Lady's Town and Country Magazine* was the following: "Those Gentlemen who are in Arrears for the Magazine, will do an essential service to the Publishers, by making a speedy payment, as a Publication of this kind, is attended with large expence." The December 1784 magazine had only Barrett's name as publisher, with a new address. Obviously, the partnership had dissolved. Unfortunately, December also was the final issue of *The Gentleman and Lady's Town and Country Magazine*, although there was no editorial indication that this was so.

Literary fame did not seem to be the goal of Weeden and Barrett, who served as editors, printers, publishers, and, most likely, writers for *The Gentleman and Lady's Town and Country Magazine*. Rather, anonymity suited these torchbearers of literature and information who tried to make this magazine a valuable repository of instruction and entertainment. "How many young ladies of Boston profited by the tales, the poems, the confessions, and the advice offered by this periodical, it is impossible to tell, but apparently no very great number found life without it unendurable, for after less than a year of life it ceased to exist."[45]

Certainly, what emerges from a study of the verbiage of *The Gentleman and Lady's Town and Country Magazine* is a composite of the nation's social life and political interests, particularly concerning the status of women following the American Revolution. Hampered by financial constraints, geographic limitations, and sometimes narrow social mores, this publication nonetheless offers an intriguing tale of changing audiences and content to the student of women's magazines in the United States. First and foremost, *The Gentleman and Lady's Town and Country Magazine* should be praised for its starting point, for including women for the first time as a viable readership, not cut off from the topics that were of interest to men also. The resulting blend of audiences made for a worthy experiment that would lead the way to American magazines dedicated solely to women.

Notes

1. Frank Luther Mott, *A History of American Magazines 1741–1850* (Cambridge: Harvard University Press, 1939), pp. 19–21, 24.

2. Ibid., p. 29.

3. Ibid., p. 21.

4. There is some confusion as to whether *The Gentleman and Lady's Town and Country Magazine* published eight or nine issues. The Union List of Serials and the American Periodicals Series 1741–1900 (APS) list nine issues, from May 1784 through January 1785. Respected researchers like Frank Mott and Lyon Richardson, however,

cite only eight issues, from May 1784 through December 1784. There are no copies of a January 1785 issue to be found at the American Antiquarian Society, the resting place of the original copies. APS microfilm copies of the magazine do not include a January 1785 issue. This researcher doubts there was a January issue since there are no extant copies, and no historians refer to it.

5. Mott, *A History of American Magazines 1741–1850*, p. 13.

6. Ibid., p. 16.

7. Richard B. Kielbowicz, *News in the Mail: The Press, Post Office, and Public Information, 1700–1860s* (Westport, Conn.: Greenwood Press, 1989), p. 24.

8. Mott, *A History of American Magazines 1741–1850*, p. 16.

9. Ibid., pp. 16–17.

10. Ibid., pp. 119–120.

11. "To the Public," July 1784, p. 83.

12. Mott, *A History of American Magazines 1741–1850*, pp. 33–34.

13. Kenneth A. Lockridge, *Literacy in Colonial New England* (New York: W. W. Norton, 1974), p. 13.

14. Ibid., pp. 38–42.

15. Lyon N. Richardson, *A History of Early American Magazines 1741–1789* (New York: Octagon Books, 1966; originally published in 1931), p. 228.

16. "Advertisement," May 1784, p. 25.

17. June 1784, p. 69; July 1784, p. 112.

18. Mott, *A History of American Magazines 1741–1850*, pp. 28–29, 70, 788.

19. Richardson, *A History of Early American Magazines 1741–1789*, p. 228. Richardson is not the only researcher to misspell Weeden's name.

20. Job Weeden and William Barrett, "To the Public," May 1784, p. 4.

21. Bertha M. Stearns, "Early New England Magazines for Ladies," *New England Quarterly* 2, July 1929, p. 422.

22. Mary Beth Norton, *Liberty's Daughters: The Revolutionary Experience of American Women, 1750–1800* (Boston: Little, Brown, 1980), p. 239.

23. Gerda Lerner, *The Majority Finds Its Past: Placing Women in History* (New York: Oxford University Press, 1979), p. 17.

24. Russell Blaine Nye, *The Cultural Life of a New Nation 1776–1830* (New York: Harper and Brothers, 1960), p. 142.

25. Norton, *Liberty's Daughters,* p. 243.

26. Ibid., p. 228.

27. Sara M. Evans, *Born for Liberty: A History of Women in America* (New York: Free Press, 1989), p. 65.

28. Norton, *Liberty's Daughters,* p. 235.

29. "On Connubial Happiness," July 1784, p. 103.

30. B. W., "On Matrimonial Felicity," September 1784, pp. 193–194.

31. Norton, *Liberty's Daughters,* p. 238.

32. Constantia, "Desultory Thoughts upon the Utility of Encouraging a Degree of Self-Complacency, Especially in Female Bosoms," October 1784, pp. 251–253.

33. Mott, *A History of American Magazines 1741–1850*, p. 14.

34. Maria Frankly, "Singular Resolution in a Married Lady," November 1784, pp. 290–291.

35. Richardson, *A History of Early American Magazines 1741–1789,* p. 231.

36. Ibid.

37. Ibid., p. 234.

38. Mott, *A History of American Magazines 1741–1850*, pp. 40–41.

39. Kathryn Weibel, *Mirror Mirror: Images of Women Reflected in Popular Culture* (Garden City, N. Y.: Anchor Books, 1977), p. 11.

40. "To the Public," July 1784, p. 84.

41. Mott, *A History of American Magazines 1741–1850*, pp. 39–40.

42. David Berkeley Updike, *Printing Types: Their History, Forms, and Use*, vol. 2 (Cambridge: Belknap Press, 1962), p. 151.

43. "To the Public," July 1784, pp. 83–84.

44. Richardson, *A History of Early American Magazines 1741–1789*, p. 2.

45. Stearns, "Early New England Magazines for Ladies," p. 425.

Information Sources

BIBLIOGRAPHY:

Mott, Frank Luther. *A History of American Magazines 1741–1850*. Cambridge: Harvard University Press, 1939.

Norton, Mary Beth. *Liberty's Daughters: The Revolutionary Experience of American Women, 1750–1800*. Boston: Little, Brown, 1980.

Richardson, Lyon N. *A History of Early American Magazines 1741–1789*. New York: Octagon Books, 1966; originally published in 1931.

Stearns, Bertha M. "Early New England Magazines for Ladies." *New England Quarterly* #2 (July 1929), pp. 420–457.

INDEX SOURCES: Union List of Serials.

LOCATION SOURCES: American Antiquarian Society, Worcester, Massachusetts; *American Periodicals Series 1741–1900*, American Periodicals 18th Century (APS I).

Publication History

MAGAZINE TITLE AND TITLE CHANGES: *The Gentleman and Lady's Town and Country Magazine; or, Repository for Instruction and Entertainment.*

VOLUME AND ISSUE DATA: Vol. 1 (May through December 1784). Monthly.

PUBLISHER AND PLACE OF PUBLICATION: Job Weeden and William Barrett (May 1784–November 1784); William Barrett (December 1784). Boston.

EDITORS: Job Weeden and William Barrett (May 1784–November 1784); William Barrett (December 1784).

CIRCULATION: Unknown; estimates for a magazine of this period would be about 500.

Sammye Johnson

GLAMOUR

Glamour of Hollywood debuted in April 1939 as a down-market companion magazine to Condé Nast's first women's magazine, *Vogue*.* The magazine was launched in response to depression-era problems with *Vogue*'s pattern business, which led Nast to bring out a cheaper line of clothing patterns modeled on the clothes of Hollywood movie stars. Hollywood Patterns was born in 1932; after seven years the *Hollywood Pattern Book* was expanded to become *Glamour of Hollywood*, Condé Nast's last entry into the field of magazine publishing.[1]

The new magazine was a cross between a movie "fanzine" and a fashion magazine, aiming at young women with jobs who were more likely to make their own clothes or buy them off a department store rack than to buy them from a designer. At its beginnings, *Glamour of Hollywood* featured articles on film stars, movie-influenced fashions, movie makeup tips, full-page color photographs of film stars (reprints suitable for framing could often be purchased), and short notices of new releases. A "Prologue" in the first issue somewhat defensively explained the magazine's philosophy:

> We women are as we are—our dispositions reflecting the vintage of our coats, our morale colored by our lipsticks, our courage bolstered by a new hat, our serenity aided by the knowledge men find us pleasant to look at. . . .
>
> Glamour is a magazine for those women who count the dollars and the hours they spend in the important pursuit of feminine loveliness—but who are just as much mothered by the old Eve as the most luxurious lady in the land.[2]

Another article promised that Hollywood would share its secrets of "remaking men and women into a closer likeness of our wishful thinking" through *Glamour*, helping each reader "cast off her drab and dull self."[3]

The magazine quickly built a substantial circulation, reaching 200,000 by the end of its first year. But *Glamour* held to its original editorial mix for only two years, gradually shifting its attention away from Hollywood and toward the lives of the younger women (especially those with careers) it targeted.[4] By September 1940, the subtitle had changed from *The Hollywood Way to Fashion Beauty and Charm* to *For Young American Moderns*. The subtitle changed again a few months later, to *For Young Women—The Way to Fashion, Beauty and Charm*. "Hollywood" was dropped from the nameplate in May 1941. By that summer, the full-page photographs of Hollywood stars had disappeared from the cover and interior pages, replaced by fashion spreads featuring anonymous models. The July 1941 cover, for example, was identified as "girl with contented cow" on the contents page, which went on to list the makers of her clothing and makeup, but not her name.[5]

By 1949, *Glamour*'s subtitle read *For the Girl with a Job*. Editorial content reflected this emphasis, with articles and special issues on careers, marriage (a short-lived marriage section was dropped in 1952), fashion, and beauty. Elizabeth Penrose, formerly the editor of *Vogue*'s British edition, served as editor for most of the decade, as the emphasis on job-related articles and, to a lesser extent, current affairs expanded. But Penrose abruptly vanished from the staff box in December 1953. Nina Kyle served as editor for a couple of issues before Kathleen Casey took charge in February 1954.

Casey had been *Glamour*'s midwest editor and had also worked at Condé Nast's *Vogue*. *Glamour*'s publisher described her as "a girl-with-a-job who successfully combines a business career with managing a happy home for her husband and young son." Casey promised readers that the magazine would be

> your fashion authority. . . . Thoughts about your job, or a better one, are
> with you every day, and your work is just that important to us. . . . Finally
> we hope to make Glamour an even more important part of your life at
> home by bringing you news in entertaining, recipes, and decorating. But
> we will always remember that this news is for a young woman with limited
> time.[6]

By September 1955, the subtitle was changed to *The Fashion Magazine for the Girl with a Job,* reflecting the heightened emphasis on fashion, which now accounted for the bulk of the magazine's advertising and editorial pages. *Glamour* grew steadily in both editorial and advertising pages throughout this period.

Glamour featured regular sections on fashion, beauty, travel, decorating, entertaining, and jobs in the 1950s, along with occasional articles on topics ranging from voting to broken hearts. Although the reference to jobs was dropped from the nameplate in 1956 in favor of the generic "for young women," careers remained a regular, if minor, theme in each issue.

A few months after the Newhouse newspaper chain bought Condé Nast Publications in March 1959, it added Street & Smith Publications to its portfolio. While other Street & Smith titles continued under Condé Nast's imprint, *Glamour* absorbed *Charm*, its closest competitor, in November 1959. Both magazines targeted young working women as readers, and, while *Glamour* held a slight edge in circulation (at 665,000), *Charm* was only 15,000 copies behind.[7] The editorial in the first merged issue promised old and new readers alike "a bigger and better Glamour that tells you 'how to' look better, feel better, live better: the magazine that appeals to the million of you who really care and are eager for the best of advice."[8] For another two years, though in smaller and smaller type, the nameplate continued to remind prospective purchasers that it had incorporated *Charm* (*Charm* continues to appear in the staff box and on the spine to this day). While the merged magazine was essentially a slightly enlarged *Glamour*, some aspects of *Charm*'s format were gradually incorporated—most notably, its proclivity for short columns on subjects ranging from news of the day to horoscopes.

While *Glamour* continued to issue a thick, ad-rich book bought by nearly 1.3 million readers, the 1960s—and the competition—were passing it by. Editor Kathleen Johnson (Casey remarried in May 1966) noted, "Our job is to portray a whole generation, not just its clothes." But the magazine's pages seemed oblivious to the revolution in lifestyles, sex roles, and expectations that was sweeping the country, let alone the decade's political ferment.[9] Ruth Whitney quietly took over as editor with the January 1968 issue, and the magazine

quickly began to change. Whitney changed the magazine's annual college contest from best-dressed women to women of achievement and generally increased
its emphasis on careers and related issues.

Twenty-five years later, Whitney pointed to the social ferment of the times
and the need to move *Glamour* beyond its traditional concerns with fashion and
beauty in order to reach the new generation:

> I wanted to move Glamour in a much more socially conscious direction.
> I was a new editor, I was eager to make that magazine mine. . . . I wanted
> that educated young audience. And I wanted all young women, not just
> those who already knew Glamour. . . .
>
> I'm not obsessed with fashion at all. . . . In the course of the years I've
> turned the magazine into a magazine I want to edit.[10]

Whitney introduced a monthly "Protest" column, which ran articles on sex
discrimination and other social and political issues. In April 1968, *Glamour*
published an article by Senator Eugene McCarthy calling for an end to the
Vietnam War. Under Whitney's direction, *Glamour* began discussing issues,
such as birth control, that had previously been taboo. For the first time, the
magazine acknowledged and ran occasional articles addressing African Americans and other minorities—including running an African American model on
the cover of its August 1968 issue, the first major women's magazine to do so.[11]

Whitney has continued her efforts to keep *Glamour* socially relevant, carefully
balancing a heavy dose of fashion and beauty articles with coverage of controversial subjects ranging from infertility to "Why Women Are Mad as Hell." In
1991, *Glamour* won the National Magazine Award for general excellence, beat-
ing out finalists such as *Time* and *Money*. In 1992, *Glamour* won the National
Magazine Award for public interest for three articles on teenage pregnancy and
abortion that documented the impact of parental consent laws on young women
and the scarcity, particularly in rural areas, of doctors willing to perform the
procedure. (A survey by the *Columbia Journalism Review* found that *Glamour*
covered abortion more than any other leading women's magazines.)[12] *Glamour*
was the target of letter-writing campaigns (for and against) after its June 1992
feature story, "Not Just Another Prom Night," on two high school students who
came out as lesbians at their high school prom. *Glamour* receives about 10,000
letters a year from its readers, and staffers reply to each.[13]

But *Glamour* has been criticized for carrying advertisements for cigarettes
and, along with other women's magazines, for its selection of models that set
almost impossible standards for physical attractiveness and thereby erode young
women's self-confidence.[14] Whitney agrees that weight and body image are important issues but says *Glamour*'s "models have been getting steadily heavier"
in recent years. She sees recent attention to this issue more as a sign of women's
increasing assertiveness than a reaction to what is actually running in contemporary young women's magazines.[15]

Despite its success, *Glamour* continues to evolve. While it continues to devote about one-fourth of its editorial pages to fashion, since 1988 it has increased the space allotted to areas such as social issues and entertainment. Fashion, beauty, and health coverage fell from 70 percent of editorial space in the mid-1980s to about half today. "I think women are less interested in fashion than they were ten years ago," Whitney says. "Women are more interested in social issues. . . . The movement into the workplace has really just changed everything." Much of the fashion coverage is now devoted to career-oriented clothing.[16] *Glamour* takes an increasingly critical approach to fashion, looking for items that will fit into readers' lives and discussing issues such as the lack of standardization in dress sizes and the growing number of designers who do not actually design the clothes carrying their labels.[17]

While *Glamour* is targeted at women between the ages of 18 and 34, the editorial focus is on women in their 20s and 30s. "We're really talking to the young woman who's left home," Whitney says, though many readers stay with the magazine in later years. The magazine is highly profitable, alternating with *Vogue* as Condé Nast's most profitable magazine.[18] Even in the difficult economic climate besetting women's magazines in the early 1990s, Condé Nast has refused to discount advertisements in *Glamour* or its other titles.[19]

Whitney sees the movement of women into the workforce and up the corporate ladder into higher-placed jobs as the major trend during her editorial tenure. In the process, she says, "The lives of women, my readers, have really been more than changed, they have been transformed."[20] As its audience has been transformed, *Glamour* has kept pace—offering its readers an increasingly career-oriented, socially conscious magazine.

Notes

1. Caroline Seebohm, *The Man Who Was Vogue* (New York: Viking Press, 1982), p. 331.

2. "Prologue," April 1939, p. 33.

3. "America's Glamour Center," April 1939, p. 35.

4. Seebohm, *The Man Who Was Vogue,* pp. 334–335.

5. This remained the magazine's regular practice. For example, a 1957 issue offered detailed credits for everything from a pleated, gray flannel skirt to the lipstick on the model's face, everything, that is, except the model herself. "The Classic on the Cover," February 1957, p. 33.

6. Perry Ruston and Kathleen Casey, "*Glamour* Has a New Editor-in-Chief," February 1954, p. 81.

7. Carl Spielvogel, "Advertising: Street & Smith to Newhouse," *New York Times*, August 26, 1959, p. 46.

8. Editorial, November 1959, p. 111. The "look better" theme was borrowed from *Charm.*

9. "Orlan Johnson Weds Mrs. Kathleen Casey," *New York Times*, May 28, 1922, p. 11; Marylin Bender, "These Are the Fashion Magazines and the Women Editors Who Run Them," *New York Times*, July 25, 1966, p. 18. Bender's article focused on how

fashion editors were responding to a changing youth market—*Glamour* appeared only late in the article, and its most notable response to the new generation was a rock 'n' roll party it had sponsored a few years before. Since then, however, it has touted jazz.

10. Talk by Ruth Whitney at Newhouse School of Communications, Syracuse University, September 23, 1993.

11. See, for example, Harriet Scavupa, "The Afro Look: What's Behind It?" July 1968, pp. 82–83; "Much More than Fashion," *Marketing Communications*, September 1987, p. 12.

12. Deirdre Carmody, "The Media Business; Editor's Story: 25 Years of Creating *Glamour*," *New York Times*, June 22, 1992, p. D8; James Warren, "Not Just a Pretty Face," *Chicago Tribune*, May 3, 1992, p. E2.

13. Whitney talk.

14. Shari Roan, "Negative Images? Twentysomethings Say Women's Magazines Can Erode Self-Esteem," *Los Angeles Times*, August 18, 1992, p. E1; Kevin Goldman, "Tobacco Ads Targeted," *Wall Street Journal*, April 8, 1993, p. B6. *Glamour* was one of several women's magazines to receive criticism from the president of the American Council on Science and Health for running articles about trivial or speculative health hazards while flooding their pages with cigarette advertisements. Elizabeth Whelan, "Alarm Clocks Can Kill You. Have a Smoke," *New York Times*, September 8, 1992, p. A19. Ruth Whitney responded by pointing to "more than 50 articles" on the dangers of smoking, including a 4,000-word feature on nine women trying to kick the tobacco habit, and to *Glamour*'s frequent treatment of a wide range of health-related subjects (ranging from chlamydia to dental care). "The American Medical Association recently awarded Glamour its 1992 Medical Reporting Award," Whitney concluded, "for an article that covered the link between a man's smoking and his future children's health." Ruth Whitney, et al., "On Matters of Health, Women's Magazines Give Solid Advice," *New York Times*, September 25, 1992, p. A32.

15. Whitney talk.

16. Ibid.

17. Cara Trager, "Condé Nast Publications Design Varying Styles," *Advertising Age*, April 4, 1985, p. 26; Deirdre Carmody, "Editor's Story: 25 Years of Creating *Glamour*," *New York Times*, June 22, 1992, p. D8.

18. Whitney talk.

19. Bernard Leser, "We Won't Give In," *Advertising Age*, October 7, 1991, pp. 1, 69.

20. Whitney talk.

Information Sources

BIBLIOGRAPHY:

Carmody, Deirdre. "The Media Business; Editor's Story: 25 Years of Creating *Glamour*." *New York Times*, June 22, 1992, p. D8.

Greene, Donna. "Changing Face of Women's Magazines." *New York Times*, May 16, 1993, p. WC3.

Peterson, Theodore. *Magazines in the Twentieth Century*. Urbana: University of Illinois Press, 1964.

Roan, Shari. "Negative Images? Twentysomethings Say Women's Magazines Can Erode Self-Esteem," *Los Angeles Times*, August 18, 1992, p. E1.

Seebohm, Caroline. *The Man Who Was Vogue: The Life and Times of Condé Nast.* New York: Viking Press, 1982.

Spielvogel, Carl. "Advertising: Street & Smith to Newhouse." *New York Times,* August 26, 1959, p. 46.

Warren, James. "Women's Magazines Go for Makeovers." *Chicago Tribune,* May 27, 1991, sec. 5, p. 1.

Whitney, Ruth, et al. "On Matters of Health, Women's Magazines Give Solid Advice." *New York Times,* September 25, 1992, p. A32.

INDEX SOURCES: Access (1973–present); Magazine Index; Popular Magazine Review; Readers' Guide to Periodical Literature (1979–present).

LOCATION SOURCES: Library of Congress and other libraries.

Publication History

MAGAZINE TITLE AND TITLE CHANGES: *Glamour of Hollywood* (April 1939–1942); *Glamour* (1942–present).

VOLUME AND ISSUE DATA: Vols. 1–(April 1939–present). Monthly.

PUBLISHER AND PLACE OF PUBLICATION: Condé Nast. New York.

EDITORS: Alice Thompson (1939–1941); Elizabeth Penrose (1941–1953, name changes to Elizabeth Penrose Hawkins in 1952); Nina Kyle (1953–1954); Kathleen Aston Casey (1954–1967, last name changes to Johnson in 1966); Ruth Whitney (1967–present).

CIRCULATION: ABC, 1993: 2,133,712 (paid, about evenly divided between subscriptions and single-copy sales).

Lisa Beinhoff and Jon Bekken

GODEY'S LADY'S BOOK

Few women's magazines or editors have been so heralded as *Godey's Lady's Book* and its editor, Sarah Josepha Hale. The magazine and Hale have been critiqued and criticized by both the popular press and scholars virtually since the magazine's first issues. The journal's ability to attract the nation's top literary names and its almost 70-year successful run were enough to guarantee *Godey's* its place in history. Yet, the magazine is remembered for something more. *Godey's*, under the firm direction of Sarah Hale, defined middle-class women's roles during much of the nineteenth century.

Godey's Lady's Book and Hale's association with the magazine resulted from an 1837 merger of two journals: the *Ladies' Magazine* and the *Lady's Book*. The former began in 1828 in Boston when Sarah Hale, a reasonably well known New Hampshire author, was offered a job by the Reverend John L. Blake to edit a new magazine.

The *Lady's Book* was begun by Louis Godey in Philadelphia in 1830. Godey began his career as a writer but discovered his talents lay in publishing instead. Godey's purchase of the *Ladies' Magazine* was one step in the expansion of his publishing interests. Godey's purchase of the journal netted him both a magazine and female editor—Sarah Josepha Hale.

Hale never intended to become a magazine editor. She came by the work unexpectedly, at the age of 40, following her husband David's death from pneumonia. He died in 1822, two days after the Hales' ninth wedding anniversary, leaving Sarah Hale with five children to support. To provide for her family, she reluctantly opened a millinery shop with her sister-in-law, Hannah Hale. Writing was a side venture, but it quickly became her lifework. In 1823, she published a book of poems. This was quickly followed by poetry and prose submissions to a variety of magazines, including *The American Monthly Magazine*, the *U.S. Literary Gazette*, *The Minerva*, and *The Boston Spectator*. The latter publication published the majority of Hale's poetry and prose throughout the 1820s.[1]

Although her poetry and prose caught the attention of editors in Boston and New York, Hale's first novel, *Northwood*, a story of the North and South, gained her real fame and her first editing job. Shortly after her novel's publication, Hale received a letter from the Reverend John L. Blake asking her to move to Boston from her New Hampshire home and take up the editorship of a new women's magazine. Hale began editing *The Ladies' Magazine* in 1828. The magazine was almost entirely literary, offering poems, short stories, biographical sketches, some fashion plates, and sheet music. *The Ladies' Magazine* lasted for nine years, then began to decline, for undocumented reasons, and was purchased by Louis Godey in 1837.

Godey's purchase of *The Ladies' Magazine* and his continuation of Sarah Hale as editor did wonders for his own *Lady's Book*. Prior to the merger, Godey had little original material in his publication. In the days before copyright laws, Godey, like most early nineteenth-century publishers, reprinted whatever interested him from books or English periodicals. He supplemented these reprints with occasional original short stories and poems, recipes, and some craft ideas.

Godey's became the most popular women's magazine of the mid-1800s under Hale. Almost all of her material was original. Most of the nation's leading authors and poets wrote for the journal before the Civil War. *Godey's* attracted such nineteenth-century literary women as Harriet Beecher Stowe, Eliza Leslie, Ann Stephens (who later edited *Godey's* competitor, *Peterson's Magazine,**) Caroline M. S. Kirkland, and Hannah F. Gould. Godey and Hale also published the leading male writers of the time, including Ralph Waldo Emerson, Nathaniel Hawthorne, Henry Wadsworth Longfellow, and Edgar Allan Poe.

Hale's real mission was to encourage and publish as many quality women writers as possible. She recalled that none of the books she read while growing up were written by women. "The wish to promote the reputation of my own sex and of my country were among the earliest mental emotions I can recollect," Hale once remarked.[2]

Godey's and Hale's selection of authors reflected more than their good taste in poetry and prose. It also represented a sound business practice. Both Godey and Hale attracted a wide circulation for their publication by promising never to publish any fiction that was less than moral and pure.[3] Furthermore, they condemned literature that, in their opinion, did not have a moral to the story.[4]

The editors' promise of wholesome literature paid off well. The two decades before the Civil War proved to be *Godey's* golden years. Circulation increased from 25,000 to 150,000, largely on the strength of the magazine's literature and poetry. Much of the increase seemed due to Hale. Two years after her arrival, Godey announced that his magazine had more subscribers than all three of his competitors' magazines combined.[5]

Godey's and Hale's content requirements resulted in a total editorial blackout of war news during the Civil War. While the conflict raged, the magazine provided its usual staple of sugary poetry, stories of gallant men and beautiful women, engravings, and music. The lack of war coverage was not surprising, as both editors viewed war news as vulgar and not of interest to women. Ten years earlier, in January 1850, Harriet Beecher Stowe had attacked *Godey's* in *The Independent* for not crusading against slavery.

Godey deserves equal credit with Hale for attracting readers. He had a clear understanding of what the middle-class Victorian woman wanted in a magazine—fashion plates, literature, decorative engravings, craft patterns, and sheet music—and he gave them to his readers. Hale, however, resented the inclusion of fashion plates, first in *The Ladies' Magazine* and later in *Godey's Lady's Book*. She wanted to use the space to write about more serious causes, particularly philanthropy. Earlier, Hale had waged an unsuccessful battle against including fashion news in *The Ladies' Magazine* during the first three years of its publication, eventually giving in to reader demand in 1831. Hale published fashion plates and news but announced: "There is no part of our duty as editor of a ladies' journal which we feel so reluctant to perform, as to quote, or exhibit the fashions of dress."[6] Her readers got their fashions but also received harsh words from Hale's pen about the foolishness of outright adoption of European fashions, which she saw as frivolous and extravagant.

The fashion plates lasted only two years in *The Ladies' Magazine*. Hale stopped publishing them for the magazine's last three years. Godey solved Hale's disdain for publishing fashion plates by making her the literary editor of his new journal, *Godey's Lady's Book*. Godey hired a fashion editor to handle Hale's former tasks. The move allowed Hale to concentrate exclusively on literature and editorials.

Through her editorials, Hale defined and promoted a role for middle-class women in American society. Her views seem narrow by today's standards and thus have received criticism from some feminist scholars. Yet, to many mid-Victorian women, Hale's views on a woman's place in society were too radical.

Hale's ideal woman served her family. A woman's domain was her home. From there a woman could be a helper to her husband, a guide to her children, and, perhaps most important, the moral center of the family. Hale reiterated these points in editorials and articles throughout her years as editor. She held up Queen Victoria as a role model of femininity, morality, and intellect. She urged the queen to encourage education for women, claiming it was "the best means of improving the moral conditions of society."[7]

From the magazine's outset, Hale consistently crusaded for education for women.[8] Women, Hale believed, had to be educated if they were to be fit companions for their husbands and competent homemakers. Hale herself had been educated by her mother to essentially a high school level. Since women were not admitted to colleges in Hale's time, she read the books her brother Horatio brought home from Dartmouth.

She believed that women, if educated, could pursue some professions outside the home, particularly teaching, missionary work, and medicine. These fields were suited for women, Hale said, because they lent themselves to women's highly moral talents. At the same time, these occupations did not invade men's traditional domains of politics and power.

Hale particularly approved of missionary and philanthropic work. A social reformer, she established a number of charitable societies, including the Fatherless and Widows' Society of Boston and the Seaman's Aid Society. She established the latter group upon discovering that sailors were paid so little that their families lived in poverty. Hale employed the sailors' wives as seamstresses, making sailors' uniforms for a fraction of the cost that merchant marine stores charged the men. The aid society also provided a library and educational opportunities for women and children. She also organized the Ladies' Medical Missionary Society and its successor, the Woman's Union Mission Society, as a means of promoting medical roles for women.[9]

Hale frowned on women's involving themselves in more masculine professions and pursuits. She was opposed to women's involvement in any aspect of the slavery issue. She believed slavery and subsequent war issues were vulgar and beneath women.[10]

Godey's began its decline after the Civil War. The journal's chief competitor, *Peterson's Magazine*, increased its expenditures and published even more fashions and literature than did *Godey's*. *Godey's* began a slow decline, and Hale and Godey stopped editing the magazine in 1877. The journal's new editors kept the same sentimental, Victorian content, despite literature's change toward realism. *Godey's* inability to reflect the times led to its demise in 1898.

Notes

1. For more information on Hale's early writings, see Isabelle Webb Entrikin, "Sarah Josepha Hale and *Godey's Lady's Book*" (Ph. D. diss., University of Pennsylvania, 1946).

2. Cited in Lawrence Martin, "The Genesis of *Godey's Lady's Book*," *New England Quarterly* 1 (January 1928), p. 47.

3. February 1840, p. 96.

4. Martin, "The Genesis of *Godey's Lady's Book*," p. 69.

5. Frank Luther Mott, *A History of American Magazines*, vol. 1 (Cambridge: Harvard University Press, 1939), p. 581.

6. *Ladies' Magazine*, September 1831, quoted in Martin, "The Genesis of *Godey's Lady's Book*," p. 53.

7. March 1838, cited in Ruth E. Finley, *The Lady of Godey's: Sarah Josepha Hale* (Philadelphia: J. B. Lippincott, 1931), p. 124.

8. December 1877, pp. 522–524.

9. Mott, *A History of American Magazines*, p. 583.

10. Martin, "The Genesis of *Godey's Lady's Book*," p. 50.

Information Sources

BIBLIOGRAPHY:

Entrikin, Isabelle Webb. "Sarah Josepha Hale and *Godey's Lady's Book*." Ph. D. diss., University of Pennsylvania, 1946.

Finley, Ruth E. *The Lady of Godey's: Sarah Josepha Hale.* Philadelphia: J. B. Lippincott, 1931.

Martin, Lawrence. "The Genesis of *Godey's Lady's Book*." *New England Quarterly* 1, January 1928, pp. 41–70.

Mott, Frank Luther. *A History of American Magazines*, vol. 1, 1741–1850. Cambridge, Mass.: Harvard University Press, 1939.

Wheeler, Edmund. *The History of Newport, New Hampshire, from 1766 to 1878, with a Genealogical Register.* Concord, N.H.: Republican Press Association, 1879.

INDEX SOURCES: Poole's, except 1830–1839 and 1883–1898.

LOCATION SOURCES: Library of Congress and other sources; American Periodical Series II, Reels 772–226 and 862–880.

Publication History

MAGAZINE TITLE AND TITLE CHANGES: *The Lady's Book* (1830–1833); *Monthly Magazine of Belles-Lettres and the Arts, the Lady's Book* (1833–1834); *The Lady's Book* (1835–1839); *Godey's Lady's Book and Ladies' American Magazine* (1840–1843); *Godey's Magazine and Lady's Book* (1844–1848); *Godey's Lady's Book* (1848–1854); *Godey's Lady's Book and Magazine* (1854–1882); *Godey's Lady's Book* (1883–1892); *Godey's Magazine* (1892–1898) (absorbed by the *Puritan*, 1898).

VOLUME AND ISSUE DATA: Vols. 1–137 (July 1830–August 1898). Monthly.

PUBLISHER AND PLACE OF PUBLICATION: Louis A. Godey and Co. (1830–1877); Godey's Lady's Book Publishing Co. (1878–1883); J. H. Haulenbeek and Co. (1883–1886); William E. Striker (1886–1887); Croly Publishing Co. (1887–1888); Godey Publishing Co. (1888–1898). Philadelphia (1837–1892); New York (1892–1898).

EDITORS: Louis A. Godey (1830–1836); Louis A. Godey and Sarah J. Hale (1837–1877); J.G.L. Brown, Charles W. Frost, and Mrs. S. A. Shields (1878); J. Hannum Jones, A. E. Brown, and Mrs. S. A. Shields (1878–1881); J. Hannum Jones and A. E. Brown (1881–1883); J. H. Haulenbeek (1883–1885); J. H. Haulenbeek and Eleanor Moore Hiestand (1885–1886); Mrs. D. G. Croly (1887–1888); Albert H. Hardy (1892–1893); Harry Wakefield Bates (1894–?). Editorship during 1888–1892 is unrecorded.

CIRCULATION: APS: 150,000 before the Civil War.

Mary M. Cronin

GOLF FOR WOMEN

Sometimes it is OK to stand alone. It is especially good to stand alone when you are tapping the largest growing area of golf. Women account for almost half of all new golfers.[1] Born of a great idea and filling a void, *Golf for Women* made its debut in July 1988. This bimonthly periodical appeared exactly one year after results of a market test indicated a need for a magazine devoted to the feminine side of the sport.[2] *Golf for Women* is still the only magazine devoted to women's interest in golf. With a circulation of 300,000, it stands alone also as the largest of *any* women's sports magazine.[3]

The idea for developing a magazine devoted to the needs of female golfers was conceived in 1985 in a place remote from business epicenters—the college classroom. Debra and Woody Brumitt, students in Samir Husni's journalism program at the University of Mississippi, put together a prototype for a women's golf magazine. Woody, a pro at a local golf club, followed Debbie's suggestion to concentrate on women, and the prototype "won a national competition for best student prototype."[4] Following through with the idea, the Brumitts raised $66,000 from family and friends to finance a direct mail campaign in 1987. Earning a 5 percent response from that campaign, the Brumitts received another $200,000 from a private investor to publish the magazine. By July 1988, *Golf for Women* was no longer just a great classroom idea, but rather a periodical on the coffee tables of female golfers.[5]

One year later, with Debbie as editorial director and Woody as marketing director in Oxford, Mississippi, the Meredith Corporation in Des Moines, Iowa, purchased the magazine.[6] Meredith Corporation, publisher of magazines targeted at female audiences, such as *Better Homes and Gardens** and *Ladies' Home Journal,** as well as non-gender-specific magazines such as *Sail*, intended to increase *Golf for Women*'s circulation from 20,000 to 300,000.[7] The company made no editorial changes until 1994, although the magazine was moved to Meredith's corporate headquarters in Des Moines. In January 1994, the editorial offices were moved again, this time to Lake Mary, Florida. In May 1994, Patricia Baldwin, business and sports marketing writer for the *Dallas Morning News*, took the helm of editorial directorship. By mid-1994, Meredith reached its goal of a 300,000 circulation.[8]

In an era when the chances are that a new magazine will fold before it is noticed by the public, why has this one succeeded? Samir Husni attributed this success to its "strong editorial."[9] Major golf magazines targeted toward male readership tend to ignore women's interest in learning more about the game of golf. Magazine founder Debra Brumitt agreed with Husni and emphasized that the content of this periodical especially targeted women: the "meat [of the editorial] is instruction" for women.[10] Five out of 15 articles written in each issue deal with instruction regarding specific aspects of the game. "It was designed to be written to improve women's knowledge of and enjoyment of the game. Women buy the magazine in order to become better golfers."[11]

Entrusted with the task of helping improve women's games are both playing editors and instruction editors. The Ladies Professional Golf Association's (LPGA) Hall of Famer Kathy Whitworth serves as the "playing" editor in chief. She contributes regularly with her articles "Eye on the Basics." The other touring professional who contributes regular articles is Missie Berteotti. From the LPGA Teaching Division of golf professionals, Sharon Miller and Joann Beddow contribute articles to help beginning, as well as advanced, female players. In each issue, articles are solicited from other touring professionals, such as Sandra Haynie and Maxine Lupo. Mike McGetrick, the Professional Golfers' Association's (PGA) 1990 Teacher of the Year, writes an article with Tom Ferrell called "Swing Analysis." This article is devoted to analyzing the swing of a current female touring pro, utilizing description and stop-action photography.

Other articles feature equipment, travel, and fashion. For example, one article discussed tips on traveling to tournaments alone. This included advice from seasoned pros on what to do when you get there for both comfort and safety. Occasionally a special interest article runs. One of these was Lois Meyers Migliorini's account of a middle-aged housewife's transformation from a nongolfer and gourmet cook to a devoted player/fan who spends three days a week on the links and orders her desserts in when she entertains.[12]

Golf for Women reaches a female audience beyond the housewife golfer. Executive Women's Golf Association is a group designed to instruct and unite professional women who are interested in networking through the game of golf. Its founder, Nancy Oliver, is impressed with how *Golf for Women* "speaks to all age groups and all types of women from the working woman to the traditional-role woman."[13]

The regular departments appeal to this diverse population. In each issue, "Law of the Links," written by a lawyer, discusses some legal aspect of the game. "To Your Health" may give advice on nutrition to aid a woman's game or on the proper use of sunscreens or insect repellents. "LPGA Profile" interviews a leading pro. "Quick Cures" adds more instruction for some of the small things that interfere with proper driving, chipping, or putting. Readers are kept up-to-date with current tournament results. *Golf for Women* lives up to its claim to be "a full service women's golf magazine."[14]

Its target audience, women who play golf, make up the fastest-growing segment in the sport. When the prototype was being tested in 1987, less than 5 million golfers were women. By 1990, that figure rose to in excess of 6.5 million. By the mid-1990s, almost half of all new golfers were women.[15]

Women golfers, in general, share several common characteristics. They come from households with average incomes of $60,000, and these women spent $3 billion in 1990 on golf itself and golf-related items. Most are married (77 percent) and are usually better educated than other women—75 percent having attended college and 35 percent having graduated from college. Subscribers of *Golf for Women* generally make the influential purchasing decisions regarding bill paying, family vacations, investments, autos, and choice of restaurants. While almost half of all new golfers are women, the subscribers have been playing the sport for some time, an average of 8.4 years, and play an average of 67 times a year.[16]

The advertisements in *Golf for Women* reflect the purchasing power and the time spent on the golf course of this target group.[17] Knowing these women are apt to spend their money on high-end products, advertisers promote luxury automobiles and watches along with the expected golf equipment, golf attire, and golf resorts.

When Meredith Corporation purchased the magazine, the ad rate for a black-and-white page doubled. By the mid-1990s, the rate for a black-and-white page had tripled from its 1988 rate. In spite of advertising price increases, Meredith reported *Golf for Women* earned a record 33 percent ad page growth in 1992. That same year, the magazine realized a 49 percent increase in ad revenues.[18] It appeared advertisers were eager to tap into the fastest growing segment of the sport. Jeanne Sherman, director of golf merchandising for the Wilson Sporting Goods Company, confirmed that Wilson places "creative messages targeted toward women" in this magazine.[19]

Subscription rates remained at $14.95 for a six-issue year through the July/August 1993 issue. The rate rose to $15.97 ($13.97 plus $2 shipping and handling) per year with the September/October 1993 issue, the first increase in subscription rates since the publication began. *Golf for Women* continues as a bimonthly publication.[20]

Catering to the needs of women golfers is an area that has been overlooked by the traditional and established golf magazines and merchandisers. When it comes to taking women golfers seriously, "change is coming—but slowly," according to golf pro Renee Powell.[21] In late 1993, *Golf Digest* hired female marketing editor Lisa Furlong. Wilson Sporting Goods Company's appointment of Jeanne Sherman as director of golf merchandising made her the first female executive for the company.

Golf for Women "still remains the only regularly published full-service national women's golf publication dedicated to helping women learn more about and improve in all facets of their golf games."[22] By following its philosophy of bringing the reader the best information about golf, editor Debra Brumitt claimed, "We have a great deal of respect for our readers."[23]

When it comes to reporting how women are treated on the golf course, Nancy Oliver agreed that *Golf for Women* showed respect for their readers. "Their story on getting equal really showed their colors. They reported the facts on how it really is out there. They didn't sensationalize or sugarcoat any of the issues."[24]

From an idea to combine a love for the sport of golf with filling a publication void in the mid-1980s comes a 1990s success story. The Brumitts are duly proud of this success. "We're delighted our prototype has turned into a full-fledged real-life magazine."[25]

No major change of focus is anticipated for the later part of the decade. According to *Golf for Women*'s publisher, David Cohen, "[I]nstruction, equipment, travel, and fashion will make up 80 percent of the editorial with instruction having the highest share of that 80 percent." The only change is a shift from emphasizing the professional golfer to more emphasis on the amateur.[26]

Justified by its success, the mission remains the same—to be a full-service magazine for the female golfer. Under new editorial leadership, *Golf for Women* broadened its reach, becoming more sophisticated in tone and image to inform as well as entertain the woman who makes golf a part of her life. What happened with the change was "not a revolution, just an evolution."[27] New editor Patricia Baldwin's vision is for *Golf for Women* to be "the premier publication in instruction in women's golf; the source of entertainment and information regarding women's involvement in golf. In other words, we want *Golf for Women* to be a 'must read' " for every woman who plays the sport.[28]

A circulation of 300,000 proves women and golf can be taken together seriously. How does *Golf for Women* compare with the other major golf magazines on the market? Long before the publication reached 300,000, Katz and Katz recommended libraries include *Golf for Women* in their collections. "A golfer is a golfer, but this publication stresses the feminine side of the sport. This title should be next to *Golf* and *Golf Digest*."[29]

Debra and Woody Brumitt knew golf and knew women enjoyed the game. They also knew women want to know as much as they can to improve their game and enhance that enjoyment. By stressing instruction, giving information about players and tournaments, and showing what is available in equipment as well as golf fashion, *Golf for Women* continues to appeal to the interests of the female golfer.

Other golf magazines may publish a regular or occasional article about some feminine aspect of the sport. However, as golf pro Renee Powell points out, *Golf for Women* is "the only golf magazine out there geared strictly for women."[30] That makes it "the premier magazine." Whether it becomes "a must read" for female golfers is the next challenge. If success is measured by offering a quality product at an affordable price to the right target, then *Golf for Women* has sunk the putt for the win. The magazine has established a par that competing publications may find difficult to match.

Notes

1. Renee Powell interview, March 25, 1994. *Golf for Women*, Media Kit.
2. Debra Brumitt interview, April 5, 1994.
3. Ibid.

4. Lambeth Hochwald, "Colleges Provide Fertile Ground for Launch Ideas," *Folio*, December 1, 1992, p. 28.

5. Ibid.

6. Ibid.

7. "Meredith Buys *Golf for Women*," *Folio,* March 1990, pp. 54, 56.

8. David Cohen interview, April 30, 1994.

9. Hochwald, "Colleges Provide Fertile Ground for Launch Ideas," p. 28.

10. Brumitt interview.

11. Ibid.

12. Lois Meyers Migliorini, "How Golf Changed My Life," December 1993, p. 74.

13. Nancy Oliver interview, March 25, 1994.

14. Media Kit.

15. Media Kit. Source: National Golf Foundation.

16. Media Kit. Source: 1990 Subscriber Study, Market Facts, Inc., National Golf Foundation, 1991.

17. Media Kit. Source: 1992 Fall MRI.

18. Media Kit. Source: Publishers' Information Bureau.

19. Jeanne Sherman interview, March 25, 1994.

20. Cohen interview.

21. Powell interview.

22. Media Kit.

23. Brumitt interview.

24. Oliver interview.

25. Brumitt interview.

26. Cohen interview.

27. Patricia Baldwin interview, May 4, 1994.

28. Ibid.

29. Bill Katz and Linda S. Katz, *Magazines for Librarians*, 7th ed. (New Providence, N.J.: R. R. Bowker, 1992).

30. Powell interview.

Information Sources

BIBLIOGRAPHY:
Hochwald, Lambeth. "Colleges Provide Fertile Ground for Launch Ideas." *Folio*, December 1, 1992, p. 28.
Katz, Bill, and Linda S. Katz. *Magazines for Librarians*, 7th ed. New Providence, N.J.: R. R. Bowker, 1992.
"Meredith Buys *Golf for Women*." *Folio*, March 1990, pp. 54, 56.
INDEX SOURCES: None.
LOCATION SOURCES: Library of Congress and other libraries.

Publication History

MAGAZINE TITLE AND TITLE CHANGES: *Golf for Women.*
VOLUME AND ISSUE DATA: Vols. 1–(July 1988–present). Bimonthly.
PUBLISHER AND PLACE OF PUBLICATION: Brumitt Publications, Inc. (July 1988–July 1989); Meredith Corporation (July 1989–present). Oxford, Miss. (July 1988–July 1989); Des Moines, Iowa (July 1989–1994); Lake Mary, Fla. (1994–present).

EDITORS: Debra Dotley Brumitt (July 1988–April 1994); Patricia Baldwin (May 1994–
    present).
CIRCULATION: ABC, 1993: 278,500 (primarily subscriptions).

Patricia E. Linder

GOOD HOUSEKEEPING

When *Good Housekeeping* published its first edition in May 1885, editor and
publisher Clark W. Bryan promised readers that he aimed to "produce and
perpetuate perfection—or as near unto perfection as may be attained in the
Household."[1] In that issue, he presented readers with a magazine that neatly
mixed fiction and poetry with domestic advice. With its earliest numbers, *Good
Housekeeping* magazine established a successful editorial tradition that has continued for more than a century (and in the unusual position of *always* being
under the direction of a man until 1994).

From a recipe for salt fish and cream, a description of a proper sitting room,
and a poem hailing "The Tired Mother" in its first number to a potato and
onion casserole, a tour of television talk show host Regis Philbin's home, and
advice on how working mothers cope with sick children in the February 1994
edition, *Good Housekeeping*'s editorial content has varied little. In more than
100 years of publication, the editorial balance of recipes, etiquette, household
advice, information features, and fiction continued to appeal to a vast number
of American women.

With a paid circulation of 5 million and a readership of 24.2 million in 1993,
Good Housekeeping held its position as one of the most popular (and tradition-
bound) of the "Seven Sisters" women's magazines. Despite declining readership and disappointing ad revenues within the industry, *Good Housekeeping*
maintained that it had "fared better than most in the advertising downturn of
recent years."[2]

In its earliest days, *Good Housekeeping* appeared as a 32-page biweekly magazine costing 10¢ an issue and available to subscribers for $2.50 annually. In
1891, it switched to monthly publication, downsized from its format a bit, and
charged $2 a year for subscriptions. In 1994, the cover price for a magazine
that often numbered more than 200 pages was $1.95, while the annual subscrip-
tion was $17.97.

Bryan founded *Good Housekeeping* after a long journalism career. He was
the regional correspondent of the *Springfield Republican*, edited and published
the *Berkshire Courier*, briefly owned the Springfield *Union*, and then founded
a trade journal, *Paper World*.[3] Under Bryan, the magazine's circulation probably
hovered at about 25,000.[4] He published *Good Housekeeping* until his death—
by suicide—in March 1898. The magazine was bought by John Pettigrew, who
passed it on to his printer, George D. Chamberlain. Within two years, it was

purchased by the Phelps Publishing Co., which hired James Eaton Tower to edit it. By the time the Hearst publishing company purchased it in 1911, *Good Housekeeping* was an established traditional woman's magazine with a circulation of about 300,000 and a solid advertising base.[5] In the 1990s, *Good Housekeeping* continues as one of Hearst's leading publications.

Under the Hearst publishing banner, *Good Housekeeping* grew in prestige and popularity. When Tower resigned as editor in 1913, Hearst tapped William Frederick Bigelow, who had been at the corporation's *Cosmopolitan** magazine. Bigelow led *Good Housekeeping* until 1942. He increased the amount of fiction and poetry and solicited work from popular writers, including Somerset Maugham, Mary Roberts Rinehart, Booth Tarkington, Edna St. Vincent Millay, Ogden Nash, and Ella Wheeler Wilcox.[6] Circulation exceeded 1 million in the 1920s, and, while other magazines felt the weight of the depression in the 1930s, *Good Housekeeping* circulation (and profits for Hearst) continued to climb.

When Herbert R. Mayes took over in 1942, he reduced the number of fiction offerings, but the magazine remained basically unchanged. Throughout the decade, the magazine continued to grow, and by the mid-1950s, gross revenues stood at about $21.5 million.[7] Wade Hampton Nichols, Jr., was named editor of the magazine in 1959. By 1966, the magazine's circulation peaked at 5.5 million.[8]

In 1975, Nichols was replaced by veteran magazine journalist John Mack Carter, who had been editor in chief at *McCall's** and *Ladies' Home Journal** and had started his magazine career at *Better Homes and Gardens.** Carter maintained a high-profile celebrity status, frequently appearing on talk shows, doling out advice over supermarket public address systems, and traveling the country to meet and woo readers. Carter probably is fated to be the last in the long line of male editors in chief at *Good Housekeeping*. Executive editor Mina Mulvey noted that "until relatively recently, women were in effect excluded from all the top jobs in publishing," but, she predicted, "It is reasonable to expect that the next editor will be a woman."[9]

The 1980s were difficult years for the venerable women's magazine group known as the "Seven Sisters." Like the others, *Good Housekeeping* saw a dip in the number of ad pages in the late 1980s.[10] Circulation also fluctuated, although it stayed slightly above the 5 million mark. Hearst reacted to the advertising downturn by offering a discounted rate for advertisers who bought space in both *Good Housekeeping* and *Redbook,** which had been bought by Hearst in 1984.[11] By the end of 1989, *Good Housekeeping* circulation ranked third among the "Seven Sisters," behind *Better Homes and Gardens* and *Family Circle.**[12] The magazine had more than 3.6 million subscribers and 1.4 million newsstand sales with estimated ad revenues at $148 million.[13]

While most of the "Seven Sisters" revamped their covers and streamlined formats to accommodate the new generation of working women and potential readers (whose mothers read these same magazines), no major changes were planned for *Good Housekeeping*. Carter said that *Good Housekeeping* has always been updated monthly.[14]

In October 1990, *Advertising Age* hailed the revival of *Good Housekeeping* as the ad page leader in women's service magazines. Between 1983 and 1988, *Good Housekeeping* ad pages had fallen 22.7 percent to 1,621 ad pages. *Good Housekeeping* finished 1989 with 1,702 ad pages. Although the 1989 figure was still far off the 1983 high of 2,097 ad pages, "the title appears headed in the right direction."[15]

One reason for the magazine's success and popularity was that, despite its huge circulation, *Good Housekeeping* maintained an intimate relationship with readers. Photographs of readers and their children were published; many letters from readers appeared each month. In his chapter on *Good Housekeeping* in the 1968 edition of *History of American Magazines*, journalism historian Frank L. Mott noted that the magazine had always solicited articles and contributions from readers. A contest in the first issue promised cash prizes for a series of six articles on "How to Eat, Drink and Sleep as Christians Should," another series on "Mistress Work and Maid Work—Which Is Mistress and Which Is the Servant?" and another article on how to make bread.[16]

While most of the copy in the 1990s was professionally written, *Good Housekeeping* remained in touch with contemporary readers through contests, polls, and letters. The February 1994 issue, for example, invited readers to "[j]oin our editorial team" by sending in ideas for coverage. The magazine promised a $100 prize "to the first person who submits any lead we follow up."[17] In 1970, the magazine began publishing its "List of the 10 Most Admired Women," an annual feature that reflects the traditional nature of the *Good Housekeeping* reader. The first list featured actress Patricia Neal, writer Pearl S. Buck, Mrs. Dwight D. Eisenhower, Mrs. Robert F. Kennedy, Mrs. Joseph P. Kennedy, Mrs. Richard M. Nixon, Mrs. Martin Luther King, Jr., Queen Elizabeth II, Mrs. Indira Gandhi, and Mrs. Golda Meir. Noting the conspicuous absence of Jacqueline Kennedy from the list, the magazine quoted a voter who said her marriage to Aristotle Onassis had put her in disfavor. In 1994, celebrating the 25th anniversary of the poll, the winners were Mother Teresa, Barbara Bush, Hillary Rodham Clinton, Janet Reno, Oprah Winfrey, Princess Diana, Marilyn Quayle, Rosalynn Carter, Katharine Hepburn, and Erma Bombeck. In 1982, the magazine also began including a Most Admired Men poll.

In general, the most striking editorial changes in *Good Housekeeping* over its long history were the introduction of color around the turn of the century and the shift since the 1950s toward more articles about celebrities and celebrity lifestyles.

In terms of artwork, the earliest issues of the magazine contained only small drawings and decorative lettering at the beginning of each article. The covers were drab, muted monochrome. After the turn of the century, however, the magazine began featuring cover drawings of women and children drawn by some of the most popular illustrators of the day. Illustrations by Charles Dana Gibson and Jessie Willcox Smith came to represent the *Good Housekeeping* image, and the covers often were reproduced as artwork. Through the 1950s, the magazine featured illustrations, especially of children, on its cover. Drawings were then replaced by photographs. In the 1960s, the magazine began featuring celebrities on its cover, a feature that continued through the 1990s. This editorial shift helped increase newsstand sales.[18]

Unlike other women's magazines (such as the competing Hearst publication *Redbook*) that, by the 1990s, focused more of their editorial content on sexuality and intimate relationships, *Good Housekeeping* preserved its traditional image and shied away from blatantly sexual editorial copy.

The February 1994 edition of the magazine featured a cover story about entertainer Mary Hart, a Weight Watchers diet, and a feature by actress Ann-Margret about "Elvis, Alcohol, My Husband & Me." The monthly departments included household hints from the syndicated columnist Heloise, Elizabeth Post's etiquette, Dr. Joyce Brothers's psychological advice, a short, humorous essay by Erma Bombeck, and medical advice. The food section included five different features, including "30 Easy Casseroles" and "Sweetheart Apple Pie." The beauty section included a makeover, a popular monthly feature, and "13 Pretty Hairdos."

The monthly magazine-within-a-magazine feature, "The Better Way," began in 1956. Printed on noncoated stock paper to emphasize its identity, this section features short articles that can be clipped and advice that women can act on immediately. In February 1994, it included a monthly list of product recalls, money advice, booklets that could be sent for, and other short features. The editorial content of the magazine clearly revolved around celebrities, home, and personal appearance.

The most recent *Good Housekeeping* advertising campaign focused on a celebration of the "new traditional" women who were the magazine's readers. The campaign, which began in 1988, included the catchy "America is coming home to *Good Housekeeping*."[19] The advertising initially encountered criticism by feminists because they argued that it subtly attempted to turn women away from the workforce and back to domestic servitude. Then, in 1993, when the magazine attempted to promote itself with an advertisement featuring an "unconventional family" of a single working woman, the gay and lesbian community protested.[20]

Yet, *Good Housekeeping* describes its readership as "the baby boom generation at its prime."[21] The magazine's demographics in the fall of 1993 indicated the median age of readers was 43.5. More than 57 percent of readers worked; 46.2 percent had one or more children at home; and only 27.1 percent of readers lived in apartments. The median household income was $33,256.[22] The magazine described its typical reader: "She is actively involved in every aspect of contemporary life because it affects *her*, her family, her work, her home. She's a doer, thoughtful, responsible, active in neighborhood and community affairs; she cares about the state of the schools, the environment, the plight of the poor; she reacts with tears and rage at stories about child abuse—and writes to her congressman [*sic*]."[23]

Social responsibility has long been an aspect of *Good Housekeeping* magazine. In 1900, the magazine created the Good Housekeeping Institute Experiment Station to improve women's lot in the home. The institute, headquartered initially in Springfield, Massachusetts, hired a small staff to research household methods and practices. A monthly column produced by the institute began appearing in the magazine and included such advice as "Poultry Keeping for the Woman of Today" and "Buttermilk as a Remedy."[24] In 1902, *Good Housekeeping* publicized its "Ironclad Contract," a money-back guarantee on all products that were advertised in the magazine. With the Pure Food and Drug Act still four years away, *Good Housekeeping* also began inspecting food products and publishing a monthly honor roll of food that had passed inspection. The magazine's guarantee of products evolved by 1910 into an oval "Seal of Approval," a forerunner of the seal that still appeared on consumer goods through the 1990s. Throughout the early years of the century, the institute grew in size and prestige. In 1912, chemist Harvey W. Wiley, who had worked with the U.S. Department of Agriculture to set standards for consumer products, joined the institute and established a Bureau of Foods, Sanitation and Health. He also contributed a column to the magazine. The institute later included departments for babies, beauty, needlework, food, engineering, fashion, patterns, and decorating.

The integrity of the Seal of Approval came under attack in the late 1930s at a time when Congress was debating whether "grade labeling" should be included on consumer goods. The Hearst Corp. vigorously opposed grading products on the grounds that it would erode the consumer's right to choose and that it would give government agencies the power to make arbitrary decisions (the magazine's Seal of Approval also would be usurped by a government grade).[25] Hearst openly lobbied against the concept, even after Congress failed to approve it. *Good Housekeeping* sponsored a monthly *Consumers Information Service* tabloid from 1936 to 1942 to lobby against increased government intervention in private industry.

Mott in his *History of American Magazines* argued that the feud with the government probably fueled Federal Trade Commission (FTC) action in 1939 against the Seal of Approval. The FTC filed a complaint charging the magazine with "misleading and deceptive acts and practices in the issuance of guarantys, seals of approval, and the publication in its advertising pages of grossly exaggerated and false claims."[26] *Good Housekeeping* fought the complaint for nearly two years. When the publisher of *Ladies' Home Journal* and the editor of *McCall's* testified against *Good Housekeeping*, it aroused "[s]uspicion that envy of competitors directed against the home magazine that had surpassed all others" also triggered the complaint. In 1941, after the FTC ordered *Good Housekeeping* to stop declaring that its advertised products were "tested and approved," the magazine introduced a "Guaranty Seal." The new seal simply promised to replace the product or refund the money if it did not live up to the advertised promises. The seal was amended in 1962 and again in 1975 to read "A Limited Warranty to Consumers—Replacement or Refund if Defective."[27] In the 1990s, the institute included a staff of 70 under the directorship of Amy Barr.

The seal represented just one aspect of a rather rigid advertising policy. "The Magazine maintains high levels of good taste and exercises strict editorial judgments in the consideration of products it will accept for advertising and in reviewing the advertising copy it publishes," according to the magazine's consumers' policy, which is reprinted each month on page 6. *Good Housekeeping* does not accept tobacco or liquor advertisements. The magazine initially banned tobacco advertisements (certainly in keeping with the idea that its readers were ladies, not smokers), then accepted these ads in the 1930s but banned them again in 1952.[28]

In its earliest years, the magazine relegated advertisements to its back pages. The advertising in the first issue was limited to two pages that contained 19 advertisements, some of them illustrated, for domestic goods, including pens, Webster's dictionary, several space heaters, stained glass windows, a lamp, wallpaper, a typewriter, and a "domestic remedy." Such patent medicine ads, however, clearly had no place in a magazine that was promoting perfection in the household, and they disappeared from print around the same time as the Good Housekeeping Institute opened its doors. Managing editor Mina Mulvey estimated that in 1993 the editorial/advertising mix was roughly 48–49 percent editorial, 52–51 percent advertisements.

In addition to the American-based *Good Housekeeping*, a British *Good Housekeeping*, owned by a Hearst British subsidiary, the National Magazine Co., was published monthly. The two magazines had no connection editorially. *Buenhogar* also was published in Spanish and Portuguese in Latin America and South America. The content, however, was not identical with that in *Good Housekeeping*.

Notes

1. "Editor's Portfolio," May 2, 1885, p. 23.

2. *Good Housekeeping* executive editor Mina Mulvey responded in writing to a detailed series of questions posed by this writer about the history and philosophy of the magazine. As part of the privately owned Hearst Corporation, *Good Housekeeping* does not publish annual reports or profits.

3. Frank L. Mott, *A History of American Magazines*, vol. 5 (Cambridge: Harvard University Press, 1968), pp. 125–126.

4. Ibid., p. 131.

5. Ibid., p. 133.

6. Ibid., pp. 134, 136.

7. Theodore Peterson, *Magazines in the Twentieth Century* (Urbana: University of Illinois, 1956), p. 204.

8. Mott, *History of American Magazines,* p. 143.

9. Mulvey response to questions. She was correct; the current editor is Ellen Levine.

10. Pat Sloan, " 'Good Housekeeping' Sees Trend," *Advertising Age*, October 17, 1988, p. 12.

11. Rebecca Fannin, "The Growing Sisterhood," *Marketing & Media Decisions,* October 1989, p. 44.

12. Deirdre Carmody, "Identity Crisis for 'Seven Sisters,' " *New York Times*, August 6, 1990, p. D1.

13. Jean Marie Angelo, "John Mack Carter: Editor, Celebrity and Southern Gentleman," *Folio,* February 1990, p. 31.

14. Ibid.

15. Scott Donaton, "Once-Sagging 'GH' Bounces Back," *Advertising Age*, October 8, 1990, p. S26.

16. "Get the Best," May 2, 1885, p. 24.

17. "Join Our Editorial Team," February 1994, p. 171.

18. Mulvey response to questions.

19. Philip H. Dougherty, "Social Analysis from *Good Housekeeping*," *New York Times*, August 11, 1988, p. D18.

20. Stuart Elliott, "*Good Housekeeping* Is Drawing Fire from Homosexuals over Ads Dealing with Family Values," *New York Times*, May 7, 1993, p. D15.

21. "Profile of a *GH* Reader," included in information sent by Mina Mulvey in response to author's questions.

22. Mediamark Research Inc. figures for 1991 as quoted in Susan Krafft, "Window on a Woman's Mind," *American Demographics*, December 1991, p. 46.

23. "Profile of *GH* Reader."

24. "A History: 90 Years of the Good Housekeeping Institute," in "The Way We Were! The Way We Are!" special section, February 1990, p. 5.

25. Mott, *A History of American Magazines*, p. 139.

26. Ibid., p. 140.

27. "Celebrating 80 Years of the Good Housekeeping Seal," in "The Way We Were! The Way We Are!" p. 10.

28. "Handling Health Problems—Then and Now," in "The Way We Were! The Way We Are!" p. 19.

Information Sources

BIBLIOGRAPHY:

Angelo, Jean Marie. "John Mack Carter: Editor, Celebrity and Southern Gentleman." *Folio*, February 1990, p. 31.

Carmody, Deirdre. "Identity Crisis for 'Seven Sisters.' " *New York Times*, August 6, 1990, p. D1.

Donaton, Scott. "Once-Sagging 'GH' Bounces Back." *Advertising Age*, October 8, 1990, p. S26.

Dougherty, Philip H. "Social Analysis from *Good Housekeeping*." *New York Times*, August 11, 1988, p. D18.

Elliott, Stuart. "*Good Housekeeping* Is Drawing Fire from Homosexuals over Ads Dealing with Family Values." *New York Times*, May 7, 1993, p. D15.

Fannin, Rebecca. "The Growing Sisterhood." *Marketing & Media Decisions*, October 1989, p. 44.

Krafft, Susan. "Window on a Woman's Mind." *American Demographics*, December 1991, p. 46.

Mott, Frank L. *A History of American Magazines*, vol. 5. Cambridge: Harvard University Press, 1968.

Peterson, Theodore. *Magazines in the Twentieth Century*. Urbana: University of Illinois, 1956.

Sloan, Pat. " 'Good Housekeeping' Sees Trend." *Advertising Age*, October 17, 1988, p. 12.
"The Way We Were! The Way We Are!" Special Section of *Good Housekeeping*, February 1990.
INDEX SOURCES: Readers' Guide to Periodical Literature; Consumers Index; Magazine Index; Popular Magazine Index; Text on Microfilm.
LOCATION SOURCES: Library of Congress and other libraries.

Publication History

MAGAZINE TITLE AND TITLE CHANGES: *Good Housekeeping* (1885–1909); *Good Housekeeping Magazine* (1909–1916); *Good Housekeeping* (1916–current).
VOLUME AND ISSUE DATA: Vols. 1–(May 2, 1885–present). Biweekly (1885–1890); monthly (1891–present).
PUBLISHER AND PLACE OF PUBLICATION: Clark W. Bryan & Co. (1885–1898); John Pettigrew (1898); George D. Chamberlain (1898–1900); Phelps Publishing Co. (1900–1911); American Home Magazine Co. (later called International Magazine Co.) (1914–1936); Hearst Magazines (1936–1952); Hearst Corp. (1952–present). Holyoke, Mass. (1885–1886); Springfield, Mass. (1887–1911); New York (1911–present).
EDITORS: Clark W. Bryan (1885–1898); James Eaton Tower (1899–1913); William Frederick Bigelow (1913–1942); Herbert Raymond Mayes (1942–1958); Wade Hampton Nichols, Jr. (1959–1975); John Mack Carter (1975–fall 1994); Ellen Levine (fall 1994–present).
CIRCULATION: ABC, 1993: 5 million (paid, primarily subscriptions).

Agnes Hooper Gottlieb

GOURMET

An old adage goes, "Timing is everything." In publishing, timing may not be everything, but it is an important element in the success or failure of the launch of a magazine. A magazine—no matter how good the concept—can fail if it is introduced too early (before there is sufficient interest in the subject) or too late (when the niche is glutted). That is why the launch of *Gourmet* is so fascinating. In hindsight, the start of *Gourmet,* the "magazine of good living,"[1] probably was ill-timed. A magazine dedicated to the epicurean delights of food and drink probably should not have been launched a few months before the United States' entry into World War II. Not only did *Gourmet* have to face the usual publishing problems associated with wartime shortages (especially of paper), but it also had to adjust its editorial content to wartime rationing of certain foods. Facing such formidable problems, *Gourmet* could have become a casualty of war, but the magazine survived. Today the magazine, now owned by Condé Nast, is successful, with demographics that make advertisers drool.

The magazine did not trigger such a reaction when it debuted in January 1941 or throughout much of the war years. During that time, *Gourmet*'s circulation was small.[2] Physically, the magazine itself was also small. The first issue had

48 pages, with color only on the cover. In fact, throughout much of the war years, the magazine seldom exceeded 56 pages.[3] The editorial content was also alien to the existing publishing field. *Gourmet* created the epicurean magazine niche; it had no real competition when it started and for many years after.

Yet, much in the magazine intrigued the advertiser—and the reader. The magazine—from its very first issue—showed potential. Its first front cover— original art by Henry Stahlhut[4]—showed a tantalizing wild boar's head garnished with holly and berries. Inside the magazine, editor Pearl Mezelthin offered a savory plate of recipes and features on cooking (including one by Louis DeGouy, *Gourmet*'s official "chef"[5]) and wine.[6] During its first years, the magazine introduced many of the features for which it became known. In February 1941, Samuel Chamberlain, writing under the name of Phineas Beck, introduced "Clementine," the enormously popular "red-cheeked Burgundian cook," to readers.[7] Clementine was so popular that *Gourmet* soon offered a book based on the magazine series. "Specialities de la Maison"—New York, still one of the magazine's departments, debuted in the first issue. (The California version did not appear until 1974.) "Gastronomie Sans Argent," a department designed to show that fine cooking did not demand a large budget, was already in existence in 1942. "Let's Eat Out," a column that listed only the "best" restaurants, debuted in 1942. In the first years, only New York restaurants were listed. As the magazine's circulation increased outside the New York City metropolitan area, this column began carrying restaurant lists from many cities across the nation and, eventually, across the world.

This, of course, was all part of Earle R. MacAusland's plan when he started the magazine. As he explained in the first issue:

> Never has there been a time more fitting for a magazine like *Gourmet* to come into being. Good food and good living have always been a great American tradition. At our very fingertips lie an abundance and variety of food [un]equaled anywhere. And our native, unquenchable thirst for discovery is now leading us daily into new and exciting channels of exploration in the realm of fine food and drink.[8]

The war, he argued, helped the magazine find its audience. As MacAusland recalled, "It was during the war . . . and there were no domestic servants, so women had to go into the kitchen and do their own cooking"[9]—presumably with a copy of *Gourmet*.

The magazine probably did help many American epicureans through the war. Although the magazine (and especially MacAusland) loathed even the term "ration recipes," the publication did offer a range of menus and recipes that could be prepared with ingredients commonly available. It was something the magazine did without fanfare. In response to a reader requesting "ration recipes," the magazine wrote:

We are indeed thinking of current food problems, and if you'll look back through our recent issues, you'll find that we have been stressing unrationed foods. But why ask for "ration recipes"—and destroy forthwith in your mind the taste of what are still very savory dishes? The recipes that we give are not for rations; they are for good food, made of the very many ingredients that are still plentiful.[10]

Gourmet's contribution to the war effort was made in its own distinctive way. MacAusland even wrote an editorial[11] urging the nongourmet to "throw away his can-opener for the duration, donate it to the scrap metal drive, and join us, month by month, in the unexplored field of gastronomy, still unrationed."

So we here at GOURMET feel that if we make the most of rationing, out of it all will come a fine appreciation of good food, less waste, and even a smaller expenditure of food. Last and not least, a patriotic contribution to our war effort and the men and women in the service.[12]

MacAusland personified *Gourmet* magazine. He founded the publication. He owned it. In 1943, he took over as editor and held the combined title of editor/publisher until his death in 1980. In 1945, the magazine moved into the penthouse of the famous Plaza Hotel in New York City with the MacAusland family. One staffer complained that MacAusland's poodles and terriers "enjoyed nipping editorial anklebones."[13]

That, however, was only a minor annoyance. The postwar years brought enormous prosperity to *Gourmet*. The momentum grew slowly. Circulation increased in the 1950s, but the reading public "discovered" *Gourmet* in the 1960s and after. The magazine's circulation soon doubled and doubled again, until it exceeded 900,000 in the 1990s.[14]

Advertising grew apace. The magazine in the 1950s had to rely almost solely on liquor/wine advertising. As circulation expanded, the advertising base diversified. By the 1960s, the magazine retained the liquor/wine advertising but welcomed airlines, upscale food products, and automotive ads as well. Since Condé Nast took over, the diversification of the advertising base has increased. In the 1980s and the early 1990s, the magazine included upscale clothing, jewelry and cosmetic advertising.

The editorial content of the magazine was shifting as well—diversifying. The recipes, menus, and wine reviews remained, but the magazine increased its travel coverage, especially after commercial jet flight became more popular and more affordable. The magazine took its readers from Hawaii to France, from Italy to Britain in the 1950s. In the 1960s and after, *Gourmet* blended European and American destinations with more exotic, less traveled locales—from Bird Island in the Seychelles to Appalachicola. That trend continued after Condé Nast acquired the magazine in 1983.

The travel pieces were always accompanied by lush photography. After the war, *Gourmet* shifted to a better-quality, coated paper stock. In the 1960s, four-color photography was regularly available in many parts of the magazine. Initially, it was reserved for food, but as the number of travel features increased, magnificent four-color photographs were used to illustrate that material as well. The magazine soon came to be known for its graphic and photographic excellence. Over the years, *Gourmet* has won many graphic awards. In 1976 alone, the Printing Industries of America gave the magazine seven national awards in its Graphic Arts Competition, more than any other publication in the nation.[15] An editor later recalled that beginning in the early 1970s, *Gourmet*'s pages "would glow with reproductions of a technical brilliance worthy of the finest art books."[16] It was little wonder why readers saved their old *Gourmet* magazines for future reference. The magazine, under Condé Nast, continues its graphic and photographic excellence.

Photography was only a part of *Gourmet*'s story. The magazine featured stories from some of the top chefs and food writers in the nation. James Beard was, for a time, a member of the staff. His tours of France still remain classics. Louis Diat, chef of the Ritz-Carlton, offered a cooking series that culminated with the publication in 1961 of *Gourmet's Basic French Cookbook*. Craig Claiborne also wrote for the publication.[17]

Gourmet also welcomed nonfood "personalities" into its pages. Those personalities had to be of a special sort—well known in their fields and of an intellectual variety. That approach could be traced to the war years, when band leader Xavier Cugat offered his own approach to food. (Cugat also illustrated his story.) Stephen Longstreet, painter, screenwriter, and playwright, offered the series "Travels with Gramps around the World." Pulitzer Prize-winning poet laureate Robert P. Tristram Coffin became one of *Gourmet*'s favorite New England writers. He covered everything from lobsters and blueberrying to life on a saltwater farm. Poet Ogden Nash and writer Leslie Charters (creator of the "Saint") offered other features.[18]

Readers seemed to love this eclectic approach. Many reported that they had subscribed for years and brought the magazine into their circle of friends by giving gift subscriptions. Among these friends, *Gourmet* magazine became a shared reference point.[19] Counting other *Gourmet* readers among their broader circle of "friends," subscribers often shared their advice and most treasured recipes with the magazine. These appeared in the regular column "Sugar and Spice," an exchange between readers and editor and among readers. This department, particularly, illustrated the magazine's strong ties to its readers.

Gourmet had become not just a magazine, but a way of life. These readers would never be satisfied with "just" a cookbook. Beginning in the 1950s, *Gourmet* began offering a pricey line of cookbooks and travelogues. Among the two earliest ones were *Bouquet de France*, based on Samuel Chamberlain's popular series "An Epicurean Tour of the French Provinces," and the "official" *Gourmet Cookbook*. Both books sold for ten dollars, a high price for cookbooks and travelogues at the time. Soon *Gourmet* offered the cookbook in two volumes (bound in opulent burgundy and gold). Other books highlighted French, Viennese, and other cuisine. Travel guides included "gastronomic tours" of Italy and France.[20]

For almost 40 years, Earle R. MacAusland was the heart of *Gourmet*. Although the magazine had grown in staff, in size, and in reputation, MacAusland was always guiding the book—as well as its various ancillary products. In 1980, at the age of 90, he died. His widow, Jean, took over as publisher; longtime executive editor Jane Montant became editor. After MacAusland's death, rumors flew about the possible sale of the magazine, although his widow denied them.[21] Two years later, however, the magazine was sold to Condé Nast for an undisclosed amount. It seemed to be an ideal acquisition. Condé Nast publishes a line of upscale magazines, many of which are aimed at women: *Vogue,* Vanity Fair** and *Bride's & Your New Home.* Gourmet*, with its emphasis on upscale food, wine, and travel, seemed to be a perfect addition to the Condé Nast family. As Robert J. Lapham, chairman of the board, explained, "We'd been interested in *Gourmet* for a number of years and felt that, although it was in a different field, it was very compatible with Condé Nast." At the time of the acquisition, *Gourmet* had a circulation rate base of 650,000. That figure had been declining for several years. Nonetheless, advertising revenue had been up in 1982, to $10.2 million. A certain portion of the circulation decline had to be attributed to the competition from *Bon Appetit** magazine. After searching for its place in the epicurean magazine niche, *Bon Appetit* had settled for a middle-class, practical approach in its editorial. By 1983, the magazine had topped *Gourmet* in circulation and in advertising revenue.[22]

Condé Nast soon moved to build *Gourmet*. Jane Montant remained as editor, but the company brought in its own publisher, Verne Westerberg, who had held the same position on the booming *Self** magazine, another Condé Nast property. Condé Nast poured money into *Gourmet*. Soon, the magazine was graphically redesigned. Condé Nast aggressively sold the magazine to advertisers. Issues in excess of 200 pages became common. In 1990, the company acquired *Cook's Magazine*, folded it, and added its subscription base to *Gourmet*'s.[23] Even before that acquisition, however, *Gourmet*'s circulation was on the upswing. Since Condé Nast acquired the magazine, its circulation has increased by more than 200,000.

In 1991, Gail Zweigenthal took over as editor. In the July issue, the first where Zweigenthal was listed as editor, a nightmare happened. It was a simple cookie recipe. *Gourmet* had printed hundreds before. But this one called for wintergreen oil, an ingredient that could be toxic. Quickly, the magazine sent letters to every one of the subscribers repudiating the recipe. Newspapers reported what seemingly was a catastrophe. In the October issue, the magazine repeated its concern about the ingredient: "Some people may be unknowingly allergic to a significant ingredient in wintergreen oil and, further, that wintergreen oil is generally not intended for internal consumption. In light of this, we strongly urge our readers not to use wintergreen oil in preparing the cookie recipe, and not to eat the cookies that have been made with wintergreen oil."[24] Yet *Gourmet* did not appear to be injured temporarily or permanently by the event. Circulation and advertising revenue continued to grow.

Today, the editorial focus remains much the same: travel, food, wine, lush photography, and close ties to readers continue to be the hallmark of *Gourmet* magazine. It may have a new editor, Gail Zweigenthal, and a new owner, Condé Nast; but the magazine has remained true to its founder and its founding mission. *Gourmet* remains the magazine for "good living."[25]

Notes

1. This has been the magazine's subtitle since its launch.

2. The magazine appeared to use some sort of combination of free and paid circulation. In 1944, for example, Ayer's reported a circulation of 44,621 free plus 12,345, apparently paid. *N. W. Ayer & Son's Directory Newspapers and Periodicals* (Philadelphia: N. W. Ayer & Son, 1944), p. 628.

3. Only late in the war did the magazine exceed this number. In December 1944, the number of pages reached 80. In early 1945, as the war wound to a close, the number of pages often exceeded that 56-page mark—but not by many pages. In January 1945, there were 64, and in February 1945, 72 pages. The magazine seldom had inside spot color. Only late in the war (March 1945) did the magazine carry a two-color Red Cross filler.

4. Stahlhut did most of the magazine's front covers until his death in the 1950s. After Stahlhut's death, the magazine hired several other artists for front covers but soon shifted to photography. *Gourmet* still uses photos on its front cover.

5. *Gourmet* was one of the few magazines launched with an editorial employee with the title of "chef."

6. Jane Montant, "Celebrate!" January 1991, p. 70.

7. Ibid.

8. Statement of purpose that appeared in the first issue, January 1941, as reprinted in "*Gourmet* at 20," January 1961, p. 1.

9. Mimi Sheraton, "Earle MacAusland Is Dead at 90; Founded *Gourmet* Magazine in '41," *New York Times,* June 6, 1980, p. D15.

10. "No Ration Recipes," March 1943, p. 3.

11. Under MacAusland, *Gourmet* seldom carried editorials. Typically, the exchange between editor and reader took place in the "Sugar and Spice" column. A "Letter from the Editor" column was added after Gail Zweigenthal took over as editor.

12. Earle R. MacAusland, "Why Worry?" May 1943, p. 6.

13. Montant, "Celebrate!" p. 73.

14. In 1951, circulation was 78,680; in 1959, 120,250; in 1963, 183,623; in 1971, 450,723; in 1979, 665,122; in 1983, 651,820; in 1987, 817,025; in 1993, 899,549. *N. W. Ayer & Son's Directory Newspapers and Periodicals* (Philadelphia: N. W. Ayer & Son, 1951), p. 673; 1959, p. 707; 1963, p. 720. *Ayer Directory Newspapers, Magazines and Trade Publications* (Philadelphia: N. W. Ayer & Son, 1971), p. 738; 1979, p. 603; 1983, p. 659. *Gale Directory of Publications* (Detroit: Gale Research, 1987), p. 679; 1993, p. 1443.

15. "Sugar and Spice," October 1976, p. 1.

16. January 1981, p. 1.

17. James Beard, "A Vintage Tour," January 1950, pp. 8–9, 25; Montant, "Celebrate!" p. 73; Sheraton, "Earle MacAusland Is Dead at 90."

18. "Cugat Cooks," January 1945, pp. 14–15; see, for example, Stephen Longstreet, "Roaming round the Equator," January 1950, pp. 10–11, 56; Montant, "Celebrate!" p. 71; Sheraton, "Earle MacAusland Is Dead at 90."

19. See comments from readers in special 50th-anniversary issue, January 1991.

20. November 1952, pp. 44–45; January 1960, pp. 36, 44.

21. Sheraton, "Earle R. MacAusland Is Dead at 90"; "Jean MacAusland Named Publisher of *Gourmet*," *New York Times*, July 28, 1980, p. D7.

22. Sandra Salmons, "Condé Nast Buying *Gourmet* Magazine," *New York Times*, September 28, 1983, p. D15.

23. Patrick Reilly, "Condé Nast Buys *Cook*'s Magazine and Will Fold It," *Wall Street Journal*, June 28, 1990, p. B8.

24. Phyllis Richman, "*Gourmet*'s Cookie Crumbles: Did Magazine Print a Toxic Recipe?" *Washington Post*, August 7, 1991, p. B1; "Attention," October 1991, p. 28.

25. Bill Katz and Linda Sternberg Katz in their book *Magazines for Libraries* note that *Gourmet* "has been slow to join the pack running with low-cal and light cuisine" (New Providence, N.J.: R. R. Bowker, 1992), p. 527.

Information Sources

BIBLIOGRAPHY:
"Jean MacAusland Named Publisher of *Gourmet*." *New York Times,* July 28, 1980, p. D7.
Katz, Bill, and Linda Sternberg Katz. *Magazines for Libraries*. New Providence, N.J.: R. R. Bowker, 1992.
Reilly, Patrick. "Condé Nast Buys *Cook*'s Magazine and Will Fold It." *Wall Street Journal,* June 28, 1990, p. B8.
Richman, Phyllis. "*Gourmet*'s Cookie Crumbles: Did Magazine Print a Toxic Recipe?" *Washington Post*, August 7, 1991, p. B1.
Salmons, Sandra. "Condé Nast Buying *Gourmet* Magazine." *New York Times*, September 28, 1983, p. D15.
Sheraton, Mimi. "Earle MacAusland Is Dead at 90; Founded *Gourmet* Magazine in '41." *New York Times*, June 6, 1980, p. D15.
INDEX SOURCES: Garden Literature; Magazine Index; Popular Magazine Review; Readers' Guide to Periodical Literature.
LOCATION SOURCES: Library of Congress; Kent State University (Ohio); other university and community libraries.

Publication History

MAGAZINE TITLE AND TITLE CHANGES: *Gourmet, the Magazine of Good Living.*
VOLUME AND ISSUE DATA: Vols. 1–(January 1941–present). Monthly (no issue published January 1942).
PUBLISHER AND PLACE OF PUBLICATION: Gourmet Inc. (1941–1983); Condé Nast (1983–present). New York City.
EDITORS: Pearl V. Mezelthin (1941–1943); Earle R. MacAusland (1943–1980); Jane Montant (1980–1991); Gail Zweigenthal (1991–present).
CIRCULATION: ABC, 1993: 906,299 (primarily subscriptions).

Kathleen L. Endres

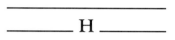

H

HARPER'S BAZAAR

The news of November 2, 1867, was not astounding. Still another Indian treaty had been signed, this one with the Cheyennes and Arrapahoes. Yellow fever was claiming new victims in Louisiana and Alabama. Immigrants in New York City were forging naturalization papers so they could vote in coming elections. It was Pennsylvania's official Thanksgiving Day.[1]

It was a sort of thanksgiving day at the New York City offices of Harper and Brothers too, for on that Saturday the publisher of books and two newsmagazines came out with a first-of-its-kind U.S. weekly called *Harper's Bazar*.[2] Although the weekly's arrival did not make the news in the *New York Times*, the *Bazar's* arrival was an event, because the *Bazar* was a distinctly different periodical. Untypically, it avoided reports of treaties and plagues and such "hard news." The 16-page tabloid "was intended largely for ladies," and it would "devote a considerable space to the matters which fall particularly under their jurisdiction, such as dress and household affairs. In this connection, the fashions are naturally an important subject," the editor wrote.[3]

The reportage on fashion and on "the useful, . . . the beautiful, . . . [and] everything that will be interesting to the family circle"[4] hit its mark in that post–Civil War period. By 1877, the *Bazar* had achieved a circulation of 80,000. It was an unprecedented publishing success.[5]

Besides being first, the *Bazar* was the biggest and the best U.S. fashion publication for decades. Then it began to seesaw in circulation and fame as competition sharpened, and its editors' inspiration at times grew dull. For instance, in 1993, it was one year into the editorship of Elizabeth Tilberis. It was then struggling to emerge from the shadow of archrival *Vogue** and trying to regain circulation and advertising losses to comparative newcomer *Elle** magazine, among others.

When Tilberis took over the magazine in 1992, *Newsweek* magazine commented that the publication "had become so wooden that even a mannequin could have redesigned it."[6] It was Tilberis's job to regain for her magazine the prestige it had commanded during the legendary, 26-year reign of editor Carmel Snow in the 1930s, 1940s, and 1950s and in the very beginning under the direction of editor Mary L. Booth.

If Booth's challenge was not easier, it was at least dramatically different from Tilberis's. In 1867, the women's market was unexploited. As it turned out, women needed and wanted a woman's publication. So did those selling cloth, sewing supplies, housewares, and such.

Some 125 years later, Tilberis faced sharp, relentless competitors scrabbling for the lion's share of a static, 6,000-page advertising market. As the *Wall Street Journal* commented at the time, one fashion magazine could "expand only by savaging another."[7] Tilberis had to re-create a publication. Booth had to create one; she was well qualified for the job.

Booth was a historian and well-known translator. One of her translations earned her a commendation from President Abraham Lincoln for "strengthening the spirit of the American people."[8] Booth was also a woman of refined taste and keen understanding of her audience. She filled her newsprint pages with woodcuts and etchings by such giants as artist Winslow Homer and cartoonist Thomas Nast. She ran their works dramatically large, often across two pages. She published serialized novels, short stories, and poems of prominent authors, along with articles about manners, diet, health, furniture, and household management.

Under a column headed, "Personal," she introduced gossip—tidbits like the story of a New York actor who announced plans to marry his 20-year-old adopted daughter, whom he had raised from infancy. Booth introduced a humor section of mostly single-panel cartoons. She ran articles on women's rights and inserted into the publication patterns for dresses and other garments readers might make at home.

Of course, she provided pictures and comments about the latest fashions, which were displayed in exclusive and elegant etchings shipped to New York by *Der Bazar*, the German fashion magazine[9] that had inspired Fletcher Harper to start his own fashion publication and that served as its namesake.[10] Booth's own staff developed reports on the latest New York styles.

Booth perfected the newspaper's formula. She emphasized quality in artwork and writing; and as historian Frank Luther Mott put it, "The paper improved consistently, through the eighties and early nineties, both in physical appearance and in literary quality."[11]

Booth died in 1889. She was succeeded by Margaret Sangster, a novelist. Sangster reduced the amount of fiction in the *Bazar* but mostly continued Booth's innovations. She stayed at the *Bazar* until 1899, when financially troubled Harper and Brothers went into receivership and was reorganized.

Elizabeth Jordan, a reporter at the *New York World* (and later a novelist and playwright) replaced Sangster. She kept the editorial content much the same as it had been but introduced a number of economies.[12] In 1901, she converted the publication from a tabloid to a booklike, octavo magazine that appeared monthly instead of weekly. The redesign and cutbacks did not generate profits.

Finally, in 1913, William Randolph Hearst bought the once-wealthy publication, paying a mere $10,000. Again it was redesigned. It emerged as a colorful, sophisticated, large-size magazine with an aura of sophistication. For years it featured the art deco sketches of the French artist Erté, whose simple, suave designs graced cover after cover.

From 1913 to 1934, six different men headed the magazine for short periods. Among them was Henry B. Sell, who flooded the publication with the latest styles, and Arthur H. Samuels, who took over in 1929, the year the second "a" was added to the name "Bazaar." Samuels had little interest in fashion. He mainly edited the fiction and literary copy, leaving the rest to his staff. Under that arrangement the magazine fared poorly against its big competitor, *Vogue.*

Vogue was then edited by Edna Woolman Chase, who had won considerable fame for fashioning the Condé Nast publication into the nation's leading U.S. fashion magazine. Chase's fashion editor—and later the editor of *Vogue*'s American edition—was Irish-born Carmel Snow, who soon became a fashion-editing prodigy and more famous than her boss.

Snow's widowed mother, Ann White, had run an exclusive dressmaking shop in New York. She sent Carmel to fine New York and Brussels schools, but it was in her mother's East 57th Street boutique that Snow learned the fine points of fashion. Snow's brother and sister were artists. They and their friends taught her design, while Condé Nast himself taught Snow editing.[13]

Snow fell into fashion reporting by chance and had some dealings with Chase, who introduced her to publisher Nast. Nast, recognizing Snow's eye for fashion, invited her to join *Vogue.* He served as her mentor and—without Chase's acquiescence—even promised Snow the editorship of all *Vogue* editions when Chase retired. However, during the Great Depression and before Chase's retirement, Snow was marked for demotion in a cost-cutting move. Rather than accept the lesser post, she accepted an offer to become fashion editor of *Harper's Bazaar* in 1932. The move shocked the magazine and fashion worlds. Nast never spoke to Snow again, and *Vogue* personnel—including old friends—were forbidden to speak to her. The order lasted 21 years.[14]

Snow was named the *Harper's Bazaar* editor in 1934. She revamped the magazine, introducing a host of innovations. She began using socialites as models. She hired pioneering Russian designer Alexey Brodovitch to design the magazine. She encouraged shooting fashion pictures in the street and on locations, thus breaking the tradition of photographing fashion only in studios. Snow also started the trend of photographing models in action—walking, running, and playing—in addition to showing them in formal poses.

She persuaded the surrealist painter Salvador Dali to produce fashion sketches for the *Bazaar.* (He painted one model with a head of flowers.) She reproduced in the magazine the art of Picasso, Chagall, Braque, Ben Shahn, and others, along with the writings of such famed authors as Virginia Woolf, Eudora Welty, Truman Capote, and Carson McCullers. (She pulled apart one issue at the last minute to run in its entirety McCullers's famed *Ballad of a Sad Cafe.*) She also "discovered" photographers who later became famous, including Richard Avedon. She had a legendary ability to spot talent and fashion trends. As the *New York Times* reported, "Under Mrs. Snow, *Harper's Bazaar* rose in the realms of fashion and the arts."[15]

Snow was arguably America's most famous fashion editor. She was lionized in the fashion world and earned medals of commendation from the Italian and French governments. She made *Harper's Bazaar* the "co-bible of the fashion industry" (with *Vogue*).[16] She picked as her successor a woman who would keep it that way for a while longer, her niece Nancy White.

White was the wife of *Fortune* magazine publisher Ralph Paine, Jr., and daughter of the general manager of Hearst's *New York Journal American* newspaper. She took command at the *Bazaar* on New Year's Day, 1958. Although less daring than Snow, White continued the policy of presenting readers with presentations of avant-garde, fanciful styles, along with solidly accepted fashions. She continued aiming the publication at fashion-conscious women across the nation, not just at the New York set.

Under White, the magazine celebrated its 100th birthday. By then it had a circulation of 424,800, and in three years that rose to 442,220. Advertising revenues were at $8 million in 1967. But times were changing. The era of elegance seemed to pass with the arrival of the so-called youth revolution and what the *New York Times* called the "thrift shop look" of the 1960s.[17] In 1970, circulation dipped; advertising was off by 30 percent.

After 14 mostly successful years, White resigned in 1971. She gave way to James Brady, former publisher of *Women's Wear Daily,* who had moved to the *Bazaar* as publisher and editorial director four months before White's departure. Brady brought with him new ideas. He wanted each issue to have a different theme, such as politics or defending city life. He wanted a 50-50 mix of fashion and nonfashion articles, with more emphasis on controversy. He said he wanted to photograph "wearable" clothes in the environments where they are worn. Fourteen months and ten issues later, in the fall of 1972, Brady was fired.

Into the editorship came Anthony Mazzola, a 40-year Hearst career man who had worked his way to editor in chief of *Town and Country* magazine. Mazzola declared he would rebuild the *Bazaar*'s fashion coverage, and he did. He created themes for each issue like "The World's Ten Most Beautiful Women." This worked for a time. From 1979 to 1984, the number of advertising pages in the magazine nearly doubled; then in 1985 they started to decrease. Critics said Mazzola overworked his editing formula. The verve and creativity introduced by Carmel Snow had vanished.

Michael Gross wrote in *New York* magazine that "*Bazaar* was in a holding pattern."[18] Patrick M. Reilly reported in the *Wall Street Journal* that the *Bazaar* "lacks spirit and pizazz" and that it was "bland" and had lost its "cachet."

The average age of the magazine's readers was, at 37 years, the oldest among the fashion magazines. Magazine advertising revenues had continued to drop from 1991 to 1992, and the *Bazaar* had the biggest advertising dip of all fashion magazines.[19]

At that point the Hearst organization determined to make "one of the biggest efforts" of recent years to resuscitate its drowning publication. As it did when recruiting Snow 30 years before, the Hearst corporation raided *Vogue*. It hired Elizabeth Tilberis, the editor of British *Vogue* and a 20-year veteran of that organization.

Tilberis swept into the magazine's Broadway offices, replaced practically the entire *Bazaar* staff, and announced, "*Harper's Bazaar* enters a new era." She stopped what the *Wall Street Journal*'s Reilly called "the typical fashion magazine's jarring, off-kilter 'street shots' in favor of a return to a classic—and more staged—fashion photography."[20] She removed the clutter of cover headlines and again introduced articles on art, architecture, and serious authors. She hired a touted Italian designer to give the magazine a new look and declared the magazine would publish "the work of some of the most influential photographers of our times."[21]

The Tilberis changes began occurring at a time of worldwide economic—and advertising—slowdown, when women reportedly were buying fewer magazines. Yet, a year after Tilberis began editing the *Bazaar*, when most other magazines were reporting advertising downturns, the *Bazaar* reported advertising gains of nearly 80 percent. Clearly, some liked what was happening at the venerable magazine. They were saying the magazine might yet succeed in what author Michael Gross called its "uncertain quest to restore itself to glossy glory."[22]

Notes

1. A survey of the *New York Times* of November 2, 1867.

2. The spelling of "Bazar" was changed to "Bazaar" in 1929.

3. "Our Bazar," November 2, 1867, p. 2.

4. Ibid.

5. Frank L. Mott, *A History of American Magazines 1865–1885* (Cambridge, Mass.: Harvard University Press, 1938), p. 388.

6. Tom Mathews and Lucille Beachy. "The Battle of the Rag Mags," *Newsweek*, September 7, 1992, p. 64.

7. Ibid.

8. Eugene Exman, *The House of Harper* (New York: Harper and Row, 1967), p. 121.

9. November 2, 1862, p. 2.

10. Mott, *A History of American Magazines*, p. 388.

11. Ibid.

12. Exman, *The House of Harper*, p. 126.

13. Carmel Snow and Mary L. Aswell, *The World of Carmel Snow* (New York: McGraw-Hill, 1962), p. 38.

14. Ibid., p. 75.

15. "Carmel Snow, Editor, Dies at 73; Headed *Harper's Bazaar* Board," *New York Times*, May 9, 1961, p. 32.

16. Philip H. Dougherty, "Advertising: *Harper's Bazaar* Playing It Up," *New York Times*, December 18, 1966, sec. 3, p. 4.

17. Charlotte Curtis, "*Vogue, Bazaar* Are Changing in Own Ways," *New York Times*, June 27, 1971, sec. 1, p. 48.

18. Michael Gross, "War of the Poses," *New York*, April 27, 1992, p. 31.

19. Patrick M. Reilly, "*Harper's Bazaar* Aims to Reclaim Lead of Slumping Fashion-Magazine Industry," *Wall Street Journal*, August 17, 1992, p. B1.

20. Ibid.

21. Liz Tilberis, "Editor's Note," September 1992, p. 33.

22. Gross, "War of the Poses," p. 31.

Information Sources

BIBLIOGRAPHY:

"Carmel Snow, Editor, Dies at 73; Headed *Harper's Bazaar* Board." *New York Times*, May 9, 1961, p. 32.

Curtis, Charlotte. "*Vogue, Bazaar* Are Changing in Own Ways." *New York Times*, June 27, 1971, sec. 1, p. 48.

Dougherty, Philip H. "Advertising: *Harper's Bazaar* Playing It Up." *New York Times*, December 18, 1966, sec. 3, p. 4.

Exman, Eugene. *The House of Harper*. New York: Harper and Row, 1967.

Gross, Michael. "War of the Poses." *New York*, April 27, 1992, p. 31.

Mathews, Tom and Lucille Beachy. "The Battle of the Rag Mags." *Newsweek*, September 7, 1992, p. 64.

Mott, Frank L. *A History of American Magazines 1865–1885*. Cambridge: Harvard University Press, 1938.

Reilly, Patrick M. "*Harper's Bazaar* Aims to Reclaim Lead of Slumping Fashion-Magazine Industry." *Wall Street Journal*, August 17, 1992, p. B1.

Snow, Carmel and Mary L. Aswell. *The World of Carmel Snow*. New York: McGraw-Hill, 1962.

INDEX SOURCES: Biographical Abstracts; Health Index; Magazine Index; Philanthropic Studies Index; Popular Magazine Review; Readers' Guide to Periodical Literature.

LOCATION SOURCES: Library of Congress and other libraries.

Publication History

MAGAZINE TITLE AND TITLE CHANGES: *Harper's Bazar* (1867–1929); *Harper's Bazaar* (1929–present).

VOLUME AND ISSUE DATA: Vols. 1–(November 1867–present). Weekly (1867–1901); monthly (1901–present).

PUBLISHER AND PLACE OF PUBLICATION: Harper and Brothers (1867–1913); International Magazine Co. (1913–1928); Harper's Bazaar, Inc. (1929–1936); the Hearst Corp. (1936–present). (International Magazine Co. and Harper's Bazaar, Inc. were both subsidiaries of the Hearst Corp.) New York.

EDITORS: Mary L. Booth (1867–1889); Margaret Sangster (1889–1899); Elizabeth Jordan (1900–1913); William Martin Johnson (1913–1914); Harford Powell (1914–

1916); John Chapman Hilder (1916–1920); Henry Blackman Sell (1920–1926); Charles Hanson Towne (1926–1929); Arthur H. Samuels (1929–1934); Carmel Snow (1934–1957); Nancy White (1957–1971); James Brady (1971–1972); Anthony Mazzola (1972–1992); Elizabeth Tilberis (1992–present).
CIRCULATION: ABC, 1993: 772,715 (paid, primarily subscriptions).

August Gribbin

HEALTH

What does it mean to be healthy? What is the nature of a family? What are women's roles in health, in the family, and otherwise? Answers to these questions have changed considerably over the years. So did the magazine *Health*, which originated in 1969 as *Family Health* and was published until 1991.

Established by Maxwell M. Geffen, also the founding publisher of *Medical World News*,[1] the magazine addressed a wide range of health topics and family concerns in its early volumes. Subjects of feature articles in the December 1969 issue included a high-technology ambulance for people with heart attacks, the importance of autopsies, how much independence to give children, and concern about the safety of food additives. Features in other issues discussed nutrition, accident prevention, and various chronic health problems. The magazine initially showed a progressive bent, publishing articles on national health insurance (December 1969, February 1971), the then-recently established Harvard Community Health Plan (September 1971), and an unmarried man's adopting a child (December 1969).

Departments in the initial volume included "Ask the Doctor," featuring editorial board member Morris Fishbein, a highly visible physician who had edited *The Journal of the American Medical Association* for many years and had written extensively for the public. This column, said to be the most popular feature in *Family Health*,[2] was later joined by "Ask the Pediatrician," "Ask the Dentist," and "Ask the Vet." The magazine thus addressed questions regarding the entire family's health—even that of the family pet.

Advertisements in early volumes touted products for managing common ailments and discomforts, as well as for maintaining a healthy and comfortable lifestyle. These products included cold medications, vitamins, support hose, contraceptive foam, hair conditioner, skin care products, a weight-reduction plan, salt substitute, margarine, vegetable oil, and cookware. Also advertised were books and periodicals on various topics, including health, science, and investment.

Various emphases emerged in the magazine's early volumes and remained throughout its more than two decades of publication. The magazine consistently devoted considerable editorial space to nutrition and food. Whether by policy or tobacco companies' choice, it apparently never ran cigarette advertisements;

and unlike various other women's magazines of the era,[3] it published material on health hazards of smoking.[4] From time to time it contained articles on sexuality and advertised publications on the subject. It also repeatedly included articles on remaining youthful. It promoted attitudes of self-reliance and consumerism, as evidenced by recurring columns bearing such titles as "The Activated Patient," "Brand News," and "Consuming Interest." The magazine likewise tended to focus on the products rather than the process of medical research, as reflected by the appearance for several years of a section titled "Breakthroughs."

Over the years, however, the magazine underwent various major changes. Most obviously, the title changed. Starting in April 1978, both the magazine cover and the masthead ran the word "Family" in much smaller type than the word "Health." Beginning with the July/August 1981 issue, the magazine became known simply as *Health*. "When this magazine started 12 years ago," editor Hank Herman explained, "its essential purpose, reflected in its name, was to tell mothers and fathers how to care for their children, wives how to care for their husbands, and couples how to care for their aging parents. But in recent years, each family member has become more independent about his or her health." Further, Herman noted, single-person households had increased 108 percent since 1965.[5] Thus, the magazine now targeted readers mainly as individuals rather than as family members.

The main individuals being targeted were more and more clearly women. In the magazine's early years, much of the content appeared suited to readers of both genders. Even then, however, it seemed slanted somewhat toward a female readership. Article titles included "A Man on the Way Up Needs a Boost" (December 1969) and "How to Get Your Husband—and Yourself—to Relax" (July 1973); features on beauty soon became frequent; and advertisements for tampons kept appearing next to the table of contents. The column "Woman, Wife, Mother," presenting advice from a gynecologist, debuted in the mid-1970s and ran for several years. By the early 1980s, credits were being published for the hairstyling and makeup in the cover photographs, and by the mid-1980s both the style and the substance of *Health* were very much those of a women's magazine.

In 1990, the managing editor of *Health* characterized the magazine's readers as "primarily women, most of them in their late 30s (including women from the mid-20s to the 50s), who are college-educated, half of whom are married and are mothers." She added that readers were "interested in every aspect of health, psyche, fitness; they want to get information that will help them look well, feel well and dress well."[6]

Indeed, another change apparent over the years was the magazine's increasingly broad concept of "health." In keeping with more widespread social trends, emphasis moved from preventing or managing disease to cultivating "wellness" and fitness in very general senses. Even in the early years, the magazine construed health broadly, as indicated by frequent attention to nutrition and to emotional well-being and as stated by Fishbein.[7] Nevertheless, the magazine maintained a biomedical emphasis. Thus, it was with little apparent difficulty that in 1976, *Family Health* incorporated the magazine *Today's Health*, which had been published by the American Medical Association for half a century and commonly graced physicians' waiting rooms.[8]

In 1979, the magazine began indicating its breadth with the subtitle *The Magazine for Total Well-Being*. Especially as the 1980s progressed, it devoted less and less space to medical topics per se and more to areas such as fitness, weight control, emotional well-being, and beauty. The mix of products advertised also changed. Although, in 1991, some advertisements for medications remained, ads for reduced-calorie and reduced-fat foods and occasionally for athletic shoes and exercise equipment seemed to predominate. The scents of Lysol and Listerine had given way to those of herbal shampoo and baby-oil moisturizer.

As the magazine focused progressively less on biomedical aspects of health, it contained less and less material by health professionals and placed less emphasis on medical credentials. The "Ask the Doctor" column ceased publication, as did its dental and other counterparts. Feature articles by health professionals became increasingly scarce. The once-prominent listing of advisory board members (who included such illustrious figures as Fishbein, transplant surgeon Christiaan Barnard, nutritionist Jean Mayer, and polio vaccine developer Albert Sabin) moved lower on the masthead and eventually disappeared. In October 1989, when former National Institute on Aging director Robert N. Butler guest-edited an issue on aging, his M.D. degree was not even listed. Editorial emphasis shifted increasingly from dependence on health professionals to self-reliance, as reflected by the magazine's slogan in latter years, "Getting the Best from Yourself."

But perhaps the biggest shift was in the role the magazine depicted for women. Again in keeping with contemporary trends, that role became considerably less family-centered. Noted the magazine in an article marking its 15th birthday:

> In the beginning, we were *Family Health*, helping women with their domestic concerns: how to keep "hubby" from heart attacks, the kids from drugs. Times changed, and so did we: Health became a personal affair, and the renamed *Health* magazine put you front and center with articles about exercise regimens, food preferences, sexual needs.[9]

Early volumes, in addition to featuring articles on giving one's husband emotional support, had contained a set of poems titled "Lady Doctor in the House: Can an MD from New York Find Happiness as a Mrs. in the Suburbs of Maryland?" (February 1972), a humor piece titled "How I Liberated Myself from Women's Liberation" (March 1973), and an advertisement titled "16 Things I Learned from my Wife . . . since she started reading *The National Observer*" (December 1969). Later volumes, however—when they dealt with family matters at all—addressed such topics as the availability of child care and even the option of remaining "childless by choice."

Perhaps in 1992, with "family values" being emphasized in the presidential campaign and elsewhere, the magazine would have again focused more on women's traditional roles. However, *Health* ceased publication in mid-1991, when its publisher, Family Media, Inc., shut down its seven magazines because of poor advertising revenues.[10] The magazine's subscribers—and the title *Health*— were promptly adopted by *In Health* magazine, a more biomedically oriented publication slanted toward women.[11]

So ended the history of *(Family) Health*. During the magazine's 22-year existence, women's concepts of health, of family, and of themselves changed substantially. The magazine's volumes provide many vivid glimpses of the changes.

Notes

1. Hy Steirman, "As We See It: On Reaching 80," August 1976, pp. 4, 9.
2. William H. White, "Editor's Letter," February 1973, p. 4.
3. Lauren Kessler, "Women's Magazines' Coverage of Smoking Related Health Hazards," *Journalism Quarterly* 66:2 (summer 1989), pp. 316–322, 445.
4. Examples: "She's Saving You from Cigarette Smoke!" October 1973; "The Fight for Breath," January 1974; "Special Section: Health's Stop-Smoking Guide," February 1986.
5. Hank Herman, "From the Editor," July/August 1981, p. 3.
6. "The Markets," *Writer's Digest*, February 1990, p. 42.
7. Morris Fishbein, "As We See It: On *Family Health* and Health Education," May 1976, p. 7.
8. Ibid.
9. Sally Cummings, "Celebrating 15 Years," October 1984, p. 31 ff.
10. Robert J. Samuelson, "The End of Advertising?" *Newsweek*, August 19, 1991, p. 40.
11. Eric Schrier, "The Last Name This Magazine Will Ever Have," February/March 1992, p. 6.

Information Sources

BIBLIOGRAPHY:
Kessler, Lauren. "Women's Magazines' Coverage of Smoking Related Health Hazards," *Journalism Quarterly*, 66:2 (Summer 1989), pp. 316–322, 445.
"The Markets." *Writer's Digest*, February 1990, p. 42.
Samuelson, Robert J. "The End of Advertising?" *Newsweek*, August 19, 1991, p. 40.
INDEX SOURCES: Academic Index; Biological Abstracts; Biology Digest; Canadian Periodical Index; Consumer Health & Nutrition Index; Cumulative Index to Nursing and Allied Health Literature; Current Literature in Family Planning; General Science Index; Magazine Index; Physical Education Index; Popular Magazine Review/Magazine Article Summaries; Readers' Guide to Periodical Literature; Sportsearch; Text on Microfilm.
LOCATION SOURCES: Library of Congress and many other libraries (collections commonly incomplete).

Publication History

MAGAZINE TITLE AND TITLE CHANGES: *Family Health* (October 1969–June 1981); *Health* (July/August 1981–July/August 1991).

VOLUME AND ISSUE DATA: Vols. 1–23 (October 1969–July/August 1991), Monthly (some years: ten times).

PUBLISHER AND PLACE OF PUBLICATION: Family Health Magazine, Inc., (1969–1975); Family Communications, Inc. (1976); Family Media, Inc. (1976–1991). New York.

EDITORS: William H. White (1969–1974); Sylvie Reice (1974); Morris Fishbein (medical editor) (1974–1976); Caroline Stevens (1976); Jim Hoffman (1976–1977); Dalma Heyn (1977–1980); Hank Herman (1980–1988); Dianne Partie Lange (1988–1990); Nan Silver (1990–1991).

CIRCULATION: ABC, 1991: 878,998 (shortly before magazine ceased publication).

Barbara Gastel

HOUSE & GARDEN

House & Garden (then called *HG*) died in 1993, the victim of an advertising downturn, increased competition in the home/decorating niche, and Condé Nast's acquisition of Knapp Communications. That acquisition was not supposed to kill *HG*, one of the oldest magazines in the Condé Nast family and one of the most respected in the decorating niche. Condé Nast president Bernard Leser had even assured media observers that *HG* would not close and could coexist with the newly acquired, extremely profitable *Architectural Digest*.[1] Taking their cue from Leser, media observers never predicted the folding; they expected *HG* to change, most likely returning to a more downscale approach.[2] However, that was not to be. On April 20, 1993, just one day after the company took title to *Architectural Digest*, Condé Nast abruptly announced the folding of *HG*. The magazine's staffers, competitors, and readers, as well as media observers, all mourned the loss.[3] *HG* had helped define refined American home decorating in the twentieth century.

The magazine started in 1901, at a time of enormous prosperity for a moneyed group. A Philadelphia businessman urged three friends, architects Wilson Eyre, Jr., Frank Miles Day, and Herbert C. Wise, to start a magazine devoted to the development of the country home. The three started the magazine as a ''pleasant diversion,'' not a serious commercial endeavor.[4] It was also not started as a publication for the general reading audience but as an architecture publication. As the editors wrote in the first issue,

Its [*House & Garden*'s] own point of view is that of the architect; but of the architect to whom the house and its garden seem so intimately related that the attempt to design the one without duly considering the other is an attempt that can never reach the highest level of success.[5]

Although the original intent differed from its subsequent, more popular version, these early issues did have much in common with the publication that would follow. *House & Garden*—in 1901 and 1993 and all the years in between—used the best-quality coated paper stock available.[6] From its first issue, likewise, *HG* used photography extensively. Of course, in the first few decades, the photographs were black and white. Once the technology and the advertising base allowed it, however, the magazine was lush with four-color photography. Until its last issue in July 1993, *House & Garden* had outstanding photography and printing. Like other Condé Nast magazines,[7] *HG* often achieved the quality of an art book.[8]

In the first years and those that followed, the magazine emphasized the home. However, during the earliest years, the magazine also featured other great architectural feats, including streets, bridges, and large institutional buildings.[9]

Earliest editorials reflected the architectural base of the magazine and seemed far removed from many of the *HG* commentaries that followed. The magazine provided suggestions for the education of future architects (travel and study in Europe were advocated over "measured drawings"), applauded Cleveland's civic improvements ("radical" solutions for urban "ugliness"), and condemned graffiti on New York City subway walls ("The time has come when all sign advertising in public places should be held in check, and arrangements should be made to do this before the next subway is built").[10]

The initial advertising base was quite different from that of the *HG* of subsequent decades. Early on, the magazine relied on advertising for the architectural and building markets. Thus, manufacturers of fine products for construction advertised in the early *HG*—lock makers, brass and bronze producers, hardware manufacturers, and the like.

The content and the approach of *HG*'s first year were dictated by the three architect/editors. Soon after, however, Herbert C. Wise took over the editor's title and duties. The magazine stayed in the hands of the architects until 1904, when the three could no longer handle the publication's growing success. The three had started *HG* as an "architectural lark"[11]; but, as Wise related at the time of the sale, the magazine had achieved a success never anticipated. It had won "unexpected friends in every locality" and received "more than enough approval to establish it on a firm basis." The architects were clearly out of their league. The three sold the publication to John C. Winston Co., Philadelphia, and withdrew from publishing. The new owner had "[P]rogressive methods, ample capital and a determination to make HOUSE AND GARDEN fully possess the broad, though unique, field it has entered."[12]

The new owner quickly repositioned the magazine.[13] Its content shifted from its narrow architectural base to more practical stories appealing to a wider variety of readers. In one of its first issues under new ownership, the magazine and its new editor—Charles Francis Osborne—began the "Home Making Series," stories clearly aimed at the nonarchitect. Nonetheless, the magazine attempted to retain its original audience as well by covering the activities of various architectural associations.[14]

The "look" of the magazine itself changed. The new *House & Garden* was slightly smaller in dimension, although not in page number. On the inside pages, the magazine continued to rely on its outstanding photography. But there was more experimentation in design. In April 1905, the magazine offered its first four-color editorial insert, picturing "Blair Eyrie," the estate of DeWitt Clinton Blair. In May 1905, the magazine experimented with a trifold insert of improvements of the Schuylkill River Banks.

The John C. Winston Co. moved to New York City in 1909 and took *House & Garden* with it. Osborne, the editor, apparently did not make the move. Henry H. Saylor became *HG*'s new editor and officer in the reorganized publishing company, called McBride, Winston & Co. Soon a young, ambitious businessman by the name of Condé Nast bought into the firm and became vice president. The publishing company was renamed McBride, Nast & Co. Finally, in 1915, Condé Nast purchased the magazine outright; it was the third "crown jewel" in Condé Nast's publishing crown. (The other two were *Vogue** and *Vanity Fair.**)

Although *House & Garden* had a relatively small circulation at the time of the acquisition (only 10,000), the magazine seemed to be an ideal complement to the other Condé Nast properties. As new editor Richardson Wright explained:

> *Vogue* tells the up-to-date woman what clothes to wear; *Vanity Fair*, what books to read, what pictures to see, what currents of modern life to touch. In the same measure does *House & Garden* tell her what architecture to choose for her house, how to furnish it, and with what garden to surround it.[15]

While the greatest portion of the editorial content emphasized the homes and gardens of the rich and famous in America, the editor insisted that affluence was not necessarily a requirement for good taste—or readership. A "man with $5,000 and the man with $50,000" could both benefit from *House & Garden*'s "practical element in all its articles."[16] Moreover, *House & Garden* encouraged interaction with readers by urging them to write with their questions and problems in home building, house furnishing, and gardening. Those letters were answered by authorities in the field.[17] This approach seemed to strike a responsive chord among readers. Soon the magazine was selling out at the newsstand.[18]

Condé Nast had acquired the magazine just as the country was going to war. During World War I, *House & Garden* was a consistent supporter of U.S. involvement. The editor often reminded readers what the war was all about ("We have gone there [France] to bring back security for our homes here"); how to help the war effort (everyone needed to "raise your bit" in the war gardens);

and what they needed to do to assure victory ("patriotism of service by living normally").[19]

The postwar years brought heretofore unequaled prosperity. Readership soared; circulation topped 130,000 by 1926. Advertisers of many expensive consumer products flocked to the magazine.[20] Nothing could stop the growth— until the Great Depression.

In 1929, *House & Garden* was enormously successful. Two-hundred-page issues were not unknown. The effects of the depression were not felt immediately. In 1930, *House & Garden* was still stuffed with advertising, although not as much as in 1929. However, the magazine may have been having problems sustaining its readership. In 1930, *House & Garden* cut its subscription price from four dollars to three dollars. Soon, advertising was off as well; 1932, 1933, and 1934 were difficult years for the magazine.

As much as possible, Richardson Wright, still editor, did everything to counter the pessimism, the hoarding, and the lack of construction. In 1931, the magazine even hired the eminent New York architect Leigh French to design a small house, "the house that grows," as the editor called it. The magazine offered blueprints free to anyone who would begin building a house "*this year.*" Throughout the depression, *House & Garden*'s message was consistent: readers had to spend to assure economic recovery. That message permeated the editorials[21] and the feature stories. Features ranged from how-to building inserts to stories about furniture (including one written by Mrs. Franklin D. Roosevelt) and a guide to Christmas giving.[22]

Advertising cutbacks and circulation problems did not stop the magazine from experimenting graphically. The nameplate was redesigned in 1931. In the December issue of that same year, although advertising was off, the magazine added an expensive fifth color to the front cover. In 1932, the magazine introduced its first photographic front cover. Anton Bruehl, a well-known photographer who contributed many of the color photos for the inside pages of *House & Garden*, took the picture and many of the others that would be featured on the front cover.

The magazine did not recover from the depression until the late 1930s. Then, graphic experimentation was the rule of the day. The magazine was by then issued in two sections. Each section had its own theme and its own front cover. In July 1939, for example, the theme for section one was "Trends for Tomorrow"; section two offered "Gardeners' Handbook." The front covers, typically, had original art. Unlike many other contemporary magazines, *House & Garden* changed its logo design to blend in with the "feel" of the art of the front cover. Thus, the magazine's name on the September 1939 cover carried out the circus motif of the art. Manipulating the typeface of the nameplate, however, stopped once the magazine turned completely to photography for its front cover.

The best-quality four-color photography became a hallmark of the magazine from the 1940s on. Some great photographers, including Edward Steichen, Anton Bruehl, and Carola Rust, did work for *House & Garden*. The excellent quality of the photography assured the magazine of a number of exclusives. *House & Garden* was the first to publish color photographs from the movie classic *Gone with the Wind*. The magazine was welcomed into the White House to photograph the interior. That same issue featured photographs of the homes of many wealthy, famous Washingtonians.[23]

World War II found the magazine bulging with advertising and reaching new circulation heights. However, it also found the magazine facing severe paper shortages. The magazine had always prided itself on using the best-quality coated paper stock.[24] In part, that was how the magazine was able to achieve such high-quality photographic reproduction. During World War II, however, the magazine had to turn to coarser paper for at least a portion of each issue. Special inserts that used drawings instead of photography were printed on coarse, noncoated stock. The magazine still used the best-quality coated stock when publishing four-color photographs.

During the war, *House & Garden* carried many stories designed to help mobilize the population. The magazine covered the "victory garden" from every conceivable angle.[25] Perhaps as helpful were the many practical, how-to stories to help women get through the war while their husbands were off fighting. The magazine offered "canning primers," a guide to home repair, how to prepare for blackouts, and preparing houses "for defense."[26] Like many other magazines of the time, *House & Garden* did its part to foster war bond sales, even featuring the bonds on the front cover on more than one occasion.[27]

After the war, things returned to normal editorially. Richardson Wright, still editor, returned the magazine to a course that had always proved successful. The stories covered decorating, building, and the finest homes in the nation, as well as getting started on a limited budget. But Wright was nearing retirement age and needed a successor. During World War II, it looked as if Henry Humphrey would win the job. In June 1943, he was named editor to Wright's editor in chief; but six months later, Humphrey was gone. In 1946, Albert Kornfeld gained the editor's title and kept it. In 1950, Richardson Wright retired after 36 years as editor of *House & Garden*. He had built it "from modest beginnings to national statute," the publisher wrote at the time.[28] Indeed he had. When he had taken over in 1914, the magazine had a circulation of less than 10,000. When he left, the circulation had reached 405,104.[29] When Wright began as editor, *House & Garden* had just started down the home/decorating editorial road. Under Wright, the magazine traveled many miles. It became the "interior design authority,"[30] competing successfully with Hearst's *House Beautiful.**

Albert Kornfeld continued the magazine down Wright's road. The magazine was a monthly of the finest decorating, although gradually content shifted. By 1953, the magazine had a new subtitle, *A Guide to the Art of Living*. That implied an editorial package of more than decorating and building. Food, entertaining, and travel were added to the editorial package.[31] However, the magazine was not growing. Circulation[32] stagnated, and advertising seemed to remain even. In 1955, *House & Garden* got a new editor and a much needed injection of energy. William H. Lowe, Jr., did two things: he introduced innovative features to the magazine and began a gradual downscaling that would eventually bring in many more readers. Lowe brought in people like poet Ogden Nash to write and Robert C. Osborn, the well-known artist/cartoonist, to draw. He introduced the first "Hallmark House," with its easy-living features.[33] While the magazine continued to offer the best in decorating, it started to downscale with special features for the less affluent. For example, the magazine offered "15 Decorating Finds under $30" in the same issue (May 1957) that cooking/wine expert James A. Beard wrote about the "pleasant surprises" of Italian wines. That direction continued in 1958 under new editor Harriet Burket, probably the first woman editor in *House & Garden*'s history.[34] Burket brought to the magazine a youthful energy, a commitment to broadening even more the magazine's appeal and editorial package, and a dedication to social improvement. She brought the magazine very much into the spirit of the 1960s. Burket continued the magazine's move toward downscaling. Many of the features appealed to the less affluent: "Gifts for Everyone" in the November 1958 issue, for example, listed 99 suggestions under $9. She introduced to *House & Garden* heretofore untried features. She introduced a series on "simple things of everyday life" written by well-known literary figures. Thus, Pulitzer Prize-winning poet Marianne Moore wrote about "The Knife"; author Aldous Huxley had much to say about "Salt"; nature essayist Joseph Wood Krutch offered his views on "Grass"; and the editor of the *London Times Literary Supplement* Alan Pryce Jones dwelled on "The Glories of Glass."[35] Burket also reminded her readership of their social responsibilities. They had to be mindful of the environment ("*House & Garden* is convinced that an intellectual awareness of the whole environment is essential to the enhancement and protection of the home") and respectful of the young ("*House & Garden* is convinced that youth's freshness of viewpoint, youth's challenges, even youth's rebelliousness are what stimulate the continual self-renewal that makes life exciting and truly worth living").[36] Those changes brought prosperity to the magazine. By 1965, the magazine's circulation exceeded 1 million,[37] and most issues bulged with advertising.

The magazine in the 1970s had a new editor, Mary Jane Pool, but the same editorial vision. *House & Garden* had become almost a lifestyle magazine. While the magazine's base remained decorating, it approached decorating through even more practical, how-to stories, advice that could be used by the middle class as well as the most affluent readers: "How to Decorate and Build for the Good Family Life," "How to Decorate for Charm and Comfort," "Decorate-It-Yourself How To," "Make Over Ideas to Give You and Your House a Lift."[38] But the magazine also became a guide to living: rearing children through the department, "Today's Child," features on crafts and releasing creativity, tax advice, exercising, cooking, and travel.[39]

Under Pool, the magazine was redesigned. The logotype was changed in 1975 to place greater emphasis on the word "House" over "Garden," although the magazine applied its practical, how-to approach to gardening as well. However, the gardening portion of the editorial package had been reduced when more lifestyle features were added. The emphasis on "House" was continued when the logotype was redesigned in 1977. In 1980, "House" and "Garden" were given equal play in yet another redesign of the logotype. In 1977, also, the dimensions of the magazine itself were changed from oversized to a standard 8½" × 11" format. Inside the magazine, although the four-color photographs remained the finest quality, the layouts seemed cluttered. The new "lifestyle" approach demanded more copy; as a result, the overall graphic appearance seemed jumbled. Nonetheless, the advertisers did not seem to mind. Each issue was choked with ads; many issues exceeded 200 pages. In the 1970s, circulation remained more than 1 million. But changes were in the offing.

House & Garden's populist approach seemed strangely out of step with the 1980s. In 1981, Condé Nast brought in a new editor, Louis Oliver Gropp, and a new editorial vision. Gropp shifted the magazine away from Pool's and Burket's middle-class lifestyle approach to the opulence of decorating and collecting of the affluent. It represented a sharp shift from earlier magazines but, no doubt, reflected changes in the marketplace. The home/decorating niche was changing. More specialized, upscale decorating and architecture books had entered the competition. Among the most notable were *Architectural Digest* and *Metropolitan Home*.* To compete, *House & Garden* was repositioned. Its populist features were shunted aside; *House & Garden*, with yet another, more elegant logotype, became upscale with a capital "U."

The graphics were a vast improvement over the clutter of the 1970s. They were sophisticated and airy. The magnificent four-color photographs (printed on even better stock paper) were enlarged; copy was kept to a minimum. The magazine took on the appearance of an art book with its heavy stock front cover and the best-quality coated stock on the inside.

The new editor took readers into the homes of the rich and the famous, including the Vanderbilts in New York and the Johnsons in Texas.[40] Collecting was highlighted, but not the collections of the middle class.[41] Gardening was almost absent in the "new" *House & Garden*. The practical aspects of gardening that highlighted the magazine from Richardson Wright on were gone. Instead, there were pictures of finely appointed gardens and commentary on their histories.[42] As expected, circulation plummeted; in 1985, it was 552,003, down from 1,035,363 in 1980.[43] The demographics of the new magazine, no doubt, were much more attractive to advertisers. The magazine was bringing in the advertisers of the most expensive products.

In 1987, Condé Nast brought in a new editor for *House & Garden*. Gropp had created a magazine that appealed to an affluent, mature audience. Anna Wintour was brought in from *British Vogue* to "revitalize" *House & Garden* and make it "younger and hipper." She did just that. Within three months, *House & Garden* had a new look, a new editorial focus, and a new name. The name was *HG*. The magazine was completely redesigned. Even the dimensions of the magazine itself changed, adopting a popular, wider look. The design, more radical than the staid, traditional look associated with the *House & Garden* of the 1980s, would appeal to a younger audience. Wintour was also out to change *HG*'s approach to home/decorating. As she explained, "[Y]ou'll find greater attention to innovative personal styles in the new HG." The magazine would feature different lifestyles and put less emphasis on decorating per se. Soon the magazine was covering a trendy old diner on the edge of the artsy New York SoHo district; photographers photographing their own homes (even the controversial artist Robert Mapplethorpe participated in the story); and the art collection of actor/comedian Steve Martin.[44] Many subscribers were appalled by the changes and left the magazine. A number of advertisers, dismayed by the change in direction, also pulled back—and this at a time of a general downturn in advertising. Jim Terminiello, advertising manager for Laura Ashley, explained, "We felt it [*HG*] was heading in the direction of *Vanity Fair*."[45] Within ten months, Wintour was gone, becoming new editor of *Vogue*. Nancy Novogrod stepped in to try to rebuild *HG*. Novogrod returned it to the direction that Gropp had set for *HG*. Under Novogrod, the magazine lost the erratic edge that seemed to characterize it under Wintour. Novogrod tried to find a balance between appealing to a younger audience and retaining the magazine's basic character. The February 1990 issue represented *HG* under Novogrod. The front cover showed supermodel Isabella Rossellini gathering roses. Inside, "The Model Apartment" took the reader into the home of model Jerry Hall. "City Lights" highlighted the Manhattan apartment of Gary Hager, who was with the decorating firm of Parish Hadley Associates. "Crystal Gazing" captured Bohemian glass. "The Fame of the Rose" took the reader back into the garden. During her five years as editor, Novogrod rebuilt *HG*'s circulation and credibility with advertisers.[46]

But it was too little, too late after Condé Nast acquired Knapp Communications. *Architectural Digest*, the upscale magazine appealing to the affluent mature market, had become a leader in the home/decorating niche after editor Paige Rense transformed it from a specialized business publication to a vibrant consumer book. The magazine was a leader in advertising pages. *HG*'s 760 advertising pages in 1992 seemed few in comparison to *Architectural Digest*'s 1,155. *HG* had the edge in circulation, but not by much: in 1992, *HG* had 695,958 subscribers, and *Architectural Digest* counted 653,648. But in the dollars behind those subscribers, *Architectural Digest* took the lead, selling the bulk of its subscriptions for $39.95; drastic discounts meant that the typical *HG* subscription sold for $12. In advertising revenue, *Architectural Digest* brought in $33 million in 1992, compared with *HG*'s $23 million.[47]

HG died with its July 1993 issue. In announcing Condé Nast's decision to close the magazine, Leser explained, "We did the [Knapp Communications] acquisition with the intention that we would continue the two magazines. But we reluctantly came to the conclusion that with the two magazines continuing as they were, both editors would be putting out redundancy." According to

Leser, the thought of repositioning/downscaling *HG* was rejected: "We considered that option but felt it was unacceptable to us as a company and to the staff and the readers." Media observers pointed out that the decision to close *HG* seemed inconsistent with holdings within Condé Nast. The company owns both *Glamour** and *Mademoiselle,** two competing fashion magazines aimed at the younger female audience.[48]

But the decision had been made. *HG* died, and it was mourned. Dorothy Kalins, former editor of *Metropolitan Home*, observed, "It was like the death of a friend." Stephen Sills, owner of a residential and commercial design firm, explained, "They [*HG*] had a beautiful sensibility about interiors and they really were always right on target about what was happening." Two writers for the *Washington Post* called *HG* the "grande dame of decorating magazines."

No eulogies could help. *House & Garden*, one of the original three "crown jewels" in Condé Nast's publishing crown, was gone forever.

Notes

1. Deirdre Carmody, "In a Reversal, Condé Nast Closes *HG*," *New York Times*, April 21, 1993, p. D1.

2. Deirdre Carmody, "Food and Design Magazines Are Bought by Condé Nast," *New York Times*, March 3, 1993, pp. D1, D17; Scott Donaton, "Condé Nast Paying Premium for Knapp," *Advertising Age*, March 8, 1993, pp. 1, 44.

3. Carmody, "In a Reversal, Condé Nast closes *HG*," pp. D1, D19; Roxanne Roberts and Patricia Dane Rogers, "Demise of *HG* Has 'Shelter' Magazines Quaking," *Washington Post*, April 21, 1993, pp. B1, B4.

4. Richardson Wright, "How *House & Garden* Began," July 1926, p. 69.

5. June 1901, p. 16.

6. For a brief time during the paper shortages during World War II, the magazine often included inserts on coarser paper stock. But even in these years the greatest portion of the magazine was printed on coated stock, although admittedly of a lower quality than in the years before or after the war.

7. See, especially, *Vogue* and *Vanity Fair*.

8. Condé Nast purchased its own printing house to assure top quality. By the late 1920s, Condé Nast Press was known for its technical excellence. Caroline Seebohm, *The Man Who Was Vogue: The Life and Times of Condé Nast* (New York: Viking Press, 1982), pp. 246–249.

9. Charles Mulford Robinson, "The Evolution of the Street," February 1904, pp. 57–62; "The Architectural Embellishments of the New Williamsburg Bridge," March 1903; "The New Gymnasium Building," January 1905, pp. 16–22.

10. December 1901, p. 34: September 1903, p. 148; November 1904, p. 260.

11. Wright, "How *House & Garden* Began," p. 69.

12. December 1904, p. 313.

13. The new owners also reduced the price of *House & Garden* from five dollars to three dollars and briefly experimented with usng the word "and" instead of the ampersand in the title.

14. "House Making Series: Choosing a Site for the House," July 1905, pp. 24–27;

John T. Comes, "The Pittsburgh Architectural Club Exhibition," August 1905, pp. 83–89.

15. "Fall Furnishings," August 1916, p. 7.

16. In these early years, the magazine made it a point to appeal to both genders. However, Condé Nast saw decorating as a woman's domain. "Announcement," September 1915, p. 64.

17. October 1915, p. 9.

18. March 1916, p. 9.

19. "Things We've Gone to France For," September 1917, p. 20; "Raise Your Bit," June 1917, p. 22; "The Hardest Part of Patriotism," February 1918, p. 16.

20. Wright, "How *House & Garden* Began," p. 69. Advertisers included a variety of car companies, producers of upscale furniture, and travel companies and resorts. In addition, the magazine drew to it retailers of expensive personal goods such as perfumes and jewelry.

21. See, for example, Richardson Wright, "The Happy Faculty of Beginning Again," October 1934, p. 38; Richardson Wright, "Good Homes—Good Investments," June 1935, p. 22.

22. See, for example, the following inserts: "*House & Garden* Presents Air Conditioning," August 1935, pp. 51–62; "Walls and Roofs," January 1936, pp. 43–47, 50; "Insulation," February 1936, pp. 51–58; Mrs. Franklin D. Roosevelt, "Adventures with Early American Furniture," January 1934, pp. 21–23; "A Portfolio for Christmas Giving," December 1933, pp. 32–33.

23. July 1940, sec. 1.

24. The only exception to this occurred during the depression, when the magazine sometimes printed certain inserts on a lower-quality paper.

25. See, for example, January 1942, pp. 9–40; June 1942, sect. 2; "50 Tips for Victory Gardeners," January 1943, front cover; January 1944, pp. 12–34.

26. June 1943, pp. 43–50; March 1943, pp. 35–42; February 1942, pp. 18–19, 25.

27. July 1943; July 1944.

28. Iva S. V. Patcevitch, "To *House & Garden* Readers," May 1950, p. 109.

29. Wright, "How *House & Garden* Began," July 1926, p. 70; *N. W. Ayer & Son's Directory Newspapers and Periodicals* (Philadelphia: N. W. Ayer & Son, 1950), p. 145.

30. Seebohm, *The Man Who Was Vogue*, p. 120.

31. See, for example, "How to Give a Good Party," May 1955, pp. 102–107; "Gaylord Hauser's 10-Day Diet," June 1955, pp. 94–95; "Complete Summer Cook Book," June 1955, pp. 96–105.

32. In 1950, *House & Garden*'s circulation was 405,104; in 1955, it was 451,302. *N. W. Ayer & Son's Directory Newspapers and Periodicals*, 1950, p. 145; 1955, p. 693.

33. "Hallmark House Number 1," February 1957, pp. 34–49.

34. Wright, in his history of the publication, reports that Margaret Greenleaf became editor in 1903; however, she is not listed as the editor in any of the issues of that year. However, the author was not able to locate and consult all of the pre-1910 issues and, thus, cannot say absolutely that a woman never edited the magazine. Wright, "How *House & Garden* Began," p. 69.

35. Marianne Moore, "The Knife," February 1963, pp. 98–99, 140; Aldous Huxley, "Salt," March 1963, pp. 116–117; Joseph Wood Krutch, "The Miracle of Grass," June 1963, pp. 112–113, 151; Alan Pryce Jones, "The Glories of Glass," May 1963, pp. 152–153.

36. "The New Boundaries of Home," February 1965, p. 87; "Why Should We Segregate Young and Old?" May 1965, p. 123.

37. In 1965, the circulation was 1,234,859. *N. W. Ayer & Son's Directory of Newspapers and Periodicals*, 1965, p. 737.

38. January 1972; February 1972; April 1972; May 1974.

39. See, for example, "You and Your Craft: How to Release Your Creativity," an interview with the popular Dr. Rollo May, May 1976, pp. 88–89, 151; Paul Gross, "Money: Take a Tax Break," May 1976, pp. 108–109, 130; Paula Rich Judeson, "Doing Your Bad Back Good," June 1976, pp. 99, 168; Marian Burros, "Good Plains Cooking for Rosalynn Carter," February 1977, pp. 118–119; special section, "Bring China Home," April 1979, pp. 146–172. Before normalization, the Chinese government had invited *House & Garden* to see the arts and crafts of China.

40. "A Very Personal Luxury: Jean H. Vanderbilt's Manhattan Apartment," January 1983, pp. 116–125; Barbara Lazear Ascher, "A Personal Tradition: Gloria Vanderbilt Layers Past and Present in Her New York Apartment," February 1984, pp. 76–87; "Family Farmhouse, Lady Bird Johnson's Texas Retreat," January 1983, pp. 126–129.

41. See, for example, Joan Larrick, "Majolica Mania," September 1982, pp. 82–85.

42. See, for example, Susan S. H. Littlefield, "The Classical Garden Goes West," April 1984, pp. 156–165; Fleur Champin,"Riviera Garden with an English Accent," May 1984, pp. 182–189.

43. *Ayer Directory Newspapers, Magazines, and Trade Publications* (Philadelphia: N. W. Ayer & Son, 1980), p. 617; 1985, p. 686.

44. "The Canal Bar," April 1988, pp. 154–155; "Robert Mapplethorpe," June 1988, pp. 158–163; "The Private Eye of Steve Martin," April 1988, pp. 142–145.

45. Carmody, "In a Reversal, Condé Nast Closes *HG*," p. D19; Roberts and Rogers, "Demise of HG has 'Shelter' Magazines Quaking," p. B4; Debora Toth, "*HG* Battles Back," *Advertising Age*, April 23, 1990, p. S14.

46. Circulation went from 589,000 to 696,000. Roberts and Rogers, "Demise of *HG* has 'Shelter' Magazines Quaking," p. B4. *HG* publisher Kevin Madden reported that the number of advertising pages was up at the time of the folding. "A Love Letter to *HG*, R.I.P.," *New York Times*, May 3, 1993, p. D7.

47. Carmody, "In a Reversal, Condé Nast Closes *HG*," p. D19; Lorne Manly, "In *HG*'s Wake, Rivals Are Ready to Move In," *Folio*, June 1, 1993, p. 20; "*Advance*'s Condé Nast Folds *HG* Magazine, Having Bought Rival," *Wall Street Journal*, April 21, 1993, p. B6.

48. Carmody, "In a Reversal, Condé Nast Closes *HG*, pp. D1, D19; Manly, "In *HG*'s Wake, Rivals Are Ready to Move In," p. 20. Roberts and Rogers, "Demise of *HG* has 'Shelter' Magazines Quaking," p. B4.

Information Sources

BIBLIOGRAPHY:

"*Advance*'s Condé Nast Folds *HG* Magazine, Having Bought Rival." *Wall Street Journal*, April 21, 1993, p. B6.

Brown, Patricia Leigh. "As the Shelter World Turns." *New York Times*, May 13, 1993, pp. C1, C8.

Carmody, Deirdre. "Food and Design Magazines Are Bought by Condé Nast." *New York Times*, March 3, 1993, pp. D1, D17.

————. "In a Reversal, Condé Nast Closes *HG.*" *New York Times*, April 21, 1993, pp. D1, D19.

Donaton, Scott. "Condé Nast Paying Premium for Knapp." *Advertising Age*, March 8, 1993, pp. 1, 44.

Ford, James L. C. *Magazines for Millions: The Story of Specialized Publications.* Carbondale: Southern Illinois University Press, 1969.

"A Love Letter to *HG*, R.I.P." *New York Times*, May 3, 1993, p. D7.

Manly, Lorne. "In *HG*'s Wake, Rivals Are Ready to Move In." *Folio*, June 1, 1993, p. 20.

Mott, Frank Luther. *A History of American Magazines, 1885–1905.* Cambridge: Harvard University Press, 1957.

Peterson, Theodore. *Magazines in the Twentieth Century.* Urbana: University of Illinois Press, 1964.

Roberts, Roxanne, and Patricia Dane Rogers. "Demise of *HG* Has 'Shelter' Magazines Quaking." *Washington Post*, April 21, 1993, pp. B1, B4.

Seebohm, Carolina. *The Man Who Was Vogue: The Life and Times of Condé Nast.* New York: Viking Press, 1982.

Toth, Debora. "*HG* Battles Back." *Advertising Age*, April 23, 1990, p. S14.

INDEX SOURCES: Art Bibliographies Modern; Avery Index to Architectural Periodicals; Biography Index, Garden Literature; Magazine Index, Popular Magazine Review; Readers' Guide to Periodical Literature.

LOCATION SOURCES: Library of Congress and many other libraries.

Publication History

MAGAZINE TITLE AND TITLE CHANGES: *House & Garden* (ampersand varies, 1901–1988); *HG* (1988–1993).

VOLUME AND ISSUE DATA: Vols. 1–165 (June 1901–July 1993). Monthly.

PUBLISHER AND PLACE OF PUBLICATION: Architectural Publishing Co. (1901–1904); John C. Winston Co. (1905–?); McBride, Winston & Co. (?–1911); McBride, Nast & Co. (1911–1915); Condé Nast & Co. (1915–1993). Philadelphia (1901–1909); New York (1909–1993).

EDITORS: Wilson Eyre, Jr., Frank Miles Day, Herbert C. Wise (1901); Herbert C. Wise (1902–1904); Charles Francis Osborne (1905–1909); Henry H. Saylor (1909–1913); William A. Vollmer, managing editor (1913–1914); Richardson Wright, managing editor, editor, editor in chief (1914–1950); Henry Humphrey, editor (June–November 1943); Albert Kornfeld, editor, editor in chief (1946–1955); William H. Lowe, Jr. (1955–1958); Harriet Burket (1958–1969); Mary Jane Pool (1969–1981); Louis Oliver Gropp (1981–1987); Anna Wintour (1987–1988); Nancy Novogrod (1988–1993).

CIRCULATION: ABC, 1993: 695,958 (paid, primarily subscriptions) (peak circulation: 1,234,859 in 1965).

Kathleen L. Endres

HOUSE BEAUTIFUL

The American 1890s have been labeled the "age of excess," the "mauve decade," and the "gilded age."[1] Victorian styles in art, architecture, fashion, philosophy, and literature, patterned after English culture, still were alive, but sparks of an emerging American way of thinking were being lit.

Winslow Homer, John Sloan, and Thomas Eakins were transforming American painting; Charles S. Peirce, William James, and John Dewey were advancing a new philosophy of practicalism and utilitarianism; and William Dean Howells, Theodore Dreiser, and Frank Norris were writing about American topics in a new, "realistic" American style.

Embedded in all these changes was a fervent protest against the excesses of Victorianism. In the fields of architecture, furniture design, and interior decoration, that meant a battle against the flagrant excesses of the rich: the bric-a-brac in crowded, heavily draped, rococo rooms; houses with fancy, but useless, gingerbread trappings, turrets, and cupolas; golden oak and heavily ornamented furniture; and other ostentatious excesses of the nouveau riche.

Leading this crusade for practical, sensible, simple, tasteful houses and interior decoration was *The House Beautiful*, a December 1896 entry into the home and shelter magazine group and subtitled *A Monthly Magazine of Art and Artisanship*. It sold for 10¢ a copy and was targeted at the middle class.

House Beautiful has remained consistent in its zealous pursuit of homes and furnishings that reflect "sound simplicities and lasting truths."

Originally titled "*The House Beautiful*" after a Robert Louis Stevenson poem, the magazine was the brainchild of Eugene Klapp, a Chicago engineer with what Frank Mott called "a flair for architecture and literature."[2] He was joined by Henry B. Harvey, who shared Klapp's beliefs about simple, utilitarian architecture and furniture design.

Other "clear-thinking people" in the 1890s rebelled against the show of wealth and the materialistic house designs of the period. One was William C. Gannett, a minister, who wrote a series of articles entitled "*The House Beautiful*" in 1895, a series printed in a deluxe volume a year later by another young Chicago revolutionary, Frank Lloyd Wright.

The new magazine, as one former editor recalled in 1946, had always been a "voice crying in the wilderness of the terrible era of golden oak, of gingerbread carving, of cozy corners, of awful lamps and the rise of mission furniture."[3] The editor noted, with pride, that the magazine had "harried the manufacturers of golden oak relentlessly, on the grounds that they were debasing the taste of the whole country by flooding the market with their atrocious, claw-footed and be-griffined designs."[4]

After about a year, Klapp and Harvey found a publisher in Herbert S. Stone Co. in Chicago. Stone received generous economic support from his father, Melville Stone, head of the Associated Press. The younger Stone, while a student at Harvard, had been a founder of the experimental *Chap-Book*, a short-lived pioneer in the "little magazine" movement in the 1890s. Stone bought *The House Beautiful* in 1897. He served as editor of the magazine for 16 years.[5] Stone had an "almost religious devotion to simple beauty, an abhorrence of display and blatancy in modern life, and a special interest in the development of new art forms and the revival of old ones as he found them within the framework of beauty and suitability,'' according to Mott.[6]

The magazine's singularity of mission led it to exclude topics that were included in other ''shelter'' magazines of the time and that are common today. As an early editor recalled, ''In the beginning it was purely house. . . . It was strictly architectural and decorative. No people wandered through the rooms or appeared on the covers. There were no recipes, no wine lists, no babies or dogs.''[7] Over the years, of course, the magazine evolved with readers' interests, adding departments and features on furniture and interior decorating and housekeeping. By 1900, the size of the magazine was increased to 64 pages, the price was doubled, and it claimed a circulation of 7,000.

In 1904, it created a marvelously juicy controversy when it began a series of essays under the daunting—and long—title, ''The Poor Taste of the Rich: A Series of Articles Which Show That Wealth Is Not Essential to the Decoration of a House, and That the Homes of Many of Our Richest Citizens Are Furnished in Execrable Taste.'' Shaking entrenched standards and families to the core, the magazine ran photographs of the houses and named the owners of these ''bad-taste'' homes.

In response to critics who denounced the series as unethical journalism, Stone replied:

> Many people recognize good things when they see them and are astonishingly ignorant as to what is bad. This series of articles was designed to point out what is bad. The intention is as moral as can be. It is a great pity that many unguided persons will try to imitate the lavish furnishings of millionaires' homes, unless someone shows them how . . . for a very much smaller investment, they can obtain better results. *The House Beautiful* acts merely as a signpost; it points the way to go; if the rich show no more taste than the poor, it merely proves that *The House Beautiful*'s mission is larger than some people suppose.[8]

About the same time, Stone began an annual competition for the best design of a house costing no more than $3,000. The price went up over the years, but the competition remained an annual staple of the magazine, and by the late 1930s, blueprints were folded into the publication.

Capitalizing on the growing success of the magazine, Stone added more departments dealing with home economics, gardening, antiques, fabrics, and household appliances. The focal point, however, remained on the house and its components, with ''modern'' architects such as Frank Lloyd Wright, Howard Shaw, and Alfred Granger being mentioned and praised. The magazine was in the forefront of the battle for ''modern'' architecture in which ''form follows function.''

Readership and advertising continued to increase. By 1904, the magazine, published on quality paper with excellent halftones, had 20,000 circulation and 20 pages of advertising. As early as 1906, it was printing three-color covers, and a few full-color plates were printed occasionally. Not until the 1930s, however, did *House Beautiful* begin extensive cover and inside use of color.

In its early years, many of its competitors were swallowed up. In 1902, it absorbed *Domestic Science Monthly*. In 1908, *Indoors and Outdoors* was absorbed. Two years later it merged with, and subsumed, *Modern Homes*. In 1911, the magazine was moved from Chicago to New York, where it was consolidated with *American Suburbs* a year later.

During its stay in New York, the magazine underwent several changes in ownership and management and began experimenting with its appearance, using new typographical designs, with initials and decorations. In 1915, the publication was moved to Boston. Virginia Robie, a longtime contributor and staff member, had become editor in 1913, the first of six successive women editors of *House Beautiful*. (Only a one-year stint by Ellery Sedgwick in 1922 disrupted the reign of women editors.)

In the 1920s, the magazine expanded thematically and geographically. It now included, on a regular basis, articles on building, furnishing, and planting. It published special issues, focusing on simple, modern, utilitarian houses in cities across the country. Its target audience was upgraded to the middle and upper middle classes. By the 1930s, it was carrying about 60 pages, half of them advertising, and its circulation was near 100,000 monthly. Mott called it "a high-class, well-produced monthly book, lavishly illustrated."[9]

During the depression, the magazine survived, but changes were in the works. In 1934, the magazine was sold to the International Magazines Co., the magazine division of William Randolph Hearst's enterprises. Hearst took his *Home and Field* and merged it into *House Beautiful*, moving the publication back to New York. The magazine remains a Hearst property today.

Over its first 40 years of existence, *House Beautiful* was bought, sold, and merged several times. Yet, as Mott noted, "the essential vitality of *House Beautiful* is attested by the fact that, though it changed hands repeatedly and three of its purchasers consolidated their own house-and-home periodicals with it, it kept its own name; and through all its vicissitudes of changing owners, editors, and places of publication, it maintained a reasonable consistency in editorial policy."[10]

Up until the years of World War II, the outstanding editor was Stone, although each editor added his or her mark on the publication. In 1941, however, the magazine was placed in the capable hands of Elizabeth Gordon, and she spent the next 24 years guiding the magazine with the same fervor and dedication as Stone. In this period, she oversaw an increasingly complex organizational structure and displayed a remarkable editorial touch, such that by the mid-1960s, the magazine was publishing 200 pages, double what it had been providing when Gordon took over. Circulation shot up from 200,000 to 700,000 to more than 900,000 by 1964. The magazine was fat with advertising, used color lavishly, and maintained its original principle of sensible spending for good construction and furnishings. Gordon, for example, dissented from the popular Bauhaus and international style structures, disdaining the "less is more" philosophy.

Gordon embraced the simple, geographically based housing design whose principles could be adapted upward or downward, depending on one's resources. The ranch-style home, featured from 1948 to 1965, became one of the most popular housing forms and enjoyed strong support from *House Beautiful*. Gordon also advocated energy conservation and an appreciation of some international housing styles, especially those from Scandinavia and Japan.

In the 1960s, four magazines dominated the home-family books: Meredith's *Better Homes and Gardens,** Downe's *The American Home*, Condé Nast's *House & Garden,** and Hearst's *House Beautiful*. The first two led in circulation (7.5 million and 3.5 million, respectively) and sold for 50¢ a copy, while the latter two, both with circulations around 1 million, sold for 75¢ per issue, indicating a search for a slightly more upscale audience. At this writing, its single-issue price is $2.50.

Similarly, in 1964, the price of a single page, full-color advertisement was quoted as $8,750. In 1994, that same single page, full-color ad was quoted at $58,445 in the magazine's rate card.

Sarah Tomerlin Lee followed Gordon as editor and was confronted by a youthful, rebellious, anti-Establishment culture. Lee advocated a "sweet-sharp" color palette and vivid contrasts to represent that culture. She embraced the work of Barbara D'Arcy at Bloomingdale's and the folk crafts decorating style of Alexander Girard.

In the early 1970s, Wallace Guenther became editor and helped develop the concept of "country chic," defined as "chrome and glass with patchwork, acrylic with Eastlake, bentwood with Rauschenberg, Breuer with basketry."[11] Later in the 1970s, with Doris Shaw at the helm, the work of such architects as Ward Bennett was popularized. His design philosophy was unity of house with surroundings, furnishings reduced to essentials.

In the 1980s, with Shaw and then JoAnn Barwick as editors, "a celebration of American ingenuity" pervaded the magazine's articles. Readers were provided again with the call for simplicity, along with "a passion for collecting crafts, a thrill for combing flea markets and rural antique shops, an appetite for homegrown food and gardening."[12]

In the late 1980s and early 1990s, an overall sluggish economy seriously cut into magazines' advertising income, and, although most "shelter" publications, including *House Beautiful*, survived, it was not without change.

In 1991, the magazine underwent a major makeover. The cover was redesigned, type size was increased, and more consumer-oriented features were published. Leading the way was Louis Oliver Gropp, brought in as editor in chief by the Hearst Corp. in early 1991. Gropp, a veteran of some 30 years in the most sophisticated aspects of decorative design and former editor of *House & Garden*, had an almost immediate impact. Indeed, within a short time, Gropp had been awarded the *Interior Design Magazine*'s Hall of Fame Award for outstanding achievement in professional magazine design.

Most competing home-oriented publications—*Better Homes and Gardens*, *Metropolitan Home*, and *Architectural Digest*—also came through the slump. But longtime nemesis, Condé Nast's *House & Garden*, did not and ceased publication in 1993.

The earlier success of most home-oriented magazines was dependent, to some extent, on the broadening of their editorial appeal. That left the door open in the 1980s for the development of specific home-related publications, including *Colonial Home*, *Country Living*, *Americana*, and *Metropolitan Home*. Ironically, today *House Beautiful* includes *Metropolitan Home* and *Colonial Home* among its chief competitors (along with *Architectural Digest*, *Home*, and *Traditional Living*, according to the spring 1994 M.R.I. report).

House Beautiful remains a major entry in its field. Its full-color pages now carry more articles about food and recipes, remodeling, and fabrics. It embraces the new developments in architecture and design, so long as they are in keeping with the magazine's audience and with practical usefulness. Like many of the other shelter magazines, it also has developed its "special" issues over the years, including "Building Manual," "Home Remodeling," "Home Decorating," "House & Plans," and "Gardening & Outdoor Living." House plans also were offered readers for $25 a set, accompanied by a "Building Ideas Kit" chock full of advertising and offers of free booklets and brochures.

The magazine's average total paid circulation has grown slowly but steadily, normally a little more than 1 million. Twenty percent of that is from single-copy sales. It claims more than 7 million readers, with a median household income of $44,830 and a median individual reader age of 46.2.

Obviously, it has grown more upscale in the past several decades, compared with its middle-class upbringing 100 years ago. It also has expanded its areas of interest from building and decoration to travel, food, entertaining, remodeling, and gardening.

Today, the Hearst Corp., publishers of the magazine since the 1930s, has expanded the offerings and departments of the magazine. It also has looked toward the future, acquiring a minority interest in the Books That Work company in early 1994. The goal, according to the *Wall Street Journal*, was for the companies to develop and market multimedia software tied to such Hearst properties as *Popular Mechanics* and *House Beautiful*.[13]

House Beautiful continues as in the past. While always looking ahead, in this case with the increasingly popular multimedia and interactive computer software, it remains bound by the same philosophy on which it was founded in 1896: construction, design, and decoration should be tasteful, sensible, simple, and useful.

Notes

1. Ray Ginger, *Age of Excess* (New York: Macmillan, 1965); Thomas Beer, *The Mauve Decade: American Life at the End of the Nineteenth Century* (New York: Vintage Books, 1960); *The Gilded Age: A Reappraisal* (Syracuse, N.Y.: Syracuse University Press, 1963).

2. Frank Luther Mott, *A History of American Magazines*, vol. 5 (Cambridge:Belknap Press of Harvard University Press, 1968), p. 155.

3. Virginia Robie, "How We Did It in the Old Days," December 1946, p. 243.

4. Ibid., p. 244.

5. Stone died in 1915, a passenger on the *Lusitania* when it was sunk by a German U-boat.

6. Mott, *A History of American Magazines*, p. 156.

7. Robie, "How We Did It in the Old Days," pp. 153, 243.

8. As quoted by Robie, "How We Did It in the Old Days," pp. 245–246.

9. Mott, *A History of American Magazines*, p. 162. The article "The" was dropped from the title in 1925.

10. Ibid., p. 162.

11. "How the Pendulum Swings from Ornateness to Simplicity: A Chronicle of Style over the Last Century," December 1986, p. 22.

12. Ibid.

13. "Hearst in 'How-to' Software," *Wall Street Journal*, February 16, 1994, p. B8.

Information Sources

BIBLIOGRAPHY:

Barwick, JoAnn. "Delving into the Past Never Fails to Bring You Face to Face with the Old Adage That 'Nothing Is Ever New.' " *House Beautiful*, December 1986, p. 21.

Buck, Genevieve. "A House Beautiful." *Chicago Tribune*, May 5, 1991, sec. 15, p. 3.

Carmody, Deirdre. "Elite Magazines Compete for a Place at Home." *New York Times*, November 5, 1990, p. D9.

————."Stylish Home Magazines Fight Ragged Times." *New York Times*, August 5, 1991, p. D6.

————. "New Publishers Are Named at Two Hearst Magazines." *New York Times*, February 22, 1992, p. A51.

Ford, James L. C. *Magazines for Millions: The Story of Specialized Publications.* Carbondale: Southern Illinois University Press, 1969.

"Hearst in 'How-to' Software," *Wall Street Journal*, February 16, 1994, p. B8.

Lande, Melissa. "Home/Lifestyle Magazines Make the Most Out of Living." *Marketing Communication*, March 1982, pp. 49–52, 55–56.

Mott, Frank Luther. *A History of American Magazines, 1885–1905.* Cambridge: Harvard University Press, 1957.

Reilly, Patrick M. "Hearst Names 3 High-Profile Editors to Bolster Sagging Magazine Division." *Wall Street Journal*, January 10, 1991, p. B6.

INDEX SOURCES: Readers' Guide to Periodical Literature; Avery Index to Architectural Periodicals; Magazine Index; Popular Magazine Review.

LOCATION SOURCES: Library of Congress and many other libraries.

Publication History

MAGAZINE TITLE AND TITLE CHANGES: *The House Beautiful* (1896–1925); *House Beautiful* (1925–present). (Names of absorbed magazines kept as subtitles for brief periods after each merger.)

VOLUME AND ISSUE DATA: Vols. 1–(1896–present). Monthly (1896–1938); irregular (1939–1942); monthly (1943–present). (January 1933 issue not published.)

PUBLISHER AND PLACE OF PUBLICATION: Klapp & Co. (1896–1897); Herbert S. Stone & Co. (1897–1906); *House Beautiful* Co. (1906–1912); G. Henry Stetson, Wallace S. Peace, Stuart W. Buck, and others, as officers and stockholders (1912–1913); Atlantic Monthly Co. (1913–1915); Atlantic Monthly Co. (1916–1934); International Magazines Co. (1934–1936); Hearst Corp. (1936–present). Chicago (1896–1912); New York (1912–1915); Boston (1916–1934); New York (1934–present).

EDITORS: Eugene Klapp and Henry B. Harvey (1896–1897); Eugene Klapp (1897–1898); Herbert S. Stone (1898–1913); Virginia Robie (1913–1915); Mabel Kent (1915–1916); Grace Atkinson Kimball (1916–1918); Mabel Rollins (1918–1920); Charlotte Lewis (1921); Ellery Sedgwick (1922); Ethel B. Power (1923–1934); Arthur H. Samuels (1934–1936); Kenneth K. Stowell (1936–1941); Elizabeth Gordon (Norcross) (1941–1964); Sarah Tomerlin Lee (1965–1969); Wallace Guenther (1969–1977); Doris Shaw (1977–1978); JoAnn Barwick (1978–1991); Margaret Kennedy (1991–present).

CIRCULATION: ABC, 1994: 1,006,488 (paid, primarily subscriptions).

Fredric F. Endres

$$\text{———— L ————}$$

THE LADIES' COMPANION

One of the subtitles used by *The Ladies' Companion* during its decade of existence (1834–1844) is indicative of the magazine's grandiose style and the ambitions of William W. Snowden, its publisher: *A Monthly Magazine Embracing Every Department of Literature. Embellished with Original Engravings and Music Arranged for the Piano Forte, Harp, and Guitar.* Published in New York, *The Ladies' Companion* became one of the leading women's magazines in the nation during this period, along with the *Ladies' Magazine* of Boston and *Godey's Lady's Book** and *Graham's Magazine* of Philadelphia. The magazine was typical of similar magazines of its time, featuring mainly "polite" literature.

Snowden's main goal was to provide entertainment for his readers and, thereby, gain new subscribers. By rewarding his contributors generously, he attracted the leading popular writers of the day, including Emma C. Embury, Frances Sargent Osgood, Elizabeth Oakes Smith (Mrs. Seba Smith), Henry Wadsworth Longfellow, Edgar Allan Poe,[1] Ann S. Stephens, Lydia H. Sigourney, and Nathaniel Willis.[2] Snowden's reputation for paying contributors well and promptly helped to attract these writers.[3] However, his devotion to boosting the *Companion*'s circulation caused conflict with some of these same contributors, who resented Snowden's preference for popular features over spiritually uplifting verse and fiction.

Correspondence between two popular women writers who contributed to the *Companion* and also were listed as editors for the magazine is indicative of the mixed feelings some contributors had for the magazine, as well as for Snowden himself. Emma C. Embury, who contributed many stories, sketches, and poems to contemporary periodicals, and Lydia H. Sigourney, perhaps the most popular versifier of the time, were distressed with the magazine's moral tenor. In one letter to Sigourney, Embury agreed with Sigourney's concerns about the magazine. She wrote, "That its tone ought to be and might be greatly elevated is most certain.''[4] In another letter, Embury wrote to Sigourney about the ''absolute necessity of our assuming the power of selection''[5] for material in the magazine.

However, Snowden seems to have ignored entreaties from both ladies, whose names he listed as editors to give the magazine prestige and respectability but from whom he allowed no editorial input. Embury's discouraged, somewhat bitter response to Sigourney's complaints in a later letter is revealing of Snowden's attitude toward his ''editors'' and, perhaps, women in general: ''I think he seems unwilling to accept any suggestions from us. . . . I think he regards them as woman's whims, to which his politeness allows him to listen, while his superior discretion can find nothing in them worthy even to be disputed, far less to be adopted.''[6]

Of all the contributors who wrote for the *Companion*, Ann S. Stephens may have been the most influential. Stephens had edited another women's magazine, *The Portland Magazine*, from 1834 to 1836[7] and was hired by Snowden soon after her family moved to New York City in 1837. She contributed many poems, essays, stories, and at least two long, serialized stories to the magazine. These serialized stories, sentimental romances that included Indian characters and described Indian life with some detail and accuracy, had the greatest impact on the public.

The first story, ''Mary Derwent: A Tale of the Early Settlers,'' was serialized beginning with the May 1838 issue as winner of a $200 story competition the magazine had advertised. The story was accompanied by an obtuse explanation of why the magazine had awarded the prize to a staff member, since Stephens was now listed as one of the magazine's editors.[8] The story, set in Pennsylvania in the Wyoming Valley of the Susquehanna River, tells the story of Lady Gordon, an English noblewoman who becomes the ''White Indian Queen'' of the Mohawk Indians. The readers followed Lady Gordon's adventures, which included a number of plot twists and several incredible coincidences, until she was killed in a massacre during the Revolutionary War.

The story was reprinted in 1840 in the May-August issues. In an editor's note that accompanied the story's second appearance in May 1840, Stephens's importance to the magazine's popularity was noted: ''[A]t the time of its former publication, there were only four thousand, five hundred copies issued; now 'The Ladies' Companion,' has a circulation of *seventeen thousand*.''[9] Another one of Stephens's Indian stories, ''Malaeska,'' which was serialized in three parts from February to April 1839 in the *Companion*, earned a significant place in literary history. The story was reprinted in 1860 as the first Beadle Dime Novel, which became a hugely popular series of paperback melodramas. *Malaeska: The Indian Wife of the White Hunter* sold 300,000 copies as Beadle's Dime Novel number one.[10]

The Ladies' Companion contained little obvious advertising, in keeping with Snowden's desire to create a refined and tasteful image for the magazine, although the *Companion* did list a rate of ten cents per line for advertising on its cover in 1838.[11] A close examination of the magazine's "Editor's Table" reveals some items that seem to be paid advertising, although they appear no different typographically from other informational items in the table. One such item praises the work of a New York carriage maker, declaring, "The extreme luxury of life appears to be centered here in this species of elegant convenience." However, the item also contains an apology for including it at all, saying that, as a rule, the magazine does not "pass beyond the province of polite literature" to include "remarks upon Mechanical productions."[12]

Like the other women's commercial magazines of the day, the *Companion* and its contributors emphasized traditional roles for women rather than stressing reform or championing women's rights. Contributors, both men and women, seemed to go out of their way to portray women as spiritual creatures devoted completely to home and family. Still, the magazine reflected recent societal changes in which women had begun to take leadership positions in morals, to participate in the nation's literary life, and to function as arbiters of fashion. The magazine prided itself as a cultural repository and did not include material devoted to practical domestic matters, filling most of its pages with romantic or spiritually uplifting poetry and prose.

Stories were almost always melodramatic and contained a strong romantic interest. Stories typical of the type appeared in a regular feature titled "Our Library," which was written by Embury. One such story, "The Manuscript of Father Aubertius,"[13] concerned Embury's alleged discovery of a scroll hidden in the frame of a religious painting that purported to reveal the secret life of a prominent bishop who lived during the Middle Ages. The story began as the title character, Father Aubertius, married and then abandoned his wife, then followed his ascendancy to bishop after a ruthless career, and ended with his inadvertent execution of a young priest whom he discovered, to his sorrow, was really his only son.

This story displays many of the characteristics common to the fiction in *The Ladies' Companion*, although it does not have the usual happy ending: an exotic setting, complex, romantic entanglements and plot twists, scandalous behavior, and amazing coincidences. Perhaps most typically, the story seems to be striving more to be popular and entertaining than morally uplifting. Although the story pays respect to conventional morality, it is not preachy. Rather, the moral lessons seem to function as a veneer that allows the author to maintain respectability while presenting as spicy, suspenseful, and exciting a plot as possible.

The poetry published in the magazine more often emphasized spiritual themes, although the accent on sentimentality and even romance in the verse was equally pervasive. A poem by Sigourney can serve as a typical illustration of both characteristics. The poem "The Sacred Minstrel" recounted how Saul, the king of Israel, found himself troubled and melancholy until his minstrel boy began to sing to him about God and nature, which changed his mood. The poem ended with an entreaty to readers to follow Saul's example and turn to music when they "feel the poison fumes/of earth's fermenting care."[14]

However, the magazine often included romantic and even sexual appeals in its verse, further evidence of Snowden's understanding of his readers' popular tastes. On the first page of the same issue where Sigourney's poem appeared, an engraving of a beautiful young woman in a rather low-cut gown was followed by a poem, "The Star of Love," which sedately but emphatically called attention to both the woman's purity and her romantic charms.

Although a majority of the magazine's editorial content was devoted to "polite" fiction and poetry, the "Star of Love" engraving represented an example of one of the many other features in the magazine. The magazine itself often touted its engravings, and at least one plate and sometimes two appeared in every issue. The plates were usually illustrations of a poem or story, illustrations of a landscape of a well-known city or scene accompanied by a prose description of the place, or fashion plates that usually focused on seasonal clothing. The plates were high-quality engravings, clear, and meticulously detailed, and Snowden frequently boasted that he used all new plates rather than reusing worn engravings from other magazines.[15]

The magazine also included a number of other features in most issues, including accounts of travel and adventure; biographies; brief historical features; reviews of books, plays, and artworks; and miscellaneous items that appeared each month in the feature called "Editor's Table." These items focused on current events, mainly cultural, obituaries, weather, and hyperbolic puff pieces about the magazine, often containing descriptions of special features planned for future issues, pleas to readers to pay their subscriptions, or calls for support from readers to aid the magazine with problems such as high postal rates.

In fact, the reviews of plays contained in a monthly section titled "Theatricals" were partly the cause of the disapproval Embury and Sigourney expressed to Snowden about the magazine's tone. Neither woman wanted her name associated with theatrical productions of popular plays of dubious morality. In Embury's letter of March 4, 1843, to Sigourney, she expressed both her hope that Snowden would "omit the theatrical reviews" and her understanding of his pecuniary nature, with the observation that such an omission would happen only if Snowden received "the assurance from you that their insertion injures the circulation of the Companion in New England."[16] Snowden's enthusiasm for the "Theatricals" may have been related to the fact that he had a financial interest in New York's Bowery Theater, whose productions were given rave reviews in every issue of the Companion.[17]

In the same letter, Embury also revealed Snowden's steadfast commitment to the popular fiction he favored for the magazine when she complained about his lack of enthusiasm for the preambles to her stories, which were intended to convey her "moral sentiments" to readers. "Mr. Snowden," she wrote, "gave me to understand that he much preferred the more practical and popular tales."[18] Despite their concerns about the magazine's moral standards, both Embury and Sigourney allowed themselves to be listed as editors of the Companion until a particularly scandalous incident rocked the literary community and threatened Snowden and the continued existence of the *Companion*.

In the September and November 1842 issues of the *Companion*, Snowden attacked Park Benjamin, calling Benjamin "a literary hedge-hog" and "literary reptile." Snowden had published a poem written by Benjamin in the *Companion* just two years earlier,[19] but Benjamin had since become the rival editor of the *New World*. These attacks had serious implications for the *Companion*'s contributors and editors, who were loath to be associated with the attack. Both Embury and Sigourney deplored the incident and worried about its effect on their good names; and Sigourney wrote a public apology to Benjamin, at his insistence,[20] which was published in the *New World*.[21]

Among Sigourney's papers is a manuscript written on unlined paper in her absolutely straight, nearly calligraphic script. At the top of the manuscript, titled "The Geranium Plant," a prose piece about the power of flowers to awaken memory, appears Sigourney's note: " 'Ladies' Companion' June 3, 1843. Used, with the exception of the first two pages."[22] So Sigourney, at least, continued to contribute to the *Companion* after the incident, although her name disappeared from the magazine as an editor. However, within a year, Snowden had sold the *Companion* "to a company of gentlemen."[23] The magazine continued publication for only six months under the new owners. The last issue appeared in October 1844.[24]

The Ladies' Companion represents a model of the successful women's magazines of the period. Typically, it portrayed the expanded role women had assumed in society but also downplayed the importance of real political and economic power for women. The magazine recognized the importance of women as arbiters of taste in literary matters and in matters of fashion. Most important, the handsome payments Snowden offered his contributors helped to establish a new professional class composed of women authors, whose work has been admired, respected, and rewarded throughout the nineteenth and twentieth centuries.

On the other hand, the magazine did little to encourage literary growth and experimentation by women authors. Contributors were encouraged to produce the same sentimental, uplifting poetry and prose, usually with happy endings, which did little either to improve their own literary skills or to portray women in anything but conventional and traditional roles. One essay in the magazine, while maintaining that it is good for a woman to become educated, argued that "woman should find the proper exercise of her faculties far retired from the busy highways of Ambition [where] she should wander in the shady, green lanes of domestic life."[25] In fact, the magazine and its contributors were apologists for a social order that ensured that its subscribers, devoted as they were to "domestic life," would continue to demand the conventional literature, music, and engravings that its creators had become so adept at producing.

Perhaps, the *Companion* and its contemporaries' greatest influence on the U.S. magazine industry was to create the model for the general circulation, monthly women's magazines that existed for the next century and a half. Magazines like the *Companion* not only convinced the industry that women's magazines attuned to popular tastes could profitably capture a mass audience but also helped to create and develop that audience.

Notes

1. Frank Luther Mott, *A History of American Magazines, 1741–1850* (Cambridge: Harvard University Press, 1938), p. 627.
2. Ann D. Wood, "The 'Scribbling Women' and Fanny Fern: Why Women Wrote," *American Quarterly* 23 (Spring 1971), p. 16.
3. Gordon S. Haight, *Mrs. Sigourney: The Sweet Singer of Hartford* (New Haven, Conn.: Yale University Press, 1930), p. 113.
4. Letter from Embury to Sigourney, April 18, 1843, Lydia H. Sigourney Collection, Connecticut Historical Society.
5. Letter from Embury to Sigourney, July 14, 1843. Lydia H. Sigourney Collection.
6. Ibid.
7. Caroline Garnsey, "Ladies' Magazines to 1850," *Bulletin of the New York Public Library* 58 (February 1954), p. 74.
8. Madeleine B. Stern, "Ann S. Stephens: Author of the First Beadle Dime Novel," *Bulletin of the New York Public Library* 64 (June 1960), pp. 306–307.
9. "$200 Prize Article," May 1840, p. 18.
10. Stern, "Ann S. Stephens," p. 163.
11. Garnsey, "Ladies' Magazines to 1850," p. 82.
12. "Editor's Table," October 1840, p. 308.
13. Emma C. Embury, "Our Library," May 1840, pp. 26–33.
14. Lydia H. Sigourney, "The Sacred Minstrel," October 1840, p. 261.
15. Mott, *A History of American Magazines,* p. 628.
16. Embury to Sigourney, March 24, 1843, Lydia H. Sigourney Collection.
17. Haight, *Mrs. Sigourney,* p. 114.
18. Embury to Sigourney, March 24, 1843.
19. Park Benjamin, "To a Boy," August 1840, p. 162.
20. Letter from Park Benjamin to Sigourney, May 8, 1843, Lydia H. Sigourney Collection.
21. Haight, *Mrs. Sigourney,* p. 117.
22. Lydia S. Sigourney, "The Geranium Plant," Lydia H. Sigourney Collection.
23. Mott, *A History of American Magazines*, p. 628.
24. Garnsey, "Ladies' Magazines to 1850," p. 88.
25. "Influence of Woman—Past and Present," September 1840, p. 245.

Information Sources

BIBLIOGRAPHY:

Garnsey, Caroline. "Ladies' Magazines to 1850." *Bulletin of the New York Public Library* 58 (February 1954), pp. 74–88.
Haight, Gordon S. *Mrs. Sigourney: The Sweet Singer of Hartford.* New Haven, Conn.: Yale University Press, 1930.
Mott, Frank Luther. *A History of American Magazines, 1741–1850*, vol. 1. Cambridge: Harvard University Press, 1938.

Stern, Madeleine B. "Ann S. Stephens: Author of the First Beadle Dime Novel." *Bulletin of the New York Public Library*, 64 (June 1960), pp. 302–322.

Wood, Ann D. "The 'Scribbling Women' and Fanny Fern: Why Women Wrote." *American Quarterly* 23 (Spring 1971), pp. 3–24.

Zuckerman, Mary Ellen. *Sources on the History of Women's Magazines, 1792–1960: An Annotated Bibliography*. Westport, Conn.: Greenwood Press, 1991.

INDEX SOURCES: None.

LOCATION SOURCES: Library of Congress; Franklin and Marshall College; and other libraries.

Publication History

MAGAZINE TITLE AND TITLE CHANGES: *The Ladies' Companion; A Monthly Magazine Embracing Every Department of Literature, Embellished with Original Engravings and Music Arranged for the Piano Forte, Harp and Guitar* (1834–1843); *The Ladies' Companion, and Literary Expositor: A Monthly Magazine Embracing Every Department of Literature, Embellished with Original Engravings and Music Arranged for the Piano Forte, Harp and Guitar* (1843–1844).

VOLUME AND ISSUE DATA: Vols. 1–21 (May 1834–October 1844). Monthly.

PUBLISHER AND PLACE OF PUBLICATION: William W. Snowden (1834–1844); "A Company of Gentlemen" (1844). New York.

EDITORS: William W. Snowden (1834–1844); Ann S. Stephens (1837); Lydia H. Sigourney (1843); Emma C. Embury (1843); (both Mrs. Sigourney and Mrs. Embury served in 1843).

CIRCULATION: Mott, vol. 1, p. 628: 17,000–22,500 (Peak, 1840).

Paul S. Belgrade

LADIES' HOME JOURNAL

On March 18, 1970, about 100 feminists stormed the editorial offices of the *Ladies' Home Journal* in New York City. During the 11-hour siege, the feminists demanded a chance to put out a "liberated" issue of the magazine, the replacement of the male editor with a woman, an all-woman editorial and advertising staff, the end of "exploitative" advertising in the periodical, and a free day-care center for employees. The protestors were only partly successful. The August issue of *Ladies' Home Journal* did include an eight-page supplement written by supporters of the feminist—then called the women's liberation—movement. Three years later, Lenore Hershey, former executive editor, was promoted to editor, although John Mack Carter retained the title of editor in chief and board chairman of Downe Communications Inc., the owner of the magazine at that time.[1]

This demonstration assured the *Ladies' Home Journal* a footnote in a history of the twentieth-century women's movement. It is unlikely it will receive little more than this passing reference. The magazine has been a conservative spokesman for the role of women in society. It never editorially endorsed suffrage and was slow to cover the women's liberation movement.

In magazine publishing history, however, *Ladies' Home Journal* has already won its place—whatever the future might hold for the magazine. The *Ladies' Home Journal* is the "grand old lady" of the women's magazine niche, still retaining a multimillion readership, although it is well into its second century of publication.

Ladies' Home Journal started, modestly enough, as a column in the weekly newspaper, *Tribune and Farmer.* From there, it grew to one page, then an eight-page supplement, and, finally, in December 1883, a distinct magazine. In the early days, the *Journal* was a ma-and-pa operation. The publisher was Cyrus H. K. Curtis; the founding editor was his wife, who was identified in the magazine by her maiden name Louisa Knapp.[2]

Under this management, the magazine grew quickly. The monthly doubled in number of pages within two years and then doubled again and again. So did the circulation. Within five months of its launch, the *Journal*'s circulation reached 31,000; 70,000 by September 1884; 100,000 by December 1885; 250,000 by July 1886; and 1 million by November 1889.[3]

Several reasons explain the phenomenal early success of the *Journal*. First, Knapp developed an editorial formula that seemed to strike a responsive chord with the readership. True to her pledge to publish "a pure and high-toned family paper,"[4] Knapp offered a combination of short stories and serialized novels written by some of the popular writers of the day, including Ella Wheeler and Margaret S. Harvey. She also offered features that are commonly associated with today's service journalism. The *Ladies' Home Journal* was becoming a woman's survival manual with departments that offered practical advice on child rearing, useful household hints, instructions for various crafts, and inspirational essays on a variety of topics.

Moreover, the magazine also had an enlightened policy with regard to advertising. From an early point in its history, the *Journal* monitored its advertisers, rejecting "[a]ll doubtful advertisements . . . ; no room for swindlers in our family."[5] The editor estimated that the magazine had lost thousands of dollars in advertising revenue because of this policy. Thus, Knapp asserted, "if you want anything advertised do not fear to buy it."[6]

The magazine was just as enlightened in some of its circulation policies. The magazine always maintained a paid circulation and ensured those paying readers by offering generous rewards to agents. In 1884, there were cash prizes of up to $500 for agents who brought in the largest number of paying subscriptions, parlor organs (for 300 subscribers), dolls (for 20), and tableware (various pieces for 4 to 20 subscribers).[7]

Throughout Knapp's six-year tenure as editor, the magazine witnessed steady growth. Yet, it was also witnessing intense competition. Although the magazine boasted that its 400,000 paid subscribers represented the largest circulation of any newspaper or periodical in the United States, the *Journal* was increasingly threatened by the *Woman's Home Companion*,* a magazine that was based in Ohio and had a national circulation.[8]

Knapp, who has been characterized as a "very domestic woman,"[9] was wearing under this pressure. She had always done her editorial work at home; and, increasingly, more and more of her time was spent on the magazine at the expense of her preteen daughter and publisher husband. Finally, Knapp had to give up the editor's title.

In January 1890, Edward W. Bok took her place as editor, although Knapp remained in charge of the "Practical Housekeeper" department. Thus began Bok's 39-year reign as head of the *Journal*. Although just 26 years of age when he took over the *Journal*, Bok soon grew into his role. His editorial vision dovetailed nicely with Curtis's business strategies. Bok's *Journal* was to be a magazine to appeal to the whole family. His would be an ideal companion for the growing number of middle-class women and their families.[10]

Bok built on Knapp's successful editorial formula. Bok's *Journal* had short stories, serialized novels, and poetry by popular writers. As the magazine grew more successful, it was able to pay even more to bring in some of the finest female and male writers of the day. Sarah Orne Jewett, Mrs. Burton Harrison, Frances Hodgson Burnett, to name but a few, contributed to the magazine. William Dean Howells, James Whitcomb Riley, and Bret Harte, at various times, published in Bok's *Journal*. The magazine even claimed it "discovered" author Rudyard Kipling and published his first "Just So" story in 1900. The *Journal* under Bok also published essays of many female reformers, including Frances Willard, Jeanette Rankin, and Anna Howard Shaw, and male politicians, including Franklin Delano Roosevelt and Herbert Hoover in their prepresidential days. Since 1905, every president has written at least one article for the *Journal*, a tradition that Bok started while he was editor.[11]

Bok's graphic judgment was as well developed as his literary sense. The *Journal* sported front covers and inside art done by some of the finest illustrators of the day. Kate Greenaway, Charles Dana Gibson, Maxfield Parrish, Howard Charles Christy, and Albert Lynch did artwork for the *Journal*.

Bok also brought important reforms to the publication. He introduced a column on American architecture to which celebrated architect Frank Lloyd Wright contributed. Bok was also responsible for the *Journal*'s college scholarship program for top subscription sellers.

In his editorial column, Bok brought a strange brand of conservatism and reform to his opinion. On one hand, he did not see any need to expand women's sphere in society. (He even editorially opposed suffrage.)[12] At the same time, he waged a long and bitter campaign against patent medicines, even urging the Women's Christian Temperance Union to join him in his battle against "the curse of the patent medicine."[13] Nonetheless, Bok could see no reason for the government to pass laws establishing Prohibition. "You cannot legislate a drunkard into an abstainer," he wrote.[14] He also waged an editorial campaign for sex education for women. That campaign caused the *Journal* to lose at least 25,000 subscribers, according to Bok's estimate.[15] His editorial campaigns met with only mixed results. In spite of his opposition, suffrage was ratified, and

Prohibition became the law of the land. Yet, his patent medicine editorials have been generally credited with mobilizing support for what became the Food and Drug Act of 1906.

When Bok retired, he soon became the brunt of criticism, primarily because of the *Journal* during World War I. Bok and the *Journal* were war supporters. Critics contended that Bok had permitted George Creel of the Committee on Public Information (CPI) too great a rein in the magazine.[16]

Once Bok left, no editor was as closely identified with the *Ladies' Home Journal*. H. O. Davis briefly followed Bok; John E. Pickett followed Davis, but with the title of managing editor. Barton Currie soon followed, as did Loring Schuler. All these editors offered the Bok editorial formula of good fiction. Dorothy Parker, Booth Tarkington, Thomas Hardy, Pearl Buck, Edith Wharton, A. A. Milne, Agatha Christie, H. G. Wells, and others wrote for the *Journal*.

Capitalizing on suffrage, the new *Journal* editors forgot about Bok's opposition and offered essays on the woman's vote for changing America's politics.[17] Yet, this does not mean that the *Journal* was in the forefront of the equal rights movement. The *Journal* would have none of that radical measure and warned that if any such amendment passed, it would spell the end of most of the gains women had achieved through labor laws.[18]

During this period, also, the ''celebrity'' was added to the magazine's editorial mix. Today, the ''celebrity'' feature remains an important staple of the magazine. In the 1920s and 1930s, movie stars and religious celebrities captured the largest amount of attention. Actress Dorothy Gish, actor John Barrymore, and the Reverend William A. (Billy) Sunday all offered essays that appeared in the magazine.

The depression brought hard times to the *Journal* and its readers. Like other magazines, the *Journal* suffered from advertising cutbacks, although those cuts were never so deep as to threaten the magazine's future. The *Journal*, as well as its sister publication the *Saturday Evening Post*, remained one of the largest circulating periodicals in the nation, even during the depth of the depression. Although the *Journal* weathered the economic reversals relatively unscathed, its editors were mindful that their readers were not so ''comfortable.'' The magazine offered a wide range of editorials and features designed to help female readers through the hard times. Loring Schuler crafted most of the early depression comment. He reminded the women that they had valuable parts to play in the recovery. They needed to have confidence in the government and spend a certain amount of money to fuel economic recovery.[19]

In 1935, Schuler was replaced with the husband-and-wife team of Bruce and Beatrice Gould. Like the editors before them, the Goulds saw the *Journal* as a conservative voice to America's women. As Beatrice Gould wrote:

I believe it is a woman's job to be as truly womanly as possible. I mean to nourish her family, and to rest them, to guide them, and to encourage them. To be as pretty as possible, as helpful as possible, as loving as possible, so that if the whole rest of the world blacks out, each family has the center of warmth and comfort and cheer and tolerant good sense.[20]

This philosophy permeated the magazine. The editorial campaigns for which the Goulds are best remembered hinged on the perspective that women were wives and mothers first. Thus, the Goulds campaigned for policies and procedures designed to lower maternal mortality, for implementation of the hot school-lunch program, and for enhancement of women's awareness of health issues.[21]

Features, similarly, often reflected traditional values and perspectives. Rose Wilder Lane wrote of her voyage from women's rights activist to one who turned her back on the reform. Clifford D. Adams, a psychologist, offered hints on keeping a marriage together. Roger Butterfield urged readers to have children early and grow up with them. Henry B. Safford warned of the physical dangers and moral reprehensibility of abortion—no matter what the reason.[22]

The Goulds were also responsible for features that gained the magazine an even stronger national reputation. The two invited First Lady Eleanor Roosevelt to write a column, which was entitled "If You Ask Me." Also under their leadership, the famous "How America Lives" series began, a highly regarded journalistic series on how ordinary Americans lived.[23]

Similarly, several departments that have come to be seen as *Journal* staples premiered under the Goulds. "Can This Marriage Be Saved," still one of the magazine's most popular offerings, debuted in 1953. The *Journal*'s "Tell the Doctor" column highlighted health concerns related to women and children.

Also under the Goulds, the slogan "Never Underestimate the Power of a Woman" premiered, a slogan that has become a part of American culture.

In 1962, after 27 years as editors, the Goulds retired, leaving the editorial leadership to Curtiss Anderson. He remained editor for two years. However, these were strange times for the *Journal*. Frequency varied. In 1962, only 11 issues came out; in 1963, 10; in 1964, 11. In 1965, the monthly cycle returned.

In his relatively brief tenure with the *Journal*, Anderson offered a range of features that dealt with some of the pressing social problems of the decade. There were stories on unwed mothers on relief and even an early special edition on the women's movement. That 1964 issue was entitled "Woman: The Fourth Dimension" and had articles written by Betty Friedan, Jessica Mitford, Rona Jaffee, and Marya Mannes.[24]

Anderson was replaced in 1964 by Davis Thomas, who, in turn, was replaced by John Mack Carter. Carter brought stability back to the *Journal* on the editorial side, but there was little stability on the business end. The frequency cycle of the early 1960s might have reflected trouble brewing at Curtis Publishing Co. In 1968, the financially troubled Curtis Publishing sold the *Journal* to newly organized Downe Communications for $5.4 million. The sale did not seem to satisfy anyone. In 1969, Curtis sued to revoke the sale, but the deal was done. In April, several editors left the *Journal* and *American Home*, another Curtis magazine that had been sold to Downe. They charged that advertising and circulation were being stressed at the expense of editorial.[25]

Carter was not among those editors. In fact, Carter seemed to solidify his position with the sale. He soon became board chairman of Downe Communications Inc. Of course, the feminists who stormed his offices in 1970 did not rejoice in his success. It was Carter's *Journal* that feminist groups protested, and it was Carter's *Journal* that added the special insert that included essays and features by women's rights activists. Protests notwithstanding, Carter's *Journal* was more progressive than the Goulds' or Bok's. It was more the creation of the tumultuous 1960s and 1970s.

Carter brought in previously excluded voices. Mrs. Medgar Evers offered a perspective from a woman of color, a group generally overlooked by the *Journal*. Carter was also responsible for using the first African American woman on the front cover.[26] However, Carter brought no radical changes to the magazine. The *Journal* did deal with the Vietnam War, by calling for a full accounting of the prisoners of war and those missing in action. As a result, more than 60,000 signed petitions were sent to Congress demanding that something be done about the situation.[27]

Carter's eight years as editor (1965–1973) were times of tremendous prosperity for the *Journal*. The magazine hit its top circulation of 7 million in 1970 and, in 1971, reached its top revenue of $45 million. But trouble was on the horizon for the publication.

The 1970s brought new competition to the *Journal*. New magazines that catered to the specialized interests of women were launched during that decade. *Ms.** offered feminist perspectives, *Working Woman** appealed to the growing number of employed women, and *Women's Sports & Fitness** addressed health concerns. The *Journal*'s audience was changing, and the magazine was finding it difficult to serve all its diverse interests. Circulation soon reflected this difficulty; subscriptions plummeted from 7 million in 1970 to 5 million in 1985.

Lenore Hershey became editor in this competitive environment. From the beginning, she seemed to grasp that her readers were changing. She promised an editorial fare to accommodate the "women who live a variety of lifestyles."[28] However, the magazine could only partially fulfill that pledge.

Hershey brought innovations to the magazine. She started the "Women of the Year" awards. In 1980, that honor expanded into a televised special program, "A Celebration of Women," honoring the *Journal*'s "Women of the Decade" and "Women of the Future." A number of features published during Hershey's editorship pointed to the variety of lifestyles that women maintained. One special report even outlined "How to Be Strong and Female."[29]

In 1981, Lenore Hershey retired. She could not have picked a better time. The magazine was about to start a roller-coaster ride on the business side. In 1982, the *Journal* was sold; this time to Family Media Inc. for an estimated $15 million. Family Media was soon facing some problems of its own, and

Ladies' Home Journal was up for sale again. In 1986, the sale was complete: the magazine was sold to Meredith Publishing for $92 million.[30]

Throughout this period and into the 1990s, Myrna Blyth, who had been former executive editor of *Family Circle*,* has been the *Journal*'s editor. She offers an editorial fare designed to appeal to the large female audience. To assure its substantial newsstand sales (averaging in excess of 750,000 per month in 1992),[31] Blyth relies on celebrity front covers. The women pictured represent a range of interests and activities. In 1993, the *Journal* offered First Lady Hillary Rodham Clinton in April and talk show hostess Kathy Lee Gifford in September, Princess Diana of England in August, and singer/actress Bette Midler in July.

Inside the magazine, Blyth offers articles designed to appeal to the wide variety of interests of her readership. Most of the departments, features, and columns deal with food and nutrition, followed by editorial material relating to beauty or fashion. Many stories deal with problems associated with rearing children and taking care of the home, but the editorial mix also includes stories on business, travel, and national and international affairs. Today, fiction accounts for only about 1 percent of the *Journal*'s editorial content.[32]

The shifts in editorial content over the *Journal*'s long history reflect changes within the readership. In 1883, the largest number of readers were middle-class women whose primary occupation was taking care of their homes and families. Today, the readers have other roles. The majority of the *Journal*'s readers are married, many with children under the age of 18. The majority of readers are also employed outside the home.[33]

The editorial fare offered by the *Journal* under Blyth seems to be appealing to its readership. After more than a decade of substantial circulation decreases, the magazine is holding its own. While others of the "Seven Sisters," the mass circulation women's magazines,[34] have witnessed substantial decreases in readership, the *Journal* remains at the 5 million circulation figure, the same as 1985.[35] Moreover, the *Journal*, now part of the Meredith Corp., may also be facing a brighter advertising future. Meredith now offers combination discounts when companies advertise in both the *Ladies' Home Journal* and *Better Homes and Gardens*,* another Meredith property.

Notes

1. Grace Lichtenstein, "Feminists Demand 'Liberation' in *Ladies' Home Journal* Sit In," *New York Times*, March 19, 1970, p. 51; "Ladies' Journal has 'Lib' Section," *New York Times*, July 28, 1970, p. 13; "*Ladies' Home Journal* Gets Its Second Woman Editor," *New York Times*, October 11, 1973, p. 60.

2. Edward W. Bok, "The Story of the *Journal*," November 1893, p. 13.

3. May 1884, p. 4; October 1884, p. 4; December 1885, p. 6; July 1886, p. 6; November 1889, p. 10.

4. January 1884, p. 4.

5. "Editorial Notes," April 1884, p. 4.

6. "Editorial Notes," June 1884, p. 4.

7. February 1884, p. 4; premium supplement, July 1884.

8. November 1886, p. 8.

9. Reprint of *New York Journalist*, October 23, 1887, in "The *Ladies' Home Journal*," December 1887, p. 5.

10. Salme Harju Steinberg, *Reformer in the Marketplace: Edward W. Bok and the* Ladies' Home Journal (Baton Rouge: Louisiana State University, 1979), p. 7.

11. Bryan Holme, *The Journal of the Century* (New York: Viking Press, 1976), p. 7.

12. Steinberg, *Reformer in the Marketplace*, p. 68.

13. "How Women Can Be Good Americans," July 1903, p. 16; "A Few Words to the WCTU," September 1904, p. 16.

14. "Suppose America Does Go 'Dry,' " February 1917, p. 9.

15. Steinberg, *Reformer in the Marketplace*, pp. 107–111.

16. Ibid., pp. 119–120.

17. Elizabeth Jordan, "New Women Leaders in Politics," December 1920, pp. 6–7, 192; Elizabeth Jordan, "Women in the Presidential Campaign," October 1920, pp. 3–4, 38.

18. "Equal Rights," July 1929, p. 22.

19. "It's Up to the Women," January 1932, p. 3; "Pocketbook Patriotism," February 1932, p. 3.

20. "How the *Journal* Runs," May 1949, p. 214.

21. "We Must All Care," December 1936, p. 4; "How the *Journal* Runs," p. 214.

22. Rose Wilder Lane, "Woman's Place Is in the Home," October 1936, p. 94; Clifford D. Adams, "Making Marriage Work," February 1949, p. 26; Roger Butterfield, "Meet a Steelworker's Family," February 1949, pp. 133–138, 195; Henry B. Safford, "Tell Me, Doctor," November 1952, p. 35, and December 1952, p. 93.

23. Holme, *The Journal of the Century*, p. 8; J. C. Furnas, *How America Lives* (New York: Henry Holt, 1941), p. 5.

24. Margaret Parton, "Unwed Mothers on Relief," October 1962, pp. 28, 30, 32, 34; special issue June 1964.

25. Henry Raymont, "Curtis Magazines Lose Top Editors," *New York Times*, April 30, 1969, p. 44; "Downe Communications," *New York Times*, May 24, 1969, p. 55.

26. Mrs. Medgar Evers, "Black Christmas," December 1968, p. 83; Holme, *The Journal of the Century*, p. 10.

27. "Editor's Diary," February 1971, p. 12.

28. "Editor's Diary," January 1974, p. 2.

29. February 1978, pp. 146–152.

30. Leonard Sloane, "Charter to Sell 3 Publishing Interests," *New York Times*, July 9, 1982, p. D4; "Meredith Buys *Ladies' Journal*," January 4, 1986, p. 33.

31. Audit Bureau of Circulations, Magazine Publisher's Statement, *Ladies' Home Journal*, Average Paid Circulation, for six months ending December 31, 1992.

32. Percentage based on "*Ladies' Home Journal* Editorial Breakdown," Media Kit.

33. "A Profile of the *Ladies' Home Journal* Readers," 1992, Media Kit.

34. *Better Homes and Gardens, Family Circle, Redbook, Woman's Day, McCall's*, and *Good Housekeeping*. Only *Good Housekeeping* did not suffer a circulation reduction from 1985 to 1993. "A Historical Perspective of Circulation Performance Rate Base Circulation, 1985–1993," Media Kit.

35. Ibid.

Information Sources

BIBLIOGRAPHY:

"Downe Communications." New York *Times*, May 24, 1969, p. 55.

Furnas, J. C. *How America Lives*. New York: Henry Holt, 1941.

Holme, Bryan (ed.). *The Journal of the Century*. New York: Viking Press, 1976.

"*Ladies' Home Journal* Gets Its Second Woman Editor." *New York Times*, October 11, 1973, p. 60.

Lichtenstein, Grace. "Feminists Demand 'Liberation' in *Ladies' Home Journal* Sit In." *New York Times*, March 19, 1970, p. 51.

"Meredith Buys *Ladies' Journal*." *New York Times*, January 4, 1986, p. 33.

Raymont, Henry. "Curtis Magazines Lose Top Editors." *New York Times*, April 30, 1969, p. 44.

Sloane, Leonard. "Charter to Sell 3 Publishing Interests." *New York Times*, July 9, 1982, p. D4.

Steinberg, Salme Harju. *Reformer in the Marketplace: Edward W. Bok and the* Ladies' Home Journal. Baton Rouge: Louisiana State University Press, 1979.

Wood, James Playsted. *Magazines in the United States: Their Social and Economic Influence*. New York: Ronald Press, 1949.

INDEX SOURCES: Abridged Readers' Guide to Periodical Literature; Consumers Index; Health Index; Magazine Index; Readers' Guide to Periodical Literature; Text on Microfilm.

LOCATION SOURCES: Library of Congress and other libraries; Dialog.

Publication History

MAGAZINE TITLE AND TITLE CHANGES: *Ladies' Home Journal* (1883–present).

VOLUME AND ISSUE DATA: Vols. 1–(December 1883–present). Monthly (1883–1910); semimonthly (1910–1911); monthly (1911–1961); 11 times (1962); 10 times (1963); 11 times (1964); monthly (1965–present).

PUBLISHER AND PLACE OF PUBLICATION: Curtis Publishing Co. (1883–1968); Downe Communications (1968–1978); Ladies' Home Journal Publishing Inc. (1978–1982); Family Media Inc. (1982–1986); Meredith Corp. (1986–present). Philadelphia (1883–1968); New York (1968–present).

EDITORS: Louisa Knapp (1883–1890); Edward W. Bok (1890–1919); H. O. Davis (1919–1920); John E. Pickett, managing editor (1920); Barton W. Currie (1920–1928); Loring A. Schuler (1928–1935); Bruce Gould and Beatrice Gould (1935–1962); Curtiss Anderson (1962–1964); Davis Thomas (1964–1965); John Mack Carter (1965–1973); Lenore Hershey (1973–1981); Myrna Blyth (1981–present).

CIRCULATION: ABC, 1993: 5,138,168 (paid, primarily subscriptions).

Kathleen L. Endres

THE LADIES' REPOSITORY

A detailed argument published in 1856 accused Leonidas Lent Hamline of seducing and having an affair with a woman other than his wife. Hamline's sensuality was blamed, in part, for causing insanity early in his life. He was mentally, if not morally, deranged, his accuser said.[1] The affair was to have taken place while Hamline was the first editor of *The Ladies' Repository and Gatherings of the West* and before he became bishop of the Methodist Episcopal Church.

Hamline, who, after retiring as bishop in 1852, admitted to having a drinking problem, was one of the more colorful, though not necessarily most controversial, of the editors to lead the staid, church-sponsored women's magazine.

Women of the mid-nineteenth century looked to Queen Victoria of England as their symbol. "That the world's most powerful empire should be ruled by a woman affected profoundly not only the way of life in that country, but also in America."[2] Women became willing recipients of efforts toward their enlightenment.

The number of women's magazines nationwide was increasing, particularly after 1830, and their content had a "remarkable sameness"—a crusading zeal, poetical, sentimental, fictional, and biographical.[3] The publications, except the newspapers, of the period were dominated by "uplift matter"—sectarian religion, personal moral reform, improvement of manners, education, and culture. "The reader was called upstairs to a higher life than his fluid desires provided."[4] To the writers and readers of women's magazines, "success meant just one thing: marriage and living happily ever afterward. The exceptions to this were few."[5]

Mortality among these periodicals was high. Some flourished, however, and the most successful of these was *The Ladies' Repository and Gatherings of the West.*[6] "For longevity and circulation there was no publication west of the [Appalachian] mountains comparable to the *Repository.*"[7] The magazine, the most elaborate literary periodical in the West, was published by the Western Book Concern, which was established by the Methodist Episcopal Church in 1820. It was one of the most important publishing houses in Cincinnati, Ohio, a city of only 48,000 in 1841 yet a hub of periodical literature. There were seven daily newspapers, 14 other papers, and nine monthly publications. It is not surprising that such a magazine would rise in the West, which was less bound by tradition than the more established and rigid East.

The subtitle, *and Gatherings of the West,* suggested the regional foundation of the publication. The principal writers of the West, mostly Ohioans, and, in fact, many of the best writers of the country contributed to this magazine.[8] The subtitle was dropped in 1848, but the *Ladies' Repository* remained a magazine of the Midwest, the concentration of Methodist power.

The *Repository* was started at the suggestion of Samuel Williams, an eminent layman of the Cincinnati area, who told the 1840 Methodist General Conference that Christian women, including Methodist women, needed an alternative to the worldly *Godey's Lady's Book** and *Snowden's Lady's Companion.** The *Repository* was designed to compete for eye appeal with *Godey's.* It was printed on quality paper and embellished with detailed engravings of the Cincinnati countryside and natural wonders of America, used a new type, and was stitched in a neat, colored cover.[9]

The *Repository* was "the most important western magazine for ladies."[10] While competing in eye appeal with *Godey's*, the magazine had different editorial intentions. Instead of teaching women to dance, sing, and flirt, the *Repository* contained earnest essays of a moral nature, poetry, articles on historical and scientific affairs, and book reviews. The *Christian Advocate and Journal* hailed the publication as "something rich."[11]

The publication sought to:

> point out the religious duty of females to God, and to others and to themselves; help women perform these duties; exemplify female virtue through the publication of female biography of high order; give short discussions on "some appropriate text;" and encourage domestic economy.[12]

Reading matter for children, husbands, sons, and fathers was included. One early subscriber wrote that she intended to "convince [females] that the 'Ladies' Repository' is far preferable to the [Godey's] Ladies' Book [*sic*]."[13]

Unlike in similar publications, its first four editors would not accept fiction. Articles had to be based on fact found either in the sciences or in the Bible. Unlike other women's magazines of the period, the *Ladies' Repository* did not emphasize that a woman's place was in the home. It was more concerned about educating men and women alike. "We do not intend simply to make the work a lady's parlor book, but hope to render it useful to every member of every family," a December 1851 issue reported. It was dedicated to overcoming the "morbid taste of the fashionable world."

"The serious, contemplative, even funereal climate into which the reader steps on opening the *Repository* may be anticipated."[14] The magazine was similar to others of the period in reflecting a nineteenth-century gentility. Historian Frank Luther Mott commented:

> In its best days, the *Ladies' Repository* was an excellent representative of the Methodistic mind and heart. Its essays, sketches and poems (which now seem quaint and stilted), its good steel engravings, and its careful moral tone give it a character of its own, and a pleasant, though slightly musty, fragrance.[15]

Awarding of the editorship of the magazine was generally well thought out by the Methodist Church, which was based in the East. It was not unusual that a man would hold the editorship of a women's periodical. However, appointments were not without controversy. In the 1876 selection process, a woman placed second on the first ballot. Frances E. Willard, founder of the

Women's Christian Temperance Union, dropped to fourth on the second ballot and lost on the third ballot to Daniel Curry, who would be the last *Repository* editor.

The magazine was a place for a Methodist minister, who kept his regular pastoral duties, to establish a power base for advancement in the church. In fact, four of the eight editors in the magazine's 36-year history became bishops, indicating the class of the men who filled the position. One editor noted the "rush for the vacant [editorship] because it was considered a regular route to the episcopacy." Not interested in being bishop, Erastus Wentworth offered to step aside if someone else felt a "divine call in that direction." Though most editors reported not seeking the editorship, lobbying did occur, and inevitably the successful candidate humbly accepted the appointment. Only one, William Clark Larrabee, really did not want the job, holding it for six months before the Methodists found a replacement.

The first editor was a lawyer by education. A native of Connecticut, Leonidas Lent Hamline spent much of his ministry in Ohio before tackling his literary assignments. The magazine was an experiment in the developing Methodist Church press. Few writers in the church were interested in supporting periodical literature, and fewer still were familiar with the demands of such an enterprise. The publishing house was poor, and payment for contributions was little known. Work essentially was volunteered. Consequently, Hamline not only edited the publication but wrote most of it in its early years. "This was deplored by the editor of the *Western Christian Advocate*, who pointed out that writing '32 pages . . . in small print' was too much for any man—especially since it consisted largely of advice to women."[16] Hamline was the "man that gave character to the *Repository*. He gave it form and fashioned it after a pure model."[17]

Hamline's purpose from the start was to educate both sexes. "No periodical published by the Methodist Episcopal Church ever called out a greater amount and variety of literary and religious talent in the sphere of popular journalism than has the *Ladies' Repository*, and none has exerted greater influence in molding and elevating character."[18] Hamline and his successors exhorted readers to promote the magazine and find additional subscribers. Because there was no advertising in the publication, it depended on subscriptions to pay its way.

At the General Conference of 1844, Hamline was elected as bishop of the church, and the friends of the Reverend Edward Thomson, a native of England, nominated him as editor. Thomson, a doctor by training, practiced medicine in Ohio, was an agnostic, converted to Methodism when he was 22, and joined the ministry. Considered more of an essayist than an editor, Thomson became known as a good writer through his articles in church periodicals.

The appointment of Thomson, a westerner, changed the direction of the publication—moving it toward a more liberal philosophy than that espoused by easterners. Thomson, a vocal antislavery advocate who refused to obey the fugitive slave law, used the magazine as a bully pulpit from which to support the government and to denounce slavery in the South. As the country rushed headlong toward civil war, so, too, was the Methodist church experiencing a break between its northern and southern branches. But Thomson deplored strife, seeking compromise instead. He wore the moderate cloak more comfortably than the radical garb easterners put him in.

Thomson saw the opportunity to be editor as a chance to preach to a larger audience than his education assignments had provided. Though the magazine was having an impact, surpassing other Methodist publications, it suffered from lack of prestige and subscriptions.

Thomson brought the same characteristics of diligence and perseverance he had shown in other positions. He had a fondness for writing, but in order to fill the publication, Thomson borrowed material from other publications, along with writing many of the articles himself. "The publication was in many ways daring and independent. . . . The content was not superficial but challenging. . . . More significant was the view that women are intelligent and literate and deserved to be recognized—under the tutelage of men, of course."[19]

The magazine grew in popularity. Thomson, the youngest *Repository* editor at 34, served only two years before the Ohio Wesleyan University trustees, who had named him president in 1842, demanded that he move to Delaware, Ohio, to take control of the school, which he did in 1846.

In August 1846, the Reverend Benjamin Franklin Tefft, a professor of Greek and Hebrew languages at Indiana Asbury University (now DePauw University), became the third editor to oversee the *Ladies' Repository*.

Tefft was called by the *Cincinnati Gazette* "one of the finest belles-lettres scholars we have among us, and a gentleman warmly devoted to the cultivation of a pure and classic literature."[20] Beginning in 1851, the magazine published a piece of music with each issue until 1855. At this time, there were two steel plate engravings in each issue. In his farewell to readers, Tefft said, "I took to transform the Western Book Concern from a book selling to a book publishing establishment." The business side of the Book Concern was the responsibility of agents, who reported directly to the Methodist Conference. Editors of specific magazines often found themselves active in other magazines of the Concern or as editors of books they or others wrote.

Tefft admitted that as a result of all his activities with the Concern, he did not devote much time to the quality of the magazine, because two-thirds of his time was spent with the publishing side of the Concern. However, he noted with some pride that the circulation of the magazine had grown during his tenure, saying that it stood at 3,000 at the end of Hamline's tenure; 5,000 when Thomson departed; and 17,000 by the end of his. The circulation "is proof enough that the *Repository* is destined to live, and do greater things hereafter for the cause of piety, purity, and truth."

After three successful editors, it is curious that the Methodists failed in their next appointment—that of the Reverend William Clark Larrabee. At the time of his selection as editor in 1852, Larrabee, a native of Maine, was a professor of mathematics and natural science at Indiana Asbury University. During the time he was editor, Larrabee, who is regarded as the founder of the public school system in Indiana, was the first state superintendent of public instruction in the state.

As other editors before and after him, Larrabee, who contributed writings to the magazine, did not actively seek the position. But unlike other editors, once appointed, he made every effort to get out of the position. He admitted in an "Editor's Table" in January 1853, his last issue, that he had visited the magazine's office only once a month and that the publication was largely put out by Erwin House, an assistant editor at the Western Book Concern.

The Book Committee of the General Conference met November 10, 1852, to select Larrabee's successor, Davis Wasgatt Clark, whose name would first appear in the February 1853 issue. If Thomson began the process of turning the *Ladies' Repository* to a more liberal and active magazine, Clark, the fifth editor, completed it. His 11-plus years as editor, the longest of any editor, were pivotal to the magazine's success and impact.

The Maine native "as a writer was clear, exact, and forcible."[21] A lifelong Methodist, Clark developed an antislavery position early in life, espousing it in his contributions to the *Christian Advocate*, *Northern Christian Advocate*, and *Christian Advocate and Journal*. He called the national Fugitive Slave Act contrary to the law of God and principles of natural justice and became the standard-bearer of the moderate Methodist antislavery movement.

Clark always had a clear idea of what he (and the church) wanted in a women's magazine.

> To impart solid intelligence, to beget habits of thought, to improve the taste, to refine and invoke the heart; . . . to cultivate the expansive virtues of the Christian faith. . . . It must be . . . attractive, lively, chaste, and instructive. . . . Strong and muscular thought must be combined with the charms of a chaste literature, and the whole must be permeated with the spirit of a pure and holy faith.

He aimed the publication at the whole family, because he thought that was what nineteenth-century church women wanted.

The six months of Clark's predecessor had hurt the magazine, as it seemed to founder and lose its way. Circulation dropped. It was Clark's job to revitalize the *Ladies' Repository*. Clark thought readers wanted more than sermons and biblical instruction written by ministers. They desired useful and enjoyable material. In order to grow, the magazine had to be "intrinsically valuable," Clark said, "worth being sought after."

The writing had to improve significantly, Clark said, "something more racy, life-like, attractive," with "originality, piquancy, force, attractiveness." Clark wanted the *Ladies' Repository* to become a "moving panorama of life." To improve marketability, Clark abandoned a long-held policy of not accepting fiction. However, the fiction had to have a moral lesson. He also sought out experienced writers and spent time and money to improve the quality of the engravings in the magazine, which had always used illustrations. The engravings and writing had to be original; Clark rejected reprinting material from other publications. He also convinced the Western Book Concern to increase the number of pages from 40 to 64 and to use better-quality paper and graphics at no extra cost to the readers. He was successful. By 1855, circulation topped 20,000; in 1856, it reached 29,580; in 1859, it was 33,400; and on the eve of the Civil War it exceeded 40,000, making it the second largest Methodist publication in the United States. It lost some circulation during the war and raised its price from $2 to $3.50.

Like Thomson before him, Clark used his position as a broad pulpit from which to preach. He had much to say about the Civil War and President Lincoln's directing of it. The war, explained in terms of religion and morality, was a fight for religious freedom as well as national survival. For Clark and the *Ladies' Repository*, the Civil War was a holy war.

The magazine was affected by the war in other ways. Its August 1863 issue was delayed because one of Morgan's raids put Cincinnati under martial law. The magazine's title page reflected its dedication to the cause. It showed a woman holding a U.S. flag standing next to a rock labeled "Constitution." The magazine's name was in stars and bars.

> The magazine sent Northern forces into battle: with a prayer on their lips and God in their hearts. If they fell in battle, they were promised eternal salvation. . . . Just the opposite was true of Southern soldiers, who fought for sin, heresy and decadence, which could be found in every aspect of Southern life, including the Methodist Church South, whose ministers had perverted God's teaching.[22]

Clark wanted readers to help the Union cause by doing more than staying at home and praying. He wanted women to mold public opinion by becoming politically involved, a new and controversial role not normally open to females. He wanted women to step out of their traditional spheres and influence the government to vigorously pursue the war and quickly free the slaves.

Clark and Thomson before him had been considered radicals in their political philosophies, but eventually the church came around to their view. Both were elected bishops at the General Conference of the Methodist church in 1864.

Finding a successor to the innovative Clark who could maintain the popularity of the magazine was a matter of serious interest to the General Conference. Clark had developed the magazine into the "one periodical in which the Church, in all parts of the country, had a common interest,"[23] except the South, of course. It was a modern, vital magazine appealing to Christian women. "Clark showed that church journalism could be dynamic and appealing to a wide range of readers."[24] The successor would have the difficult task of keeping the same quality and popularity of the magazine. It had grown to be not only the most widely circulated magazine in the Midwest but one of the largest women's periodicals in the nation. Delegates, who at one point considered delaying the appointment, recognized immediately the difficulty they were going to have.

They selected Isaac William Wiley, a Pennsylvania native who had graduated from the University of New York and, like Thomson, studied medicine. He was not widely known in the church. Wiley was a missionary to China and had appeared infrequently in the church press. As a result, Wiley did not bring extensive editorial experience to the office. "To those who study Methodism from without, this custom of intrusting the interests of an important paper or magazine to one who is without editorial experience must seem somewhat perilous."[25] Six of the 12 editors named to church publications in 1864 did not have editorial experience.

Wiley's appointment represented a move toward the right of center, under the control of eastern philosophy, and away from the more radical leanings of Clark and the westerners. With the end of the Civil War, the *Ladies' Repository* lost one of its major issues. However, the disposition of freed slaves, uniting of the splintered church, and squelching the demon rum became the issues Wiley addressed. Wiley was expected to be forceful and popular in his writing. It was an exacting, delicate, and difficult position.

Daniel Curry, who would become the last editor of the *Ladies' Repository*, evaluated Wiley's tenure:

> When it passed into the hands of Dr. Wiley, though somewhat changed in its character, it was still an able and instructive magazine. The decline in its circulation during his term of office was certainly not the result of a corresponding deterioration in the character of the publication—but to a change in the public taste, and to the better character of other periodicals, both those of the Church and those of the secular press.[26]

A large part of Clark's success was his aggressiveness in pursuit of readers and a willingness to compete against other publications. Unlike Clark, Wiley did not understand his audience. Where Clark and his predecessors promoted the magazine for the entire family as well as urging women to expand their interests outside the home, Wiley did the opposite. "Surely the duties and responsibilities of wife and mother are occupation enough for any woman."

Magazine literature for a number of years had formed two distinct classes—

illustrated and nonillustrated. Partly because of the war, the taste for immediate woodcut engravings in illustrated magazines increased. The high-quality steel engravings used by the *Repository* were artistically excellent but lacked popular interest. Woodcuts attracted general readers to the stories they illustrated that steel engravings could not. To reach that audience, woodcuts appeared in the *Repository* from 1869 to 1872.

Wiley, who also chaired the Committee on the Book Concern for the General Conference, allowed the publishers to change the magazine, essentially giving up some measure of editorial control and turning a deaf ear to the wants of the readers. Wiley decided not to compete in the general market. That decision sounded the death knell for the *Ladies' Repository*. Wiley thought that the church demanded a religious magazine and that such a publication would be generously supported, but he failed to see that he was limiting his audience and subscriptions, thus hurting the magazine financially. Before Wiley could pursue his plans for the magazine, which had increased its pages to 80, he was elected bishop in 1872. His eight-year tenure as editor was second only to Clark's in length.

By the time the General Conference named Connecticut native Erastus Wentworth as editor in July 1872, the *Repository* was well on the road to decline. A teacher of natural science, college president, and missionary, Wentworth reduced the page size and did away with the "ugly woodcuts," though he added serial fiction and art notes. Four years later, Wentworth's leadership was rebuked by the General Conference. Though he sought reappointment, it was clear on the first ballot in 1876 that Wentworth would not remain as editor. He placed fourth on a ballot of six candidates, finishing behind, of all people, a woman.

In the face of declining popularity and financial losses of its most popular publication, the General Conference in 1876 ordered a committee to consider the propriety of making changes in the *Ladies' Repository* to make it a magazine of wider interest and more extended usefulness. One delegate said the best they could do was to make the magazine what its name purported to be and elect a woman as editor. Another said the name was a "millstone about its neck." Women did not want a ladies' magazine. Others questioned why the church was trying to compete with general circulation magazines like *Scribner's* and *Harper's*. Neither man nor woman could save the publication. "The *Ladies' Repository* is as sure of death as death itself. It has now a galloping consumption."

After a long debate, delegates appointed Daniel Curry, a former educator and editor of *The Christian Advocate*, as editor in July 1876. Curry, the oldest person at 67 to serve as editor, blamed Wentworth, in part, for the *Repository*'s condition, saying he had refused to listen to readers. The magazine was in moribund condition and was passed to Curry to be killed or made alive with different literary material and a different form. Curry reintroduced woodcuts, used the same type and paper, and expanded the publication to 96 pages.

The changes apparently had a dramatic effect, but perhaps not in the way the church anticipated. Readers were left wondering what was to become of their magazine. An August 1876 issue admitted the publication's future was uncertain. The magazine was barely self-supporting, and circulation had dropped to 10,000.

By the end of 1876, the magazine's name was changed to *The National Repository*, but it remained monthly and devoted its pages to general and religious literature for the entire family. But differences between the publishers and the editor became evident. Curry wrote that "more money and a broader policy were needed" for a successful magazine, but "the publishers chose to pursue the old and beaten track." Curry continued as editor until the General Conference of 1880 voted to discontinue publication of *The National Repository*. The *Ladies' Repository*, the jewel of Methodist Episcopal journalism, died.

Virginius Hall concluded that here was a "periodical with body, and a bouquet. Cointreau is not my favorite liqueur, but it seems preferable to some of the raw corn now coming off the press."[27]

Notes

1. L. D. Harlan, *Case of Bishop Hamline Explained; His Lunacy, etc., etc.* (Cincinnati: A. Watson, 1856).

2. James Penn Pilkington, *The Methodist Publishing House, A History* (New York: Abingdon Press, 1968), p. 277.

3. Caroline John Garnsey, "Ladies' Magazines to 1850, The Beginning of an Industry," *Bulletin of the New York Public Library* 58:2 (February 1954), p. 80.

4. Virginius C. Hall, "To *The Ladies' Repository*," *Bulletin of Historical and Philosophical Society of Ohio*, Vol. 7:3 (July 1949), p. 188.

5. Garnsey, "Ladies' Magazines to 1850," p. 81.

6. The Universalist Church also published a *Ladies' Repository* under various names in Boston from 1832 to 1873.

7. Hall, "To *The Ladies' Repository*," p. 188.

8. Charles T. Greve, *Centennial History of Cincinnati and Representative Citizens*, Vol. 1 (Chicago: Biographical Publishing, 1904), p. 802.

9. Ibid.

10. Garnsey, "Ladies' Magazines to 1850," p. 80.

11. Pilkington, *The Methodist Publishing House*, p. 278.

12. Ibid.

13. Ibid., p. 279.

14. Hall, "To *The Ladies' Repository*," p. 189.

15. Frank Luther Mott, *A History of American Magazines, 1850–1865*, vol. 2 (Cambridge: Harvard University Press, 1938), p. 305.

16. Pilkington, *The Methodist Publishing House*, p. 279.

17. F. G. Hibbard, *Biography of Rev. Leonidas L. Hamline* (Cincinnati: Hitchcock and Walden, 1880), p. 98.

18. Ibid., p. 100.

19. Frederick A. Norwood, "Who Was Edward Thomson?" Unpublished manuscript, Ohio Wesleyan University, Office of Public Relations, July 1993.

20. Quoted, October 1850, p. 351.

21. Matthew Simpson, *Cyclopedia of Methodism* (Philadelphia: Louis H. Everts, 1880), p. 224.

22. Kathleen L. Endres, "Davis Wasgatt Clark," *Dictionary of Literary Biography*, vol. 79 (Ann Arbor, Mich.: Gale Research, 1989), p. 110.

23. Richard S. Rust, ed., *Isaac W. Wiley, A Monograph* (Cincinnati: Cranston and Stowe, 1885), p. 73.

24. Endres, "Davis Wasgatt Clark," p. 110.

25. Rust, *Isaac W. Wiley, A Monograph*, p. 75.

26. Ibid., pp. 80–81.

27. Hall, "To *The Ladies' Repository*," p. 189.

Information Sources

BIBLIOGRAPHY:

Endres, Kathleen L. "The Women's Press in the Civil War: A Portrait of Patriotism, Propaganda, and Prodding." *Civil War History* 30:1 (March 1984), pp. 31–53.

———."Davis Wasgatt Clark." *Dictionary of Literary Biography*, vol. 79. Ann Arbor, Mich.: Gale Research, 1989, pp. 107–111.

Garnsey, Caroline John. "Ladies' Magazines to 1850, The Beginning of an Industry." *Bulletin of the New York Public Library* 58:2 (February 1954), pp. 74–81.

Greve, Charles T. *Centennial History of Cincinnati and Representative Citizens*, vol. 1. Chicago: Biographical Publishing, 1904.

Hall, Virginius C. "To *The Ladies' Repository*." *Bulletin of the Historical and Philosophical Society of Ohio* 7:3 (July 1949), pp. 188–189.

Harlan, L. D. *The Case of Bishop Hamline Explained: His Lunacy, etc., etc.* Cincinnati: A. Watson, 1856.

Harmon, Nolan B., ed. *The Encyclopedia of World Methodism*, vol. 2, Nashville: United Methodist Publishing House, 1974.

Hibbard, F. G. *Biography of Rev. Leonidas L. Hamline*. Cincinnati: Hitchcock and Walden, 1880.

Leete, Frederick D. *Methodist Bishops*. Nashville: Parthenon Press, 1948.

Mott, Frank Luther. *A History of American Magazines*, vol. 1. New York: D. Appleton, 1930.

———. *A History of American Magazines*, vol. 2. Cambridge: Harvard University Press, 1938.

———. *A History of American Magazines*, vol. 3. Cambridge: Harvard University Press, 1938.

Pilkington, James Penn. *The Methodist Publishing House, A History*, vol. 1. New York: Abingdon Press, 1968.

Rust, Richard S. (ed.) *Isaac W. Wiley, A Monograph*. Cincinnati: Cranston and Stowe, 1885.

Simpson, Matthew (ed.) *Cyclopedia of Methodism*. Philadelphia: Louis H. Everts, 1880.

Stroup, J. Martin. "The Story of 'Mother' Stoner and the Making of a Bishop" (six-part series). *The [Lewistown, Pa.] Sentinel*, May 1964, clippings in the Methodist Collection, Archives, Ohio Wesleyan University, Delaware, Ohio.

Thomson, Edward. *The Life of Edward Thomson.* Cincinnati: Cranston and Stowe, 1885.
INDEX SOURCES: None.
LOCATION SOURCES: Ohio Wesleyan University Archives; Cincinnati Historical Society; and other libraries.

Publication History

MAGAZINE TITLE AND TITLE CHANGES: *The Ladies' Repository and Gatherings of the West: A Monthly Periodical Devoted to Literature and Religion* (1841–1848); *The Ladies' Repository: A Monthly Periodical Devoted to Literature and Religion* (1849–June 1872); *The Ladies' Repository: A Monthly Periodical Devoted to Literature, Art and Religion* (July 1872–1876); *The National Repository: Devoted to General and Religious Literature, Criticism and Art* (1877–1880).
VOLUME AND ISSUE DATA: Vols. 1–36 (January 1841–December 1876). Monthly.
PUBLISHER AND PLACE OF PUBLICATION: Western Book Concern, Methodist Episcopal Church. Cincinnati.
EDITORS: Leonidas Lent Hamline (1841–1844); Edward Thomson (1844–1846); Benjamin Franklin Tefft (1846–1852); William Clark Larrabee (1852–1853); Davis Wasgatt Clark (1853–1864); Isaac W. Wiley (1864–1872); Erastus Wentworth (1872–1876); Daniel Curry (1876).
CIRCULATION: magazine reports: 3,000 (1844); 5,000 (1846); 17,000 (1852); 40,000 (1862); 35,000 (1864); 10,000 (1876).

Paul E. Kostyu

LEAR'S

Lear's, founded as a style magazine "for the time of your life," carved out a niche for women who had outgrown *Vogue** and were too sophisticated for the "Seven Sisters."[1] In six years, it gained recognition for providing solid information, as well as entertainment, for its audience of affluent, educated women over 40.[2] Recognition was not enough, however, and the magazine ceased publication with its April 1994 issue.

Lear's had a tumultuous beginning, and much of the tumult is associated with its founder and first editor in chief, Frances Lear. Although she had worked on issues that concerned women and had formed an executive-search firm for the placement of women, she had no publishing experience. Still, she decided to devote $25 to $30 million of her $112 million divorce settlement from Hollywood producer Norman Lear to starting a magazine she named for herself. She has said she did no demographic studies before deciding to launch the magazine in 1988; she simply recognized there were no magazines for women like her.[3]

The magazine sold out its first printing of 475,000 copies in March 1988. It was a bimonthly for its first year and went monthly with its first-anniversary issue. Its audited circulation was 505,020 in 1993—91.2 percent in subscriptions.[4]

In the fifth-anniversary issue, Frances Lear defined the magazine she had envisioned:

> *Lear's* mission was—and still is—to be an entertaining and thoughtful magazine for women who are updating the way we think about ourselves, our country and the world around us. *Lear's* stands outside the tradition of women's magazines.[5]

Lear, known for her mercurial personality, oversaw a rapidly changing staff where some employees lasted only a few months. After four years, she moved to the position of founder on the masthead, from editor in chief, but her presence was still strong. Her photo appeared on the cover of the first- and fifth-anniversary issues (*"Lear's* at five: Frances Lear at 70''). She has said she did not intend to name the magazine for herself, but, after trying out other names, she eventually decided to go the route of other entrepreneurs, such as Malcolm Forbes.[6]

Lear's, which used the slogan "For the Woman Who Wasn't Born Yesterday'' on its premiere issue, both highlighted its orientation for women in their middle years and danced around the target age of its audience. Its Standard Rate and Data listing said *Lear's* "blends entertainment and information to present that which is good in this rewarding stage of life,'' without saying what that stage was.[7] Although *Lear's* 1993 media kit identified 35 to 54 as the "Lear's Years,'' Frances Lear bristled at the idea that the magazine was aimed at any age group. "I do not target any age; I never have,'' she said.[8]

Interestingly, it was not age that distinguished *Lear's* readers from those of many other women's magazines; it was affluence. *American Demographics* listed the median age of *Lear's* readers as 43.1, comparable to the age of readers of all the "Seven Sisters'' except *Redbook*.* By contrast, *Lear's* readers had twice the household income of that of the readers of the "Seven Sisters.''[9] This difference in demographics translated into the editorial content of *Lear's*, which, unlike the more traditional "Sisters,'' emphasized career over home. Closest to *Lear's* in demographics was the fashion magazine *Mirabella*.* By appealing to professional women in midlife, *Lear's* and *Mirabella*, according to *American Demographics*, were "poised to ride a huge demographic wave of aging baby boom women.''[10]

Despite that rosy prediction, *Lear's* financial situation was never secure. In 1990, *Lear's* dismissed 24 of 83 staff members, a move that Frances Lear said was required for financial reasons.[11] She predicted in 1990 that the magazine would show a profit in 1992, but it still was referred to as financially troubled in the trade press a year after that deadline.[12] In 1994, less than a month before the magazine folded, Frances Lear refused to discuss whether the magazine had ever made a profit.[13] At the time of *Lear's* closing, *New York* magazine estimated the losses were $500,000 an issue, or $6 million a year.[14]

The content of the magazine itself changed less in its first six years than staff producing it. Each month's issue was a mixture of feature stories on social and political issues of interest to women; profiles of newsmakers, including authors, government officials, and entertainers who were past 40; fiction; and essays. The "style" section was devoted to fashion, primarily designer clothes and cosmetics. Departments provided traditional women's magazine fare (beauty, health, travel, the arts, relationships, and horoscopes), along with those that defined *Lear's*: "Lunch," Frances Lear's Q&A column with a prominent person of interest to her; "Money & Worth," advice on investing; "Shopping," an essay; and "A Woman for *Lear's*," an interview with a woman who was not a celebrity but who embodied the attributes celebrated by Frances Lear.

Like *Mirabella*, *Lear's* was for women with beauty and brains, but *Mirabella* is a high-fashion magazine that also covers social issues, while *Lear's* was a lifestyle magazine that included fashion. *Lear's* also represented greater geographic diversity in its editorial than does the New York-oriented *Mirabella*. Most of *Lear's* diversity came from its "Woman for Lear's," which featured women ranging from a strategic planner for private schools, who lives in Tulsa, Oklahoma, to a conservationist in Edgecomb, Maine.

Frances Lear dismissed *Mirabella*, her competition, as "a contrived magazine to get fashion advertising—not comparable to *Lear's*." She described *Lear's* as "feminist, but not anti-men" and "the only magazine for intelligent, active, involved American women—women who like to read."[15]

She said the magazine was different from other women's magazines because it did not talk down to readers. It confronted difficult issues, as in its February 1992 cover story on incest, for which a half-million reprints were sold. "This was the first serious piece on incest," she said. "We opened it up in a responsible way."[16]

Lear said the magazine was significant because its founding marked the beginning of the end of the youth culture for baby boomers. The magazine, which brought some models out of retirement for its pages, redefined beauty, she said, as "character, experience and personality."

In its early years, *Lear's* used gray-haired models and those who clearly looked over 40. By 1993, issues revealed a shift to models who looked as if they were in their 30s. As *Lear's* blurred the age distinctions to reach a larger audience, gray-haired models all but disappeared from the fashion pages, even though they continued to appear in ads. Editor in chief Caroline Miller acknowledged in early 1993 that part of her mission was to make *Lear's* less about age.[17] A September 1993 redesign was heralded by Miller as giving the magazine a bolder and more energetic visual voice. "It reflects the fact that women who read *Lear's* are more confident, more accomplished, more influential, and more involved than ever before," Miller wrote.[18]

Most of the attention showered on *Lear's* in the magazine industry dealt with its flamboyant founder and questions of whether a magazine targeted to women in midlife would survive. In the academic community, *Lear's* was criticized for suggesting a link between financial worth and self-worth and for postponing, rather than enhancing, the transitions of aging. Its ads were cited as glamorizing the youth culture.[19] Frances Lear countered: "This is the farthest from the truth in my philosophy."[20]

Women's magazines traditionally rely on clothing and fragrance advertisers as their strongest categories of advertising, and those were important ones for *Lear's*, but the magazine surprised industry analysts at its launch because its strongest ad category was automotive.[21] The magazine also carried ads for financial planning, cosmetics, pharmaceuticals (especially estrogen replacement drugs), and liquor. "We talked about marketing to women before anyone else understood it," Frances Lear said.[22]

The first issue had 76 pages of ads in 206 pages—37 percent advertising. In the fifth-anniversary issue, advertising made up 41 percent of the book, but total pages were down to 138. Even with the increase, *Lear's* was still shy of the industry average of 48.4 percent advertising in consumer magazines.[23] At the end of 1993, *Lear's* was showing a decline in ad pages, and its rival, *Mirabella*, was showing an increase. Further, *Mirabella* had almost twice the advertising pages of *Lear's*.[24] Industry observers blamed the closing of *Lear's* on the decision to abandon the magazine's target age, a move that confused advertisers, on Frances Lear's management style and abrasive personality, which alienated advertisers and employees, and on Lear Publishing Co.'s position as a single-title company in the competitive women's/fashion category.[25]

Despite the decline in advertising, Frances Lear bypassed the magazine's finances in explaining in an early 1994 interview why she wanted to reposition *Lear's* as a personal finance magazine for women. It was time to change the magazine, she said, because women themselves had changed since the magazine was founded.

"I believe the most important need in women is information about money," she said. "Then it was becoming familiar with aging."[26] At the style magazine's closing three weeks later, Lear said she had decided at the last moment that a repositioning was not feasible.[27]

Despite its financially troubled history and short life span, *Lear's* awakened the industry to an important niche—educated, affluent, career-minded women over 40.

Notes

1. The "Seven Sisters": *Ladies' Home Journal*,* *Good Housekeeping*,* *Redbook*,* *Better Homes and Gardens*,* *McCall's*,* *Family Circle*,* *Woman's Day*.*

2. Bill Katz and Linda Sternberg Katz, *Magazines for Libraries* (New Providence, N.J.: R. R. Bowker, 1992).

3. *Current Biography Yearbook* (New York: H. W. Wilson, 1991).

4. *Magazine Publisher's Statement, Lear's* (Schaumburg, Ill.: Audit Bureau of Circulations, 1993)—average paid circulation for six months ending June 30, 1993.

5. Frances Lear, "Founder's Letter," March 1993, p. 8.

6. *Current Biography Yearbook.*

7. *Consumer Magazine and Agri-Media Rates and Data* (Wilmette, Ill.: Standard Rate and Data Service, September 1992).

8. Frances Lear interview, February 17, 1994.

9. Susan Kraft, "Window on a Woman's Mind," *American Demographics,* December 1991, pp. 44–50.

10. Kraft, "Window on a Woman's Mind," pp. 44–50.

11. Deirdre Carmody, "*Mirabella* vs. *Lear's*: Stylish Fight," *New York Times*, November 26, 1990, p. D8.

12. Carmody, "*Mirabella* vs. *Lear's*," "*Lear's* Does Executive Shuffle," *Folio*, June 1, 1993, p. 13.

13. Lear interview.

14. Jeanie Russell Kasindorf, "Still Very Crazy after All These Years," *New York*, March 28, 1994, pp. 78–84.

15. Lear interview.

16. Ibid.

17. Mary Huhn, *Lear*'s Looks to the Future with Eyes on Fortysomethings," *Mediaweek*, January 18, 1993, p. 4.

18. Caroline Miller, "*Lear's*: The New Look," Media Kit, September 1993.

19. Caroline Wang, "*Lear's* Magazine 'For the Woman Who Wasn't Born Yesterday': A Critical Review," *The Gerontologist* 28: 4 (April 1991), pp. 600–601.

20. Lear interview.

21. Patrick Reilly, "*Lear's* Second Issue Off and Running," *Advertising Age*, April 18, 1988, p. 28.

22. Lear interview.

23. "Relationship of Advertising to Editorial Pages in Consumer Magazines" (New York: Magazine Publishers Association, 1992).

24. Publishers Information Bureau figures reported in *Advertising Age*, January 3, 1994, p. 27.

25. Keith J. Kelly, "Innovative '*Lear's*' Sinks in Sea of Red Ink," *Advertising Age*, March 14, 1994, p. 3; Kasindorf, "Still Very Crazy after All These Years," pp. 78–84.

26. Lear interview.

27. "*Lear's* Magazine Is Closed," *New York Times*, March 11, 1994, p. D16.

Information Sources

BIBLIOGRAPHY:

Carmody, Deirdre. "*Mirabella* vs. *Lear's*: Stylish Fight." *New York Times*, November 26, 1990, p. D8.

Kraft, Susan. "Window on a Woman's Mind." *American Demographics*, December 1991, pp. 44–50.

Reilly, Patrick. "*Lear's* Second Issue Off and Running." *Advertising Age*, April 18, 1988, p. 28.

Wang, Caroline, "*Lear's* Magazine 'For the Woman Who Wasn't Born Yesterday': A Critical Review." *The Gerontologist* 28:4 (April 1991) pp. 600–601.

INDEX SOURCES: Readers' Guide to Periodical Literature; Women's Studies Abstracts.

LOCATION SOURCES: Library of Congress and other libraries.

Publication History

MAGAZINE TITLE AND TITLE CHANGES: *Lear's*.
VOLUME AND ISSUE DATA: Vols. 1–7 (March/April 1988–April 1994). Bimonthly
(March/April 1988–January/February 1989); monthly (March 1989–April 1994).
PUBLISHER AND PLACE OF PUBLICATION: Lear Publishing Co., Inc. New York.
EDITORS: Frances Lear (1988–1992); Caroline Miller (1992–1994).
CIRCULATION: ABC, 1993: 505,020 (paid, primarily subscriptions).

Ann B. Schierhorn

M

MADEMOISELLE

In 1938, *Mademoiselle* might have joined the legions of other failed magazines had Barbara Phillips, a Boston nurse, not been so unhappy with her looks. Editors at *Mademoiselle* treated her to a whirlwind New York shopping tour and a complete makeover. The resulting publicity revitalized circulation and scored an important success for the magazine's new editor, Betsy Blackwell.[1]

Blackwell's next idea became the cornerstone of *Mademoiselle*'s fame: let college women write and edit an issue of the magazine during summer vacation. This time the resulting publicity not only spurred the popularity of the magazine (circulation moved from 178,057 in May 1939 to 241,740 in August)[2] but also firmly linked *Mademoiselle* to an image of mentoring young college women who were not afraid of being both beautiful and intelligent.

From its launch in 1935, when it billed itself as "the magazine for smart young women," *Mademoiselle* sought to link brains with beauty in the minds of its readers. Its awards for fiction and poetry and its guest editor program brought prestige while furthering *Mademoiselle*'s intention to nourish "readers' minds as well as provide fashion and beauty information."[3]

Aimed at young women (originally 18–34, now 18–29), "*Mademoiselle* tried to be a completely rounded guide, philosopher, and friend to intelligent young women."[4] Yet, the magazine always placed itself firmly in the genre of fashion (later called "lifestyle") magazines. Its main appeal to advertisers has been that its readers "admire so many beautiful things. And acquire them."[5]

Mademoiselle approached serious subjects in its feature content, including articles relating to current events in politics and the arts, to stay current with the interests of its young female readers. "At the same time, this audience must not be allowed to forget its crucial role in the consumption of beauty and fashion products or *Mademoiselle*'s advertising might decline."[6]

The original publisher of *Mademoiselle* was Street & Smith, which had prospered in the nineteenth century as a publisher of dime novels and other popular, inexpensive publications, including the works of Horatio Alger, Jr., and reprints of books by Conan Doyle and Rudyard Kipling. Magazine publishing was familiar territory for Street & Smith; they brought out *Ainslie's* in 1898 and *Popular Magazine* in 1903. By the 1920s and 1930s, Street & Smith was a major publisher of pulp magazines. *Mademoiselle* represented a conscious effort to move into quality publishing, followed by *Charm* in 1941 and *Living for Young Homemakers* in 1947. By the end of the 1940s, Street & Smith had stopped publishing pulp magazines.[7]

The original idea of creating *Mademoiselle* apparently belonged to two editorial staffers at Street & Smith, F. Orlin Tremaine and Desmond Hall, who had in mind creating a junior *Vogue*.* With start-up costs funded by Street & Smith, the first issue, February 1935, "was such a flop that Editor Tremaine gave up and went back to Street & Smith. Editor Hall stayed on, but skipped the March issue entirely."[8] By 1937, Hall resigned, to be replaced by *Mademoiselle*'s fashion editor, the young Betsy Blackwell. By 1940, *Mademoiselle* (a monthly) was outselling *Vogue* and *Harper's Bazaar*.* (both published twice a month).[9]

This success established *Mademoiselle* as a magazine worth watching in the publishing industry. The May 1940 issue, with 159 pages of advertising, led all monthly magazines, tripling the May 1939 total of 54 pages. Its circulation rose from 16,000 in May 1935 to 97,000 in May 1938, almost doubling in a year to 178,000 in May 1939 and almost doubling again to 340,000 in May 1940.[10]

Famous stunts, like the Barbara Phillips makeover, were not the only reason for this early success. It resulted from a combination of the magazine's "emphasis on the 'younger generation' of women, and a great deal of 'leg work' by the magazine's staff in New York dress houses. . . . The magazine . . . has a tie-in with about 100 retail stores throughout the country . . . [and] the magazine has reader acceptance and wields considerable influence on stores."[11]

In August 1941, *Mademoiselle* started another famous tradition that furthered its image of pairing intelligent writing with articles on beauty and fashion: a short story contest. The first year it drew 2,492 entries from writers under 30, with the first prize of $500 going to a young man.[12] In 1943, the magazine started sponsoring an annual college forum, which brought together student speakers and politicians to discuss significant issues of the day.

From the early 1940s through the 1980s, *Mademoiselle* was remarkably stable in its editorial direction. It stood out from its competitors by developing a reputation for finding new talent, fostering the professional development of young women, and publishing exceptional fiction. The first published works of Joyce Carol Oates and Sylvia Plath appeared in *Mademoiselle*, along with fiction by authors such as James Baldwin, Flannery O'Connor, Barbara Kingsolver, Mona Simpson, Perri Klass, and Alice Munro.[13]

"There was a wonderful time in the fifties when Marguerita Smith was the fiction editor of *Mademoiselle* and published work by her sister, Carson McCullers, by William Faulkner, Tennessee Williams, Katherine Anne Porter, and a young writer she discovered, Truman Capote, as well as many others."[14] Perhaps the most famous fiction associated with *Mademoiselle* was only indirectly fostered by the magazine. Sylvia Plath's autobiographical novel, *The Bell Jar*, reported many unflattering details of her 1953 guest editor experiences. Plath's suicide attempt two months after her editorship ended also became associated with the magazine.[15] The drama of Plath's experiences at *Mademoiselle* only seemed to enhance its literary cachet, however.

Betsy Blackwell continued as its editor for 33 years, though the magazine was sold to Condé Nast when it bought Street & Smith in 1959 from the founding families.[16] When Edie Lock replaced Blackwell as editor in 1971, the magazine maintained its editorial course.

At a 1991 reunion of *Mademoiselle* staffers, Nancy Comer, who was at *Mademoiselle* from 1968 to 1980 and went on to become managing editor of *Mirabella*,* described the working climate at *Mademoiselle*:

> We shared a special, stimulating, exciting time; we were writing for ourselves, showing clothes we ourselves liked. We also shared a time of intellectual challenge, an interest in levels of writing not normally found in mass magazines. We published Truman Capote and Solzhenitsyn, and even though we said ''gal'' in some pieces, we were feminist before anyone used the word.[17]

Despite the editorial stability, during this time *Mademoiselle* gained a reputation for innovation. It became the first mainstream fashion magazine to break the color barrier. The August 1961 issue included ''a Negro girl . . . in the pages of a major fashion magazine for what is believed to be the first time.''[18] Willette Murphy, a June graduate of the University of California at Los Angeles, was selected from a group of students by a *Mademoiselle* editor and photographer for the traditional August feature on campus fashions.[19]

In 1972, *Mademoiselle*'s guest editor program reflected the changes occurring on college campuses when it selected two males to join its 18 female college editors. That same year the magazine stopped referring to its female college editors as ''girls'' and, at the visiting editors' insistence, reset a page to call them ''women.''[20]

In 1981, a year after Amy Levin Cooper became the third female top editor at *Mademoiselle*, the magazine was more successful than ever. Advertising pages increased 5 percent over the previous year, to 1,525, with revenues reaching $17 million. Circulation rose to 950,000 in August and topped 1 million by early 1982. Joseph Fuchs, the publisher, declared, ''It's our best year in 47 years.''[21]

Mademoiselle's success continued to rely on the nuts and bolts of beauty advice that complemented advertisers' interests. The advice, however, was often a potpourri of messages that suited the magazine's commercial purposes. An analysis of *Mademoiselle* issues from 1982 found the magazine sending contradictory messages to its young female readers. For example, articles about diet and exercise appear in the same issue with an article about the delights of ice cream, followed by an ad for Tab (a diet soft drink).

> Readers are to vacillate between eating and dieting. Regardless of these contradictions, the main purpose of the "Home and Food" section is fulfilled—to secure advertising revenue from the makers of food and home products for a magazine whose editorial material relates principally to beauty and fashion.[22]

A content analysis comparing the nonfiction in *Mademoiselle* with that in *Redbook** and *Ms.** from 1966 to 1974 found it did not substantially change its role portrayals of women to reflect societal changes. However, it did identify *Mademoiselle* as most consistently presenting "a balanced image of woman as homemaker, career person and individual."[23]

A decade later, Condé Nast showed interest in freshening the editorial approach to *Mademoiselle*. In September 1991, the president of Condé Nast Publications, Bernard Leser, appointed Julie Lewit-Nirenberg as publisher of the magazine, saying she "brings to *Mademoiselle* a new pair of eyes, new attitudes, a different personality."[24] He went on to emphasize that the appointment did "not have as its aim a change of direction" for *Mademoiselle*.[25]

Less than six months later, however, Lewit-Nirenberg announced that *Mademoiselle* would break with its own traditions and no longer publish fiction, at least "for the time being."[26] To distinguish itself from *Glamour*,* another Condé Nast publication, *Mademoiselle* was lowering its target age to women in their 20s, "too old for *Seventeen* and too young—or, too poor—for *Vogue*."[27] *Mademoiselle*, feeling the effects of an industrywide advertising slump, had its ad pages fall 16 percent in 1991, with its circulation holding at 1.1 million. A design change would accompany the change in editorial policy.[28]

For the next year, *Mademoiselle* experienced editorial upheaval. In October 1992, Amy Levin Cooper ended her 12-year editorship when she was replaced by Gabé Doppelt, who had been an associate editor for *Vogue*. The stories and layout reflected a more daring editorial style, including an article titled "Young Lesbians—They're Fresh, They're Proud. They're Comfortable with their Sexuality" and an article alerting readers to the carcinogenic dangers of hair dyes. Advertisers, known not to welcome articles critical of their products in fashion and lifestyle magazines, watched warily.[29]

Gabé Doppelt lasted exactly one year before she resigned due to "conceptual differences" with the chairman of Condé Nast, S. I. Newhouse.[30] Although ad pages had held even for the year, circulation was down 7.6 percent, with newsstand sales dropping 13.5 percent.[31] The changes in editorial policy were seen as too innovative, and Leser "made it clear that the time had come to rein in the magazine."[32] A vice president of an advertising agency responded to the change by saying, "*Mademoiselle* was always a little funkier than *Glamour* and younger than *Vogue*. . . . But maybe *Elle* has taken its place."[33]

On October 1, 1993, Elizabeth Crow, formerly editor in chief of *Parents** magazine, replaced Doppelt. Crow's task was to bring the magazine closer to the mainstream. "Any magazine of over one million circulation has to acknowledge that although it can be as edgy as all get out . . . it is a mass magazine. . . . Your focus should not be on a special segment of your audience."[34]

By the time Crow took over, *Mademoiselle* was starting to feel a negative reaction from advertisers to Doppelt's changes. Following the October and November issues, which were edited by Doppelt before she left, ad sales fell 18 percent in the first quarter of 1994,[35] including a 22.6 percent plunge in February.[36]

Despite the defection of advertisers, members of the "twentysomething" generation appear to be loyal. Circulation appears to be at least holding steady at 1.2 million, and Crow has set the circulation goal at 2 million.[37] If this goal is realized, it will approach the circulation of its closest competitors, *Glamour*, with 2.3 million, and *Cosmopolitan*,* with 2.6 million.[38]

Under Crow, *Mademoiselle* developed a new cover line, "Fashion-Beauty-Relationships."[39] In later issues, "Health-Fitness" was added. According to the *New York Times*, "Virtually everything in the magazine is new, and the emphasis is on relationships. It uses a question-and-answer format in six of its regular features—about love, men, sex, friends, work and money. Ms. Crow also likes first-person articles by women in their 20's because readers can identify with them."[40]

In January 1994, Condé Nast named James Truman, the 35-year-old editor of its magazine for young men, *Details*, to succeed Alexander Liberman as the company's editorial director. This followed by two weeks the replacement of Bernard Leser, the company's president, by Steven Florio, the former president of the *New Yorker*. Although the editorial director has only advisory power, *Mademoiselle* was expected to be among the first of the Condé Nast magazines to receive his attention.[41]

The discussions of new direction do not appear to include a return to the fiction and poetry contests or guest editorships of the earlier years of *Mademoiselle*. In 1994, "49 percent of its readers attended college, slightly less than *Glamour*'s 50 percent and just ahead of *Cosmo*'s 46 percent."[42] The strategies of attracting the young female audience have changed. Articles are organized under the cover line topics, with self-discovery and entertainment added. Virtually all articles offer advice or nonfiction information; most fit on one page. *Mademoiselle* appears to be maintaining its tradition of offering opportunities to women in the publishing industry. The listing of staff members reveals few male names, even among its advertising staff.

Times have changed since *Mademoiselle*'s guest editors stayed at the Barbizon Hotel. Has the magazine changed? An analysis of the magazine's content in the 1970s concluded: "Who is the American woman revealed in this fashion magazine? She is educated, ambitious, career-oriented, independent, successful and believes she should look well and fit; she has a full future ahead.''[43] As a young reader's magazine that celebrated its 60th anniversary in 1995, *Mademoiselle* pursued rejuvenation to determine and reflect its youthful audience's tastes.

Notes

1. "The Press," *Time*, April 15, 1940, p. 55.

2. Ibid.

3. Sarah Duffy Edwards and Kathryn McManus, *Mademoiselle* Fact Sheet, June 1994, p. 2.

4. Roland E. Wolseley, *Understanding Magazines* (Ames, Iowa: Iowa State University Press, 1965), pp. 259–260 as cited by Dorothy D. Prisco, "Women and Social Change as Reflected in a Major Fashion Magazine," *Journalism Quarterly* 59:1 (Spring 1982), p. 131.

5. Ellen McCracken, *Decoding Women's Magazines: From Mademoiselle to Ms.* (London: Macmillan, 1993), p. 150.

6. Ibid.

7. Theodore Peterson, *Magazines in the Twentieth Century* (Urbana: University of Illinois Press, 1964), pp. 200–201.

8. "The Press."

9. Ibid.

10. "Advertising News and Notes," *New York Times*, May 14, 1940, p. 34.

11. Ibid.

12. "Short Story Trend Noted in Contest," *New York Times*, March 31, 1942.

13. Deirdre Carmody, "*Mademoiselle* Is Seeking a Fashionable New Look," *New York Times*, February 3, 1992.

14. Amy Janello and Brennan Jones, *The American Magazine* (New York: Harry N. Abrams, 1991), p. 102.

15. "*Mademoiselle* Reunion," *New York Times*, February 27, 1979, sec. III, p. 6.

16. Peterson, *Magazines in the Twentieth Century*, p. 200.

17. Nadine Brozan, "Former Editors Reune," *New York Times*, November 20, 1991, p. B9.

18. "A Negro Student Models for Fashion Publication," *New York Times*, July 21, 1961, p. 26.

19. Ibid.

20. Angela Taylor, "Until Now, These Jobs Were Strictly for Coeds," *New York Times*, June 14, 1972, p. 52.

21. Philip H. Dougherty, "Advertising: 'Life Style' Magazines Prospering," *New York Times*, November 17, 1981, sec. 4, p. 30.

22. McCracken, *Decoding Women's Magazines*, pp. 149–150.

23. Carole Ruth Newkirk, "Female Roles in Non-Fiction of Three Women's Magazines," *Journalism Quarterly* 54:4 (Winter 1977), p. 782.

24. Eric Pace, "Chronicle," *New York Times*, September 19, 1991, p. B13.

25. Ibid.

26. Carmody, "*Mademoiselle* Is Seeking a Fashionable New Look," p. D8.

27. Ibid.

28. Ibid.

29. Patrick M. Reilly, "*Mademoiselle*'s Editor Tries the Look of the Twentysomething on for Size," *Wall Street Journal*, February 12, 1993, p. B8.

30. "*Mademoiselle* Editor Quits in Clash over Concepts," *Wall Street Journal*, September 30, 1993, p. B13.

31. Deirdre Carmody, "Top Editor Resigns at *Mademoiselle*," *New York Times*, September 30, 1993, p. D21.

32. Ibid.

33. Ibid.

34. Deirdre Carmody, "*Mademoiselle* Names a New Editor in Chief," *New York Times*, October 1, 1993, p. D16.

35. Meg Cox, "*Mademoiselle*'s New Editor Is Guiding Magazine's Return to the Mainstream," *Wall Street Journal*, February 7, 1994, p. A9.

36. Deirdre Carmody, "New Makeover for *Mademoiselle*," *New York Times*, March 21, 1994, p. D8.

37. Cox, "*Mademoiselle*'s New Editor Is Guiding Magazine's Return to the Mainstream."

38. Carmody, "New Makeover for *Mademoiselle*."

39. Ibid.

40. Ibid.

41. Meg Cox, "James Truman Gets Star Status at Condé Nast," *Wall Street Journal*, January 26, 1994, pp. B1, B12.

42. Carmody, "New Makeover for *Mademoiselle*."

43. Prisco, "Women and Social Change as Reflected in a Major Fashion Magazine," p. 134.

Information Sources

BIBLIOGRAPHY:

"Advertising News and Notes." *New York Times*, May 14, 1940, p. 34.

Brozan, Nadine. "Former Editors Reune." *New York Times*, November 20, 1991, p. B9.

Carmody, Deirdre. "*Mademoiselle* Is Seeking a Fashionable New Look." *New York Times*, February 3, 1992, p. D8.

———. "Top Editor Resigns at *Mademoiselle*." *New York Times*, September 30, 1993, p. D21.

———. "*Mademoiselle* Names a New Editor in Chief." *New York Times*, October 1, 1993, p. D16.

———. "New Makeover for *Mademoiselle*." *New York Times*, March 21, 1994, p. D8.

Cox, Meg. "James Truman Gets Star Status at Condé Nast." *Wall Street Journal*, January 26, 1994, pp. B1, B12.

———. "*Mademoiselle*'s New Editor Is Guiding Magazine's Return to the Mainstream." *Wall Street Journal*, February 7, 1994, p. A9.

Dougherty, Philip. "Advertising: 'Life Style' Magazines Prospering." *New York Times*, November 17, 1981, sec. 4, p. 30.

Janello, Amy, and Brennan Jones. *The American Magazine*. New York: Harry N. Abrams, 1991.

"*Mademoiselle* Editor Quits in Clash over Concepts," *Wall Street Journal*, September 30, 1993, p. B13.

"*Mademoiselle* Reunion." *New York Times*, February 27, 1994, sec. III, p. 6.

McCracken, Ellen. *Decoding Women's Magazines: From Mademoiselle to Ms.* London: Macmillan, 1993.

"A Negro Student Models for Fashion Publication." *New York Times*, July 21, 1961, p. 26.

Newkirk, Carole Ruth. "Female Roles in Non-Fiction of Three Women's Magazines." *Journalism Quarterly* 54:4 (Winter 1977), pp. 779–782.

Pace, Eric. "Chronicle." *New York Times*, September 19, 1991, p. B13.

Peterson, Theodore. *Magazines in the Twentieth Century.* Urbana: University of Illinois Press, 1964.

"The Press," *Time*, April 15, 1940, p. 55.

Prisco, Dorothy. "Women and Social Change as Reflected in a Major Fashion Magazine." *Journalism Quarterly* 59:1 (Spring 1982), pp. 131–134.

Reilly, Patrick. "*Mademoiselle*'s Editor Tries the Look of the Twentysomething on for Size." *Wall Street Journal*, February 12, 1993, p. B8.

"Short Story Trend Noted In Contest." *New York Times*, March 31, 1942, p. 25.

Taylor, Angela. "Until Now, These Jobs Were Strictly for Coeds," *New York Times*, June 14, 1972, p. 52.

Wolseley, Roland. *Understanding Magazines.* Ames, Iowa: Iowa State University Press, 1965.

INDEX SOURCES: Biography Index; Consumers Index; Health Index; Magazine Index; Media Review Index; Media Review Digest; Readers' Guide to Periodical Literature; TOM (Text on Microfilm).

LOCATION SOURCES: Columbia University: Journalism School Library, Teachers College Library; William Paterson College Sarah B. Askew Library; and other libraries.

Publication History

MAGAZINE TITLE AND TITLE CHANGES: *Mademoiselle.*

VOLUME AND ISSUE DATA: Vols. 1–(February 1935–present). Monthly (No number issued March 1935).

PUBLISHER AND PLACE OF PUBLICATION: Street & Smith (1935–1959); Condé Nast (1959–present). New York.

EDITORS: Desmond Hall and F. Orlin Tremaine (1935); F. Orlin Tremaine (1935–1937); Betsy Blackwell (1937–1971); Edie Lock (1971–1980); Amy Levin Cooper (1981–1992); Gabé Doppelt (1992–1993); Elizabeth Crow (1993–present).

CIRCULATION: ABC, 1993: 1,101,220 (paid, primarily subscriptions).

Diana Peck

THE MAGNOLIA: A SOUTHERN HOME JOURNAL

If he had tried, Charles Bailie could not have picked a worse time to start a southern "home journal." The North and South were waging a Civil War. Soon paper and the necessities of publishing would become scarce. Inflation would drive subscription costs sky-high. Militia duty would call editors away; as a result, publication delays would be inevitable.

At the time, however, it seemed like a logical idea. Although a variety of southern ladies' magazines had been started in the antebellum period,[1] none had achieved the success of the northern *Godey's** or *Peterson's,** the two largest circulating women's publications of the day. With the war raging and the mails disrupted between the sections, the time seemed right to start a newspaper for female readers in the Confederacy. Thus, on October 4, 1862, the weekly newspaper, *The Magnolia: A Southern Home Journal*, premiered in Richmond, the capital of the Confederacy.

Bailie never saw his newspaper as serving only one city. His was designed to be a ''national'' newspaper for Confederate women. In his opening editorial, he wrote, ''[W]e are anxious to circulate *The Magnolia* in every portion of the Southern Republic.'' Nonetheless, even Bailie realized that there might be economic problems ahead for his weekly. As he continued: ''In order to achieve this end [a circulation throughout the Confederacy] the terms of subscriptions are exceedingly low, considering the disjointed state of affairs which pervade every branch of human industry. Even the miserable paper which we are compelled to use, has more than doubled in value since the advent of 'gumvisaged' war.''[2] *The Magnolia*'s opening subscription price was in keeping with costs for women's periodicals throughout the nation. For $2.50 per year, the southern woman would receive a four-page weekly.[3]

Bailie had designed the paper to appeal to women. That message was clear from the nameplate to his weekly editorials. The nameplate showed a woman with pen in hand at a desk. She was surrounded by cherubs, dashing off with papers. His paper would also ''protect'' his female readers, providing the ''right'' type of reading material. Bailie promised, ''Nothing of a political or sectarian nature will be published, but every article must be of a highly moral tone.''[4] He was true to his word.

The Magnolia, under Bailie, was a chatty, informal exchange between the editor and his readers, who frequently contributed letters, short stories, and poetry. While Bailie avoided, as much as possible, news from the political arena, he did not ignore the war. Each week he carried news of campaigns and Confederate victories.[5] The war themes permeated the publication. Fiction became a propaganda tool—capturing all the romance of the war, the gallantry of the Confederate soldier, and the depravity of the Yankee. *Nellie Graves*, a serialized novel, showed how just one brave woman could ensure a Confederate victory— and romance.[6]

Bailie, however, had a limited view of what a Confederate woman should do to ensure victory—and his newspaper reflected that view. He perceived the Confederate woman's role primarily as a *passive* one. The soldiers fought gallantly primarily because the women back home were brave and kind and moral. ''Let it [southern female support] be ours, and we can brave the cannon's mouth or face danger in ten thousand forms.''[7]

Although the periodical received "flattering notices" from the press,[8] the weekly quickly faced a series of crises. On December 27, 1862, the weekly carried the announcement that its founder, Charles Bailie, had died from a disease contracted "in the memorable campaign on the Peninsula."[9]

In the next issue, however, the unnamed "new management" pledged to carry on *The Magnolia* and improve it, to make it a "literary representative of the Confederacy, and a fit companion for every Southern home."[10] That commitment seemed genuine. Soon the weekly sported a new size—and a new price. *The Magnolia* doubled in size—to eight pages—and almost tripled in price— to six dollars per year. The quality of the literature improved as well. William Gilmore Simms, one of the leading novelists of the Confederacy, contributed a novel to be serialized.[11]

W.A.J. Smith and Oakley P. Haines, the new owners, were behind the changes. The two had purchased *The Magnolia* and its 270 subscribers for $50 from the Bailie estate.[12] Haines acted as editor initially.

More changes were coming to the weekly. By March, *The Magnolia* had a new nameplate, a new name, and yet a higher price, ten dollars. *The Magnolia: A Southern Home Journal* became *The Magnolia: A Home Journal of Literature and General News*. The nameplate showed a more warlike woman with a helmet surrounded by globe, easel, writings, and books. She was the type of woman who might take an active part in a war effort. She would have been pleased with the new editorial direction of the weekly.

Unlike Bailie, whose editorials stressed a *passive* role for female readers, the new owners had a different vision of Confederate women. Beginning January 10, 1863, *The Magnolia* offered up-to-date political and military news in a new column, "Notes on the War." Although this column contained some criticism of the war and politicians, it reported primarily on the inevitable success that the Confederacy had to eventually attain. Or, as Haines predicted in March 1863, the summer would bring victory to the battlefield. " 'Weary of battle' are words unknown to the Southern camps—ever eager, ever anxious to press on, and fight, and fight, and fight, our soldiers cannot repress the spirit which inspires them any more than they can divest themselves of the indomitable nerve which Heaven has given them, to bare their bosoms to the battle, and pass the ordeal of privation and fatigue which falls to the lot of armies everywhere."[13]

However, by June, the editorial duties were wearing on Haines, who retired from *The Magnolia*. Smith brought in a new editor, James D. McCabe, Jr., a novelist, playwright, and contributor to *The Magnolia* since its first issue.[14] Like Haines, McCabe saw only success on the Confederate horizon. Or, as he wrote, "To us the issue does not seem doubtful. We cannot bring ourselves to believe that the God who has so long and so triumphantly upheld our cause, will permit the armies upon whose success so much depends to suffer defeat at the hands of our enemies."[15]

Beyond his staunch support for the Confederate cause, McCabe also did much to improve the literary quality of the journal itself. Simms contributed periodically, as did Edward S. Joynes, a well-known educator at William and Mary College who dabbled in fiction writing, and father-and-son authors John C. and William G. McCabe. Women contributors were more difficult to identify. As was the custom of the day, many female writers preferred that their names not be used. However, Mrs. Burton Harrison, a well-known post–Civil War short story writer, admitted in her autobiography that she had contributed to *The Magnolia*.[16]

Although the literary quality improved, the weekly was plagued with problems. Increased costs of paper and publishing meant yet another subscription rate increase; by the end of 1863, the cost doubled, to $20.[17] That was not the only problem facing the editor of *The Magnolia*. The July 18, 1863, issue was delayed because of militia duty.[18] This, however, represented only the beginning of the militia problems that editors of *The Magnolia* would face.

In early 1864, McCabe moved on, and young Charles P. Dimitry took over as editor. Dimitry, only 27, faced militia duty on a fairly regular basis because of new state regulations that made editors of religious and literary journals eligible for military work. The June 11, 1864, issue was delayed three weeks because of Dimitry's military duty "in defiance of all justice and governmental honor,"[19] he complained. Throughout 1864, Dimitry reported delays because of militia duty.[20] In late 1864, Dimitry observed that the state's requirement of military duty for editors of literary publications "has had the effect of retarding most seriously the prosperity of the organs of our Literature."[21] *The Magnolia* seemed to illustrate that comment. Although the founders and proprietors saw the weekly as a means to cultivate a southern literature, increasingly the weekly was relying on British works, including those by Charles Dickens and William Thackeray. By December 1864, the weekly was cut to four pages because of Dimitry's "almost constant employment on military duty."[22]

In 1865, the weekly came out irregularly, due no doubt to added militia duty as the war ground to a close. April 1, 1865, was *The Magnolia*'s last issue. However, even then, just eight days before General Robert E. Lee surrendered at Appomattox, *The Magnolia* remained a supporter of the Confederate cause— "[O]ur chances of success, so far as the question of battle is concerned, are at least as favorable as those of the enemy," wrote Dimitry.[23]

The Magnolia survived wartime inflation, paper shortages, and militia duty, but it could not survive peace and Union occupation. But for two and a half years, *The Magnolia* had served two important purposes: it was a valuable ally of the Confederate cause on the home front, and it was the solitary southern voice aimed specifically at women during the Civil War.

Notes

1. Bertha-Monica Stearns, "Southern Magazines for Ladies (1819–1860)," *South Atlantic Quarterly* 31:1 (1932), pp. 70–87.

2. "Editorial Chit Chat," October 4, 1862, p. 2. *The Magnolia* used a continuous page numeration throughout each volume.

3. October 4, 1862, p. 1.

4. "Our Paper," October 4, 1862, p. 2.

5. "The Winter Campaign," October 4, 1862, p. 2.

6. "Nellie Graves," November 29, December 6, and December 13, 1862.

7. T. J. M'C. "Woman," December 13, 1862, p. 42.

8. "Acknowledgments," October 18, 1862.

9. December 27, 1862, p. 50.

10. January 3, 1863, p. 54.

11. "Announcement," February 21, 1863, p. 82.

12. "The Close of the Volume," September 26, 1863, p. 320.

13. "Notes on the War," May 2, 1863.

14. McCabe was also a supporter of secession. For his attitudes, see James D. McCabe, Jr., *Fanaticism and Its Results: or, Facts versus Fancies, By a Southerner* (Baltimore: Joseph Robinson, 1860).

15. "Notes on the War," November 14, 1863, p. 52.

16. Mrs. Burton Harrison (Constance Cary), *Recollections Grave and Gay* (New York: Charles Scribners' Sons, 1911), pp. 118–119.

17. "To Our Patrons," November 28, 1863, p. 68.

18. "Delay in Our Paper," July 18, 1863, p. 240.

19. "To Our Subscribers," June 11, 1864, p. 260.

20. "The Magnolia Weekly—Its Third Year," October 1, 1864, p. 356; "To Our Subscribers," October 29, 1864, p. 13.

21. "The Magnolia Weekly—Its Third Year."

22. "To Our Subscribers and Patrons," December 10, 1864, p. 35.

23. "Notes on the War," April 1, 1865.

Information Sources

BIBLIOGRAPHY:

Harrison, Mrs. Burton (Constance Cary). *Recollections Grave and Gay*. New York: Charles Scribners Sons, 1911.

McCabe, James D., Jr. *Fanaticism and Its Results: Or, Facts Versus Fancies by a Southerner*. Baltimore: Joseph Robinson, 1860.

Stearns, Bertha-Monica. "Southern Magazines for Ladies (1819–1860)." *South Atlantic Quarterly* 31 (1932), pp. 70–87.

INDEX SOURCES: None.

LOCATION SOURCES: Harvard University Library and other libraries, primarily in the South.

Publication History

MAGAZINE TITLE AND TITLE CHANGES: *The Magnolia: A Southern Home Journal* (October 4, 1862–March 24, 1863); *The Magnolia: A Home Journal of Literature and General News* (March 31, 1863–April 1, 1865).

VOLUME AND ISSUE DATA: Vols. 1–3 (October 4, 1862–April 1, 1865). Weekly, but irregular cycle in 1865.

PUBLISHER AND PLACE OF PUBLICATION: Charles Bailie (October 4–December 1862); Haines & Smith (January 1863–June 1863); W. A. Smith (June 1863–January 1864); Smith & Barrow (January 1864–July 1864); Smith & Robertson (July 1864–April 1865). Richmond, Va.

EDITORS: Charles Bailie (October 4–December 1862); Oakley P. Haines (January–June
    1863); James D. McCabe, Jr. (June 1863–February 1864); Charles P. J. Dimitry
    (March 1864–April 1865).
CIRCULATION: Self-reported, 1862: 270; unreported after.

Kathleen L. Endres

THE MAGNOLIA; OR, SOUTHERN APALACHIAN

Philip C. Pendleton's career as a literary editor was short and to the point. It
lasted from January 1840 to June 1843, a tempestuous three-and-a-half-year
interlude when his journal lived constantly under the threat of collapse. The
publication, which started life in Macon, Georgia, as *The Southern Ladies' Book*,
was subsequently published under three titles and in three locations: from January 1840 until June 1840, it was issued through a publishing house in Macon,
Georgia. When this adventure proved unsuccessful, he moved the journal to
Savannah, Georgia, where it became *The Magnolia; or Southern Monthly*. In
its final transformation, it was published in Charleston, South Carolina, as *The
Magnolia; or, Southern Apalachian*. Until June 1840, Pendleton shared the editing duties with the Reverend George F. Pierce, a Methodist cleric and educator
who had a special interest in female education. With Pierce's departure, Pendleton assumed the editorial and publishing duties alone until January 1843. At
that time, he convinced William Gilmore Simms, the South's most prominent
literary figure, to assume the editorship. When Simms and Pendleton parted
company in June of that year, the journal ceased publication.[1]

   As the original title indicated, Pendleton and Pierce were determined to seek
out and publish the best literature that the South's womanhood had to offer. The
editors were convinced that the journal was a critical factor in their desire to
advance female education in the South.[2] In keeping with many other periodicals
with similar missions in both the North and South, the journal was to have a
decidedly religious, Protestant, and, in particular, Methodist perspective on
world and national issues. However, both Pendleton and Pierce had a second
and more noble objective:

> That the South should have a Literature of her own is a proposition, if
> not self-evident in its truth, at least too clear and decisive for controversy.
> Necessity is laid upon us in this matter, unless we are willing to occupy
> before the world, the singularly consistent position of boldly asserting our
> natural and constitutional rights in politics and commerce, and yet tamely
> submitting to a more inglorious dependence for all the agencies by which
> taste is to be refined and sentiment cultivated.[3]

Southern writers and, in particular, those of the caliber of Simms had always
worked within the shadows cast by more popular northern writers. In his early

years, Simms published almost exclusively in northern publishing houses.[4] In fact, many Americans revered 1821 as the birth of the American literary tradition, convinced that two northerners, Nathaniel Hawthorne and Henry Wadsworth Longfellow, were responsible for its rise. Northern writers consistently set their southern counterparts on the defensive in savage criticisms of both their writings and their unique culture.[5] As John C. Guilds pointed out, ''Simms' Old South . . . has, until recently, too frequently been looked upon as a curiously separate land of sentimentality, chauvinism, and racial bigotry—its people devoid of, and incapable of, serious intellectual and artistic accomplishment.''[6]

Southerners were not prepared to accept the thesis that their plantation economy ''made against the creation of literary centers.''[7] In fact, as H. V. Wooten, a physician from Lowndesboro, Alabama, argued in *The Southern Ladies' Book*,

> No people are more favorably situated for the cultivation of literature than we are. A large portion of the educated part of our population are entirely free from the exactions of necessity upon their time and labor; and nothing is wanting but a proper direction of the mind, to lead it into the pleasing field of Literature, where it will at once be entertained and instructed, and when it will import both usefulness and pleasure to others around.[8]

When Pendleton and Pierce decided to launch their literary adventure, they turned to Simms for support. Simms was reluctant to lend his name to their cause. The writer was not pleased with the overall editorial direction of the journal. He believed that the financial pressures inherent in printing and distribution would force Pendleton and Pierce to compromise their content expectations. This, in turn, would force them to publish what he called ''that inoffensive sort of commonplace, which is usually furnished by young Misses from their school exercises, and young Masters when they first begin to feel the startling sensations of the tender passion.''[9] Having acted as editor for a number of southern magazines, he had serious doubts that the two editors could make *The Southern Ladies' Book* a success. Simms spoke from bitter experience. He had been deeply involved in the publication of the *Southern Review*, a quarterly that emanated from Charleston, South Carolina, from February 1828 until February 1832. It had attracted the best and the brightest of the southern literary establishment but sank in the face of ever-increasing debt and reader apathy. Pendleton and Pierce ignored Simms's advice and embarked on a campaign to get him involved with their work. In spite of his pessimism, he eventually became a contributor and finally an editor under Pendleton in 1843.

Under the direction of Pendleton and Pierce, *The Southern Ladies' Book* genuinely attempted to reach and cultivate a female constituency. With the move from Macon and the eventual retaining of Simms as editor, the successor editions became more strongly identified with literary, as opposed to gender, issues. As a consequence, for those interested in exploring the range of ideas on gender relationships, the first nine months of the publication are critical. Although some of the journal's views on gender were repeated in the Savannah editions, by the time that the journal had settled in the coastal city, it was apparent that Pendleton was suffering from some editorial uncertainties from which his publication never recovered. The initial concept that Pendleton and Pierce professed in early 1840 died with the appointment of Simms as editor in January 1843.

The mandate for *The Southern Ladies' Book* was outlined by Pierce in his address at the opening of the Georgia Female College in 1839. Pierce's main point was that females needed to be "summoned to the promotion of knowledge, patriotism and religion,"[10] a position obviously shared by his cohort Pendleton. In every respect, the content of Pierce's address demonstrated that his feminism was bound by literary considerations. Pierce concluded his remarks by attacking those who had kept the Bible out of secular learning institutions. Here he revealed his real agenda. "With education, divorced from Christian morals, we hold no fellowship, and unto the assembly of its advocates, we would not unite our honor."[11]

Pierce's vision on the role of women in southern society was strengthened by subsequent submissions in *The Southern Ladies' Book*. Another contributor, Daniel Chandler, argued that female education was critical if young children were to receive a moral and Christian upbringing. In his view, ignorant women were unable to provide such services to the sons of the South.[12] In all fairness to Pierce, Pendleton, and the like, the division of gender roles within the Christian home was not uncommon in these years prior to the Civil War.[13] Religiously inspired feminism divided men and women by their perceived worldly roles. Men were providers, and women were nurturers. However, many religious editors refused to accept that women should be denied life's rewards simply because of this division of labor. They believed that women should be able to enjoy the fruits of education and literary experience. In particular, females were advised to study history and natural philosophy.[14] However, lest there be any confusion, it remained that equality in this period was confined almost exclusively to intellectual experiences.

A writer who contributed to the journal under the name "Vindex Veritatis" argued that Southern women should not be sent North for their formal training since it only resulted in an appreciation of things described as frivolous, discouraging "a taste for the solid information and learning."[15] The correspondent continued, arguing that it was the duty of the South to encourage and build new institutions of learning that could respond to the needs of both males and females. "By doing so, our fair ladies will not only be better prepared to discharge the high and weighty offices of their station, but the whole South will experience from it beneficial effects."[16]

When the editors of *The Southern Ladies' Book* stated that women needed the benefits of education, they had very clear ideas of what kind of woman would be qualified to receive it. Pendleton believed that women were unaware of the influence that they held over important, worldly events, not to mention the influence they held over men.[17] Women were first and foremost moral and enlightened creatures who could soften and temper the more coarse aspects of male behavior. Women were the mothers of the nation. They implanted in their children, both male and female, those characteristics that determined the mind and manners of the future generations. This was a critical and important obligation, according to Pendleton. He noted, "We are prone to forget, that as the items, so are the aggregates; that society is constituted of individuals, and if the formation of personal character be neglected, the whole mass will become depraved."[18]

The moral female in conflict with the immoral male provides interesting and constant reading through *The Southern Ladies' Book* and to a certain, but lesser, degree, its successors. The conflict had one of two resolutions. In the first, the immoral man abandoned his wife and children, throwing them on the mercy of charity. The courageous female carried on in spite of severe hardship to raise her brood with some success. The male in these cases was universally condemned. The second case had a happier ending. With the perseverance of the strong female, eventually the male abandoned his evil ways—normally drinking and gambling—and returned to the family hearth a changed man. In both these case studies, the morality of the female was apparent, as was the immorality of the male.

Abandonment was the theme of the poem "The Wife to Her Husband," which appeared in the May 1840 issue:

But I would ask some share of hours that you on clubs bestow,
Of Knowledge which you prize so much, might I not something know?
Subtract from meetings amongst men, each even an hour for me,
Make me companion of your soul, as I may safely be.
If you will read, I'll sit and work; then think when you're away,
Less tedious I shall find the time, dear William, of your stay,
A meeting companion soon I'll be for e'en your studious hours,
And teacher of those little ones you call your cottage flowers;
And if we be not rich and great, we may be wise and kind,
And as my heart can warm your heart, so may my mind your mind.[19]

In all respects, the journal was not prepared to blithely accept female submission to the whims of the male. Pendleton referred to such a social arrangement as "a doctrine no less injurious to him, than degrading to her."[20] Pendleton believed that in these circumstances, while women appeared, on the surface, to be submissive, they were, in practice, manipulative. Thus, while the male actually believed that he was the lord and master of his domestic relationship, he was no better than a slave to his wife and family. His desire to control his situation forced him to be a tyrant reigning over what the editor called "the weaker vessel."[21] In the final analysis, men were responsible for depriving women of "the means of acquiring that knowledge which would induce her to demand equality as her right."[22]

In spite of the seemingly one-sided arrangement that surfaced in mid-nineteenth-century marital relationships, Pendleton was convinced that young southern women should marry and make families. However, the appeal was accompanied by the belief that marriage was more necessary for males than for females. Women had an obligation to marry in order to ''save'' the male from his own selfish desires. Pendleton believed that ''man never becomes a member of society until he is married. Unmarried, he is looked upon with distrust. He has no home, no abiding place, no anchor to hold him fast, but is a mere piece of floatwood, on the great tide of time.''[23]

Pendleton's ideal marriage contained elements of gender equality that were bound to be seen as radical in their time. The editor complained that laws that forbade married women from owning property in their own right were unjust and unfair. He wrote:

> In this age of universal reform, why has not this matter arrested the public attention, and demanded, if not change, at least investigation, if not a law to secure her property entirely, at least some portion thereof, in order to save her and her hapless offspring from degradation and want. Because the oppressed parties do not constitute the public—they do not compose any part of the political world—because they are not clamorous for their rights. There has [sic] been instances where woman has dared to assert her rights, but how has she been derided and ridiculed—how has the finger of scorn been pointed at the unfortunate, who strove to assert the dignity of her sex.[24]

Yet, Pendleton saw clear gender divisions in the marriage contract. Men were to ensure, first and foremost, the financial well-being of the unit as well as contribute to the overall welfare of the community at large. The female member was commissioned to look after the moral and emotional commitments that came with the family. ''It is hers to comfort and cheer the spirits of her partner amidst life's toils and perplexities, and by her devotion and loveliness of character, to throw around his home all those charms and endearments that can make it attractive.''[25] In the final analysis, she was to care for her offspring, in charge of the moral development that was to characterize future generations.

Pendleton also believed that middle-class women had a duty to elevate the status of their poor female counterparts. He called on southern women to form associations through which the benefits of female education could be extended to all women regardless of status. In this instance, of course, he was referring solely to white women, ignoring the needs of blacks, who were almost exclusively bonded by slavery.[26] Within marriage or beyond, educated or not, as a writer from Milledgeville, Georgia, wrote, the final result was to produce a cast of female writers who could contribute with intelligence to journals such as *The Southern Ladies' Book*. In this respect, Pendleton enjoyed one of his few successes. Following the move to Savannah, the journal attracted a stable cast of female contributors, women such as Caroline Lee Hentz, a transplanted New Englander whose husband taught at the University of North Carolina at Chapel Hill.[27] Another significant change took place in Savannah. Pendleton, now sole editor, changed the journal's name to the *Magnolia; or Southern Monthly*. The journal ceased addressing women's issues with the intensity it had in Macon. Pendleton announced that his publication had "assumed a more manly character."[28] It was beginning its transformation to a literary journal, a process that was to be completed when William Gilmore Simms assumed the editorship in January 1843.

The character and design of the Savannah edition were summed up in an article in a Richmond newspaper, the *Virginia Whig*. It reported the emergence of the journal in Savannah and was pleased by the contributions of Mary E. Lee of Charleston, South Carolina, Simms, Professor Haderman, Dr. W. A. Caruthers, and the Honorable R. H. Wilde. The reviewer noted:

> The two numbers before us contain a traditionary tale of the cocked-hat gentry in the Old Dominion, styled the "Knights of the Golden Horse-Shoe," by the authors of the "Cavaliers of Virginia." The scene is laid in and about Williamsburg whilst Sire Alexander Spotwood, who figures largely in the tale, was Governor of the Province. We have read enough of it to take a deep interest in the continuation and accordingly, with impatience the receipt of the March No.[29]

Not long after the move to Savannah, it became apparent that Simms was about to become a regular contributor in both prose and poetry. Editorially, the journal was an ideal outlet for the South's most famous literary personality. Pendleton had moved to carrying long, full-length serializations of stories, such as Simms's "The Loves of a Driver," Professor Mark Anthony Ponder's "Tales of Packolette Hall," and Professor C. J. Hadermann's translation of Schiller's "The Ghost-Seer." As Pendleton noted, "Subscribers we hope will be gratified instead of displeased as the plan we are pursuing in giving them stories of length continuing from month to month, even though they should amount to the dignity and length of an ordinary novel."[30] These tales were complemented by epic poems written by a contributor named John Love Lawrie and numerous, shorter pieces, in the main composed by female writers.[31]

In spite of the support of the some of the South's most public literary figures and complimentary reviews in a number of journals, the *Magnolia; or Southern Monthly* continued to stagger from issue to issue. Pendleton appealed to his subscribers to "try us one year more—cast the mantle of charity over the past seeming negligence, and non-compliance with our promises—make a strong effort in our behalf—send us subscribers."[32] In part, the appeal was successful. The journal limped on until late 1841, when Pendleton realized that he had to take drastic measures to ensure the future of the magazine. In February 1842, he announced that he was prepared to share his editorship with Simms. He was confident that his readers would approve.

> They will, at once, estimate it as a very great addition, and it now only remains for those who are disposed to lend a helping hand to the permanent success of this Magazine, to do so at once, and with effect, if it is their purpose ever to aid in this enterprise."[33]

Simms finally joined the Pendleton team in May. However, his entry was short-lived. He temporarily withdrew when his young daughter died unexpectedly.[34] Simms was the final editor in the history of the *Magnolia; or Southern Monthly*. In July 1842, he moved the journal to Charleston, South Carolina, and changed the name to *The Magnolia; or, Southern Apalachian*. The publication was a mix of fiction, poetry, and criticism written both by Simms and by members of his literary cohort in the South.

Simms was a native southerner, born in Charleston, South Carolina, on April 17, 1806, the son of a failed businessman. The young Simms grew up with a love of books and composed his first lines at the age of seven. Upon leaving school, he became a clerk in a drugstore. Finding the work unsatisfying, he decided to study law. Before being admitted to the bar, Simms married. A year later, he published his first volume of poetry, *Lyrical and Other Poems*. In 1827, the young advocate opened a law practice and earned the princely sum of $600 in his first year, poor by even southern standards. Discouraged by law, Simms abandoned the practice a year later and became a full-time literary scion. He became editor of the *Tablet or Southern Monthly Literary Gazette*, an experience that left him dubious about the viability of southern literary magazines. However, he became an editor again between 1849 and 1854, when he took charge of the *Southern Quarterly Review*. Following the collapse of the journal, Simms, in partnership with E. S. Duryea, purchased the Charleston newspaper *City Gazette* in 1830. The new journalist/editor found himself on the opposite side of too many issues in the city; and within two years, the newspaper died. At this point Simms enjoyed the success of his first novel, *Martin Faber*. His joy had been tempered by the premature death of his first wife in 1832. He did not remarry until 1836. His second marriage ended in 1863, when his second wife died.

Although he was an ardent Unionist in the 1830s, Simms had become a secessionist by the 1850s, albeit a nonviolent one. Simms's dedication to the Confederate cause forced him into literary obscurity with the northern victory in the Civil War. He spent his remaining days editing newspapers in and around Charleston.[35]

If Simms showed no interest in women's rights, he was not loath to make known his feelings about African Americans, views that in modern terms would certainly brand his attitudes as racist. He recycled an 1810 volume of arguments on racial equality written by H. Gregoire, bishop of Blois in France, in which the cleric argued that race was only skin-deep. In the area of literature, Bishop Gregoire believed that black artists were capable of producing substantive art equal to that of white communities. Simms begged to differ:

Our firm conviction is that, the African race is and has ever been, far inferior, in natural powers of intellect, to the white man; and that those "Writings," which are paraded as brilliant specimens of genius, bear in themselves intrinsic evidence of a mental source at once dull, feeble and jejune. . . . The negro, wherever found, unchecked and unguided by the white man exists in a state of barbarism, sensuality and ignorance.[36]

Yet, Simms was not without some compassion for America's black citizens. When a local official in Charleston reported to the city authorities that the majority of free blacks were living in squalor and on the verge of starvation, Simms used the journal to call for assistance.

We should hardly have supposed that any question could be made as to the relative claim of colored and white—when starving—to the humane consideration of a Christian community. Man is the subject of the charity. Shall we ask, when he craves bread—what is his complexion? Surely not.[37]

The never-ending chaos that seemed to plague Pendleton finally caught up with Simms in the spring of 1843. Writing to his friend Major Benjamin Franklin Perry on May 26, the editor announced that he was leaving the journal:

Under the existing conditions of the Proprietorship the work cannot possibly continue long, and I am unwilling that it should perish in my hands. The proprietors are squabbling among themselves and are accordingly either doing nothing for the magazine or positively injuring it. Messers Pendleton and Burges do not agree. The former is a sensitive suspicious person,—I verily believe an excellent good creature, but somewhat deficient in calm-prudence & good common sense. The latter is a cool, rather cold business man, who does not yield much deference to nervous sensibilities of any kind, and thinks chiefly of the means to make the pot boil.[38]

James Burges, Pendleton's partner and printer, had decided to relinquish his shares on July 1, 1843. Simms believed the journal would cease publication since Pendleton was deeply in debt, with no hope of getting out. Yet, Simms refused to reveal his reasons for his resignation in the last issue he edited. He invited contributors to send their works directly to Pendleton following the May issue.[39] Pendleton managed to publish a June issue in which he carried a spirited editorial denouncing capital punishment.[40] However, no July issue appeared, and

The Magnolia; or, Southern Apalachian became one more entry in America's press history.

Notes

1. Jean Hoornstra and Trudy Heath (eds.), *American Periodical Series*, vol. 2 (Ann Arbor: University of Michigan Microfilms, 1979), p. 128.

2. *The Southern Ladies' Book.* July 1840, p. 1.

3. Ibid., p. 53.

4. Samuel Albert Link, *Pioneers of Southern Literature*, vol. 1 (Nashville, Tenn.: M. E. Church, 1899), pp. 179–181.

5. Ibid., pp. 155–156.

6. John C. Guilds (ed.), *Long Years of Neglect* (Fayetteville: University of Arkansas Press, 1988), p. 8.

7. Link, *Pioneers of Southern Literature*, p. 204.

8. *The Southern Ladies' Book*, April 1840, p. 216.

9. Mary C. Simms Oliphant, Alfred Taylor Odell, and T. C. Duncan Eaves (eds.), *The Letters of William Gilmore Simms*, vol. 1 (Columbia: University of South Carolina Press, 1952), p. 197.

10. *The Southern Ladies' Book*, January 1840, p. 6.

11. Ibid., p. 14.

12. Ibid., p. 56.

13. For a similar view, see the account of *The Universalist and Ladies' Repository* contained in this book.

14. *The Southern Ladies' Book*, June 1840, p. 364.

15. Ibid., p. 1.

16. Ibid., p. 2.

17. *The Southern Ladies' Book*, April 1840, p. 255.

18. *The Southern Ladies' Book*, March 1840, p. 154.

19. *The Southern Ladies' Book*, May 1840, p. 302.

20. *The Southern Ladies' Book*, June 1840, p. 364.

21. Ibid.

22. Ibid.

23. Ibid., pp. 342–343.

24. Ibid., p. 363.

25. *The Southern Ladies' Book*, July 1840, p. 1.

26. *The Southern Ladies' Book*, April 1840, p. 222.

27. Link, *Pioneers of Southern Literature*, p. 279.

28. *The Magnolia; or Southern Monthly*, April 1841, p. 193.

29. Ibid.

30. *The Magnolia; or Southern Monthly*, January 1841, p. 43.

31. The listings here are too numerous to cite. However, Pendleton, Pierce, and, later, Simms published complete yearly summaries of both articles and contributors to which researchers may refer.

32. *The Magnolia; or Southern Monthly*, February 1841, p. 96.

33. *The Magnolia; or Southern Monthly*, February 1842, p. 124.

34. *The Magnolia; or Southern Monthly*, May 1842, p. 320.

35. The biographical information has been extracted from three sources: Mary C.

Simms Oliphant et al. (eds), *The Letters of William Gilmore Simms*, vol. 1 (Columbia: University of South Carolina Press, 1952), pp. ix–xxxix; David Moltke-Hansen, ''Ordered Progress: The Historical Philosophy of William Gilmore Simms,'' in John Caldwell Guilds (ed.), *Long Years of Neglect* (Fayetteville: University of Arkansas Press, 1988), pp. 126–147; and Link, *Pioneers of Southern Literature*, pp. 149–221.

36. *The Magnolia; or Southern Monthly*, May 1842, pp. 265–267.
37. *The Magnolia; or, Southern Apalachian*, February 1843, p. 139.
38. Oliphant et al., *The Letters of William Gilmore Simms*, p. 351.
39. *The Magnolia; or, Southern Apalachian*, May 1843, p. 336.
40. *The Magnolia; or, Southern Apalachian*, June 1843, p. 340.

Information Sources

BIBLIOGRAPHY:
Guilds, John Caldwell (ed.). *Long Years of Neglect: The Work and Reputation of William Gilmore Simms*. Fayetteville: University of Arkansas Press, 1988.
Link, Samuel Albert. *Pioneers of Southern Literature*. Nashville, Tenn.: M. E. Church, 1899, p. 439.
Oliphant, Mary C. Simms, Alfred Taylor Odell, and T. C. Duncan Eaves (eds.). *The Letters of William Gilmore Simms*, vol. 1. Columbia: University of South Carolina Press, 1952.
INDEX SOURCES: None.
LOCATION SOURCES: University of Western Ontario, D. B. Weldon Library; University of Michigan at Ann Arbor, Xerox Microform Centre; American Periodical Series.

Publication History

MAGAZINE TITLE AND TITLE CHANGES: *Southern Ladies' Book* (1840); *Magnolia; or Southern Monthly* (1841–1842); *Magnolia; or, Southern Apalachian* (1842–1843).
VOLUME AND ISSUE DATA: Vols. 1–4 (1840–1842); Vols. 1–2 (new) (1842–1843).
PUBLISHER AND PLACE OF PUBLICATION: Philip C. Pendleton. Macon, Ga. (1840); Savannah, Ga.(1840–1842); Charleston, S. C.(1842–1843).
EDITORS: Philip C. Pendleton and George F. Pierce (1840); Philip C. Pendleton (1841–1842); William Gilmore Simms (1842–1843); Philip C. Pendleton (1843).
CIRCULATION: Unreported.

David Spencer

McCALL'S

McCall's was founded as a fashion sheet to advertise the clothing patterns of tailor James McCall. Called *The Queen: Illustrating McCall's Bazar Glove-Fitting Patterns*, it first appeared in the fall of 1873. This catalog contained four small folio pages, featuring woodcuts of the styles of McCall's patterns. Its pink pages made the journal highly visible. In the space not given over to McCall's patterns, the editor ran notes about current fashions. Initially, the paper appeared ten times a year, skipping the summer months.[1]

McCall, an immigrant from Scotland, had started his pattern-making business with his wife. Their business prospered, both because of the superiority of the McCall patterns and because the McCalls promoted their patterns through *The Queen* and other publications. By the late 1880s, for the subscription price of a dollar, a homemaker could receive a combined package of (1) ten monthly issues of *The Queen*; (2) two numbers of the *Bazar Dressmaker*, showing illustrations of the latest fashions from New York, Paris, London, Berlin, and Vienna; (3) spring and fall fashion catalogs; and (4) two colored fashion plates. This promotional tactic worked well, as the pattern business and the fashion magazine business both targeted the same market.[2]

McCall died in 1884. In that year, the McCall Co. claimed a circulation of 300,000.[3] The magazine's pages had been reduced in size but increased in number to eight. The journal still consisted primarily of fashions and patterns.

Mrs. McCall became president of the company, and Mrs. George Bladsworth (better known by her pen name of "May Manton") filled the editorial spot, a position she held until 1891. Mrs. Bladsworth's husband, George, already a member of the McCall organization, succeeded to the presidency of the McCall Publishing Company in 1890.

With the accession of Bladsworth to the editorial seat, the content of the magazine broadened to include more household information, homemaking tips, and ideas on handiwork. In 1891, the magazine acquired a new name, becoming *The Queen of Fashion*. The previous year, the journal had been expanded to 12 pages, and for the first time readers could buy this magazine separately from the other fashion sheets of the company, at the comparatively low price of 30¢ a year. The new management proved ineffective, however, and the magazine changed ownership in 1892, when Page & Ringot purchased it. At this time, audited circulation figures had fallen to 12,000 (although this drop in circulation may also reflect the inflation of the earlier figures reported by the publisher but unverified). Decreases in the fashion magazine's circulation affected the pattern business of the company as well.

A change in leadership was needed; Bladsworth yielded the editorial role to Frances Benson, who held the position for four years. However, no notification of this switch appeared in the pages of the magazine.

In 1893, businessman James Henry Ottley took over the McCall Co., offering the company good financial management. Ottley raised the subscription price of the magazine to 50¢ annually (5¢ per issue) and increased the number of pages to between 16 and 30 per issue.[4] He accelerated the trend toward content expansion. Fiction, one of the major components of women's magazines, appeared for the first time in *McCall's* in 1894, the result of a contest with a ten-dollar prize. Editorial columns on a variety of topics, including children's interest, literary notes, and jokes, began appearing, as well as columns on health and beauty and foreign travel.[5]

Ottley also focused on the pattern business. He cut pattern prices to 10¢ and 15¢, establishing agencies around the country to sell them. By concentrating on both the pattern and the magazine business, Ottley brought the publication and the company back to financial stability. Circulation picked up again, hitting 75,000 by 1894.[6] The magazine contained several pages of small advertising, placed at the back, for items such as powder, soaps, and the ubiquitous patent medicines. McCall Co. offered premiums for subscribers, and the gifts available appeared in the back pages, amid the other advertisements.[7]

In the September 1897 issue, the magazine took the name of its founder, becoming known as *McCall's Magazine—The Queen of Fashion*. The editor explained that this change of name reflected the greater range of articles in the magazine, which contained more than simply fashions (although it still published a large number of patterns).

The publication's low price and its fashions continued to be its chief attractions, although it was slowly improving editorially. In 1913, the banking firm White, Weld & Co. bought the magazine and formed the McCall Corporation. In 1917, the price was raised to 10¢, putting it in the same price group with the other general women's magazines. Simultaneously, *McCall's* stopped using premiums to gain subscriptions. This temporarily hurt circulation, which dropped in 1918. Advertising declined a bit as well, but both picked up by 1920, when White, Weld & Co., after several years of floundering for a strategy, found the man who would set the magazine on a successful course.[8] William Bishop Warner, a man with a merchandising background who had worked at department stores J. L. Hudson and Filene's in Boston, was hired in 1919. Warner moved quickly and effectively to build up the company in both the publishing and the pattern businesses.

Warner was willing to spend money to improve *McCall's* and give it an identity. Myra G. Reed (editor from 1916 through 1918) and well-known foreign correspondent Bessie Beatty (editor from 1918 through 1921) both failed to find a steadily winning mix for the journal. However, with the hiring in 1922 of Harry Payne Burton, another former foreign correspondent, *McCall's* found an editor who could consistently win readers. Burton did this (as did other women's magazine editors of these years) by filling the magazine with big-name fiction writers, including Kathleen Norris, Harold Bell Wright, Zane Grey, Booth Tarkington, and Mary Roberts Rinehart. Burton mixed the stories with nonfiction articles, service features, and the ubiquitous McCall fashions and patterns, in color by the mid-1920s.[9] During the 1920s, circulation practically doubled, to more than 2.5 million, and advertising quadrupled, to almost $8.5 million.[10]

Associate editor Otis Wiese took over Burton's seat in 1928. Called the "boy editor" because of his youth (23) when given the top editorial position, Wiese quickly demonstrated a flair for the job that belied his youth. He continued Burton's strategy of including big-name writers in the magazine, and the patterns and fashions remained a fixture. To this mix Wiese added his own ideas, including an inventive redesign of the magazine into three parts in 1932: "Fiction and News," "Home Making," and "Style and Beauty." Each was complete with its own advertising, which was now located throughout the book. Another innovation was borrowed from sister McCall publication *Redbook** (bought with *Blue Book* by the McCall Co. in 1929): printing a complete novel in an issue. This feature proved extremely popular with readers.

In the 1920s, *McCall's* envisioned its readers as ordinary, middle-class citizens, whom it referred to as living on "McCall Street." The company sponsored extensive reader research in the 1930s and 1940s on its own and its competitors' audiences. Shrewd editing, attention to readers, and a healthy company allowed *McCall's* to survive the depression with its circulation only pausing, and its advertising significantly recovered by the end of the 1930s.[11]

McCall's was the first of the women's magazines to respond to U.S. entry into World War II, in part, because the magazine had anticipated American participation and established a bureau in Washington and a defense section in the magazine in 1940.[12] The magazine's initial response appeared in February 1942, with articles on national defense inside and a cover showing a young woman who had joined *McCall's* consumer campaign, boasting a button saying "I've enlisted." Readers could enlist as well, if they signed the pledge and sent in the coupon printed in the magazine (more than 150,000 did so within the first three weeks).[13] *McCall's* effort was part of the government's "Consumer's Pledge for Total Defense" campaign.

Throughout the war *McCall's* featured stories about women juggling war work and home, managing with husbands overseas. It also published guidelines about food and clothing conservation and tips on how to run a household under rationing. When the war was nearing its end, the magazine discussed ways individuals and society could help veterans adjust to peacetime society.

After the war longtime editor Wiese continued his successful editorial pattern, while simultaneously trying to find something to make the magazine stand out, especially as television posed a threat to advertising dollars. Wiese published and promoted the new memoirs of former First Lady Eleanor Roosevelt. He featured a cake on half the covers of one issue of the magazine and a girl on the other half, asking readers to vote on which they liked better. He established editorial offices on the West Coast.[14]

Wiese's biggest innovation, however, came with his "togetherness" campaign. Announced with great fanfare, this strategy to get men more involved in the household and women more involved in men's activities was designed, in part, to attract more advertising as well as to boost circulation. Editorially, it meant more service material featuring men in home-related activities, more articles on sex and marriage, and more novels complete in one issue.[15] Unfortunately, despite (or because of) the press the campaign generated, the campaign failed to push *McCall's* past the circulation-leading *Ladies' Home Journal.**

Ownership of the company was changing in these years. Norton Simon, a West Coast financier and head of a group of investors, had begun purchasing shares of McCall Corp. in 1953. By 1956, this group had control of the company's board.[16] In 1958, when Simon passed over Wiese for the position of president of the company (awarding it instead to former Washington state governor Arthur B. Langlie), Wiese and a number of loyal staffers resigned. (Wiese had become a vice president of the organization in 1949, as well as holding positions as both editor and publisher of the magazine.) Instead of caving in to Wiese's demands, Simon hired Herbert Mayes, longtime *Good Housekeeping** editor who had recently been dismissed by Hearst management in an argument over editorial control.[17]

Both Mayes and *McCall's* were invigorated by the change. Mayes brought a new look to the magazine, which had been in Wiese's hands for almost 30 years. Mayes threw out a substantial amount of inventory purchased by his predecessor, valued at $400,000. He redesigned *McCall's* pages, introduced bold graphics and many bleed pages (color all the way to the edge), created a new slogan (''first magazine for women'') to replace the disastrous ''togetherness'' idea, brought in the concept of product testing he had overseen at *Good Housekeeping*, and thrust *McCall's* headlong into competition with circulation leader *Ladies' Home Journal*.[18] Backed by Norton Simon's dollars and aided by some of his staffers from *Good Housekeeping*, Mayes succeeded mightily, passing the *Journal* in circulation in 1960 and increasing circulation to 8 million by the end of 1961. Advertising followed suit and exceeded the *Journal*'s revenues in 1960 by $2.6 million.

Norton Simon backed Mayes in his redesign, giving him the funds and promotion to bring the magazine to the top. Simon encouraged Mayes to spend money if it would bring good publicity and circulation to the magazine. Features published by Mayes included columns by writer/political figure Clare Booth Luce and the duchess of Windsor, celebrity biographies and autobiographies, and photographs by Richard Avedon of model Twiggy. The magazine was provocative, up-to-date, visually exciting.[19]

Mayes became president and chief executive officer of McCall Co. in 1961, a position he held through July 1965. He continued as editor of *McCall's* briefly, then in 1962 turned the job over to executive editor John Mack Carter. Under Carter, circulation rose, reaching over 8.4 million in 1965. Advertising revenues were sound, and in 1965, *McCall's* led its competition in this area; *McCall's* took in $51.4 million in ad dollars compared with $32.7 million for *Good Housekeeping* and $29.2 million for *Ladies' Home Journal*.[20]

When Carter departed in 1965 to take over at *Ladies' Home Journal* (and get out from under the thumb of Mayes, still hankering for the editorial role), editors followed in rapid succession for several years.[21] Robert Stein, who had been editing the sister publication *Redbook*, took over at *McCall's* in 1965, followed by running expert James Fixx in 1967. Norman Cousins, editor of *Saturday Review* (now owned by McCall Co.) and on the McCall Co. board, also exerted direction over the magazine. *McCall's* began to lose its identity with this quick turnover of male editors, and new McCall Co. president Edward Fitzgerald decided to try a woman. Fitzgerald first hired *Life* staffer and columnist Shana

Alexander, who held the editorial spot briefly in 1970 and attempted to make the magazine more responsive to changes in women's lives. However, Alexander had no experience either as an editor or on a women's magazine, and she left the job in 1971.[22] In that year the magazine's size was cut to match that of sister publication *Redbook*. With advertisers unwilling to pay for subscribers gained through sharp discounts, the rate based was dropped from 8.5 to 7.5 million.[23]

Patricia Carbine, executive editor of *Look*, followed Alexander. During Carbine's one-year tenure, feminist Gloria Steinem often appeared in the magazine. The appointments of Alexander and Carbine may have been in response to the heated-up women's movement, and, indeed, under these women the magazine became broader, more intellectual. However, Carbine left in 1972 to work on the newly created *Ms.** After her departure Robert Stein returned and stayed in the editorial position until 1986. Under Stein the magazine took on a subtitle reflecting demographic shifts among its readers: *The Magazine for Suburban Women*. The magazine's content increasingly showed an awareness of the growing number of working women, particularly in its monthly column devoted to working mothers. Eventually, this segment of readers was considered important enough for McCall Corp. to spin off a new publication called, appropriately enough, *Working Mother*. Begun in 1978, this magazine became bimonthly and by 1981 had become a monthly. This highly targeted publication enabled *McCall's* to focus more tightly on its traditional franchise, while allowing the company to meet the needs of female readers who were working mothers.

Owners shifted, as well as editors, in these years. In 1973, Norton Simon, Inc. sold *McCall's*. After being privately owned, McCall's Publishing Co. was taken over in 1986 by a partnership of Time, Inc. and Lang Communications. (Sister publication *Working Mother* and Lang's original journal, *Working Woman*,* were also part of the group.) The new group, called the Working Woman/McCall's Group, had advertising run by Lang and circulation by Time, Inc. Elizabeth Sloan took over as editor of *McCall's*.

The Lang-Time partnership proved unhappy, and in 1989, *McCall's* was sold to the New York Times Magazine Group, which already owned *Family Circle*.* The New York Times Co. paid $80 million for the acquisition. The new owner redesigned *McCall's* and brought in new editor Anne Mollegen Smith. In 1990, the title had a circulation of 5 million.

At this writing (1994), Kate White edits the magazine, which attracts women in their early 40s. *McCall's* has responded to changes in women's lives and interests with more columns on health and legal issues, fewer and shorter pieces of fiction, and a greater emphasis on celebrities; diets, exercise, beauty tips, and parenting advice are all standard fare. This magazine, which began as a pattern catalog, stopped publishing patterns in its pages in the mid-1980s, over a hundred years after its creation.

In June 1994, Gruner + Jahr, the publishing division of the German media company Bertelsmann, announced plans to buy the New York Times' Women's Magazine division, including *McCall's*. Gruner + Jahr International Publishing president Axel Ganz predicted a major repositioning for the publication. As part of that makeover, the magazine would be directed at a slightly younger readership.[24]

Notes

1. Frank Luther Mott, *A History of American Magazines*, vol. 4: 1885–1905 (Cambridge: Harvard University Press, 1957), p. 580.
2. John Tebbel and Mary Ellen Zuckerman, *The Magazine in America, 1741–1990* (New York: Oxford University Press, 1991), pp. 99, 100.
3. Mott, *A History of American Magazines,* p. 581.
4. See various issues for the year 1894.
5. See various issues 1894; Mott, *A History of American Magazines*, p. 580.
6. Tebbel and Zuckerman, *The Magazine in America*, p. 100.
7. See various issues 1894.
8. John Drewry, "*McCall's*—Three Magazines in One," *The Writer*, October 1938, p. 304.
9. Mott, *A History of American Magazines,* pp. 584–585.
10. Lenore Hershey, "The Pace and the Pattern," McCall Corp. promotional brochure, 1950: n.p.
11. Mott, *A History of American Magazines*, pp. 585–586; Hershey, "The Pace and the Pattern," n.p.
12. Mott, *A History of American Magazines*, p. 586.
13. "Women's War," *Business Week*, March 7, 1942, p. 58.
14. Theodore Peterson, *Magazines in the Twentieth Century* (Urbana: University of Illinois, 1964), p. 204.
15. "Accent on 'Togetherness,' " *The Writer*, October 1955, p. 322.
16. Peterson, *Magazines in the Twentieth Century*, pp. 204–205.
17. "Rival Women's Magazines Near Hair-Pulling Stage," *Business Week*, October 1, 1960, pp. 88, 89, 95, 96.
18. Herbert Mayes, *Magazine Maze* (Garden City, N.Y.: Doubleday, 1980), pp. 298–314.
19. Peterson, *Magazines in the Twentieth Century*, p. 205; Mayes, *Magazine Maze*, p. 304.
20. "Magazine Puts Seal on Its Own Success," *Business Week*, March 19, 1966, p. 191.
21. Mayes, *Magazine Maze*, p. 324.
22. "Lady at the Top," *Newsweek*, April 29, 1969, p. 88; "The Feminine Eye," *Time*, April 25, 1969, p. 78.
23. William Taft, *Magazines for the 1980s* (New York: Hastings House, 1982), p. 104.
24. Keith J. Kelly, "Gruner & Jahr Thinks Younger," *Advertising Age*, June 27, 1994, p. 4.

Information Sources

BIBLIOGRAPHY:
Drewry, John. "McCall's—Three Magazines in One." *The Writer*, October 1938, pp. 304–305.

Mayes, Herbert. *Magazine Maze*. Garden City, N.Y.: Doubleday, 1980.
Mott, Frank Luther. *A History of American Magazines*, vol. 4: 1885–1905. Cambridge: Harvard University Press, 1957.
Nourie, Barbara. "McCall's," in Alan Nourie and Barbara Nourie (eds.), *American Mass-Market Magazines*. Westport, Conn.: Greenwood Press, 1990.
Tebbel, John, and Mary Ellen Zuckerman. *The Magazine in America, 1741–1990*. New York: Oxford University Press, 1991.
INDEX SOURCES: Health Index; Magazine Index; Media Review Digest; Popular Magazine Review; Readers' Guide to Periodical Literature; TOM (Text on Microfilm).
LOCATION SOURCES: Cleveland Public Library and other (primarily community) libraries.

Publication History

MAGAZINE TITLE AND TITLE CHANGES: *The Queen* (1873–1891); *The Queen of Fashion* (1891–1897); *McCall's Magazine* (1897–present).
VOLUME AND ISSUE DATA: Vols. 1–(September 1873(?)–present). Monthly. (Early volumes (1–14?) combined January and February and July and August each year; vols. 15–21 combined July–August each year.)
PUBLISHER AND PLACE OF PUBLICATION: James McCall and Co. (1873–1890); McCall Publishing Co. (1890); Bladworth and Co. (1890–1892); Page and Ringot (1892–1893); J. H. Ringot and Co. (1893); McCall Co. (1893–1936, James H. Ottley, 1893–1913, and White, Weld and Co., 1913–1936); McCall Corp. (1936–198?); Time Inc. and Lang Communications (198?–1989); New York Times Women's Magazines (1989–1994); Gruner + Jahr USA (1994–present). New York City.
EDITORS: James McCall and wife(?) (1873–1884); May Manton (Mrs. George H. Bladworth) (1885–1891); Frances M. Benson (1892–1896); E. B. Clapp (1897–1911); William Griffith (1911–1912); Alice Manning (1912–1916); Myra G. Reed (1916–1918); Bessie Beatty (1918–1921); Harry P. Burton (1921–1927); Otis L. Wiese (1918–1959); Herbert R. Mayes (1959–1962); John Mack Carter (1962–1965); Robert Stein (1965–1967); James F. Fixx (1967–1969); Shana Alexander (1969–1970); Patricia Carbine (1971–1972); Robert Stein (1972–1986); A. Elizabeth Sloan (1986–1989); Anne Mollegen Smith (1989–1991); Kate White (1991–1994); Sally Koslow (1994–present).
CIRCULATION: ABC, 1993: 4,605,441 (paid, primarily subscriptions).

Mary Ellen Zuckerman

METROPOLITAN HOME

In 1969, the Woodstock nation met at White Lake, New York; Charles Manson and his family went on a murder spree; and Neil Armstrong walked on the moon. McDonald's introduced the Big Mac; Sesame Street aired for the first time; and a new magazine from Meredith Corporation, *Apartment Ideas*, made its debut. The magazine featured pop art, day-glo colors, orange crate bookcases, wood paneling, and zebra print wallpaper, all designed to improve the looks of the readers' "pads."

In 1981, Lady Diana Spencer became Princess Di, and Ronald Reagan became president. The youngest baby boomers were now in the workplace, and the oldest were eyeing a frightening new concept: middle age. Kellogg introduced NutriGrain cereal, and *Apartment Life* (formerly *Ideas*) magazine underwent a metamorphosis into *Metropolitan Home*. The new magazine featured pomegranate walls, sleek window shades, projection televisions, and framed art prints, all geared to what editor Dorothy Kalins called "a generation of change."

The history of *Metropolitan Home* is the history of its audience, those baby boomers who were recent college grads in 1969 and successful professionals by 1981. The "apartmentsia"—as they were called in the first issue of *Apartment Ideas*—had become urban landowners.

In the introductory editorial of *Apartment Ideas*, editors explained the new magazine:

> In the more than a year that went into planning and producing this premier issue we've been in touch with millions who want to live in apartments ... and millions make what might be called a social movement. With only a little effrontery, *Apartment Ideas* hereby knights itself Number One Spokesman for that movement. (In all honesty, we're also the only spokesman.)[1]

The magazine was an advocate for renters' rights, starting with its first editorial, "Apartment People Are Treated like Second-Class Citizens."[2] In an introductory memo, publisher Charles Coffin said *Apartment Ideas* would treat "the apartment like a permanent home rather than in the traditional manner of a stop-gap until a house is affordable." Average reader income was $8,000 a year.[3]

The magazine carried the tag line *The Magazine of Better Apartment Living from Better Homes and Gardens* and was promoted as one of the many special-interest publications under the name of Meredith's flagship magazine, *Better Homes and Gardens*.* There was no indication on the magazine itself nor on promotional materials as to the magazine's planned frequency. In 1970, it became quarterly, still under the *Better Homes and Gardens* name. It sold for $1.35, with a 9½" × 12½" format—standard for magazines of the late 1960s. The format was reduced to 8½" × 11" in early 1971, and the cover price was dropped to $1. With the fall 1973 issue, the magazine's name changed to *Apartment Life*, and the price dropped a nickel, to 95¢. In March 1977, the magazine became monthly, with a circulation of 800,000. Later that year the *Better Homes and Gardens* name was dropped from the cover; *Apartment Life* stood on its own, this time with the motto underneath the logo, "Liberty and the Pursuit of Happiness."

Editorial director of the first issue was Jim Autry, and contributing editor was Jean LemMon. Jim Hufnagel became editor in 1971, with David Jordan succeeding him in 1973. Dorothy Kalins joined the magazine as a contributing editor from New York in 1970 and became executive editor in 1974 and editor in 1978.

In 1980, *Apartment Life* took in $9 million in advertising—an 11.9 percent rise over 1979. But the audience and its needs were changing, and the magazine was planning one of the most significant metamorphoses in magazine history— to a new name and new look to "keep up with and stay a bit ahead of the young movers and shakers" in its audience.[4]

Apartment Life became *Metropolitan Home* in April 1981, with 700,000 paid circulation, a 50/50 editorial-advertising balance, and a cover price of $1.25. Kalins was editor in chief. In defining the new magazine, the editors tracked the changes in the magazine's audience:

> The magazine saw its readers become, by turns, militantly anti-institution and anti-war, resolutely anti-materialistic; saw them turn back to the land and then back up from that; saw them never trust anyone over thirty only to wake up one day over thirty themselves.[5]

Following research done by Daniel Yanklevich and Florence Skelly, editors created *Metropolitan Home* for "an increasingly rooted way of life," offering "longer, in-depth pieces; increased national coverage of real estate, professional interior design, money and food."[6] According to audience surveys, more than half the magazine's readers owned homes. The term "apartment," promotional material noted, was limiting—"only an apartment is an apartment; but houses, co-ops, condos, lofts, townhouses and apartments are all Metropolitan Homes."[7]

The first issue profiled design "superstar" Angelo Donghia; offered tips on shopping for Shirvan rugs and art nouveau silver; showcased the Metropolitan Home of the Month with the headline "Looking Forward into the Past: Post-modern"; and ran tidbits about Cher's new house and Princess Caroline's new apartment.

In 1986, the first baby boomers turned 40, and *Metropolitan Home* celebrated with a facelift, becoming one of the country's top upscale magazines. In the September 1986 issue, Kalins said the change, which indicated the "maturing of the magazine," created a design package that better matched the editorial package readers had grown to expect. It meant a wider format—9" × 10¾"— heavier, glossier paper, and thicker, glossier inks. Kalins emphasized audience input in the decision:

> I spoke with readers across the country as we prepared our new package and the message was clear: "We don't mind if you make *Met Home* bigger. Just don't change the important things—its usefulness, its friend-liness, its taste." Rest assured. Because inside this oversized package with its super-heavy paper and extra-shiny inks is Classic *Met Home*. The qual-ities that make us special—and unique in our field—we'd be crazy to abandon.[8]

The issue represented the changing lifestyle of readers, with an article entitled "10 Years After. From 1970s Radical to 1980 Refined, Two Funky Artists Settle In—Without Selling Out." Other articles were on comfort food ("substantial meals that made you feel good back when Mom made 'em"), Jeep chic, and Eurostyle design.

The median household income of readers was $81,900, and the median home value was $184,200. Steve Burzan, publisher, explained the magazine's new focus:

> So here we have the audience becoming very affluent, the advertising base becoming very affluent, and instead of competing with middle-class magazines, we find ourselves competing with *Architectural Digest, Town & Country, Gourmet, New Yorker*—the upscale giants.[9]

Metropolitan Home was on a roll. It ran a total of 1,220 advertising pages in 1989, an increase of 15 percent from the previous year. From 1987 to 1988, ad pages grew by 32 percent. It was named one of *Adweek's* "Ten Hottest Magazines" for 1987 and 1988. The magazine won the National Magazine Award for General Excellence in 1990 and was a finalist in general excellence in 1989 and a finalist in design in 1988 and 1989. *Adweek* named Kalins Editor of the Year in 1988.[10]

All that changed in the sobering 1990s, when a lingering recession was especially hard on upscale magazines. *Metropolitan Home*'s ad page count in 1990 dropped to 888, a 27.2 percent slide from 1989. Circulation remained strong, however, increasing 11 percent, to 738,973, in 1990.[11]

Meredith considered redesigning the magazine, selling it, or closing it down completely. In November 1992, Meredith sold *Metropolitan Home* to Hachette Magazines for an estimated $10 million. Donna Warner succeeded Kalins as editor in chief; Kalins stayed at Meredith to work on magazine development. Hachette, publisher of *Elle Decor* and *Home*, changed the magazine to a bimonthly and cut its rate base to 600,000 but retained its upscale look and philosophy.[12]

In 1991, Jim Autry, who was by then president of the Magazine Group of Meredith Corporation, spoke of the magazine's history. *Metropolitan Home*, he said, had grown in what he called a golden age of magazines, in the late 1970s and early 1980s. In the final analysis, he noted, the magazine had become "as establishment as a magazine can be."[13] That Establishment continues into the challenges of the 1990s, with its baby boomer audience looking wistfully at retirement. From orange crates to Shirvan rugs . . . to rocking chairs?

Notes

1. "Apt Ideas," 1969, p. 21.
2. Ibid., p. 54.
3. Chuck Coffin, "*Apartment Ideas*—First Edition," memo dated April 23, 1969.

4. *"Metropolitan Home*: The Prospectus," Meredith Corporation, 1981.

5. "Editorial Plan: The Premise of Change," planning memo attached to letter from Dorothy Kalins, editor, *Metropolitan Home*, January 20, 1981.

6. Dorothy Kalins, "The Editors' Page: Something Different Matters Here," April 1981, p. 9.

7. *"Metropolitan Home*: The Prospectus," Meredith Corporation, 1981.

8. Dorothy Kalins, "Same Guts, New Glory," September 1986, p. 11.

9. "The Remodeled *Metropolitan Home*," *Imprint*, March 1986, p. 9.

10. "Tenth Anniversary Year: A Decade of Design: Facts," Media Kit.

11. "Upscale Titles," *Advertising Age*, November 2, 1991, p. 1.

12. "In HG's Wake, Rivals Are Ready to Move In," *Folio*, June, 1, 1993, p. 20.

13. Jim Autry, "Magazines: Dinosaurs or Survivors," Meredith Magazine Lectureship, Drake University, Des Moines, Iowa, April 1991.

Information Sources

BIBLIOGRAPHY:

Autry, Jim. "Magazines: Dinosaurs or Survivors." Meredith Magazine Lectureship. Drake University, Des Moines, Iowa, April 1991.

   "The Remodeled *Metropolitan Home*." *Imprint*, March 1986, p. 9.

   "Upscale Titles." *Advertising Age*, November 2, 1991, p. 1.

INDEX SOURCES: Access, the Supplementary Index to Periodicals; Index to How to Do It Information; Magazine Index; Popular Magazine Review Search.

LOCATION SOURCES: Library of Congress and other libraries.

Publication History

MAGAZINE TITLE AND TITLE CHANGES: *Better Homes and Gardens Apartment Ideas* (1969–1973); *Better Homes and Gardens Apartment Life* (1973–1977); *Apartment Life* (1977–1981); *Metropolitan Home* (1981–present).

VOLUME AND ISSUE DATA: Vols. 1–(1969–present). Quarterly (1969–1973); monthly (1977–1992); bimonthly (1992–present).

PUBLISHER AND PLACE OF PUBLICATION: Meredith Publishing (1969–1992); Hachette Magazines (1992–present). New York City.

EDITORS: Jim Autry (1969–1971); Jim Hufnagle (1971–1973); David Jordan (1973–1978); Dorothy Kalins (1978–1992); Donna Warner (1992–present).

CIRCULATION: ABC, 1993: 778,606 (paid, primarily subscriptions).

Patricia E. Prijatel

MIRABELLA

An upscale publication touting itself as the magazine for the woman who "reads and thinks"[1] was launched in June 1989, one year after the eponymous Grace Mirabella found herself out of *Vogue*.* In the seemingly saturated market of fashion magazines, *Mirabella* has survived. Marketing slick glamour imagery alongside an eclectic array of text, the Murdoch publication has attempted to define the niche of the affluent American woman in order to secure a hold on the 1990s.

From the outset, publication director Grace Mirabella has maintained that purely demographic considerations such as age did not define the target of this magazine's marketing: "The idea that a person who is 50 thinks differently about things doesn't make sense to me."[2] *Mirabella* set out to embody the sophistication of its intended audience, to redefine fashion in terms of style:

> *Mirabella* is about style and how it pertains to every aspect of a woman's life—the fashion she wears, the books she reads, the theater and film she enjoys, her travels, her home, her favorite restaurants, her health and sports activities.[3]

In the language and the subjects of its articles, the magazine appeals to a college-educated readership. With its upscale advertisements, it aims for a population with means to participate in the marketplace with more than the price of a subscription. The magazine aims at the 30- to 50-year-old female reader, an older population than for most fashion magazines, such as *Glamour*,* *Mademoiselle*,* *Elle** or *Vogue*. A magazine often compared with *Mirabella* was *Lear's*.*[4] *Lear's*, which has since folded, was aimed at an audience of women over 40.

For *Mirabella*'s first calendar year—1990—the amount of space devoted to editorial (as opposed to advertising) attested to its play for educated females more than the merely fashionably literate. Keeping promises of offering readers "a lot of copy," the first issue contained 269 pages, over half of which were devoted to editorial, which still left 120 pages of advertising.[5] Its 54.4 percent editorial placed it between magazines such as *Condé Nast Traveler* with 54.8 percent and *House Beautiful** with 53.2 percent and well above *Vogue*'s 38.2 percent, which defined the baseline for comparison.[6]

As editor in chief of *Vogue*, Mirabella had worked 17 years building that magazine into the leading women's fashion and beauty magazine. In 1988, *Vogue*'s search for the eternally youthful market prompted Mirabella's dismissal,[7] which she found out about on a television newscast.[8] After she left, *Vogue* actively pursued a younger audience in order to compete with relative newcomer *Elle*.[9]

Even before *Vogue* replaced her and shifted to a younger focus, Mirabella had a more mature audience in mind. "I felt it was time to reposition the fashion magazine from a book of endless pages of clothes to a style magazine that readers would pick up and stay with for a few hours," she said of the magazine she envisioned, which became *Mirabella*.[10] Media magnate Rupert Murdoch had a similar vision. With *Vogue* repositioning itself, a niche opened; Mirabella would have the chance to help create the magazine she envisioned. In November, less than six months after her ouster, Mirabella accepted Murdoch's offer that she provide direction for a new fashion magazine for the 30- to 50-year-old woman. One media director addressed this positioning as key to its success: "They're marketing against a niche in that 30- to 45-year-old marketplace that has somewhat of a void."[11] It was not Mirabella but Murdoch and John Evans, Murdoch Magazines president, who suggested the "fashionably" recognized name *Mirabella* for the stylish new venture.[12]

Murdoch's investment, combined with Mirabella's savvy, garnered the magazine a stunningly successful first year in terms of advertising. However, the magazine lost $6.13 million its first fiscal year. Swept along with the general downturn of the economy, the magazine lost $15.7 million its second fiscal year.[13] Since the first fiscal year was based on only two issues, the second is perhaps a more accurate indicator of its launch. Mirabella came to the realization that, at least for their first few years, "endeavors like this just don't" show a profit.[14] Yet, she remained hopeful; the January 1992 issue was not in deficit.[15] She wrote in the third-anniversary issue that the magazine not only survived its second year but "thrived."[16] Mirabella readily shared credit for *Mirabella*'s success with her staff,[17] particularly those she hired away from *Vogue*, creative director Jade Hobson Charnin and features editor Amy Gross.[18] In 1991, Rebecca W. Darwin from Playboy Enterprises was appointed publisher.[19]

In its mission to cover style for the mature modern woman, the magazine has variously segmented editorial material into news, features, and style departments. Pages devoted to fashion provide paradoxical guidance; what one month is extolled as sublime may be critiqued as ridiculous the next. For instance, September 1992 ran "Platforms: What This Year's Clothes Beg For," but in October the magazine recanted with "High Rise: Platforms Get Silly." Fashionable fluctuations notwithstanding, the magazine regularly covers the industry side of fashion, often highlighting women designers, from Donna Karan to Sonia Rykiel. For example, in the November 1991 issue, women fashion designers shared their views on evening wear. When fashion bows to style, "fashionable" means a wider focus: females other than those in the fashion industry. A profile of author Eudora Welty and articles on the women who served in the Persian Gulf War constitute the type of editorial content that adds that breadth and some depth.

During the 1992 election year, *Mirabella* sponsored events in larger cities across the nation that went beyond wardrobe considerations, focusing on political issues that affected women. These forums did not subside after the election and have become a hallmark of *Mirabella*.[20] Articles profiled women with clout. Television producer Linda Bloodworth-Thomason turned out to be as political and as powerful as conservative columnist George Will. Thomason's convictions were backed up by her connections: Bill Clinton's brother was her production assistant on "Designing Women"; First Lady Hillary Rodham Clinton provided the poetical title for her later television show, "Evening Shade."[21] *Mirabella* also reviewed everything from mandatory makeup to media. As with many modern women's magazines, *Mirabella* did not cater to the thinking woman's appetite for short stories, but it did occasionally run fiction and recommended readings. "Trust Us: Rantings and Ravings" is a quick pickup at the back of the book, with a swatch of unusual information about this and a patch of text about that. Another one-page, regular offering is "Travel Debriefings," which offers hints and insight for the female sojourner. Mirabella speaks through her column "Dictu."

While editorial content may keep readers anticipating the next issue, advertisers have kept the publication alive. Advertisers have ranged from Gucci cologne to Givenchy handbags, from Tanqueray to Tiffany, all presented in a sumptuous package for the urban female elite. Full-page ads flow cover to cover, the bulk of them retail fashion, beauty, and jewelry. The spectrum of upscale consumer desires is completed with shoes and accessories, alcoholic beverages, automobiles, cigarettes, travel fitness, entertainment, and a few packaged goods such as coffee and chocolate. The magazine spelled out much of its policy for advertisers: "*Mirabella* reserves the right to reject or cancel at any time any advertising which the Publisher deems unacceptable for any reason."[22] According to Mirabella, her magazine must reflect the things she stands for; however, *Mirabella* is a business venture, and preferences of the publication director cannot always be reflected in the advertising.

Mirabella found this out with tobacco advertising. Although she would prefer that the magazine not run tobacco ads, she said that the magazine does accept advertising for tobacco products. "We take it, but it doesn't stop us from doing . . . articles on how bad smoking is for you."[23] Cigarette manufacturer Philip Morris was one of *Mirabella*'s first advertisers, and in the 1990s the magazine still numbered at least six tobacco products among its advertisers. Such patronage opened the door for ads, such as the Dolce & Gabbana ad in the November 1992 issue, which, despite a culturally chilly climate for cigarettes, appeared to have had postproduction enhancement to depict the models inhaling.

Advertisers have patronized *Mirabella* because of its readers' buying power. The magazine estimated the net worth of each subscriber at $750,800, and the advertising rate base effective with the September 1991 issue reflected a 122 percent increase since the magazine's launch.[24] Initial guaranteed circulation was 225,000.[25]

Developing its advertising base by including the new magazine in innovative group packages, Murdoch strongly supported *Mirabella*. For example, he offered a joint advertising deal in 1991 with Meredith's *Metropolitan Home*.* *Mirabella* was also added to advertising packages of Murdoch magazines that were being sold to another company.[26] Then-publisher Julie Lewit-Nirenberg also offered incentives. Advertisers were extended a package for the first and second issues. Those who wanted to advertise in the first issue also had to advertise in the second, but they would receive a 50 percent discount on the second.[27] Advertising strategies such as these afforded *Mirabella* a successful foothold in a highly competitive market, even though initial rates were more than 30 percent higher than those of other fashion magazines.[28]

Despite its early success, *Mirabella*'s continued loss of revenue discouraged the once-supportive Murdoch. By 1991, he was said to have spent $25 million on the magazine.[29] In a divestiture that year, he kept *Mirabella* in his portfolio solely because the buyer did not want it. In that sale, he let go eight of his other U.S. magazines to K-III Holdings, a company controlled by Kohlberg, Kravis, Roberts & Company, a firm known for buyouts of troubled companies. Initially, *Mirabella* was included in the $650 million sale, which also included the highly successful publications *Seventeen*,* *New York Magazine*, *Soap Opera Digest*,* and *New Woman*.*[30] Although *Mirabella* showed an increase in advertising pages and anticipated a break-even point in June 1993, K-III Holdings was not willing to invest in it. Upon the rejection, Murdoch kept the youngest of his proffered magazines. *Mirabella* did not ring in a profit with the new year, but circulation was said to be two years ahead of its original business plan.[31]

In an attempt at name recognition for a magazine entering a seemingly glutted market, a script similar to Mirabella's own penmanship scrawled the magazine's name prominently across the top of each cover. At first, nothing could stop it— not even the cover model, the name often running across her forehead. But later issues have allowed the model to intrude on the script, such as the model Manon on the cover of the April 1994 issue. Clad in a $1,200 slip-dress, she strolled in the surf. Although her satin and silk were to evoke "[t]he eternal appeal of the bare summer dress," the largest headline, "Waif Goodbye: Return of the Real Woman," left the reader wondering which this model embodied. Between the covers, "the reintroduction of bigger models (at least by waif standards)" used models such as Cindy Crawford to cite this curvaceous trend.[32]

Author Tina Gaudoin penned the provocative article that acknowledged the sigh of relief as American women exhaled from sucking in their collective gut for at least a decade. She pensively drew the reader into the question of whether the return of the curve was but a different (and equally as unattainable) stereotype, stating that the transition should not merely replace one with another but broaden acceptance: "What the waif has done is to force us to reassess the way society makes value judgments based on body shape. So, let's applaud the 'return of the curve,' but only if it's a step on the road to embracing all body types."[33]

Such thoughtful pieces are usually sandwiched by shorter articles, which often rely on a montage style of presentation, whether showcasing shoes, evening wear, or designers themselves. Since the montage effect is one of raw, candid presentation, the pieces set themselves apart from the polished pool of the purely promotional, seeming to capture a reality that the poised perfection of the advertising eluded.

Although covers have the seduction that consumers have come to expect— flawless features luring the customer toward the contents—the "look" of *Mirabella* suffered a setback in the advertising downturn of the 1990s. After differentiating itself in the marketplace with the large format that was in keeping with Mirabella's feeling that fashion magazines were generally "too squat,"[34] *Mirabella* went to a smaller format with its August 1991 issue—to cut production costs. *Mirabella* downsized from 11⅞" × 9" to 10⅞" × 8⅜". Heavier-weight paper was used for the cover, increasing from 100-pound to 128-pound stock in the hopes of giving the impression of exchanging size for a certain "richness."[35] Despite the downsizing, shifts in design have kept the *Mirabella* of the mid-1990s elegant while making it more approachable: cover articles are easier to find than in earlier issues, and departments have become regularized in both theme and placement.

At the time *Mirabella* hit the scene, only two out of every ten magazines launched made it to its fourth year, a year considered crucial.[36] *Mirabella* cleared that hurdle with grace amid tough competition for both advertising and circulation. In developing the niche for stylish women over 30, *Mirabella* has employed the glamour vernacular of the 1980s. However, as of March 1995, *Mirabella* had yet to turn a profit; that month, Hachette Filipacci Magazines bought the magazine for an undisclosed amount.

Notes

1. Media Kit.
2. Grace Mirabella, quoted in N. R. Kleinfield, "Grace Mirabella, at 59, Starts Over Again," *New York Times*, April 30, 1989, sec. 3, p. 13.
3. Media Kit.
4. For example, see Deirdre Carmody, "*Mirabella* vs. *Lear's*: Stylish Fight," *New York Times*, November 26, 1990, sec. 9, p. 8. In an interesting twist of fate, former rival Frances Lear appeared in a 1994 computer ad campaign run in *Mirabella*.
5. Lenore Skenazy, "Mirabella's Debut: Editor Makes Her Mark with New Title," *Advertising Age*, June 12, 1989, p. 60.
6. Advertising/Editorial Ratio, Media Kit. Source: Hall's Magazine Reports.
7. Kleinfield, "Grace Mirabella, at 59, Starts Over Again," p. 13.
8. Mary Cronin, "A Fresh Take on Fashion," *Time*, April 1, 1991, p. 69.
9. Geraldine Fabrikant, "The Jury's Out on the Hipper Vogue," *New York Times*, April 30, 1989, sec. 3, p. 13.
10. Grace Mirabella, quoted in Cronin, "A Fresh Take on Fashion," p. 69.
11. Bob Zach, vice president/New York media director, Chiat/Day, quoted in "Media Buyers Praise 'Mirabella,' " *Advertising Age*, June 12, 1989, p. 54.
12. Grace Mirabella interview, August 6, 1992.
13. Anthony Ramirez, "Magazines Murdoch Is Selling, and One He Is Not," *New York Times*, April 27, 1991, p. 40.
14. Mirabella interview.
15. Ibid.
16. Grace Mirabella, "A Letter from Grace Mirabella," June 1992, p. 22.
17. Grace Mirabella, publication director, speech to the Magazine Division of the Association for Education in Journalism and Mass Communication, Montreal, Quebec, August 6, 1992. Mirabella made this acceptance speech upon receipt of the Outstanding Magazine Professional Award.
18. Cronin. "A Fresh Take on Fashion," p. 69.
19. Deirdre Carmody, "A Publisher Is Appointed at *Mirabella*," *New York Times*, October 10, 1991, p. D19.

20. For example, see Genevieve Buck, "Looking Good on the Outside, Feeling Good on the Inside," *Chicago Tribune*, September 30, 1993, sec. 5, p. 11D; Mary O'Neill, "Mirabella's Saving Grace Is a Mix of Style, Substance," *Detroit News*, September 23, 1993, p. E1.

21. "The Producers," September 1992, pp. 76, 78.

22. Rate card.

23. Mirabella speech.

24. Circulation information, Media Kit.

25. Skenazy, "Mirabella's Debut," p. 60.

26. Deirdre Carmody, "Murdoch Keeps Ties to Eight Magazines," *New York Times*, May 17, 1991, p. D15.

27. Kleinfield, "Grace Mirabella, at 59, Starts Over Again," p. 13.

28. Ibid. Rates figured at cost per thousand.

29. George Lazarus, "Mirabella Hangs On with Murdoch," *Chicago Tribune*, May 1991, sec. 3, p. 4. However, other estimates are higher; less than one year later, Grace Mirabella, in her interview with the author, estimated that Murdoch had invested $45–$50 million in the magazine.

30. Geraldine Fabricant, "Murdoch Gets a Generous Price," *New York Times*, April 27, 1991, p. 37.

31. Deirdre Carmody, "Can 4 Magazines Stay in Fashion?" *New York Times*, January 27, 1992, p. D1.

32. Tina Gaudoin, "The Return of the Real Woman," April 1994, p. 44.

33. Ibid.

34. Kleinfield, "Grace Mirabella, at 59, Starts Over Again," p. 13.

35. Len Egol, "Cutting Trim Size: Is Less More?" *Folio*, August 1, 1991, p. 26.

36. Kleinfield, "Grace Mirabella, at 59, Starts Over Again," p. 13.

37. Deirdre Carmody, "Sale Planned for *Mirabella* After 6 Years of Losses," *New York Times*, March 23, 1995, p. D8; Lawrie Mifflin, "Murdoch Publishing Unit Sells *Mirabella* to Hachette," *New York Times*, March 31, 1995, p. D5.

Information Sources

BIBLIOGRAPHY:

Carmody, Deirdre. "*Mirabella* vs. *Lear's*: Stylish Fight." *New York Times*, November 26, 1990, sec. 9, p. 8.

———. "A Publisher Is Appointed at *Mirabella*." *New York Times*, October 10, 1991, p. D19.

———. "Can 4 Magazines Stay in Fashion?" *New York Times*, January 27, 1992, p. D1.

Cronin, Mary. "A Fresh Take on Fashion." *Time*, April 1, 1991, p. 69.

Kleinfield, N. R. "Grace Mirabella, at 59, Starts Over Again." *New York Times*, April 30, 1989, sec. III, p. 13.

Matthews, Tom, and Lucille Beachy. "The Battle of the Rag Mags." *Newsweek*, September 7, 1992, pp. 64–65.

Ramirez, Anthony. "Magazines Murdoch Is Selling, and One He Is Not: No Glass Slipper or Invitation for Mirabella." *New York Times*, April 27, 1991, p. 40.

Skenazy, Lenore. "Mirabella's Debut: Editor Makes Her Mark with New Title." *Advertising Age*, June 12, 1989, p. 60.

INDEX SOURCES: Access.

LOCATION SOURCES: Library of Congress and many public libraries.

Publication History

MAGAZINE TITLE AND TITLE CHANGES: *Mirabella.*
VOLUME AND ISSUE DATA: Vols. 1–(June 1989–present). Monthly.
PUBLISHER AND PLACE OF PUBLICATION: Murdoch Magazines (1989–1995);
  Hachette Filipacchi (1995–present). New York.
EDITORS: Gay Bryant (1989–1995; Dominique Browning (1995); Amy Gross (1995–
  present).
CIRCULATION: ABC, 1993: 607,655 (paid, primarily subscriptions).

Therese L. Lueck

MS.

Ms. magazine, created as the voice of the reemerging feminist movement of the 1970s, sailed on shaky waters for much of its history. The magazine broke new publishing ground at the same time it butted heads with a publishing and advertising community that tried to fit it into existing and often inappropriate categories. Patricia Carbine, one of the first editors of *Ms.*, said the magazine required a new definition of an old term: women's magazine. "We are more like *Harper's*, *The Atlantic*, *The New Republic*, *Esquire* and *Rolling Stone* than like any other magazine for women," she said in 1983.[1]

Ms. was never a Madison Avenue favorite because the magazine never played by the traditional advertising rules. In fact, the magazine's stormy relationship with advertisers was one of the reasons for its death in 1990. Conversely, the magazine's rebirth in 1991 put *Ms.* on the map as an advertising-free pioneer. Through it all, though, *Ms.* could depend on one group for support, encouragement, and well-targeted criticism: its readers.

The launching of *Ms.* was unique. Clay Felker, editor of *New York* magazine and a friend of founding editor Gloria Steinem, agreed to publish 44 pages of *Ms.* material as a supplement in *New York* magazine in December 1971. *Ms.* received more than 20,000 letters from across the world from that issue. The magazine appeared as a self-standing monthly in the spring of 1972. Within six months, it had a circulation of 395,000.[2] The editorial staff included Carbine, Steinem, Suzanne Levine, and Letty Cottin Pogrebin.

Feminists of the late 1960s and early 1970s had been lobbying for the use of the term "Ms." as a title for women that has no reference to marital status, so the name became an apt one for a magazine that was built on the feminist movement. In fact, the spring 1972 preview issue offered a definition of "Ms.," noting that secretarial handbooks had recommended the use of the term for 20 years.

It was obvious early on that the magazine had tapped into the heart of its audience. By 1973, it was receiving 1,000 letters a week,[3] many highly personal. Mary Thom, who has been with the magazine in various positions since the first issue and is executive editor of the new *Ms.*, says the magazine created its own community of readers who often used the letters column as their personal forum.

Through this forum, women shared how their lives were changing. In 1982, one woman wrote: "In 1972, I asked 'What's wrong with me?' Now, at thirty-three, I ask 'What the hell is the matter with them!' "[4]

The magazine's initial design was straightforward and unpretentious, with small headlines, functional line art, and little white space. Newsprint or uncoated stock was used, full color was usually reserved for the cover and interior ads, and photos most often were black and white. Writers used first person and a relaxed, personal tone and incorporated personal anecdotes and autobiographical information in articles to add to the sense of community and to bring an immediacy to the material.

Ms. incorporated the feminist philosophy in its offices as well as in the magazine. New mothers brought their babies to work, and flexible hours and part-time jobs gave working mothers some latitude. On the masthead, the typical hierarchical magazine structure, with staff members listed in order of importance, was avoided. In its place, names were listed alphabetically, putting Gloria Steinem's name near the bottom.

The magazine also applied for—and won—nonprofit status as an entity of the *Ms.* Foundation and used magazine funds and contributions to help promote the feminist agenda and provide financial support for the women living that agenda. One such project, a children's record and television special entitled "Free to Be . . . You and Me," spearheaded by actress Marlo Thomas in 1973, was a moneymaker for the foundation.[5]

The founding editors of *Ms.* made a decision to limit advertising to products and product messages consistent with the feminist movement. The editors, however, felt they had an editorial product that would provide an excellent forum for advertisers and strove to make advertising part of their magazine, while maintaining their editorial integrity.

It was a long battle.

In a speech before the American Association of Advertising Agencies in 1987, Steinem assessed the magazine's relationship with advertisers:

> *Ms.* won reader support and jeopardized advertiser support for exactly the same reason: the editorial content wasn't dictated by the ads. The readers loved it; many advertisers loved it less. I suggest to you that there's something wrong in a world in which women readers and advertisers trying to reach them don't want the same thing.[6]

Three years later, in the first issue of the advertising-free *Ms.*, Steinem said, "Advertisers—not readers—have always been the problem for *Ms.*" She contended that the magazine did not play by the accepted women's magazine rules, in which the magazine creates a "supportive editorial atmosphere" for advertising. *Ms.* editors created a dynamic unacceptable to the advertising world, she said, by expecting audience quality and loyalty—rather than editorial control—to draw advertising support.[7]

Because the magazine was so closely tied to the women's movement, Steinem saw any failure on its part as symbolic of a failure of the movement itself: "We knew that if we closed our doors, that we could wrongly be seen as damaging the women's movement. Like losing the Equal Rights Amendment."[8]

But, by Steinem's own admission, the magazine changed editorial content to satisfy advertisers—changing "Porsche" to "car" in an article on Nazi symbolism, for example, because a valued advertiser, Volkswagen, manufacturer of the Porsche, was skittish about being connected with Nazi Germany.[9]

In 1986, the *Ms.* Foundation began looking for a buyer for the magazine as a way to keep it alive. Australian publisher John Fairfax bought the magazine in October 1987 and named Anne Summers editor. Summers and other editors then formed Matilda Publications to keep control of *Ms.* and the newly started *Sassy.** Steinem and other founding editors made no profit from the sale and moved into the background as new editors took over.

Ms. was redesigned several times, the most obvious changes being the European-size page—nine inches wide—and an upgraded paper stock, when the magazine was taken over by Fairfax in 1987. Full-color photos replaced black and whites, design became livelier, and metallic ink even popped up occasionally—a gold logo set off the October 1988 cover.

Summers tried to create an editorial environment conducive to advertising, adding a gardening column and a fashion section. She acknowledged that the fashion section turned both readers and advertisers off, but for different reasons—readers because they did not care to read about fashion in *Ms.*, advertisers because the women featured had the gall to wear their own clothes.[10]

Eventually, even the magazine's covers began to be influenced by advertisers. Summers planned to put abused woman Hedda Nussbaum on the cover and lost seven advertisers, although four said they would come back if she changed the cover. She did, to a "naked woman, a grainy picture that said: 'Dangerous Liaisons: Women & Estrogen, Hedda & Joel, the Supreme Court & Abortions.' "[11]

Researchers Jill Hicks Ferguson, Peggy J. Kreshel, and Spencer Tinkham concluded that the editorial content in *Ms.* changed so much by the mid–1980s that it resembled that found in traditional women's magazines. However, they acknowledged, the women's movement itself had changed through the years, and society had changed along with it. What had been considered radical became more and more acceptable; at the same time, behavior that had once been tolerable became unacceptable as the definition of sexism was broadened and refined.[12] Feminism became more widely accepted as more and more traditional magazines—such as *Glamour** and *Good Housekeeping*—began dealing with feminist issues, and more magazines were developed based on a feminist foundation—such as *Working Woman** and *Savvy.* Women's titles were specialized further with publications such as *Women's Sport & Fitness,** started in 1974, before women were even allowed to run in Olympic marathons, and *Essence,** for African American women.

Summers said she was worried about "tampering with this American institution" and conceded the magazine was "too soft." But, she said, business worries were a major focus in the two years she edited the magazine.[13] Robin Morgan, speaking of what she calls the magazine's "Australian period," said, "The sheer effort of trying to be everything to everybody meant reaching a lowest common denominator to some degree."[14]

Ms. was not profitable under Fairfax or Matilda ownership. From 1985 to 1988, ad pages dropped 38 percent. Significantly, however, circulation rose, peaking at 548,708 in 1988, a gain of 18 percent from 1985. Advertising rose slightly—11 percent—in 1989, while circulation dropped by a tiny 1 percent.[15] In 1989, Dale Lang, owner of *Working Woman** and *Working Mother,* bought Matilda Publications.

The magazine's 17th-anniversary issue, August 1989, featured a giant cover line, printed in blood red on a black background: "It's War!" in reaction to the Supreme Court's decision in the Webster case, allowing states the latitude to limit abortion rights. In her editor's essay, Summers said it was time to "really fight" for reproductive freedom. What was most notable about the issue was its lack of advertising. Advertisers complained that the magazine was too strident and pulled their advertising. Subsequent issues got thinner and thinner, with ad pages dwindling, until October 1989, when Lang shut down the magazine entirely.

Less than a year later, the magazine was republished by Lang as *Ms.: The World of Women.* The "new" *Ms.* is free of advertising. Morgan, the new editor, promised "no slick pages and no slick thinking." She now refers to the revised magazine as "the liberated *Ms.*"[16]

The magazine polled readers for content suggestions and learned, not surprisingly, that readers did not want to read about fashion, celebrities, gardening, or makeup. They did want to read about lesbian issues, relationships, parenting, international news, spirituality, health, environmental issues, fiction, older women, politics, child care, profiles of women, reproductive rights, feminist theory, humor, and literary reviews. Morgan promised more reader involvement.

In fact, Morgan had accepted the position as editor with reluctance. She says she told Lang executives:

I will come back this time and run the magazine, but on the following grounds: It must be completely free of all advertising. It must be editorially autonomous from Lang Communications—which is not true of any of the other magazines there—in other words, no one at Lang sees this magazine until it's in the mail to subscribers. And, I want to make it international, I want to make a minimum of six pages of international news in each issue plus at least one major feature. I want to do in-depth investigative journalism, and I want to name names, because now I could if I didn't have advertisers. And, I want to bring back world class fiction and poetry. And, I would suggest not a quarterly but six issues a year, but each to be a double issue of 100 pages of solid copy and art, and those are my terms.

And, to my absolute horror they met them, and I have not had a chance to wash my hair since.[17]

The first two issues of the ad-free *Ms.* sold out on the newsstands; by the third issue, the magazine had more than 100,000 subscribers. Subscribers actually paid more than newsstand buyers—a one-year subscription for six issues ran $40 ($30 with a discount for former subscribers), with the per-copy cost at $4.50. Publisher Ruth Bower, interviewed in the fall of 1990, after two issues of the magazine had been printed, said she was confident the magazine would survive its first year. To survive, she said, the new magazine had to have top editorial quality because it was entirely subscriber-driven.[18]

Like the original *Ms.*, the republished version has no full color inside the magazine, paper stock is uncoated, and the design is direct and straightforward, although sophisticated graphics and the use of spot color indicate the magazine is geared to a visually literate readership. Many of the original writers are back—Alice Walker, Gloria Steinem, Toni Morrison.

The magazine even had the confidence to make fun of its former self. Its classic "No Comment" department, showcasing "bad ads," was reinstated; in the premier issue, the bad ads either had appeared in, or were ads for, *Ms.* magazine in the 1980s.

In July 1993, the advertising-free *Ms.* celebrated its third anniversary. The magazine by this time had 250,000 subscribers in 117 countries. In her opening editorial, Morgan summed up the magazine's success by quoting a feminist proverb: "Only she who attempts the absurd can achieve the impossible."

Also in that editorial, Morgan announced her resignation. She turned the reins of the magazine over to its first editor of color: Marcia Ann Gillespie, former editor of *Essence** and a *Ms.* contributing editor since 1981. Morgan will continue as a contributing editor for international issues. In telling readers farewell, she said what she would miss most at the magazine would be the readers' "wonderful, funny, vulnerable, honest, cranky, tender, brave letters."[19] Readers will no doubt write on, as a new editor spends her evenings reading the words of a continually changing feminist audience.

Notes

1. "Behind the Lines: Carbine: The Misunderstood *Ms.*," *Folio*, February 1983, p. 43.

2. Marcia R. Prior, "*Ms.*: The Magazine Whose Time Was Right," paper presented to the Association for Education in Journalism and Mass Communication Annual Convention, 1977.

3. Martin Arnold, "*Ms.* Magazine, a Success after 16 Issues, Now Tries Other Business Ventures," *New York Times,* September 21, 1973, p. 38.

4. Mary Thom, *Letters to Ms.* (New York: Henry Holt, 1987), p. xviii.

5. In the early 1980s, the foundation began the *Ms.* University Program, providing free copies of the magazine for use in college classes. Eventually, *Ms.* was used in

English, journalism, women's studies, political science, sociology, psychology, econom-ics, and communications courses in nearly 3,000 colleges. Class copies were funded through contributions to the *Ms.* Foundation.

6. Michael Hoyt, "Damsels in Distress," *Columbia Journalism Review*, March/April 1990, p. 41.

7. Gloria Steinem, "Sex, Lies and Advertising," July/August 1990, p. 18.

8. Peggy Orenstein, "*Ms.* Fights for Its Life," *Mother Jones*, November/December 1990, p. 81.

9. Steinem, "Sex, Lies and Advertising," p. 27.

10. Orenstein, "*Ms.* Fights for Its Life," p. 81.

11. Steinem, "Sex, Lies and Advertising," p. 28.

12. Jill Hicks Ferguson, Peggy J. Kreshel, and Spencer Tinkham, "In the Pages of *Ms.*: Sex Role Portrayals of Women in Advertising, *Journal of Advertising*, 19:1, 1990, p. 49.

13. Orenstein, "*Ms.* Fights for Its Life," p. 82.

14. Robin Morgan, "It Feels like Journalism." Meredith Magazine Lectureship, Drake University, Des Moines, Iowa, April 15, 1992.

15. Michael Hoyt, "When the Walls Come Tumbling Down," *Columbia Journalism Review*, March/April 1990, p. 41.

16. Morgan, "It Feels like Journalism."

17. Ibid.

18. "No Ads? No Sweat. *Ms.*'s Ruth Bower Is '100 Percent Confident' That the Title Will Fly," *Folio's Publishing News*, November 15, 1990, p. 23.

19. Cosmic Laughter," July/August, 1993, p. 1.

Information Sources

BIBLIOGRAPHY:

Ferguson, Jill Hicks, Peggy J. Kreshel, and Spencer Tinkham. "In the Pages of *Ms.*: Sex Role Portrayals of Women in Advertising. *Journal of Advertising*, 19:1 (1990), pp. 40–51.

Hoyt, Michael. "Damsels in Distress." *Columbia Journalism Review*, March/April 1990, pp. 40–41.

———."When the Walls Come Tumbling Down." *Columbia Journalism Review*, March/April 1990.

Morgan, Robin. "It Feels like Journalism." Meredith Magazine Lectureship, Drake University, Des Moines, Iowa, April 15, 1992.

Orenstein, Peggy. "*Ms.* Fights for Its Life," *Mother Jones*, November/December 1990, pp. 32–36+.

Prior, Marcia R. "*Ms.*: The Magazine Whose Time Was Right." Paper presented to the Association for Education in Journalism and Mass Communication Annual Convention, 1977.

Thom, Mary. *Letters to Ms.* New York: Henry Holt, 1987.

INDEX SOURCES: Academic Index; Book Review Index; Child Book Review Index; Consumers Index; Current Index in Family Planning; Film Literature Index; Health Index; Magazine Index; Media Review Digest; Middle East, Abstracts and Index; Personnel Literature; Popular Magazine Review; Readers' Guide to Periodical Literature; Studies on Women Abstracts: TOM (Text on Microfilm); Women Studies Abstracts.

LOCATION SOURCES: Library of Congress and other libraries.

Publication History

MAGAZINE TITLE AND TITLE CHANGES: *Ms.* (1972–1989); *Ms.: The World of Women* (1990–present).

VOLUME AND ISSUE DATA: Vols. 1–(Spring 1972–present). Monthly (1972–1989); bimonthly (1990–present).

PUBLISHER AND PLACE OF PUBLICATION: Ms. Magazine Corp. (1972–1979); Ms. Foundation (1979–1987); Fairfax Ltd. (1987–1988); Matilda Publications (1988–1989); Lang Communications, Inc. (1989–present). New York.

EDITORS: Gloria Steinem and Patricia Carbine (1972–1987); Anne Summers (1987–1989); Robin Morgan (1990–1993); Marcia Gillespie (1993–present).

CIRCULATION: 1993: 250,000 (paid).

Patricia E. Prijatel

THE NATIONAL MAGAZINE; OR, LADY'S EMPORIUM

In 1830, when fashion, "female" advice, and sentimental fiction dominated the women's magazine market, a contrary editor in Baltimore tried to appeal to the serious and sensible side of her sex by publishing political commentary, a category not found in her competition. Though she would have bristled at the label, Mary Barney was a political animal who was willing to challenge the status quo and offer articles with intellectual depth. She was not interested in editing and publishing a "ladies" magazine primarily concerned with home life and fashion trends, a formula made successful by her contemporaries Sarah Josepha Hale (*Ladies' Magazine*, established in Boston in 1828) and Louis Godey (*Lady's Book*,* established in Philadelphia in 1830). Instead, Barney's *National Magazine; or, Lady's Emporium* offered a forum for women to express their views on matters both political and literary.

Barney made her intentions clear on page 1 of the premier November 1830 issue of *The National Magazine; or, Lady's Emporium*. In her letter "To Patrons," she admitted:

> Many persons both friendly and otherwise, have objected more particularly to the political part of my prospectus. On this subject I have not been properly understood, and I now wish to be more explicit. I did not intend to propose myself as a championess in the political arena; for I will engage in no *party* warfare, more especially in such a contest as that which is now raging throughout the land, and which promises to increase in bitterness and be lastingly severe. This I feel would be unsuited to me.

Yet Barney already had insinuated herself into the political scene the year before when she wrote a letter criticizing President Andrew Jackson for removing her husband as naval officer at Baltimore. (Jackson was the first president to remove civil employees who had opposed him from their appointed government posts and replace them with those who had conspicuously supported him.) Called "the most remarkable protest published at the time," Barney's attack on Jackson's "reform policy" was "narrated with the eloquence of sorrow and indignation."[1] Barney's letter was "so highly regarded by local politicians that they circulated large editions of it, printed on satin, throughout the country."[2] Barney, then, already had a national reputation as a fighter when she established *The National Magazine; or, Lady's Emporium.* In her closing editorial in that first issue, Barney again referred to her need to speak out:

> In the struggle which is now going on between civil liberty and wild anarchy, under the garb of democracy, she will sometimes raise her feeble voice; not as a disputant in the arena of party, but as an advocate for certain great principles which it may become her sex and condition to feel a lively and deep interest in maintaining, in these times of miscalled "reformation." As a victim of "proscription," she has suffered too much, and knows too much, to permit her entire silence. Upon that subject she cannot avoid speaking feelingly—she will try, however, to speak discreetly. If there are any who would still frown upon this last struggle of a mother for her family, they are at liberty to withhold their support.—A Daughter of the Revolution and the grand-children of Revolutionary Heroes, will perish ere they beg in the land where they should live in honour.[3]

The 46-year-old Barney informed her readers that "necessities" forced her to put aside her duties of a wife and mother of eight children and to start this magazine as editor and publisher. Despite a greater number of career options for women in 1830, many Americans still believed the "gentler sex" should stick to feminine occupations. The prevailing view was that the field of literature was "not women's sphere by nature but by circumstances only."[4] Economic need, as experienced by Barney, was the only justification for women becoming writers or editors. Yet, after a cursory nod to social conventions, the feisty Barney expounded: "But why speak in the language of apology? Is literary labour unbecoming the female pen; is it incompatible with the dignity of the female character, or repugnant to feminine delicacy? I trust not . . . .The region of letters is a pure Republic, where there is no distinction but that of talent; sex presents no barrier to literary eminence, and female brows have worn the garland and the wreath."[5]

Having dismissed that stereotype, Barney proceeded to challenge another convention: the topics that women could discuss. "Women writers had a very real limitation in the common feeling that feminine talents did not present learned treatises on such abstract subjects as philosophy, religion, government, and history. The areas considered proper for women were juvenile texts, stories for children, hints for the home, etiquette, moralistic stories, pious poems, and novels of deep and elevating sentiments."[6] Barney was not having any of that; *The National Magazine; or, Lady's Emporium* would be "generally literary, and occasionally political . . . nor shall the lucubrations of science, in any of its branches, be neglected."[7]

By selecting a double name for her magazine, Barney showed her twofold purpose. She would include the sciences, though "there are some who regard the sciences, among which they rank government and politics, as too masculine to engage the attention of female writers however mildly and humbly they may be treated." Hence, the "National" in her title, because "no knowledge . . . should be withheld from those who may be wives, mothers, and companions of the hardier sex, and because we have no voice in the government, have we no voice in the nation?"[8]

As for the "Lady's Emporium" portion, Barney was bowing to the prevailing taste of the day. Use of the word "lady" or "ladies" was a reflection of the ideals of piety, purity, and genteel domesticity preached by magazines of the 1830s as the model of American femininity. "Mass circulation newspapers and magazines made it possible to teach every woman how to elevate the status of her family by setting 'proper' standards of behavior, dress, and literary tastes."[9] Such magazines were read by middle-class women who wanted the "ladylike" status formerly reserved for the upper classes, who had long been devouring periodicals. "Emporium" signaled the diversity of Barney's editorial content and was similar to the use of such popular magazine title words as "Repository," "Cabinet," "Museum," and "Casket." Accentuating the title duality was the use of two different typefaces, with "National Magazine" in a strongly bold serif on one line and "Lady's Emporium" in a delicately outlined italic beneath it.

Despite the implied miscellany, Barney seemed to have a loose editorial formula. Every issue of the 80-page *National Magazine* featured a serious historical article, at least two travel pieces, several thoughtful essays, a biography, criticism of plays, books, or architecture, and lengthy discussions of current political issues at home and abroad, with a half-dozen poems scattered throughout. Most distinctive was the use of "apt quotations," which can be likened to the filler paragraphs found in *Reader's Digest.*

Articles ran consecutively, separated only by a short, hairline rule. The body copy was 8-point Scotch Roman, with each article topped by a bold 10- or 12-point, all-caps headline. Some attention seemed to be paid to rudimentary layout principles in terms of placement of text on the 6¼" × 9¾" page. There was at least an inch of white space surrounding the copy, which was set in a one-column width, resulting in a booklike format. Consequently, despite the scarcity of illustrations, *The National Magazine* did not seem type-heavy or boring. Barney assured readers, "This work will be comprised in eighty octavo pages, on fine paper, in new type, handsomely stitched, and coloured cover—making two handsome volumes a year."[10] The paper quality was good, still white and thick, the typeset copy still easy to read more than 160 years later.

The cover, usually a pale blue paper of a lighter weight, featured a bust of Sappho framed by garlands of flowers. That, in turn, was set off by several ruled borders and masthead information (volume, month, number, title, editor and publisher, location and printer address). In her use of the seventh-century B.C. lyric poet on the cover every month, Barney clearly was making a statement about the intellectual and literary qualities of her publication. She also may have been wishing for her magazine's ultimate success since classical writers praised Sappho as the tenth muse. Barney also paid homage to Minerva, offering an engraving of the goddess of wisdom with an owl, books, and lyre as an accompaniment to the January 1831 issue. The inside front cover page of *The National Magazine* featured the table of contents, while the inside back cover and back cover pages listed the magazine's subscription terms and agents. No advertisements were placed on any of the cover pages, nor were any ads to be found inside the magazine's editorial pages.

From the start, Barney's editorial selections were discerning and thought-provoking, not the pious and sentimental page-turners anticipated by the ladies of the day. The lead article in the premier issue was "Historical Parallels," a scholarly analysis of the historical traditions that sabotaged and supported the Stuart (British) and Bourbon (French) monarchies.[11] "Another historical piece, "Napoleon and His Army," detailed the Waterloo military campaign of 1815.[12] Not content to cover European and military history, Barney even printed religious history, offering two articles on "The Inquisition."[13]

To balance these longer, weightier essays, Barney included numerous shorter pieces that were both informative and light in tone. Charming travel articles took readers to Paris ("The Flower-Market of Paris," November 1830, pp. 46–50), Ireland ("An Irish Wedding," July 1831, pp. 165–173), and Georgia ("Southern Scenery," June 1831, pp. 117–120). Short compositions covered such varied topics as "Decline of the Drama,"[14] "Good Teeth,"[15] and "Refinement."[16] Longer essays (up to six pages in length) were devoted to concerns of special interest to women: female education (a hot topic at the time), female heroism, female character, and the cornerstone of all ladies' books, a mother's love (one of the few occasions when Barney followed the editorial lead of her competition).

Biographies were popular in all magazines of the period, and *The National Magazine* likewise published short sketches of a diverse group of individuals such as English portrait artist Sir Joshua Reynolds, Italian opera singer Angelica Catalani, American judge George Hay, and American poet Lydia Huntley Sigourney. Equally eclectic was the poetry, mandatory periodical fare on such scintillating topics as faded bluebells, fireflies, thunderstorms, and the widowed mother.

The "apt quotations" offered layout variety (being used to fill space when the close of an article did not reach the bottom of the page), as well as information and amusement. These fillers were always less than three paragraphs in length and showed a refreshing sense of humor on Barney's part. One example, "On the Word Impartial," was from the December 1830 issue:

> The word *impartial* will admit of being applied in a variety of cases; but one of the most curious applications of it occurred some time since in a Connecticut paper, in which a person advertises an "*impartial* account of a hail storm!"[17]

Criticism was a staple of *The National Magazine*, with reviews of recently published books, as well as older editions, critiques of plays being performed in Philadelphia and New York, and discussions of the architecture of opera houses in Italy. There was even an interpretation of the design of "The Baltimore Monument," which included a lithograph of the massively marbled structure so readers could compare details for themselves. A review usually included pages and pages of dialogue from the novel or dramatic script, offering a solid sense of language, pacing, and content. The liveliest reviews were provided by Clara Jones in an ongoing series titled "The Circulating Library." Found in five of the nine issues[18] published, "The Circulating Library" featured Jones, her aunt, and an elderly bachelor named Beverly Barnacle. The series combined witty dialogue about social mores and narrative analysis of celebrated novels and their authors. These included discussions of such familiar names as Sir Walter Scott (*Waverly*, 1816) and Samuel Richardson (*Pamela* and *Clarissa*, though written in 1740 and 1747 respectively, were still very popular), as well as less-remembered novelists—Miss Edgeworth, Mrs. Opie, Miss Porter, and Mrs. Green. Averaging more than 20 pages, or one-fourth of each issue, "The Circulating Library" was probably the most anticipated feature of the magazine, though it is difficult today to discern whether it was fiction or fact. One could make a case either way; at any rate, that one series would provide social historians with much information.

Equally insightful were commentaries found in every issue about the current concerns of the day, in all their ramifications—political, economic, social, religious, and legal. These lengthy articles about the United States and Europe assumed a level of intelligence and interest in female readers not acknowledged by other women's magazines. For example, the first issue offered "Baltimore and Ohio Rail Road," which began: "We do not know that we can refer our readers to a subject more interesting to them in every relation which binds them to the interests of their country than [this] magnificent project." The article discussed the background leading up to the adoption of a railroad instead of a canal along the intended route, described some of the viaducts and bridges that were constructed, and concluded with excerpts from the fourth annual report to the stockholders of the Baltimore and Ohio Rail Road Company.[19] The article was a solid precursor to other comprehensive pieces, such as "The State of Europe," which analyzed the warlike news arriving from overseas.[20] Articles dealing with America were appropriately political, investigating "The Post Office Department"[21] and "The Indians."[22]

Despite her initial promise to avoid party politics, Barney published the first of several critical articles about her nemesis, Andrew Jackson, beginning in March 1831. The early pieces, about correspondence between Jackson and John C. Calhoun, the newly instigated spoils system, and the Eaton affair, were straightforward in their presentation of Barney's viewpoint (though lacking by-lines, these articles were most likely penned by Barney). However, the language became censorious by June 1831 with publication of "The Deranged Cabinet" (pp. 126–142) and downright vituperative with July's "General Jackson." In the latter, Barney wrote that Jackson was depraved, obstinate, and frivolous.[23] These were strong words in a magazine intended for polite, upper-class female readers.

Although few pieces were signed, "The American System," an excellent discussion of free trade, manufacturing, employment, taxation, and monopolies, ended with the revelation that it was written by a woman, Clayonie. She concluded, "We have endeavoured to render the subject plain to every capacity, by divesting it of unmeaning technicalities and bewildering sophistries. To those who would object to us, that the subject is unsuited to a 'Lady's Emporium,' we reply, that its appropriate place is 'The National Magazine.' "[24]

Readers did object. There were no advice columns on hairdos or conversational gambits to try with shy young men, no love stories, and nothing about the duties or proper conduct of wives. Only two pieces even mentioned dress, and they were about "Circassian Women" and "Oriental Females." By the third issue, Barney was defending her approach in an editorial titled "Editress in a Dilemma." Responding to some of the magazine's young women who exclaimed, "Oh! I like Mrs. Barney's 'National Magazine,' very much—but there's no love in it," Barney noted in a fussy tone (after listing 14 different kinds of love) that it would be "impossible to please all classes of persons, their whims, wants and caprices. We would willingly exert our faculties to satisfy all—but we cannot make love for all." Therefore, Barney added, planting tongue firmly in cheek, "We would advise our young readers of both sexes, but particularly those of our own, *to make love for themselves*. We are certain they will have helpmates—but we are too far advanced in life, under all circumstances, to give them our assistance." Then, relenting and addressing the real issue, the inclusion of sentimental love stories, Barney vowed, "We assure them however, that should we be so fortunate as to catch a love effusion on the wing, they shall enjoy the benefit of it."[25]

In that same issue, subscriber Sibylla whined that she had looked in vain for "an enigma, a rebus, or a conundrum, which from 'time immemorial' have been considered as appropriate 'trifles' for a Lady's Magazine . . . .I cannot suppose you mean to become so entirely *Blue* [as in a "bluestocking," who shuns frivolous things], as to exclude altogether such innocent sources of amusement, since you must know that a great portion of our sex have neither leisure nor inclination for any deeper or more *puzzling* studies.'' Assuming that Barney had received no puzzles from her writers, Sibylla created ''Enigmatical List of Wise Men,'' which Barney published along with the letter.[26]

Acquiescing to reader tastes, later issues of *The National Magazine* included enigmas, and a romantic ''effusion'' was featured in the March 1831 magazine, possibly to balance Barney's first critical article about Jackson. In choosing a sentimental romance, Barney stayed away from swooning, flighty damsels in distress, offering instead ''The Young Italian.'' This is a short story worth reading even today, as its eerie coincidences are reminiscent of Poe and Hawthorne; the author was identified only as Bolingbroke. This incomplete author identification was frequent in *The National Magazine*, with most writers using only a single name or initials. However, content and tone made it clear that the majority of pieces were written by women. More significant, about two-thirds of the material was original rather than ''selected'' from other publications by Barney in her role as a ''gleaner.''

Barney nurtured her writers, which was shown through extensive individual comments in the May 1831 issue, where she praised and thanked them for their contributions. After all, Barney admitted, ''The editor, it is true, has not been able to *command* all the variety of talent necessary to please every taste, because it has not been in her power to offer the high *premiums* which are given by some of her richer contemporaries; but it has been her happiness to find that *all the talent of the country* is not 'on sale'—there are still a few generous, gifted spirits, to whom the pleasure of communicating amusement or instruction to others is sufficient reward.''[27]

Barney especially urged ''Marylanders of both sexes to lend a generous aid'' since ''her sons and daughters have contributed but sparingly'' to original literary productions.[28] While *The National Magazine* can be considered one of the earliest monthly periodicals for southern ladies, it really transcends identification as a regional publication. The topics were not ''southern'' by any means, and at least one-third of the writers indicated residence in cities north of Baltimore. Furthermore, Barney obviously intended the magazine to have a national scope in terms of subscribers as well as content since she listed agents in the District of Columbia and 22 states.

Feisty, fussy, farsighted, and fierce in her role as an editor and publisher, Barney became despondent as her magazine moved into its seventh month of publication. She shared her disappointment with readers in the May 1831 issue, writing in the third person: ''She relied, more perhaps than was justifiable or prudent, upon the hope that the intrinsic merits of her work would be the best and surest passport to the public favour; and that public favour would be, necessarily followed by the only unequivocal evidence of it—patronage and support.''[29] Adding quite frankly that she was unable to ''even gain her living'' from her occupation as editor and publisher, Barney quickly regained her usual tone of righteous indignation to argue:

> It has been thrown up to her by some, who are much more ready to give advice than assistance, that she has forfeited the pretensions of the Magazine to public support, by the introduction of *Political* subjects into its pages!—Can this be possible? Can *the public* so soon have forgotten the syllabus of her proposed course to which their attention was *originally invited*? . . . She promised that her work should be *"generally* literary and occasionally political."* She feels conscious that she has not been unfaithful to this promise—that if she has erred at all, it has been in not devoting a larger portion of the Magazine to the discussion of political questions. Politics is, in fact, a branch of general literature, which, in this country more especially, should form a part of the study of *every individual*. Education begins *in the cradle*; and the first and most lasting impressions of the mind are those imparted by *the mother*. Shall it be said, then, with a sneer, that a *female* has no right to meddle with politics? Has she no motive for desiring to understand the principles of a science in which the interests and happiness of her children are concerned?[30]

Barney rightfully stated that "the appearance, typographical execution and general character of *The National Magazine*, as a repertory of useful and elegant literature . . . has exceeded rather than fallen short of the expectations which the public were authorised to form. . . . And her ambition was limited to the humble hope of making a *respectable book* that should be *worth the money she asked for it*."[31] This sum was five dollars a year, payable in advance, or 75¢ per issue. That Barney was having collection problems was hinted at as early as the December 1830 issue, when she urged agents "to exert themselves" in forwarding the names of subscribers. Each subsequent issue included pleadings to agents to collect names and payments for circulation and subscription records.

Whether it was the cost—Hale and Godey each charged only three dollars for their more feminine books[32]—or the political content, *The National Magazine* struggled for just two more issues. Certainly, a factor had to be Barney's inability to attract advertising, as not a single advertisement appeared during the nine months of publication. The July 1831 magazine, featuring the bitterest attack on President Jackson, was Barney's final one.

It always has been easy to start a magazine, and never more so than at the dawn of the "golden age of magazines" (1825–1850), when thousands of publishers took advantage of the rapid growth of a more literate population, an increase in leisure time, and improved printing technologies.[33] But it is difficult to keep a magazine going, especially if the editor is defiantly marching while her readers are daintily strolling.

Barney's *National Magazine; or, Lady's Emporium* has been ignored by noted magazine historians.[34] Feminists fail to include Barney in their biographies of significant female editors, though it is obvious to this researcher that she was a woman to be reckoned with. Though *The National Magazine; or, Lady's Emporium* was short-lived, Mary Barney should be admired for her determination to treat women as thinking, sentient beings in 1830 and not as housewifely appendages or fashion plates.

Notes

1. James Parton, *Life of Andrew Jackson*, vol. 3 (New York: Mason Brothers, 1860; reprinted by Johnson Reprint Corporation, 1967), p. 222. For the text of Mary Barney's letter, see pp. 222–224.

2. Bertha-Monica Stearns, "Southern Magazines for Ladies (1819–1860)," *The Southern Atlantic Quarterly* vol. 31:1 (January 1932), p. 75.

3. Mary Barney, "Proposals," November 1830, p. 78. Her Revolutionary references were to her father, Samuel Chase, a signer of the Declaration of Independence, and her father-in-law, Commodore Joshua Barney, noted for his military exploits at sea from 1776 to 1812.

4. Robert E. Riegel, *American Women: A Story of Social Change* (Rutherford, N.J.: Fairleigh Dickinson University Press, 1970), p. 160.

5. Mary Barney, "To Patrons," November 1830, p. 1.

6. Riegel, *American Women*, p. 162.

7. Barney, "Proposals," p. 77.

8. Barney, "To Patrons," p. 2.

9. Gerda Lerner, *The Majority Finds Its Past: Placing Women in History* (New York: Oxford University Press, 1979), p. 26.

10. Barney, "Proposals," p. 78.

11. November 1830, pp. 5–16; December 1830, pp. 81–88.

12. February 1831, pp. 298–303.

13. December 1830, pp. 156–158; July 1831, pp. 198–205.

14. November 1830, pp. 44–45.

15. December 1830, pp. 159–160.

16. March 1831, p. 382.

17. December 1830, p. 95.

18. The five issues: December 1830, January 1831, February 1831, March 1831, and June 1831.

19. November 1830, pp. 67–75.

20. January 1831, pp. 229–233.

21. May 1831, pp. 26–35.

22. February 1831, pp. 293–298.

23. Mary Barney, "General Jackson," July 1831, pp. 210–211: "Putting *goodness* out of the question, he does not seem to possess a single *great* quality. His mind, in every respect appears to be of the lowest order—utterly incapable either of generating or comprehending an elevated or liberal idea. . . . If he had been bribed by the crown heads of Europe to use his best endeavours to bring republican institutions into ridicule

and disrepute, he could not have accomplished the object more effectually.''

24. Clayonie, "The American System," January 1831, p. 180.

25. "Editress in a Dilemma," January 1831, pp. 194–195.

26. Sibylla, "To, the Editor of the Lady's Emporium," January 1831, p. 210.

27. Mary Barney, "Prolegomena," May 1831, p. 3.

28. Barney, "To Patrons," p. 3.

29. Barney, "Prolegomena," p. 1.

30. Ibid., pp. 2–3.

31. Ibid., p. 3.

32. Helen Woodward, *The Lady Persuaders* (New York: Ivan Obolensky, 1960), p. 28.

33. Frank Luther Mott, *A History of American Magazines 1741–1850* (Cambridge: Harvard University Press, 1939), pp. 339–343.

34. Mott, in his Pulitzer Prize-winning seminal work, has only a fragmented mention of Barney's magazine as one of several Baltimore periodicals established during the era of magazine expansion. Theodore Peterson, author of *Magazines in the Twentieth Century* (Urbana: University of Illinois Press, 1964), a magazine text used for many years by departments and schools of journalism and mass communication, does not include Barney or her magazine in his historical discussion of women's magazines. *The American Magazine*, published in 1991 under the auspices of the Magazine Publishers of America and American Society of Magazine Editors to celebrate the 250th anniversary of magazine publishing in America, does not even include *The National Magazine; or, Lady's Emporium* in its historical time line of magazines.

Information Sources

BIBLIOGRAPHY:

Mott, Frank Luther. *A History of American Magazines 1741–1850.* Cambridge: Harvard University Press, 1939.

Parton, James. *Life of Andrew Jackson*, vol. 3. New York: Mason Brothers, 1860; reprinted by Johnson Reprint Corporation, 1967.

Stearns, Bertha-Monica. "Southern Magazines for Ladies (1819–1860)." *The Southern Atlantic Quarterly* 31:1 (January 1932), 70–87.

INDEX SOURCES: Union List of Serials.

LOCATION SOURCES: American Antiquarian Society, Worcester, Mass.; Peabody Institute Library, Baltimore, Md.; *American Periodical Series, 1741–1900,* American Periodicals (APS II).

Publication History

MAGAZINE TITLE AND TITLE CHANGES: *The National Magazine; or, Lady's Emporium.*

VOLUME AND ISSUE DATA: Vols. 1–2 (November 1830–April 1831). Monthly.

PUBLISHER AND PLACE OF PUBLICATION: Mary Barney (November 1830–July 1831). Baltimore.

EDITORS: Mary Barney (November 1830–July 1831). (Some sources have incorrectly spelled Mary Barney's name as Burney. The correct spelling is Barney. In some references she is referred to as Mary Chase Barney, including her maiden name.

However, nowhere in *The National Magazine* did she refer to herself as Mary Chase Barney; she identified herself in all issues as Mary Barney.)
CIRCULATION: Unknown.

Sammye Johnson

NEW WOMAN

New Woman magazine was just that when it was born—a magazine aimed at the new women who were entering the workplace following the latest wave of the women's movement. Born as a bimonthly in 1970, *New Woman* was the brain-child of publisher Margaret Harold Whitehead.[1] In its infancy, the magazine had the largest circulation rate base of any magazine aimed at working women, with 1 million readers.[2] *New Woman* sought to create a niche that was somewhere between the more radical *Ms.** magazine and traditional women's magazines.

Indeed, *New Woman*'s intent in its first few years was to reinforce the self-esteem of working women, who may have faced their obstacles with some fear and trepidation. Its articles were described as those that would "boost the psyche."[3] Former associate editor and publisher Wendy Danforth attributed the magazine's success to its ability to help women "find out who they want to become and then helping them become what they want."[4] The editors provided new women with information on dressing for success and dealing with sexism, among other useful topics.

By 1980—ten years after its birth—*New Woman* was one of the most successful working women's magazines. Midway through that year, it was able to increase its rate base by 20 percent to 1.2 million.[5] The magazine had found a formula that worked, and it grew rapidly. In the summer of 1982, *New Woman* went from bimonthly to monthly publication,[6] which only added to its popularity.[7] Increasing newsstand sales were attributable, in part, to the models who appeared on the cover and resembled the working woman and to the strand of equal rights that ran through the magazine's articles.

For advertisers, *New Woman* had a special attraction. Since its inception, *New Woman*'s pages promoted automobiles, insurance, and travel, in addition to the traditional cigarette and liquor advertisements.[8] In late 1982, however, the magazine announced its new technique designed to attract readers to advertisements. Called "subliminal synergism," the technique consisted of continuing the dominant colors from a four-color advertisement across the fold to editorial tints of headlines or graphics, which supposedly moved the readers' eyes from the editorial to the ad.[9] *New Woman* was unique in its use of this technique, and magazine officials advertised it as a way to get two pages for the price of one. Although there was no scientific support for this practice, subliminal synergism remained with *New Woman* through its subsequent ownership and editorial changes.

Adolescence brought drastic changes to *New Woman*. In May 1984, News America Publishing, owned by Rupert Murdoch, purchased the magazine.[10] Whitehead and Danforth, the original publishers, were replaced. Murdoch hired

Pat Miller, a 49-year-old Englishwoman, as the publisher and editor.[11] Miller was fresh from running the international editions of *Cosmopolitan*,* and her experience there soon began to creep into the pages of *New Woman*. She intended to position the magazine somewhere between *Cosmopolitan* and the traditional "Seven Sisters" of women's magazines, adopting the rather enigmatic slogan "The *New Woman* is the new woman." New special sections such as a horoscope guide for the new year and a travel issue started to shift the focus of *New Woman* from that of career to a contemporary women's magazine concerned with beauty and relationships.

The most notable change in *New Woman* during Miller's tenure, though, was the huge increase in articles about sex. While *New Woman* had previously received little coverage in other media, the number and variety of these articles drew the attention of several newspaper columnists.[12] But the most popular sex features were the surveys, most notably the March 1986 survey designed to investigate how women had adjusted to the sexual revolution; among its findings, the survey revealed that women valued their sexual freedom but believed sex was a barrier to true intimacy. Its results appeared in the October 1986 issue, then in a wide variety of other media.[13] About 34,000 *New Woman* readers answered the survey, which seemed to support senior editor Stephanie von Hirschberg's justification of the extensive space devoted to it: "We know that sex is a very important part of our lives," von Hirschberg said. "We run lots of articles on sex and relationships. It's one of the mainstays of our magazine."[14] The years since have regularly produced similar provocative surveys, such as use of contraceptives and the "*New Woman* Infidelity Report," which appeared in the March 1994 issue.

Whether the primary audience left *New Woman* when its focus shifted away from business and career is unclear. A 1985 readership study found that the magazine's average reader was 31 years old and college-educated.[15] Circulation appeared to slip briefly around the time Murdoch Magazines bought the periodical, perhaps because of a shifting readership due to content changes. Circulation and advertising figures during the years Miller served as publisher and editor, however, indicate that the new content stimulated sales. Under Miller's leadership, *New Woman*'s circulation rate base returned from 1 million to 1.2 million readers in just over two years, most of whom bought the magazine off the newsstand.[16] Advertising pages increased 30 percent from 1985 to 1986 and more than 10 percent from 1986 to 1987.[17] Late in 1987, *New Woman* began a television and outdoor print advertising campaign to raise those figures even further, using the slogan "Nobody knows you like *New Woman*."

Pat Miller left *New Woman* in January 1988, and associate publisher Janice Grossman took over as publisher,[18] with Gay Bryant named editor in chief.[19] When Bryant became *Mirabella*'s editor in May 1990, she was replaced by Karen Walden.[20] During Grossman's two-year stint, *New Woman* became the third largest contemporary women's magazine in the United States, with circulation of more than 1.34 million, when Grossman resigned from the magazine to publish *New York Magazine* in January 1991.[21] No significant changes appeared in editorial content during this period.

As *New Woman* reached adulthood, it experienced yet another publisher and owner. Lori Zelikow Florio, then 31 and former advertising director of *Seventeen*,* became publisher in January 1991.[22] K-III Magazines purchased *New Woman* from Murdoch Magazines as part of a nine-publication, $650 million package in early 1992.[23] Walden remained in place as editor in chief. This publisher-editor combination was to last (at least until spring 1994).

By the early 1990s, *New Woman* was positioned just behind *Cosmopolitan* and *Glamour** in the contemporary women's magazine market. Miller's editorial adjustments in the mid-1980s had left *New Woman* with the reputation of being a ''*Cosmo* clone,'' according to Florio.[24] Florio immediately sought to better define *New Woman* with a new advertising campaign using the theme ''*New Woman* magazine. For the woman who loves life.'' That Florio herself provided a new mind-set for the magazine was evinced by her preference for the title ''Ms.''; Miller and Grossman preferred to be called ''Mrs.''[25]

One reason that *New Woman* may resemble *Cosmopolitan* more than its own original incarnation was the turnaround in advertising content from the magazine's early days. As a working women's magazine, *New Woman* had mostly promoted automobiles and insurance, products about which a newly liberated working woman would need to know. In the 1990s, though, beauty products—particularly cosmetics and hair care—constitute the largest portion of advertisements. Weight loss products and exercise equipment are the second most frequently occurring advertisements, with automobiles, computer software, and business association ads rarely appearing. This shift toward beauty also included the addition of typical women's magazine columns on dieting and cosmetics.

Celebrities began to replace the career-minded models who appeared on the magazine's cover during its first decade. Actresses such as Jane Seymour (February 1994) and Heather Locklear (March 1994) graced the *New Woman* cover, then were profiled briefly inside. Actress Halle Berry was one of the rare women of color to appear in the editorial pages, as well as on the November 1993 cover. Women of color are seldom (if ever) used as models in editorial illustrations, and they generally appear in advertisements only when teamed with white women.

New Woman's articles retain a bit of the ''*Cosmo* clone'' image that publisher Florio disdained. For example, the January 1994 issue contained articles on finding one's inner child, what men are afraid of sexually, the lack of a man shortage in the 1990s, and beauty ideas for the new year. Articles on women leaders and sabotaging one's career by lacking self-confidence, however, displayed an attempt to reach women concerned about their careers. The March 1994 issue contained a complaint from a reader who wrote, ''Over the past couple of years, [*New Woman*] seems to have changed from an informative professional magazine to a women's *Playboy*.'' Tellingly, that same issue included a photo analyst examining celebrity love lives, meeting men through personal computer networking, and, as mentioned before, an extensive report on *New Woman*'s infidelity survey.

Despite its emphasis on sexuality, *New Woman* still promotes career and independence. The "People of the Year" are selected annually in the December issue; women who have made strides for women's rights or society in general are honored. Investing, stress reduction, and health issues are regular topics. Popular monthly features called "Sounds like a New Woman . . . " and "A Thump on the Head to . . . " compile quotations by celebrities and politicians that either celebrate women or insult them. *New Woman*'s favorite bits from these features were collected in a 1994 Penguin paperback titled *Sounds like a New Woman: A Decade of New Women, Old Ladies and Thumps on the Head.*[26] Thus, actor Kirk Douglas is immortalized as saying, "Why can't a woman be more like a dog, huh? So sweet, loving and attentive?"

Under Florio and Walden's leadership, *New Woman*, along with the National Association for Female Executives (NAFE), implemented an annual contest for female entrepreneurs in 1990. The concept was designed to help women start or expand their own businesses. The magazine and NAFE offered $50,000 in prize money for the three best entries, based on originality, feasibility, and presentation. Such a contest helps to set *New Woman* apart from contemporary women's magazines. Additionally, *New Woman* was a major sponsor of the 1994 album "Red Hot + Country," a release produced to benefit various acquired immunodeficiency syndrome (AIDS) organizations.[27]

New Woman magazine has undergone growing pains in its first quarter-century, all the while maintaining its position as one of the most successful nontraditional women's magazines in the United States. Its primary focus shifted midway through life from a working women's magazine to a contemporary women's publication, with the usual emphasis on sex, relationships, and appearance. With its wide range, *New Woman* may be more closely related to women than are other, better-defined magazines. Pat Miller, the former publisher and editor who directed *New Woman*'s most dramatic change, may have best analogized the magazine's philosophy when she said: "Women are constantly rearranging themselves. They are not defined chronologically anymore."[28]

Notes

1. "Baker's Dozen in Women's Magazines," *Marketing & Media Decisions*, October 1979, p. 132.

2. Ibid.

3. "Magazines Targeted at the Working Woman," *Business Week*, February 18, 1980, p. 150.

4. "Baker's Dozen."

5. *New York Times Information Bank Abstracts*, March 31, 1980, p. 6.

6. "Addenda," *New York Times*, August 20, 1981, p. D16.

7. "Circulation in Mid-1982 Was Up to 1.3 million, with Seventy Percent from Newsstand Sales, According to the *New York Times*," *New York Times*, September 7, 1982, p. D12.

8. "Baker's Dozen."

9. Karla Vallance, "Does 'Subliminal Synergism' Trick Magazine Readers?" *Christian Science Monitor*, October 28, 1982, p. 6.

10. "Murdoch Buys a Magazine," *New York Times*, May 26, 1984, p. 34.

11. Philip H. Dougherty, "*New Woman* Magazine Picks O.&M. Partners," *New York Times*, January 30, 1985, p. D19.

12. For example, *Los Angeles Times* columnist Al Martinez was inspired to write his August 22, 1985, column about a *New Woman* article titled "Too Busy for Sex?" (August 1985, part 9, p. 2). Ten years later, a *Buffalo News* columnist mentioned the magazine in an advice column about relationships, describing it as a "peevish, neo-feminist *New Woman* magazine—which seems to like no men at all" ("Dr. Love," *The Buffalo News*, April 1, 1994, p. 7).

13. Reuters carried the survey results on its wire service on September 19, 1986. It subsequently appeared, among other places, in the *Chicago Tribune* under the headline "1980s Women Sexually Confident, but Cuddling Counts Too" (October 19, 1986. Domestic News sec., p. 5).

14. Beth Austin, "Read All about Work and Sex," *Chicago Tribune*, October 19, 1986, p. 2.

15. "Dougherty, "*New Woman* Magazine Picks O.&M. Partners," p. D19.

16. Philip H. Dougherty, "*New Woman* Gets a New Campaign," *New York Times*, December 23, 1987, p. D15.

17. Ibid.

18. "New Publisher for New York," *New York Times*, January 5, 1991, p. 32. Miller left *New Woman* to publish *Woman*, which folded in two years.

19. Randall Rothenberg, "*Mirabella* Editor Named," *New York Times*, May 17, 1990, p. D26.

20. Ibid.

21. "New Publisher for New York."

22. "Executive Moves," *Crain's New York Business*, January 14, 1991, p. 14.

23. Stuart Elliott, "*New Woman* to Clarify Its Identity," *Press Association Newsfile*, February 5, 1993, p. D7.

24. Ibid.

25. Dougherty, "*New Woman* Gets a New Campaign."

26. Lois M. Blinkhorn, "Can You Believe They Said That about Women?" *Sacramento Bee*, March 7, 1994, p. B5.

27. Edward Morris, "Mercury to Release 'Red Hot + Country,' " *Billboard*, October 2, 1993, p. 31.

28. Dougherty, "*New Woman* Gets a New Campaign."

Information Sources

BIBLIOGRAPHY:

"Addenda." *New York Times*, August 20, 1981, p. D16.

Austin, Beth. "Read All about Work and Sex." *Chicago Tribune*, October 19, 1986, sec. Tempowoman, p. 2.

"Baker's Dozen in Women's Magazines." *Marketing & Media Decisions*, October 1979, p. 132.

Blinkhorn, Lois M. "Can You Believe They Said That about Women?" *Sacramento Bee*, March 7, 1994, p. B5.

Dougherty, Philip H. "*New Woman* Picks O.&M. Partners." *New York Times*, January 30, 1985, p. D19.
———. "*New Woman* Gets a New Campaign." *New York Times*, December 23, 1987, p. D15.
Elliott, Stuart. "*New Woman* to Clarify Its Identity." *Press Association Newsfile*, February 5, 1993, p. D7.
"Executive Moves." *Crain's New York Business*, January 14, 1991, p. 14.
"Magazines Targeted at the Working Woman." *Business Week*, February 18, 1980, p. 150.
Martinez, Al. "There Ought to be a Little Magic to the Moment . . . Which Would Preclude Appointment Books and Tuna Sandwiches." *Los Angeles Times*, Westside sec., p. 2.
Morris, Edward. "Mercury to Release 'Red Hot + Country.' " *Billboard*, October 2, 1993, p. 31.
"Murdoch Buys a Magazine." *New York Times,* May 26, 1984, p. 34.
"New Publisher for New York." *New York Times*, January 5, 1991, p. 32.
New York Times Information Bank Abstracts, March 31, 1980, p. 6.
"1980s Women Sexually Confident, but Cuddling Counts Too." *Chicago Tribune*, October 19, 1986, Domestic News sec., p. 5.
Rothenberg, Randall. "*Mirabella* Editor Named." *New York Times*, May 17, 1990, p. D26.
Salmans, Sandra. "Access: A Storybook Catalogue." *New York Times*, September 7, 1982, p. D12.
Vallance, Karla. "Does 'Subliminal Synergism' Trick Magazine Readers?" *Christian Science Monitor*, October 28, 1982, p. 6.
INDEX SOURCES: Readers' Guide to Periodical Literature.
LOCATION SOURCES: Lexis/Nexis; Linebaugh Public Library (Murfreesboro, Tenn.); Todd Library (Middle Tennessee State University) and other libraries.

Publication History

MAGAZINE TITLE AND TITLE CHANGES: *New Woman.*
VOLUME AND ISSUE DATA: Vols. 1–(1970–present). Bimonthly (1970–1982); monthly (1982–present).
PUBLISHER AND PLACE OF PUBLICATION: Margaret Harold Whitehead (1970–1984); Pat Miller (1984–1988); Janice Grossman (1988–1991); Lori Zelikow Florio (1991–present). Palm Beach, Fla. (1970–1984); New York (1984–present).
EDITORS: Margaret Harold Whitehead (1970–1984); Pat Miller (1984–1988); Gay Bryant (1988–1990); Karen Walden (1990–present).
CIRCULATION: ABC, 1993: 1,314,292 (60 percent subscriptions, 40 percent newsstand) (peak circulation, 1990: 1,340,540).

Julie L. Andsager

NEW YORK WOMAN

Students of the magazine form have long recognized that the editorial personas of many magazines—the tonal style of their editorial voices, their values and worldviews, the nature and focus of their primary concerns—are, to some extent, reflections of the personalities of their chief editors.[1] This coincidence between the character of a magazine and its editor in chief is often particularly true when the chief editor is also the original founder of the publication. Certainly, the instance of *New York Woman* (*NYW*) bears out the point.

Though raised in Miami and educated at the University of Michigan, Betsy Carter had lived and worked in New York City for more than 15 years before she founded *NYW* in September 1986, and she served as editor in chief during the magazine's entire five-and-a-half-year existence. In describing her view of life in the city, she also summed up the editorial attitude of her magazine: ''I think most New York women's personalities are certainly shaped by living here. It's a matter of urban survival. You have to notice everything, and you have to be smart. You also have to put up with a lot, so it helps to be irreverent and funny.'' Reflecting on *NYW*'s persona, she said: ''We thought of the magazine as our reader's older sister who, though she didn't know all the answers, did know all the questions. And she could talk about it because she had been there.''[2]

Despite its title, the magazine was edited for urban women in general, not just residents of New York, and almost a third of its 110,000 circulation was outside the city. Nevertheless, *NYW* was explicit in its assumptions about a particular kind of urbanity, if not exactly sophistication, on the part of its readers, and these helped to differentiate it from many other glossy women's magazines of the late 1980s. ''We assumed a level of intelligence, curiosity, and energy in our readers,'' said Carter. ''But few had the luxury of doing just one thing; most had both personal and professional lives. I used to tell people that our model was the smart and funny character played by Julie Kavner, the sister on the television show, 'Rhoda.' Additionally, our readers' belief in feminism was simply another assumption we were willing to make.''[3]

The idea for *NYW* came to Carter in the mid-1980s, while she was editorial director of *Esquire* magazine. At the time, she already had a wealth of experience as a magazine editor, having worked at *Newsweek* for ten years, followed by five years as a member of *Esquire*'s senior editorial staff.[4] The original concept for the magazine arose from a special women's issue of *Esquire* that Carter was responsible for in 1985. ''The special issue was very well received,'' she recalled, ''especially because it brought, perhaps for the first time, *Esquire*'s literary quality to women's interests.''[5] Based on the success of the women's issue, Carter proposed *New York Woman* as a freestanding magazine to Philip Moffitt, the editor of *Esquire* and the president and chief executive officer of its parent company. With Moffitt's encouragement, she then produced a ''dummy'' issue, a mock-up of her editorial ideas for the magazine. Further development of the concept was included in two additional dummy issues, and the final proposals for bimonthly publication were presented to the executive committee of Esquire Magazine Group, Inc. on February 3, 1986. With the committee's approval, the cover date of the premier issue was set for September/ October 1986. Carter was appointed editor in chief, and Julie Lewit Nirenberg became the publisher. The cover price would be $2.50, and the ad rates, $3,975 for a four-color full page and $3,150 for a black-and-white page.[6]

Predictably, as the tasks of staffing and producing the first issue began in earnest in March 1986, the pace quickly turned hectic. "We must have interviewed every magazine person in New York," Carter said, "but without being able, for reasons of confidentiality, to tell them what the magazine was going to be. Mostly, I think we just said it would be a 'woman's *Esquire.*' It was a very exciting time, but also personally trying, because during that same period my house burned down and my marriage ended." Working closely with the new staff, Carter began to refine her ideas. Two individuals she relied on for significant contributions to the magazine's conception were Helen Rogan, executive editor, and Ann Kwong, originally associate art director but soon promoted to art director.[7]

As a point of editorial departure, it was clear from the start that *NYW* would not be a conventional "women's service" magazine. Its title notwithstanding, neither would it focus on the kind of useful service information typically found in city/regional magazines. In large measure, this was due to Carter's editorial sensibilities, but competitive considerations also played a role. The traditional women's service field was crowded to the point of virtual saturation, and there were already a number of city/regional publications—*7 Days, New York,* the *Village Voice*—that provided service information on living in New York. *NYW* would clearly be a women's magazine, but it would be something altogether different, and it was hoped that it would define a new niche in the women's publication market.

During the planning for the first issue, even though it was apparent that *NYW*'s structure would be departmentally driven to a degree, much effort was put into coming up with feature article ideas that would signal the magazine's intended editorial positioning. "We operated mostly on our own instincts. We certainly weren't scientific about it, and we didn't use surveys," said Carter. "We talked a lot to our friends and neighbors, and the magazine evolved out of our sense of what we thought was missing in women's magazines. Our story meetings were like the conversation at a slumber party, because all of the ideas we came up with were ideas from our own lives."[8]

Despite the magazine's loftier literary aspirations, however, *NYW* would not be an intellectual's magazine. Every article would not only have to have a clear entertainment value, but would also, in Carter's words, "have to deal with issues on an emotional level." Stylish art direction, moreover, was deemed essential. The design would be chic and elegant, but not arch or overly refined. Touches of four-color, bold headlines and generous white space around the text would give it an urbane but accessible look. "The late 1980s were filled with too much stuff," said Carter. "We had to think of new ways of communicating or no one would need us."[9]

While the new staff worked to produce the first issue, a special advisory committee for the magazine was recruited. Comprising more than 60 professionally prominent women, committee membership was largely honorary, but the list did add a certain cachet of accomplishment and credibility to the publication. Public relations research consultant Dorothy Gregg and retired *Ladies' Home Journal** editor Lenore Hershey were the committee's cochairpersons, and among the members were Letitia Baldridge, the corporate consultant; Rena Bartos of J. Walter Thompson; actress Polly Bergen; the Reverend Joan Campbell of the World Council of Churches; Donna De Varona, chair of the Women's Sports Foundation; Eileen Ford of Ford Models; Neale Godfrey of the First Women's Bank; Gracie Mansion, the gallery owner; Marcella Maxwell, chair of the New York City Commission on Human Rights; the investment banker Muriel Siebert; Beverly Sills of the New York City Opera; Madelon Devoe Talley, chair of the Women's Economic Roundtable; and the chair of the New York City Commission on the Status of Women, Kay J. Wright.[10]

The contents and form of the 176-page premier issue of *NYW*, which appeared in the early fall of 1986, were true to its charter. The six feature articles in the issue were "Who Do They Think We Are: Local Luminaries Try to Figure Us Out" by Lenore Hershey, "Their Town: Actresses Swoozie Kurtz and Judith Ivey Have an Intimate Chat" by Tracy Breton, "Anna's Tangled Destiny: A Defiant Woman's Pride Defines Her Harsh Existence" by Ursala Obst, "Getting Done: The Tyranny of Hairdressers" by Patricia Bosworth, "The Eyes Have It: Mary Alice Williams Makes It Big at CNN" by Geoffrey Stokes, and "What We Won't Tell Our Children: Forget about Sex, Today's Real Taboo Is Much Dirtier" by Viva. The issue also had a separate "Fashion" section, which in later issues was renamed "Style."[11]

One unusual aspect of the magazine's structure was that many of the dozen or so departments included in each issue would change from issue to issue. "We thought that the departments were very important," recalled Carter. "We put a great deal of effort into them, experimenting, changing them, keeping what worked, discarding what didn't." Over time, the most successful included "Power of the City," profiles of successful women; "Neighbors," a sort of celebrities-in-the-laundromat department; "Neighborhoods," *NYW*'s way of looking at the city as a collection of hometowns; and "Loose Lips," a gossip column filled, Carter said, "with bitchy, girl stuff."[12]

The success of the first issue of *NYW*, however, did little to reverse the failing fortunes of its parent company, Esquire Magazine Group. By the end of the year, it was clear that Philip Moffitt's publishing firm was in serious trouble, and on January 1, 1987, it had to sell off all of its assets. Of its two most important properties, *Esquire* was purchased by Hearst Corporation, and *NYW* was bought by American Express Publishing Corporation, a unit of American Express, which already owned a number of magazines, including *Travel & Leisure* and *Food & Wine*, as well as the city publications *Dallas*, *Atlanta*, and *LA Style*.[13]

At the time, the purchase by American Express Publishing, a wealthy, multititle publisher, seemed to secure *NYW*'s financial future. With the first-anniversary issue in September 1987, the magazine's publishing frequency was increased from bimonthly to ten times a year, and an extensive television and print advertising campaign to promote *NYW* to both potential advertisers and subscribers was launched.[14] Unfortunately, only a few months later a major recession of unusual depth and length (1988–1991) hit the American magazine industry, and it especially affected those publications, such as *NYW*, that relied heavily on upscale retail advertising. No matter how well Carter and her fellow editors succeeded in maintaining the distinctive editorial vitality of their magazine, its long-term economic prospects for profitability remained uncertain.

In an effort to increase revenues, American Express appointed *NYW*'s original fashion advertising manager, Amy Rappeport, publisher in 1988,[15] and two new group advertising directors, Patti Friedman and Joanne Halev, were brought in the next year.[16] Unique circulation and advertising promotions were implemented that attempted to capitalize on American Express's ownership of the publication. In early December 1989, American Express cardholders were admitted free to six specially marked "Holiday Shoppers' Express" buses, which circulated in downtown Manhattan, stopping at 45 stores that advertised in the magazine. In addition to encouraging cardholders to subscribe, it was hoped that the promotion would, in the words of a company official, "carry out *New York Woman*'s promise to the advertiser that we are able to bring American Express card members to the store."[17] For one issue in late 1991, copies of the magazine were sent free to 190,000 selected American Express gold card holders.[18]

Despite all the activity on the business side, however, advertising income continued to be seriously affected by the ongoing recession. Moreover, circulation did not meet the company's expectations. "Our circulation was around 110,000, with about half sold on the newsstand," said Carter, "which may have been our correct size. Even at the very beginning I never imagined that we would ever be any bigger, than say, the *New Yorker*."[19] As the recession deepened, and the balance-sheet problems mounted on many of its magazines, American Express appointed a corporate editorial director, Pamela Fiori, the former editor of *Travel & Leisure*.[20] "When our advertising lineage began, along with everyone else's, to decline, there was pressure to change the editorial, perhaps make it a bit more mainstream," recalled Carter. "American Express may have viewed us as subversive because editorially we didn't really care about the women who shopped at Bloomingdale's. It also may have been easier to sell ads if we'd been a more narrowly defined city/regional magazine." As editor, Carter resisted the pressures. "I was certain that it would be wrong to change the fundamentals. It simply was not a conventional service book, and that was the problem. Perhaps it should have had more."[21]

By late 1991, it was apparent that the editors' battle might be won, but their war was likely to be lost. In November, it was reported that American Express was trying to sell *NYW*, as well as some of its other titles.[22] Facing severe advertising losses—a 34 percent decline in ad pages in 1991 alone—and unable to find a buyer, on January 10, 1992, American Express ceased publication of *New York Woman*.[23]

In retrospect, it was not *NYW*'s business failure, but rather its editorial originality that may be most important. It was, for example, one of the first upscale women's magazines to deal with subjects such as the new immigrants, adoption, and issues of age and class. "We tried very hard to make sure that the point of view in all our stories was original," said Carter, "and visually we were certainly quite different from other women's magazines." As with most historically significant publications, the quality of the writing was paramount. "We didn't have the funding to put anyone on a retainer, but we were able to attract good writers such as Merrill Markoe, Marcel Clements, and the playwright Wendy Wasserstein because we could offer them a chance—indeed insisted—they write in an original voice. And I think we had a reputation of treating writers really well. We were never violent in our editing."[24]

Though it lasted less than a half-dozen years, *NYW* was certainly an interesting, often compelling magazine. The result of a single editor's vision, it spoke in its own distinctive voice and shared a unique sensibility with its readers. When asked to reflect on its contribution to the field of women's magazines, Carter's perspective was, in all likelihood, quite close to the mark:

> In editorial terms, including our art direction, we probably were ahead of our time. In a way, we may have been more a 1990s than a 1980s magazine. We were always more interested in substance than the superficial. During the late 1980s that probably was, from a marketing point of view, not the best position to take. But I think that *New York Woman* left an important legacy, largely the result of its unique perspective. It was the first woman's magazine to talk up to women. Its voice was both smart and funny, both worldly and naive. The attitude was: I've seen it all, but I'll never be cynical. And our commitment to addressing the entire woman probably influenced other women's magazines including *Glamour* and *Mirabella*, and the field is probably the better for it.[25]

Notes

1. See David Abrahamson, "The Rise of the Special-Interest Magazine," in "The Other 1960s: An Economic and Sociocultural History" (Ph.D. diss., New York University, 1992), Chapter 6.

2. Betsy Carter interview, September 24, 1992.

3. Betsy Carter interview, November 11, 1988.

4. Before starting *NYW*, Carter's editorial career included editorial assistant, McGraw Hill (1967–1968); editor of a Washington, D.C. bank's in-house magazine (1968–1969); editorial assistant, *Atlantic Monthly* (1969–1970); researcher, assistant editor, and associate editor, *Newsweek* (1971–1980); senior editor, executive editor, and senior executive editor, *Esquire* (1980–1983); editorial director, *Esquire* (1983–1985). In 1993, after the demise of *NYW*, she became executive editor of *Harper's Bazaar*. See *Marquis Who's*

Who, 1992 ed., s.v. "Betsy Carter," Dialog file 234, item 09987850; Diana B. Henriques, "Hearst Picks Betsy Carter for *Bazaar*," *New York Times*, March 24, 1993, p. D18.

5. Carter interview, September 24, 1992.

6. Philip H. Dougherty, "*New York Woman* Magazine," *New York Times*, April 17, 1986, p. D25; see also "Betsy Carter," *USA Today*, August 26, 1986, p. B4.

7. Carter interview, September 24, 1992.

8. Ibid.

9. Carter interview, November 11, 1988.

10. September/October 1986, pp. 4, 6.

11. September/October 1986, p. 24.

12. Carter interview, September 24, 1992.

13. Lee A. Daniels, "Hearst Gets *Esquire* Magazine," *New York Times*, January 1, 1987, sec. 1, p. 43; see also *Wall Street Journal*, January 2, 1987, p. 6.

14. Philip H. Dougherty, "Promoting *New York Woman*," *New York Times*, October 29, 1987, p. D26.

15. Geraldine Fabrikant, "New Publisher Named at *New York Woman*," *New York Times*, August 30, 1988, p. D39.

16. Randall Rothenberg, "Patti Friedman and Joanne Halev," *New York Times*, December 6, 1989, p. D23.

17. Isadore Barmash, "Bus to Stores by American Express," *New York Times*, October 10, 1989, p. D20.

18. Deirdre Carmody, "*New York Woman* Opens Its Gold-Card Mine," *New York Times*, July 1, 1991, p. D8.

19. Carter interview, September 24, 1992.

20. Andrea Rothman, "Amex Goes for the Glossies," *Business Week*, October 23, 1989, p. 66.

21. Carter interview, September 24, 1992.

22. Scott Donaton, "Amex Talks to Time Warner," *Advertising Age*, November 11, 1991, pp. 1, 74; "American Express Company Is Hoping to Sell *New York Woman* Magazine," *Wall Street Journal*, November 15, 1991, p. B5; "Buyer Sought for a Magazine," *New York Times*, November 18, 1991, p. D10.

23. Deirdre Carmody, "Ad Drop Forces Closing of *New York Woman*," *New York Times*, January 11, 1992, p. A37; Kevin Goldman, "American Express Shuts Magazine, *New York Woman*," *Wall Street Journal*, January 13, 1992, p. B6; Scott Donaton, "Titles Tortured in 1991," *Advertising Age*, January 20, 1991, p. 46.

24. Carter interview, September 24, 1992.

25. Ibid.

Information Sources

BIBLIOGRAPHY:

"American Express Company Is Hoping to Sell *New York Woman* Magazine." *Wall Street Journal*, November 15, 1991, p. B5.

Barmash, Isadore. "Bus to Stores by American Express." *New York Times*, October 10, 1989, p. D20.

Carmody, Deirdre. "*New York Woman* Opens Its Gold-Card Mine." *New York Times*, July 1, 1991, p. D8.

———. "Ad Drop Forces Closing of *New York Woman*." *New York Times*, January 11, 1992, p. A37.

Daniels, Lee A. "Hearst Gets *Esquire* Magazine." *New York Times*, January 1, 1987, pp. 1, 43.

Donaton, Scott. "Amex Talks to Time Warner." *Advertising Age*, November 11, 1991, pp. 1, 74.

Dougherty, Philip H. "*New York Woman* Magazine." *New York Times*, April 17, 1986, p. D25.

———. "Promoting *New York Woman.*" *New York Times*, October 29, 1987, p. D26.

Fabrikant, Geraldine. "New Publisher Named at *New York Woman.*" *New York Times*, August 30, 1988, p. D39.

Goldman, Kevin. "American Express Shuts Magazine, *New York Woman.*" *Wall Street Journal*, January 13, 1992, p. B6.

Henriques, Diana B. "Hearst Picks Betsy Carter for *Bazaar.*" *New York Times*, March 24, 1993, p. D18.

ooRothman, Andrea. "Amex Goes for the Glossies." *Business Week*, October 23, 1989, p. 66.

INDEX SOURCES: None.

LOCATION SOURCES: Library of Congress and other sources.

Publication History

MAGAZINE TITLE AND TITLE CHANGES: *New York Woman.*

VOLUME AND ISSUE DATA: Vols. 1–6 (September/October 1986–July/August 1987), bimonthly; (September 1987–December 1991/January 1992), ten issues per year.

PUBLISHER AND PLACE OF PUBLICATION: Esquire Magazine Group, Inc. (September 1986–January 1987); American Express Publishing Corporation (January 1987–January 1992). New York.

EDITOR: Betsy Carter (1986–1992).

CIRCULATION: Gale's, 1993: 100,000 (paid).

David Abrahamson

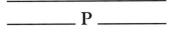

P

PARENTS

"There are magazines devoted exclusively to the raising of cattle, hogs, dogs, flowers, and what not, but until now none of the most important work of the world—the rearing of children."[1]

This statement heralded the birth of a new magazine entitled *Children: The Magazine for Parents* in October 1926. The voice behind this statement was also the guiding voice behind the new magazine. George Joseph Hecht took his vision of a magazine that would provide parents with practical guidelines and inspiration for rearing children and made it into a powerful publication that was the only one in its field, that published articles by some of the leading personalities of its time, and that quickly developed a loyal following. Today, that magazine—known simply as *Parents*—continues to be the leader in its field, with the largest circulation of any child care magazine.[2]

Between the covers of one of the early issues of the magazine, which was at that time entitled *The Parents Magazine* (its name until 1976), were articles entitled "Guiding the Adolescent in a Changing World," "Are Parents Bad for Children?" "No One Need Have Scarlet Fever," "Special Schools for Different Children," "Add Cheese to the Child's Diet," "Books for Boys and Girls," and "Things for Children to Do and Make."[3] Its subhead advertised the magazine as a guide "on rearing children from crib to college." Special features of that early issue included a reference to articles of particular interest to fathers and a key to guide parents to articles that referred to specific ages. It boasted a board of editors consisting of nine staff members, three consultants, and 50 advisory editors (child care experts). Typical advertisements included ones for medicines, private schools, and baby clothing. An issue cost just 25¢, and at the time of the issue's publication, in May 1930, circulation for *The Parents Magazine* stood at around 200,000.[4]

Jump ahead more than 60 years, and you see a magazine that retains a similar mission but that tackles different issues and reaches a broader audience. The table of contents of an issue of *Parents* in the 1990s included articles entitled "Will You Need Another Cesarean?" "Ten Essentials for a Safe Nursery," "Latchkey Kids," "Kitchen Express," "When a Child Dies," and "When Parents Expect A's."[5] Its age-by-age guide is more extensive, with departments directed to ten different age groups; it also has departments on fashion and beauty, something strikingly different from early issues. Today, its mission statement proclaims that *Parents* provides "expectant, new, and experienced parents with the information they need to raise healthy, happy children . . . also gives readers practical and emotional support in their multiple roles in and out of the family."[6] Its staff box boasts 77 members, including contributing editors (similar to the early issue's advisory editors). Advertisements now include—in addition to the expected baby products, toys, and clothes—items geared specifically to women. The cover price now runs $3.50, circulation has recently topped at 1.8 million paid subscribers.[7]

When George Joseph Hecht founded *Children: The Magazine for Parents*, under the auspices of his Parents Corporation, he devoted himself to issues of education and other reform. His influence on the magazine was immense and continued until 1978, when he died at the age of 83; he was still listed on the masthead as publisher.

Soon after the publication began, Hecht removed himself as editor in chief and devoted himself to serving as president and publisher. Clara Savage Littledale, who had come in as managing editor with the inception of the magazine, became editor in 1931. Under her guidance, *The Parents Magazine* became known as an accessible publication that cared deeply about its audience. She was known to take mothers' calls in her office and to dole out parenting advice freely. Although she took the magazine through the years in which a woman's place was still, primarily, in the home, Littledale herself was a strong supporter of expanded women's rights and roles. She began her career as a woman suffrage editor at the *New York Evening Post*; at *The Parents Magazine*, she fought for social action that would improve the lives of children (i.e., school lunches and more accessible child health care) and wrote of issues that affected her readers not only as mothers, but as women.

The July 1954 issue illustrated Littledale's expanded editorial mission for her magazine. It contained stories that dealt with social issues and included articles that focused on a child's personal well-being ("Are We Expecting Too Much from the New Polio Vaccine?" and "First Steps to Self-Confidence"). It also showed Littledale's interest in her readers' roles as modern women, with articles on fashion and beauty.

After Littledale died in 1956, *The Parents Magazine* began a period of numerous staff changes. The years were also marked by only slight editorial change; its focus remained essentially the same as it was during Littledale's tenure.

Mary E. Buchanan, a former managing editor and Littledale assistant, took the helm from Littledale in 1956. Nine years later in 1965, she retired and was followed by Dorothy Whyte Cotton. In 1971, Genevieve Millet Landau became editor; she was followed by Peter Jannsen, who served for only four months.

In 1979, Elizabeth Crow became editor. Under her leadership, *The Parents Magazine* underwent a complete editorial and graphic overhaul. Its redesign created what we know today as *Parents*.

The changes at *The Parents Magazine* were precipitated by the acquisition of the magazine by the West German publishing house of Gruner + Jahr in 1978. The new owners were concerned with making the magazine "more responsive to the needs of men and women who are raising children today," as well as making it "more lively and stimulating to look at."[8]

The first and most noticeable change was its new name. Now *Parents*, the magazine sported a new, livelier look and expanded editorial coverage. The benchmark of the new editorial tone was a new section called "As They Grow." Today, still the magazine's most popular feature, the section consisted of columns that discussed problems and issues associated with particular children's ages. Other editorial features began to focus more on the lives of mothers and fathers outside the home. Articles typical of this time, which would not have been found in earlier issues, included ones on such issues as work tactics, financial concerns, and marital and sexual tips. Because of this focus, *Parents* is characterized as not only a child care and parental guidance magazine but a women's magazine.

The new owners were also concerned with revitalizing its sales. When Gruner + Jahr acquired the magazine, more than 99 percent of its circulation came directly from subscriptions. Emphasis began to be placed on single-copy sales. This change, along with the editorial ones, helped circulation rebound from the gradual decline it had experienced over the years.[9]

With the takeover by Gruner + Jahr, the magazine's family grew. The corporation began the formation of sister publications and complementary business ventures. Today, the enterprise includes *Expecting* magazine (a quarterly prenatal publication), *Parents Baby Care* (a series of age-specific publications distributed to families at five intervals in their new baby's life), and the Ser Padres Network of magazines. The Ser Padres Network provides Hispanic parents with information similar to that found in *Parents*; the network consists of the magazines *Ser Padres*,* *Embarazo*, and *Una Nueva Vida*. Today, *Ser Padres* is the largest Spanish-language consumer magazine in the United States.[10]

In addition to this impressive line of publications, Gruner + Jahr operates Parents Books and produces a line of educational toys and videos.

Since 1988, the editor of *Parents* has been Ann Pleshette Murphy. The magazine's look remains as it was with the redesign in 1976, yet the editorial focus continues to adapt to changing societal times. With Murphy's guidance, *Parents* has expanded its coverage of such issues as family and work concerns, health and medical information, family and marital relationships, nutrition, and personal concerns for women.

The same year that Murphy joined the staff of *Parents*, the publication was recognized with the magazine industry's highest editorial honor—the General Excellence Award. It had already been recognized three times as a finalist for the National Magazine Award.

Notes

1. James L. C. Ford, *Magazines for Millions: The Story of Specialized Publications* (Carbondale: Southern Illinois University Press, 1969), p. 29.
2. From fact sheet in Media Kit.
3. Table of Contents, May 1930, p. 4.
4. Barbara Nourie, "Parents," in Alan Nourie and Barbara Nourie (eds.), *American Mass-Market Magazines* (New York: Greenwood Press, 1990), p. 357.
5. Table of Contents, March 1994, pp. 5, 7.
6. From mission statement in Media Kit.
7. Mark Garvey (ed.) *1994 Writer's Market* (Cincinnati: Writer's Digest Books, 1994), p. 344.
8. "A Fresh Start: Notes on Our New Look," November 1978, p. 11.
9. William H. Taft, *American Magazines for the 1980s* (New York: Hastings House, 1980), p. 118.
10. From fact sheet in Media Kit.

Information Sources

BIBLIOGRAPHY:
Ford, James L. C. *Magazines for Millions: The Story of Specialized Publications*. Carbondale: Southern Illinois University Press, 1969.
Mott, Frank Luther. *A History of American Magazines. Vol. 5: Sketches of 21 Magazines 1905–1930*. Cambridge: Harvard University Press, 1968.
Nourie, Barbara. "Parents." Alan Nourie and Barbara Nourie (eds.), *American Mass-Market Magazines*. New York: Greenwood Press, 1990, pp. 352–359.
Taft, William H. *American Magazines for the 1980s*. New York: Hastings House, 1980.
INDEX SOURCES: Magazine Index; Readers' Guide to Periodical Literature.
LOCATION SOURCES: Amelia Gayle Gorgas Library, University of Alabama, Tuscaloosa, Ala., and other libraries.

Publication History

MAGAZINE TITLE AND TITLE CHANGES: *Children: The Magazine for Parents* (October 1926–January 1929); *Children: The Parents' Magazine* (February 1929–July 1929); *The Parents' Magazine* (August 1929–December 1965); *Parents' Magazine and Better Homemaking* (January 1966–October 1969); *Parents' Magazine and Better Family Living* (November 1969–June 1977); *Parents' Magazine* (July 1977–December 1978); *Parents* (January 1979–present).
VOLUME AND ISSUE DATA: Vols. 1–(October 1926–present). Monthly.
PUBLISHER AND PLACE OF PUBLICATION: Parents Corporation (October 1926–July 1978); Gruner + Jahr (August 1978–present). New York City.
EDITORS: George J. Hecht (1926–1931); Clara Savage Littledale (1931–1956); Mary E. Buchanan (1956–1965); Dorothy Whyte Cotton (1965–1970); Genevieve Mil-

let Landau (1971–1978); Peter A. Janssen (August 1978–December 1978); Elizabeth Crow (1979–1988); Ann Pleshette Murphy (1988–present).
CIRCULATION: ABC, 1993: 1,755,283 (paid, primarily subscriptions).

Cheryl Sloan Watts

PETERSON'S MAGAZINE

Although not well remembered today, *Peterson's Magazine* was once the most widely read women's publication in America. From the 1860s to the 1880s, it led the circulation race over its chief competitor, *Godey's Lady's Book.** The journal lacked consistently high-quality literature, however, and faded in the 1880s and 1890s as new, more elaborate women's magazines, such as *The Ladies' Home Journal,** came into existence. *Peterson's Magazine*'s chief value for researchers today is its depiction of middle- and upper-class Victorian women's home life and literature.

The magazine was founded by Charles J. Peterson in 1842. Peterson was already co-owner and comanager (with George R. Graham) of the *Saturday Evening Post* and an editor at *Graham's Magazine*. Peterson kept his old positions for a year until he was convinced that his new venture would be a success. He then sold his interest in the *Post* and resigned his editor's position at *Graham's Magazine* in 1843.

Peterson priced his magazine at two dollars and offered high-quality, hand-colored fashion plates to compete with *Godey's*, which sold for three dollars a year. This new journal billed itself as "a magazine of choice American literature." Over the years, it grew both in length and in content into a full-fledged magazine for the Victorian homemaker. By the mid-1860s, the magazine offered recipes, patterns, craft ideas, parlor game instructions, and piano music, as well as the literary and fashion fare that marked its beginning.

Like its rival *Godey's*, *Peterson's* provided women with an outlet for literary expression. Women accounted for about three-quarters of the authorship of the magazine's poetry, short stories, and serialized novels. Despite the diversity of authors, the literature was often similar in themes: romance pieces and adventures of heroes and heroines. The magazine gained a prolific coeditor and author in Ann S. Stephens in 1843. She had been an associate editor at *Graham's* before taking the editing job at *Peterson's*. Stephens was a poet and short story and short novel writer. She became one of the best-known women writers of the mid-1800s due to both her volume and quality. Although the cover of *Peterson's* prominently billed Stephens as the journal's editor, historian Frank Luther Mott noted that Peterson always was the magazine's real editor. Stephens, said Mott, should be considered as an associate editor since she appeared to have written the "Editor's Table" column, besides contributing literature.[1]

Peterson's also published other well-known women authors of the time, including Elizabeth Oakes Smith, Mary V. Spencer, and Lydia June Pierson, as well as some noted male authors and poets, including such luminaries as Long-fellow and Tennyson.[2]

Unlike *Godey's*, *Peterson's Magazine* offered little editorial commentary. The monthly ''Editor's Table'' column often focused on literature or crafts. Stephens did occasionally address the question of what role women should play in society. Her answer was unswerving throughout her ten years at *Peterson's*: a woman's home was her domain. Stephens did encourage women to pursue literary careers, however, largely because women usually stressed in their writings the theme that women were dignified and refined. Furthermore, through their literature, women authors helped make home life even lovelier and more feminine, Ste-phens added. Women authors, she said, ''exalted [a] woman in her own sphere, but never [enticed] her beyond it.''[3]

Stephens noted that women as writers were a largely new phenomenon in literature. She praised early nineteenth-century women authors, explaining that they were brave to enter a field that had largely been a man's domain: ''For at that time a woman who wrote books was considered almost a rival to masculine intellect, and regarded as something strange and unapproachable by her sister women.''[4]

Besides writing, Stephens saw few career fields for women. She believed most other careers would degrade women.[5] Stephens was opposed to any notions of equality for the sexes. She also was against the early women's rights movement, believing women's roles in society had been divinely established. Women who sought to dress differently or who wanted to engage in political discussions found themselves severely rebuked by Stephens for sacrificing the ''dignity and delicacy'' of their sex.[6]

Competition for women readers was fierce by the mid-1800s. Many publications, including *Godey's*, *The Lady's Friend*, The Methodist-Episcopal *Ladies' Repository*,* the *Mothers' Magazine*, and a host of others, vied for the same middle- and upper-class audience. Many of these magazines, including *Peterson's*, relied on the home club subscription system as a means of attracting more readers. The club system offered subscription discounts when groups of at least five purchased the magazine.

Competition, therefore, was Charles Peterson's main concern for the maga-zine's first 20 years. Peterson attracted readers and created a national magazine in part by hiring authors from across the country. His magazine was filled with regional tales.

The publisher also raced to be the first to print the latest fashion plates from Paris and London. Throughout the 1840s and 1850s, the publication's editorial column frequently stated that its European fashion plates were published three weeks or more before any of its competitors. Peterson also claimed his maga-zine's literature was more lively and of a higher quality than any produced by three-dollar magazines, a thinly veiled reference to *Godey's*. As added proof to its readers that *Peterson's* was striving to be the best women's magazine, Pe-terson gave bylines only to authors who wrote exclusively for his publication.

Peterson's editorial column frequently commented that the publisher spared no expense in hiring the best steel, copper, and wood engravers to reproduce the magazine's European and American fashion plates. Despite the magazine's pride in its fashion plates, publisher Peterson mildly rebuked American women's desires for European fashions. "Too little attention is paid by our ladies to the variableness of climate, but we hope that this evil will soon be corrected. A slavish imitation of foreign fashions, without regard to their fitness to our climate, is not to be recommended."[7]

Competition forced the magazine and its contents to grow throughout the decades. When *Peterson's Magazine* first began, its 32-page issues offered largely literature and poetry, two or three fashion plates, and an occasional scenic engraving. By the 1850s, the magazine had expanded to approximately 48 pages per issue. The magazine's content changed over the years as well. *Peterson's* offered more fashion plates and introduced crafts, embroidery and sewing patterns, and recipes by mid-decade as a means of attracting more readers. The middle-class Victorian woman now had patterns for rugs, baby boots, and purses, among other items. When not busying herself with crafts, she could follow the magazine's recipes for mock turtle soup or roast pigeon.

By the start of the Civil War, the magazine had increased to approximately 80 pages and featured a lavishly engraved cover. Fashion plates were moved to the back. The front-page story was now always fiction, boasting engraved illustrations of scenes from the narrative.

The war years brought articles on how women could care for injured soldiers. Readers learned how to treat dysentery, fevers, and other war-related diseases. *Peterson's* also offered war literature. Most of the stories were highly romantic, focusing on gallant soldiers and the women they left behind.[8]

By 1864, *Peterson's Magazine* became the largest-circulation women's magazine in America. It continued to be sold at two dollars.[9] Historian Frank Luther Mott noted the magazine's circulation was advertised as 140,000 in the first *Rowell's Directory*, published in 1869. By the mid-1870s the magazine claimed a circulation of 165,000.[10]

Peterson's included various supplements, such as full-size folded patterns, as enticements aimed at keeping its top circulation position.

Despite its leading circulation, the magazine continued to use extremely cheap paper and a small, hard-to-read typeface until shortly before its demise in the 1890s. The magazine's two-dollar cost undoubtedly contributed in limiting the publisher's production choices.

Advertisements began appearing in the back pages in the 1850s. By the mid-1860s, advertisements in *Peterson's* went beyond small classified and display advertisements for patent medicines, hairbrushes, and corsets to full-page advertisements offering products of interest to the whole family. Book publishers and piano makers frequently advertised their wares. The Illinois Central Railroad

Company placed a full-page advertisement in the February 1865 issue offering 1 million acres of land for sale.

The magazine changed publishers in 1887 upon Peterson's death. His wife, Sarah, continued the magazine until 1892, when she sold it to Roderic Penfield. Penfield envisioned a quite different magazine from the one he had bought. He changed the publication's name to *The New Peterson Magazine*, expanded the literature section, and added art and theater articles. Penfield had to drop the magazine's price to one dollar a year in 1894 to compete with the growing number of cheap, high-quality magazines. He also renamed the publication *The Peterson Magazine of Illustrated Literature* and moved the publication to New York, taking it away from its longtime Philadelphia home.

Under Penfield's editorship, the magazine tried, but failed, to adapt to the rapidly changing world of publishing. The editors added halftone illustrations, expanded its news and commentary on theater, and began featuring biographies of famous Americans from political, literary, and military circles. Despite these changes, the magazine continued to decline in circulation. *Peterson's* ceased to exist for all intents and purposes in 1898, when publisher Frank Munsey purchased it and merged *Peterson's* into his magazine, *The Argosy*.

Notes

1. Frank Luther Mott, *A History of American Magazines*, vol. 2 (Cambridge: Harvard University Press, 1938), p. 307.
2. See March 1842, pp. 76–79 and June 1842, p. 176, for examples.
3. Ann S. Stephens, "Literary Ladies," April 1843, p. 98.
4. Ibid.
5. Ibid., p. 99.
6. Ibid.
7. "The Fashions," January 1842, pp. 1–2.
8. See various issues of 1860–1862 and Kathleen L. Endres, "The Women's Press in the Civil War: A Portrait of Patriotism, Propaganda, and Prodding," *Civil War History*, 30:1 (March 1984), p. 43.
9. "Editor's Table," December 1864, p. 478.
10. Mott, *A History of American Magazines*, p. 309.

Information Sources

BIBLIOGRAPHY:
Endres, Kathleen. "The Women's Press in the Civil War: A Portrait of Patriotism, Propaganda, and Prodding." *Civil War History* 30:1 (March 1984), pp. 31–53.
Mott, Frank Luther. *A History of American Magazines*, vol. 2 (1850–1865). Cambridge: Harvard University Press, 1938.
Oberholtzer, Ellis Paxson. *The Literary History of Philadelphia*. Philadelphia: George W. Jacobs, 1906.
INDEX SOURCES: None.
LOCATION SOURCES: Library of Congress and other libraries; American Periodical Series II, Reels 1292–1308.

Publication History

MAGAZINE TITLE AND TITLE CHANGES: *The Lady's World of Fashion* (1842);
    The Lady's World (January–May 1843); *The Artist and Lady's World* (June 1843);
    The Ladies' National Magazine (July 1843–1848); *Peterson's Magazine* (1849–
    1892); *The New Peterson Magazine* (1892–1894); *The Peterson Magazine of
    Illustrated Literature* (1894–1898) (merged into *The Argosy*, 1898).
VOLUME AND ISSUE DATA: Vols. 1–113 (January 1842–April 1898). Monthly.
PUBLISHER AND PLACE OF PUBLICATION: Charles J. Peterson (1842–1887); Pe-
    terson Magazine Co. (1888–1893); Penfield Publishing Co. (1894–1895); The
    Peterson Co. (1895–1898). Philadelphia (1842–1895); New York (1895–1898).
EDITORS: Charles J. Peterson (1842); Charles J. Peterson and Ann S. Stephens (1843–
    1853); Charles J. Peterson (1854–1887); Sarah Peterson (1887–1892); Frank Lee
    Benedict (1892–1893); Roderic Campbell Penfield (1894–1898).
CIRCULATION: Rowell's Directory, 1869: 140,000.

Mary M. Cronin

PICTORIAL REVIEW

In 1929, *Pictorial Review* was one of the "Big Six," mass circulation magazines
aimed at a middle-class female audience.[1] It was among the biggest of the six,
with advertising revenue and circulation that rivaled even those of the *Ladies'
Home Journal** and the *Woman's Home Companion.** Ten years later, however,
Pictorial Review died. Its suspension came as a surprise to media observers, for
this was the biggest magazine (in terms of circulation and advertising revenue)
ever folded in the history of American journalism until that point. But *Pictorial
Review* had always been a magazine of surprises.

The enormous success of *Pictorial Review* was a surprise. The magazine was
never designed for huge circulations or editorial acclaim. It was designed to sell
dress patterns. Like *The Delineator** and *McCall's,** *Pictorial Review* was
launched to show the array of dress patterns available through the American
Fashion Co., owned by William Paul Ahnelt, a German immigrant. Its first issue
reflected its modest aspirations; it (September 1899) was nothing but fashion
drawings, with little editorial material. The magazine was highly departmentalized. For example, one department was called "About Furs," with illustrations
of seals and polar bears. The page, however, had no editorial copy, although
space had been allotted for a story. The same was the case for the "Corset"
department: a drawing portrayed a corseted woman without any copy explaining
the fashion advances in the undergarment. The magazine even failed to provide
the "Boudour Gossip" promised in the headline.[2]

By the next month, however, the magazine had plenty of copy. It introduced
its first fiction serial (written by Alexander McArthur) and book reviews. But
the real staple of the magazine was fashions. The magazine was loaded with
drawings of the latest designs and stories of what was popular in Paris. Almost

as important, the magazine was carrying much more advertising, primarily for stores located in New York.

In its earliest years, the *Pictorial Review* was primarily a fashion magazine—and for good reason. The magazine was advertised and sold as "A MONTHLY MAGAZINE of practical fashions for dressmakers and the Home. Useful information and illustrations for Tailors and Furriers."[3] True to its word, the magazine carried fashion drawings on almost every other page. Between the illustrations, the unidentified editor[4] placed brief stories on everything from etiquette to decorating, from the theater to recipes, from child rearing to children's stories.[5] The magazine grew slowly in size and circulation.

In its earliest years, the magazine never seemed to aspire to greatness. The fiction that was carried was poor in comparison to the short stories in the *Ladies' Home Journal, Woman's Home Companion,* and *Delineator.* Even the departments offered little in comparison with the other women's magazines. Nonetheless, the readers and the advertisers (then primarily for fashion and sewing supplies) seemed to like the mix. But things would soon change—in editorial content and advertising prosperity.

In 1907, Arthur T. Vance, former editor of the *Woman's Home Companion,* came aboard to lead the fashion magazine. The *Pictorial Review* was never the same again.

Vance had been eminently successful at the *Companion.* While there, he had developed an editorial formula that blended the best in fiction with practical household and child care advice and a strong reform sense. Vance brought that editorial formula to the *Pictorial Review* and transformed the magazine from a small, unassuming little monthly into a publication for the thinking, reform-minded, middle-class woman—and a circulation and advertising success.

Vance brought controversial new writers to the magazine. Reformer Charlotte Perkins Gilman wrote about divorce;[6] an unidentified woman wrote about leaving her husband;[7] and muckraking journalist Rheta Childe Dorr explained why women wanted to be self-sufficient.[8] During the muckraking period (1902–1912), the magazine conducted a number of investigations, the most notable of which looked into the general welfare of children.[9]

Given Vance's commitment to social change, as evidenced by the editorial content of the *Pictorial Review,* it came as no surprise when the magazine editorially supported suffrage, one of the few mass circulation women's magazines to do so. As Vance wrote, "The Editor of the PICTORIAL REVIEW believes in Equal Suffrage." Women, who were responsible for home care and child rearing, "might just as well be entrusted with National Housekeeping and National Housecleaning."[10]

Vance explained the *Pictorial Review*'s bold new direction:

We appeal to women who want to think and to act as well as to be entertained. It is a feminine age. Women are taking more and more part in affairs and our idea is this: that a magazine correctly to represent the women of this country must keep its readers in close touch with questions of public interest, and guide and direct this feminine activity in the most useful and practical channels.[11]

That approach struck a responsive chord among the reading public. Vance witnessed the magazine's enormous growth in terms of circulation and advertising. When Vance took over in 1907, the magazine had a respectable circulation of 200,000. Three years later, that figure passed 500,000; by 1912, 900,000 subscribed. By 1915, the figure was 1.1 million; three years later, 1.5 million. The magazine celebrated the end of World War I with a 2 million circulation. In 1922, the figure reached 2.2 million, and in 1923, 2.5 million.[12]

National advertisers rushed to the thriving magazine. Advertising for household and furniture products dominated; Victrola, Johnson Wax, Bon Ami, Congoleum, Armstrong Linoleum, and Kroehler Furniture took out full-page ads, some in color. Advertising for food products also found a home in *Pictorial Review*: Quaker Oats, Heinz, Crisco, Pillsbury, Swift, and Wesson. Advertising for clothing was only of secondary importance and illustrated how far Vance had taken the magazine from its original fashion roots.[13]

The tremendous growth in the magazine's circulation and advertising could not be credited solely to Vance's commitment to social reform or the muckraking investigations. It was due to the entire editorial package. Fiction represented an important component of that mix. Vance realized the importance of fiction to the success of any woman's magazine. Accordingly, he brought some of the top short story writers to the *Review*. In fact, he promised his readers the best fiction "that time, money and energy can buy."[14] "Time, money and energy" brought P. G. Wodehouse, Zona Gale, Edna Ferber, Hamlin Garland, Irving S. Cobb, Kathleen Norris, and many others to the magazine.[15] Likewise, he initiated a new serial policy. While other women's magazines dragged serials out for half a year or more, the *Review* provided the complete novel in only three or four parts; so that over one year, a subscriber would get four novels instead of just two.[16]

Under Vance, the *Review* also improved graphically. Its front covers began to rival those of the other magazines in its niche. Well-known artists Rose O'Neill Wilson, Bessie Pease Gutmann, Howard Chandler Christy, and Harrison Fisher, among others, provided art for the covers and the inside pages of the *Review*.

Fashion remained an important component of the magazine. However, it was no longer scattered throughout the book. It was departmentalized and centralized. If a reader wanted to see the latest fashions, she would look at the back of each issue to find the newest illustrations and accompanying stories.

Vance spent lavishly on the fiction and art. The *Review*'s editorial budget rivaled any in its class. In 1914, for example, the magazine spent $200,000 on editorial costs alone: $50,000 for serial stories; $50,000 for short stories;

$40,000 for illustrations; $15,000 for special articles; and $15,000 for departments.[17]

Vance remained editor until 1930. During that tenure, he never seemed to lose his knack for editorial innovation. In 1916, the magazine looked into birth control. Although Vance never took an editorial stance on this topic, he invited readers to submit letters on birth control. Thousands responded. Letters were reproduced in the March 1916 issue; some could be reprinted even today. One reader wrote of a mother who lost a child. She concluded, "Every mother should be scientifically instructed regarding birth control." Another subscriber, a welfare worker, explained, "All normal women want children, but they want them when *they* want them—not just as it may happen."[18]

World War I found Vance and the *Pictorial Review* ready to do their part to help the war effort. The magazine was filled with any number of articles designed to help women adjust to the demands of wartime: from how-to stories to inspirational features about women at the front written by the *Pictorial Review*'s reporter, Mabel Potter Daggett. The war carried into the art of the magazine with front covers of women in Red Cross garb as well as battlefield illustrations within the magazine.[19]

The *Pictorial Review* did not seem to have any difficulty adjusting to postwar America. The magazine was fat with advertising, and its circulation continued to race forward. Prosperity, however, did not stop the magazine from dealing with the controversial social and sexual issues facing the nation. The magazine carried stories about birth control in 1920[20] and new attitudes toward marriage[21] and editorially supported a national divorce law.[22]

Yet, there was often an undercurrent of conservatism in some of the features. A story on the "sex-stuff" in the movies written by Benjamin B. Hampton[23] was a case in point. The story was extensively quoted by magazines, ministers, and women's clubs throughout the nation. As a result, movie moguls met to keep "salacious pictures" out of the theaters.[24]

Pictorial Review put an emphasis on publicizing women and their contributions to American life. Like other magazines in its niche, the *Review* offered a range of features on prominent women. However, the magazine did more. It polled women on various issues. By eight to one, women favored a national uniform marriage and divorce law; by six to one, they favored birth control; and by "overwhelming sentiment," they approved of a federal amendment to abolish child labor, one survey showed.[25]

Beginning in 1924, the magazine began awarding $5,000 to the "American Woman Who Makes the Greatest Contribution to American Civilization Each Year."[26] The first winner was Mrs. Edward MacDowell, founder of the Peterborough Artists Colony in New Hampshire. (Controversial birth control advocate Margaret Sanger was a finalist for the award.) Other winners included Cora Wilson Stewart, for work in eliminating illiteracy in the United States, and Sara Graham-Mulhall, for her work in fighting drug abuse.

The next year, the *Review* began offering a $10,000 prize for the best first novel. Not only did the novelist win the money, but the book was serialized in the *Pictorial Review* and published by Dodd, Mead & Co. A motion picture was also to be produced.[27] Although the prize assured the magazine the pick of the best new writers, the *Review* relied primarily on well-known, well-established writers for the greatest portion of its fiction. In the 1920s, Wallace Irwin, Hugh Walpole, Booth Tarkington, Edith Wharton, and Theodore Dreiser offered novels and short stories.

The 1920s also found *Pictorial Review* adding stories and features on vaudeville celebrities and movie stars to its editorial mix. Movie mogul Samuel Goldwyn wrote about the "Intimate, Personal Story of the Motion-Picture Industry,"[28] vaudeville producer Florenz Ziegfeld, Jr., updated readers on the "Ziegfeld" girls,[29] and writer Jim Tully offered the inside story on movie comedian Charlie Chaplin.[30]

On its editorial pages, the magazine never seemed to lose its edge. In the early 1920s, Ida Clyde Clarke, who had written a column for the *Review* during World War I, offered a woman's perspective in the magazine's editorials. By the late 1920s, Vance was writing the editorials again. Even in the later years of his career, Vance's commitment to reform never seemed to wane. He came out against capital punishment just as Mrs. Ruth Snyder went to her death in the electric chair for murdering her husband.[31] In 1927, he editorially supported the equal rights amendment,[32] one of the few mass circulation magazines to do so.

The 1920s were the high mark for the *Pictorial Review*. Although the magazine reached greater circulation figures in the 1930s, it never regained its editorial energy once Vance left.

In late 1930, Percy Waxman, who had been managing editor under Vance, took over as editor. His first issue (November 1930) included an interview with Colonel Charles Lindbergh; that story included pictures of the new baby, who would soon be kidnapped and murdered.[33]

After this spectacular beginning, however, Waxman was unable to sustain that same level of editorial energy—or circulation gains or advertising levels. The magazine's circulation remained high through the depression period, at 2.5 million. However, the advertising plummeted. In 1932, Ahnelt sold to George S. Fowler, an advertising man, and Lee Ellsmaker, formerly the publisher of *Liberty*. Soon after, Ellsmaker alone was listed as owner and publisher. Waxman was out, replaced by three editors, Theodore Von Ziekursch, Helen Duer Walker, and Morgan Steinmetz. But three editors were no better than one in stemming the decline of the *Review*.

In 1934, the magazine was sold again, this time to Laurelton Corp.[34] The details of the transaction were never revealed, yet *Time* later reported that the deal "presumably permitted him [Hearst] to ignore its [*Pictorial Review*'s] back debts unless it made money."[35]

Nonetheless, Hearst seemed committed to revitalizing the magazine. Herbert R. Mayes, who was editor of *American Druggist* (another Hearst property) and would soon go on to *Good Housekeeping*,* took over as editor. The budget for

Pictorial Review appeared to increase substantially. More four color was used, and the quality (and quantity) of the fiction improved substantially.

Mayes also strengthened nonfiction and the departments of the *Review* in a new "Book of Service," an insert with a separate four-color front cover. Many of the departments were the same but with better graphic presentation under the new package.

Under Mayes, prospects looked better for the *Review*. By 1936, advertising seemed to increase, and the average number of pages for the magazine reached into the 80s. By November 1936, the typical issue was around a hundred pages. In large part, this was due to an editorial innovation introduced that month. Beginning in November, the magazine offered a book-length novel in each issue. That novel was published at the end of the issue and was printed on a cheaper, uncoated stock of paper. Typically, no advertising was included within that text.

The *Review* got another boost when Hearst acquired the *Delineator* in 1937. The *Delineator* was folded into the *Pictorial Review*. In the process, the *Review* got the *Delineator*'s circulation of almost 1.5 million. This, added to the *Pictorial Review*'s circulation of just over 2.1 million, assured the combined magazine (now called the *Pictorial Review combined with Delineator*) a circulation well in excess of 3 million. That figure meant that the *Review* (in its combined form) became number one (in terms of circulation) in its niche.[36] Newsstand figures merely enhanced *Pictorial Review*'s position in the market.[37]

Mayes also continued to improve the editorial quality of the magazine. Yet, clearly, the magazine's mission differed strikingly from its glory days under Vance. Mayes had limited its goals, aspirations, and mission. The job of *Pictorial Review* was to

> convey a semblance of extra experience to normal, average, American people; some romance, some adventure, some adolescent love, some pathos, a touch—once in a while—of tragedy. It is our job to help such people live larger emotional lives, not to vote right; to enable such people, who haven't much money to spare, to touch far horizons, not to show how to make more money, which we don't know much about anyway.[38]

In spite of the innovations, in spite of the improved editorial content, in spite of the circulation gains, the advertising began to slip again. The magazine got a new editor, Mabel Search, the fiction editor under Mayes; but advertising continued to decline.

The magazine's March 1939 issue was its last. Nothing in that issue suggested that the *Pictorial Review* would die. Readers were left without the end of two serials. The editors never explained the rationale for the folding—nor did the Hearst corporation. The announcement provided no reason for the action, only an explanation that the magazine's "circulation and editorial features will be, as far as practicable, absorbed by other publications."[39]

Thus ended the 40-year life of *Pictorial Review*. In its day it stood for editorial excellence, the finest fiction, innovative graphics, and progressive (with or without the capital ''P'') ideas. Unfortunately, after Vance's departure and Ahnelt's sale, the magazine fell on hard times. It floundered. It became yet another casualty of the advertising cutbacks of the depression years.

Notes

1. The other five were *Ladies' Home Journal, Woman's Home Companion, The Delineator, Good Housekeeping*, and *McCall's*.

2. See September 1899.

3. Advertisement, January 1902, p. 41.

4. The editor, at least, in 1903 was a woman. She was pictured in the prospectus offering. However, she was not identified. August 1903, p. 6.

5. See, for example, January 1902.

6. "A Square Deal for the Divorced Woman," November 1909, pp. 13, 75.

7. "Why I Left My Husband," October 1909, pp. 15, 84.

8. "Why Women Want to Be Self-Supporting," May 1912, p. 6.

9. See, for example, Helen Christine Bennett, "The Story of Your Easter Hat," April 1910, pp. 18–19.

10. "An Editorial Declaration," March 1913, p. 3.

11. "The Editor's Page," August 1910, p. 3.

12. "The Editor's Page," April 1910, p. 3; April 1923, p. 1.

13. Advertising is based on the October 1919 issue. The advertising in this issue is typical of the ads in the *Pictorial Review*.

14. "Breaking Away from Traditions," July 1914, p. 1.

15. Ibid.

16. "Our New Serial Policy," September 1914, p. 1.

17. "Price Going Up!" March 1915, p. 2.

18. "Results of Birth Control Letter Contest," March 1916, pp. 24–25.

19. See, for example, Carl Vrooman, "The Family Balanced Ration," August 1917, p. 1; "Knitting for the Red Cross," November 1917, p. 28; Herbert Hoover, "What Every Woman Can Do to Help the Government," October 1917, p. 1. Mabel Potter Daggett, "An American Woman at the Front," August 1917, pp. 5–7, 42; Mabel Potter Daggett, "The Woman in Khaki," November 1917, pp. 13–14, 36, 38–39; front cover, July 1917; Lucien Jones, drawings from the battlefield, pp. 38–39.

20. "Where Do You Stand on Voluntary Parenthood?" May 1920, p. 16, and Eleanor Kinsella McDonnell, "Keeping the Stock in His Place," January/February 1920, pp. 21, 49, 55. In February 1924, the magazine reported that its poll of women revealed that six to one, women favored birth control. Ida Clyde Clarke, "Now We Know Where the Women Stand," February 1924, p. 1.

21. "What's the Matter with Marriage?" January 1921, pp. 25, 48.

22. In 1922, *Pictorial Review* in cooperation with the General Federation of Women's Clubs and other groups had congressmen introduce into both houses the so-called Capper Amendment, which was a resolution to empower Congress to regulate marriage and divorce. That amendment was not passed. Genevieve Parkhurst, "A Great Necessity," February 1930, p. 1.

23. Benjamin B. Hampton, "Too Much Sex-Stuff in the Movies?" February 1921, pp. 11, 13.

24. "A Splendid Victory," May 1921, p. 1.

25. Ida Clyde Clarke, "Now We Know Where the Women Stand," February 1924, p. 1.

26. "$5,000 Award," March 1924, p. 1.

27. "16,500.00 Prize-Novel Contest," February 1926, p. 1.

28. See March 1923, pp. 22–23, 28, 32.

29. "What Becomes of the Ziegfeld Follies Girls?" May 1925, pp. 12–13, 48.

30. Jim Tully, "Charlie Chaplin, His Real Life Story," January 1927, p. 2.

31. "Is There No Other Way?" August 1927, p. 1.

32. "Significant!" October 1927, p. 1.

33. Percy Waxman, "An Interview with Colonel Charles A. Lindbergh," pp. 14–15, 90.

34. "*Pictorial Review* Is Sold," *New York Times*, August 10, 1934, p. 15.

35. "Biggest End," *Time*, January 30, 1939, p. 47.

36. At the time, *Woman's Home Companion* placed first with a circulation in excess of 2.8 million and *Ladies' Home Journal* with more than 2.7 million. *McCall's* circulation was 2.5 million. "Ladies' Line Up," *Time*, February 15, 1937, p. 50.

37. "Town Hall," March 1938, p. 4.

38. Ibid.

39. "The *Pictorial Review* to Suspend," *Time*, January 21, 1939, p. 18.

Information Sources

BIBLIOGRAPHY:

"Biggest End." *Time Magazine*, January 30, 1939, p. 47.

"*Delineator* to Be Sold." *New York Times*, February 5, 1937, p. 19.

"Ladies' Line Up." *Time Magazine*, February 15, 1937, p. 50.

"Magazine Merger Ratified." *New York Times*, February 16, 1937, p. 42.

Peterson, Theodore. *Magazines in the Twentieth Century*. Urbana: University of Illinois Press, 1956.

"The *Pictorial Review* to Suspend." *New York Times*, January 21, 1939, p. 18.

INDEX SOURCES: Readers' Guide to Periodical Literature.

LOCATION SOURCES: Library of Congress; Cleveland Public Library; and other libraries.

Publication History

MAGAZINE TITLE AND TITLE CHANGES: *Pictorial Review* (1899–1937); *Pictorial Review Combined with Delineator* (1937–1939).

VOLUME AND ISSUE DATA: Vols. 1–40 (September 1899–March 1939). Monthly (December 1919 not issued. January/February 1920 was a combined issue due to a labor strike. July/August 1920 also combined because of a paper shortage and railroad strike.)

PUBLISHER AND PLACE OF PUBLICATION: William Paul Ahnelt (under corporate name of American Fashion Co. and Pictorial Review Co.) (1899–1932); Lee Ellsmaker (1932–1934); Hearst (under corporate name of Pictorial Review Co.) (1934–1939). New York.

EDITORS: First editors are unknown; Arthur T. Vance (1907–1930); Percy Waxman

(1930–1932); Theodore Von Ziekursch, Helen Duer Walker, and Morgan Steinmetz (1932–1934); Herbert R. Mayes (1934–1938); Mabel Search (1938–1939).
CIRCULATION: Ayer, 1936: 2,145,922 (paid).

Kathleen L. Endres

PLAYGIRL

Playgirl marked its 20th anniversary in June 1993. In her editor's column of
Playgirl in August 1993, editor in chief Charmian Carl stated:

Sexuality in the '90s. Or perhaps more *apropos*, Sexuality for Women in
the '90s. It seems to be a topic I either see in the media or am asked about
frequently. What better voice for this subject than PLAYGIRL? Now that
we're 20 years old, PLAYGIRL has reached a new level of maturing and
sophistication. In that spirit we're looking forward to bringing you the
best in entertainment for women—not to mention, the hottest men anywhere—for years to come.[1]

There is no doubt that the history of *Playgirl*, "the first erotic magazine for
women,"[2] illustrates how the early 1970s provided a sociopolitical and magazine journalism setting for several new women's periodicals, including *Playgirl*,
that featured nude males.

Playgirl, according to a 1976 study,[3] was made possible by three major contributing forces in American society. First, the women's liberation movement in
the 1960s led American women to assert their roles in society by helping them
to "move from dependence to independence, from ignorance of the way society
worked to knowledge of its machinations, from housewife status to labor force
status."[4] Second, the study has argued that the sexual revolution, expedited by
the development of birth control methods and by the growing use of sex coun-
seling, changed the perceptions of large numbers of women toward sex from
"a risk with dubious returns" to "fun."[5] Finally, the sociopolitical changes had
started to attract the attention of the editors of women's magazines in the United
States, while "most women's magazine editors had still failed to realize the true
depth and breadth of the changes which were taking place."[6]

The first 130-page issue of *Playgirl* (June 1973), which was characterized as
"the first magazine to offer attractive male nudes for American women to look
at on a regular basis,"[7] was out on May 15, 1973. It was for "today's liberated,
independent, self-aware, sensual woman."[8] One *Playgirl* reader was quoted as
saying in 1975: "Being a *Playgirl* in the modern sense means not having to
apologize for my lifestyle and options. Being a liberated women [*sic*] today is
an art, demanding tact, insight, self-confidence, and a consciousness of one's
sexuality."[9]

Playgirl sold out its first issue with 600,000 copies at one dollar each,[10] which

Playgirl, Inc., claimed to indicate "[j]ust how serious women were about having their own erotic publication."[11] It was published by Fawcett Publications Corp. in New York on credit with Douglas Lambert, owner of the Playgirl Club in Garden Grove, California, and two friends investing $250,000 into the *Playgirl* venture.[12]

Lambert's source of inspiration for his venture came from the success of *Cosmopolitan*,* the April 1972 issue of which ran a nude photo of actor Burt Reynolds. Lambert said, "When I saw Burt Reynolds naked in *Cosmo*, and saw what a winner that was, it came to me, that's what women want. If a woman says to me she wants to see a man's smile, his eyes, I say, 'Don't lie to me— you want to see a man's dong, that is if you're normal.' "[13]

The first issue of *Playgirl* contained the male nude photos, three features, and eight articles, including two on sexual subjects: "Fall (and Rise) of Virginity" and "Compulsions of the Promiscuous Woman."[14] One thoughtful commentator distinguished *Playgirl* from *Cosmopolitan* in focusing on why male nudes are emphasized. She observed:

> *Cosmo* used a nude male feature as an occasional gimmick to attract read-
> ers and advertisers. It was as if the staff looked at nudity as a cooking
> spice. A little attracted their readers to the kitchen but too much spoiled
> the dinner. *Playgirl*, of course, would use male nudity as a regular feature
> on its menu. Then, too, *Playgirl* was aimed at the woman who was at
> least trying to establish her personhood independent of any male. *Cosmo*
> was still directed at the woman who defined herself through a male.[15]

Playgirl is also different from Bob Guccione's *Viva*, the only other women's magazine to feature nude males, which was beaten by *Playgirl* to the stands by four months. Most notably, for example, *Playgirl* uses the centerfold format, while *Viva* does not. Guccione said: "There will be no centerfold beefcake. That would be demeaning to men and women don't like men who have been demeaned that way."[16] *Playgirl* strongly disagreed:

> *Playgirl* covers the full gamut of women's interests: from the latest word
> on relationships and how to please men, to the best in sexual fantasies
> and beyond. And of course, it does all this every month in addition to
> serving up a hearty helping of the most erotic and tantalizing nude male
> pictorials to be found anywhere. *In fact, the Playgirl Centerfold has be-
> come synonymous with the word "hunk" the world over* [emphasis
> added].[17]

Playgirl, which editor in chief Carl called the "one free forum for a purely female sexual voice that exists in the marketplace," still tries to serve as the "ultimate venue for women and their sexuality."[18] It is often considered the female version of *Playboy*. But *Playgirl* is described as "more of a raunchy

Cosmopolitan, lack[ing] the flair and style of *Playboy*, not to mention its literary aspects."[19]

It is especially noteworthy, however, that among the provocative periodicals, *Playgirl* is one of the only two deserving consideration for any library wishing to add a "nudie magazine," because of its "redeeming social value" for its topical variety and wide audience appeal.[20] (*Playboy* is the other magazine.) *Playgirl* articles and features deal with women's issues and male pictorials, arts and entertainment, politics and fiction. While maintaining its original focus on allowing women to rejoice in their own sexuality by offering erotic entertainment, education, and fantasy, the magazine has published a number of controversial interviews with diverse subjects, including Jimmy Carter, Henry Kissinger, and Margaret Thatcher.[21]

Since the very first issue in June 1973, two nude male features, *Playgirl*'s "Man of the Month" and "Discovery," have stood out as more permanent fixtures of the women-oriented magazine than any other. As a *Playgirl* editor stated:

> There are two just to get more nude pictures in there. . . . In the past we tried to make the "Man of the Month"—the centerfold—a distinctive personality rather than someone that we just haul in off the street. But it certainly doesn't always work that way. In fact it usually doesn't work that way. It just turns out that whoever is better looking goes in the centerfold and whoever is left goes in the "Discovery."[22]

In 1993, *Playgirl*'s "Man for August" centerfold featured ten nude photos and about one page of copy about chlorine technician Drew Ricciardi on eight pages.[23] There were six photos and a page of copy about skater Gary Hartwell in the "*Playgirl* August Discovery."[24] All the pictures were in color, and the men were sometimes completely clothed.

The "Man of the Month" and "Discovery" features were included in the "pictorials" section of the August 1993 issue. Also included were photos of six nude males, such as exercise guru Ed Gaut, star-to-be Scott Smith, surf meister Rudy Mosier, and Jackyl's front-man Jesse Dupree. One of the nude males was on a "fantasy trip" for sex with Wendy Wild. As a matter of policy, *Playgirl* publishes no photos of "*actual* sexually explicit conduct" (emphasis added).[25]

Another section of the editorial content of the *Playgirl* of August 1993 had four feature stories: "Rock 'n' Roll Fantasy: PLAYGIRL Picks the 10 Sexiest Rockers for 1993," "Swing Time: A Report from the Swingers' Club Scene," "Racing the Biological Clock: Coping with the Motherhood Imperative," and "Ending the Sexual Drought: Sometimes the Best Sex Is Worth Waiting For."

Departments in a magazine are called so "because they are supposed to appear issue after issue. In older magazines, departments come or go very seldom and only after great deliberation."[26] When it comes to *Playgirl*, however, one journalism researcher claimed in 1976 that the departments "have come and gone with bewildering speed'' since the magazine's founding in June 1973. The August 1993 issue offered 14 departments, including "The Editor's Page: What's Up with This Issue" and "Letters." Among other departments were "Quickies: Late-Breaking Health and Fitness News," "Sex Talk: Intimate Issues and Answers," "Quiz: What's Your Breaking Point?" and "Women Now: For the Pleasure of Women?"

As an entertainment source for the contemporary woman, *Playgirl* is designed for 18- to 34-year-old females.[27] The *Playgirl* reader is slightly younger than the reader of *Cosmopolitan, Glamour,** or *Mademoiselle.** The median age of the *Playgirl* reader is 27 years, compared with 30.4 for *Cosmo*, 28.6 for *Glamour*, and 28.8 for *Mademoiselle*.[28]

The 1992 circulation of *Playgirl* stood at 300,000.[29] The 1992 advertising rate of the magazine was $3,500.[30] *Playgirl* is published every 28 days by Playgirl, Inc. Its subscription rate in 1993 in the United States was $38 for one year and $68 for two years. For the foreign subscription, *Playgirl* is $46 for one year and $78 for two years.[31] As of August 1993, the single copy was priced at $3.95. According to an early study of *Playgirl*, "[m]ost of *Playgirl*'s readers buy the magazine issue by issue."[32] At present, about 20–25 percent of *Playgirl*'s readers are regular subscribers to the magazine.[33]

Notes

1. Charmian Carl, "Editor's Letter," August 1993, p. 1.
2. Press Release, "The History of Playgirl," 1993, p. 1.
3. Jean Marie McMahon, "*Playgirl*: New Player, Old Game," M.A. thesis, University of Oregon, 1976. This master's thesis is an outstanding analysis of the early history of the 20-year-old *Playgirl* in the context of the magazine's sociopolitical and magazine journalism. Among the several questions pursued in the 149-page study were "What forces in American society and in magazine journalism led to the creation of *Playgirl*?" "What was the original editorial formula?" "How did it compare to that of other women's magazines and to *Playboy*'s?" and "Which businesses have advertised in *Playgirl* and what problems have they caused the staff?" I am enormously indebted to this excellent study for preparing this chapter.
4. Ibid., p. 9.
5. Ibid.
6. Ibid.
7. Ibid., p. 97.
8. "The History of Playgirl," p. 1. See also Philip H. Dougherty, "Advertising: Big Accounts Shift," *New York Times*, May 3, 1973, p. 61.
9. "The History of Playgirl," p. 2.
10. "The Girls' Magazines Claw at Each Other," *Business Week*, May 11, 1974, p. 36.
11. "The History of Playgirl," p. 1.
12. "The Girls' Magazines Claw at Each Other," p. 37. Lambert called his magazine *Playgirl* because readers would obviously compare it with Hugh Hefner's successful *Playboy*. He was also aware of a possibility that Hefner would sue him over his magazine title, as he did when Lambert named his Garden Grove nightclub the Playgirl Club.

Lambert won the suit because the court ruled against Hefner in monopolizing the word "playgirl" as well as the word "playboy." McMahon, *"Playgirl,"* p. 28.

13. McMahon, *"Playgirl,"* p. 4, quoting Douglas Lambert as saying to *New York Times* writer Marcia Seligson (footnote omitted). Burt Reynolds, while wearing only a cigar, was not revealingly naked in that his left arm was strategically placed. Judy Klemesrud, "She Picks the Men Who Pose in Magazine's Centerfold," *New York Times*, October 2, 1973, p. 38.

14. McMahon, *"Playgirl,"* p. 29.

15. Ibid., pp. 30–31.

16. Philip H. Dougherty, "Advertising, Erotica for Women," *New York Times*, January 18, 1973, p. 68, quoted in McMahon, *"Playgirl,"* p. 35.

17. Press Release, "Happy Birthday *Playgirl*! 20 Years of Giving Women What They *Truly* Want . . . And Still Going Strong!" 1993.

18. Carl, "Editor's Letter," August 1993, p. 1.

19. *"Playgirl," Serials Review* 9 (Winter 1983), p. 9.

20. Ibid., p. 10.

21. "The History of Playgirl," p. 2.

22. McMahon, *"Playgirl,"* p. 38, quoting Robin Tucker, *Playgirl*'s managing editor (footnote omitted).

23. "Centerfold: Home Improvements," August 1993, p. 48.

24. "Discovery: Slap Shot!," August 1993, p. 12.

25. August 1993, p. 128.

26. McMahon, *"Playgirl,"* p. 53.

27. Mark Kissling (ed.), *Writer's Market: Where & How to Sell What You Write* (Cincinnati: Writers Digest Books, 1992), p. 697.

28. "Changes at *Playgirl*," *New York Times*, January 24, 1978, p. 51.

29. Beth R. Nussbaum interview, August 2, 1993.

30. *Bacon's Publicity Checker: Magazines*, 40th ed., vol. 1 (Chicago: Bacon's Information, 1992), p. 636.

31. August 1993, p. 128.

32. McMahon, *"Playgirl,"* p. 95.

33. Todd Gershon interview, August 2, 1993.

Information Sources

BIBLIOGRAPHY:

"Changes at *Playgirl*." *New York Times*, January 24, 1978, p. 51.

Dougherty, Philip H. "Advertising, Erotica for Women." *New York Times*, January 18, 1973, p. 68.

———."Advertising: Big Accounts Shift." *New York Times*, May 3, 1973, p. 61.

———."Playgirl Enters New Ad Arena." *New York Times*, July 21, 1976, p. 51.

"The Girls' Magazines Claw at Each Other." *Business Week*, May 11, 1974, p. 36.

Press Release. "Happy Birthday *Playgirl*! 20 Years of Giving Women What They *Truly* Want . . . And Still Going Strong!" 1993.

———. "The History of Playgirl." 1993.

Kissling, Mark (ed.). *Writer's Market: Where & How to Sell What You Write*. Cincinnati: Writers Digest Books, 1992.

Klemesrud, Judy. "She Picks the Men Who Pose in Magazine's Centerfold." *New York Times*, October 2, 1973, p. 38.

McMahon, Jean Marie. "*Playgirl*: New Player, Old Game." M.A. thesis, University of
    Oregon, 1976.
"Playgirl." *Serials Review.* 9 (Winter 1983), pp. 9–10.
INDEX SOURCES: None.
LOCATION SOURCES: University of Arizona Library and other libraries.

Publication History

MAGAZINE TITLE AND TITLE CHANGES: *Playgirl.*
VOLUME AND ISSUE DATA: Vols. 1–(June 1973–present). Monthly.
PUBLISHER AND PLACE OF PUBLICATION: Playgirl, Inc. (1973–present). New
    York.
EDITORS: Charmian Carl (1973–present).
CIRCULATION: Gale, 1994: 300,000.

Kyu Ho Youm

PREVENTION

The magazine *Prevention* was the vision of a man who believed that a healthy,
holistic way of natural living could be achieved even in the midst of the chemical
revolution of the 1950s. Sickly as a young man, J. I. Rodale was motivated to
investigate health information and to share his findings. He had already founded
the magazine *Organic Gardening*, which reflected what he saw as the connection
between gardening and health. Nevertheless, he was strangely out of step with
a culture determined to synthesize, or analyze and reproduce chemically, what
nature offered. His *Prevention: The Magazine for Good Health* attempted to
counter that impulse. Launched in 1950, the magazine has grown steadily since
then in circulation and advertising revenue.

The small-format magazine featured articles on the benefits of eating well
without chemicals and other food additives. He touted the benefits of herbs and
spices while railing against such commonly accepted and unquestioned staples
as salt and sugar. He wrote about the health benefits of having a positive outlook
on life and high self-esteem as the cornerstone of good health.

Rodale wrote many of the articles himself, often making proposals that put
him at odds with the federal government, the medical associations, and the
chemical industry. He scoured medical journals and other specialized
publications, finding health-related information too obscure or too technical to
have made it into the newspapers, and he regularly summarized it in readable
language. When the established industries did not go far enough, he did not
hesitate to research, experiment, and, in some cases, manufacture what he (and
his readers) needed.[1] He shared adventures, including his vacation with his wife
in Nassau in July 1957. A person with an abundance of energy and inventive-
ness, he used *Prevention* as a forum for plays and skits that made biting jabs at
the Establishment.

But *Prevention* made its name with its well-researched, clearly written feature

articles. Topics ranged from the benefits of vitamin C to the overcommerciali-
zation of white leghorn hens in the 1950s, from the need for vitamin D to linking
sugar with heart disease in the 1960s, from fiber to vitamin E in the 1970s, from
cholesterol to envisioning a national preventive health plan in the 1980s, and
diet and exercise in the 1990s.

The magazine has always had an upbeat, positive tone, encouraging habits to
attain a healthy body and lifestyle, yet some of his favorite campaigns and the
stands he took flew in the face of the time's conventional wisdom. For instance,
he was against fluoridation of tap water, which was widely accepted as a dental
cure-all; he railed against salt, sugar, and other highly refined substances, which
were the very symbol of a generation's purity;[2] he urged legislation against
pollution—air, water, and even noise—at a time when industry was going
through a postwar resurgence.

The magazine addresses the mature reader. For example, in its 40th-
anniversary issue, the magazine reported that newswoman Connie Chung, 47,
kept fit by taking "catnaps."[3] The magazine speaks even more directly to the
mature woman, with articles on subjects such as having children: "Encouraging
News (and Timely Advice) for the Fortyish Mother-to-Be."[4] Recognition of its
predominantly female audience has often shifted the contents to more superficial
fare in recent years, with "diet" taking on the more contemporary meaning of
"slimming down." While the magazine was founded by taking on the government and powerful industries such as the chemical industry, today's magazine
concerns itself almost exclusively with diet and exercise. Diets touted on almost
every cover promise to shed pounds. Walking is promoted in each issue, as well
as stretching exercises.

Rodale headed the magazine until his fatal heart attack while on Dick Cavett's
evening television show in 1971.[5] His son, Robert Rodale, immediately took
over. The vision had not changed—it just became more popular. Society, it
seems, caught up with *Prevention*. The younger Rodale, as editor in chief, kept
the magazine on the same course his father had. The staff grew. Rodale appointed editors to deal with everything from recipes to walking.

The younger Rodale no longer leads the magazine. He, like his father, faced
a tragic end. He died in a car accident while he was in the Soviet Union in
1990. He was there working against hunger by introducing "a magazine that
would teach Russian farmers the techniques of regenerative farming."[6] Since
then, Mark Bricklin, who had been editor under the younger Rodale, took over
as the main editor. He did not make any major changes in the publication;[7] and
he kept Rodale's name on the mast as editor in chief, adding the dates he served
in that position.

Not only has this magazine differed from much of American magazine fare,
but it also looks different. It retains its smaller dimensions and has not used
competitive cover tactics such as "cover girls." Perhaps these characteristics
have contributed to the general notion that it is a magazine for "older" people,
a notion the magazine attempts to dispel. One reader's letter used for promotion

reads: "PREVENTION was a gift subscription from my aunt. I had always considered it for 'older' readers. I'm happy to admit I couldn't have been more wrong and look forward to each new issue."[8] The largest portion of its readers are 35 years or older (77 percent).[9]

Although not traditionally classified as a "woman's magazine," *Prevention* nevertheless has a predominantly female audience (74 percent).[10] Recognizing such, the magazine has recently featured, almost exclusively, women on the cover. These women are generally white and middle-aged, youthful and healthy, a reflection of its readership.

Prevention has introduced readership surveys (a recent eight-page survey garnered over 16,000 responses) charting the health-related habits of its readership, such as whether they permit smoking in their homes and how much they walk each week. The staff has often found that they have not only an informed readership but a proactive one. The magazine has earned a comfortable place in the health and fitness niche, with a circulation of over 3 million and a monthly readership of over 9 million.[11]

The magazine keeps up with the times and does not shy from all controversy. It published facts to dispel myths about acquired immunodeficiency syndrome (AIDS). While it relies on medical advisers and some medical authors, the magazine maintains an adamant nonsurgical stance. The September 1991 cover read, "When to say 'Wait' when the Doctor says 'cut.' " Its primary concern remains health, the subtitle now reading, *America's Leading Health Magazine*. It still looks at new research, often spotlighting medical issues of interest to women, such as self breast examinations and mammography. When surgery is the call, the magazine still seeks "kinder" options, such as myomectomy, "a procedure . . . in which the fibroids are surgically removed, leaving the uterus intact," instead of hysterectomy.[12]

While advertising still maintains its billion-dollar mail-order market, the magazine also has many color and full-page ads. The advertisers are a varied lot— from the predictable vitamins and walking shoes, to more general-audience ads, such as those for midsize cars. Evident in the advertising is the targeted female audience, from panty hose that are "just my size" to Tums, which reminds the reader that it contains calcium.

Rodale Press concentrates on magazines focused on health and fitness. *Prevention* has inspired spin-offs, such as *Quick & Healthy Cooking*, *Men's Health*, and *Women's Health*.[13] The press's other publications include activity-based magazines *Bicycling* and *Scuba Diving*. Advertising revenues for the Rodale magazines totaled over $28 million for the first half of 1992, up over 10 percent from the previous year.[14] Although admittedly slow at adopting electronic publishing,[15] Rodale Press, cited as a $240 million company,[16] has a book division, which, like its magazine division, concerns itself primarily with health (physical and spiritual) and fitness (personal and environmental).

A magazine that blends sophisticated medical research with traditional natural curatives, *Prevention* has always looked toward the future, and it has cited that in the next century a personalized version of *Prevention* may be available for its readers.[17]

Notes

1. For an account of his dissatisfaction with industry's support of synthesized vitamin C and how he eventually had a natural alternative grown, harvested, manufactured, and made available to his readers, see Harald J. Taub, "J. I. Rodale, Father of Natural Food Supplements," September 1971, pp. 69–75.

2. For example, "In Review: Just a Pinch of Salt—Too Much?" declared, "*Prevention* editors believe all of us eat too much salt—the white crystallized chemical that is actually not necessary at all for good health," p. 11, and "What's Wrong with Sugar?" stated, "Sugar is a drug," July 1957, p. 34.

3. "Special Report: Feel Fit & Fabulous at 40-Plus," June 1990, p. 62.

4. Denis Foley and Susan Godbey, "Prime-Time Pregnancy," October 1991, p. 52.

5. Robert Rodale, "J. I. Rodale In Memoriam," August 1971, p. 14.

6. The staff of *Prevention,* "Honoring Robert: 1930–1990," September 1990, p. 7. See obituaries and *in memoriam* articles in other Rodale publications, including George A. Hirsch, "The Inside Track," *Runner's World,* December 1990, pp. 2–3; John Viehman, "The View from Here," *Backpacker,* February 1991, p. 3; also outside publications such as Maria Simson, "Bob Rodale and Sierra Club Fight World Hunger," *Publishers Weekly,* August 2, 1991, pp. 20–21.

7. See Scott Donaton, "Rodale Carries On: Few Changes Seen after Leader's Death," *Advertising Age,* October 1, 1990, p. 53.

8. Carolyn Fullerton, letter, Media Kit.

9. Ibid.

10. Ibid.

11. "Congratulations: We're on the Dean's List," May 1991, p. 29.

12. "Case of the Kinder Option," December 1992.

13. Scott Donaton, "Rodale Press Nurtures Growth with Spinoffs," *Advertising Age,* September 14, 1992, p. 48.

14. Ibid.

15. Jim Milliot, "Rodale Press Book Group Has 10% Sales Increase," *Publishers Weekly,* March 21, 1994, p. 10.

16. Donaton, "Rodale Carries On," p. 50.

17. Robert Rodale, "With the Editor: Health Facts in the Year 2000," January 1990, p. 23.

Information Sources

BIBLIOGRAPHY:

Donaton, Scott. "Rodale Carries On: Few Changes Seen after Leader's Death." *Advertising Age,* October 1, 1990, p. 53.

Hirsch, George A. "The Inside Track: Robert David Rodale—1930–1990." *Runner's World,* December 1990, pp. 2–3.

Simson, Maria. "Bob Rodale and Sierra Club Fight World Hunger." *Publishers Weekly,* August 2, 1991, pp. 20–21.

Viehman, John. "The View from Here: The Man Who Planted Trees." *Backpacker,* February 1991, p. 3.

INDEX SOURCES: Consumer Health & Nutrition Index; Environmental Periodicals Bibliography; Health Index; Junior High Magazine Abstracts; Magazine Index; Popular Magazine Review (now Magazine Article Summaries).

LOCATION SOURCES: Library of Congress; Kent State University, and other libraries.

Publication History

MAGAZINE TITLE AND TITLE CHANGES: *Prevention.*

VOLUME AND ISSUE DATA: Vols. 1–(June 1950–present). Monthly.

PUBLISHER AND PLACE OF PUBLICATION: Rodale Press, Inc. Emmaus, Pa.

EDITORS: J. I. Rodale (1950–1971); Robert Rodale (1971–1990); Mark Bricklin (1990–present).

CIRCULATION: ABC, 1993: 3,255,998 (paid, primarily subscription; 136,422 nonpaid).

Therese L. Lueck

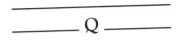

QUILT WORLD

Quilt World, a bimonthly magazine subtitled *A Quilter's Dream Come True*, has served quilt makers since 1976—a period in which the craft expanded from a private domestic skill to a publicly recognized art form. Readers of *Quilt World* also changed: the image of a thrifty homemaker, piecing a warm and functional bedcover from scraps of well-worn fabric, has gradually broadened to include the fabric designer, working with fiber as a creative alternative to oil and canvas. The magazine targets both the traditional and the contemporary quilter.[1]

Quilt World was founded in April 1976, as the first major handicraft magazine of House of White Birches, a spin-off of Tower Press in Seabrook, New Hampshire. Tower Press, operated by brothers Edward and Michael Kutlowski, was a small but successful publisher of nostalgia and women's magazines, then in its 19th year. Edward, the more enterprising of the two partners, had pushed the company to develop new titles for a growing market in American handicrafts—especially quilting. Alice Jankauskas, general manager of White Birches from 1974 to 1987, recalls, "In the seventies there were plenty of how-to publications like *Popular Mechanics* for men, but none for women hobbyists."[2] Indeed, the only competitor in the quilter's market was a publication called *Quilter's Newsletter*, which was sold by subscription only.[3] Furthermore, needlework patterns of all kinds were hard to come by, according to Jankauskas. Quilters traditionally circulated patterns among themselves or purchased occasional and expensive patterns sold at fabric shops. But even these promising indicators failed to win family approval for a new quilter's magazine, so in 1974, Edward Kutlowski split off his own local company, which he named House of White Birches, and, two years later, launched *Quilt World* on his own. The magazine was an immediate success; at 60¢ a copy, three dollars a year, it had a start-up circulation of about 11,000. Within the first year, circulation rose to 78,000; two years later, it had doubled to 145,000.[4]

Quilt World's success was probably influenced by several related events that took place during the decade of its founding. In 1971, the Whitney Museum of Art had mounted an exhibit called ''Abstract Design in American Quilts.'' The exhibit revitalized the craft by stressing its creative and artistic side, an aspect frequently downplayed by women quilters. After the Whitney show, many women—and a few men—who saw quilting as an art form gave the craft an exciting new direction. A second key event was the celebration of the American Bicentennial in 1976, which helped to attract a larger audience to quilting—and to quilt publications.[5]

To keep costs down, both Kutlowskis printed their magazines in black and white on inexpensive newsprint, limiting color to covers only. But *Quilt World* began using color and coated stock on its inside pages as early as 1980. This was not a lavish gesture on the part of the publisher, but rather a necessity. Quilt patterns, unlike those of other types of needlework—such as crochet— cannot be reproduced effectively in black and white.[6] By the early 1980s, about a third of *Quilt World*'s 68 pages were printed in color; currently, about half of the magazine is in color.[7]

Quilt World's first editor was Barbara Hall Pederson, who turned the magazine into a showcase of original quilt designs created and executed by readers. Contributors earned a byline plus a moderate payment, an arrangement that delighted readers and helped White Birches to hold down editorial costs.[8] *Quilt World* also featured a lively reader's exchange—letters from readers to readers in search of patterns, advice, and materials. This strong interaction among readers became a hallmark of all White Birches craft magazines; it gave them a warmth and intimacy—and a market niche—that still differentiate them from higher-circulation competitors.[9]

In 1982, a mere six years after *Quilt World*'s launch, House of White Birches was publishing a string of successful craft magazines with corresponding special annual issues, and Ed Kutlowski was able to make a bid for his then-floundering parent company, Tower Press. Accompanied by some antagonism between the longtime employees of the older company who lost their seniority to the ''new'' staff, Tower Press was absorbed into House of White Birches. The two brothers were, once again, partners in a single enterprise.[10]

By then, *Quilt World* had reached a circulation of 161,000, which was to be its highest point.[11] In the mid-1980s, the magazine was apparently beginning to fall victim to its own success. The booming quilt market had attracted many other publications to the field; White Birches itself had introduced a competitor called *Stitch 'N Sew Quilts*, a variation of an older Tower Press magazine called simply *Stitch 'N Sew*. There were also the quarterly and annual book-length collections of quilt patterns that White Birches had pioneered with great success.[12] Even noncraft magazines on the White Birches list promoted quilt patterns. For example, its flagship family magazine, *Women's Circle*,* created by the brothers in 1957, issued the *Women's Circle Patchwork Quilter* early in 1983. It offered a collection of 12 full-size quilt patterns for $3 at a time when a single issue of *Quilt World* magazine cost $1.35.[13] The craft was certainly growing, but it seemed that the number of publications it could support was limited.

In 1985, after 30 years of publishing, separately and in partnerships, the Kutlowskis retired and sold House of White Birches to another pair of brothers—Indiana printers Carl and Arthur Muselman. The Muselmans moved the operation to their hometown of Berne (pop. 4,000) in the northeast corner of the state. In the shuffle of personnel, *Quilt World* got a new editor, Sandra Hatch, who was editor of *Quilt World Omnibook*, a White Birches quarterly publication. Like some other White Birches editors at the time of the sale, she elected to remain in her East Coast home.[14] Today, working from her office in Maine, Hatch prepares *Quilt World* copy by computer, sending typeset copy and some photos to Berne to be printed.

Under her direction, several regular *Quilt World* features have been added or expanded. "Pieces & Patches" is a long-running column that reports on the fiber artists who create wall hangings, high-style clothing, and other fabric works of art. "Tools of the Trade" teaches needlework techniques and evaluates new products such as quilt frames. "Quilt Bookshelf" reviews new books about the craft, or as many as possible. This is another branch of quilt publishing that has exploded along with the craft, according to Hatch. "I never dreamed there would be so many books on the subject. I have catalogued at least 1000 titles on all aspects of quilting; recently I added 20 new titles in just one month."[15]

Other regular columns include "Quilters' Chronicles," a chatty collection of personal anecdotes written by Canadian author Ethel Austin Rondpre, and the "Quilt Show Directory," a calendar of the major shows in the United States and overseas. The proliferation of competitions sponsored by craft associations or by tourism promoters makes the directory an important feature of the magazine. Hatch publishes follow-up features on show prizewinners and their work, selecting articles on the quality of the writing and the photographs submitted.[16]

The magazine strives for a mix of features to attract both traditional and contemporary quilt makers. A recent story about a quilter who graduated from traditional patterns into one-of-a-kind works of art was balanced by a report on the native quilters of the Cook Islands, whose work follows the historic Hawaiian Island patterns.[17] Although women make up 98 percent of her readership,[18] Hatch also features the work of male quilters. She published four profiles of male quilters during 1993.[19]

In her regular "Editorial," Hatch attempts to keep readers informed about developments in the craft, particularly its expansion into big business. She notes that while quilters make up only a small percentage of all craftspeople, they spend more money than most. "Pioneers made quilts of scraps; some still do, but most quilters buy all new materials and they're not cheap. You can crochet a coverlet for a few dollars, but a quilt is expensive."[20] Readers confirm this; they report spending over $40 per project; about half of the 1992 survey respondents said they complete between 5 and 20 projects per year.[21]

Interestingly, as the craft of quilting becomes more costly, the quilt publication business has moved steadily in the other direction. Hatch says there were at least 16 quarterly quilt publications on the market in 1993. ''Anyone with desktop publishing equipment can start up a quilter's magazine for almost nothing,'' she says. ''When *Quilt World* started, quilters bought all of the publications then being printed and saved them all. Today there are so many magazines and books on the subject, no one could possibly do that.''[22]

In this saturated market, *Quilt World* does well. Standard Rate and Data Service reported 50,000 paid *Quilt World* subscribers out of a total circulation of about 70,000 for the first half of 1993.[23] The magazine's 1993 price of $2.95 per issue still gives good value; both the traditional quilter and the contemporary fiber artist find plenty of information about patterns and materials, plus a perspective of the history and development of the craft, a mix that seems likely to preserve *Quilt World*'s position among House of White Birches publications.

Notes

1. Sandra Hatch interview, October 31, 1993.
2. Alice Jankauskas interview, November 20, 1993.
3. Hatch interview.
4. Jankauskas interview.
5. Willow Ann Soltow, *Quilting the World Over* (Radnor, Pa.: Chilton Books, 1991), pp. 17–20.
6. Jankauskas interview.
7. July 1993.
8. Jankauskas letter to the author, January 17, 1994.
9. Marjorie Pearl interview, March 23, 1993. According to House of White Birches 1992 *Update* newsletter, the company currently publishes 23 titles—mostly craft, cooking, and nostalgia magazines. It mails a total of 6.6 million copies worldwide and has an overall newsstand circulation of 10 million copies.
10. Jankauskas letter to the author.
11. Hatch interview.
12. Jankauskas interview; Jankauskas letter to the author, February 6, 1994.
13. April 1983.
14. Hatch interview.
15. Hatch interview. Hatch herself coauthored a 1991 book: *Putting on the Glitz: Unusual Fabrics & Threads for Quilting and Sewing* (with Ann Boyce) (Radnor, Pa.: Chilton Book Company), which has sold over 15,000 copies to date.
16. Ibid.
17. July 1993, pp. 8–9.
18. *Quilt World's Reader's Survey*, 1992.
19. Hatch interview.
20. Ibid.
21. Survey, 1992.
22. Hatch interview.
23. Standard Rate and Data Service, *Consumer Magazine and Agri-Media* (Skokie, Ill.: Standard Rate and Data, 1993) p. 717.

Information Sources

BIBLIOGRAPHY:
Soltow, Willow Ann. *Quilting the World Over*. Radnor, Pa.: Chilton Books, 1991.
———. *Update*. House of White Birches newsletter, undated, 1992.
INDEX SOURCES: None.
LOCATION SOURCES: Library of Congress and other sources.

Publication History

MAGAZINE TITLE AND TITLE CHANGES: *Quilt World*.
VOLUME AND ISSUE DATA: Vols. 1–(April 1976–present). Biweekly.
PUBLISHER AND PLACE OF PUBLICATION: House of White Birches. Seabrook,
    N.H. (1976–1985); Berne, Ind. (1985–present).
EDITORS: Barbara Hall Pederson (1976–1985); Sandra Hatch (1985–present).
CIRCULATION: ABC, 1993: 71,668 (paid, primarily subscriptions).

Jean E. Dye

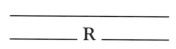

REDBOOK

Redbook magazine, the baby sister of the "Seven Sisters" women's service magazines, is a good example of how modern consumer magazines, especially women's magazines, are constantly redefining their market niche. Launched in Chicago in 1903, *Redbook* has undergone many changes. It began as an all-fiction magazine geared toward both men and women. After it was purchased in 1929 by the McCall Corporation, it evolved into a general-interest magazine, featuring a blend of fact and fiction pieces. Due to changing demographics after World War II, it was transformed in 1949 into a service magazine aimed at young adults. It continued to carry a lot of fiction, despite television's devastating impact on most magazine fiction.

By the mid-1950s, *Redbook* had steered to an all-female audience and eventually became one of the "Seven Sisters" (the others are *Better Homes and Gardens*,* *Family Circle*,* *Good Housekeeping*,* *Ladies' Home Journal*,* *McCall's*,* and *Woman's Day**) which, despite recent declines in circulation numbers, still boast an impressive combined circulation of 40 million.[1] Beginning in the 1950s and continuing on into the 1960s and 1970s, *Redbook*'s editors tackled many controversial issues while remaining commercially viable. According to Robert Stein, a former editor, "*Redbook* led sort of a charmed life in the '50s, '60s, and even into the '70s."[2]

In the 1970s, *Redbook* published more fiction than any other magazine in the field. At the same time it became an outspoken advocate of the women's movement, providing a forum for discussion of issues such as the equal rights amendment, sexual harassment on the job, and equal pay for equal work. Some observers have argued that the male-edited issues in the 1970s were more feminist in tone than the female-edited publication of the next decade. The focus in the 1980s was no longer on women's struggle for equality. The magazine was now a handbook for women juggling career and family responsibilities. It still ran fiction pieces, but the majority of its articles were nonfiction. To let its audience know about the magazine's new agenda, *Redbook*'s advertising department came up with "The Juggler" ad campaign in the 1980s.

When the current editor, Ellen Levine, joined the *Redbook* staff in January 1991, some more changes were made. Her audience still consisted of working women with children, but Levine felt that women in the 1990s were more experienced than they had been when "The Juggler" campaign began. "They don't need the same information anymore. [Working mothers] used to be the minority in the neighborhood; now they are the neighborhood."[3] The new *Redbook* acknowledged family needs but focused on the special attention Levine felt women should give themselves.

Today's *Redbook* is quite different from the *Red Book* that was begun in May 1903 by Stumer, Rosenthal, and Eckstein, a firm of Chicago retail merchants, under the leadership of Louis Eckstein.[4] Founded at the height of the so-called fiction craze, it was called *The Red Book Illustrated*, but it changed its name to *The Red Book Magazine* shortly thereafter. It was edited from 1903 until 1906 by Trumbull White, who in his first editorial wrote that the name of the magazine was appropriate because "red is the color of cheerfulness, of brightness, of gayety."[5] Subtitled *The Great Ten Penny Short Story Magazine*, *Red Book* offered short fiction by famous authors, many of whom were women. The covers, always in red, featured a painting of a beautiful young woman and continued to do so through the 1920s.

Each *Red Book* issue began with a frontispiece or illustration of an inside story, which was aimed to entice the reader into the book. The next section, entitled "Photographic Art Studies," was a gallery of photographs of popular actresses in either costume or modern dress.[6] Occasionally, attractive heiresses, operatic prima donnas, dancers, and vaudeville stars were featured as well. Next came the short stories, which were accompanied by several illustrations by some of the top artists of the day. At the end of the book, a regular feature—"Some Dramas of the Day"—was illustrated by photos of individual actors and actresses or scenes from plays.

At the end of its first two years, *Red Book* under Trumbull White's leadership, was successful and had a circulation of approximately 300,000.[7] White, a brilliant young journalist, had been a newspaper editor, war correspondent, explorer, and author of ten books prior to coming to *The Red Book Magazine*.[8] When White left to edit *Appleton's Magazine*, Karl Edwin Harriman took over and edited the magazine and its sister publications, *The Blue Book* and *The Green Book*, from 1907 until 1912.[9]

Under Harriman's stewardship, the magazine touted itself as "the largest illustrated fiction magazine in the world" and increased its cover price to 15¢. The advertising section claimed to be "the great shopping window of America." An in-house ad proclaimed, "*The Red Book* reaches the home because it is editorially wholesome." The ad pictured a mother and her teenage son and daughter framed in the front window of their substantial home as they waited for the return of the head of the household, who was shown walking up the porch steps with the latest copy of *Red Book* peeking out of his jacket pocket.[10]

In other words, *Red Book* was trying to convey the message that it offered something for everyone, and, indeed, it did. It was an entertainment magazine, and its contents were not too dissimilar from those of modern television programming. There was short fiction by talented writers such as Jack London, Sinclair Lewis, Edith Wharton, and Hamlin Garland. Stories were about love, crime, mystery, politics, animals, adventure, and history (especially the old West and the Civil War). As an example of the variety of themes, the April 1909 issue included stories that dealt with "an emigrant father's sacrifice for his little boy,"[11] "the trial of a young man's strength in the crucible of a great city,"[12] "an old man's adherence to the church of his fathers,"[13] and "the story of a famous crime, a defense, and the *corpus delicti* that wasn't."[14]

Harriman also ran some nonfiction pieces. One, "Billions for Bad Blue Blood," was about the trend of American heiresses' marrying impoverished, titled Europeans.[15] The author, who was billed by *The Red Book Magazine* as "the greatest investigator of his day," described one nobleman as follows: "He is what you call in America a 'dope-fiend.' Most of his kind are 'dope-fiends.' He wears corsets, paints his face, and the most honest way he has of making a living is by borrowing money from silly Americans who are proud of being fleeced by a nobleman."[16] This feature and others belied *Red Book*'s claim of being "editorially wholesome."

Harriman continued the photography and theater sections, but he tried a few innovations. There were contests. For example, in December 1909, a "$500 reward" was offered for answering questions in that issue. Other additions included monthly features such as "Parisian Modes" (photographs of the latest fashions from France) and "In Ye Olde Print Shop," a section that featured longer works of both nonfiction and fiction. (Novelist George Bernard Shaw was a contributor.) They were printed and illustrated in styles reminiscent of fine printing of earlier centuries.

Harriman was succeeded by Ray Long, who was editor from 1912 until 1918. Long discarded Harriman's format, eliminating the nonfiction pieces and focusing on fiction. A typical Long-edited issue included "The Three Best Serial Novels of the Year" and "The Best Short Stories of the Month." In addition, Long ran the one-page "Bruce Barton's Common Sense Editorial" and a poem each month. The "Photographic Art Studies" section was still there, but Long called it "Beautiful Women." While it used to include as many as 28 photographs, it was now reduced to 7 photos per issue. In recognition of the growing popularity of moving pictures, many photographs were of "Film Play Stars." The "Some Dramas of the Day" section was a victim of the rise of the movie industry and was eliminated.

Indiana-born Long had worked on newspapers in Indianapolis, Cincinnati, and Cleveland and edited *Hampton's Magazine* before he became editor of *Red Book* and Eckstein's other publications, *Blue Book* and *Green Book*.[17] While

Long did an excellent job with *The Red Book Magazine*, he really made his name when he took over the editorship of William Randolph Hearst's *Cosmopolitan*.* *Fortune* magazine in Long's 1931 obituary, however, suggested that Long's career at *Red Book* was actually more brilliant than his more celebrated stint at *Cosmopolitan*.[18]

Long's strongest suit had been his ability to recognize fiction that would please the general magazine audience. Although he was writing about his experience at *Cosmopolitan*, the following probably applies to his work at *Red Book* as well.

> I happen to be an average American who has the opportunity to read a tremendous number of manuscripts. From these I select the stories I like, publish them within the covers of a magazine, and through the facilities of our circulation department put that magazine where people may see it; and there are enough other average Americans who like to read the same thing that I like to read to buy the magazine in sufficient quantities to make me worth my salary.[19]

When Long became editor of *Cosmopolitan* in January 1918, Harriman went back to work as editor of *Red Book*. He did not revert to his old editorial format but retained Long's, with a few minor modifications. His audience still consisted of both men and women, but the woman reader for whom Harriman was editing was changing. She was a flapper. This flapper and her male counterpart continued to read *Redbook* primarily for the fiction it delivered.[20] One coup was a series of complete short stories by Edgar Rice Burroughs, in which Burroughs described the "exploits of Tarzan the Untamed."[21] During Harriman's second stint as editor, the magazine increased in both size and price. When he took over in 1918, the price per issue was 20¢; by the 1920s it cost 25¢.

The price remained the same during the 1930s and 1940s, when Edwin Balmer was editor. A short story writer who had written for both Harriman and Long, Balmer took over from Harriman in the spring of 1927. Balmer was *Red Book*'s last midwestern editor.[22]

In the summer of 1929, the McCall Corporation bought *Red Book* and *Blue Book*, and Balmer and the magazines moved to New York.[23] *Redbook*, under Balmer, ran short stories by authors such as Booth Tarkington and F. Scott Fitzgerald. The Grand Duke Alexander contributed nonfiction pieces about the Prince of Wales and Alfonso of Spain. Celebrities of the day took their hand at magazine writing as well. Gertrude Temple, Shirley's mother, wrote an article about what her daughter ate, and First Lady Eleanor Roosevelt wrote an article entitled, "The Ingredients of an Ideal Wife." Two very different pieces about the stock market crash appeared in the 1930s: industrialist Cornelius Vanderbilt, Jr.,'s "Farewell to Fifth Avenue" and singer Eddie Cantor's "Selling at the Top." Cantor wrote that after the crash, " 'sugar daddies' were only men with diabetes."[24] With articles like these, Balmer made *Redbook* a general-interest monthly for men and women while continuing the tradition of running a lot of fiction.

Balmer also included complete book-length novels in each issue. Dashiell Hammett's *The Thin Man* (1934), for instance, was published in *Redbook*. More fiction was run in the "Encore of the Month" section, which featured reprints of short stories by well-known authors that, for whatever reason, had not received wide circulation. *Redbook* also sponsored photographic, letter, and short story contests, as well as two novel contests with Dodd, Mead and Company.

Redbook's formula worked, and although the magazine never outstripped its main competition (Crowell-Collier's *American* and Hearst's *Cosmopolitan*), under Balmer's leadership, sales passed the million mark in 1937.[25] For many of the years he edited the magazine (1927–1949), Balmer was successful. Then two things almost put an end to *Redbook*: television and demographics. While television was just beginning to be a threat, changing demographics resulted in plunging circulation figures. Balmer, who always had a knack for attracting what he referred to as "the little old ladies in Kokomo,"[26] was losing "the little old ladies" and did not know how to reach a younger audience. Increasing the ratio of fact to fiction in the 1940s did not help, and the magazine continued to lose readers. It lost $400,000 in 1948, and Balmer was replaced by Wade Hampton Nichols in 1949.[27]

The 34-year-old Nichols had made a reputation for himself by increasing the circulation of *Click* and *Modern Screen*. Unlike that of his predecessors, Nichols's career revolved exclusively around magazines. Nichols had been the editor of *Screen Guide* (1938), *Stardom* (1941), *Click* magazine (1942), and *Modern Screen* magazine (1948). He was editor of *Redbook* from 1949 to 1958 and, between 1953 and 1955, was also associate editor of *Bluebook*.[28]

With Phillips Wyman, the magazine's new publisher, Nichols looked at the post–World War II demographics and then aimed the editorial content at "young adults" between the ages of 18 and 34.[29] This tactic turned the magazine around. In 1949, the year both men began working for *Redbook*, the magazine had a circulation of 1.8 million and advertising revenue of $1,467,128. By 1950, circulation reached 2 million.[30]

In 1951, the subtitle *The Magazine for Young Adults* was added in recognition of *Redbook*'s new audience. The newsstand price was raised to 35¢. According to Robert Stein, a staffer under Nichols as well as his successor as editor, the price hike did not stop readers from buying the magazine in increasing numbers. "What they were getting was an honest, if not distinguished, magazine. Amid the conventional fiction and the treacle about movie stars, there was a vein of reporting that reflected social and moral concern: about racial prejudice in the churches and elsewhere, about the damage that McCarthyism was doing to the country, about the dangers of nuclear weapons, about public-health problems such as air pollution and the indiscriminate use of pesticides and food additives."[31]

These efforts were recognized in 1954, when the magazine received the Benjamin Franklin Award for public service for three articles that dealt with government security, academic freedom, and integration.[32] Wyman died in the spring of 1955, just as the magazine was becoming profitable and as it began to steer toward a female audience. Nichols left three years later to edit *Good Housekeeping* magazine.

The new editor was Robert Stein, who recalls that he

> was only in third position on the staff hierarchy at that time, thirty-four years old and philosophically uncongenial to Langlie [*Redbook*'s president]. In addition, in its 88 years of existence, the McCall Corporation had never had a Jew as editor-in-chief of one of its magazines. Although I was fully prepared to see the executive editor or an outsider become the new editor, Langlie called me in and after an hour's conversation, gave me the job.[33]

In addition to being *Redbook*'s first Jewish editor, Stein was the first to be born and educated in New York. Stein had a magazine background, having worked for the *Alumnus* magazine at City College and *Argosy* magazine.

According to Stein, his first two years as editor of *Redbook* were the most productive he ever had as a magazine editor. He wrote:

> Langlie gave me the kind of confidence and support that editors dream about but seldom get. When I asked for better schedules and more press capacity from our printing plant, Langlie spent two days backing my demands against the plant managers who wanted to reserve their best equipment for outside customers. When the magazine was given an award by the Family Service Association for supporting Federal welfare programs, about which I knew he had personal reservations, Langlie stood next to me during the ceremony and expressed his pride in the magazine. After we published an article criticizing frozen-food manufacturers for slipshod practices, Langlie greeted an industry delegation with the remark, "I suppose you've come here to thank us for trying to raise the standards of your business," and brushed aside suggestions that members might withdraw advertising from both of his company's magazines.[34]

Stein's editorial content was aimed at an all-female audience, between 18 and 34. Stein believed his readers were women who were "above average in income, awareness, sophistication, and education."[35] One of his first major pieces was entitled "Why Young Women Feel Trapped." He also recruited Dr. Benjamin Spock and celebrated anthropologist Margaret Mead as regular contributors and started a special monthly feature called "Dialogue," which was an intriguing conversation between two famous people.[36]

During Stein's tenure as editor, he tried to integrate the regular light fare with a whole range of political and social issues. When Stein had been a staffer under

Nichols in the 1950s, the magazine was already heading in this direction. This was an unusual tack for a women's magazine, says Stein, adding that Nichols had switched the magazine's focus in order to attract younger women, who Nichols believed would be more open-minded and better educated.[37]

Stein felt he, too, was successful in covering controversial issues, especially in the 1960s. When he left in 1965, he said his successor, Seymour Chassler, "continued in that general direction with his particular cast of mind. We [Nichols, Stein, and Chassler] were fairly young and idealistic and tried to see how far we could push a mass circulation magazine. We did fairly well with it."[38]

Stein was particularly proud of *Redbook*'s coverage of racial issues. *Redbook* was the first national magazine to run a story on civil rights leader Martin Luther King. Stein was also interested in the threat of nuclear war, which he said most editors of women's magazines found "a little off-putting." He initiated a joint interview of John F. Kennedy by a handful of editors of women's magazines just before Kennedy's assassination in 1963. Stein also did a follow-up with Kennedy on the Test Ban Treaty. The article came out in the November issue, the same month Kennedy was killed.[39]

None of this type of coverage was done without some struggle, says Stein. "Editing for a mass women's magazine is like doing pirouettes in a telephone book. It's limiting. And the pressure from advertisers is nothing compared to limitation from some readers. Editing during a period of social change we did as much as we could have done and kept the magazine successful."[40]

He was rewarded for his persistence. *Redbook* not only garnered many public service awards but was also financially successful, more than tripling the amount of its advertising in just six years. By 1963, *Redbook* carried more than $10.2 million of advertising, and circulation had shot up to almost 4 million.[41] Stein left to edit *McCall's* in 1965.

Seymour (Sey) Chassler, the next editor, brought a lot of experience with him to his new job. He had been associate editor of *Coronet*, a writer for *March of Time* films, and a picture editor for *Pageant* and *Colliers*. Chassler began his career with *Redbook* as executive editor in 1960.

Fiction remained a mainstay, and *Redbook* published more fiction than any other women's magazine. Each issue carried about three short stories, and the August issue, which was always jam-packed with fiction, ran nine short stories. Novels were also carried. Judith Guest's *Ordinary People*, for example, was published in *Redbook*. The magazine was also the first periodical to win the National Magazine Award for fiction twice.

Chassler also ran nonfiction pieces about nontraditional subjects, such as women farmers and women blue-collar workers. He also had an impressive group of contributing editors and columnists. In addition to Spock and Mead, pediatrician T. Berry Brazelton, poet Judith Viorst, sex researchers Masters and Johnson, and consumer advocate Bess Myerson wrote frequently for the magazine. Chassler opened *Redbook*'s pages not only to experts such as these but to its readers as well. The magazine frequently ran questionnaires ("How Do

You Feel about God and Religion?'' and ''How Do You Feel about Being a Woman?'') to determine who its readers were.

This typical reader could be described as a young woman between 18 and 34 who ''may or may not be married, may or may not be a mother.''[42] Above all, she was a feminist. Chassler was himself a feminist. As a child he had always been aware that his twin sister had been treated differently than he was treated. In the pages of his magazine he ran articles geared toward reversing this imbalance between male and female. He was able to carry highly politicized articles about feminist issues without losing his advertisers.[43]

In 1976, the bicentennial year, Chassler spearheaded an effort to use the combined power of the women's magazines to promote passage of the equal rights amendment (ERA). He talked 35 magazines into running something about the ERA in their July 1976 issues.[44] His own magazine ran companion pieces by Republican Maureen Reagan and by Democrat Cathleen Douglas supporting passage. There were also boxed quotes of women like athlete Billie Jean King, columnist Ann Landers, and actresses Jean Stapleton, Marlo Thomas, Brenda Vaccaro, and Susan Seaforth Hayes and a ''Special Message from Betty Ford.''[45]

Chassler was also very concerned about civil rights. He used African American models and carried many articles of interest to African American women, including one entitled, ''Black Feminism'' and another about California congresswoman Yvonne Braithwaite Burke, as well as a piece on black English by an African American scholar.[46] One month when there were no African Americans featured in the issue, Chassler insisted that a short story about a family use an illustration of a black family. Chassler also insisted that ''Black'' always be capitalized in the copy.[47] According to Chassler, his was also the first magazine to use female pronouns in place of male pronouns. He recalled that when he introduced this policy, monthly columnist Margaret Mead, who was by no means antifeminist, asked, ''What for?''[48]

He wanted to do it because, as he wrote in a 1977 editorial: ''We stand for the forward movement of women. . . . we are proud of the stand and the leadership position we have taken in behalf of ratification of the Equal Rights Amendment.''[49] Taking such a stand did not hurt the magazine. By the late 1960s, *Redbook*'s advertising pages went up from 813 to 910, and it had a circulation of 4.5 million.[50] The inflation of the 1970s, however, affected printing costs and the cover price, which jumped from 35¢ to 60¢ by 1974 and to 90¢ by 1976. Chassler remembered, '' 'This is a magazine for young mothers; you can't do that.' Our audience was having to make decisions between a box of crackers and buying our magazine.''[51]

In addition to editing, Chassler was active in the women's movement. Among many other things, he served as a member of the advisory committee of the National Women's Political Caucus, was an honorary trustee for the Elizabeth Cady Stanton Foundation, and won the Headliner Award from Women in Communications, Inc.

Therefore, it was appropriate that his successor was *Redbook*'s first woman editor—his former fiction editor, Anne Mollegen Smith. In keeping with her expertise in fiction, there was an emphasis on short stories, novellas, and novels during her short tenure (February 1982–April 1983). Nonfiction articles about topics such as sex and celebrity interviews ran alongside old standbys such as columns by Viorst and Brazelton. Although the tone of the magazine was not as strongly feminist as it had been, *Redbook* under Smith continued to carry articles relevant to the changing status of women in society. For instance, in the June 1982 issue she ran a "Special *Redbook* Report on Alcohol."

The Hearst Corporation bought *Redbook* in 1982. Smith was fired shortly after and was replaced in 1983 by Annette Capone, who had been with *Seventeen** magazine, *Ladies' Home Journal*, and *Mademoiselle*.* Under Capone, the magazine de-emphasized the traditional fiction, featured more celebrity covers, and gave a lot of coverage to exercise, fitness, and nutrition. The main focus was on the young woman who was balancing family, home, and career. *Redbook*'s advertising department described her as "the juggler." During this period, a lot of *Redbook* features began with the words "How to."

Unlike most mass circulation magazines, *Redbook* did not totally abandon fiction. However, of the approximately 35,000 unsolicited fiction manuscripts *Redbook* received annually, only about 40 short stories were published each year.[52] Rebecca Boroson, a *Redbook* employee who read approximately 250 manuscripts a week during Capone's tenure, wrote that "when a woman reads the *New Yorker*, she may enjoy spare vignettes, glimpses into lives, a touch of irony. But when the same woman puts her tired feet up and opens *Redbook*, she wants a story, a narrative. She wants to disappear for a while into a fictional world where things happen, where she may be able to identify with exciting events—both large and intimate—with the main character."[53]

Fiction has taken the back seat under current editor, Ellen R. Levine, former editor of *Woman's Day*. She joined the *Redbook* staff in January 1991 and had an impressive résumé. Educated at Radcliffe, she had been a newspaper reporter and magazine editor since 1964. Along with then-publisher Gregory Dunn, Levine refocused the magazine shortly after her arrival. "We couldn't be the magazine we wanted to be with such a big audience, you have to lose your older readers," said Levine. "We did it the minute I walked in the door. It was part of the deal."[54] Out went "the juggler." In came a new kind of young mother. She loves her children, but she takes time out to take care of her needs. "When a woman buys *Redbook*, I want that to be something she does for herself. Sex is a part of it; love and personal relationships are, too," said Levine.[55]

Going on the assumption that to survive in the 1990s meant narrowing your market niche, Levine redefined not only *Redbook*'s reader but how she addressed her editorially. Forty-five percent of the magazine became editorial, with its top editorial categories being fashion, beauty, and personal relationships. From January to December 1993, *Redbook* delivered more than 200 pages of parenting editorial, more than any of the other "Seven Sisters." Other top editorial categories included health and fitness, food and nutrition, entertainment and celebrity profiles, fiction, national affairs, and home furnishings. Sex has also played a part. Under Levine's direction, it is not unusual to see a man on the cover (e.g., Mel Gibson), a sharp departure from traditional covers of women.[56] But the ultimate goal was to attract a younger, more affluent reader in order to turn *Redbook* into a transition magazine between two other Hearst publications— *Cosmopolitan* and *Good Housekeeping*. "We want it to be a bridge, and not just between *Cosmo* and the Sisters, but between *Glamour* and the Sisters," said Levine.[57]

Levine's strategies seemed to work. "There's been a shift on the newsstand, which is up significantly, and the reader is younger."[58] With a median age of 38.9, *Redbook* readers are the youngest among women's service magazines.[59] The median age has continued to drop as the editorial attracts a younger reader. Even though median age has gone down, individual employment incomes have gone up since 1991, from $15,897 in 1991 to $18,986 in 1994. This was true of household incomes as well. *Redbook*'s 12 million readers—working women 25 to 44 years old—have a median household income of $40,348, which, according to *Redbook*'s rate card, is "the most influential consumer group today accounting for nearly 50% of all products and services purchased."[60]

In 1991, *Redbook* was ranked number one of the "Seven Sisters" on an index in delivering women between 18–34 and 25–34 and number one in reaching women with children. It was positioned between fashion and beauty books and women's service magazines.[61] As a consequence of all this, *Redbook*'s ad pages continued to climb. Beauty was the largest advertising category, but fashion was the fastest growing advertising category.[62]

The pages of *Redbook* have reflected changes in America for almost a century. What lies ahead? "I don't know where women will be five years from now," Levine said. "They don't know where they'll be five minutes from now. The important thing is to not get caught in cement."[63]

Notes

1. Circulation among the "Seven Sisters" fell from 1978 to 1988 (*Redbook*'s circulation was down 11 percent; *Ladies' Home Journal*, 15 percent; *McCall's*, 18 percent; *Woman's Day*, 28 percent; *Family Circle*, 32 percent). Eric Schmuckler, "Sob for the Sisters," *Forbes*, April 4, 1988, p. 112.

2. Robert Stein interview, May 27, 1994.

3. Therese Kauchak, "Dominant Color? Try Red; Once Full of Fiction, *Redbook* Puts Service First," *Advertising Age*, October 6, 1991, p. 40.

4. John Tebbel and Mary Ellen Zuckerman, *The Magazine in America, 1741–1990* (New York: Oxford University Press, 1991), p. 74.

5. "*Redbook*'s First Sixty Years," May 1963, p. 76. This article is not a narrative history. Instead, it consists of illustrations and short excerpts from previous issues and spans the period from 1903 until 1949.

6. These included actresses Billy Burke, Anna Held, and Ethel Barrymore.

7. Frank Luther Mott, *A History of American Magazines*, vol. 4 1885–1905 (Cambridge: Harvard University Press, 1957), p. 116.

8. After he was editor of *The Red Book*, he edited *Appleton's Magazine*, 1906–1909; *Adventure*, 1910–1911); and *Everybody's*, 1911–1915. *Who Was Who in America*, vol. 1 (Chicago, A. N. Marquis, 1942), p. 1336; Maxine Block (ed.), *Current Biography 1942* (New York: H. W. Wilson, 1942), p. 888.

9. *Blue Book* was a fiction magazine and ran stories by writers such as Mary Roberts Rinehart, James Oliver Curwood, and H. Rider Haggard. In the 1920s, personal experience articles and serialized autobiography by contributors such as Admiral Richard E. Byrd and André Maurois began to appear. In the 1940s, *Bluebook* increased the number of nonfiction articles and began to call itself a men's magazine. By the 1950s, it was losing money. It was finally suspended in May 1956. Theodore Peterson, *Magazines in the Twentieth Century* (Urbana: University of Illinois Press, 1964), p. 209.

10. *The Red Book Magazine*, 1907–1912.

11. John S. Lopez, "Love of Offspring," April 1909, p. 994.

12. Michael Williams, "The Alembic," April 1909, p. 1014.

13. John Barton Oxford, "The Reconciliation," April 1909, p. 1024.

14. Barton Wood Currie, "The Great Jones Ham Case," April 1909, p. 962.

15. Charles Edward Russell, "Billions for Bad Blue Blood," October 1908, p. 786.

16. Ibid., p. 787.

17. Frank Luther Mott, *A History of American Magazines*, vol. 5 1905–1930 (Cambridge: Harvard University Press, 1968), p. 497.

18. "The *Cosmopolitan* of Ray Long," *Fortune*, March 1931, p. 502.

19. Doris Ulmann, *A Portrait Gallery of American Editors* (New York: W. E. Rudge, 1925), p. 92.

20. John Tebbel, *George Horace Lorimer and the Saturday Evening Post* (New York: Doubleday, 1948), pp. 46, 82.

21. March 1919, p. 19.

22. *Who's Who in America 1940–1941* (Chicago, A. N. Marquis, 1940), p. 244.

23. *Redbook* and *Blue Book* were the McCall Corporation's first attempt at publishing something other than women's magazines or patterns. The *Green Book*, originally a theater magazine and later a periodical for career women, ceased publication in 1921. Peterson, *Magazines in the Twentieth Century*, p. 208.

24. *The Red Book Magazine* 1927–1929; *Redbook Magazine*, 1929–1949.

25. Peterson, *Magazines in the Twentieth Century*, p. 208.

26. John Tebbel, *The American Magazine: A Compact History* (New York: Hawthorne Books, 1969), p. 211.

27. Peterson, *Magazines in the Twentieth Century*, p. 208.

28. *Who's Who in America*, (Chicago: Marquis's Who's Who, 1990), p. 2423.

29. Robert Stein, *Media Power: Who Is Shaping Your Picture of the World?* (Boston: Houghton Mifflin, 1972), pp. 138–139.

30. Tebbel, *The American Magazine*, p. 211; Peterson, *Magazines in the Twentieth Century*, p. 208.

31. Stein, *Media Power*, p. 140.

32. Robert Stein interview, May 27, 1994.

33. Stein, *Media Power*, p. 134.

34. Ibid., pp. 135–136. In reference to Stein's problems with the printing plant, it is

worth noting that the McCall Corporation plant was printing more than 50 magazines for other publishers in the early 1960s.

35. Tebbel and Zuckerman, *The Magazine in America*, p. 269.

36. Ibid.

37. Stein interview.

38. Ibid.

39. Ibid.

40. Ibid.

41. Peterson, *Magazines in the Twentieth Century*, p. 209.

42. Seymour Chassler interview, June 2, 1994.

43. Ibid.

44. Ibid.

45. July 1976.

46. In this article, which was part of a series of essays by women for the bicentennial year, Braithwaite Burke said, "As we took our baby daughter home from the hospital, a swarm of reporters greeted us. 'Do you want your child to be a congresswoman someday?' they asked. 'Oh, no!' I replied. 'One day she'll be President!' " May 1976, p. 79.

47. Chassler interview.

48. Ibid.

49. January 1977, p. 22.

50. Tebbel, *The American Magazine,* p. 250.

51. Chassler interview.

52. Boroson, "Over the Transom and out of the Woods," p. 15.

53. Ibid.

54. John Motavalli, "Sex and the Married Reader," *Inside Media,* November 18, 1992, p. 43.

55. Kauchak, "Dominant Color?" p. 40.

56. January–December 1993 Hall's Reports.

57. Motavalli, "Sex and the Married Reader," p. 43.

58. Ibid.

59. *Better Homes and Gardens* 42.3; *Good Housekeeping* 42.8; *McCall's* 43.5; *Woman's Day* 43.9; *Ladies' Home Journal* 44.1; and *Family Circle* 44.7.

60. *Redbook* National Advertising Rate Card #104 (Source: 1993 Fall MRI).

61. *Mademoiselle* 27.3; *Glamour* 30.7; *Self* 31.6; and *Cosmopolitan* 32.

62. *Redbook* rate card.

63. Kauchak "Dominant Color?" p. 40.

Information Sources

BIBLIOGRAPHY:

Block, Maxine (ed.). *Current Biography 1942*. New York; H. W. Wilson, 1942.

Boroson, Rebecca. "Over the Transom and out of the Woods," *The Writer*, January 1985, pp. 13–15, 43.

"The *Cosmopolitan* of Ray Long," *Fortune*, March 1931, p. 51.

Donaton, Scott. "Donna Galotti: Rising to Power among Seven Sisters." *Advertising Age*, November 27, 1989, p. 90.

———. "*Redbook* Narrows in on New Look." *Advertising Age*, June 3, 1991, p. 37.

———. "Media Reassess as Boomers Age." *Advertising Age*, July 15, 1991, p. 13.

Kauchak, Therese. "Dominant Color? Try Red; Once Full of Fiction, *Redbook* Puts Service First." *Advertising Age*, October 6, 1991, p. 40.

Krafft, Susan. "Unhappy New Year: Publishers See No Ad Rebound in January." *Advertising Age*, November 18, 1991, pp. 1, 46.

———. "Window on a Woman's Mind." *American Demographics*, December 1991, pp. 44–50.

Motavalli, John. "Sex and the Married Reader." *Inside Media*, November 18, 1992, p. 43.

Mott, Frank Luther. *A History of American Magazines, vol. 4 1885–1905.* Cambridge: Belknap Press of Harvard University Press, 1957.

———. *A History of American Magazines, vol. 5*: *Sketches of 21 Magazines 1905–1930.* Cambridge: Belknap Press of Harvard University Press, 1968.

Peterson, Theodore. *Magazines in the Twentieth Century*, 2d ed. Urbana: University of Illinois Press, 1964.

Reilly, Patrick. "Marketing to Women: Service Magazines Adapt to Market." *Advertising Age*, March 7, 1988, pp. 66, 610.

———. "Magazines: Single-Copy Sales Fight Downward Trend." *Advertising Age*, October 24, 1988, p. 66.

Rich, Cary Peyton. "Thinking Green." *Folio*, February 1, 1991, pp. 81–95.

Schmuckler, Eric. "Sob for the Sisters." *Forbes*, April 4, 1988, pp. 112–113.

Stein, Robert. *Media Power: Who Is Shaping Your Picture of the World*? Boston: Houghton Mifflin, 1972.

Tebbel, John. *George Horace Lorimer and the Saturday Evening Post.* Garden City, N.Y.: Doubleday, 1948.

———. *The American Magazine: A Compact History.* New York: Hawthorne Books, 1969.

———, and Mary Ellen Zuckerman. *The Magazine in America, 1741–1990* New York: Oxford University Press, 1991.

Ulmann, Doris. *A Portrait Gallery of American Editors.* New York: W. E. Rudge, 1925.

Who's Who in America, 1940–1941. Chicago: A. N. Marquis, 1940.

Who's Who in America, 1960–1961. Chicago: A. N. Marquis, 1986.

Who's Who in America, 1990–1991. Wilmette, Ill.: Marquis' Who's Who, 1990.

Who Was Who in America, vol. 1. Chicago: A. N. Marquis, 1942.

INDEX SOURCES: Current Literature in Family Planning; Health Index; Magazine Index; Popular Magazine Review; Readers' Guide to Periodical Literature.

LOCATION SOURCES: Cleveland Public Library and other libraries.

Publication History

MAGAZINE TITLE AND TITLE CHANGES: *The Red Book Illustrated* (1903); *The Red Book Magazine* (1903–1929); *Redbook* (1929–present).

VOLUME AND ISSUE DATA: Vols. 1–(May 8, 1903–present). Monthly.

PUBLISHER AND PLACE OF PUBLICATION: The Red Book Corporation (1903–1909); Consolidated Magazines Corporation (1909–1929); McCall Corporation (1929–1982); Hearst Corporation (1982–present). Chicago (1903–1929); New York (1929–present).

EDITORS: Trumbull White (1903–1906); Karl Edwin Harriman (1907–1912); Ray Long (1912–1918); Karl Edwin Harriman (1919–1927); Edwin Balmer (1927–1949); Wade Nichols, Jr. (1949–1958); Robert Stein (1958–1965); Seymour Chassler

(1965–1982); Anne Mollegen Smith (1982–1983); Annette Capone (1983–1990); Ellen Levine (1991–present).
CIRCULATION: ABC, 1994: 3,345,451 (paid, primarily subscriptions).

Victoria Goff

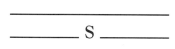

SASSY

In his grand survey of popular culture, *The Unembarrassed Muse*, the late Russel Nye argued that "popular art has been an unusually sensitive and accurate reflector of the attitudes and concerns of the society for which it is produced."[1] More specifically, contemporary communication theorists such as John Pauly have suggested that all of the popular media in America represent "shared systems of meaning [in which both] senders and receivers compete and collaborate in constructing reality." As a result, all communication media, including magazines, have an important societal dimension, both reflecting and shaping the social actualities of their time.[2] If persuasive evidence of a single magazine's role in altering the social construction of a particular reality were needed, the 1988 launch of *Sassy* magazine could perhaps suffice.

At stake was America's fundamental definition of much of its postpubescent female population, those 14 million women 14 to 19 years old who traditionally have been the objects of society's deepest instincts of parental protectiveness. What *Sassy* did—to its everlasting shame or credit, depending on one's point of view—was to suggest not only that these teenage girls had sexual lives but that it was a proper editorial mission for a magazine to address their urgent informational needs about sex. The result was gasps of shock and horror from the other magazines aimed at young women, an advertising boycott organized by the fundamentalist Religious Right, and, perhaps unsurprisingly, an immediate success with its teenage readers.

John Fairfax Ltd., a prominent Australian magazine publishing company, got the idea for *Sassy* from *Dolly Magazine*, one of the firm's major successes in its home market. Founded in 1970, *Dolly*'s sexual candor, as well as its clearly teenage editorial tone, made it immensely popular; indeed, its owner claimed that it was read by one out of every four young women in Australia. In the United States, the company reasoned, a similar sort of success would be immensely profitable. In the mid-1980s, there were 14 million American young women between the ages of 14 and 19; but only 4 million, less than 30 percent of them, at any one time read teenage magazines.[3] Even more attractive from an advertising-sales point of view, the most affluent two-thirds of the female teenage population, 9 million girls in all, spent an average of $65 in disposable income on themselves each and every week. ''More parents are working or divorced and away from home, so they are giving kids more money,'' said Helen Barr, 38, Sassy's first publisher, who oversaw the publication's debut. ''It is the payoff generation.''[4]

By mid-1987, Fairfax Publications (U.S.) Ltd., the firm's American subsidiary, had completed its plans for launching *Sassy* in early 1988. In addition to the publisher, Barr, whose background included sales experience at *Woman's Day,** the advertising directorship of *Ms.,** and a brief stint as the publisher of *Success Magazine,* the staff included Patricia Cantor, the former marketing director of *Harper's Bazaar,** and, as editor in chief, Jane Pratt, a 24-year-old former associate editor on a short-lived magazine called *Teenage.* The fact that *Sassy* would be a different kind of young women's magazine was signaled by a prototype issue prepared during the summer of 1987; the lead article's title was ''Sex for Absolute Beginners.'' Moreover, a $500,000 advertising promotion campaign, designed by Della Femina, Travisano & Partners, that appeared in late 1987 directly challenged the competition; its theme was ''I'm too *Sassy* to read *Teen.*'' When the premier issue (March) appeared in mid-February 1988, it had a cover price of $2, a yearly subscription price of $13.98, a guaranteed circulation of 250,000, a four-color advertising page rate of $6,950, and 55 pages of advertising.[5]

Most notably, the first issue contained a feature story entitled ''Losing Your Virginity—Read This Before You Decide,'' as well as a full-page condom advertisement. The degree of departure from other teen magazines that both the article and the ad represented was suggested by the reactions of *Sassy*'s publishing competition. Sarah Crichton, the editor of *Seventeen,** with a circulation of 1.8 million and the largest magazine for teenage girls, acknowledged that few young women were still ''sweet Sandra Dee types,'' but she also said, ''When it comes to teenage sexuality, this is still quite a puritanical country.'' Robert Brown, the associate publisher of *'Teen,** the second largest publication in the category, with 1.2 million circulation, was less restrained: ''I don't think the feature was responsible. I think it's offensive.'' Milt Franks, the publisher of *YM** (circulation: 825,000), took exception to the condom ad: ''It's wrong. We're not saying kids don't have sex. But kids drink, and we don't carry beer ads, and kids get pregnant, and we don't carry maternity ads.''[6]

In response, *Sassy*'s publisher pointed out provocative advertisements, including a Godiva-like image used to promote Oggi shampoo, that the other teen magazines had been willing to run. Additionally, it was proclaimed that, in Barr's words, ''There are things we don't think are right.'' These included sexually assertive ads for Calvin Klein's Obsession perfume and No Excuse jeans ads featuring Donna Rice, the woman involved in the collapse of Senator Gary Hart's 1988 presidential ambitions.[7] Speaking for the editorial department, however, Pratt was far from apologetic. Referring to the condom ad, she said, "It was done very intentionally. The United States has twice as much teenage pregnancy as countries where there is mandatory sex education."[8] The problem, in her judgment, was the timidity of *Sassy*'s competition: "Other magazines have a stereotypical or idealized view of teenagers. Maybe what parents or teachers would like. Not really what teenagers are about."[9]

The controversy, of course, did little to detract from *Sassy*'s appeal to its target audience, and within six months of its debut, its circulation rose 60 percent, from 250,000 to 400,000.[10] It can be argued that the magazine was, in many ways, less of a departure from the standard teen fare than some imagined. Commenting on the premier issue, John Gabree, with telling insight, noted:

> The writing, with few exceptions, runs to giggly, [and] is either embarrassingly mediocre or odiously condescending. The staff interrupt each other's articles with cute bracketed asides. The reviews and service pieces read like they were transcribed at a pajama party. The most daring person on the staff is the one composing the cover teasers.[11]

Despite its early success with its readers, financial uncertainty and management instability characterized the first year of the magazine's life. There were two major problems, originating from two markedly different sources. First, its parent company in Australia encountered financial difficulties and was forced to sell off a number of its publishing properties. In May 1988, *Sassy* and another Fairfax-owned title, *Ms.*, were sold to a new firm, Matilda Publications, founded by Sandra Yates, the former president of Fairfax Publications (U.S.) Ltd.[12]

Far more troubling, however, was a letter-writing campaign that began in July 1988 that threatened *Sassy*'s advertisers with boycotts if they continued to advertise in the magazine. Organized by the *Liberty Report*, a newspaper published by the Reverend Jerry Falwell's Moral Majority, a Christian Fundamentalist lobby, the campaign accused *Sassy* of promoting "teenage promiscuity" and "homosexuality." Three advertisers in particular were targeted—the makers of Cover Girl cosmetics, Levi's jeans, and Maybelline beauty products—and ultimately all three ceased advertising in the magazine.[13] When a similar newsstand boycott reduced single-copy sales by 30 percent, Pratt knew that unflinching resistance was no longer possible, and for the next six months she worked to tone down the sexual content.[14] Making matters worse, in the middle of the difficulties the publisher, Helen Barr, resigned, publicly declaring that she had long believed that *Sassy* had been wrong to deal candidly with teenage sexuality. In response, Matilda President Yates issued a statement stating that the magazine was taking a "more balanced editorial approach."[15]

Though circulation continued to grow, it was clear that the underlying financial health of the publication had been dealt a severe blow by the boycott. In mid-1989, the institutional investors who had underwritten the purchase the year before from Fairfax withdrew their support of Matilda Publications, and *Sassy* was once again put up for sale.[16] By late summer, a controlling half-interest had been purchased by Dale W. Lang, a magazine publisher and investor, and it soon became part of a new publishing company, Lang Communications, which also published *Ms.*, *Working Woman*,* and *Working Mother* magazines.[17]

It was soon apparent that in Lang, *Sassy* had a cautious but essentially supportive new owner. Lang stated that he believed that the magazine had been ''blind-sided by the Moral Majority'' but that the previous owners had reacted by trying ''to do nothing and ride it out.'' He offered assurances that *Sassy* would keep its irreverent outlook and tone but also added that he would ''keep a close watch on the editorial content of the magazine.''[18] Shortly after its purchase by Lang, *Sassy*'s circulation passed 500,000, and by the end of 1990, it had increased by another 10 percent.[19] The next three years saw extraordinary growth in the magazine's readership, no doubt greatly assisted by Pratt's supplementary career as the host of a television talk show for young women that debuted in early 1992. Though she continued to serve as editor in chief of the magazine, Pratt quickly became a figure of some celebrity, and, perhaps as an indirect result, *Sassy*'s circulation reached 715,000 in mid-1993.[20]

Despite its evident success, the magazine remained, at least to some observers, something of an enigma, particularly when judged against the other, more conventional magazines for young women. For example, a spokesperson for Coty, a cosmetics company, offered the following comparison: ''*Seventeen* is more conservative. *YM* is more celebrity-oriented and provides more information for older teens. *'Teen* is for younger girls, very conservative and very Midwest. *Sassy* is off the curve, out of the mainstream and a little more offbeat.''[21]

Perhaps closer to the mark and certainly more explanatory of *Sassy*'s success was a comparison by Martin Walker, chairman of Walker Communications, a magazine consulting firm. Referring to *Sassy*'s mildly irreverent and risqué cheekiness, he said: ''*Seventeen* and *'Teen* give you advice, and their voice is always that of Mother. *YM* is better, but often it's the voice of your older sister. *Sassy* is the voice of a friend.''[22]

Notes

1. Russel B. Nye, *The Unembarrassed Muse: The Popular Arts in America* (New York: Dial Press, 1970), p. 4.

2. John J. Pauly, ''A Beginner's Guide to Qualitative Research in Mass Communications,'' *Journalism Monographs* 125 (February 1991), pp. 2–3. See also James W. Carey, *Communication as Culture: Essays on Media and Society* (Boston: Unwin Hyman, 1989).

3. John Gabree, ''A Monthly That Speaks Teentalk,'' *Los Angeles Times*, February 18, 1988, sec. 5, p. 1.

4. Geraldine Fabrikant, ''Magazine to Pursue Teenagers,'' *New York Times*, August 24, 1987, p. D7.

5. Richard W. Stevenson, "First Issue of *Sassy* Due Out Next Week," *New York Times*, February 11, 1988, p. D25. See also Fabrikant, "Magazine to Pursue Teenagers," p. D7.

6. Cynthia Crossen, "Sexual Candor Marks Magazine for Teen Girls," *Wall Street Journal*, February 17, 1988, p. 31.

7. Ibid.

8. Marilyn Gardner, "Controversial Magazine for Teen-Age Girls Hits Sensitive Subjects," *Christian Science Monitor*, March 7, 1988, p. 24.

9. Suzanne Daley, "*Sassy*: Like, You Know, for Kids," *New York Times*, April 11, 1988, p. D8.

10. Isadore Barmash, "Addenda: *Sassy* Magazine's Circulation," *New York Times*, August 24, 1988 p. D15.

11. Gabree, "A Monthly That Speaks Teentalk," sec. 5, p. 8. For an interesting analysis of changes in the social roles of young women, see also Kate Peirce, "The Socialization of Teenage Girls through Teenage Fiction: The Making of a New Woman or an Old Lady?" (presented at Association for Education in Journalism and Mass Communication Annual Conference, Kansas City, Mo., August 14, 1993).

12. Cynthia Crossen, "Fairfax Discussing Sale of Ms. *Sassy* to Management," *Wall Street Journal*, March 18, 1988, p. 32; Geraldine Fabrikant, "Fairfax Executives Purchase *Ms.* and *Sassy*," *New York Times*, May 3, 1988, p. D26; "Management of *Ms.*, *Sassy* to Acquire Both Magazines," *Wall Street Journal*, May 3, 1988, p. 36. See also Leslie Wayne, "*Ms.* Magazine Is Changing Hands Again," *New York Times*, March 18, 1988, p. D5; Claudia H. Deutsch, "The *Ms.* on the Masthead Wants the Magazine," *New York Times*, April 3, 1988, sec. 3, p. 7.

13. Cynthia Crossen, "More Advertisers in *Sassy* Are Targeted in Moral Majority's Letter Campaign," *Wall Street Journal*, September 6, 1988, p. 36; Garry Abrams, "Jerry Falwell Starts a Drive against *Sassy*," *Los Angeles Times*, September 15, 1988, sec. 5, p. 1.

14. Dinitia Smith, "Jane's World! Jane's World!" *New York*, May 25, 1992, p. 69.

15. Randall Rothenberg, "Resignation and Boycott at *Sassy*," *New York Times*, November 3, 1988, p. D19.

16. Joe Sharkey, "Matilda's Founder Quits; Firm Is Put on Auction Block," *Wall Street Journal*, May 30, 1989, p. B7.

17. Albert Scardino, "Magazine Investor Buying 50% Stake in *Ms.* and *Sassy*," *New York Times*, August 4, 1989, sec. D, p. 5; "Lang to Be Joint Owner of Publisher of *Ms.*, *Sassy*," *Wall Street Journal*, August 4, 1989, p. B3; Scott Donaton, "Lang Buying Spree," *Advertising Age*, August 7, 1989, p. 60. See also Patrick M. Reilly, "Gruner + Jahr Thinks 'Sassy,' " *Advertising Age*, June 5, 1989, 2, p. 74. Lang completed the purchase of *Sassy* in February 1993; see "Lang Communications: Company Is Buying Back Ownership of 3 Magazines." *Wall Street Journal*, February 19, 1993, p. B5.

18. Patrick M. Reilly, "New Publisher of *Ms.*, *Sassy* Moves Boldly," *Wall Street Journal*, October 19, 1989, p. B6.

19. Laurie Freeman, "People to Watch," *Advertising Age*, April 15, 1991, p. S12.

20. Kevin Goldman, "Media: Sassy Talk Show Targets Young Women," *Wall Street Journal*, March 9, 1992, p. B1; Sarah Lyall, "Jane's Excellent Adventure: 'Oprah' for Teen-Age Girls," *New York Times*, April 15, 1992, sec. C, p. 1; David Wharton, "When the Editor Is Sassy," *Los Angeles Times*, September 18, 1992, sec. E, p. 1. See also Smith, "Jane's World! Jane's World!" pp. 60–71. Even though Pratt's television career

suffered a small setback when the Fox Network did not renew her show, it soon returned in syndicated distribution; see George Russell, "Jane: No Fox, but Still Sassy?" *Variety*, June 15, 1992, pp. 1, 78.

21. Deirdre Carmody, "Reaching Teen-Agers, without Using a Phone," *New York Times*, January 18, 1993, sec. D, p. 6.

22. Martin S. Walker interview, October 29, 1993.

Information Sources

BIBLIOGRAPHY:

Abrams, Garry. "Jerry Falwell Starts a Drive against *Sassy*." *Los Angeles Times*, September 15, 1988, sec. 5, p. 1.

Barmash, Isadore. "Addenda: *Sassy* Magazine's Circulation." *New York Times*, August 24, 1988, p. D15.

Carmody, Deirdre. "Reaching Teen-Agers, without Using a Phone." *New York Times*, January 18, 1993, p. D6.

Crossen, Cynthia. "Sexual Candor Marks Magazine for Teen Girls." *Wall Street Journal*, February 17, 1988, p. 31.

———."Fairfax Discussing Sale of Ms. *Sassy* to Management." *Wall Street Journal*, March 18, 1988, p. 32.

———."More Advertisers in *Sassy* Are Targeted in Moral Majority's Letter Campaign." *Wall Street Journal*, September 6, 1988, p. 36.

Daley, Suzanne. "*Sassy*: Like, You Know, for Kids." *New York Times*, April 11, 1988, p. D8.

Deutsch, Claudia H. "The *Ms.* on the Masthead Wants the Magazine." *New York Times*, April 3, 1988, sec. 3, p. 7.

Donaton, Scott. "Lang Buying Spree." *Advertising Age,* August 7, 1989, p. 60.

Fabrikant, Geraldine. "Magazine to Pursue Teenagers." *New York Times*, August 24, 1987, p. D7.

———."Fairfax Executives Purchase *Ms.* and *Sassy*." *New York Times*, May 3, 1988, p. D26.

Freeman, Laurie. "People to Watch." *Advertising Age*, April 15, 1991, p. S12.

Gabree, John. "A Monthly That Speaks Teentalk." *Los Angeles Times*, February 18, 1988, sec 5 pp. 1, 8.

Gardner, Marilyn. "Controversial Magazine for Teen-Age Girls Hits Sensitive Subjects." *Christian Science Monitor*, March 7, 1988, pp. 23–24.

Goldman, Kevin. "Media: *Sassy* Talk Show Targets Young Women." *Wall Street Journal*, March 9, 1992, p. B1.

"Lang to Be Joint Owner of Publisher of *Ms.*, *Sassy*." *Wall Street Journal*, August 4, 1989, p. B3.

"Lang Communications: Company Is Buying Back Ownership of 3 Magazines." *Wall Street Journal*, February 19, 1993, p. B5.

Lyall, Sarah. "Jane's Excellent Adventure: 'Oprah' for Teen-Age Girls." *New York Times*, April 15, 1992, p. C1.

Peirce, Kate. "The Socialization of Teenage Girls through Teenage Fiction: The Making of a New Woman or an Old Lady?" Presented at Association for Education in Journalism and Mass Communication Annual Conference, Kansas City, Mo., August 14, 1993.

Reilly, Patrick M. "Gruner + Jahr Thinks 'Sassy.' " *Advertising Age*, June 5, 1989, pp. 2, 74.

———."New Publisher of *Ms.*, *Sassy* Moves Boldly." *Wall Street Journal*, October 19, 1989, p. B6.

Rothenberg, Randall. "Resignation and Boycott at *Sassy*." *New York Times*, November 3, 1988, p. D19.

Russell, George. "Jane: No Fox, but Still *Sassy*?" *Variety*, June 15, 1992, pp. 1, 78.

Scardino, Albert. "Magazine Investor Buying 50% Stake in *Ms.* and *Sassy*." *New York Times*, August 4, 1989, p. D5.

Sharkey, Joe. "Matilda's Founder Quits; Firm Is Put on Auction Block." *Wall Street Journal*, May 30, 1989, p. B7.

Smith, Dinitia. "Jane's World! Jane's World!" *New York*, May 25, 1992, pp. 60–71.

Stevenson, Richard W. "First Issue of *Sassy* Due Out Next Week." *New York Times*, February 11, 1988, p. D25.

Wayne, Leslie. "*Ms.* Magazine Is Changing Hands Again." *New York Times*, March 18, 1988, p. D5.

Wharton, David. "When the Editor Is *Sassy*." *Los Angeles Times*, September 18, 1992, p. E1.

INDEX SOURCES: None.

LOCATION SOURCES: Library of Congress and other libraries.

Publication History

MAGAZINE TITLE AND TITLE CHANGES: *Sassy*.

VOLUME AND ISSUE DATA: Vols. 1–(March 1988–present). Monthly.

PUBLISHER AND PLACE OF PUBLICATION: Fairfax Publications (U.S.) Ltd. (March 1988–May 1988); Matilda Publications, Inc. (May 1988–August 1989); Lang Communications (Sassy Publishers, Inc.) (August 1989–present). New York.

EDITORS: Jane Pratt (March 1988–present).

CIRCULATION: ABC 1993: 732,835. (paid, primarily subscriptions).

David Abrahamson

SELF

Riding the crest of the health/fitness craze of the late 1970s and early 1980s, with a nod toward that era's self-improvement zeitgeist, Condé Nast launched *Self* magazine in January 1979 as one of the first magazines devoted to women's health and fitness. As its original audience has grown, however, and as women's concerns of the 1970s and 1980s have been replaced somewhat by their more integrated concerns of the 1990s, *Self* has attempted to reposition itself as more than "just" a fitness magazine—while remaining true to its original focus.

Self magazine originated as a result of strong reader response to articles on physical and emotional fitness presented in other Condé Nast publications, such as *Glamour** and *Mademoiselle*,*[1] and it was an immediate success. The first-year (1979) advertising page goal was set at 250; the circulation projection, 500,000.[2] These forecasts proved to be far too low. In fact, *Self* ran 520 ad pages in 1979 (of 1,550 total pages); this total rose to 710 (of 1,702 total) in 1980 and pushed 900 (of 1,788) in 1981.[3] As for circulation, *Self* could boast 900,000 readers by the end of 1979[4]; in another year and a half, it had surpassed the 1 million mark and was being celebrated in the industry as "one of the most successful magazine launches since World War II."[5]

From the beginning, *Self* has consistently asserted to readers (and advertisers) that it is not merely a physical fitness publication but one designed to address women's overall fitness, encompassing physical, emotional, sexual, and mental health.[6] Indeed, one is struck by how early, how often, and how insistently *Self*'s publishers and editors have argued this point.[7] One is left with the impression that advertisers did not quite know what to do with a women's publication that was neither strictly beauty/fashion- nor family-oriented. As a result, the magazine has sometimes been pigeonholed as a "health" publication by advertisers, particularly in its earlier years.[8]

Along with some marketplace uncertainty about its identity, *Self* has also fought the criticism that it feeds on, and contributes to, the self-indulgent side of popular culture. Even before the first issue had been published, commentators were making much of the magazine's title and how it seemed to fit in with "the current life-style trend exemplified by *self*-examination, *self*-indulgence, and *self*-fulfillment."[9] Articles in *Self* have consistently countered this complaint by suggesting that self-improvement should not be equated with selfishness.[10] Nevertheless, five years into its life, *Self* was still defending itself against such reproach,[11] and the association of *Self* with self-indulgence in the popular consciousness has never quite faded.[12]

Self's target audience is the 25-to-40-year-old professional woman.[13] Advertisements have consistently been for products middle-class women can afford; more "everyday" items (Dannon Yogurt, Diet Sprite, Hanes) share space with popular but not particularly upscale beauty items (Revlon, Estée Lauder, Oil of Olay). The ads generally strike a balance between the "tony" (i.e., Gucci) and the "lowbrow" (i.e., Kraft Macaroni and Cheese), though more toward the upper end. Surveys have shown that the women who read *Self* are professional, college-educated "achievers" who are "interested in taking control of their lives."[14] As its audience has found achievement and taken further steps toward independence and power, *Self* has attempted to change and grow with them.

In *Self*'s first issue, then-editor Phyllis Star Wilson promised readers that the magazine would focus on women's "exuberant concern for body and mind,"[15] and early issues of *Self* fulfilled that pledge. With recurring departments such as "Fitness," "Money," "Good Looks," "Emotion," "Love/Sex," "Health," and "Food," *Self* provided women with information about a wide variety of topics inevitably tied to their physical and emotional fitness. For the first several years of publication, virtually each issue of *Self* featured at least two physical fitness (i.e., exercise) articles, most with 15–20 accompanying "how-to" photos.[16] Health issues were covered in abundance, most offering practical advice on how to improve one's personal health.[17] In particular, breast health received early and extensive coverage, culminating (in *Self*'s beginning years) with 12 pages of related news in the January 1981 issue. Indeed, this subject has always been something of a cause célèbre at *Self*, which has faithfully publicized all aspects of breast health (self-examination, prevention, treatment) throughout the years.

In articles such as "Love Versus Work: How to Handle Women's No. 1 Challenge" (July 1979), *Self* examined how women's relatively new choices— both personal and professional—affected their physical and emotional health. Early issues of *Self* also found ways to link health with such topics as food, travel, and fashion. Recipes were not just for good-tasting food but for healthy food; fashion articles tended to explain how to dress for success or health as well as for style (e.g., "A Smart Shopper's Guide to Healthy, Great Looking Shoes," March 1980); even travel features might discuss how a solo trip could boost one's self-esteem.

By 1981, *Self* had hit upon the technique of featuring several articles about a special topic each month. For example, the November 1981 "mood-shaping" report featured articles on positive thinking, how moods affect job success, and exercises to improve mood and mental outlook. Generally, *Self* devoted 20–25 pages of each issue to its special monthly topic, filling the rest of each issue with its familiar blend of health, fitness, beauty, relationship, and career items. Although during this time *Self* sometimes featured articles such as the May 1981 piece about retaining the right to make personal choices, "Who Plays Politics with Your Private Life," such political or issue-oriented articles were the exception rather than the rule. Instead, the magazine spent its formative years focusing intently on its readers, their immediate environment, and how that environment related to their overall well-being.

Self's initial design was plain-spoken and user-friendly. One feature much appreciated by readers[18] was the virtual absence of "jump" pages: longer articles were continued on succeeding pages, rather than buried in the back of the issue. The first couple of years saw occasional tinkering with the look of the contents page (February 1980, May 1981), but otherwise the design changed little until late 1982, when a bit more color and typeface experimentation began.

By the mid-1980s, *Self* had settled into a comfortable combination of regular departments—"Good Looks and Fitness," "Love and Sex," "Health," "Food-Diet," "Money and Careers," and "Parents and Kids"—woven around the monthly special topic. The 1983–1984 issues continued the trend toward a more colorful internal design with more photos, graphics, and screen tints than in previous years; during this time the table of contents was expanded to two pages. By 1984, brief monthly summaries of various health/fitness topics (e.g., "Beauty Watch," "Health Watch," "Mind Watch,") had also become a regular feature of the magazine.

By *Self*'s fifth anniversary, beauty and fashion coverage had become prominent.[19] If there were somewhat fewer physical fitness articles than previously, the health coverage remained strong, with at least three or four articles (averaging four to five pages each) in every issue.[20] Several articles on breast health continued to appear every year; typical among these was the "Breast Confidence Check" in the September 1985 issue. Relationships (i.e., love and sex) also received strong coverage during this period, generally related toward either physical or emotional health.[21] Money/career guidance—heavily skewed toward the first-time investor or first-time job holder—was also prominently featured, perhaps best typified by the regular column "New Job Wise-Ups—What Nobody Teaches You That You're Supposed to Know."

The promotion of Valorie Griffith Weaver to editor in March 1987 occasioned a slight shift in *Self*'s editorial and ad content. Responding to her readers' perceptions that "it is easier to do something in your kitchen than to go out and run for an hour," Weaver began focusing more on health and nutrition issues while somewhat downplaying physical fitness.[22] Appropriately enough, food products became *Self*'s second biggest advertiser during this period (behind health and beauty aids but surpassing fashion),[23] in contrast to previous years, when fashion had been number two.[24]

Total ad pages remained in the 1,150–1,200 range during the mid-1980s,[25] rising to a record 1,248 pages in 1988 (up 4.5 percent from 1987).[26] However, as *Self* approached its tenth anniversary, a certain sameness had begun to creep into the editorial content. Topics had begun repeating themselves (e.g., fashion and makeup tips to look confident, advice on how to juggle job and relationships, guides to perfect skin). Despite some moves toward a stronger design and increased use of color, the look of the magazine had not radically changed.

The late 1980s and early 1990s, however, ushered in a period of unprecedented design and editorial experimentation for *Self*, as it took steps toward becoming the very visual, design-driven publication it is in the mid-1990s. *Self*'s first major retooling occurred under Anthea Disney, who succeeded Weaver as editor in October 1988. Disney's impact was immediate. Her first cover (October 1988) featured a seductively posed Brooke Shields; her second, a similarly posed Kim Basinger (November 1988). The November issue featured a new department, "The A List," which essentially consisted of gossip and brief blurbs about celebrities (e.g., Candice Bergen's debut as "Murphy Brown"; meet the new "James Bond girl"; whatever happened to actress Shelly Long?). Though celebrities had never been absent from *Self*'s pages (the very first issue featured athletes Guillermo Vilas and Nancy Lopez on "how to be winners"), the magazine had never before presented them so prominently. Even *Self*'s traditional topics were often tied in to celebrities—for instance, readers were treated to a profile (with accompanying fashion layout) of actress Kelly Preston (December 1988) and "second baby shape-up" advice from model Andie McDowell (September 1989).

In December 1988, the slanting, full-cover-width *Self* typeface (used since the magazine's inception) was replaced by a narrow, elongated typeface pushed into the cover's left corner. Even more striking was the cover model, looking more casual than "made up" and shot in natural light, not a photographer's studio.[27]

The goal was to create a "smart, sophisticated, though not airbrushed" look more in touch with readers' broadened interests.[28] Internally, an increased use of stronger, bolder primary colors and design elements was being introduced.

Initial responses to the new *Self* were strong: the magazine's ad pages increased by 8 percent between 1988 and 1989, more than for such publications as *Cosmopolitan,** *Elle,** *Glamour,* and *Mademoiselle*; in addition, circulation increased 3.4 percent (to 1.2 million) from June to December 1989.[29] More than 100 new advertisers, such as Haagen-Dazs ice cream—impressed by the "lifestyle" image of the magazine—were also attracted to the new-looking *Self* (though some clients, such as Lenox Crystal, were less enthusiastic).[30] Despite this success, by January 1990 the design—along with the editor—had changed again.

Alexandra Penney's ascension to editor introduced revisions to the design and editorial changes Disney had inaugurated 15 months earlier. Under Penney, *Self*'s art director, Alexander Liberman, was given free rein to introduce his "color-blocking" concept to *Self*'s cover and internal design. Drawing on sources as disparate as television's "*Miami Vice*" and MTV and the collage styles of Picasso and Braque,[31] Liberman continued the transformation of *Self* into a very visual magazine, in compliance with his belief that "words and their shapes can communicate quicker in today's world than moody photographs or traditional illustration."[32]

Extensive internal use of silhouetted and oddly angled photos, great swathes of bold, bright colors (both on the cover and internally), and pages featuring an abundance of colored shapes became commonplace. The effect created by Liberman's design was motion, as if there were so much material to squeeze into each issue and so little time to read it. As such, the design dovetailed perfectly with Penney's edict that no story in *Self* should be more than 1,500 words, in response to "the time-constraining reality of women's lives in the 1990s."[33]

Editorially, the *Self* of the 1990s has kept very close to the vision Penney laid out in her first letter from the editor in January 1990, when she promised that *Self* would be a publication that "focuses on the nurturing bases of living, approves of smart luxury, promotes mind/body fitness and healthy hedonism, [and] recognizes social responsibility."[34] Indeed, an increased focus on the larger community—though never entirely lacking in earlier years—is perhaps the most striking feature of the *Self* of the mid-1990s. Articles began to appear on such topics as "Women, Power, and Politics" (March 1993), environmental activism ("How Can I Make a Difference?" March 1993), "Animal Testing" (February 1993), and pornography ("Lipless Sex: or Why Men Love Pornography," November 1992). It is very difficult to imagine such topics being covered to any great degree in *Self*'s early years.

In the 1990s, *Self*'s traditional topics (fitness, health, beauty, fashion, career) have been featured at about the same rate as in the late 1980s, though with decidedly less celebrity tie-in. If anything, breast health awareness has been even more highly promoted than ever before; in 1993, for example, *Self* entered into partnership with Estée Lauder to promote breast cancer research and early detection—a campaign lauded by First Lady Hillary Rodham Clinton in the October 1993 reader response column.

Another development (January 1990) has been the establishment of a fax number to allow readers to give quick, direct feedback to Self staffers; the goal, according to Penney, was to produce a magazine constantly in touch with readers' perspectives.[35] Hoping to expand this communication with readers, a 24-hour phone system ("Interactive Self") was added in 1993, allowing readers to leave messages to various staffers, hear news about Self subjects, and renew subscriptions—the intent being to make Self "the first magazine that is in daily, hourly, constant contact with its readers."[36]

The biggest differences between the Self of the early 1980s and the magazine of the mid-1990s, however, can probably best be ascertained by examining the lives and outlooks of American women then and now. Self's early issues—at least through the mid-1980s—presented articles from something of a "you-can-do-it" perspective, not militant or activist but encouraging, reassuring women that it was all right to have a career, participate in sports, seek sexual pleasure, and so forth. One comes away with the sense that Self was attempting to teach women about themselves: how to find a job (and juggle it with relationship/family concerns), how to buy a car, how to maintain and improve self-esteem.

In the 1990s, however, it no longer seems a novelty that women should have, or want to have, fully integrated lives; and today's Self does not present issues in that way. Editor Penney had spoken of her "mandate to bring male/female relationships into the magazine on a post-feminist, equal basis,"[37] and, indeed, Self does not advocate equality; it is simply assumed. Self seems to be attempting to motivate women rather than merely encouraging them. Whether it be publishing articles about environmental activism, promoting breast cancer awareness by encouraging readers to wear pink ribbons (a campaign created by Self), or sponsoring seminars on health or sports,[38] the emphasis is on activity. Activity is reflected in the interactive self-concept, which suggests that readers should not simply absorb information passively but should respond, give feedback, do something. It is even reflected in Self's "active" design and shorter articles, which assume that readers are busy.

Like any publication, Self is not without its flaws and contradictions. For instance, one issue may celebrate the diversity of women's body shapes; another issue may illustrate a swimsuit piece with only picture-perfect models.[39] The magazine also has carried a surprisingly high number of cigarette ads for a fitness magazine. Some advertisers have voiced concerns about creeping trivialization, worrying that Self may be losing its "competitive edge" in health coverage and that the magazine's past balance between health and beauty tips may be losing out in favor of beauty.[40]

There is also currently something of a "cause of the day" aspect to the magazine's politics: one month, readers are warned that acquired immunodeficiency syndrome (AIDS) is America's number one threat; the next, they are told that illiteracy is the biggest menace. This tendency has been noted by *Mediaweek* magazine, which critiqued the [June 1991] issue's cover story on AIDS:

> Just to make sure I knew that this was the SERIOUS interlude, there, right there in the middle of the magazine, was the letter from the editor (marked URGENT in red) accompanied by her concerned-looking picture. Read this story, it says, or you will die. Which is followed by a headline and subhead that take up two whole pages. And finally, barely two pages of copy about "The AIDS Outrage." Gee, I guess there wasn't that much to say after all.[41]

As *Mediaweek*'s criticism suggests, the generally shorter articles favored by today's *Self* tend to discourage in-depth analysis and discussion. Critics have also complained that by placing undue attention on reader reaction, *Self* has become a follower rather than a leader.[42] *Self*'s recent experiments with fax numbers and interactive phone lines contribute to this impression.

Despite such criticism, the creators of *Self* have much to be proud of. They have virtually created a new genre of magazine[43] and have inspired many competitors.[44] They have presented—and continue to present—information about issues vital to American women. Their efforts on behalf of breast cancer awareness have been strong and unwavering. It will be interesting to follow the course of this influential publication in the years to come.

Notes

1. "Condé Nast's New Arrival Dovetails with Fitness Craze," *Product Marketing*, September 1978, p. 11.

2. Ira Ellenthal, "*Self* Surprises Everyone with Unpredictable Success," *Product Marketing*, January 1980, p. 26.

3. Ira Ellenthal, "Westerberg Meets *Self*'s Challenge; Plans Beauty Emphasis, Wide Visibility," *Product Marketing*, January 1981, p. 25.

4. Ellenthal, "*Self* Surprises Everyone with Unpredictable Success," p. 26.

5. Stuart J. Elliot, " 'Self,' Near 5, Still Fights Skeptics," *Advertising Age*, September 26, 1983, p. 41.

6. Phyllis Star Wilson, "Letter from the Editor," January 1979, p. 6.

7. "Condé Nast's New Arrival Dovetails with Fitness Craze," p. 11; Elliot, " 'Self,' Near 5, Still Fights Skeptics," p. 41; Stuart J. Elliot, " 'Self': A New Emphasis on Nutrition," *Advertising Age*, February 16, 1987, p. 34.

8. Elliot, " 'Self,' Near 5, Still Fights Skeptics," p. 41.

9. "Condé Nast's New Arrival Dovetails with Fitness Craze," p. 11.

10. Benjamin DeMott, "Who's Afraid of the Me Generation," December 1979, pp. 64–65.

11. Elliot, " 'Self,' Near 5, Still Fights Skeptics," p. 41.

12. "Buzzword on Post-Yuppies: *Self*-Absorbed," *Folio*, February 15, 1993, p. 18.

13. Patrick Reilly, "New Editor Guides 'Self' to a New Look," *Advertising Age*, January 2, 1989, p. 24.

14. Elliot, " 'Self,' Near 5, Still Fights Skeptics," p. 41.

15. Wilson, "Letter from the Editor," p. 6.

16. For instance, "Quick-Time Fitness," November 1979, p. 34; "Exercises That Build a Strong Heart and Steady Nerves," November 1979, pp. 82–85.

17. Sally Wendkes Olds, "How to Calm a Stress-Sensitive Stomach," December 1979, pp. 70–72; Deidre Laiken, "How Anxiety Affects Fertility," December 1979, pp. 92–95.

18. See Letters to the Editor, March 1979.

19. Elliot, " 'Self,' Near 5, Still Fights Skeptics," p. 41.

20. Typical examples include Lorraine Daigneault, "Stress Self-Defense—Decoding the Body's Chemical and Emotional Defenses," January 1984, pp. 112–113; Rochelle Green, "Do-It-Yourself Diagnosis—How Accurate and Safe Are Take-Home Health Tests?" October 1986, pp. 122–126; and Jennifer Cook, "Bone Strength: Crucial Guide to Building Yours," December 1986, pp. 114–119.

21. Candace Campbell, "Desire Dullers—Ever Think Your Cough Drops or Allergy Pill Could Dampen Your Lovemaking?" June 1984, pp. 54–60; Jennifer Cook, "Learning to Trust Again—After Divorce . . . Yourself and Men Too," December 1986, pp. 110–113.

22. Elliot, " 'Self': A New Emphasis on Nutrition," p. 34.

23. Ibid.

24. Ibid., p. 41.

25. Ibid., p. 34.

26. Reilly, "New Editor Guides 'Self' to a New Look," p. 24.

27. Ibid.

28. Ibid.

29. Deborah Toth, "Wider Focus Proves 'Self' Serving," *Advertising Age*, April 23, 1990, p. S18.

30. Ibid.

31. Iris Cohen Selinger, "Liberman's 'Self': A Debt to Braque, Picasso," *Adweek*, December 10, 1990, p. 22.

32. Ibid.

33. Ibid.

34. Alexandra Penney, "Yes, It Is Possible," January 1990, p. 93.

35. Alexandra Penney, "Memo from the Editor-in-Chief," January 1990, p. 91.

36. "Let's Talk," February 1994, p. 24.

37. Selinger, "Liberman's 'Self,' " p. 22.

38. For instance, "Women's Health Day" seminars (May 1993) or "Hit the Slopes with Self" ski outings (March 1994).

39. Amy Clyde, "The Brave New Body," April 1993, pp. 126–131; "Heatwaves," June 1993, pp. 136–141.

40. Toth, "Wider Focus Proves 'Self' Serving," p. S18.

41. David Granger. "The Nutley Reader: The Best of What You Could Be Missing," *Mediaweek*, June 3, 1991, p. 10.

42. Nina Darnton. "*Vogue, Self, Allure*—Alex," *Newsweek*, April 8, 1991, p. 56.

43. Elliot, " 'Self,' Near 5, Still Fights Skeptics," p. 41.

44. Lorne Manly. "Women's Fitness Titles Pump Up in Shrinking Market," *Folio,* November 15, 1993, p. 22.

Information Sources

BIBLIOGRAPHY:

"Buzzword on Post-Yuppies: Self-Absorbed." *Folio,* February 15, 1993, p. 18.

"Condé Nast's New Arrival Dovetails with Fitness Craze." *Product Marketing,* September 1978, p. 11.

Darnton, Nina. "*Vogue, Self, Allure*—Alex." *Newsweek,* April 8, 1991, p. 56.

Ellenthal, Ira. "*Self* Surprises Everyone with Unpredictable Success." *Product Marketing,* January 1980, p. 26.

———. "Westerberg Meets *Self*'s Challenge; Plans Beauty Emphasis, Wide Visibility." *Product Marketing,* January 1981, p. 25.

Elliot, Stuart J. " 'Self,' Near 5, Still Fights Skeptics." *Advertising Age,* September 26, 1983, p. 41.

———" 'Self': A New Emphasis on Nutrition." *Advertising Age,* February 16, 1987, p. 34.

Granger, David. "The Nutley Reader: The Best of What You Could Be Missing." *Mediaweek,* June 3, 1991, p. 10.

Manly, Lorne. "Women's Fitness Titles Pump Up in Shrinking Market." *Folio,* November 15, 1992, p. 66.

Reilly, Patrick. "New Editor Guides 'Self' to a New Look." *Advertising Age,* January 2, 1989, p. 24.

Selinger, Iris Cohen. "Liberman's 'Self': A Debt to Braque, Picasso." *Adweek,* December 10, 1990, p. 22.

Toth, Deborah. "Wider Focus Proves 'Self' Serving." *Advertising Age,* April 23, 1990, p. S18.

INDEX SOURCES: Readers' Guide to Periodical Literature; Business Periodical Index; ABI Inform Index; InfoTrac General Periodical Index.

LOCATION SOURCES: Library of Congress; Hamilton County [Cincinnati] Public Library; and other libraries.

Publication History

MAGAZINE TITLE AND TITLE CHANGES: *Self.*

VOLUME AND ISSUE DATA: Vols. 1–(1979–present). Monthly.

PUBLISHER AND PLACE OF PUBLICATION: Condé Nast Publications. New York.

EDITORS: Phyllis Star Wilson (January 1979–February 1987); Valorie Griffith Weaver (March 1987–September 1988); Anthea Disney (October 1988–December 1989); Alexandra Penney (January 1990–present).

CIRCULATION: ABC, 1993: 1,314,315 (paid, primarily subscriptions).

Thomas N. Lewis

SER PADRES

At the beginning of 1990, Gruner + Jahr USA's *Parents Magazine** introduced the Ser Padres Network.[1] However, not until January 1991 was the new magazine network for the young Hispanic family introduced in the United States. The postponement of the launching of the Ser Padres Network appeared to have been of benefit for Gruner + Jahr. The publishing company learned from others who were entering the Spanish-language family magazine segment. Before introducing *La Familia de Hoy*, a Spanish-language family magazine, Whittle Communications explored the market to assess its potential for this type of publication.[2] Results of Whittle's research showed potential for success. It seems that Whittle's experience pleased Gruner + Jahr. The publishing company launched the Ser Padres Network almost one year after *La Familia de Hoy* entered the market.

The Ser Padres Network, "a new series of controlled-circulation magazines in Spanish targeted at today's Hispanic parents,"[3] counted mostly on the experience of *Parents Magazine*, a publication that had been in the market long enough to know success. The idea of *Parents Magazine* was first introduced in 1925, when George J. Hecht noticed that there was no magazine dealing with the subject of child rearing. In October 1926, Hecht introduced *The Magazine for Parents*, which became *Parents Magazine* in August 1929.[4] *Parents Magazine* was a commercial success from the beginning. The increasing birthrate and the growing interest in child rearing explained the magazine's success. Hecht expected to attract perhaps 100,000 readers. He reached that many by the end of the first five years and many more than that by 1957.[5]

Ser Padres (Being Parents), the flagship of the Ser Padres Network, drew upon this background. It followed the editorial quality and breadth of *Parents Magazine*, but it was adapted to the Hispanic market. With the introduction of *Ser Padres*, Gruner + Jahr also introduced two other magazines to complete a package of publications on related topics: *Embarazo* (Pregnancy) and *Una Nueva Vida* (A New Life).

Ser Padres is issued six times a year. Each issue has a minimum of 68 pages. It aims at Spanish-speaking mothers between 18 and 44 years of age who live in the United States. It contains a "broad range of articles on all aspects of parenthood, and offers features on food and beauty topics as well."[6] The magazine is developing in a niche that was virtually nonexistent several years ago. The foreign-language family magazines category has suddenly become one of the hottest media segments in the market.[7]

Although *Ser Padres* was conceived to mirror *Parents Magazine*, most of the staff at the magazine are Latinoamerican. The publication presents articles that are written exclusively for *Ser Padres* and others that are adapted from *Parents Magazine*. However, the commitment of *Ser Padres* is to tailor those articles "to meet the specific informational needs of Hispanic parents."[8] The efforts of *Ser Padres* to fulfill its mission of providing Hispanic parents with specific, reliable, and helpful information and practical guidance are accomplished in the articles written by sociologists, psychologists, educators, therapists, pediatricians, gynecologists, and psychiatrists.

The content of *Ser Padres*, however, not only is based on scientific matters but also focuses on different topics such as children's games, practical measures to prevent accidents, real-life experiences, creative ideas to integrate children and parents in different activities, and children and school. Additionally, the magazine addresses beauty, nutrition, and skin and hair care for the young Hispanic mother. For example, in one issue, *Ser Padres* dedicated four pages to beauty and health for mothers and their children; specifically, a four-color article presented a rationale on why it is important to protect child's and mother's skin against the sun. The article also offered suggestions on how to get a tan without causing skin damage or burn.[9]

Elvia Delgado, chief editor of *Ser Padres*, *Embarazo*, and *Una Nueva Vida*, addresses in each issue of *Ser Padres* topics that help build confidence and communication between parents and children. Delgado covers subjects that range from what appropriate toys for a specific age to how to establish an open, serious conversation with children about any problem.

The Ser Padres Network does not wait for readers to find it. The *Ser Padres* magazine is brought to the places where Hispanics go to obtain the information contained in the publication. Therefore, doctors' waiting rooms, clinics, and hospitals are the primary places of distribution for *Ser Padres*. The magazine is distributed free of charge.[10]

When the Ser Padres Network was introduced in 1991, Frank Kelez, publisher of special projects for Gruner + Jahr Publishing, had already identified about 40,000 doctors' offices frequented by Hispanics.[11] *Ser Padres* was going to be available nationwide at nearly 3,000 locations. However, by March 1993, the magazine was reaching 5,000 doctors' offices. Projections of annual circulation for *Ser Padres* were then estimated at 900,000 issues. By January 1991, approximately 90 percent of the annual circulation was 1,350,000 or 225,000 per issue.[12] Results, however, seem to have been better than expected. Sam Pagan, advertising sales director of the Ser Padres Network, indicated that circulation reached 325,000 per issue in the first quarter of 1993.[13] The remaining 10 percent of total circulation came from subscriptions that were marketed via cards and advertisements in all three network magazines of *Embarazo*, *Una Nueva Vida*, and *Ser Padres*.[14]

Main competitors of *Ser Padres* are *La Familia de Hoy* and *Mundo Infantil*, both published by Whittle Communications. The two publications were introduced in the market at the beginning of 1990. More emphasis seems to have been placed on *Mundo Infantil*, which is published ten times annually and claims a circulation of 400,000 issues. It is sent free to anyone requesting it in writing, and, like *Ser Padres*, *Mundo Infantil* is delivered to hospitals and doctors' offices.[15]

Distribution efforts for *Ser Padres*, as well as for the other two Spanish-language publications of the network, have focused on cities where there is a high concentration of Spanish-speaking individuals. *Ser Padres* reaches 83 percent of the Hispanic population in Chicago, Miami, New York, and cities in

Southern California and Texas. However, the Ser Padres Network is looking for new markets and new consumers. Thus, the network is working on expanding the circulation of *Ser Padres* to other Spanish-speaking countries, including Puerto Rico.[16]

Advertising is also increasing. Advertisers include Procter and Gamble, Gerber Products Company, Colgate-Palmolive Co., Eastman Kodak Company, Kraft General Foods, Inc., Ford Motor Company, Toyota Motors, La Compania de Walt Disney, and AT&T. Most advertise baby food and care products. However, there are also some ads from the automotive industry highlighting family cars. The magazine dedicates approximately 28 percent of its 64 regular pages to advertising.

The Ser Padres Network strategy of launching three family publications aimed at the Hispanic market was based on the strategy of *Parents Magazine*. Each one of these three new publications has its counterpart in English.

Embarazo's American counterpart is *Expecting*. *Embarazo* is a semiannual publication that presents "vital information on all aspects of pregnancy and birth."[17] It is distributed free to Hispanic mothers-to-be in a carefully selected number of obstetricians' and gynecologists' offices. Also, it is delivered to childbirth education and community health centers. *Embarazo*'s editorial content focuses on prenatal and postnatal infant development, diet and nutrition during the waiting months, health and beauty of the mother-to-be, and maternity fashions. Additionally, the magazine includes regular features on products for mothers and babies. *Embarazo*'s current circulation is 175,000.[18]

The American counterpart for *Una Nueva Vida* is *Baby Care*. The magazine is an annual publication that offers young Spanish-speaking mothers "supportive information and advice on how to nurture their babies during the first months of life."[19] *Una Nueva Vida* magazine is given to Hispanic mothers at hospitals and is also included in a hospital gift pack that mothers receive after giving birth. Editorial content focuses on a wide range of topics important to the new parents, such as proper feeding habits, infant development, and common ailments. During its first year, *Una Nueva Vida* was distributed to 450,000 new mothers via First Moments Hispanic New Parent Sampler.[20]

The Ser Padres Network successfully launched its three magazines by combining the quality, credibility, and experience of *Parents Magazine*. Using a precisely timed Spanish-language vehicle to reach the untapped Hispanic market in the United States, these three new publications offer readers a variety of important information on taking care of children and educating parents on raising children in an atmosphere of warm and affectionate love that must be shown to the children from the very moment they are conceived. At the same time, these three magazines offer marketers of baby and new mother products an opportunity to reach the growing Hispanic market in the United States through their advertising campaigns.

Whether the *Ser Padres*, *Embarazo*, and *Una Nueva Vida* publications will be successful depends on the expertise of the Gruner + Jahr group in tapping the growing Hispanic market. As Ashley Shomaker, vice president/publisher of Whittle Communications, claims, "Two-thirds of the market's growth will come from monolingual Spanish-speaking immigrants. . . . Spanish is here to stay."[21] Additionally, success of Gruner + Jahr's Spanish publications will be influenced by the economic developments of the 1990s.

Notes

1. Ed Fitch, "Family Magazines Are Springing to Life," *Advertising Age*, February 26, 1990, pp. 45–46.
2. Ed Fitch, "People to Watch," *Advertising Age*, February 12, 1990, p. S13.
3. Media Kit.
4. Theodore Peterson, *Magazines in the Twentieth Century* (Urbana: University of Illinois Press, 1956).
5. Ibid.
6. Media Kit.
7. Fitch, "Family Magazines Are Springing to Life," pp. 45–46.
8. Rate Card.
9. Carol Straley, "Un Nuevo Sentido del Sol," June/July 1991, pp. 44–47.
10. Media Kit.
11. Fitch, "Family Magazines Are Springing to Life," pp. 45–46.
12. Rate Card.
13. Sam Pagan interview, March 23, 1993.
14. Rate Card.
15. Fitch, "Family Magazines Are Springing to Life," pp. 45–46.
16. Pagan interview.
17. Media Kit.
18. Ibid.
19. Ibid.
20. Fitch, "Family Magazines Are Springing to Life," pp. 45–46.
21. Fitch, "People to Watch," p. S13.

Information Sources

BIBLIOGRAPHY:

Fitch, Ed. "People to Watch." *Advertising Age*, February 12, 1990, p. S13.
———. "Family Magazines Are Springing to Life." *Advertising Age,* February 26, 1990, pp. 45–46.
Peterson, Theodore. *Magazines in the Twentieth Century.* Urbana: University of Illinois Press, 1956.
INDEX SOURCES: Infotrac—General Periodical Index.
LOCATION SOURCES: Library of Congress and other libraries.

Publication History

MAGAZINE TITLE AND TITLE CHANGES: *Ser Padres.*
VOLUME AND ISSUE DATA: Vols. 1–(January 1991–present). Bimonthly.

PUBLISHER AND PLACE OF PUBLICATION: Gruner + Jahr USA (1991–present).
New York.
EDITORS: Elvia Delgado (1991–present).
CIRCULATION: BPA, 1993: 327,213 (primarily nonpaid).

Norys C. De Abreu-Garcia

SEVENTEEN

When *Seventeen* magazine was born in September 1944, its readers were promised a publication of their own, a magazine covering everything that concerns, excites, annoys, pleases, or perplexes the teenage girl. The first issue cost 15¢ and sold 400,000 copies.[1]

Walter Annenberg, president of Triangle Publications and founder of *Seventeen*, wrote in a letter to the reader of the anniversary issue 40 years later: "That September 1944 issue promised to demonstrate to you, the reader, a devotion to what you do and a consuming interest in how you look, dress, feel and think. 'We are interested in the kind of human being you are,' we said in that inaugural issue. And truly, though the world has changed many times since that day, the primary objective of *Seventeen* hasn't really changed all that much. Our aim remains the same: to strive always to serve our millions of young readers in an intelligent, enlightening, sympathetic way."[2]

It did not take long for the magazine to have millions of readers. By 1949, its circulation was 1 million, and *Time* magazine reported that the publication had grown from a gangling kid to something of an Amazon. The newsmagazine credited publisher Alice Thompson and editor Helen Valentine with turning *Seventeen* into a money-making monthly by "taking dead aim on teenage readers. The magazine gives them low-priced fashions, fiction, sensible articles such as 'how to get along with parents' and frank discussions of teenage problems which other magazines shy away from."[3] By 1961, the magazine had a circulation of 1.15 million, a cover price of 50¢, and 162 pages of advertising in its September issue.[4]

Seventeen, over 50 years old now, is still the leader of the teen-magazine pack. Its circulation of 1.9 million is 43 percent more than that of its nearest competitor, *YM*; its 948 advertising pages for January–December 1992 were 52 percent more than those of its nearest competitor; and its 943 editorial pages for that period were 24 percent more.[5] Because of its huge circulation base and because it skews older than its competitors, *Seventeen* is considered more of a mass magazine than a niche magazine.[6]

Midge Richardson, editor of *Seventeen* from 1975 to 1994, says part of the magazine's success comes from the fact that it does not talk down to teenagers but instead talks to them the way they want to be talked to. While the target audience is 12–19 years old, the median age is 16.8, so the magazine is edited for the 16–18-

year-old.[7] This puts *Seventeen* in a different category from the teen magazines that are edited for a younger audience. The magazine is read by one out of two female teens in the United States[8] and one out of five females between 18 and 24.[9]

Seventeen is demographically represented across the United States, appealing to all teenagers regardless of interests, background, or race, and this diversity of the audience, in part, influences the topics covered and the way they are covered. About 40 percent of the editorial content is devoted to both light and serious subjects.[10] Another 40 percent of the magazine is devoted to fashion and beauty, and the rest to health, entertainment, food, decorating, columns, and fiction.[11]

Richardson says *Seventeen* succeeds because it is able to change with the times. In the beginning, *Seventeen* reflected society's view of a young woman by depicting her as a "very precious commodity"; this view did not change until the 1960s, when "she emerged as a real person who could think and speak for herself."[12] The magazine reflected society's view of sex, too. In the 1950s, kissing was discouraged, and "going all the way" was never mentioned. In the 1960s, kissing was openly discussed, and readers were given helpful hints about how to make themselves more kissable. Stories in the 1970s included "going all the way" and its possible consequences, and in the 1980s, a column called "Sex and Your Body" found its way into the publication.[13]

The magazine discussed careers in the 1950s, but the assumption remained that women's primary role was domestic. By the 1960s, both *Seventeen* and society let girls know that housewife was not the only occupation open to them.[14] Now, in the 1990s, the magazine has a strong emphasis on academic and social questions relating to education beyond high school, so it includes profiles of universities and stories on other educational topics.[15]

Seventeen keeps up with teen trends and changes in teen attitudes by conducting major surveys every other year. The research found, for example, that teens in the 1970s were interested in causes and the environment but in the 1980s were describing themselves as greedy, Richardson says. But altruism has made a comeback in the 1990s, and teens are more interested in such issues as the environment, politics, and health and health care.[16] The magazine responded to this change in the teen population with, among other things, a page in the November 1992 issue devoted to the presidential election and an annual environmental issue. The magazine's food pages have evolved to include discussions of vegetarian diets, the scoop on ice cream, and planet-friendly food. In an attempt to raise readers' self-esteem, the staff has added more articles on psychological issues, including those that celebrate individual differences. Richardson says that in the 1940s and 1950s, teens wanted to be like everyone else, but now the philosophy of the magazine is to encourage them to like themselves the way they are and to be comfortable with diversity.[17] The philosophy of the magazine also includes respecting the diversity of attitudes of the public at large and trying to educate rather than editorialize. "So when we write about abortion we're very careful when we say this is what it is, this is what it's all about. It isn't for everyone. It isn't something that we would be encouraging or saying this is what you should do."[18] According to Richardson, no subject is off-limits; the magazine has covered, and will cover, such topics as condoms, incest, contraception, and homosexuality.

Advertisers are not so lucky. Cigarette and liquor ads are always rejected, and Calvin Klein ads with naked people in them are, too. The ads are rejected only in part because they are not appropriate for the publication. *Seventeen* can be found in every school, city, and state library in the United States, and its editor does not want anything jeopardizing its school connection. She accepts fashion and beauty-related ads that do not include naked people, and, indeed, about 40 percent of the advertising in *Seventeen* is devoted to fashion and beauty.[19] Advertisers in this category include major clothing manufacturers such as Esprit, Benetton, DKNY, Gap, and Guess, shoe manufacturers such as Nike, Keds, and Reebok, and cosmetic companies—Richardson does not know of a single cosmetic company that *does not* advertise in *Seventeen*. This, she says, is one difference between *Seventeen* and its competitors.[20] Other advertising content includes music, entertainment, health, and education/career-oriented ads. *Seventeen* leads its competitors in advertising space to total space—57 percent— and in total number of different ads.[21]

Since the late 1970s, advertisers have been capitalizing on two things: the spending power of teenagers and the fact that teens with working mothers do much of the shopping for the family. According to former publisher Frank Wolf, the teenage girl with working parents has more money to spend on cosmetics, toiletries, and clothes because she is being rewarded for doing more of the cooking and other chores. This also means she is spending for food and other household items. Thus, major marketers "are coming to realize that getting to this young woman is not a future activity but a now activity." Increased advertising has come from the cosmetics, fashion, toiletries, and food industries. From 1977 to 1982, retail advertising—primarily Sears, Penney's, and K-Mart— increased significantly.[22]

Other changes in the magazine include new owners. Murdoch Magazines took over from Triangle Publications in 1989, and K-III Magazines took over from Murdoch in 1991. At the time of purchase, Harry A. McQuillen of K-III said *Seventeen* had fantastic potential but had been underdeveloped on the sales and marketing side. K-III made a $1 million commitment to the magazine to work on the marketing side.[23]

Along with the most recent change in ownership have come changes in design and new columns. In August 1992, the magazine created a new logo, redesigned the front section and some departments, such as "College," "Earth Talk," and the food pages, and added a regular auto column in response to reader interest and in an effort to attract more automobile advertisers.[24] In March 1993, *Seventeen* came out with a whole new wardrobe: expanded departments, new sections, and new typefaces. New departments include "Spin," a section of hard news; "Voice," a reader-generated section; "GuyZine," an expanded version of "Guy Talk," a regular column written by young men; and "Body Line," a department on health. "With young people, you have to change in order to stay current," Richardson said. "If you're going to stay with them, you're going to have to make some changes along with them."[25]

No one at *Seventeen*, however, believes that change alone will keep or attract teen readers. The magic ingredient, former publisher Frank G. Wolf said in 1982, is trust. Readers must believe the magazine is something they can rely on.[26] Richardson says it is. "They write us all the time, saying they just simply adore us, they trust us, they feel we're really a friend. If we were off target they'd be the first to tell us."[27]

Seventeen has been recognized not only by its many readers but by colleagues in the media. It has won the American Society of Magazine Editors (ASME) Elephant Award for fiction, which is to magazine fiction what the Oscar is to movies. Richardson is adamant that fiction in *Seventeen* is not intended to teach or to preach but to provide readers with good writing. She wants themes that appeal to young people—but no sappy love stories. While well-known writers such as Stephen King and Margaret Atwood contribute stories to the magazine, unknown writers do, too. In addition to its fiction award, *Seventeen* has been nominated four times for general excellence in the million-plus category. Richardson was thrilled to be nominated; winners in that category include *Time*, *Newsweek*, and *National Geographic*.[28]

Notes

1. *Printers' Ink*, August 25, 1961, p. 10.
2. Walter Annenberg, letter to the reader, September 1984, p. 3.
3. *Time*, May 16, 1949, p. 57.
4. *Printers' Ink*.
5. Media Kit.
6. Scott Donaton, "Teen Titles Grow Up," *Advertising Age*, June 11, 1990, p. 41.
7. Midge Richardson interview, April 30, 1993.
8. Ibid.
9. Media Kit.
10. Richardson interview.
11. Ellis Evans, et al., "Content Analysis of Contemporary Teen Magazines," *Youth and Society*, September 1991, pp. 99–120.
12. Richardson, quoted in Stuart J. Elliott, "Seventeen Hits 40: Numbers Tell the Story," *Advertising Age*, August 30, 1984, p. 24.
13. Landon Jones, "How Much Have Teens Changed?" September 1984, pp. 160–165.
14. Ibid.
15. Judy Massey, "Girl Talk Magazines," *School Library Journal*, October 1992, p. 54.
16. Richardson interview.
17. Ibid.
18. Ibid.
19. Evans, et al., "Content Analysis of Contemporary Teen Magazines," pp. 99–120.
20. Richardson interview.
21. Evans, et al., "Content Analysis of Contemporary Teen Magazines," pp. 99–120.
22. Mary McCabe English, "How to Stay 17 and Keep Growing," *Advertising Age*, August 2, 1982, pp. M27–28.

23. Scott Donaton, "K-III Picks New Titles for Investment," *Advertising Age*, February 24, 1992, p. 43.

24. Mary Huhn, "At *Seventeen*, Teens Look a Little Older: Redesign to Reflect Sophistication," *MediaWeek*, June 15, 1992, p. 4.

25. Ibid., p. 2.

26. English, "How to Stay 17 and Keep Growing," pp. M27–28.

27. Richardson interview.

28. Ibid.

Information Sources

BIBLIOGRAPHY:

Donaton, Scott. "K-III Picks New Titles for Investment." *Advertising Age*, February 24, 1992, p. 43.

Elliott, Stuart J. "Seventeen Hits 40: Numbers Tell the Story." *Advertising Age*, August 30, 1984, p. 24.

English, Mary McCabe. "How to Stay 17 and Keep Growing." *Advertising Age*, August 2, 1982, pp. M27–28.

Huhn, Mary. "At *Seventeen*, Teens Look a Little Older: Redesign to Reflect Sophistication." *MediaWeek*, June 15, 1992, p. 4.

———."*Seventeen* Gets a More Newsy Design." *MediaWeek*, January 4, 1993, p. 2.

INDEX SOURCES: Abridged Readers' Guide to Periodical Literature; Health Index; Junior High Magazine Abstracts; Magazine Index; Media Review Digest; Magazine Article Summaries; Readers' Guide to Periodical Literature.

LOCATION SOURCES: Many libraries throughout the United States.

Publication History

MAGAZINE TITLE AND TITLE CHANGES: *Seventeen.*

VOLUME AND ISSUE DATA: Vols. 1–(September 1944–present). Monthly.

PUBLISHER AND PLACE OF PUBLICATION: Triangle Publications (September 1944–July 1989); Murdoch Magazines (August 1989–July 1991); K-III Magazines (August 1991–present). New York.

EDITORS: Helen Valentine (1947–1950); Alice Thompson; Enid A. Haupt (1965–1972); Merrill Panitt, editorial director (1973–1975); Midge T. Richardson (1975–1994); Caroline Miller (1994–present).

CIRCULATION: ABC, 1993: 1,940,601 (paid, primarily subscriptions).

Kate Peirce

SOAP OPERA DIGEST

Soap operas entertain us, serve as a diversion from our own loves and miseries, and give us information on social issues such as acquired immunodeficiency syndrome (AIDS), single parenthood, prescription drug addiction, problems facing Vietnam veterans, Alzheimer's disease, and even the U.S. involvement in Somalia. Their plots sometimes offer alternative views of certain population groups, such as portraying older people in realistic story lines.

Because of their broad and varied topics, soap operas draw viewers from every walk of life. Sometimes these viewers become too busy to keep track of their favorite soap operas. In 1975, Jerome and Angela Shapiro, owners of Digest Publishing, came to the rescue. Their company, with founding editor Ruth Gordon, launched the first publication of its kind, *Soap Opera Digest*. Keeping soap opera followers in touch with their favorites was an idea whose time had come. In two months the Shapiros sold 400,000 subscriptions to their new publication.[1]

Their idea was a semimonthly magazine, printed on newsprint, geared toward the young working woman with income under $24,000.[2] Its design provided a day-by-day synopsis of every show by reviewing daytime and prime-time soap operas. The magazine also looked behind the scenes through personal interviews with the soap opera actresses and actors, delving into what they do off the set, which stars are going on to movie stardom, who is dating whom.

Another tradition Jerome Shapiro introduced is the Soap Opera Digest Awards, a yearly television presentation. The awards program began in 1976 and ran in syndication until 1988, when it was picked up by a network. Soap Opera Digest Awards presents the magazine's readers an opportunity to vote for their favorites in 21 daytime and prime-time categories. The top three vote-getters in each category become finalists. These categories are based on the magazine's editors' nominations for best soap opera, best actress, best actor, best writer, and so on.[3]

Most of the advertising during the Shapiros' ownership was for beauty products and cigarettes. The cost of advertising for a full black-and-white page was $3,000 and for a full page in color, $3,600.[4]

By the time Jerome Shapiro sold *Soap Opera Digest* in 1980 to the Journal Company, publishers of the *Providence Journal-Bulletin*,[5] the magazine was trying to increase circulation from 500,000 to 650,000.[6] The Journal Company tried several new ideas. It offered retailers two free pages for promotion and advertising.[7] It increased publishing frequency from 18 to 26 times per year.[8] It also tried to increase the base circulation rate from 650,000 to 675,000 and to increase advertising rates 8.5%.[9] By 1986, the Journal Company decided to downsize and diversify. *Soap Opera Digest* was sold to a magazine consultant, Gerry Ritterman, and his company, Network Publishing Corporation.[10]

Ritterman paid $20 million and took over as publisher. Under Ritterman, *Soap Opera Digest*'s target market was still young working women with incomes between $25,000 and $27,000.[11] Approximately 80% of the magazine's revenue came from sales at grocery store checkout lines. The other 20% came from advertising beauty products and cigarettes. Revenue from subscriptions was minimal. The price of *Soap Opera Digest* was $1.75. It was printed mainly on newsprint, with a four-color, one-page advertisement costing $14,300.[12]

While Ritterman was publisher, he experimented with the cover design and new ad campaigns. He had success with the cover design, but the other proved to be a legal failure.

In 1988, with sales slumping or staying the same, Ritterman decided to buck the system. Most of the magazine industry was changing from multi-image covers to simplified covers in the hopes of luring new buyers to test their magazines. Ritterman, on the other hand, went in the opposite direction. He removed nighttime soap opera stars from the cover, added inset photos, used sensational headlines, started new specialty issues such as "Best & Worst" and "Fall Preview," and began creating multi-image covers.

The makeover was a hit. There was a 17% growth in single-copy sales compared with the same period in 1987. This made single-copy sales 71.4% of total sales and 1,059,522[13] copies in total sales for the first half of 1988. When asked about *Soap Opera Digest*'s rise in sales, Ritterman responded, "We tried what has been done successfully at other magazines. We are just increasing our chances of drawing a reader."[14]

On June 6, 1988, *Soap Opera Digest* launched a new $500,000 ad campaign based on parodies of ads run by *Cosmopolitan*,* *McCall's*,* and *Rolling Stone*. The campaign, with ads running in several magazines, celebrated the average working woman with the tag line "where the forgotten consumer is remembered."[15]

The parodies of these upscale publications resulted in a strongly worded letter from *Rolling Stone*'s lawyers warning *Soap Opera Digest* that the parodies were nothing less than a rip-off and that they had to stop.

The *Soap Opera Digest* ad to which the *Rolling Stone* lawyers objected was based on a "Perception vs. Reality" ad campaign and showed "a middle class mother at a grocery store with her overweight son, a thumb sucking daughter and a cart full of groceries" under the headline, "Perception." The photograph was repeated under the headline "Reality" on the opposite page. In the *Rolling Stone* print ads, a different photograph appears on each page except in one instance where singer Bob Dylan appears on both pages. Because of this, *Rolling Stone* felt the ad campaigns were too similar.[16]

By the time the *Rolling Stone* lawyers wrote *Soap Opera Digest*, several magazines running the parody ads had stopped using them. Ritterman decided to halt the print campaign, saying, "We hadn't seen that particular ad . . . but I think *Rolling Stone* is taking itself a little too seriously. They should know that parody is the highest form of compliment."[17]

During Ritterman's tenure, *Soap Opera Digest* had a suit brought against it by a newsletter called *Soap Opera NOW!*, which claimed that *Soap Opera Digest* was trying to create a monopoly in soap opera publications by refusing to print any more of *Soap Opera NOW!* ads. The agreement to publish the ads, which *Soap Opera Digest* had been printing since December 1983, was canceled in April 1985, then reinstated and canceled two more times before the suit was brought against *Soap Opera Digest* in February 1988. *Soap Opera NOW!* sought $400,000 in damages, and, since their research showed that the ads were very successful, the publication wanted the right to publish their ads in *Soap Opera Digest*. The judge granted *Soap Opera NOW!*'s request and ordered *Soap Opera*

Digest to continue advertising *Soap Opera NOW!* in its publication. *Soap Opera Digest* had used late payments, reader complaints, and fear that *Soap Opera NOW!* would obtain its customer lists as reasons for canceling the advertising contract, but *Soap Opera NOW!* successfully proved that *Soap Opera Digest* had been printing *Soap Opera NOW!*'s ads for four years and that *Soap Opera NOW!* had been paying its bills on time. The judge also ruled that *Soap Opera NOW!* was "too small to be considered a competitive threat to *Soap Opera Digest*."[18]

Soap Opera Digest was sold to News Corporation, owned by Rupert Murdoch, in June 1989 for $70 million.[19] The Australian-born media baron added *Soap Opera Digest* to Murdoch Magazines, which consisted of *Automobile, European Travel & Life, Mirabella,* * *New Woman, New York Magazine, Premiere, Seventeen,* * *Soap Opera Weekly, TV Guide,* and *The Daily Racing Form.*

Total circulation of *Soap Opera Digest* at time of purchase was 2,100,508,[20] and the cost of a full-page black-and-white ad was $20,910. The same ad in color cost $25,480.[21] Murdoch did not change the format of *Soap Opera Digest.* The major advertisers were still beauty products and cigarettes. The target audience was still young women.

But Murdoch had overextended himself, and by 1990, he was under pressure from his bankers to restructure his debt. News Corporation agreed to reduce its $8.2 billion debt to $800 million by February 1991. The assets Murdoch sold for $650 million were nine U.S. publications: *Automobile, European Travel and Life, New Woman, New York Magazine, Premiere, Seventeen, Soap Opera Digest, Soap Opera Weekly,* and *The Daily Racing Form.*[22]

The buyer, K-III Holdings, is a management buyout specialist. At the time of purchase, K-III Holdings's philosophy when taking control of a magazine was to leave the editorial staff and policies intact and to hold on to everything they bought. In *Soap Opera Digest*'s case they have done just that. The magazine is still owned by K-III Holdings, it targets the same audience, and the majority of the advertisers are beauty products and food products.

Soap Opera Digest's current editor, Lynn Leahey, has tried some new ideas. In 1993, the magazine abandoned all newsprint pages for glossy paper, incorporated color into every page, and moved the late-breaking news section to the front of the magazine. These changes have allowed colored ads to be placed throughout the magazine. The cover remains multi-image, as when Ritterman owned the magazine.

At the end of 1993, total circulation was 1,437,758, up 2.97% from the previous year.[23] *Soap Opera Digest*'s latest trend is to have an even higher percentage of its advertising for beauty and fashion products. They also are attempting to branch into automobile advertising.

The most interesting thing Leahey added to the soap opera scene was Monday appearances on CNN's soap segment at 10:45 A.M. EST, barring preemption by a late-breaking news story. She takes calls from listeners and answers the questions they have about soap operas or *Soap Opera Digest.*

Notes

1. Ron Wood, "New TV Shopping Show Will Offer Discounted Magazine Subscriptions; 'The Sweepstakes Channel' Debuts in January," *DM News*, December 1, 1986, p. 1.

2. Dan Thomas, "Soap Opera Update Targets Yuppies," *DM News*, September 1, 1987, p. 45.

3. Knight-Ridder Newspapers, "Soap Opera Awards Set," *Chicago Tribune*, TV Week, p. 31.

4. Philip Dougherty, "Advertising," *New York Times*, January 22, 1979, sec. 4, p. 8.

5. Thomas, "Soap Opera Update Targets Yuppies," p. 45.

6. Dougherty, "Advertising," January 22, 1979, p. 8.

7. "GM's Bright Picture Has Some Cloudy Edges; General Merchandise, Non-Food, 1985 Super Market Sales Manual," *Progressive Grocer*, July 1985, p. 143.

8. Philip Dougherty, "Advertising," *New York Times*, September 30, 1980, sec. 4, p.15.

9. Philip Dougherty, "Advertising," *New York Times*, February 29, 1984, p. D20.

10. Allan Kozinn, "Musical America Magazine Announces Reorganization," *New York Times*, April 3, 1991, p. C15.

11. "Special Report," *Advertising Age*, September 19, 1988, 1988 Consumer Magazine Directory, p. S3.

12. Eleanor Blau, "Soap Opera Magazines Fight for Fans' Hearts and Dollars," *New York Times*, October 24, 1988, p. D10.

13. "Special Report," *Advertising Age*, October 24, 1988, Magazines, Data Bank, p. S30.

14. Patrick Reilly, "Single-Copy Sales Fight Downward Trend," *Advertising Age*, October 24, 1988, Special Report, Magazines, p. S6.

15. "Ads Parody Upscale Market," *Crain's New York Business*, June 6, 1988, p. 25.

16. Bruce Horovitz, "Bruce Horovitz/Marketing: Top Ad Jobs Are Hard to Come by for Women," *Los Angeles Times*, July 12, 1988, Business, part 4, p. 6.

17. Ibid.

18. Kim Dennis and Brian Zabcik, "U.S. District Court—Who's Suing Whom," *Manhattan Lawyer*, June 7, 1988, p. 20. "Soap Opera Magazine Sues Rival over DR Advertising Agreement," *DM News,* March 15, 1988, p. 30.

19. Lisa I. Fried, "McQuillen Writes K-III's Next Chapter," *Folio's Publishing News*, December 15, 1991, p. 9.

20. "Cover Story," *Advertising Age*, December 24, 1990, Data File, p. 20.

21. Joe Mandese, "New Ad Rates," *Advertising Age*, December 9, 1991, p. 34.

22. Deirdre Carmody, "Surprise Choice to Head Magazines," *New York Times*, October 30, 1991, p. D1.

23. Scott Donaton, "Magazines Limp at Newsstand; Fret over Rate Bases; Goal to Pare Bonuses, Up Profits," *Advertising Age*, February 21, 1994, p. 25.

Information Sources

BIBLIOGRAPHY:
"Ads Parody Upscale Market," *Crain's New York Business*, June 6, 1988, p. 25.

Blau, Eleanor. "Soap Opera Magazines Fight for Fans' Hearts and Dollars." *New York Times*, October 24, 1988, p. D10.

Carmody, Deirdre. "Surprise Choice to Head Magazines." *New York Times*, October 30, 1991, p. D1.

"Cover Story." *Advertising Age*, December 24, 1990, Data File, p. 20.

Dennis, Kim, and Brian Zabcik. "U.S. District Court—Who's Suing Whom." *Manhattan Lawyer*, June 7, 1988, p. 20.

Donaton, Scott. "Magazines Limp at Newsstand; Fret over Rate Bases; Goal to Pare Bonuses, Up Profits." *Advertising Age*, February 21, 1994, p. 25.

Dougherty, Philip. "Advertising." *New York Times*, January 22, 1979, sec. 4, p. 8.

———. "Advertising." *New York Times*, September 30, 1980, sec. 4, p. 15.

———. "Advertising." *New York Times*, February 29, 1984, p. D20.

Easton, Nina J. "Caller Clash Reflects TV's Challenge on AIDS." *Los Angeles Times*, December 3, 1988, part 5, p. 1.

Fried, Laura. "Issues Now Take Plots beyond Perfect Hair and Designer Clothes." *Calgary Herald*, March 6, 1994, p. B7.

"GM's Bright Picture Has Some Cloudy Edges; General Merchandise, Non-Food, 1985 Super Market Sales Manual." *Progressive Grocer*, July 1985, p. 143.

Horovitz, Bruce. "Bruce Horovitz/Marketing: Top Ad Jobs are Hard to Come by for Women." *Los Angeles Times*, July 12, 1988, Business, part 4, p. 6.

Huhn, Mary. "Soap Book Goes Glossy; Seeks More, Better Ads; Soap Opera Digest." *MediaWeek*, February 1, 1993, p. 6.

Knight-Ridder Newspapers. "Soap Opera Awards Set." *Chicago Tribune*, TV Week, p. 31.

Kozinn, Allan. "Musical America Magazine Announces Reorganization." *New York Times*, April 3, 1991, p. C15.

Mandese, Joe. "New Ad Rates." *Advertising Age*, December 9, 1991, p. 34.

Reilly, Patrick. "Single-Copy Sales Fight Downward Trend." *Advertising Age*, October 24, 1988, Special Report, Magazines, p. S6.

Sloan, Pat, and Stuart J. Elliott. "Adwhirl." *Advertising Age*, July 13, 1987, p. 88.

"Soap Opera Magazine's Refusal to Publish Advertisements of Soap Opera Newsletter Does Not Violate Antitrust Laws Because Publishers Are Not Competitors." *Entertainment Law Reporter*, January 1991, p. 14.

"Soap Opera Magazine Sues Rival over DR Advertising Agreement." *DM News*, March 15, 1988, p. 30.

"Special Report." *Advertising Age*, October 24, 1988, Magazines, Data Bank, p. S30.

"Special Report." *Advertising Age*, September 19, 1988, 1988 Consumer Magazine Directory, p. S3.

Thomas, Dan. "Soap Opera Update Targets Yuppies." *DM News*, September 1, 1987, p. 45.

Wood, Ron. "New TV Shopping Show Will Offer Discounted Magazine Subscriptions; 'The Sweepstakes Channel' Debuts in January." *DM News*, December 1, 1986, p. 1.

INDEX SOURCES: The Serials Directory; Lexis-Nexis.

LOCATION SOURCES: Middle Tennessee State University's Todd Library and other libraries; Business Information On-line Services—Educational Program.

Publication History

MAGAZINE TITLE AND TITLE CHANGES: *Soap Opera Digest.*
VOLUME AND ISSUE DATA: Vols. 1–(December 1975–present). Semimonthly.
PUBLISHER AND PLACE OF PUBLICATION: Jerome and Angela Shapiro (1975–1980); The Journal Company (1980–1986); Gerry Ritterman (1986–1989); Rupert Murdoch (1989–1991); K-III Holdings, now known as K-III Magazines (1991–present). New York City.
EDITORS: Ruth Gordon (1975–1982); Meredeth Brown (1982–1987); Meridith Berlin (1988–1991); Lynn Leahey (1991–present).
CIRCULATION: ABC, 1993: 1,437,758 (paid, primarily newsstand)(peak circulation, 1989: 2,100,508).

Jean Nagy

SOUTHERN ACCENTS

In Atlanta in 1977, just two doors from offices where Jimmy Carter had launched his presidential campaign, W.R.C. Smith Publishing Company, a small but respected trade publisher, prepared to take on one of the best-known names in the commercial market. James A. Hooton, editor of *Electrical South* and a talented interior designer, had devised a plan to merge his two areas of expertise.

Hooton met with Walter M. Mitchell, Jr., president of W.R.C. Smith, and proposed a magazine based on slick upscale publications like *Architectural Digest* and *House Beautiful.** This magazine also would cater to a high-income readership, using the best photography, paper, and printing technology available. However, Hooton envisioned a magazine with one distinct difference: it would showcase what those other publications overwhelmingly ignored—the South.

The board of W.R.C. Smith believed the future lay in trade publishing and hesitated to venture into the commercial arena, but Mitchell convinced them to produce a promotional brochure to test interest. Hooton, on a limited budget, prepared a four-color brochure on the proposed *Southern Accents.* The brochure featured the Georgian-style home of Ruben Jones, a well-known antiques dealer in Atlanta. Unfortunately, response was lukewarm, and the project was tabled until two socialites became involved.

Lisa Newsom, the wife of a prominent Atlanta physician, saw the brochure while browsing in an antiques shop and wanted to purchase a copy of the magazine. She called Mitchell and was told that interest in such a publication had been nominal, to which she pointed out an obvious problem: the mailing list must not have been well focused or she would have been on it. Newsom was "reasonably horrified" to learn the company had mailed the brochure to the names on its trade journal list.[1]

Also interested was a former W.R.C. Smith employee, Helen (Nena) Candler Griffith, of the Coca-Cola Candlers, who offered her help. Meanwhile, Newsom "demanded, insisted, begged and pleaded for the magazine"[2] and prepared a list of advertisers and potential subscribers—persons in high-income occupations, garden clubs, historical societies, and the Junior League. The response to a second direct-mail piece was tremendously favorable, but pushing the idea over the top, according to Sally Smith, daughter of W.R.C. Smith, were the approximately 7,000 signatures Griffith and Newsom collected from people who wanted a regional upscale magazine on interiors and gardens.[3]

The timing was perfect for such a regional magazine. Carter's successful bid for the presidency had made the South a national news topic, and, consequently, those living below the Mason-Dixon line basked in a newfound cultural pride. The rest of the country was discovering new aspects of the South: the existence of an educated, wealthy class of people with refined tastes and a great deal of disposable income. Striving to create a magazine to appeal to that market, Hooton, Griffith, and Newsom produced a first issue, fall 1977, which was mailed free to the prospect list. Fifteen thousand copies were printed, 1,500 of those distributed to newsstands with a cover price of $2.95.[4]

For obvious reasons the first issue focused its editorial and advertising primarily, though not entirely, on Atlanta. Featured with an Atlanta decorator's apartment, the gardens of eight Atlanta residences, and an Atlanta townhouse were a historic New Orleans landmark, a Birmingham, Alabama, home, and the house of a Washington, D.C., ambassador.

Advertising manager Sims Bray, Jr., armed with ad pages from *Architectural Digest*, landed national names Baker Furniture and Scalamandré Silks, along with about 45 local companies. Waterford Crystal and Henredon Furniture purchased space in future issues. Advertising with *Southern Accents* at the time involved little risk on the part of those advertisers: a full-page color ad sold for just $1,100.[5] Still, the magazine's advertising base was limited for a few years as advertisers shied away from regional magazines. To further entice advertisers, Mitchell—against Bray's advice—offered a three-year rate protection to advertisers in the premier issue. Bray was concerned, but only a few of the 48 advertisers who bought 30 pages in that magazine took the deal, and by year's end the number of advertising pages had nearly doubled.

Editorially, *Southern Accents* lived up to its billing as "the magazine of fine Southern interiors and gardens." Its pages glowed with dramatically vibrant photographs of opulent residences and historic landmarks. Truly, these represented the most elegant homes of any region of the country. But the editors were banking on one factor, summarized by a contributing editor, Maryon Allen: "I have found appreciation for all things beautiful in absolutely endless supply in the South. Southerners own beauty . . . they collect beauty, they cherish beauty."[6]

Southern Accents proclaimed itself to be a publication for "all people who enjoy the art of living gracefully,"[7] but its popularity stemmed from the regionalism. That was—and still is—the deciding factor, according to past and present editors. With only the South, the states, and border states of the old Confederacy as its original editorial coverage area, the magazine devoted itself not just to a region but to a lifestyle. Letters poured into the offices on Peachtree praising this "magazine devoted to Southern class," an "excellent vehicle for showing the world what it is like to be a part of the South," and also raving about the fine printing quality and beautiful photography.[8] Newsstand copies of the first issue sold out in a few weeks, and accolades streamed in from designers and persons in related fields. The response "staggered" the editors.[9] About half of the people who had received the initial issue subscribed,[10] and the print order was doubled for the second issue. Newsstand coverage was increased to include distribution to larger cities in each of the 12 states covered by the publication. By the time volume 2 came out, the print order was 50,000, and volume 1, number 1 had become a collector's item of sorts: readers willing to part with their copies offered them to the highest bidder, often for charity, through the magazine's "Letters" section.

But the magazine encountered its share of problems. Diane Burrell, the magazine's production coordinator, was at the time editing the company's one-shot trade publications on a freelance basis. Professional freelance writers were not yet being used, and Mitchell, a University of Georgia journalism school graduate, knew that for this magazine to succeed, the writing had to be of equal quality to the photography. He approached Burrell with a manuscript and by volume 2, number 2 (Spring 1979), she took over as the copy editor of *Southern Accents*.

The magazine, slated for quarterly release, experienced significant production problems as well—no spring 1978 issue was printed. Mitchell then made Burrell the managing editor, with instructions to improve the writing and photography and get the magazine out on time. The print order began a steady climb as the editorial staff of five settled into their roles. With the second volume, editorial content extended beyond interiors, accessories, and gardens "to encompass more dimensions of the gracious lifestyle so special to the South."[11] The editors introduced a continuing series on southern artists with a feature on *Jericho*'s Hubert Shuptrine. The first nonresidential interior appeared with a photo essay on Atlanta's Fox Theatre. Plans to enter the book market with *Historic Southern Homes and Restorations* were announced.

But subject matter like "Victorian Townhouse on Capitol Hill," "Classic Background in Modern Design," "City Garden in the English Manner," "Dallas Designer's Retreat," and "Casual Sophistication in Nashville" formed the cornerstone of the magazine's appeal, complemented by departments on related topics such as art, table settings, and southern gardening. Hooton professed one unifying element: "Taste . . . it's what *Southern Accents* is all about . . . we shall pursue it vigorously in word and picture."[12] The magazine also claimed a depth beyond design, gardens, architecture, and southern history. "It's also about people—Southern people—whose creations these are."[13]

The current editorial director, Katherine Pearson, claims the magazine "brings attention to the good work that is being done in the South but that is overlooked by national publications."[14] Southern designers and artists, as well as the general "affluent" public, have responded overwhelmingly in favor of the magazine's decidedly biased philosophy. Apparently, the founders were correct in assuming a "need to explode at least one popularly held misconception . . . that Southern culture and lifestyles are somehow less sophisticated than their Northern or Western counterparts."[15]

The magazine early evidenced its popularity. During the first Christmas season, according to Smith, the company had to hire eight extra persons just to handle the gift card subscriptions that flowed in.[16] Circulation grew 103 percent between 1978 and 1979 (the cover price rose to $3.50, and the following year the rate of circulation growth was 68 percent, second in the nation).[17] National advertisers became much easier to land, although ad rates rose steadily with circulation increases. Still, the rates of *Southern Accents* stayed significantly lower than those of *Architectural Digest*,[18] and soon such companies as Kohler, Beefeater Gin, Mercedes Benz, and Cadillac began to advertise on the pages of the regional magazine. In a trend that holds true today, a substantial number of advertisements were for southern products and services, including designers, portraitists, other artists, and resorts. The market these companies expected to reach was evidenced by ads in 1981 issues for oceanfront condominiums starting at $275,000.

Not surprisingly, the activity from this trade publishing house caused the South's preeminent magazine publisher to take note. Southern Progress Corporation, home to *Southern Living** and *Progressive Farmer*, watched the events in Atlanta closely. Mitchell wisely established rapport with executives at Southern Progress early. Despite the initial success of *Accents*, Mitchell kept a cautious attitude, worried that someone might eventually have to bail out the small company.[19] Southern Progress did become enamored of the publication, and several unsuccessful offers were put forth.

By mid-1982, Hooton resigned because of health problems, and Newsom became editor. The circulation of *Southern Accents* had expanded to 100,000, and in the next year the decision was made to publish bimonthly beginning in 1984. The print order in 1983 reached almost 220,000, due primarily to an overwhelming subscription rate base of 140,000.[20] *Inc.* magazine named *Southern Accents* one of its top 500 (331st) fastest growing, privately held smaller businesses in the country. Whereas at one time subscriptions provided 60 percent of the total revenue, by 1985, advertising accounted for almost 70 percent.[21] A four-color page in the spring 1982 issue brought $4,305; in 1985, that ad commanded $6,590. A Mendelsohn Media Research Survey named *Southern Accents* the number one affluent publication in the country that same year.[22]

Southern Progress, meanwhile, decided not to allow this lucrative market to go untouched by its vast resources, and the company launched a rival. The competitor, *Southern Living Classics*, hit newsstands in mid-1985 with a rate base of 160,000. With this magazine's release, W.R.C. Smith began to seriously consider selling, intimidated by the power of Southern Progress, which itself had just been acquired by Time Inc. *Classics* did well with its first issue with subscribers, but according to current chief executive editor John Floyd, "Southern Progress let the W.R.C. Smith folks know that the door was still open for continued negotiations."[23]

In October 1985, Southern Progress Corporation purchased W.R.C. Smith Publishing for $16 million. "They were so powerful moneywise that it was a great scare to us," Mitchell said. "We intended to still be in business to this day, but they just put too much money on the table."[24] W.R.C. Smith's last magazine, the November–December 1985 issue, was, ironically, Griffith's first as editor. Cofounder Newsom stepped down to spend time with family and to pursue other interests.

Southern Progress sold the only remaining trade publication, *Sports Merchandiser*, to Shore Communications, an Atlanta-based company. Southern Accents Press, the book division, was absorbed into Oxmoor House. Editorial offices for *Southern Accents* remained in both Atlanta and Birmingham for a time; by 1987, the base of operations was moved to Birmingham. Southern Progress merged the staffs and mailing lists of the two magazines, and *Classics* itself was absorbed into *Southern Accents*. Burrell was the only staff member to relocate, although Griffith was persuaded to stay on as editor. Even today she contributes to the publication.

Because the "major players" did not change, the transition was relatively smooth; and the magazine showed little or no visible effects. However, the combining did produce a more competitive rate base. *Accents* benefited by becoming part of a well-established, successful publishing firm that brought not just money but experience in circulation and ad sales. Former publisher Tony Glaves, who became publisher in 1989, blamed high-end production costs and advertising page rates that were too low in relation to the rest of the market for the magazine's limited profitability before Southern Progress acquired it.[25]

"The fact that Southern Progress had taken over the magazine generated a lot of publicity and a lot of favorable trade coverage," former publisher Jim de Vira said. "And, I think we brought a much deeper commitment to taking the magazine to where we thought it should be."[26] Although stating that, editorially, W.R.C. Smith was producing a good product, de Vira believes the small company's inexperience in the commercial arena limited it in terms of circulation and advertising. "I think they were a little overwhelmed getting involved in the consumer area. We thought we could do with *Accents* what we did with *Southern Living*, only directed at a much more affluent, upscale audience who were interested in interior design and homes."[27]

Southern Progress combined its staff and other resources with its credibility in the marketplace to push *Accents* ahead. With such luxuries as full-time copy editors and proofreaders, the editorial product improved, although feature subjects and departments, such as "Tablescapes," "The Visual Arts," "Design Sources," and "Travel," remained unchanged. In geographic scope the magazine added Maryland, Delaware, Oklahoma, and Missouri to its coverage region.

An annual "Holidays" issue was added in 1987 to feature Christmas in the

South, and in 1990, publication frequency became ten times per year—a move that soon was regretted. According to Pearson, it was the right decision at the wrong time. The need for greater frequency existed to attract more national advertising, but just as *Southern Accents* increased its schedule, "the bottom fell out of the home furnishings market," the magazine's "bread and butter."[28] After two years the magazine reverted to bimonthly. It simply was more profitable to produce six 200-page magazines rather than ten 120-page magazines.[29] Pearson cited a drop in newsstand sales across the board in 1990 and 1991. *Southern Accents* was hurt in addition by smaller issues being on the newsstand for shorter sales periods.[30]

Back on a bimonthly schedule, *Southern Accents* is on strong financial ground. Newsstand sales are up considerably: in 1993, they almost doubled 1991 figures—even at five dollars a copy. Broad-based national advertising has come in, and the home furnishings market is making a comeback. In addition, several competitors—for advertising dollars, not subscribers—have downgraded or ceased publication. The number of ad pages has dropped from 724 in 1989 to 551 in 1993, but ad revenue has risen about half a million dollars over that same period. The September 1993 issue was the largest revenue issue to date.[31]

Southern Accents also has begun to succeed outside the traditional confines. The magazine has become more promotion-minded, with special sections appearing regularly on topics such as rugs, arts, and antiques—even travel. Increased interaction with designers and manufacturers, in such venues as seminars and trade shows, has proved financially sound, especially with the dwindling advertising dollar. Smith, who still contributes to the magazine in a scouting capacity, said such interaction allows the magazine to remain "on the edge" of everything in the field, which fits the magazine's less traditionally minded readership.[32]

In addition to growing profitability, *Southern Accents* enjoys a national credibility for its journalistic and design qualities, which have gained stature in the mid-1990s.[33] Although expanding editorial coverage beyond the South has been discussed, Pearson says that will not happen soon.

We know the magazine is popular across the nation just like it is, and we are more aggressively pursuing circulation outside the South. The Southern readership is enormously loyal to us because of our attention to and presentation of the South as a source of pride. But our magazine also appeals as just a comfortable living style to the affluent outside the South, and I think there is a mystique and charisma about the South that work for us there.[34]

Notes

1. Helen Candler Griffith interview, May 2, 1994.
2. Walter M. Mitchell, Jr., "Letter from the Publisher," Fall 1977, p. 64.
3. Sally Smith interview, July 11, 1994.

4. Walter M. Mitchell, Jr., "Letter from the Publisher," Fall 1978, p. 112; Diane Burrell interview, April 6, 1994.

5. Sims Bray, Jr., interview, April 6, 1994.

6. Maryon Allen, quoted by Jim Hooton, "Editorial," Fall 1977, p. 5. Maryon Allen contributed to the magazine for two years; she was also the wife of Alabama senator James Allen.

7. Jim Hooton, "Editorial," Fall 1977, p. 5.

8. "Letters," Winter 1978, p. 8.

9. Griffith interview.

10. Sharron Hannon, "Magazine Publishers Here Gambling with Slim Chance of Profit," *Atlanta Business Chronicle*, November 28, 1983, pp. 6, 27.

11. Jim Hooton, "Editorial," Summer 1979, p. 6.

12. Jim Hooton, "Editorial," Spring 1979, p. 6.

13. Jim Hooton, "Editorial," Fall 1978, p. 6.

14. Katherine Pearson interview, April 4, 1994.

15. Smith interview.

16. Lisa B. Newsom, "Editorial," July–August 1985, p. 8.

17. Andria Krewson, "*Southern Accents* Ranks 2nd in Growth," *Atlanta Journal*, July 31, 1981, p. 3D.

18. Bray interview.

19. Walter M. Mitchell, Jr., interview, April 6, 1994.

20. "Statement of Ownership, Management and Circulation," Fall 1983, p. 164; Lisa Newsom, "Editorial," Spring 1983, p. 12.

21. Tom Walker, "Accenting Life in the South Was a Winner," *Atlanta Journal and Constitution*, January 21, 1985, pp. 1C, 6C.

22. Bray interview.

23. John Floyd, letter to author, June 10, 1994.

24. Mitchell interview.

25. Tony Glaves, July 11, 1994. Glaves was associate publisher at *Sunset* until June 1994. Bill Carey is the current publisher.

26. Jim de Vira interview, July 5, 1994.

27. Ibid.

28. Pearson interview.

29. Ibid.

30. Pearson, letter to author, June 10, 1994.

31. Pearson notes, Design Conference, March 1994.

32. Smith interview.

33. Pearson letter.

34. Ibid.

Information Sources

BIBLIOGRAPHY:

Bell, Elma. "Editor Designed a Magazine with Southern Accent." *Birmingham News*, July 9, 1984, p. 1D.

Elliot, Stuart J. "Time Heads South for Winner." *Advertising Age*, February 25, 1985, p. 1.

Hannon, Sharron. "Magazine Publishers Here Gambling with Slim Chance of Profit." *Atlanta Business Chronicle*, November 28, 1983, p. 27.

Krewson, Andria. "*Southern Accents* Ranks 2nd in Growth." *Atlanta Journal*, July 31, 1981, p. 3D.

LeRoux, Margaret. "Publication Accents Genteel South." *Advertising Age*, August 23, 1984, p. 18.

Riley, Sam G. "Southern Accents." In *Magazines of the American South*. Westport, Conn.: Greenwood Press, 1986, pp. 209–212.

"*Southern Accents*." *New York Times*, March 29, 1978, p. IV, 9.

"*Southern Accents* Slows Frequency." *Advertising Age*, February 24, 1992, p. 33.

"The Inc. 500: America's Fastest Growing Private Companies." *Inc.*, December 1983, pp. 113, 124.

Walker, Tom. "Accenting Life in the South Was a Winner." *Atlanta Journal and Constitution*, January 21, 1985, pp. 1C, 6C.

INDEX SOURCES: Avery Index to Architectural Periodicals Supplement, Columbia University.

LOCATION SOURCES: University of Alabama, William Stanley Hode Special Collections Library; Southern Progress Corporation; Library of Congress; and many other libraries.

Publication History

MAGAZINE TITLE AND TITLE CHANGES: *Southern Accents.*

VOLUME AND ISSUE DATA: Vols. 1–(Fall 1977–present). Quarterly (1977–1983); bimonthly (1984–1990); ten issues (1990–1992); eight issues (1992); bimonthly (1993–present).

PUBLISHER AND PLACE OF PUBLICATION: W.R.C. Smith Publishing Company (1977–1986); Southern Accents, Inc. (1986–present). Atlanta, Ga. (1977–1986); Birmingham, Ala. (1987–present).

EDITORS: James A. Hooton (1977–1982); Lisa B. Newsom (1982–1985); Helen C. "Nena" Griffith (1985–1987); Karen Phillips Irons (1987–present).

CIRCULATION: ABC, 1993: 289,048 (paid, primarily subscriptions).

Kelly Saxton and Carrie Brown

SOUTHERN LIVING

Immensely profitable, with a distinctive niche carved out among middle- and upper-class, mostly female southerners, *Southern Living* magazine has a circulation of 2.3 million. The monthly magazine's success is built upon its distinctive appeal to southern tastes.

Called by some writers a "Dixiefied version of *Better Homes and Gardens*," *Southern Living* was founded in 1966 by the Southern Progress Corp., as an offshoot of a special section in the company's flagship publication, the century-old *Progressive Farmer*. "In the mid-1960s, we began to realize that we needed more head room to grow than we would probably have with the farm magazine," remembered Emory Cunningham, founding publisher of *Southern Living* and longtime president of Southern Progress.[1]

Cunningham, who retired in 1988, was the guiding force behind *Southern*

Living. An Alabama native and graduate of Auburn University, he began work at *Progressive Farmer* in 1948, working variously as an editor, advertising manager, advertising director, and, finally, publisher. In 1965, Cunningham proposed a new magazine tailored to southern tastes but also catering to changing southern readers, who increasingly lived in urban, not rural, areas. Potential advertisers in New York were initially skeptical about the magazine's prospects. "They thought we were a bunch of crazy amateurs," Cunningham recalled. "People didn't realize we'd been publishing a regional farm magazine since 1886. Of course, we didn't have millions to start with, so we had to put things on a break-even basis in a hurry."[2]

Southern Living, in fact, did begin to make money in a hurry. The magazine showed a profit after just 18 months of publication. It began with an initial press run of 256,000 copies but increased to a circulation of 1.4 million within a decade. *Forbes* estimated in 1977 that the magazine's profit margin was as high as 30 percent, making it the most profitable magazine in the United States, or, in *Forbes*'s terms, a "down-home equivalent of the U.S. mint."[3]

The magazine's profitability, in fact, led to the sale of Southern Progress Corp. in 1985 to Time Inc., which had had its eye on *Southern Living* since 1970. The $480 million sale package was the highest price paid for a magazine company until that time. The sale included not only *Southern Living* but also other Southern Progress companies, including *Progressive Farmer* and Oxmoor House, a book-publishing subsidiary.[4]

Time Inc.'s interest in *Southern Living* goes a long way toward explaining the magazine's appeal. One reason Time wanted *Southern Living* was the latter's high readership among females. Another was the magazine's unique pull among magazine readers in the South, traditionally a region underrepresented in the circulation patterns of most national publications. As Time Inc. president J. Richard Munro put it in 1985, the Southern Progress Corp. magazines "have achieved success because their staffs are close to their readers, recognize their needs and serve them more effectively than the national magazines with which they compete."[5]

With a circulation area that stretches from Virginia to Texas and covers 17 southern and border states, *Southern Living* blankets the South. States with the highest circulation are, in order: Texas, Florida, North Carolina, and Virginia. Only about 100,000 subscribers live outside the South or in the states that border the region. Average income of *Southern Living* subscribers is $69,110.

Southern Living is written to appeal to the middle-class, urbanized southerner, particularly the southern woman. Articles focus heavily on southern homes and decorating, gardens and landscaping, travel and recreation, foods and entertaining. The magazine emphasizes places and things more than people in its articles, though *Southern Living* now includes a "Southerners" column, which focuses upon interesting residents, and a "Southern Journal," which details life in the South. Columns such as "On the Light Side" and "Quick!" are a regular staple of the food columns. Travel features include "Weekends Away" as well as more lengthy travel pieces. *Southern Living* consistently accents the positive about the South; seldom does it feature advocacy journalism. The magazine is out to save the South, an editor for the magazine once observed, but only "one front yard at a time."[6] The magazine's layout and color photography are superior.

Most *Southern Living* articles are staff-written. The magazine's 550 employees work in Birmingham, Alabama, home of the Southern Progress Corp. since 1911. Standing among a grove of evergreens, oaks, and dogwoods, the company's modern steel-and-glass structure includes kitchens in which recipes are tested before they are published in *Southern Living*. Writers and other employees come from eclectic and diverse backgrounds and include home economists, landscapers, and architects. Don Logan, president and chief executive officer of Southern Progress since Cunningham's retirement in 1988, has worked toward a doctorate in mathematics. *Southern Living* editor John A. Floyd, Jr., has a doctorate in plant physiology.

Floyd is only the third editor of *Southern Living*. The founding editor was Otis Copeland (1966–1969), who was succeeded by Gary McCalla, who held the editor's job from 1969 until Floyd took over in 1990. The current president and chief executive officer is Jim Nelson.

The magazine reaches out to its readers in several unique ways. Since 1988, *Southern Living* has built and opened "Idea Houses," homes built with products and services of *Southern Living* advertisers and then opened for public tours. More than half a million people have toured the idea houses, which both promote the advertisers' products and give visitors ideas for home decorating and landscaping. The houses are promoted by special sections in the magazine. The magazine has also operated *Southern Living* cooking schools around the South since 1975 as part of a promotional tie-in with advertisers. The 90-minute cooking lessons are held in 40 cities each year; each attracts an average of 3,000 people.[7]

Advertising rates for *Southern Living* are high. A full-page, black-and-white ad cost $50,350 in 1994; a full-page color ad cost $71,000. Ads can be purchased by geographic editions or by state. In 1992, ad pages totaled 1,397.[8] In 1993, *Folio* magazine ranked *Southern Living* 29th among the nation's magazines in total revenues. The newsstand price of the magazine is hefty; individual copies are $3.95 each. A yearly subscription costs $32.

Southern Progress continues to publish *Progressive Farmer*, as well as three other monthly magazines—*Southern Accents*,* *Cooking Light*,* and *Travel South*. But *Southern Living* is clearly the company's mainstay. Cunningham once said he believed *Southern Living* to be the best magazine success story of the 1960s and 1970s. "I thought it would be very successful, but we didn't anticipate this," he said. "I thought it would do well and it had the potential of being bigger than the *Progressive Farmer*, but I never dreamed it would be this much bigger."[9]

Notes

1. Kurt Franck, "*Southern Living:* Giant Success Story, Dixie-Style," United Press International, November 8, 1981.

2. "The Most Profitable Magazine in the U.S.," *Forbes*, June 15, 1977, pp. 30–31.

3. Ibid.

4. Alex S. Jones, "Time Inc. Will Buy Magazines," *New York Times*, February 22, 1985, p. D1.

5. Richard Zoglin, "New Additions, Southern Style," *Time*, March 4, 1985, p. 72; Time Inc., after its purchase by Warner Communications, Inc., in 1989, is now known as Time Warner Inc.

6. "The Most Profitable Magazine in the U.S.," pp. 30–31.

7. *Southern Living* press release, March 16, 1994, PR Newswire; Philip H. Dougherty, "Southern Admanship Comes to New York City," *New York Times*, August 3, 1978, p. D13.

8. Paul McDougall, "The Best and the Biggest," *Folio*, September 15, 1993, p. 54.

9. United Press International, November 8, 1981.

Information Sources

BIBLIOGRAPHY:
Dougherty, Philip H. "Southern Admanship Comes to New York City." *New York Times*, August 3, 1978, p. D13.
Franck, Kurt. *Southern Living*: Giant Success Story, Dixie-Style." United Press International, November 8, 1981.
Jones, Alex S. "Time Inc. Will Buy Magazines." *New York Times*, February 22, 1985, p. D1.
McDougall, Paul. "The Best and the Biggest." *Folio,* September 15, 1993, p. 54.
"The Most Profitable Magazine in the U.S." *Forbes*, June 15, 1977, pp. 30–31.
Zoglin, Richard. "New Additions, Southern Style." *Time*, March 4, 1985, p. 72.
INDEX SOURCES: Access: The Supplementary Index to Periodicals.
LOCATION SOURCES: Library of Congress and other libraries.

Publication History

MAGAZINE TITLE AND TITLE CHANGES: *Southern Living.*
VOLUME AND ISSUE DATA: Vols. 1–(February 1966–present). Monthly.
PUBLISHER AND PLACE OF PUBLICATION: Southern Living Inc. (part of the Southern Progress Corp.) (1966–present). Birmingham, Ala.
EDITORS: Otis B. Copeland (1966–1969); Gary E. McCalla (1969–1990); John A. Floyd, Jr. (1990–present).
CIRCULATION: ABC, 1994: 2.3 million (paid, primarily subscriptions).

David Davies

SOUTHERN WOMAN'S MAGAZINE

Southern Woman's Magazine was launched in 1913.[1] A regional periodical edited by women for a predominantly female audience, the magazine can be looked at as a genuine regional expression, distinctly female in character. The magazine targeted the southern homemaker (and future homemaker), while acknowledging the broadening range of the modern woman's sphere. As the publisher explained:

> While the magazine's appeal is primarily to the homemaker, its publishers realize how wide the interest is that goes toward the [perfecting] of woman's work in these alert and broadminded days of ours.[2]

The new southern woman—a white woman of the middle or upper class—was the primary audience, although the magazine often boasted of a demographically diverse readership, with the southern experience as the common bond.[3] One article suggested that the magazine arose from this commonality. Because of the South's

> great community of interests—the need and desire arose for a community magazine. The *Southern Woman's Magazine* is the result. It is the canvas upon which the life of the South is shown month after month. The audience which watches it is varied. The old people love it for the pictures of the old South. The young people love it because it reflects the vivid life of the South of today. The children love it for the hope and promise it foretells of the wonderful South to come.[4]

Its regular departments addressed tradition through housekeeping, gardening, cooking, fashion, domestic hints, and often a children's page, along with memories of the old South most vividly seen in the early columns of the United Daughters of the Confederacy. But the complexities of the new southern woman were also explored, through interviews with successful women in public life as well as features on working girls, canning clubs, and, increasingly, news of women's clubs.

Adopted as the official organ of the League of Southern Writers when that league was about one year old,[5] the magazine kept personal ties with prominent writers. For instance, one contributor gleaned encouragement from Dorothy Dix.[6] The magazine brimmed with fiction, introducing pieces and authors that became award-winning. In ranking short stories of 1916, a Boston literary critic, Edward J. O'Brien, chose "The Knitter of Liege" by Beth Slater Whitson (April 1916) for inclusion in the volume *Best Short Stories of 1916*. He also ranked "with distinction" nine other stories published in the *Southern Woman's Magazine* in 1916. He placed the magazine itself among the top 20, "ranked according to distinction in the quality of fiction published at this time."[7] At this time, also, a new breed of poets had emerged, and their "new poetry" often appeared on its pages.[8] The magazine also fostered its literary legacy by sponsoring frequent writing contests.

A prizewinning essay[9] on "The Woman of the New South" drew the con-

nection between the old South's gentility and its fit in the modern life of the
southern woman:

> The real woman of the New South is not at all new—in the vernacular,
> she is her great-grandmother. . . . Ladies they were . . . who held woman-
> liness their crown and reason for being. . . . whose sacrifices, beautiful and
> fruitful, rebuilded [sic] civilization there in the wilds . . . a-pioneering gal-
> lantly, no less joyously, into the wilds of a workaday world.[10]

The author, a southern woman, discounted the myth of "the 'lazy Southern
woman' so dear to our Northern critics" as but "a figment of sectional imagination."[11] Then, perhaps with a "sectional imagination" of her own, she compared the bygone plantation mistress to a queen possessed of qualities that
enabled her to succeed in business as well as the home by virtue of gracious
command.

> She's nobody's waiting maid, of course, but having all her life com-
> manded, to some extent, she knows the exceeding beauty and virtue of
> doing that which is set her to do as well as she possibly can. . . .
> [W]hatever her calling, her occupation, she is first and foremost a gentle-
> woman.[12]

Typically, articles profiling successful women in traditional male realms reflected this same womanly standard.[13] A woman could attain success in the
public world, but only by retaining her femininity. A typical article lauded a
successful businesswoman for not having succumbed to manly ways in order to
achieve her goals.

> Her manners are in no way mannish, though she can talk business straight
> to the point. In fact, she is the quintessence of feminine gentleness, and
> often, when not busy with matters of business, you will find her busy with
> crochet needle and thread, a wonderful web of lace in her lap to show for
> her labors.[14]

Education for women was encouraged throughout the issues, in advertisements, articles, and even poetry written with the student in mind.[15] With a cover
sketch by illustrator Alice Barber Stephens depicting a girl holding her younger
brother by the hand, both of them dressed and ready for school, the September
1916 issue was called the "School Girl Number." It targeted its regular columns
to her, with "Beauty Helps for the School Girl" and "Just the Sort of Play
That School Girls Like." Also in that issue the best essays solicited that summer
from schoolgirls and schoolboys on "What I Like and What I Do Not Like
about the *Southern Woman's Magazine*" were printed.

Widening the woman's sphere was in keeping with her abilities as well as the times. She had mobility afforded by the train and the automobile, which was already transforming the culture. The freedom of the road echoed in magazine-sponsored contests, travel articles, and regular features devoted to auto maintenance, such as "Her Ladyship—The Motorist."[16]

The editor often tied the home to the community. Women needed to be involved, particularly in ensuring pure food quality and good education. Each woman was charged with keeping the children clean and healthy; advice columnists, including medical doctors, told readers how to do so. The reader also had to ensure the food she fed her family was pure.

Articles highlighted women's organizations, using their "united strength to make better homes, better schools, better surroundings, better scholarship, and better lives."[17] News of women's clubs, with a focus on those of the South and their accomplishments, became a regular feature of the magazine.

Public education was treated as an extension of the home and was often linked to the vote.[18] The second vice president of the National Woman's Suffrage Association wrote that despite the fact that a mother's legal right of guardian to her children was not recognized by most states, she nevertheless had a moral responsibility to educate and train her offspring.

What does it profit a mother to have performed her duty within the limited sphere that used to be considered hers, within the four walls of her own home, if the child has gone out from that home into conditions to which he has succumbed? . . . Does she not know then that her sphere . . . followed her child wherever her child went—into the school, into the town, into the State?[19]

Although the magazine concentrated on woman-as-mother,[20] other causes were also translated as women's concerns, including the use-more-cotton movement. "It is essentially a woman's movement and . . . women of no section of the country are so qualified to understand the cotton situation as the women of the South."[21] This movement operated at many levels, from a New York cotton ball to a girl's cotillion in Nashville.[22]

Even before the United States entered World War I, war accounts ran throughout the issues, often written by women living in Europe. One article noted that a woman was honored for her "bravery by her husband's side in the trenches."[23] More typical, though, was a domestic-based emphasis of woman's peace work in the United States and, later, war work. In keeping with the traditional sphere of womanhood, women were encouraged to knit. Directions were given for specific articles, especially clothing needed by the soldiers and sailors.

Once the United States entered the war, more columns and fiction dealt with war-related aspects from a decidedly patriotic tone. The magazine particularly emphasized the homemaker's role in conserving food. Gone was the strident feminist philosophy of columnist Anne Sherrill Baird that had been with the magazine since its inception. Her last column had railed against antisuffrage forces (particularly those that relied on biblical justification); but what may have been her death knell was her strongly voiced racial sentiment in this last hurrah: "No race of people was ever designed by nature to be peasants or to be servants."[24]

Women of color were by no means absent from the pages. When a young black woman was featured in a fictional story, she was shown in her "place," or through misadventures, to recognize her proper social position—for example, a young woman who, in her desire to acquire white woman's status, bleached her facial skin until it was raw, and she nearly died from blood poisoning. But the near fatal experience taught her a lesson and her place.[25] Although young black women were not numerous in the magazine, images of mammy abounded, glorifying the traditional traits of the house slave: wise matriarch of her black family, compassionate caretaker of her white children, and submissive servant to her white masters. Although nostalgic, mammy was considered an image worth preserving; therefore, the magazine ran numerous accounts in its early years of white women's recollections of mammies.[26]

A mammy-type regular was an "Aunt Jemimy" creation showcased to voice her opinion as if she were in direct, confidential conversation with the reader. This character was given opinions on current issues as a clever mouthpiece for editorializing that might otherwise have been untoward coming from a new southern woman. For example, "Aunt Jemimy" shared her insights on rich women's wartime work, observing, "I reckon dars nuff knittin' goin' on heah en dar to wrap up dis ole earth in a wool sweatuh dis wintuh."[27]

An article about three women successfully pursuing a cottage industry since the 1890s described a literal re-creation of mammy. The three sisters made and marketed a black mammy doll, "whose perfectly molded cheeks, chin, forehead, nose, ears and lips follow identically the African cast of feature."[28] Although hit hard by competition with "Teddy Bear," the business nevertheless introduced black girl (dressed like mammy) and black boy dolls.

Revered but servile, mammy had her place, but outside the pages of the magazine there was no mammy; the new southern household was minus this cook and housekeeper, the magazine complained. With racial difference as its cornerstone, "the servant question" was posed, revealing the editorial stance:

> The question of domestic service is daily becoming more and more one of vital importance. . . . Here in the South we have a race of God-created servants already in our midst. It only remains for the intelligence and the determination of our Southern woman to make use of the material with which Providence has blessed us.[29]

The servant question was one that persisted throughout the life of the magazine. In a unique response to the editorial call for commentary on "The Servant Problem" came a letter by an educated black man from Alabama. In his letter, which was run as a full-page story, he called it *"a very human problem,"* advocating that domestic service "be put on a business basis."[30]

Business was an emerging theme in the magazine.[31] The homemaker was made aware of her buying power. With "the purchasing power of the world," the southern woman had an enormous responsibility, with an equally enormous potential for guilt: "Her responsibility is great. She owes it to those for whom she is steward to make the best of her opportunities and to do her part in bringing about the general prosperity of the country."[32]

Certainly, part of her responsibility was to patronize the magazine advertiser. The greatest amount of advertising was for cooking and cleaning products, but women's colleges and seminaries also formed a mainstay of *Southern Woman's Magazine* advertising, particularly in the fall issues. For instance, the full-page ad for Nashville's Ward-Belmont College advocated a well-rounded education: "In work and play the girls of Ward-Belmont are stimulated to their FINEST interest, enjoyment and achievement in all that leads to their physical, social, intellectual and moral development."[33] Like many other women's magazines of the day, the *Southern Woman's Magazine* guaranteed the advertising run on its pages.

Despite steady advertising and a dramatic increase in circulation, the magazine ceased publication in 1918, five and a half years after its launch. The growing circulation was blamed for an erratic production schedule.[34] A Chicago address had been added to the publishers' box, spreading the publishing and editorial effort among Chicago, St. Louis, and Nashville. Although the editor remained, and the covers were done by many of the same artists, many original contributors were gone. The magazine folded during World War I, although nearly every article was devoted to the South's role or women's role in that effort. Miscellaneous extant issues attest to attempted start-ups after that date, such as an issue dated March 1921, which ran primarily reprinted stories from earlier issues; no editor was listed for that issue.

Notes

1. This would place the *Southern Woman's Magazine* in the early stages of increased southern magazine start-ups. Sam G. Riley and Gary Selnow in "Southern Magazine Publishing, 1764–1984," *Journalism Quarterly* 65 (1988), pp. 898–901, observe that in the period 1881–1914, 782 southern magazines were started, with mean start-ups per year at 23. From 1915 to 1944, they note, "the pace quickened," with 1,099 start-ups and a mean of 36.6 start-ups per year for that period (p. 900).

2. "What You Will Like in This Number," publisher's note, March 1915, p. 3.

3. Published for the most part in Nashville, Tennessee, the magazine covered the southeastern states (Alabama, Florida, Georgia, Louisiana, Mississippi, North Carolina, South Carolina, Tennessee, Virginia), including Mason-Dixon states Maryland and Kentucky. It also covered Arkansas, Texas, and Missouri (especially when publishing moved to St. Louis) and occasionally New Mexico and Oklahoma. The magazine also circulated to women reared in the South living outside the South.

4. Laura Norvell Elliott, "The South's Own Magazine," December 1917, p. 34.

5. "The League of Southern Writers," May 1915, p. 8.

6. Vera Morel, "Does It Pay? Being a Face-to-Face Interview with a Dream," February 1915, p. 16.

7. The *Boston Transcript*, quoted in "A New Honor for the South," April 1917, p. 3. All 30 stories published in the *Southern Woman's Magazine* in 1916 were indexed, and the Whitson story was abstracted in Edward J. O'Brien, *The Best Short Stories of 1916* (Boston: Small, Maynard, 1917). In the succeeding two annual volumes of best short stories, the *Southern Woman's Magazine* was listed, but it does not appear that its fiction was indexed.

8. Poetry published in the *Southern Woman's Magazine* by authors including Grace Cook Allen, Jane Belfield, Sara Day, and Adele E. Shaw is indexed in Editorial Board (eds.), *Index to Poetry in Periodicals, 1915–1919* (Great Neck, N.Y.: Granger, 1981).

9. Dorothy Dix, "Mrs. Williams and the Dixie Club," March 1915, p. 10. Dix noted that this was the best of 97 essays submitted to the Dixie Club of New York.

10. Martha McCulloch Williams, "The Woman of the New South: A Record of Beliefs and Opinions," March 1915, p. 10.

11. Ibid.

12. Ibid.

13. See "The Story of a Southern Business Woman," January 1915, p. 18.

14. May Selley, "The Little Office and How It Grew: Being the True Story of a Successful Southern Business Woman," January 1915, p. 18.

15. For example, see Adele E. Shaw, "The Girl Graduate," June 1914, p. 29.

16. For example, see C. P. Christopher, "Her Ladyship—The Motorist/Things of Interest to Women Gathered from the Automobile World," January 1917, p. 38, which focused on maintenance of tires and tubes.

17. From the pledge of the Woman's Health Protection Association of Galveston, Texas, "The Women of Galveston," June 1914, p. 10.

18. Although the editorial stance was ambiguous about suffrage, various staffers were pro-suffrage. The November 1914 issue was dedicated as the Suffrage Convention Number to highlight coverage of the convention in Nashville. Antisuffrage voices could also be heard in the magazine, such as Katharine Atherton Grimes, "Are Southern Women Ready to Vote—A Protest," March 1915, p. 14.

19. Madeline McD[owell] Breckenridge, "A Mother's Sphere," February 1915, p. 10.

20. Particularly in the "Better Mothers" campaign begun in September 1916 ("Better Mothers," August 1916, p. 3).

21. Genevieve Champ Clark, "The Cotton Crusade and What It Means," December 1914, p. 14.

22. "Cotton Gowns the Southern Women Wear/Recollections of Two Cotton Balls," January 1915, p. 15.

23. "Women at the Front," January 1915, p. 4.

24. Anne Sherrill Baird, "A Little Window on the World," September 1916, p. 16.

25. Maria Thompson Daviss, "The Bleaching of Clarabel Ella," May 1915, p. 7.

26. For example, Harriet Parks Miller, "Black Mammy Emily," June 1915, p. 20; also the series by Florence Workman, "Chronicles of Mammy," for example, "When Mammy Chaperoned," December 1914, p. 15. In what was perhaps the magazine's longest-running series devoted to a black, the Uncle Remus character Aunt Dice was given chapter after chapter of a noble servant's life until her death in Chapter 18 (Nina Hill Robinson, "Aunt Dice—The Story of a Faithful Slave," May 1915, p. 19).

27. Cally Ryland, "Aunt Jemimy Talks about the War," January 1915, p. 8.

28. Mattie Lee Hausgen, "The Original Black Mammy Doll," October 1914, p. 16.

29. "The Question of Servants," editorial note, April 1915, p. 15.

30. Isaac Fisher, "What We Know about Servants/A Discussion of the South's Servant Problem/By the Son of a Slave," October 1916, p. 8.

31. For example, the column "Women and Finance" by May Shelley was begun in July 1916 (p. 28).

32. Clark, "The Cotton Crusade and What It Means," p. 14.

33. September 1916, p. 2, inside front cover.

34. "Announcement," June 1918, p. 3. (The May issue was omitted, and the year's later numbers combined into bimonthlies.)

Information Sources

BIBLIOGRAPHY:

O'Brien, Edward J. *Best Short Stories of 1916*. Boston: Small, Maynard, 1917.

INDEX SOURCES: Index to Poetry in Periodicals; American Poetic Renaissance, 1915–1919.

LOCATION SOURCES: The State Library of Virginia; Tennessee State Library and Archives and other libraries, especially in the South.

Publication History

MAGAZINE TITLE AND TITLE CHANGES: *Southern Woman's Magazine.*

VOLUME AND ISSUE DATA: Vols. 1–10 (1913–1918). Monthly (except 1918: omitted May issue, combined July/August, September/October. Vol. 10, nos. 1–2 omitted in numbering; many issues carry no volume or number).

PUBLISHER AND PLACE OF PUBLICATION: Southern Woman's Magazine Company. Nashville, Tenn. (listed with St. Louis in 1917; Chicago added in 1918).

EDITORS: Anne P. Rankin (1913–1918).

CIRCULATION: Magazine Cover, 1918: 125,000.

Therese L. Lueck

T

'TEEN

Since 1957, *'Teen* has successfully marketed a stable vision of a mostly white, middle-class teenage culture for its 12-to-18-year-old female readers. In the *'Teen* universe, little has changed since the postwar boom of the 1950s that created a new youth market stimulated by singer/actor Elvis Presley and actor James Dean. Acne, clothes, dating, sex, celebs, and family squabbles seem to have lost none of their fascination. With its chief competitors—*Seventeen*,* *Sassy*,* and *YM*—*'Teen* sustains the myth of a common language and a stable identity for all American teenagers.

'Teen is owned by the Petersen Publishing Company, founded by Robert E. Petersen, who in 1948 began targeting magazines to hobby enthusiasts, mostly teenage boys. The son of an automobile mechanic, Petersen based his publishing empire on America's postwar obsession with cars—*Hot Rod, Motor Trend, Rod & Custom*, and others. He diversified with other hobby magazines like *Guns & Ammo* and *Skin Diver*. Because of the hobby market's faddish nature, Petersen kept staff small and expenses low, always ready to suspend publication if his audience's interest waned. *'Teen* proved an exception. Petersen was committed to making the magazine "stable" in advertising, circulation, and presentation.[1]

Under the editorship of Charles Laufer, a former Beverly Hills high school teacher who proclaimed himself the "world's oldest teenager," *'Teen* began with an unsure sense of audience. In content and tone, the magazine resembled an expanded high school newspaper and was aimed at both boys and girls. Accompanied by black-and-white photos, lengthy features covered an eclectic mix of sports, fashion, beauty, humor, entertainment, education, careers, and, above all, celebrity gossip aimed at devotees of Elvis and other teen idols. Few pages were devoted to advertising.

In its early years, the magazine formed an identity that would remain constant despite a major shift in audience. Its letters section, "We Get," and its advice column, "Dear Jill," established *'Teen* as a popular forum, encouraging reader response. Over the years, *'Teen* has continued to elicit that response through beauty contests, opinion surveys, teenage guest editors and correspondents, and other write-in columns on beauty, health, interpersonal relationships, and pets. Indeed, *'Teen* markets itself as a magazine for teenagers "that is all their own."[2] In 1957, fully half of the letters written to *'Teen* were by boys, who seemed just as interested as girls in acne, dating, clothes, the singing duo the Everly Brothers, and James Dean's demise.

By the early 1960s, the number of boys writing to *'Teen* had declined dramatically, as the magazine sought a more meaningful union between its audience and the cosmetics industry. To establish a concrete advertising base, the magazine shifted its focus to its female audience, though many of its themes remained the same. For example, *'Teen*'s early issues devoted nearly 10 percent of their pages to football, boxing, and cars, clearly aimed at a male audience. One of *'Teen*'s quirks is its abiding interest in the automobile, apparently stemming from its publishing roots. Early issues featured a spread on Fords and a photograph of "Denver's Prettiest Hotrodder"; over the years, feature articles have discussed safe driving, car purchasing, women's motocross clubs, and even a supposed national plot to take away teenage drivers' licenses.

Sports have also maintained a place in *'Teen*. Women's sports were once treated humorously. The November 1957 issue featured black-and-white snapshots of the "Judo Janes," members of a high school judo club who tossed men over their shoulders. The article explained that this was not a frightening, defeminizing show of strength but merely an example of "leverage." *'Teen* continued its coverage of girls' sports, but in a different vein as it began to take its young female audience seriously. By November 1963, "Judo Jane" had become a "top karate expert." In the mid-1970s, the magazine held an "Athlete of the Year" contest and in 1989 began an annual "Sportsgirl of the Year" contest.

The contest has been a feature of *'Teen* since its beginnings. Its first, in 1957, was the James Dean Scholarship in the Dramatic Arts Competition, which sent young men to study at the Pasadena Playhouse. Educational importance was abandoned in 1959 when the annual Miss *'Teen* Contest was established with the help of celebrity judges Robert Wagner, Paul Newman, Janet Leigh, and Shirley MacLaine. The Miss *'Teen* Contest, along with an increasing emphasis on health, beauty, and fashion, helped the magazine solidify its audience and solicit advertising from the cosmetics industry. By the late 1960s, acne medications and blemish-free teenage models were featured in page after slick page. Articles on women's health attracted advertisements for Kotex and Pursettes; sewing and craft instructions were joined by advertisements from Singer and Simplicity.

A most regular and important part of *'Teen*, beauty contests ("Great Model Search," "Miss Teenage America," "Superface") have consistently attracted major advertisers, evoked a massive reader response, and reinforced a uniform vision of teenage identity, cosmetically enhanced and, with few exceptions, white. (Although Asian American and African American faces appear more frequently in the *'Teen* of the 1990s, they are still rare.) *'Teen*'s marketing strategy not only reinforces advertising with articles and columns on beauty, health, and sewing but urges teenagers to fully participate through endless contests. Thus, a young woman might dream of seeing her "superface"—enhanced by Clearasil and Neutrogena—on the pages of *'Teen* next to other "top teenage models." The magazine boasts that its 1992 "Superface" contest elicited 15,600 entries, and its 1992 "Great Model Search," 20,000 entries.[3] *'Teen* is careful not to alienate less-than-perfect teenagers: "Sportsgirl of the Year" nominees are allowed to wear glasses and braces.

While in the late 1950s teenage boys were active participants in *'Teen*, they were reduced to heartthrobs with the "Mr. *'Teen* Contest" of 1961. Teenage boys do not directly participate in *'Teen*'s annual "guy" contests: they are nominated by girlfriends or sisters. Like the celebrities who pepper *'Teen*'s pages—from Earl Holliman and Van Johnson to Luke Perry and Johnny Depp—teenage boys are represented as aloof and nearly godlike, passing horrific judgment on girls with never-ending complexion, hair, and personality problems. For example, in "He Tells You What He Hates" (June 1993), a "group of guys" gave *'Teen* readers advice on "Hair Hassles," "Makeup Mistakes," "Nail No-No's," and even "Hygiene Horrors": "I avoid sloppy looking girls." Under this severely critical eye, teenage girls frantically write to *'Teen* advice columnists and take "personality quotient" tests.

'Teen recognized early its audience's buying power, valued in 1993 at $32 billion.[4] *'Teen* devotes nearly half of its pages to advertising, often indiscernible in design from the features, columns, and fashion spreads. Despite the wealth generated by this market, *'Teen* has always catered to lower-middle- to middle-class teenagers with limited individual spending power. *'Teen* has the least expensive cover price among its competitors. Bargain shopping, money-saving crafts projects, and income-earning schemes are often featured. Advice on careers stresses realistic preparation and practical vocations, like robot repair and nursing. Advertised products are in the low to moderately priced range—Noxzema and Cutex.

Still, the rich and famous are omnipresent in *'Teen*: a continual parade of romantic, strong-jawed, bedroom-eyed male stars, "dreamy" or "hunky," depending on the vernacular, and nearly interchangeable over the last few decades. This libidinous aspect of *'Teen* is often reinforced in its romantic fiction: "[M]y boyfriend's bare legs felt strong and muscular as I drowsily rested my head on them."[5] But *'Teen*'s features, which most frequently cover dating and sex, are ambiguous and often admonishing. As its August 1986 cover announced, *'Teen* attracts readers with "Boys! Sex! Problems! Answers!" By the 1980s, under the editorship of Roxanne Camron, the magazine had moved beyond discussions of dating etiquette to explicit articles on rape, sexually transmitted diseases, teenage pregnancy, prostitution, and physically abusive boyfriends. In September 1981, *'Teen* ran "Your Body and His," a "sex education guide" with textbook diagrams of male and female genitalia, a glossary of proper terms, and advice on "surviving the first pelvic exam." The magazine takes its educational function seriously, though its sex articles, drawn from popular sources, are sometimes confusing and misleading. Its initial coverage of acquired immunodeficiency syndrome (AIDS) in June 1987, for example, was unenlightening for anyone who had never bought or used a condom.

For most controversial topics, *'Teen* has traditionally relied on reader opinion polls. Over the years, *'Teen* readers have been surveyed on smoking, national service, the voting age, the Vietnam War, integration, abortion, and interracial and interfaith dating. Thus, *'Teen* has generally avoided politics in its editorial content, presenting, instead, an uninformed set of readers' opinions. In September 1970, *'Teen* reached its nadir when it called its fashion spread, featuring all white models, a "civil writes [*sic*] movement." In the mid-1970s, in the wake of the second-wave feminist movement, *'Teen*'s feature content briefly strayed into overtly political territory. Its October 1975 issue's "Guide to Careers" centered on an interview with a *Ms.* editor who advocated passage of the equal rights amendment (ERA) and encouraged young women to enter nontraditional jobs. That same issue included a weighty discussion of Alvin Toffler's *Future Shock* and forecasts for the year 2000 on careers, education, law, medicine, and science. Such high seriousness was quickly abandoned.

'Teen prefers lighter and more stable subjects than politics, subjects like dating, friendship, and hair. Brief, serious articles on drug abuse, television violence, and herpes are interspersed with exposés of Satanism and instructions in astrology, psychic powers, and palmistry. Short, undemanding blocks of text, easy to read and absorb, are interspersed with bold, colorful headlines and subtitles. *'Teen* claims that it is concerned about young adult literacy and suggests that its letters sections and beauty contest applications *"encourage* readers to communicate (in writing) as part of a 'honing' process."[6]

While *'Teen* is sold mostly through annual subscriptions, it targets a narrow audience whose average age is 15. Since its age-bound readership changes regularly, *'Teen* can frequently replay its primary themes, with little innovation, slightly adapted to the fashion and mores of the day. Mother-daughter relationships are a perennial topic. *'Teen* has some stake in resolving intergenerational conflict, since it has created a singular teenage identity, blithely sailing across generations through the changing winds of history and culture. Presumably, the mothers of today—incomprehensible to their teenage daughters—were once *'Teen*-reading teenagers themselves. *'Teen* likes to promote alliances between mothers and daughters, thus encouraging a stable consumer base. In its editorial profile, the magazine claims that it provides parents with "a common ground of communication with their daughters."[7] Constantly examined in letters, poems, and features, female friendship is also integral in *'Teen* world. In 1993, the magazine had a rate base at over 1 million, but it claimed a readership of over 4 million[8]; thus, *'Teen* and its advertisers rely on teenage girls' friendship and exchange.

'*Teen* has been highly successful at promoting its vision of happily dating, acne-free American teenage girls. Its strategy of combining editorial content and advertising with reader response has worked well to create a conventional '*Teen* culture based on beauty and health product consumption. '*Teen* claims to "serve the total needs of girls 12–19"[9]; clearly, those needs are created and sustained by the magazine itself.

Notes

1. Robert E. Petersen, quoted in "Driving Down a New Road," *Business Week*, October 10, 1964, p. 144.
2. " 'TEEN-GRAM," Media Kit.
3. " 'TEEN Readers Respond," Media Kit.
4. " 'I Bought What's on Sale," *Brandweek* February 22, 1993, p. 12.
5. Vicki Grove, "Love's Little Ups and Downs," June 1993, p. 26.
6. "Ill-literate: Publishers Have a Problem," 'TEEN *Tested Topics* (supplement to '*Teen* magazine) 37:5, p. 3.
7. Rate Card #41, p. 1.
8. Ibid.
9. Ibid.

Information Sources

BIBLIOGRAPHY:
"Driving Down a New Road." *Business Week*, October 10, 1964, pp. 143–144, 148.
Harris, Dixie Dean. "And This, Dear God, Is What They Read." *Esquire*, July 1965, pp. 50–51, 105–106, 108.
———. " '*Teen* Magazine," in R. Gordon Kelly (ed.), *Children's Periodicals of the United States*. Westport, Conn.: Greenwood Press, 1984.
"Hot-Rod Journalism." *Fortune*, February 1957, p. 184.
"Hot Magazine." *Time*, October 21, 1957, p. 87.
Paris, Ellen. "Know Thy Readers." *Forbes*, August 29, 1983, p. 54.
"Rich on Wheels." *Time*, June 24, 1966, p. 98.
INDEX SOURCES: Magazine Index; Popular Magazine Review (1984–present); Readers' Guide to Periodical Literature; Readers' Guide Abstracts.
LOCATION SOURCES: Library of Congress and other libraries. All issues are available on microfilm from University Microfilms International, Ann Arbor, Mich.

Publication History

MAGAZINE TITLE AND TITLE CHANGES: '*Teen.*
VOLUME AND ISSUE DATA: Vols. 1–(June 1957–present). Monthly.
PUBLISHER AND PLACE OF PUBLICATION: Petersen Publishing Company. Los Angeles.
EDITORS: Charles Laufer (1960–1965); Robert Macleod (1965–1973); Roxanne Camron (1973–present).
CIRCULATION: ABC, 1993: 1,100,000 (paid, primarily subscriptions).

Ann E. Larabee

TODAY'S CHRISTIAN WOMAN

As the mass magazine market was fragmenting in the 1970s, evangelical Christian women looked elsewhere than the "Seven Sisters," the fashion books, and the supermarket checkout display for magazines to support their traditional values, provide role models, and give them practical support for family, church, and career. The agreement among 39 women's magazine editors to devote their July 1977 issues to a discussion of the equal rights amendment may have underlined the feeling of cultural estrangement these women felt from the political feminism being covered in the mass magazines. In reflecting on that decade, longtime editor Dale Hanson Bourke said in a published interview, "The seventies held a lot of negative manifestations of feminism. Christian women were looking for a magazine they could identify with, one that understood they couldn't relate to some of the values that permeated secular women's magazines."[1]

Into this climate appeared *Today's Christian Woman's* first issue, fall/winter 1978–1979. Singer Anita Bryant, who had a year earlier spearheaded a campaign that resulted in repeal of a controversial homosexual rights ordinance, was featured on the cover. A blurb promised to explore "America's Love-Hate Relationship with Anita Bryant." The publisher was the respected religious book publisher, Fleming H. Revell Co., Old Tappan, New Jersey. In a page one introduction, its president, William R. Barbour, Jr., wrote:

> You won't find everything in *Today's Christian Woman* that you find in secular women's magazines. We have no bedroom hints (unless you're looking for decorating ideas), no astrology charts, no personality profiles (unless it's of a Christian with something to say), no gossip.
>
> But you will find in *Today's Christian Woman* many of the good things you've come to expect from women's magazines and a good deal more. Sure, we cover budgeting, travel, food, plants, beauty, decorating, and so forth, but our feature articles are about women who are different—some well known, but even more who could be your neighbors.
>
> The women who write for us or whom we feature have encountered God through Jesus Christ.[2]

The editor on the masthead was Jerry Bruce, a pseudonym for Jerry Bruce Jenkins, then an editor with *Moody Monthly* magazine in Chicago. In the magazine's tenth-anniversary edition, he revealed his identity and how his magazine idea became reality after he had talked with Barbour.[3] Because he was not ready for a job change or geographic change, he freelanced the project, using his first and middle names. His Moody employer agreed as long as the magazines did not compete for the same advertisers. When Revell had to seek advertisers after the first two issues, Jerry decided to remain with his old job. As the vice president of publishing for Moody Bible Institute, Jenkins reflected in 1988 on the beginnings of *Today's Christian Woman*, his fascination with its growth, and the decision, which he never regretted, to turn over the editing of the new magazine to others.

Others who were involved in the beginnings of the magazine were Hugh Barbour, William's brother and Revell vice president; consultant Richard Baltzel, then editorial director for Revell; Davis W. Schultz, who ran the marketing efforts as publication director; and Dorianne R. Perrucci, who was managing editor after Bruce (Jenkins) left.[4]

An early issue of *Today's Christian Woman* gained the attention of Dale Hanson Bourke, who was then a marketing consultant in Washington, D.C. After the publisher repeatedly told her he was not ready to promote the magazine aggressively, he finally said that what the publication really needed was an editor. Because Bourke seemed more enthusiastic about it than anyone else, he asked her to consider the position.[5] She accepted and continued on the masthead for more than ten years. She wrote a back-page column, "Reflections," through November/December 1991.

Bourke frequently interviewed Christian music stars, authors, television personalities, or wives of high-profile evangelical leaders. In one of her columns, she summed up her editorial perspective and the direction of the magazine: "I read the daily newspaper for information, but I still turn to the Bible for direction and inspiration. And I know that there are many women in the world like me. . . . We know that the world seems more complicated than ever. We realize that women today have to deal with changing roles. But we also believe with all of our hearts that some things never change."[6]

Today's Christian Woman features cover photographs and lead profiles of the evangelical elite. It is a sort of *People* magazine for Christians. Former First Lady Rosalynn Carter was the subject of a profile in 1980.[7] Cover profiles have included Ruth Bell Graham, wife of evangelist Billy Graham; Elizabeth Dole, wife of senator Robert Dole and president of the American Red Cross; and Marilyn Quayle, wife of the former vice president. Christian music stars are also frequent subjects. Joni Eareckson Tada, artist, radio personality ("Joni and Friends"), and spokeswoman for the disabled, has appeared on the cover three times. There are no regular fashion or home decorating features. Hospitality is emphasized rather than entertaining. Practical information has been offered in articles on topics such as shopping for a home computer, choosing a church, creating memorable family events, making friends, and raising emotionally healthy kids. Provocative guest columnists are given opportunity to express ideas that may vary from the editorial views. During the 1980s that feature was titled, "The Way I See It." In the 1990s, the standing head "Viewpoints" publishes reader responses to a question posed in an earlier issue. Readers respond to questions such as "Do you think sex education should be taught in the schools? Why or why not?" and "What advice would you give to a woman ten years

younger than you?'' and "How do you decide which ministries to support?''
Responses indicate a variety of views.

Advertisements in *Today's Christian Woman* are mostly for Christian colleges, books, psychological therapies, music, videos, and international relief organizations. A small "Marketplace" section publishes classifieds for employment and services. Single copies of the magazine are available at Christian bookstores.

Notes

1. Sharon Donohue, "Can a Woman Have It All?'' July/August 1988, p. 37.
2. William R. Barbour, Jr., "Welcome to *Today's Christian Woman*," Fall/Winter 1978/79, p. 1.
3. Jerry Bruce Jenkins, "In the Beginning . . . ,'' July/August 1988, p. 8.
4. Ibid.
5. Donohue, "Can a Woman Have It All?'' p. 36.
6. Dale Hanson Bourke, "The New Traditional Woman,'' March/April 1987, p. 5.
7. Edna Langford, "My Friend Rosalynn,'' Fall 1990, pp. 63–65.

Information Sources

BIBLIOGRAPHY:
Board, Stephen. "Moving the World with Magazines: A Survey of Evangelical Periodicals.'' In Quentin J. Schultze (ed.), *American Evangelicals and the Mass Media*, Grand Rapids, Mich.: Academie Books, 1990, pp. 119–142.
INDEX SOURCES: Christian Periodical Index; Current Thoughts & Trends (before August 1990 known as Current Christian Abstracts).
LOCATION SOURCES: Library of Congress; Dallas Theological Seminary, Tex.; Moody Bible Institute, Chicago; Trinity Evangelical Divinity School, Deerfield, Ill.; and other libraries.

Publication History

MAGAZINE TITLE AND TITLE CHANGES: *Today's Christian Woman*.
VOLUME AND ISSUE DATA: Vols. 1–(Fall/Winter 1978/1979–present). Quarterly (Fall/Winter 1978/79–1983); six times a year (November/December 1983–present).
PUBLISHER AND PLACE OF PUBLICATION: Fleming H. Revell Co., (1978–July/August 1985); Christianity Today, Inc. (September/October 1985–present). Old Tappan, N.J. (1978–1985); Carol Stream, Ill. (1985–present).
EDITORS: Jerry Bruce (pseudonym for Jerry Bruce Jenkins) (1978–1979); Dorianne R. Perrucci (1979–1980); Dale Hanson Bourke (1980–1988); Sharon Donohue (1988); Rebecca K. Grosenbach (1989–1990); Julie A. Talerico (1990–1994); Ramona Cramer Tucker (1994–present).
CIRCULATION: Gale, 1994: 180,000 paid, 4,730 nonpaid.

Anna R. Paddon

TRUE STORY

In 1919, flamboyant publisher Bernarr Macfadden introduced a new magazine, *True Story*. In the process, he changed the woman's magazine niche forever. It was not necessarily a change for the better, critics contended. One contemporary branded the enormously successful "confessional" *True Story* "the catharsis for the sex urge of the multitudes" and Macfadden with having the "intuitive knowledge of what the mob desires and amazing lack of good taste."[1] Another charged that Macfadden was "an influence cheapening the public taste."[2] Yet another credited *True Story* with creating the "I'm Ruined! I'm Ruined! school of belles lettres."[3] Another saw hope; perhaps Macfadden and his *True Story* would be only a passing fancy, a postwar distraction.[4]

Of course, the magazine was not a postwar (World War I) distraction. It has survived the Great Depression; another world war; McCarthyism; the Korean, Vietnam, and Persian Gulf wars; the civil rights, women's rights, and peace movements; and the "me" decade of the 1980s. Indeed, each of these moments in history has spurred its own "real-life" narratives for *True Story* readers. Researchers now look to Macfadden's creation to gauge what women of the wage-earning class read during pivotal periods in American history.[5] That kind of scholarly examination has not necessarily brought the magazine respectability. Few community or university libraries retain back issues of the magazine.[6]

Bernarr Macfadden probably would not have been surprised by that. He and his *True Story* achieved enormous financial success but always remained controversial figures in American magazine publishing circles.

The story of *True Story* could be the stuff of the magazine itself. It is not just the dry tale of advertising and circulation gains—and declines. It is the amazing, dramatic, "real-life" narrative of a magazine and its editors that overcame all conventional wisdom in publishing and became a success (the happy ending).

Who came up with the idea for *True Story* remains a point of much debate. Both Bernarr Macfadden and his wife claimed credit for the idea. Both pointed to the letters sent by women to *Physical Culture*, the original Macfadden magazine, as the trigger for *True Story*. These letters, according to both of the Macfaddens, pointed to problems of "conduct and human relations" that these women were experiencing at the end of World War I.[7] Either Bernarr or Mary Macfadden saw the publishing potential there, and plans were laid for the launch.[8] Yet another version had Bernarr Macfadden coming up with the idea for the magazine after attending a publishers conference where he learned of the enormous profitability of pulp magazines and launched *True Story* as his version.[9] Wherever the idea for *True Story* came from, Macfadden borrowed $1 million and launched the magazine.

True Story was not an overnight success. In spite of a lurid cover with such headlines as "And Their Love Turned to Hatred," the first issue sold only a respectable 60,000 issues on the newsstand for 20¢, about double the going rate for popular magazines of the day. The first issue contained 12 letters that had been written to *Physical Culture*. The stories were illustrated by photographs, an innovation at the time. While the first issue was filled with letters that had been sent to *Physical Culture*, *True Story* soon had its pick of "real-life" romance manuscripts. Additional editorial material poured into the editorial offices in response to advertising soliciting such material in *Physical Culture* and contests with large prizes in *True Story*.

The editor in these early years was John Brennan, a longtime associate of Macfadden and former editor of *Physical Culture*. However, his control over the magazine was minimal. Brennan was not allowed to select the stories used, nor could he edit them closely. He was charged solely with "Get the book out—on *time*."[10] The power to select stories was left to Macfadden (and his wife before the divorce), an ever-changing editorial board of working-class women,[11] and a panel of clergymen.

The editorial selection at *True Story* differed from the process followed at most magazines of the time. The manuscript went initially to a board of "girl readers" who rated the manuscript between 90 and 100 for reader appeal. Macfadden (and his wife before the divorce) read the highest-rated manuscripts and made the final decision.

Another layer of review was added after some clergy began to denounce the magazine as "lewd" and "pornographic" and organized boycotts; Macfadden responded initially by hiring a clergyman as an associate editor. Subsequently, Macfadden organized a "ministerial advisory board": a rabbi, a priest, and Methodist, Presbyterian, and Congregationalist ministers. That board mitigated much of the criticism of the magazine.[12]

The ministers had much to comment upon. Many of the early "real-life" narratives dealt with changing moral codes in America. Anonymous, first-person narratives carried such titles as "The Wages of Sin," "The Easiest Way," "Woman with a Past," and "Keeping up with the Crowd."[13] Photographs illustrated these stories. The staged photos initially featured members of editor Brennan's family, but eventually professional models, some dramatic unknowns, took over. Thus, at one time, actor Fredric March and actresses Norma Shearer and Jean Arthur appeared in photos illustrating one lurid tale or another.[14]

True Story always paid well for its first-person narratives. Not only did the magazine offer a $1,000 monthly prize for the most compelling first-person account, but it paid well to its nonwinners. That meant that the magazine drew manuscripts not only from working-class women and men but also from professional writers. For example, reporter/editor Emile Gauvreau sold three stories to *True Story* in the 1920s for $150 apiece, more than he was making in one week as a newspaper reporter.[15] The high rates and the monthly prizes triggered a flood of manuscripts—70,000 to 100,000 a year.[16] The magazine, while generous with its editorial rates, scrimped on production. The magazine initially was printed on cheap pulp paper. Once the magazine achieved some success, however, Macfadden switched to a better-quality paper.

Although the magazine struggled initially, its days of uncertainty were limited. Newsstand sales accelerated. Within six years, the magazine's circulation exceeded 2 million. Circulation hovered around the 2-million mark throughout much of the 1920s. Those figures were not lost on the competition—or Macfadden himself. Soon there was a whole school of "confession" magazines. *True Confessions, I Confess*, and *Modern Romances* came from competitors. Macfadden launched *True Romances, True Experiences*, and *Love and Romance*. None, however, really challenged *True Story*'s dominance in the market. *True Story* remains the leader in the "confession" women's magazine niche.

The depression, however, did take its toll. Circulation declined. In 1933, *True Story*'s circulation was 1,597,247. By 1936, the magazine recovered somewhat to 1,896,456. However, Macfadden had to reduce its price during the period—from $2.50 in 1933 to $1.50 in 1936.

Subscription prices were not the only thing to reflect the hard times the readership was facing. Macfadden and his new editor, William Jourdan Rapp, offered stories designed to appeal to readers facing economic crises. The stories included "The Test of His Family's Love," "When Help Came from Heaven," and "When I Needed Her Most."[17] The importance of family could also be seen in such regular features as "Home Problems Forum" and "True Story Homemaker."[18] The lurid sexual materials that had characterized some of the stories during Brennan's tenure had long before disappeared. Rapp, when he joined the magazine in 1926, shifted the magazine from "sex to social significance" and de-emphasized the sexual aspects of the magazine's content.[19] That repositioning served the magazine well during the depression, when the publication emphasized the power of faith and family life.

World War II found *True Story* committed to building morale. Its narratives reflected war themes: "Army Nurse," "I Was a Nazi Wife!" and "We Shall Build Good Ships."[20] War workers were prominently featured—and were heroines. As one anonymous writer explained, "I was so thrilled to be learning aircraft production that I didn't know anything else existed."[21]

Rapp left *True Story* in 1942. Henry Lieferant, who had been editor of *True Story*'s sister publication *True Romances*, took over. *True Story*, under Lieferant, began its upward circulation climb. By the time he left in 1947, circulation exceeded 2.2 million. But that was just the beginning of *True Story*'s recovery. The magazine's circulation peaked in the 1950s; by 1958, it topped 2.6 million. *True Story* was the largest periodical in Macfadden's Women's Group and the biggest romance/confession publication in the nation.

True Story's narratives of the 1950s showed the power of love and romance; but, as had been the case, especially since Rapp had been editor, the magazine also emphasized traditional values and norms winning out in the end. A mother's love was paramount in "Flood! A Story of a Mother's Deathless Courage."

Teens seemed to be a recurring worry as *True Story* mothers read "Truant Teens" and "Wild Prom Party."[22] Nonetheless, the message remained the same: women needed to adhere to traditional moral standards—or face the consequences.

That kind of moral imperative greatly affected the *True Story* of the 1960s. Nonetheless, the magazine could not ignore the events that were affecting the lives of women in America. The Vietnam War began to figure into the narratives of the magazine. The televised coverage of the war offered the slant for the story, "On My TV set . . . I Saw My Husband Shot Down in Vietnam! Is He Alive or Dead?"[23]

Shifting moral standards were challenging the 1960s *True Story* reader. She looked to the magazine to help her resolve some of these challenges—and found a traditional moral resolution to her problems. Anonymous first-person narratives offered "My Priest Is My Husband," "Married to 2 Men—but I Wasn't a Bigamist!" "Is My Mother after My Man?" "I Was Hypnotized into Pregnancy," and "He Was Innocent, yet I *Had* to Tell the Police: *HE ATTACKED ME!*" Although many of the stories seemed improbable, they seemed to strike a responsive chord among the readers. *True Story* continued to appeal to a large audience. Although the magazine failed to match the record numbers in the 1950s, it still had a respectable circulation of 2 million or more throughout the 1960s. This was not a level that editors could sustain in the 1970s. During that decade, the magazine began a rapid downward spiral, which continues today.

The magazine began the 1970s with a circulation of 2,153,862. By 1978, its circulation had slipped to 1,554,156. The 1980s did not stop the decline, although the pace had slowed. In 1988, the magazine's circulation was 1,405,087. In the 1990s, the magazine has seen its circulation decline even more. Audit Bureau of Circulations statements indicate that the magazine's circulation no longer reaches 1 million. Nonetheless, the magazine carries on with its brand of "real-life" narratives.

The 1970s were the decade of the sexual revolution and the women's movement. The decade challenged women at every turn. *True Story* reflected the tumult in its narratives. Stories (still first-person and without a byline) included "White Girl on the Black Side of Town," "The Only Boss I Want Is My Husband: A Working Wife Tells Why," "I Sued My Girl for Custody of Our Child," "If I Want to Hold Our Marriage Together . . . I *Have* to Forgive Him!"[24]

Although the magazine continued to be a bastion of traditional values and mores, there was some latitude for experimentation—particularly before marriage. Virginity was not necessarily required for marriage—as long as sexual intercourse was with a marriageable man.[25] Even if the woman had been wronged by a married man, she was likely to be rescued by a "good" man. When a pregnant woman blurts out that the father of the child was a married man, she is comforted by her new lover:

I closed my eyes, braced myself for angry, accusing words. The next moment he was holding me close in his arms. "Poor little girl," he crooned softly, "I knew you had something on your mind all this time. Now that you've told me you'll feel better."[26]

Those attitudes continued into the 1980s. Women in marriage were expected to be forgiving, kind, and true. Even in divorce, women had to think of the children first—and always. Heroines in "The Husband Stealer," "Mommy, I Want to Live with Daddy," and "My Husband's Pillow Talk"[27] all showed the positive attributes of women as wives and mothers.

In the 1990s, much of the narrative fare remained the same. A certain latitude of premarital sexual experimentation was allowed; but, in the end, the narrator—still typically a woman—achieved a traditional balance in her life. "My Twin Babies Have 2 Different Fathers" was typical. Although the narrator had carried on a sexual relationship with two men, she refused to marry either until the paternity of her children was determined. When tests revealed that each man had fathered one child, the narrator opted to marry her first lover, who cares for both boys as his own. As she reflected:

Today I'm living a good life, one that is filled with honest hard work and a faithful marriage to a man I love. Most of all, I think I've learned to be a mature, responsible mother to the two little boys God blessed me with. And that's the most important thing when you come right down to it.[28]

The *True Story* of the 1990s acknowledges that the lives of women of the wage-earning class have changed. The narratives, although allowing for a latitude of premarital behavior and divorce, continue to reflect traditional values and mores.

That editorial formula has not changed substantially in years. The "real-life" narratives, the confessions, remain *True Story*'s bread and butter. Departments—beauty, health, horoscopes, puzzles, recipes, pets, and child care—continue to make up between 10 and 20 percent of each issue. The content and the writing style encourage female readers to identify closely with the magazine. Indeed, editor Sue Weiner once wrote that *True Story* has become a female tradition; "the *True Story* family has grown in just this same way—it's a tradition passed lovingly along from friend to friend, mother to daughter, woman to woman."[29]

Notes

1. Allen Talmey, "Millions from Dumb-Bells: Portrait of Bernarr Macfadden," *Outlook and Independent,* June 4, 1930, pp. 164, 166.

2. Henry F. Pringle, "Another American Phenomenon," *World Work*, October 1928, p. 660.

3. Alva Johnston, "The Great Macfadden," in John E. Drewry (ed.), *Post-Biographies of Famous Journalists* (Athens: University of Georgia Press, 1942), p. 259.

4. Oscar Garrison Villard, "Sex, Art, Truth, and Magazines," *Atlantic Monthly*, March 1926, p. 398.

5. See, for example, Lee Rainwater, Richard P. Coleman, and Gerald Handel, *Workingman's Wife: Her Personality, World and Life Style* (New York: Oceana Publications, 1959); Maureen Honey, *Creating Rosie the Riveter: Class, Gender and Propaganda during World War II* (Amherst: University of Massachusetts Press, 1984); George Gerbner, "The Social Role of the Confession Magazine," *Social Problems*, 6:1 (Summer 1958), pp. 29–40.

6. Macfadden Holdings, New York, has the most complete run of the magazine. The author wishes to thank Susan Weiner, editorial director of *True Story*, for her assistance in the preparation of this entry.

7. *History & Magazines* (New York: True Story Magazine, 1941), unnumbered page.

8. Who came up with the idea depends on the individual telling the story. Bernarr Macfadden's official biographers, Fulton Oursler and Clement Wood, gave all credit to Bernarr. Nor surprisingly, Mary Macfadden claimed the credit in her biography of her ex-husband, written with Emile Gauvreau, onetime editor of Macfadden's New York *Graphic*. Clement Wood, *Bernarr Macfadden, A Study in Success* (New York: Beekman, 1974), p. 117; Fulton Oursler, *The True Story of Bernarr Macfadden* (New York: Lewis Copland, 1929), pp. 207, 214; Mary Macfadden and Emile Gauvreau, *Dumbbells and Carrot Strips* (New York: Henry Holt, 1953), pp. 218–219.

9. Harold Hersey told his story in *Pulpwood Editor* (New York: Frederick A. Stokes, 1937), pp. 205–206, as reported in Robert Ernst, *Weakness Is a Crime: The Life of Bernarr Macfadden* (Syracuse, N.Y.: Syracuse University Press, 1991), pp. 75–76.

10. This comment was attributed to Bernarr Macfadden, in Oursler, *The True Story of Bernarr Macfadden*, p. 216.

11. This panel was a topic of great discussion. Critics made light of it. Pringle noted that it was composed of "Men and women . . . from the mental strata to which the magazine caters." Pringle, "Another American Phenomenon," pp. 664–665. A more objective analysis of the panel can be found in Bruce M. Swain, "Bernarr Macfadden," in Sam Riley (ed.), *Dictionary of Literary Biography, vol. 91, American Magazine Journalists, 1900–1960*, Detroit: Gale Research, 1990, pp. 205–215.

12. Ernst, *Weakness Is a Crime*, pp. 77–78.

13. *History & Magazines*, unnumbered page; "Keeping up with the Crowd," October 1989, p. 30. The October 1989 issue was a special anniversary edition, reproducing many stories from earlier decades.

14. Robert Lewis Taylor, "Profiles Physical Culture III: Physician, Heal Thyself," *New Yorker*, October 28, 1950, p. 42.

15. Emile Gauvreau, *My Last Million Readers* (New York: E. P. Dutton, 1941), p. 100.

16. Swain, "Bernarr Macfadden," p. 210.

17. *History & Magazines*, unnumbered pages.

18. Ernst, *Weakness Is a Crime*, pp. 79–80.

19. *Tide*, February 1, 1942, as cited in Theodore Peterson, *Magazines in the Twentieth Century* (Urbana: University of Illinois Press, 1964), p. 81.

20. *History & Magazines*, unnumbered pages.

21. "Each Moment a Memory," March 1943, as reprinted in Maureen Honey, "The Working-Class Women and Recruitment Propaganda During World War II: Class Differences in the Portrayal of War Work," *Signs* 8:4 (Summer 1983), p. 677.

22. October 1989, front cover, p. 36.

23. Ibid., p. 38.

24. October 1989, front cover, p. 40.

25. Muriel Cantor and Elizabeth Jones, "Creating Fiction for Women," *Communication Research*, 10:1 (January 1983), p. 116.

26. "Romance Special," March 1979, p. 71, as reprinted by Penni Stewart, "He Admits . . . but She Confesses," *Women's Studies International Quarterly*, 31:1 (1980), p. 109.

27. October 1989.

28. "My Twin Babies Have Different Fathers," May 1994, p. 77.

29. Sue Weiner, "Editor's Note," October 1989, p. 2.

Information Sources

BIBLIOGRAPHY:

Cantor, Muriel, and Elizabeth Jones. "Creating Fiction for Women." *Communication Research* 10:1 (January 1983), pp. 111–137.

Ernst, Robert. *Weakness Is a Crime: The Life of Bernarr Macfadden*. Syracuse, N.Y.: Syracuse University Press, 1991.

The Fifth Dimension. New York: Macfadden Publications, 1948.

Garrett, Oliver H. P. "Another True Story." *New Yorker*, September 19, 1925, pp. 9–10.

Gauvreau, Emile. *My Last Million Readers*. New York: E. P. Dutton, 1941.

Gerbner, George. "The Social Role of the Confession Magazine." *Social Problems* 6:1 (Summer 1958), pp. 29–40.

History & Magazines. New York: True Story Magazine, 1941.

Honey, Maureen. "The Working-Class Woman and Recruitment Propaganda during World War II: Class Differences in the Portrayal of War Work." *Signs* 8:4 (Summer 1983), pp. 672–687.

———. *Creating Rosie the Riveter: Class, Gender and Propaganda during World War II*. Amherst: University of Massachusetts Press, 1984.

How to Get People Excited: A Human Interest Textbook. New York: True Story, 1937.

Johnston, Alva. "The Great Macfadden." In John E. Drewry (ed.), *Post Biographies of Famous Journalists*. Athens: University of Georgia Press, 1942, pp. 258–289.

Macfadden, Mary, and Emile Gauvreau. *Dumbbells and Carrot Strips: The Story of Bernarr Macfadden*. New York: Henry Holt, 1953.

Manchester, Harland. "True Stories." *Scribner's Magazine*, August 1938, pp. 25–29.

Oursler, Fulton. *The True Story of Bernarr Macfadden*. New York: Lewis Copland, 1929.

Peterson, Theodore. *Magazines in the Twentieth Century* 2d ed. Urbana: University of Illinois Press, 1964.

Pringle, Henry F. "Another American Phenomenon." *World's Work*, October 1928, pp. 659–666.

Rainwater, Lee, Richard P. Coleman, and Gerald Handel. *Workingman's Wife: Her Personality, World and Life Style*. New York: Oceana Publications, 1959.

Stewart, Penni. "He Admits . . . But She Confesses." *Women's Studies International Quarterly* 3:1 (1980), pp. 105–114.

Swain, Bruce. "Bernarr Macfadden." In Sam Riley (ed.), *Dictionary of Literary Biography, vol. 91, American Magazine Journalists, 1900–1960*. Detroit: Gale Research, 1990, pp. 205–215.

Talmey, Allene. "Millions from Dumb-Bells: Portrait of Bernarr Macfadden." *Outlook and Independent,* June 4, 1930, pp. 163–166, 196.

Taylor, Robert Lewis. "Profiles Physical Culture III: Physician, Heal Thyself!" *New Yorker*, October 28, 1950, pp. 37–51.

Villard, Oswald Garrison. "Sex, Art, Truth, and Magazines." *Atlantic Monthly*, March 1926, pp. 388–398.

Wood, Clement. *Bernarr Macfadden, A Study in Success.* New York: Beekman Publishers, 1974; reprint of 1929 edition.

INDEX SOURCES: None.

LOCATION SOURCES: Macfadden Holding, New York; scattered issues found in various libraries.

Publication History

MAGAZINE TITLE AND TITLE CHANGES: *True Story*.

VOLUME AND ISSUE DATA: Vols. 1–(May 1919–present). Monthly.

PUBLISHER AND PLACE OF PUBLICATION: Macfadden Publications (1919–1962); Macfadden Bartell Corp. (1962–1975); Macfadden Group Inc. (1975–1988); Macfadden Holdings Inc. (1988–present). New York.

EDITORS: John Brennan (1919–1926); William Jourdan Rapp (1926–1942); Henry Lieferant (1942–1947); E. V. Heyn (1947–1950); Helen Irwin Littauer (1950–1951); Fred R. Sammis (1951–1953); Nina Dorrance (1953–1963); Ben Merson (1963–1964); Suzanne Hilliard (1965–1976); Helen Vincent (1976–1987); Sue Weiner (1987–present).

CIRCULATION: ABC, 1993: 825,060 (paid, primarily subscriptions) (peak circulation, 1958: 2,614,396).

Kathleen L. Endres

TWINS MAGAZINE

Barbara Unell has had the unique advantage of watching her twins grow along with her magazine. When the first *Twins Magazine* was published in July 1984, with a circulation of 6,000,[1] the Unell twins were four years old. Unell and her husband, Robert, started with a goal of having 10 percent of the 500,000 parents of twins subscribing. In 1993, they had 45,000 subscribers, 5,000 short of that 10 percent goal.

It is no surprise that *Twins* has experienced such success. Parents of twins, or multiples as they are known in "twin-speak," must purchase twice as many sweatshirts, car seats, and diapers as parents of singletons.

Twins entered the market at an auspicious time. Out of 3,046,162 live births in 1988, 65,136 were twin births.[2] In the United States alone, "the 1988 ratio [of live twin births to overall live births was] the highest ratio observed in the last four decades."[3] The growth of twinning is attributed to both the aging of women as they wait longer to have babies and the wider use of contraceptive and fertility drugs.[4]

What does come as a surprise in the lighthearted-but-serious-about-twins magazine is that there is so much diversity in the issues surrounding the rearing of twins. Said Unell:

> There's a thread to multiple-birth thinking which concerns very specific twintype issues. These issues reach across the years and affect every parent of twins or other multiples. The decisions parents make, or decide not to make, such as whether to dress them the same or different, should they share the same room, and should they always participate in the same activities, really do impact the twins. These decisions affect the messages parents give the kids about their identity of being twins and their individuality.[5]

Unell stated in her inaugural editorial, "In *Twins*, you'll find the answers you've been looking for," by which she meant general information that applies to twin-specific family situations. "*Twins* does more than *maybe* give a line or two to the subject of multiples. It talks twins from cover to cover."[6]

Cover the issues it does, from every possible viewpoint. *Twins Magazine*, based in Kansas, is "a bimonthly international magazine designed to give support and information to parents of multiples and those professionals who care for them."[7] That is exactly what the magazine is: a rendering of the latest in scientific research and developments for twin-specific and multiple-birth issues, written and presented in easy-to-understand language so parents and others can apply the findings to practical situations.

Research is explained by the many professional authors of the bimonthly columns. The "Research" column in the March/April 1993 issue asked the question, "If I'm bald, will they be too?" Written by Nancy L. Segal, an associate professor in the department of psychology and director of twin studies at California State University, Fullerton, California, the article focuses on the medical and genetic studies of baldness in families. Segal states that "twin studies of baldness have not been undertaken" but that another study of twins reared apart indicates that identical male twins experience similar patterns of baldness. As with the other seven research-based columns, the author ends with a note to parents: "Parents who have experienced hair loss themselves may be concerned as to the appearance of this trait in their children. There is no evidence of a one-to-one correspondence for this trait between parents and children."[8] Other professionals fill out the authorship of the remaining research-based columns. Along with these research-based columns are regular features, a series of developmental columns called "Double Focus," mostly written by freelance writers who are parents of multiples, and informational departments.

Twins takes great pride in having parents of twins—or twins themselves—write informational columns for each bimonthly issue. The columns are not recycled information meant for the parents of singletons. Each column is written especially with twins or other multiples in mind and takes into account the problems children of the same age, but not the same temperament, encounter.

Features in the March/April 1993 issue included "A View from the Other Side of the Fence: How Singletons Perceive Multiples," a report about how singletons' attitudes about multiples have changed over the years, and how those attitudes can affect twins socially, both in life and within the family.[9] The author, Alice Vollmar, is the mother of six children, including fraternal twins. "Double Focus" presents advice applicable to the different stages of twin development, from pregnancy through adolescence. These authors are professional practitioners in their field and, more often than not, parents of twins or other multiples. Georgia Lewis, author of the "Adolescence" column, is a parent education specialist for the Montgomery County (Maryland) Public School System and the mother of seven children, including fraternal twins. Adam P. Matheny, Jr., author of the "Infancy" column, is a professor of pediatrics at the University of Louisville (Kentucky) School of Medicine and director of the Louisville Twin Study.[10]

From the start, *Twins Magazine* captured the hearts of its readers with its celebrity twins parents. The inaugural issue featured a story written by Jane Brody, then *New York Times* personal health columnist. She wrote "candidly about her twins' growing-up years." Her story not only reinforces the positive outlook that *Twins Magazine* emphasizes on the twin experience but also shows, through her examples, how different in temperament twin boys can be.

Over the years, other features in *Twins* have included twin postcards; articles from notables such as advice columnists (and identical twins) Ann Landers and Abigail Van Buren; separation strategies that work; and twin trend stories ("Twins in Sports: All Fun and Games?" "Year of the Twins in the Movies, 1988," "Are Mothers of Twins at Odds with the 'Working Mother' Trends?"). The features often include short bibliographies and short, individual, true-life anecdotes. Through all of the features and columns, however, comes one basic philosophy from *Twins Magazine*: twins are a positive happening in a couple's life.

Twins Magazine is not available on newsstands and credits word of mouth, along with the cooperation of pediatricians, obstetricians/gynecologists, nurses, and childbirth educators throughout the country, for its subscription success. The magazine claims an international base for its readership and is endorsed by the Center for the Study of Multiple Births, located in Chicago, as the only source for international twin information.[11] The National Organization of Mothers of Twins Clubs, Inc. (NOMOTC), also endorses the magazine: "*Twins Magazine* is a unique publication geared to the multiple-birth family. . . . NOMOTC endorses this magazine as a guide to developing and maintaining healthy attitudes toward the rearing of multiple-birth children."[12] *The Joy of Twins*, a book written by Pamela Patrick Novotny and published by Crown Publishers, New York, in 1988, lists *Twins Magazine* as the only periodical available for the parents and families of twins. Only one other magazine serves the parents and families of twins: *Mothers of Multiples*; similar to a newsletter in editorial style, it was started in 1992.

Most *Twins* readers are female and mothers of multiples, according to Jean Cerne, managing editor. When the magazine is passed along to two or more other readers who are not subscribers, advertising exposure is most assuredly more than doubled.

> The mother of twins has to be a heavy buyer–she needs twice as much as the mother of singletons. Products for twins get heavier use and so buying less expensive products doesn't always pay. She's loyal to brands that meet her special requirements. She's extra–busy so she wants features that save her time, are easy to operate, prevent spills, etc.[13]

Advertising is one of the interesting facets of the publication. It is estimated that the cost of outfitting a baby's first year is about $5,800; parents of twins could, quite conceivably, spend approximately $12,000 getting the babies clothed and fed and healthy their first year.[14] The majority of paid advertisements are for twin specialty items, items that emphasize the uniqueness of twins or those of multiple birth such as special T-shirts, double-billed caps, posters, cards, and books. Next on the list of priorities of advertising is the double-stroller, that unusual stroller phenomenon that impresses all of single birth. "Our advertisers come from hard work and trying to keep them happy," said advertising director Brenda Schifman. *Twins* does not encourage advertisers to use strictly a twins-oriented context. "It is too expensive for most advertisers to develop a separate ad for each publication," said Schifman. Some advertisers utilize one of their twin-oriented products, while keeping the rest to single-use, thereby increasing, they hope, sales of both.[15] Advertisers who find their way into *Twins Magazine* include Kodak film, toy manufacturer Step 2, furniture manufacturer Cosco, and baby food producer Gerber.

"Advertisers in general are becoming more specialized and highly targeted," said Betty Kuhnlein, media supervisor at the J. Walter Thompson advertising agency in New York, which has placed ads for Kodak film in *Twins Magazine*. "When you talk to people in their own language, they respond more favorably to the product. *Twins* is the best example of a narrowly targeted market," added Kuhnlein.[16] Along with the cover photo and various photos and other depictions of twins throughout the magazine, Kodak film sponsors a photo feature called "Double Takes," always strategically located across from the company's advertisement. The contest always features photos of twins and multiple-birth children from around the world, identified by name and where they live. This feature enhances attempts by Unell to depict the different twin types that exist.

Twins was launched after more than two years of studying the viability of a twins specialty magazine. Unell and Associates, a Kansas-based marketing research firm that Robert Unell owns, publishes the magazine. The company also includes an advertising agency, the publishing house that produces *Twins Magazine*, and other more professionally based publications and twin information.

Unell herself organizes an approximately one-minute-long radio talk segment for parents on Associated Press Network.

Since its inception, *Twins Magazine* has always featured twins or siblings of multiple births as its cover photo. There is no specific percentage of identical twins to fraternal twins for the cover photo, nor for twins versus other multiples. This holds with Unell's philosophy that twins should be portrayed in many different forms, numbers, genders, and races to illustrate the diversity of twin types.[17]

One exception to a single set of twins or other multiples for the cover photo was made for the magazine's fifth-anniversary issue. The July/August 1989 issue featured a group photo of twins attending the annual Twins Days Festival, held in Twinsburg, Ohio. The photo, taken from a high-lift crane during the traditional gathering of the 2,356[18] sets of twins who converged on the site for the celebration that year, tied in with a feature story on the Twins Days Festival itself.

This only long-running magazine providing information and advice on the raising and parenting of twins and children of other multiple births has enjoyed its own niche of the trade.

Notes

1. *Ulrich's International Periodical Directory, 1992–93* (New Providence, N.J.: R. R. Bowker, 1993), p. 1245.

2. Susan Tassel, "Health and Demographic Characteristics of Twin Birth: U.S., 1988," *Vital and Health Statistics*, June 1992, p. 11.

3. Ibid., p. 2.

4. Ibid., p. 13.

5. Barbara C. Unell interview, June 3, 1993.

6. Barbara Unell, "Hungry for Information," July/August 1984, p. 5.

7. "Audit Report: Controlled Magazine," *Audit Bureau of Circulations*, July 1992.

8. Nancy L. Segal, "If I'm Bald, Will They Be, Too?" March/April 1993, pp. 27–28.

9. Alice M. Vollmar, "A View from the Other Side of the Fence," March/April 1993, pp. 24–26.

10. March/April 1993.

11. Donald M. Keith and Louis Keith, Media Kit.

12. Media Kit.

13. Ibid.

14. "Parents of Twins/Hot Products and Hot Markets," *Adweek*, November 4, 1991, p. 22.

15. Brenda Schifman interview, June 23, 1993.

16. Joyce E. Smith, " 'Twins' a Winner in Magazine Market," *Kansas City Star*, August 13, 1989, p. F4.

17. Unell interview.

18. Sandy Miller interview, June 4, 1993.

Information Sources

BIBLIOGRAPHY:

Collins, Glenn. "Twin Business: Expert Advice." *New York Times*, September 23, 1984, sec. 1, p. 66.

"Parents of Twins/Hot Products and Hot Markets." *Adweek.* November 4, 1991, p. 22.

Smith, Joyce E. " 'Twins' a Winner in Magazine Market." *Kansas City Star.* August 13, 1989, p. F4.

INDEX SOURCES: Not indexed.

LOCATION SOURCES: Library of Congress and other libraries.

Publication History

MAGAZINE TITLE AND TITLE CHANGES: *TWINS Magazine.*

VOLUME AND ISSUE DATA: Vols. 1–(July/August 1984–present). Bimonthly.

PUBLISHER AND PLACE OF PUBLICATION: Twins Magazine, Inc. Shawnee Mission, Kans.

EDITOR: Barbara C. Unell (1984–present).

CIRCULATION: ABC, 1993: 32,949 (paid, primarily subscriptions).

Jean Moyle Rogers

——— U ———

THE UNIVERSALIST AND LADIES' REPOSITORY

The Universalist movement in the United States was well known for its dedication in publishing its doctrines. *The Universalist and Ladies' Repository* was only one of 2,096 books and pamphlets and 182 periodicals, along with numerous weekly, monthly, and quarterly newspapers and magazines, that began rolling off the church's presses in the early years of the nineteenth century. Many of the society's publications were short-lived, but some survived for a multitude of decades, due, in part, to mergers with more successful Universalist publications.[1]

The Universalist and Ladies' Repository first appeared in 1832 as *The Universalist* under the editorship of the reverends B. Whittemore, C. Gardner, J. H. Bugbee, L. S. Everett, and S. Streeter. With the commencement of volume 2 in 1833, the Reverend D. D. Smith assumed control of the journal. With volume 3, it became *The Universalist and Ladies' Repository*, a title it retained until the issuing of volume 12, when it became simply *The Ladies' Repository*. With the 51st volume, it became *The Repository*, a name it retained until its demise in 1874.

When the Reverend D. D. Smith left the journal in May 1836, he was succeeded by the Reverend A. A. Folsom. Folsom's term of office was short-lived. In September 1836, he gave way to the Reverend Henry Bacon, who remained with the monthly until his death in March 1856. Bacon set the editorial tone of the journal for its remaining years. Bacon shared the editing duties with Sarah C. Edgarton from 1840 to 1843. She was the first in a long line of middle-class, literary women who left their mark not only on the Universalist Church but also on its publications. E. A. Bacon, Henry's wife, edited volumes 25–29, making the Bacon perspective dominant for nearly 25 years of the journal's 42-year life span. Caroline Sawyer, wife of the Reverend Thomas J. Sawyer, was responsible for the 30th to the 33rd volumes. Mrs. Sawyer was a regular contributor as well as the New York correspondent during Henry Bacon's term as editor. She was succeeded by Sarah A. Nowell, who worked on volume 34. Phebe H. Hanaford, who became one of the Universalist Church's first female clerics, edited volumes 35 through 40. The journal's final editor was Henrietta A. Bingham, who remained with the periodical until 1874.[2]

In comparison to other women's magazines in the United States in the mid-nineteenth century, *The Universalist and Ladies' Repository* could not be described as a roaring success. In its only reported circulation figure, that of 1845, the periodical sold 2,000 copies monthly. Its rival and namesake, the Methodist-Episcopal *Ladies' Repository*,* was read by 35,000 subscribers in 1864. One of the largest known circulating woman's journals of the day, *Godey's Lady's Book*,* had 150,000 subscribers in 1860.[3] There is no evidence to indicate that the Universalist publication enjoyed any more success following the Civil War than it did prior to it. The Universalist publishing house subsidized it for most of its life.[4] In many ways, it is somewhat surprising that the church continued to support the journal as long as it did.

In part, the limited appeal of *The Universalist and Ladies' Repository* can be explained by the fact that Universalism stood outside the mainstream of American religious practice in the nineteenth century. This placed the journal at a considerable competitive disadvantage to those published by the more popular Methodists and Episcopalians. The Universalists were regarded as an iconoclastic sect, cursed, on one hand, by a loose, virtually nondogmatic structure and, on the other, by a seemingly endless need to experiment with both social relations and religious doctrines.[5]

Universalism took aim at the very foundations of Christian belief and practice, specifically, the theological sanctity of the Trinity and the widely held view that God was a vengeful spirit. In a continuing series written under the title ''The Utility of Universalism,'' the church announced:

> Universalism rejects the Trinity and gives a principle of interpretation that alone can make the scriptures harmonious, and their doctrine concerning the Deity satisfying to the mind and the heart of man. The principle is, that God is the infinite and universal Father whose nature is love. In opposition to this, stand the doctrines of vicarious atonement, total depravity, endless punishment, and uncertainty in reference to man's final destiny. All these doctrines injure man's virtue and happiness. They never could and never can supply the deep wants of the soul.[6]

Universalism was not content to remain exclusively a theological heretic. It took its reforming zeal to the secular arena when it assumed a leading role in both the abolitionist movement and the nascent women's rights organizations that began to emerge in the three decades prior to the Civil War. In the Universalist mind, the need to abolish slavery and to ensure equality for women had many of the same characteristics. As David Robinson has argued, ''[H]ere the ideal of self-development bumped into the iron restrictions of custom, legal inequalities, and male self-interest, forcing both a philosophical rethinking of the sex roles and a political assertiveness to try to change them."[7]

Universalist feminism was born in the soul of Judith Sargent Murray, wife of the movement's founder, John Murray. Mrs. Murray was writing on gender questions as early as 1790, when she argued that sexual inequality was anti-Christian. She pointed out that both male and female souls were created equally by God, and, thus, it was a sin to discriminate on the basis of sex. Murray and religious feminists who followed her were as anxious to explain their bondage in religious terms as they were to seek religious convictions for their potential freedom.[8]

The reading of feminist rhetoric as it emerged in *The Universalist and Ladies' Repository* would appear to have a strikingly reactionary tinge to many modern activists. Yet, to the established institutions of the mid-nineteenth century, Universalist demands for gender equality must have seemed as threatening as some of the more outspoken modern proponents appear to established authority in this day.

As Henry Bacon began to assert his editorial perspective on the journal following his appointment in 1836, there is little evidence to indicate that this Universalist clergyman-journalist initially had any real interest in women's issues beyond acquiring their readership loyalty. Bacon was more concerned with establishing the legitimacy of a journal, which, by his notes, appears to have survived in spite of a very rocky beginning. In the summer of 1837, Bacon solicited the advice of a number of friends, who freely offered suggestions to the new editor. The majority argued that while the journal should retain its religious and literary perspective, it should do so with "a cheerful tone."[9] It became Bacon's calling to publish and interpret the Universalist creed through a number of different avenues. In his mission statement, the new editor declared:

We shall aim to present our patrons a good variety. Laboured and sound articles on the true sense of scripture passages, in defence of the great truth of Universal Salvation, and to point out and enforce the duties of the Christian's life; also, Tales, Sketches, Essays, Poetry, Music, Notices of Passing events proper to our work, and of Publications, will contribute to fill our pages, and to make the work acceptable to its patrons.[10]

The majority of the articles published early in Bacon's career carried titles such as "The Gospel," "Benevolence," "Worship by the Rose Tree," "Christian Freedom," and "Durable Riches and Righteousness."[11] Yet, beyond the obvious desire to preach the Universalist version of the Christian gospel, the first indication that the church was not purely patriarchal, at least in its literary policies, came under Bacon's leadership. Contributions about women and by women were commonplace after 1836. The July 1837 edition carried three chapters of a story called "Early Friendship" by a woman named Mary-Ann Dodd. A poet named "Ellen" contributed a six-stanza composition under the title "Thou Winding Stream." Invariably, these tales all dealt with some form of moral dilemma. Caroline, the heroine of "The Mother," sets out to rescue her wayward husband from a life of sin and depravity that was precipitated by the birth of a blind son. As in all tales of this nature, the moral strength of the female prevails, and the reformed sinner is returned to his home and family a changed person.[12] These themes were to be repeated again and again until the periodical ceased publication in December 1874.

The Universalist journalists, beginning with Bacon, had strong, preconceived notions of what a good Universalist, Christian woman should be. In admonishing lovers who presented their betrothed as expressions of excellence itself, Bacon noted that female frailties were numerous. "She has her imperfections, her weaknesses and her vices."[13] Yet, in the main, the female was a gentle and timid creature who only rarely threw these virtues aside to pursue a life of sin or, in the extreme, crime. In contrast to the male, noted for being powerful in prosperity and weak in adversity, the woman was "feeble in prosperity; but mighty when adversity comes upon her. Indeed her powers are never fully displayed, except in cases of great extremity, in times of real and deep disaster. Then, she appears in her might, and exhibits her vast superiority over man."[14]

There was little doubt in the minds of those who contributed to *The Universalist and Ladies' Repository* that religion played a key role in the development of the female character.[15] It was argued on numerous occasions that, prior to the introduction of Christianity, women were forced to play subservient roles to men. In fact, Universalists believed that non-Christian women were no more than chattels, imprisoned in a life of servitude to "gratify the brutal passion of men."[16] As a consequence, these "pagan" women were denied the benefits of civilized society, such as education. The Reverend Elbridge G. Brooks wrote, "We see her degraded, trampled upon, despised; in many instances looked upon as a soulless creature, given only to serve man's interest and man's pleasure, and everywhere treated as a slave and the lowest menial."[17]

When Bacon announced a technical redesign of the journal's typesetting in the May 1838 issue, he did not change his editorial direction. The periodical was still to be published for the benefit of Universalist evangelism and, specifically, for women who he felt could benefit from "the sanctifying and comforting influence of the doctrine of illimitable grace."[18] He introduced a series of salutes to famous women of the world, the first of whom was Josephine, the wife of Napoleon Bonaparte. The author, one C.L.E. of New Haven, wrote of "her angelic sweetness, her untiring devotion, her firm integrity, her generous and self-sacrificing love; that while Napoleon lives long in the memory of the head, Josephine may live forever in the memory of the heart."[19]

The appearance of Sarah C. Edgarton as coeditor in May 1839 was instrumental in defining an early nineteenth-century feminist perspective for *The Uni-*

versalist and Ladies' Repository. Edgarton, a devoutly religious and literary woman, began to address issues that had not been prevalent during Bacon's first term as editor. Edgarton spent considerable time discussing two major themes, the role of women in marriage and the right of females to obtain an education equivalent to that of men. As with all her writings, her insights and inspirations evolved from theological perspectives. In the spirit of Edgarton, subsequent editors found it impossible to separate seemingly secular questions from religious ones. This is hardly surprising. The Universalist world was a religious world first and foremost. Secular issues could not be separated from their divine origins.

Edgarton defied convention when she argued that women were not necessarily born to marry. She wrote, "Though it may be *expedient* for her to marry, it is her *privilege* to be single."[20] Two editions later, one of Edgarton's essayists stated:

I candidly believe that a good old maid is one of the happiest creatures alive. I entertain great respect for worthy women who have had sufficient firmness to escape the snares of mercenary or vapid wife-hunters, and who fear not the sneers of thoughtless fashionable.[21]

Edgarton was adamant that her young and eligible readers not confuse romance with love. In "A Lesson on Romance," Edgarton related the tale of a woman named Emma De Vay, who received some serious matrimonial advice from a friend named Isadore Southey. Mrs. Southey had conjured the vision of an ideal marriage in her mind. When Mr. Southey appeared on the horizon, she leaped at the chance to marry him. Too late, Mrs. Southey realized that her emotions had overruled her common sense, and she found herself in an unhappy union. Speaking to Emma, she stated, "Let your affections be moderate and rational, subdued ever to judgment. It is your only chance of passing through life with a heart unwrecked."[22]

Choosing a mate in Edgarton's world was to be a cautious, well-conceived plan. An ill-thought relationship would not deliver what Universalist journalists felt were the two essential characteristics of a religious marriage, continuing affection and happiness. Although Edgarton was by no means opposed to marriage, she reflected the conservatism of her theological upbringing in cautioning young women to be resistant to the courtship pattern that seemed to be prevalent in this age. The concept of romance was on her mind when she wrote, "The charms of moonlight rambles, talking of poetry, discussing the merits of novels, and revelling in 'unwritten music,' or unuttered feeling and sentiment will not give this."[23]

Edgarton and her contributors were not content to define the limits of courtship alone. When a male writer corresponded to argue that he could never marry a woman of genius, Ann B. Stephens took him to task.

If you would cultivate genius aright, cherish it among the most holy of your household gods. Make it a domestic plant. Let its roots strike deep into your hoe, nor care that its perfume floats to a thousand casements besides your own, so long as its greenness and its blossoms are for you. Flowers of the sweetest breath, give their perfume most lavishly to the breeze, and yet, without exhausting their own delicate urns.[24]

Edgarton's interest in the emancipation of females from numerous bondages, which ranged from heathenism to unhappy marriages, led her to explore the question of education for women. Edgarton and those who wrote for journals such as *The Universalist and Ladies' Repository* were a small community in the years before the Civil War. Very few working-class women had ever acquired any form of formal education, leaving literate females almost exclusively entrenched in the middle and upper classes. These women were normally exposed to subjects such as rhetoric, literature, and manners, all intended to cast them in the specialized role as the wives of successful men. They were seen strictly as appendages to their mates, deriving the benefits and attractions of life itself from their matrimonial choices. It was a situation that Sarah C. Edgarton found a little more than uncomfortable.

Women were born to exert influence in the moral sphere of worldly existence, at least in the Universalist way of thinking. For this onerous life duty, the female could not afford to be illiterate in both written and verbal skills, not to mention the ways of the secular world. Throughout the history of *The Universalist and Ladies' Repository*, not one contributor cast a shadow of a doubt on the influence of women. "From the cradle to the grave, its magic wand is extended over 'the sterner sex,' leading them as by a silken thread, and giving shape and consistency to their moral sensibilities and habits."[25] Certainly, this was not a feminist expression that divorced the destiny of the female from that of the male in both single and married life. Each had a role to play, and the roles were interdependent.

For Edgarton, education was the key to ensure success in this exclusively female role. She deplored the fact that men had ignored proper education for their women but urged them to realize the importance that she attached to it. In her "Illustrations of Female Education," she wrote:

One thing only is wanting—a proper cultivation of our minds and hearts for this greatest of all earthly enterprises. We must *feel our divinity*—feel that we are not subordinate agents in the high providence of Heaven— that our mission is one of toil, of danger, and blessed by God! of great and glorious reward.[26]

Edgarton dismissed arguments that because middle- and upper-class women were confined to the domestic sphere, they did not need to be educated. It was not the number of years or the quantity of books needed to educate a woman that was an issue to the editor. She approached her campaign from a purely qualitative aspect. Part of the problem, she felt, lay with women themselves, and they would have to support the need for female education. "[A]nd if the same money which is individually expended for worthless articles of finery, or what is perhaps even more deleterious to an ardent mind, popular modern novels, were saved for the purchase of valuable and *instructive* books, should we not have the reason to be proud of the intelligence, instead of blushing for the follies of our sex?"[27] The so-called follies of "our sex" dominated the pages of the journal throughout its history. Edgarton was only one of the many writers who complained that middle- and upper-class women were idlers who enjoyed such luxuries as breakfast in bed, sleeping until afternoon, after which they proceeded to city shops to indulge themselves on expensive clothes and rare perfumes. This was not an ideal readily accepted in the Universalist way of thinking.[28]

In spite of the obvious class bias of *The Universalist and Ladies' Repository*, Edgarton and Bacon were not oblivious to the plight of other less lofty females. In the summer of 1839, their journal reported on an attempt by Philadelphia clothing workers to reserve that industry exclusively for poor and industrious women who appeared to have no other means of support. The reporter, who signed her name as "Benevolencia, Boston, Massachusetts," noted that the poorer classes in the Pennsylvania city were predominantly occupied by widowed women who had great difficulty finding and keeping employment. For the writer, the poverty that resulted from this dilemma penalized women to the benefit of men, who believed that poor men would be hired over women. She continued:

If they procure employment, how are they paid? How does it happen that in a civilized land, the gentle sex, the weak who are unable to protect themselves, are turned off with a miserable pittance for performing the same amount of labour which is performed by men and for which the latter received liberal wages. Is woman to be trampled upon because she is not beautiful, because she has not learned to express her words with affected precision, and because she knows nothing of the frivolous accomplishment that show so well on the surface of character, while all within is vulgar, unintellectual, and unfeeling?[29]

This is one of the earliest recorded arguments for the now-familiar appeal for equal pay for work of equal value.

In December 1841, Edgarton recognized one of the first working-class journals written by women. The *Lowell Offering*, which billed itself as "a repository of original articles, written by Factory Girls," was the inspiration of two Universalist ministers, the Reverend Abel C. Thomas and the Reverend Thomas B. Thayer. These two clergymen had been instrumental in developing societies for "mutual improvement" in the New England mill town of Lowell. Their constituency was almost exclusively made up of young female millworkers whom they taught to read and write. The journal became a window to the world for these women, many of whom suffered from the same indignities experienced by their Philadelphia counterparts.[30]

Edgarton compared the works in the *Lowell Offering* with more sophisticated and popular journals targeted to female readers. She wrote:

> Has any writer in the *Ladies' Book*, or the *Ladies' Companion* or even in the *Ladies' Repository*, advanced more rationale or philosophical views of woman's sphere and woman's rights than has "Ella" in No. 5 of the *Factory Girl's* "Offering"? Found ever Salvarietta a more eloquent eulogist than the gentle yet martial-spirited "Adelaide"? Among the hundreds who have declaimed and written and sung of the magic heroism of Joan of Arc, who has offered a nobler tribute to her memory than the writer in a recent number of the "Offering"? God bless the guardians and the writers of the "Lowell Offering," and make it an instrument of incalculable good.[31]

Edgarton left *The Universalist and Ladies' Repository* following the publication of the December issue of volume 11. Some of the Universalist hierarchy believed that she removed herself because of editorial differences with Henry Bacon. The journal continued to publish articles that reflected traditional Universalist views on women following Edgarton's departure, but there were no more correspondents who reported on working-class women, the condition of women in the workplace, and the need for female education beyond those traits valued by males. Bacon attributed her departure to pressures involved in editing and publishing her annual journal, *The Rose of Sharon*. Caroline Sawyer, later to become an editor of *The Universalist and Ladies' Repository*, succeeded Edgarton as editor of this religious annual. Edgarton did, as she promised, continue to contribute to the periodical for a number of years following 1843.

Following Edgarton's departure, *The Universalist and Ladies' Repository* began to look a lot like the periodical that preceded her coeditorship. Bacon and his successor, Mrs. E. A. Bacon, stayed true to the Universalist line on the place of the female in the overall universe. Bacon continued to publish new and primarily female and clerical writers who often commented on the overall power and morality of the female character. Bacon revived his famous women-in-history series, paying tribute to the likes of Mary Queen of Scots and Lady Rachel Russell. With his death in 1856, the journal was never edited by a male again.

Caroline Sawyer followed Mrs. Bacon as editor with the 30th volume at the outbreak of the Civil War. Sawyer was married to the Reverend Thomas Jefferson Sawyer, a leading intellectual in the church during much of the nineteenth century.[32] In keeping with other reform journals of the period, *The Universalist and Ladies' Repository* moved away from the purely theological considerations that had characterized its earlier years. While not ignoring the longtime dedication to women's rights, Sawyer dedicated a large portion of its editorial perspective to the abolitionist cause. She had good training for her mission. She had grown up in the home of her grandfather John Kendrick, a known northern antislavery advocate. White southerners fared poorly in Sawyer's literature. She regularly portrayed them as more ignorant than the slaves whom they held in bondage.[33]

Sawyer was outraged when President Abraham Lincoln was assassinated. She wrote, "It is the fitting *finale* of a long series of wrongs and atrocities of which the rebels have been guilty."[34] The editor condemned a number of southern practices during the war, including the barbarity of their prison camps. Yet, she remained optimistic that the outcome of the war would result in one nation united peacefully under one flag. Sawyer had no patience for a state divided among east, west, north, and south.[35]

When Sawyer left *The Universalist and Ladies' Repository*, she was succeeded by Sarah Nowell, who stayed only long enough to edit the 34th volume. At the conclusion of the Civil War, women's journals were addressing new causes, in particular, the right of franchise. By the late 1860s, the Universalist Church was tiring of the constant money drain that the journal had become.[36] There were other and more influential journals campaigning for similar causes, in particular, its namesake published by the Methodist-Episcopal congregations in the United States. The Methodist-Episcopal journal was a larger, more impressive volume that contained numerous etchings to enhance its physical appearance. It was considered the most important of the reform publications dedicated to women.[37]

Following Nowell's departure in 1866, she was succeeded by the Reverend Phebe Ann Coffin Hanaford. In every respect, Hanaford was the last hope for the journal. Known for her literary works of fiction, poetry, children's stories, and biographies, she attempted to return the publication to a more feminist perspective. She had become the first female minister ordained in the Universalist Church. Although Hanaford was primarily interested in the evangelistic zeal that attracted her to the Universalist Church, she was determined that both the church and secular society recognize her quests for gender equality. She was a well-known figure in the American Woman Suffrage Association and the Association for the Advancement of Women. In 1877, she published a collection of biographies of American women under the title *Women of the Century*.[38]

When Hanaford left, following publication of the 40th volume, she was succeeded by Henrietta A. Bingham, the journal's last editor. By the time of her succession, the journal, now known simply as *The Repository*, had surrendered its right to speak for reform-minded American women. The world was changing, although the Universalist Church itself was having difficulty reconciling itself to its own rhetoric, in particular in the field of women's rights. Boston's Tufts College, where Thomas J. Sawyer was dean of divinity, was still an all-male institution in 1875, the year after *The Ladies' Repository* ceased publication. Elizabeth M. Bruce, an ordained Universalist minister, chided members of the church's Reform League at its meeting in 1875 for refusing to encourage women to join the ministry. She noted that of the 700 Universalist preachers active in the sect, only 10 were women.[39] It appears that the years of championing the rights of women, from Bacon to Hanaford, had fallen on deaf ears.

Notes

1. Joseph Henry Allen and Richard Eddy, *A History of the Unitarians and the Universalists in the United States* (New York: Christian Literature, 1894), pp. 471–472.

2. Eddy, *A History of the Unitarians and the Universalists in the United States*, vol. 11, p. 593.

3. Kathleen L. Endres, "The Women's Press in the Civil War: A Portrait of Patriotism, Propaganda, and Prodding," *Civil War History* 30:1 (March 1984), p. 30, fn. 1.

4. Russell E. Miller, *The Larger Hope* (Boston: Unitarian Universalist Association, 1985), p. 237.

5. David Robinson, *The Unitarians and the Universalists* (Westport, Conn.: Greenwood Press, 1985), p. 127.

6. November 1840, p. 201.

7. Robinson, *The Unitarians and the Universalists*, p. 85.

8. Ibid., p. 127.

9. June 1837, p. 31.

10. Ibid.

11. July 1837, pp. 45, 72–73.

12. Ibid., pp. 54–60.

13. July 1837, pp. 51–52.

14. Ibid. The theme was repeated in a poem called "Is There Poetry in Woman" (March 1841, p. 376) by a writer who wrote under the pseudonym Julia and who was a regular contributor to the periodical throughout the early years of the journal. The last verse reads:

There is poetry in a woman's smile
What hath the sunny earth more fair?
There is poetry in a woman's mind,
The *many* deep thoughts hidden there.
Too much of the poetry hath a part
Amid the wealth of a woman's heart.

15. August 1837, p. 96.

16. February 1838, pp. 345–346.

17. June 1841, pp. 6–7. Later that year a writer identified only as S.P.L. of Worcester offered virtually the same argument. See October 1841, p. 196.

18. May 1838, pp. 474–475.

19. April 1839, p. 403.

20. December 1841, p. 249.

21. February 1842, p. 347.

22. February 1840, p. 335.

23. November 1839, pp. 210–211.

24. January 1841, p. 303.

25. March 1842, p. 379.

26. June 1839, p. 15.

27. July 1839, p. 65.

28. Representative was a series "Sketches of Fashion's Eccentricities" by the Reverend J. M. Austin, which commenced in the journal with March 1838 on page 389. Austin argued that fashions were designed not to promote the beauty of the wearer but to hide natural deformities in the human body.

29. June 1839, p. 28.

30. Harriet H. Robinson, "The Lowell Offering," *The New England Magazine*, December 1884, pp. 463–464.

31. December 1841, pp. 278–279.

32. Robinson, *The Unitarians and the Universalists*, p. 319.

33. Endres, "The Women's Press in the Civil War," pp. 33–34.

34. Ibid., p. 39.

35. Ibid.

36. Miller, *The Larger Hope*, p. 237.

37. Endres, "The Women's Press in the Civil War," p. 33.

38. Robinson, *The Unitarians and the Universalists*, pp. 272–273.

39. Miller, *The Larger Hope*, p. 464.

Information Sources

BIBLIOGRAPHY:

Eddy, Richard. *Universalism in America: A History*, vol. 11. Boston: Universalist Publishing House, 1886.

Endres, Kathleen L. "The Women's Press in the Civil War: A Portrait of Patriotism, Propaganda, and Prodding," *Civil War History* 30: 1 (March 1984), pp. 31–53.

Miller, Russell E. *The Larger Hope*, Boston: Unitarian Universalist Association, 1985.

Robinson, David. *The Unitarians and the Universalists*, Westport, Conn.: Greenwood Press, 1985.

INDEX SOURCES: Union List of Serials.

LOCATION SOURCES: The University of Western Ontario Library and other libraries.

Publication History

MAGAZINE TITLE AND TITLE CHANGES: *The Universalist* (1832–1833); *The Universalist and Ladies' Repository* (1834–1842); *The Ladies' Repository* (1843–1873); *The Repository* (1873–1874).

VOLUME AND ISSUE DATA: Vols. 1–52. (1832–1874). Monthly (with the exception of vol. 2, which was issued bimonthly temporarily). No Vol. 31.

PUBLISHER AND PLACE OF PUBLICATION: The Universalist Church. Boston.

EDITORS: B. Whittemore, C. Gardner, J. H. Bugbee, L. S. Everett, S. Streeter (1832–1833); D. D. Smith (1834–1836); A. A. Folsom (1836); Henry Bacon (1836–1839); Henry Bacon and Sarah C. Edgarton (1839–1843); Henry Bacon (1843–1856); Mrs. E. A. Bacon (1856–1860); Caroline Sawyer (1860–1865); Sarah A. Nowell (1865–1866); Phebe A. C. Hanaford (1866–1868); Henrietta A. Bingham (1869–1874).

CIRCULATION: Unreported except for 1845 when it was 2,000 monthly.

David Spencer

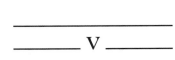

V

VANIDADES CONTINENTAL

The 1980s witnessed the growth of Hispanic print media. American and Latinoamerican publishers based in the United States realized the potential of the untapped Hispanic market and moved to capitalize on it. Publishers had little difficulty convincing leading advertisers of the advantages of exploring this market. The estimated 24.9 million Hispanics currently living in the United States had a buying power estimated at $172 billion per year. The median Hispanic household income had reached $25,200.[1] Publishers introduced a number of new magazines targeted to the Hispanics living in the United States. The new magazines (those launched since 1980) include *Harper's Bazaar en Espanol*, with a circulation of 82,774; *Vista* 1,200,000; *TU Internacional* 267,598; *TV y Novelas* 1,157,918; *Imagen* 100,000; *PC Magazine en Espanol* 150,937; *Mas* 630,000; *Medix* 118,287; *Marie Claire en Espanol* 174,106; and *Ser Padres* 325,000.[2]

Publicity has focused on the boom in the Hispanic magazine market. However, this publicity has failed to look at another Latinoamerican magazine, which has weathered revolutions, hostile takeovers, political barriers, and internal battles over its long, rich history.

Vanidades, a Spanish-language women's magazine, came into the market more than 50 years ago to serve the particular interests of contemporary Latinoamerican women. *Vanidades*, known today by its readers as *Vanidades Continental*, was launched in February 1937 in Havana, Cuba, by Editorial Carteles, S.A. In the controversial political environment of Cuba in the 1930s and 1940s, Isabel M. Ordetx, chief editor of *Vanidades*,[3] saw the chance to create a monthly magazine for those females who, without ignoring their country's current situation, had particular interests in specific women's topics such as parenting, fashion, and marriage. It was an unusual move, especially for a woman. Cuba in the 1930s and 1940s was a patriarchal society. However, Cuba did represent an oasis in Latin America for political rights for women. Cuba was one of the few Latin American countries, with the exception of Argentina and Uruguay, where women achieved a high level of equality. Cuban women had had the right to vote since 1934, before women of most Latin American countries could.[4]

The magazine was aimed at women in a privileged social class. The reader of *Vanidades* was affluent and well educated. She was the exception in Cuba. Before 1959, about one-fifth of the Cuban population over school age could not read or write,[5] there were no secondary schools in the countryside, and, as late as 1971, secondary rural enrollment was as low as 3,000 students.[6]

In this environment of privileged social class, Ordetx continued bringing her readers the most up-to-date information on fashions, beauty, and decoration, without a word of politics. In 1952, the magazine was sold. Miguel Angel Quevedo and Francisco Saralegui became the new owners of *Vanidades*. Quevedo was a well-known journalist and the founder of *Bohemia*, the largest magazine published in Cuba. Saralegui was a wealthy businessman and magazine distributor in Cuba. Saralegui bought 33 percent of the magazine's shares, and Quevedo bought 66 percent from Alfredo T. Quiles, owner of Editorial Carteles, S.A. Quiles kept 1 percent of the business to distribute the magazine through Editorial Carteles.[7] Herminia del Portal, who came back from Paris, where she was working with Andres Guide, one of the most important Latinoamerican writers of the time, was named editorial director of *Vanidades*.

When Quevedo and Saralegui acquired *Vanidades*, the publication had a circulation of 40,000. The number one women's magazine in Cuba was *Romance*, with a circulation of 102,000. *Cine Grafico* was in second place, with 70,000, and *Ellas*, with a circulation of 50,000, was in third place. A year later, *Vanidades* became the best-selling women's magazine in Cuba and in other Latinoamerican countries. Its circulation reached 140,000.[8]

Quevedo, as editor in chief, Herminia Del Portal, as editorial director, and Saralegui maintained the same editorial mix and kept the same sections in the publication. The magazine remained a traditional women's magazine, aimed at the women of the highest social class. The new owners revitalized the magazine. They acquired better printing equipment and changed *Vanidades*'s appearance by using "perfect binding." The magazine also capitalized on its new ties to *Bohemia*. *Vanidades* benefited from *Bohemia*'s distribution channels. In addition, *Vanidades* expanded its distribution to Argentina and Chile. (At this point, distribution to United States was limited.) One thing, though, was always clear for the different owners of *Vanidades*: no politics was ever a part of the publication. Jorge Saralegui, son of Francisco Saralegui and later owner of the magazine, also believes that a key point in *Vanidades*'s success was its being completely divorced from politics.[9] It was a fortunate choice since Cuba was on the verge of revolution. Fidel Castro, billed as a reformer, led the revolution that overthrew Fulgencio Batista. Castro presided over Cuba's transformation into a Communist state.

Francisco Saralegui soon retired from the publishing business. His son Jorge took his place at Editorial Carteles, S.A. and at *Vanidades*. Although the younger Saralegui and Quevedo sympathized with Castro's political ideology at the beginning of his term, the sympathy soon turned to opposition. Quevedo and Saralegui were forced to leave Cuba in mid-1959, six months after Castro took over the country. Both men left the country without even having the opportunity to take their belongings. Quevedo went to Venezuela, and Saralegui flew to the United States. Although in different countries, Saralegui and Quevedo kept their ties. But Quevedo, separately, also established business ties with Armando De Armas, one of the most powerful magazine publishers in Latin America. Saralegui, in Miami, followed his father's steps and established, in 1960, Editorial America, S.A. and introduced *Vanidades* into the United States market.[10]

The new *Vanidades* was almost a women's city/regional magazine. It was distributed primarily in the New York and Miami areas, where the highest concentrations of Hispanics were located. Saralegui could not afford to expand distribution beyond these cities. He introduced *Vanidades* to the American market with a budget of $750. Saralegui was the publisher, editor, advertising director, and manager of the magazine. He added "Continental" to *Vanidades*'s name in order to differentiate it from the old Cuban magazine (*Vanidades* had folded in Cuba with Saralegui and Quevedo's exile). Saralegui invited Del Portal as well as Quevedo, who had settled in Venezuela, to join him in this venture. In the new corporation, Saralegui owned 50 percent of the shares, Del Portal had 25 percent, and Quevedo, who came back from Venezuela to join Editorial America, owned the remaining 25 percent. The trio projected a circulation of 72,000 for the 112-page publication. Five years later *Vanidades Continental* reached a circulation of 400,000.[11]

The editorial format of the "American" version of *Vanidades* did not differ markedly from that of the Cuban product. The magazine was aimed at the affluent female Cuban exile. The monthly avoided politics, extensively covering fashion, beauty, and decoration as it had always done. Of course, the magazine was printed in Spanish by an editorial staff of Cuban exiles. The magazine ever reminded readers of their rich Latino culture. It was an important tie to a life left behind in Cuba.

The word of *Vanidades*'s success flew to Venezuela; and Armando De Armas, a Venzuelan businessman who owns Bloque De Armas, the largest magazine distributor in Venezuela and in Latin America, intrigued by the prospect of breaking into the American market, offered to buy Saralegui's shares for $1 million in 1961. Saralegui refused. De Armas established business relations with Miguel Angel Capriles, another Venezuelan businessman and journalist, owner of the second largest magazine distributor in Venezuela. In alliance with Capriles, De Armas changed strategies. If Saralegui would not sell, maybe his partners would. De Armas and Capriles persuaded Del Portal and Quevedo to sell their shares. Quevedo agreed to sell in exchange for cancellation of a debt he had with De Armas.

De Armas and Capriles, who together now held control of 50 percent of

Editorial America, S.A., pressured Saralegui to sell.[12] This time Saralegui agreed. When Saralegui owned Editorial America, *Vanidades Continental* was the company's only property. Under De Armas, Editorial America was converted into the leader in Spanish-language publications in South America. De Armas, however, had advantages Saralegui never enjoyed. He had a distribution system in place, access to sophisticated printing, and capital to bring improvements to the magazines.

At the end of 1961, De Armas and Capriles split their partnership. De Armas became the sole owner of Editorial America, S.A. and *Vanidades Continental*.[13]

De Armas shifted the direction of *Vanidades Continental* somewhat. The anticipated audience remained the affluent, well-educated Latinoamerican woman. However, the readership was not necessarily based in the United States or from Cuba. Capitalizing on the distribution system he already had in place, De Armas expanded the audience from the United States to other Spanish-speaking countries. He retained much of Saralegui's old American readership but increased it considerably with affluent readers in Venezuela, Argentina, and other Spanish-language countries. Editorial content remained much the same: fashion, beauty, and decoration, without politics.

The magazine continued thus until 1983, when De Armas made his move into the United States market in earnest. By 1983, the United States had come to realize the buying power of the Hispanic population. More important, American advertisers had come to see the Latinoamerican buying power and were ready to invest. Of course, *Vanidades Continental* already had a small but affluent, well-educated American audience. *Vanidades Continental* and De Armas's other 15 magazines became part of De Armas Hispanic Magazine Network in the United States in 1983.[14] With the opening of the network, *Vanidades Continental* began to carve its niche in the United States.

The magazine industry boom in the decade of the 1980s offered De Armas the opportunity to attract new audiences and create a new market. Early in the decade, it was apparent that a new and growing market was beginning to gain importance. A large audience of Spanish-speaking people coming from Cuba, other Caribbean islands, Latin America, and Mexico was building in the United States. It seemed that the time was appropriate to explore new markets, find new audiences, and attract new and more advertisers. Capitalizing on this, De Armas launched the De Armas Hispanic Magazine Network to distribute *Vanidades Continental* and 15 other publications that were Spanish-language versions of well-known magazines in the United States.[15] The largest number of these was aimed at a predominantly female market: *Harper's Bazaar en Espanol, TU Internacional, Marie Claire en Espanol, Cosmopolitan en Espanol,* and *Buenhogar.*

The timing was perfect. According to Kenneth Wylie, Hispanics were the fastest-growing minority in the country. The 1980 census showed a count of 14.6 million Hispanics in the United States.[16] Moreover, by 1984, the population had grown 5.4 percent to 20 million.[17] Projections for the year 2020 predict that

"Hispanics will surpass blacks as the largest minority in the country—46.6 million Hispanics and 44.4 million blacks."[18] De Armas redirected the marketing of its number one Spanish-language women's publication. The objective was to encompass a larger existing audience. De Armas was out to make *Vanidades Continental* the magazine that Saralegui envisioned.

Today's *Vanidades Continental* continues its beauty, fashion, and decoration specialties. It is defined as "a complete magazine that also has regular sections on food and cooking, travel and tourism, movies and TV, medicine, health, and nutrition and children. In-depth articles and photographs of international and local personalities, regionalized sections on local events and happenings."[19] This De Armas flagship magazine is now a biweekly publication aimed at 25- to 50-year-old, college-educated Latin American women.[20]

Of the 15 magazines that De Armas Network is currently distributing in the United States, *Vanidades Continental* is the company's best-selling women's magazine, with a total circulation of 488,392. From this total, 430,738 goes to Latin America and 57,654 to the United States.[21]

What differentiates *Vanidades Continental* from the other De Armas publications distributed in the United States is its originality. It has no American counterpart. The three other De Armas women's magazines, *Cosmopolitan en Espanol*, *Harper's Bazaar*, and *Buenhogar* (similar to *Good Housekeeping* *) base their editorial content on their English-language counterparts.

Vanidades Continental is still edited by Latinoamerican professionals. Editorial content is generated by a Latinoamerican staff under the supervision of Sara Barcelo de Castany, director of *Vanidades Continental*. These professionals understand how important it is for Hispanics to preserve their culture. At *Vanidades Continental*, they know that Hispanics interact with media in their own language as a way of preserving that culture. *Vanidades* plays an important role in recognizing that Hispanics are proud of their culture and their language and that they are a distinct minority that deserves a high-quality Spanish-language magazine. On the other hand, *Vanidades* editors seem to be effectively maintaining the positive bond created between the magazine and its readers when they are addressed in the language of their own roots.

Although *Vanidades* focuses mainly on beauty, fashion, and decoration, the magazine often offers in-depth articles, giving a touch of news to its editorial material to comply with Hispanics' economic and cultural demands. In January 1992, the reader was introduced to an extraordinary project that was being almost secretly developed. "Biosfera 2, dos años a puerta cerrada" (Biosfera 2, Two Years under Closed Doors) is the name of a series of experiments undertaken by biologists, botanists, agricultural engineers, and an administrative technician in the Sonora Desert in Tucson, Arizona. In simple words, yet using good Spanish, readers discovered how these professionals were reproducing each one of the different environments already existing on the earth: desert, jungle, and tropical forest.[22]

In February 1993, *Vanidades Continental* combined, with fashion and social manners, the serious matter of the transfer of the power from President George Bush to President Bill Clinton. The article showed with descriptive photography the elegance displayed in the clothing Bush, Clinton, and their wives were wearing. Also the article showed the harmony in both families, and the text related how rivalry in politics dissipates in such an important moment as when a new period of democracy begins for the United States. This was, however, not a political move for *Vanidades Continental*.[23]

In March 1989, rumors spread about the possible sale of De Armas publishing group to Alianza Editorial or Grupo Anaya. Carlos Gonzalez, De Armas vice president and general manager, denied the reports. Two months later, Gonzalez confirmed the news: Editorial America was sold for $55 million. Grupo Anaya, based in Madrid, would control all of the Editorial America publications except for the Venezuelan and Miami operations for *Vanidades Continental*. Although De Armas retained *Vanidades Continental*, negotiations were under way to introduce the magazine into the European market.[24]

The success of *Vanidades Continental* is openly shared by all those people who made it happen, from its director Mrs. Barcelo de Castany to its secretary. On May 28, 1991, Editorial America, S.A., celebrated *Vanidades Continental*'s 30th anniversary, an event that ignored the Cuban birth as well as its life under Saralegui. Likewise, *Vanidades Continental* chose to ignore the hostility related to the sale to De Armas. To mark the occasion, staff members, clients, advertising agency representatives, and other personalities celebrated in the Vizcaya Palace in Miami to honor 30 years of work and success. Not surprisingly, Saralegui and others from the early days of *Vanidades Continental* were not invited.

In the 30th-anniversary issue, *Vanidades Continental* reviewed events and happenings that had marked the history and the lives of many Latinoamerican people. All had been covered in *Vanidades*, thus reinforcing the magazine's reputation of being concerned not only with the way women look but also with their education and knowledge of important historical events. During those 30 years, *Vanidades* covered such news as the first man on the moon, the Persian Gulf War, the debut of the Beatles in England, the assassination of President John F. Kennedy, Mickey Mouse's 60th birthday, and the death of Pope John XXIII.[25]

Vanidades Continental has the strength to draw national advertisers. Offered as part of a package with the other De Armas publications aimed at Spanish-speaking women, *Vanidades Continental* brings in a large number of advertisers marketing upscale products. Advertisements include ads from the beauty, tobacco, automotive, mail order, medical care, and jewelry companies. Cosmetic advertisers are well known. Clinique, Estée Lauder, and Lancome Paris all advertise in *Vanidades Continental*. Advertisements come from Giorgio Armani, Yves Saint Laurent, Cassini, and Fendi. Fashion advertisers include Lanvin, Chanel, YSL, Lacroix, Valentino, and Versace. All offer upscale products to the affluent, well-educated Latinoamerican readers. *Vanidades Continental* benefits from ad packages offered through the De Armas publication network.

Editorially, *Vanidades Continental* supports Latinoamerican designers and products. Carolina Herrera, for example, is a Venezuelan designer whose success in fashion has been outstanding. Her dresses, accessories, and jewelry have been pictured in the pages of the magazine. Stories cover other Latinoamerican designers as well.

The image that De Armas has created for the company's best-selling publication, through the magazine's format, its editorial content, its slick color ads, and its glamour, has made it possible for *Vanidades Continental* to develop the solid niche it has carved in the Hispanic contemporary women's market, both in the United States and in South America. *Vanidades Continental* seems to have become such a well-known and profitable property that De Armas kept the distribution of *Vanidades Continental* in Venezuela and Miami even when Editorial America was sold to a Madrid-based publisher, Grupo Anaya, in 1989.[26]

Today *Vanidades Continental* is the number one Spanish-language women's magazine in the Americas. It is now published in Mexico, under new ownership. Mexican media magnate Emilio Azcarraga Milmo, owner of Televisa, the largest supplier of Spanish-language programming in the world, purchased Editorial America (and *Vanidades Continental*) in 1992.[27] Azcarraga plans to expand the magazine's distribution through heavy advertising in the Televisa network, which holds 90 percent of Mexico's viewership and provides shows to Latin America, the United States, Europe, and the Republic of China.[28]

By covering "traditional" female topics of beauty, fashion, and decoration, *Vanidades* has survived. By skirting political topics, it has endured. By including women within its editorial direction, it has succeeded.

Notes

1. Christy Fisher, "Study: Separate Ad Buys Needed to Reach Hispanics," *Advertising Age*, April 29, 1991, p. 54.

2. *Ulrich International Periodicals Directory 1993–1994* (New Providence, N.J.: R.R. Bowker, 1993).

3. Jorge Saralegui interview, March 14, 1993.

4. Jose A. Moreno, "From Traditional to Modern Values," in Carmelo Mesa-Lago (ed.), *Revolutionary Change in Cuba* (Pittsburgh: University of Pittsburgh Press, 1971), pp. 471-497.

5. Dudley Seers, Andres Bianchi, Richard Jolly, and Max Nolf (eds.), *Cuba: The Economic and Social Revolution* (Chapel Hill: University of North Carolina Press, 1964).

6. Claes Brundenius, *Revolutionary Cuba: The Challenge of Economic Growth with Equity* (London: Westview Press, 1984).

7. Saralegui interview.

8. Ibid.

9. Ibid.

10. Ibid.

11. Ibid.

12. Ibid.

13. Ibid.

14. John Tebbel and Mary Ellen Zuckerman, *The Magazine in America 1741–1990* (New York: Oxford University Press, 1991), p. 254.

15. Ibid.

16. Kenneth Wylie, ''Hispanic Cable TV Strives to Reach Its Potential,'' *Advertising Age*, March 19, 1984, p. M38.

17. Craig Endicott, ''Making the Most of Media,'' *Advertising Age*, March 19, 1984, p. M9.

18. Renee Blakkan, ''Reaching a Growing Market Where It Lives,'' *Advertising Age*, March 19, 1984, p. M10.

19. Advertising, Circulation, and Market Data: Selling to 18,000,000 Latin Americans. Source: Editorial America, S.A.

20. Editorial America, S.A.

21. Ibid.

22. ''Biosfera 2, Dos Años a Puerta Cerrada,'' January 1992, pp. 76–77.

23. ''Elegancia y Democracia,'' February 1993, pp. 82–83.

24. Ed Fitch, ''Spanish Conquest Puts Magazines in New World,'' *Advertising Age*, May 29, 1989, pp. 32–34.

25. ''Vanidades, 30 Aniversario,'' May 28, 1991.

26. Fitch, ''Spanish Conquest Puts Magazines in New World,'' pp. 32–34.

27. Alejandro Quintero interview, March 22, 1993.

28. Ibid.

Information Sources

BIBLIOGRAPHY:

Brundenius, Claes. *Revolutionary Cuba: The Challenge of Economic Growth with Equity.* London: Westview Press, 1984.

Jaben, Jan. ''Arturo Villar: Championing the Hispanic Audience.'' *Folio*, November 1988, pp. 125–127.

Moreno, Jose A. ''From Traditional to Modern Values.'' In Carmelo Mesa-Lago (ed.), *Revolutionary Change in Cuba.* Pittsburgh: University of Pittsburgh Press, 1971, pp. 471–497.

Seers, Dudley, Andres Bianchi, Richard Jolly, and Max Nolf (eds.). *Cuba: The Economic and Social Revolution.* Chapel Hill: University of North Carolina Press, 1964.

Tebbel, John, and Mary Ellen Zuckerman. *The Magazine in America 1741–1990.* New York: Oxford University Press, 1991.

INDEX SOURCES: Infotrac—General Periodical Index.

LOCATION SOURCES: Library of Congress and other libraries.

Publication History

MAGAZINE TITLE AND TITLE CHANGES: *Vanidades* (1937–1960); *Vanidades Continental* (1960–present).

VOLUME AND ISSUE DATA: Vols. 1–(February 1937–present). Monthly (1937–1962); biweekly (1962–present).

PUBLISHER AND PLACE OF PUBLICATION: Editorial Carteles, S.A. (1937–1959); Editorial America, S.A. (1959–present). Havana, Cuba (1937–1959); Miami (1959–present).

EDITORS: Isabel M. Ordetx (1937–1952); Francisco Saralegui (1952–1959); Jorge Saralegui (1959–1961); Sara Barcelo de Castany (1962–present).
CIRCULATION: ABC, 1993: 58,878 (U.S. circulation only, 489,000 worldwide).

Norys C. De Abreu-Garcia

VANITY FAIR

When publisher Condé Nast launched a fashionable new monthly magazine for the carriage trade in 1913, he may never have envisioned its successful rebirth in the 1980s under editor Tina Brown. *Vanity Fair* evolved from a fashion magazine to an arts monthly in the era between world wars before losing its voice during the depression, lying dormant for nearly five decades, and then being revived and repositioned as a celebrity magazine of the booming 1980s.

Nast, who pioneered in publishing periodicals aimed at affluent audiences, bought a fashion magazine called *Dress* that threatened to compete with *Vogue*,* which he had acquired in 1908. He also bought rights to the *Vanity Fair* name from a social and political journal popular in the late nineteenth century that was likened to the *Police Gazette* in its sensationalism.[1] The first issue of *Dress & Vanity Fair* debuted in September 1913 with the subtitle *Fashions, Stage, Society, Sports, the Fine Arts.* Just like its reincarnated version 47 years later, the magazine floundered with its initial issues until the publisher recruited a strong editor to bring it much needed editorial focus.

Magazine veteran Frank Crowninshield agreed to become editor but felt the monthly should move away from fashion and, instead, cover the entertainment topics people like to talk about such as parties, the arts, sports, theater, and humor. His editorial philosophy was similar to what Brown would say in the 1980s about creating articles reducible to a few provocative but easily summarized ideas someone could repeat at a party.[2]

Crowninshield insisted that the word ''Dress'' be dropped from the nameplate and women's fashions removed from the magazine's contents. In his first editorial, in the March 1914 issue, Crowninshield wrote: ''For women, we intend to do something in a noble and missionary spirit, something which, so far as we can observe has never before been done for them by an American magazine. We mean to make frequent appeals to their intellect.''[3]

Under his stewardship, *Vanity Fair* became a pacesetting magazine for a new generation coming of age in the new century. By 1915, it was the leader in advertising linage of all American monthlies.[4] The magazine became known for its eye-catching layouts, good writing, and appreciation of the avant-garde in art. *Vanity Fair*'s editorial experiments included publishing an article all in French, producing an entire issue without using capital letters, and printing controversial works of artists Picasso and Matisse. The use of a photograph of fighter Jack Dempsey posing as Rodin's *Thinker* was replicated on the November 1993 cover featuring actor Sylvester Stallone. Crowninshield employed photographer Edward Steichen and stole writers Dorothy Parker and Clare Boothe Brokaw (later Luce) from *Vogue*. Other new writers in his stable included P. G. Wodehouse, Edna St. Vincent Millay, Collette, Walter Winchell, Aldous Huxley, e. e. cummings, and Edmund Wilson. In addition, he published the work of the already famous F. Scott Fitzgerald, Anita Loos, and Heywood Broun. The magazine prided itself on its outrageousness, which included drawing world financier J. Pierpont Morgan in his underwear. A 1935 caricature of Japanese emperor Hirohito shown pulling a scroll, presumably representing his Nobel Peace Prize, on a gun carriage caused an international incident. *Vanity Fair* was banned in Japan, and its editor had to write a letter of apology to the Japanese ambassador in Washington after the diplomat complained to the State Department about the depiction. The magazine ceased publication later that year. Despite the controversial editorial material that may have boosted circulation, advertising linage had dropped 39 percent in 1935, the worst business performance of any of the Condé Nast magazines.[5]

Nast had been financially overextended for several years, and ownership of the magazines had been transferred to others. As early as 1931, Brokaw had recommended that Nast buy the rights to *Life* magazine, then a humor magazine that had just faded, and turn *Vanity Fair* into a picture journal. Her future husband, Henry Luce, followed her suggestion when he acquired *Life*. But Nast had other ideas. Desperate to keep *Vanity Fair* afloat, he considered transforming it into a beauty magazine but postponed the idea while paving the way "by presenting . . . more editorial features of interest to women."[6] But before the repositioning could be tested, the *Vanity Fair* staff was informed that, with its March 1936 issue, the magazine would be merged with *Vogue*. *Vanity Fair's* circulation was under 90,000. The merger did not last, as the sister publications were not aimed at the same elements of café society. Only 4.8 percent of *Vanity Fair* readers renewed their subscriptions to *Vogue* after their original *Vanity Fair* subscriptions expired.[7]

Times had changed from the promise of prosperity when *Vanity Fair* was launched. The shifting sociopolitical climate caused by the depression made the magazine seem irrelevant. Also, it had not been able to respond quickly to new competition for advertising and readers from the *New Yorker* and *Esquire* magazines started in the 1930s. Nevertheless, for nearly 50 years the Condé Nast publishing group (bought by S. I. Newhouse in the 1950s) clung to the once-famous nameplate in the hopes a revival might occur.

The 1980s version of *Vanity Fair* was not a resuscitation of the pre–World War II magazine but was reintroduced as a general-interest magazine, bucking the trend of specialty publications. It was aimed at affluent Americans primed for boom times. The readership was difficult to categorize demographically, but *Vanity Fair* was clustered often in "fine living," "lifestyle," and "cultural" magazine classes with competitors including *Town and Country, Fame, Connoisseur*, and *House & Garden*.*

Vanity Fair's 732,000 premier copies (with 600,000 charter subscribers) seemed quite robust compared with the paltry 90,000 copies during its last days of the mid 1930s, but the stakes were higher. Newhouse spent 18 months and $10 million to reintroduce *Vanity Fair*. One of the biggest burdens of the new version was trying to live up to what people remembered or heard about the first version in its heyday. The first issue of the relaunch, in October 1983, was critically panned.

Its relaunch was under the editorship of former *New York Times Book Review* editor Richard Locke, who envisioned the magazine as an "amalgam of the best of the *New Yorker*, the *New York Review of Books* and *Rolling Stone*."[8] He was roundly criticized for being too narrowly literary. The 290-page first edition of the reborn *Vanity Fair* included a short novel by Gabriel García Márquez and articles by Gore Vidal and Stephen Jay Gould. Locke was aware of the legacy that befell him:

> The old *Vanity Fair* was an exciting combination of high culture and low entertainment and seriousness that seemed to capture the spirit of the times. But that was the twenties. We can't bring them back, and have no interest in doing so. But we hope to be able to put together a magazine that is as much a product of this time as the original was to its.[9]

Nevertheless, the first new issue featured an illustrated cover reminiscent of its prewar image and an article by James Cain about Malibu Beach reprinted from a 1933 edition.

While the magazine was planning to cover everything from culture both high and low to public affairs, politicians, the arts, and fiction (the latter had been opposed by Crowninshield), it was not promoted to advertisers as a journal of ideas. Rather, it was touted as a luxury magazine like Condé Nast's *Vogue* and *Gentleman's Quarterly*, reaching the recession-proof reading rich willing to pay up to three dollars per issue. *Newsweek* characterized the new *Vanity Fair* as the first attempt in a decade to publish a substantial magazine that would appeal to both sexes.[10] Despite those claims, the color advertising seemed decidedly female-oriented, with page after page of fashion, cosmetics, jewelry, and luggage spreads along with liquor and tobacco advertising.

Early reviews of the ambitious relaunch were devastating. One scorched-earth critique in the *New Republic* did a point-by-point analysis comparing the old and new versions of *Vanity Fair* and proclaimed the rebirth stillborn: "the lousiest, most confusing layout with which any glossy magazine can ever have appeared . . . a magazine whose publisher and editor . . . have no ideas why it is needed, what they have to tell, or even in what time or place they have their being."[11] The review concluded: "It has no other reason for being but to make money for the publishing corporation, its accountants, and the advertisers."[12] *New Republic* characterized *Vanity Fair*'s target audience as the "fretful rich" and, "from start to finish, a magazine of status anxiety."[13]

Editor Locke was fired after the third issue and succeeded by Leo Lerman, who lasted only eight months until he was promoted out of the editorship. Tina Brown was recruited by Newhouse from the *Tatler*, described as the British version of *People* for the society set. In January 1984, Brown had moved from London to New York to help the flagging *Vanity Fair* find its niche. A *New York Times Magazine* article summed up the challenge that awaited her: "[I]t was the laughingstock of the publishing world—a critical flop on the one hand, savaged for its lack of editorial focus; a financial disaster on the other, hemorrhaging money and attracting almost no advertising."[14]

Brown soon shaped her editorial mix into an " 'intellectual cabaret,' a saucy, literate celebrity magazine featuring profiles of Hollywood aristocrats and parvenues, ballasted with some weightier and newsier pieces."[15] She paid homage to Crowninshield by resurrecting features he created, including "Letter from London" and celebrity profiles (using *Vanity Fair* photographs from the 1930s) in a section she called "Flashback." Brown also revived one of the magazine's original goals, to cultivate new talent. She is credited with attracting good writers. While Locke started out paying one dollar per word, she raised it to two dollars in a magazine market where 10¢ to 12¢ a word had been a tradition. She went out of her way to woo writers. She signed many to annual contracts and gushed over her favorites in print and at lavish parties. Brown was out to make her mark and told early interviewers, "I don't want to be editor in brief."[16] She lasted almost a decade until she was tapped by Newhouse to take over the editorship of the *New Yorker* in 1992.

During Brown's tenure at *Vanity Fair*, she pioneered in making it more topically competitive than most monthlies by taking advantage of modern satellite printing technology. She was able to send about one-third of her editorial pages out one week before the magazine appeared (as opposed to the typical two- to three-month production lead time at most monthlies). *Forbes* credited the success of *Vanity Fair* to Brown as well as Newhouse, whom it said possessed "not easily deflected determination and deep pockets,"[17] as one of the largest privately held multimedia conglomerates in the United States.

Piggybacking *Vanity Fair* with other Condé Nast publications aimed at the same affluent, educated readers helped draw advertisers, while bookstore sales increased its newsstand exposure to new readers. With nearly one-third of *Vanity Fair* readers drawn from impulse purchases, great emphasis was placed on covers to attract their attention. Brown brought the *Tatler*'s style editor with her to revamp the layout into a coffee-table magazine. Good designs and provocative photographs by Richard Avedon and Annie Liebovitz soon achieved the desired effects of increased circulation and advertising, as well as publicity. Brown's first *Vanity Fair* cover featured a statuesque actress, Daryl Hannah, blindfolded in a tight red dress. Her most famous covers involved actress Demi Moore in the nude. The August 1991 issue featured a quite pregnant pose; while one year later, Moore's then svelte body was covered only in a suit fashioned from body paint.

Brown did not seem to mind blending advertising with editorial content. Two of her covers featured designers and major *Vanity Fair* advertisers, Ralph Lauren and Calvin Klein. In October 1991, *Vanity Fair* scored an advertising coup when it included a 116-page Calvin Klein supplement touted as the largest of its kind for a consumer magazine in U.S. history. Reported to cost close to $1 million to produce, the ad supplement was wrapped in a polybag with the magazine to 250,000 of 850,000 subscribers and key newsstands.[18]

While Brown boasted that circulation surpassed the 1 million mark in 1992, and advertising revenue nearly quadrupled under her editorship, critics charged that the high-priced writer's contracts and the production costs associated with last-minute editorial changes negated any revenue increase. Newhouse was estimated to have lost from $50 to $100 million over the decade of the revived *Vanity Fair*.[19]

Between 1980 and 1990, the number of magazines on American newsstands doubled, but most newcomers failed. *Vanity Fair* succeeded because Brown was able to capture the spirit of the times: "greed on Wall Street, a couple in the White House who loved pomp and style, and an economic boom that sharpened the taste of millions for conspicuous consumption."[20] Brown said she liked to mix the pace and news to keep readership high. In her September 1992 sign-off letter as *Vanity Fair* editor, she summed up her winning formula:

> *Vanity Fair* is the quintessential postmodern magazine. It is the great high-low show, able to deliver Roseanne Barr mud-wrestling side by side with Chancellor Kohl cogitating, or Demi Moore's pregnant belly side by side with Martha Graham's dance aesthetic.

Brown boasted of a "cross-cultural" editorial mix that included 15,000-word articles, stories on the first ecology martyr, the search for the source of acquired immunodeficiency syndrome (AIDS) in Africa, William Styron's essay on depression, Norman Mailer's reporting on the Gulf War, and Gail Sheehy's reports on presidential candidates and health issues. For all its emphasis on personalities and gossip, *Vanity Fair*, under Brown's helm, had been likened to an upscale *People*. However, managing editor Pamela McCarthy said, "*Vanity Fair* is smarter and more sophisticated than *People*. And I think it's nicer than *Spy*."[21]

Brown's successor, E. Graydon Carter, came to *Vanity Fair* indirectly from *Spy* magazine, which he cofounded before taking over the editorship of a sassy weekly called the *New York Observer*. He knew he had a hard act to follow, and ad linage in *Vanity Fair* declined when a clique of loyal advertisers followed Brown to the *New Yorker*. Nevertheless, he prided himself on producing four of the ten best-selling covers in the history of *Vanity Fair* during his first year, including Madonna, Princess Diana, Julia Roberts, and an August 1993 issue featuring model Cindy Crawford giving a shave to lesbian singer k. d. lang in keeping with the magazine's tradition of controversy and celebrity. An editorial experiment in printing two March 1993 covers split between a newly elected

Bill Clinton and actress Andie MacDowell paid off. The Clinton cover became the best-selling cover featuring a male in the magazine's history.[22]

In the tenth-anniversary issue of *Vanity Fair* in October 1993, Carter reiterated the successful formula of the not-easily classifiable magazine:

> Month after month, *Vanity Fair* has hit the newsstands with a riot of color, revolution, and excess, still impervious to any kind of definition. Its title has its roots in Bunyan's pilgrimage and in Thackeray's romp: life can be a moral tale or a comedy of manners, but it takes a deal of wit and a deal of care to devise either one.

Only time will tell whether Carter or other editors have the care or wit to move *Vanity Fair* into the next century.

Notes

1. Caroline Seebohm, *The Man Who Was Vogue: The Life and Times of Condé Nast* (New York: Viking Press, 1982), p. 104.

2. Elizabeth Kolbert, "How Tina Brown Moves Magazines," *New York Times Magazine*, December 5, 1993, pp. 70–71.

3. March 1914, p. 15.

4. Seebohm, *The Man Who Was Vogue*, p. 118.

5. Ibid., p. 318.

6. Ibid., p. 323.

7. Ibid., p. 327.

8. Craig Unger, "Can 'Vanity Fair' Live Again?" *New York*, April 26, 1982, p. 28.

9. Ibid.

10. Charles Kaiser, "The Making of a Magazine," *Newsweek*, January 3, 1983, p. 65.

11. Henry Fairlie, "The Vanity of 'Vanity Fair,' " *New Republic*, March 21, 1983, p. 27.

12. Ibid., p. 29.

13. Ibid., p. 30.

14. Kolbert, "How Tina Brown Moves Magazines," p. 70.

15. Laurence Zuckerman, "The Dynamic Duo at Condé Nast," *Time*, June 13, 1988, p. 52.

16. Charles Leerhsen, "A New Editor for *Vanity Fair*," *Newsweek*, January 16, 1984, p. 71.

17. Malcolm Forbes, "Progress Report on Three Picked as Winners," *Forbes*, January 12, 1987, p. 24.

18. Alex Prud'homme, "What's It All about, Calvin?" *Time*, September 23, 1991, p. 44; "Klein 'Outsert' New Trend?" *Advertising Age*, September 9, 1991, p. 12.

19. Kolbert, "How Tina Brown Moves Magazines," p. 97.

20. Tom Mathews, "High Gloss News," *Newsweek*, May 1, 1989, p. 54.

21. Ibid., p. 58.

22. Lisa Anderson, "Now He's Fair Game," *Chicago Tribune*, September 29, 1993, sec. 5, p. 2.

Information Sources

BIBLIOGRAPHY:

Anderson, Lisa. "Now He's Fair Game." *Chicago Tribune*, September 29, 1993, sec. 5, pp. 1, 2.

Boo, Katherine. "Vanity Fare." *Washington Monthly*, September 1991, pp. 21–26.

Crowther, Prudence. "Inanity Fair." *New Republic*, November 4, 1991, p. 14.

Edel, Richard. "Mags' Graphic Design Sets Style." *Advertising Age*, October 3, 1985, pp. 18–19.

Elliott, S. J. "*Vanity Fair* comes out for round three." *Advertising Age*, March 11, 1985, p. 83.

————. "Publisher Is Only Change at *VF*." *Advertising Age*, June 3, 1985, p. 3.

Fairlie, Henry. "The Vanity of 'Vanity Fair.' " *New Republic*, March 21, 1983, pp. 25–30.

Forbes, Malcolm. "Progress Report on Three Picked as Winners." *Forbes*, January 12, 1987, p. 24.

Goldsborough, Robert. "Second Chance Sweet at *VF*, *Life*." *Advertising Age*, October 6, 1991, p. 48.

Huhn, Mary. "Fanfare for the Common Man: Carter's First Change Hits *VF*." *Mediaweek*, August 17, 1992, p. 4.

————. "The House That Si Built." *Adweek*, March 1, 1993, pp. 26–28.

Janello, Amy, and Brennon Jones. *The American Magazine*. New York: Abrams, 1991.

Kaiser, Charles. "The Making of a Magazine." *Newsweek*, January 3, 1983, p. 65.

"Klein 'Outsert' New Trend?" *Advertising Age*, September 9, 1991, p. 12.

Kolbert, Elizabeth. "How Tina Brown Moves Magazines." *New York Times Magazine*, December 5, 1993, pp. 65–72, 85–87, 97.

Leerhsen, Charles. "A New Editor for *Vanity Fair*." *Newsweek*, January 16, 1984, pp. 70–71.

Lippert, Barbara. "Calvin's Endlessly Art-Directed Sex." *Adweek*, September 16, 1991, pp. 36–37.

Mathews, Tom. "High Gloss News." *Newsweek*, May 1, 1989, pp. 54–56.

Prud'homme, Alex. "What's It All about, Calvin?" *Time*, September 23, 1991, p. 44.

Reilly, Patrick. "Mags: 'Fair' Game for Miracle Worker." *Advertising Age*, October 24, 1988, pp. S1–S4.

"Resurrecting a legend." *Time*, February 21, 1983, p. 62.

Richardson, Diana Edkins (ed.). *Vanity Fair: Photographs of an Age, 1914–1936*. New York: Clarkson Potter, 1982.

"Salescall: Media Executives Give a *Vanity Fair* Shake to a Livelier, Focused Magazine" [panel discussion]. *Madison Avenue*, October 1985, pp. 109–116.

Seebohm, Caroline. *The Man Who Was Vogue: The Life and Times of Condé Nast*. New York: Viking Press, 1982.

Stackpole, Henrietta. "It's a Small W." *Nation*, October 12, 1985, pp. 2–4.

Tebbel, John, and Mary Ellen Zuckerman. *The Magazine in America, 1741–1990*. New York: Oxford University Press, 1991.

Trillin, Calvin. "Uncivil Liberties." *Nation*, March 5, 1990, p. 298.

Unger, Craig. "Can 'Vanity Fair' Live Again?" *New York*, April 26, 1982, pp. 28, 31.

INDEX SOURCES: Access; Music Ind. Readers' Guide to Periodical Literature (Cumulative Index, September 1913–February 1936, by publisher).

LOCATION SOURCES: Illinois State University; Des Moines Public Library; Indiana University; University of Virginia; University of Wisconsin. Available in microform.

Publication History

MAGAZINE TITLE AND TITLE CHANGES: *Dress and Vanity Fair* (September–December 1913); *Vanity Fair* (January 1914–February 1936); *Vanity Fair* (March 1983–present).

VOLUME AND ISSUE DATA: Vols. 1–(*Dress and Vanity Fair*, vol. 1, nos. 1–4, September–December 1913; *Vanity Fair*, vol. 1, no. 5–vol. 45, no. 6, January 1914–February 1936; vol. 46, no. 1–present, March 1983–present). Monthly.

PUBLISHER AND PLACE OF PUBLICATION: Condé Nast Publications, Inc. New York.

EDITORS: Unknown (September 1913–February 1914); Frank Crowninshield (March 1914–February 1936); Richard Locke (March–June 1983); Leo Lerman (July 1983–March 1984); Tina Brown (April 1984–September 1992); E. Graydon Carter (October 1992–present).

CIRCULATION: ABC, 1993: 1,157,725 (paid, primarily subscriptions).

Norma Green

VICTORIA

Founded March 17, 1987, *Victoria* captured the essence of a period that had ended almost exactly a century earlier. Readers eagerly embraced the magazine's modern variation on the nineteenth-century Victorian lifestyle. A short two years after its birth, John Mack Carter, Hearst Corporation's magazine development director, summarized *Victoria*'s phenomenal success: "Nothing is so powerful as an idea whose time has gone . . . and come again."[1]

Indeed, its time had come again. *Victoria*, the magazine that espoused "a more romantic approach to living,"[2] was considered unique in a market that boasted a number of successful women's magazines. About its competitors, Carter wrote:

They all required so much effort. . . . It was as if the magazine makers were on a treadmill to make women busier and busier. . . . *Victoria* allows women to get off the world that others are creating and into their own secret world.[3]

In *Victoria*, Carter and editor Nancy Lindemeyer created a magazine that broke away from the glut of magazines devoted to converting "still more readers into superwomen striving to have it all."[4] Unrelated to either of its namesakes (the Canadian literary magazine published from 1847 to 1848 or the contemporary city magazine published in Victoria, British Columbia),[5] *Victoria* was titled "Victoriana" in the original mock-up.[6] However, the name was shortened to *Victoria*. It carried the ''parental overline''[7] on the cover until summer 1988, when *Good Housekeeping's Victoria* officially became *Victoria*.

Victoria was designed with a Victorian theme at its core, to celebrate the romantic and the feminine. Sue Woodman, writing in *Working Woman** magazine, described *Victoria* as ''a pastel-shaded publication of domestic bliss,'' with an image of women that was ''unabashed femininity.''[8] However, the magazine's concept of femininity was clearly defined and distinct from that portrayed in its contemporaries such as *Cosmopolitan** or *Playboy*.

Regina Joseph compared *Victoria* with *Martha Stewart Living (MSL)*, noting that *Victoria* was ''*MSL*'s closest competitor,'' with *MSL* being ''urbane and house-in-the-country,'' and *Victoria*, ''truly homey.'' Joseph said, ''Where *MSL* is stark and designed, *Victoria* is warm and fuzzy.''[9]

From the pastel-shaded colors that replicated the 1840s' newly developed chromolithography printing techniques[10] to the magazine's feminine image, *Victoria* was soft-spoken. *Victoria*'s publisher, Katherine W. Mountain, said: '' 'The magazine doesn't tell you how to do anything better. There are no mandates, no dictates, no shouting. What we provide is balance. We show the other, more private side of the hardworking life. That's why it's working. That's what people want.' ''[11]

Kim Foltz said, ''Some researchers think that *Victoria*'s formula, which relies heavily on the fantasy of a more gracious era, works because it tells successful women it is all right to call time out.'' She summarized the results of an early 1990s study that reported ''an increasing number of women were tired of having to steal time for themselves and were beginning to demand it.''[12] She also quoted Ann Clurman, associate director of strategic services at Grey Advertising, who said:

> Because of the stress of work and running a household, more women said they were trying to focus on little things to make their lives better. . . . It may be something as simple as taking the time to make potpourri. It could be just the luxury of indulging in a fantasy. It may seem sort of old-fashioned, but it makes many women comfortable again with their softer side.[13]

From the outset, the magazine covered everything from fashion to architecture, from teas to famous Victorian writers and poets. The magazine did not confine its pages to American Victoriana, taking the reader to writer Charlotte Brontë's England, the royal gardens of Luxembourg, and breakfast in old Irish country houses.

Victoria editorial director Tricia Foley told writer Eileen Swift, ''I think people have been through such a stark, severe period, with everything so high-tech, that they are looking for something they can relate to more personally.''[14] Peter Wilson observed in the entertainment section of the *Vancouver* (Canada) *Sun* that *Victoria*'s pages held ''the promise of a better time and a better place,'' a place where "roofs never leak. Breakerboxes never smoulder. It is forever 1888, with central heating and electricity."[15]

If the magazine was unique, so, too, was its birth. In 1987, marketing research was considered essential to a successful magazine start-up. However, 400,000 copies of *Victoria*'s first issue were put on the newsstands "on a hunch." The issue sold 320,000 copies. Carter described this 80 percent sell-through rate as "remarkable." More than 50,000 newsstand buyers became subscribers. The second issue, dated the fall of 1987, was similarly successful: almost 70 percent (more than 400,000) of the 600,000 copies shipped to newsstands sold. Subscription cards again poured into *Victoria*'s offices.[16]

Carter described *Victoria*'s start-up as the most successful launch in Hearst's history.[17] This was no small feat for the 100-year-old company, which had been viewed in its centennial years by some as "the stodgy old man of the media world."[18] The launch was successful by industry measures as well. Within three years, *Victoria*'s start-up was widely acclaimed in the magazine publishing industry. Butcher called it "the most successful magazine launch in publishing history"[19] and compared the magazine's early success with the launches of Hearst's own *Country Living* and Rupert Murdoch's American edition of France's *Elle*,* in 1978 and 1984, respectively.

Responding to increasing sales, Hearst in 1988 increased *Victoria*'s publication frequency, from quarterly to bimonthly. By the time the first bimonthly issue appeared in the fall of 1988, the magazine had garnered 300,000 subscribers and 300,000 single-copy sales.[20] With the August 1989 issue, the magazine moved to monthly publication.[21]

Carter said *Victoria*'s advertising acceptance moved more slowly than reader acceptance.[22] "The premier issue carried 12 pages of advertising; the average in 1989 (was) 52 pages per issue."[23] However, he described this as a strategy, not an unexpected problem. Claeys Bahrenburg, executive vice president of the Hearst magazines division, agreed, "Our philosophy is to establish a readership before we bring it to the advertising community." *Advertising Age*'s Patrick Reilly suggested that the strategy, which he called the Hearst method, "might be the most successful way to launch a magazine."[24]

The magazine's early issues averaged 20 to 30 advertising pages per issue, offering a wide variety of products ranging from goods and domestic furnishings to fashion and automotive items. Within a short two years, the advertising rate base was increased to 750,000.[25]

Advertising continued to increase. In 1989, *Adweek* magazine voted *Victoria* "hottest new magazine"; in 1990, it rated the magazine number three in that same category. The Publisher's Information Bureau reported a 74 percent increase in *Victoria*'s advertising pages in the first half of 1990, compared with an average loss in advertising pages of more than 10 percent at the best-known women's magazines.[26] While other magazines were dying as a result of low advertising revenues, *Victoria* increased its advertising rate base again, from 750,000 to more than 800,000; its revenues increased by 45 percent.[27] In 1990,

New York Times writer Kim Foltz reported that *Victoria* was "one of the most unusual success stories." Foltz said, "There are a few [women's] publications that have not lost their charm."[28]

Carter said Hearst carefully measured the audience from the outset. Each newsstand copy of the first issue carried "subscription offers, price tests and questionnaires designed to develop a precise profile of the reader." Using information gleaned from responses to the first issue, the staff determined how much to commit to a second issue[29] and guided the development of future issues.[30]

Data collected on *Victoria* readers indicated that reader demographics remained consistent as the magazine grew.[31] Just over 70 percent of the magazine's female audience worked outside the home. A similar percentage were married and owned their homes. More than 50 percent were college-educated. Their median income was higher than the median household incomes for *House & Garden,** *Vanity Fair,** and *Vogue** readers. Simmons Market Research Bureau's 1989 data supported the magazine's internally collected demographic findings. Libby Morse noted, "*Victoria*'s readers are not just Marabel Morgan throwbacks or latter-day Blanche DuBoises." She said most of the readers were "employed at something they consider a career" and "live in and around urban areas."[32]

Despite the positive hoopla, *Victoria* failed with some audiences. Carol Powers of the *Los Angeles Times* labeled the magazine "Hearst's phenomenally successful ode to romanticism and femininity."[33] Born when the feminist movement of the last half of the twentieth century was struggling to maintain its momentum, the magazine was attacked for "not being dialectically sound on feminism."[34] Robin Wolaner of *Parenting* magazine vividly summed up her assessment of the magazine: "*Victoria* might make us all puke."[35]

M. G. Lord gave *Victoria* its most scathing attack in her widely quoted *Newsday* article, "This Magazine Is Hazardous to Feminism's Health." Reporting on a Betty Friedan conference, "Women, Men and Media," at Columbia University, Lord said the magazine was unpopular, "to say the least," with conference-goers, who described the magazine as a "sinister, retrograde, no-good subversive rag." Lord wrote:

> It's not hard to understand the success of "Victoria's Secret." Churchgoing wives with a taste for pornographic underwear could hardly be expected to go to 42nd Street to buy it. But *Victoria* the magazine is about something dirtier than sex: class. It codifies the right tea services, Tiffany knock-offs, needle-point doodads, "collectibles" and pathetic cultural pretensions a housebound petite bourgeoise [*sic*] requires to assert her superiority over a mere member of the working class.[36]

A reader responded:

> I felt I had to respond to M. G. Lord's column . . . .I read the column and was hysterical. She hit the nail right on the head.

I am a white, Jewish, single working mother who has no time to collect antique pansy memorabilia, either. And as for an obsession with ancestors, mine fled the czar in Russia, and most of them have disappeared. But I must tell you one thing that you will really find strange. I read this magazine quite often.

I shouldn't say "read," because that is not the right word. I really enjoy breezing through it from time to time, because I find a sort of calmness about the whole thing that is unexplainable. It is a soft magazine and I find it very peaceful because every other woman's magazine out there is always screaming at me about my body, my love life, my working conditions, etc., and what I can do to improve.

At the end of a hard day's work, when I come home to a house full of children and I start my second job taking care of them and everything around sometimes what I need is a peaceful glance through this mindless magazine.

I'm not defending it, but I'm trying to point out another side. Maybe some women think this magazine is reality. I certainly don't and Lord certainly doesn't, but maybe, just maybe, it fits in somewhere.[37]

The lack of pressure to perform was intentional. Editor Nancy Lindemeyer said, "*Victoria* is a place for women to stop for a moment and revel in being women. It is a celebration of femininity. We present no imperatives. We show our readers beautiful things and they take away what they want."[38] Lindemeyer joined Hearst in 1985 to develop the magazine concept, which was similar to one she had offered former employer and competitor Meredith Publishing in Des Moines, Iowa, two years earlier, in 1983.[39]

In 1989, Carter forecast the magazine's circulation would plateau "at near two million"[40]—2 million readers not offended by tea services, doodads, or alleged class implications.

In his biography of Lindemeyer, writer Philip Dougherty reported that, in response to *Victoria*, "Ms. Lindemeyer has received a relative flood of reader mail. One of her favorites starts with, 'Dear gentle people. How did you know?' "[41]

Lindemeyer, born Nancy Canevari of Bridgeport and Greenwich, Connecticut, married into the Lindemeyer family of Strawberry Point, Iowa. She maintained the quintessential late twentieth-century long-distance marriage to spouse Robert (Bob) Lindemeyer, a staff member of Media Resources at Iowa State University in Ames. Dougherty described the Lindemeyer family as "the kind of people who value their possessions from earlier times, like family quilts, china, tea-spoons."[42] Perhaps these influences played a part in her creation of *Victoria*, which undeniably influenced the rebirth of a love affair with all that represented the long-lost era.

The Victorian revival afforded people the opportunity to step away from everything "high-tech." Publisher Mountain said, "We cannot lay claim to starting a trend but we can take credit for leading the way."[43] *Victoria* was credited with a rise in interest in things Victorian: everything from tea parties and Victorian gardens to vintage purses and greeting cards.[44] By the 1990s, Hearst had begun to publish books on the same, under the *Victoria* magazine label. Within three years of its founding, *Victoria*'s impact could be seen throughout the fashion and cultural world.[45]

Interior designer Steven Bengel said the Victorian influence represented a "more personal way to live." Reflecting on the modernist perspective that had dominated twentieth-century design, Bengel said, "Anything that was ornamental or decorative was considered excess baggage. . . . We got into form and function so much that we forgot beauty and esthetics."[46] But gradually, just as the Bauhaus designers' clean, functional lines in the 1920s had replaced the Victorian era's gingerbread of the late nineteenth century, by the end of the twentieth century, the romantic modernism's[47] new gingerbread began to supplant the Bauhaus influence in furniture, fashion, and architecture. However, until *Victoria*, contemporary 1990s readers were scarcely disposed to think of the Victorian era as functional. Foley did, however. Of her book on the British colonial style, she said, "What I'm trying to show in this is that there's a very romantic yet functional style that evolved from this period: the sisal rugs that rolled up, the hurricane lamps and the bungalow style of architecture with its verandas."[48]

Women's fashions changed. Newman quoted Embroidery Council of America's executive vice president Leonard Seiler: "Women's clothes are becoming more feminine and form-fitting, in reaction to the earlier man-tailored, broad-shouldered 'power' look."[49] Fashion designer Nancy Johnson emphasized lace for women in the boardroom, saying: "Lace is appealing to women who have reached a certain point in their lives and careers. . . . They don't feel the need to dress according to a standard that businessmen have set. They allow themselves the luxury of dressing more femininely." Johnson said her customer "treasures the sort of classics seen in the magazine."[50]

The cosmetics company Coty Inc. developed the fragrance L'Effleur, influenced by the period revival. *Victoria* contributing editor Cynthia Hart designed the perfume's packaging.[51] Randy Rolston, founder of Victorian Papers, a "tiny mail-order greeting card company" in Kansas City, said, "We are kind of riding on their success."[52] Rolston allocated almost two-thirds of his company's advertising budget, a reported $45,000, to buying space in *Victoria*.

Victoria splashed into the women's magazine market with phenomenal success. It blatantly touted femininity in a way that sold magazines and alarmed feminists. Whatever its faults and shortcomings, the publication found an audience that found something likable about the call to fantasy and to *Victoria*'s brand of femininity.

Notes

1. John Mack Carter, "Launches, Learning from the Pros: 'Victoria: Celebrating a Kinder and Gentler Time,' " *Folio*, July 1989, p. 112.

2. "Fast Facts," Media Kit, 1993.

3. Patrick Reilly, " 'Victoria' Era at Hearst," *Advertising Age*, June 27, 1988, p. 80.

4. Carter, "Launches, Learning from the Pros," p. 101.

5. Cf. *Victoria Magazine*, Easy Living Promotions Ltd., 214 Westminister, B.C., CN ISSN 0845-9770.

6. Carter, "Launches, Learning from the Pros," p. 101.

7. Reilly, " 'Victoria' Era at Hearst," p. 80.

8. Sue Woodman, "Victoria Reigns . . . Again," *Working Woman*, September 1991, p. 77.

9. Regina Joseph, "The Nutley Reader," *Mediaweek*, December 2, 1991, p. 19.

10. Lynn Van Matre, "Victorian Color Made Life's Throwaways Worth Keeping," *Chicago Tribune*, February 25, 1990, sec. Home, p. 16.

11. Quoted in Woodman, "Victoria Reigns," p. 77.

12. Kim Foltz, "*Victoria* Uses Old Charms on Readers," *New York Times*, July 31, 1990, p. D17.

13. Ibid.

14. Eileen Swift, "A Dream Job for a Designer," *Newsday*, October 20, 1991, Brookhaven Edition, p. 3.

15. Peter Wilson, "Ah, Life through Rose-Colored Pages," *Vancouver Sun*, September 19, 1991, p. C7.

16. Carter, "Launches: Learning from the Pros," p. 101.

17. Pat Guy and Stuart Elliot, " 'Victoria' Will Reign as Monthly," *USA Today*, February 2, 1989, p. B2.

18. Paul Richter, "Hearst Corporation Has Gained Vigor by Changing Focus," *Los Angeles Times*, November 2, 1989, p. D2.

19. Lola Butcher, "Nostalgia for an Era That Never Existed Is Hallmark for KC's Other Card Maker," *Kansas City Business Journal*, November 5, 1990, sec. 1, p. 1.

20. Carter, "Launches: Learning from the Pros," p. 101.

21. Ibid., p. 100.

22. Ibid., p. 101.

23. Ibid., p. 112.

24. Reilly, " 'Victoria' Era at Hearst," p. 80.

25. Alecia Swaay, "Noted . . . Magazines," *Wall Street Journal*, March 31, 1989, p. B6(W).

26. Foltz, "*Victoria* Uses Old Charms," p. 17.

27. Woodman, "*Victoria* Reigns," p. 77.

28. Foltz, "*Victoria* Uses Old Charms," p. 17.

29. Reilly, " 'Victoria' Era at Hearst," p. 80.

30. Carter, "Launches: Learning from the Pros," p. 100.

31. Ibid., p. 112.

32. Libby Morse, "Victor: *Victoria* after Five Years," *Chicago Tribune*, August 12, 1992, p. 1 (zone C).

33. Carol Powers, "Milliners Go Back in Time," *Los Angeles Times*, November 3, 1989, sec. View, p. E1.

34. M. G. Lord, "This Magazine Is Hazardous to Feminism's Health," *Newsday*, October 28, 1990, sec. Ideas, p. 9.

35. Ibid.

36. Ibid.

37. Eileen Dobrin, "A Victorian Tranquilizer?" *Newsday*, November 11, 1990, p. 11.

38. Foltz, "*Victoria* Uses Old Charms," p. 17.

39. Joel Brenner, "Ex-Meredith Force Launches *Victoria*," *Des Moines Register*, June 25, 1988, p. S6.

40. Carter, "Launches: Learning from the Pros," p. 112.

41. Philip H. Dougherty, "The Media Business: Advertising; Celebration of All Things Victorian," *New York Times*, June 24, 1988, p. D5.

42. Ibid.

43. Butcher, "Nostalgia for an Era That Never Existed," p. 1.

44. Dee Stone, "Beverages: Drink in Knowledge of Your Favorite Brews with These Gift Books," *Atlanta Constitution*, November 20, 1991, p. W20; Lynn Van Matre, "The British as Gardeners, Creating Tropical Paradises, Quaint Cottage Gardens, Formal Estates," *Chicago Tribune*, November 10, 1991, sec. Home, p. 8; Constance Crump, "Preserve, Protect, Defend: Franklin Shop Gives Vintage Purses Back Their Sparkle," *Crain's Detroit Business*, October 21, 1991, p. 3; Butcher, "Nostalgia for an Era That Never Existed," p. 1.

45. See Robin Pogrebin, "Victoriana Befits a Cottage Industrialist," *New York Times*, May 29, 1990, sec. 12CN, p. 35; Fairchild Publications, "Styles Span Times, Territory," *HFN—The Weekly Home Furnishings Newspaper*, March 19, 1990, p. 14.

46. Quoted in "Victoriana Returns as a Soft, Feminine Approach to Living," *Chicago Tribune*, July 5, 1987, p. NW17.

47. Term attributed to designer Milo Baughman by Elaine Markoutsas, "A Touch or Two Can Make Rooms More Romantic," *Star Tribune*, February 9, 1992, p. H1.

48. Swift, "A Dream Job for a Designer," p. 3.

49. Judith Newman. "Romantics," *Adweek's Marketing Week*, November 13, 1989, pp. HM 18–20.

50. Paddy Calistro, "New World Entrepreneur Focuses on Nostalgia," *Los Angeles Times,* June 2, 1989, sec. View, p. 7.

51. Cosmetics International, "Coty Out to Reinforce U.S. Market Presence," *Cosmetics International*, Information Access Company, August 15, 1990, p. 7.

52. Butcher, "Nostalgia for an Era That Never Existed," p. 1.

Information Sources

BIBLIOGRAPHY:

Brady, James. " 'Victoria'/Victorious." *Advertising Age*, May 1, 1989, p. 44.

Brenner, Joel. "Ex-Meredith Force Launches *Victoria*." *Des Moines Register*, June 25, 1988, p. S6.

Butcher, Lola. "Nostalgia for an Era That Never Existed Is Hallmark for KC's Other Card Maker." *Kansas City Business Journal*, November 5, 1990, sec. 1, p. 1.

Calistro, Paddy. "New World Entrepreneur Focuses on Nostalgia." *Los Angeles Times*, June 2, 1989, sec. view, p. 7.

Carter, John Mack. "Launches: Learning from the Pros: 'Victoria: Celebrating a "Kinder and Gentler" ' Time." *Folio*, July 1989, p. 112.

Dobrin, Eileen. "A Victorian Tranquilizer?" *Newsday*, November 11, 1990, p. 11.

Fairchild Publications. "Styles Span Times, Territory." *HFD—The Weekly Home Furnishings Newspaper*, March 19, 1990, p. 14.

Foltz, Kim. "*Victoria* Uses Old Charms on Readers." *New York Times*, July 31, 1990, p. D17.

Joseph, Regina. "The Nutley Reader." *Mediaweek*, December 2, 1991, p. 19.

Lord, M. G. "This Magazine Is Hazardous to Feminism's Health." *Newsday*, October 28, 1990, sec. Ideas, p. 9.

Morse, Libby. "Victor: *Victoria*, after Five Years." *Chicago Tribune*, August 12, 1992, p. 1 (zone C).

Newman, Judith. "Romantics." *Adweek's Marketing Week*, November 13, 1989, pp. HM18–20.

Pogrebin, Robin. "Victoriana Befits a Cottage Industrialist." *New York Times*, May 20, 1990, sec. 12CN, p. 35.

Powers, Carol. "Milliners Go Back in Time." *Los Angeles Times*, November 3, 1989, sec. view, p. E1.

Reilly, Patrick. " 'Victoria' Era at Hearst." *Advertising Age*, June 27, 1988, p. 80.

Richter, Paul. "Hearst Corporation Has Gained Vigor by Changing Focus." *Los Angeles Times*, November 2, 1989, p. D2.

Swift, Eileen. "A Dream Job for a Designer." *Newsday*, October 20, 1991, Brookhaven Edition, p. 3.

Van Matre, Lynn. "Victorian Color Made Life's Throwaways Worth Keeping." *Chicago Tribune*, February 25, 1990, sec. Home, p. 16.

"Victoriana Returns as a Soft, Feminine Approach to Living." *Chicago Tribune*, July 5, 1987, p. NW17.

Wilson, Peter. "Ah, Life through Rose-Colored Pages." *Vancouver Sun*, September 19, 1991, p. C7.

Woodman, Sue. "Victoria Reigns . . . Again." *Working Woman*, September 1991, p. 77.

INDEX SOURCES: None.

LOCATION SOURCES: Library of Congress and other libraries. Reprint service available from University Microfilms International.

Publication History

MAGAZINE TITLE AND TITLE CHANGES: *Good Housekeeping's Victoria* (1987–1988); *Victoria* (1988–present).

VOLUME AND ISSUE DATA: Vols. 1–(March 1987–present). Quarterly (1987–1988); bimonthly (1988–1989); monthly (1989–present).

PUBLISHER AND PLACE OF PUBLICATION: Hearst Magazines (1987–present). New York.

EDITORS: Nancy Lindemeyer (1987–present).

CIRCULATION: ABC, 1993: 913,691 (paid, primarily subscriptions).

Marcia R. Prior-Miller and Melody Ramsey

VIRTUE

Virtue, the Magazine of Christian Womanhood, debuted in the fall of 1978 and was edited by Devi Titus, the wife of pastor Larry Titus of Bethesda Christian

Center in Wenatchee, Washington. In an editor's column reflecting on the magazine's first year of publication, Titus explained: "*Virtue* is sponsored by a church. It is entirely published by Christian ladies who volunteer their time. The articles are not written by professionals; . . . We boast no degrees or fancy titles, only possessing a burning desire to serve God and be an example to Christian women across our nation." With the column were a photo of the "ladies of our volunteer mail crew" and an announcement that in the future, instead of relying on volunteers, the printer would label, sort, and deliver to the post office the 13,000 magazines that constituted the circulation at that time.[1]

The magazine's editorial formula focused on food, family, fashion, home interiors, and special features. The faces on the covers during the first year displayed an ethnic and age diversity that many other magazines had not yet realized. Diane Yashuhara, of the gospel music duo The Hawaiians and of Japanese ancestry, appeared on the first cover. Danniebelle Hall, an African-American gospel singer, was the cover personality and lead profile subject for the second issue. The white-haired Rachel Titus, mother-in-law of the editor and a speaker, teacher, and author, appeared on another cover. Bobbie Evans, wife of Seattle Seahawk Norm Evans; Beverly LaHaye, founder of Concerned Women for America; and ballerina Debbie Durham were other cover subjects that first year of publication.

These personality subjects reflect the magazine's emphasis—how to live as an attractive, gracious, involved, spirit-filled Christian woman in contemporary American culture. During the 1980s, fewer high-profile women appeared on the covers. Instead, *Virtue* covers featured the faces of women who could be in an adjoining pew on Sunday morning. The women were identified, members of their families were listed, and their local church affiliation was mentioned. Clothing and makeup of the cover models were usually credited.

The magazine title comes from Proverbs 31, a biblical description of the "virtuous woman," who is characterized as not only a good wife who has the trust of her husband and praise of her children but also a competent businesswoman, philanthropist, and wise teacher. Although the readership of the magazine in the beginning was 65 percent full-time homemakers, by the mid-1990s the demographics had shifted so that employed women constituted that same percentage of the readership. Even during the first year, however, an article offering help to a single working mother was published.[2]

Virtue's roots are in the Assemblies of God and, geographically, in the Pacific Northwest and California. However, as denominational lines are becoming blurred among evangelical Christians, circulation has spread east, and *Virtue* now has broader appeal. The Pentecostal emphasis on spirit-filled living, spiritual gifts, and guidance by the Holy Spirit is reflected in its pages. One example of this is early advice to would-be-freelance contributors to "[a]llow the Holy Spirit to be creative through you." How to manage a household economically, establish healthy and godly family relationships, dress appropriately, and pray effectively are all subjects that have been repeatedly included. *Virtue*'s articles focused on the building of Christian character and spirituality rather than relig-ious/political/theological issues.

With the September/October 1990 issue, *Virtue* introduced a new editor, Mar-lee Alex. New departments and some design innovations also appeared. The previous editor, Becky Durost Fish, continued with a column titled "Women Like Us." The column of longtime copublisher Nancie Carmichael was retitled "The Deeper Life." The "Good Health" department expanded into a broader focus on nutrition, fitness, and health, and its new standing head was "Good for You." The homey column of household hints, called "Sage Hen," that began in the first issue was given the updated title "Working Smarter (Not Harder)." Three new departments appeared: "Real Men," "Romancing the Home," and "Intimate Choices."

According to longtime copublisher William Carmichael, "There is a high degree of evangelical censorship on the part of readers." Any discussion of Halloween, even a feature on how to plan a community or home party to keep children from the dangers and mischief of neighborhood trick-or-treat activity, brings strong negative response from readers because for them the holiday is associated with demonism and occult activities. Although food and cooking features appear less frequently, earlier, any recipe that listed wine as an ingre-dient brought reader objections.

When country music star Barbara Mandrell was featured in a *Virtue* person-ality profile, she was quoted as saying, "Yes, I sing cheatin' songs, and I still will continue to do so. A lot of people question that, but that's my job. I'm an entertainer and I sing about life."[3]

"Readers went ballistic," Carmichael said. "They were critical of her and critical of our editors." Some accused the magazine of promoting marital infi-delity. Some questioned Mandrell's faith commitment. Others thought the edi-tors should have excised the quotation. Editors claimed it would have been journalistically dishonest to omit it.

Editors do not flinch from other controversial topics or from frankly discuss-ing social issues—a first-person abortion experience, home schooling, sex ed-ucation. A cover blurb on the May/June 1994 issue promotes an article on "When You Learn Your Husband Is Gay."

In the 1990s, an occasional piece has supported political movements that fight pornography, and the ramifications of the RU 486 abortion pill were discussed. Attention is given to international Christian activities in places like Russia and Irian Jaya. Recent issues have placed more emphasis on Christian service to women in prison, battered wives, molested children, and the unemployed. Fam-ily and relationship articles are still featured. Contemporary Christian musicians and artists are frequently profiled. Fiction is published.

An editorial innovation that appears to be drawing high reader involvement is "A Safe Place," begun in 1994. These two pages publish letters from readers who "need to talk about a problem or heartache and know that someone is listening." The letters appear on heavier paper just inside the back cover, and a postcard is supplied in the front of the magazine for anyone who wishes to "commit myself to pray for my sisters in Christ whose letters I've read in A SAFE PLACE." Writers share difficulties and personal tragedies like family violence, miscarriage, childhood sexual abuse, and suicide attempts.

Advertising, except for a few house ads and some from local businesses in Wenatchee, was absent from the first volume. But by the beginning of the second year, a Chicago sales representative appeared on the masthead. The ads in the 1990s are mostly for evangelical books, videos, sound recordings, world relief organizations, and Christian telephone help lines.

Circulation of *Virtue* is promoted by direct mail and the card promotions in the magazine itself; a two-for-one offer for those renewing who send a subscription to a friend has been popular. Christian bookstores have available individual issues. *Virtue* can also be found on Lasting Value displays, carousels that hold inspirational publications and that are often placed in large supermarkets and discount stores. Although *Virtue* was included by the Association of Christian Librarians in its listing of recommended titles for a Bible College library,[4] because it has not been indexed, it is infrequently selected as a library subscription or retained and bound for research.

Notes

1. Devi Titus, "Our Editor . . . Answering a Few Questions," July/August 1979, p. 4.
2. "Priorities for the Single Working Mother," January/February 1979, p. 37.
3. [Clare Forward], "Barbara Mandrell: Her Family, Her Faith and Her Future," January/February 1983, p. 32.
4. "A Core Periodicals Collection for Bible College Libraries," *The Christian Librarian*, November 1984, pp. 12–13.

Information Sources

BIBLIOGRAPHY:
Board, Stephen. "Moving the World with Magazines: A Survey of Evangelical Periodicals." In Quentin J. Schultze (ed.), *American Evangelicals and the Mass Media* Grand Rapids, Mich.: Academie Books, 1990, pp. 119–142.
INDEX SOURCES: None.
LOCATION SOURCES: Library of Congress; Dallas Theological Seminary; Evangel College, Springfield, Mo.; Moody Bible Institute, Chicago; Trinity Evangelical Divinity School, Deerfield, Ill., and other libraries

Publication History

MAGAZINE TITLE AND TITLE CHANGES: *Virtue.*
VOLUME AND ISSUE DATA: Vols. 1–(September/October 1978–present). Bimonthly (vol. 1; 1978–1979); five times (vols. 2–3, 1979–1981); six times a year (volumes 4–6, 1981–1983); eight issues (vol. 7, 1984–1985); ten issues (vol. 8, 1985–1986); nine issues (vol. 9, 1986–1987); eight issues (vols. 10–11, 1987–1989); six times a year (1990–present).
PUBLISHER AND PLACE OF PUBLICATION: Bethesda Christian Center (1978–

1980); Virtue Ministries, Inc., William L. and Nancie Carmichael (1980–1988); Good Family Magazines, Sisters (division of David C. Cook Publishing) (1988–1994). Wenatchee, Wash. (1978–1980); Sisters, Ore. (1980–1994); Colorado Springs, Colo. (1994–present).
EDITORS: Devi Titus (1978–1980); Laurie Masten (1981–1982); Clare Forward (1982–1984); Lee Zanon (March–August 1984); Mari Hanes (1984–1985); Becky Durost Fish (1985–1990); Marlee Alex (1990–present).
CIRCULATION: Gale, 1994: 112,548 paid; 37,452 unpaid.

Anna R. Paddon

VOGUE

Vogue magazine has been called the "supreme symbol of sophistication,"[1] the "nation's number one fashion book,"[2] and " 'the bible' of fashion,"[3] serving "the ministry [of] fantasy and fashion guidance."[4] In fact, it has been each—or all—of those things during much of its existence.

As it entered its second century in the early 1990s, *Vogue* led all fashion magazines with a 1.2 million circulation and a 43 percent share of "beauty, fashion, and retail" magazine advertising, the staples of such publications.[5] But its grip on the ad market was beginning to slip. It was accused of pursuing younger readers at the expense of its faithful, affluent, older audience,[6] and it was criticized for letting the pursuit of advertising interfere with editorial coverage.[7]

Moreover, in a period of static or declining magazine circulation and advertising, ancient rival *Harper's Bazaar,** along with new competitors like *Allure,* *Elle,** *Mirabella,** and *W,** were desperately trying to usurp *Vogue*'s dominance. As *Newsweek* magazine reported, "[T]he fashion action" was "heating up."[8] *Vogue*'s perch was shakier than it had been in decades.

However, if a magazine's past previews its future, *Vogue*'s competitors had little reason to rejoice. The magazine has survived many serious threats in tough economic times. One such test came in the late 1890s.

Vogue was not a fashion magazine then; it was a weekly society sheet. It had been founded in 1892 by socialite Arthur Baldwin Turnure (Princeton, class of 1876) with 56 rich, prominent backers, including shipping magnate Cornelius "Commodore" Vanderbilt and engineer inventor Peter Cooper Hewitt, scion of a steel tycoon. As Turnure put it, *Vogue* was to be a "dignified, authentic journal of society, fashion and the ceremonial side of life."[9] It contained fiction, poetry, and pages of jokes. There were reports about fashionable New York and departments with such titles as "Seen in the Shops," "On Her Dressing Table," and "Play House Gossip."

Josephine Redding edited the publication initially. She was mainly remembered for suggesting the title of the publication, for hating fashions, and for always wearing a broad-brim hat—even when sick in bed. Redding's *Vogue* was amateurishly produced yet pictorially interesting. It attracted a small, prestigious following, but not much money. Within a couple of years, Turnure was keeping the magazine afloat by borrowing from his mother's estate. About that time a number of the publication's backers sold their shares, leaving Turnure in control with "advertising . . . wallowing in the doldrums."[10]

To remedy the situation, Turnure hired a precocious 19-year-old "grindstone" named Tom McCready and made him advertising manager.[11] McCready convinced Turnure the publication could attract more advertising if it focused on fashion and shopping instead of society reporting and if it sold reduced-rate blocks of space that advertisers would illustrate instead of the traditional agate lines of space. McCready was right. The finances improved, and that crisis ended.

But even after Marie Harrison, Turnure's sister-in-law (and one of America's first female golf champions), replaced the contentious Redding in 1907, the editorial operation stayed largely unprofessional. For instance, illustrations had no relation to the stories they illustrated, and pictures of dresses appeared without captions and totally without explanation. The situation resulted partly from using amateur help—socialites recruited as part-time "editorial assistants."

Yet, there was on staff an intensely interested, full-time worker named Edna Martin—much better known later as Edna Woolman Chase. Chase had been hired in 1895 to address envelopes in the circulation department. She was infatuated with the magazine, eagerly undertook extra duties, and, in the process, learned publishing. In the informal atmosphere of the early *Vogue,* Chase apparently became an indispensable aide to Redding, Harrison, and Turnure.

Turnure died in 1906. For three years the staff ran the operation for his family, gradually improving the operation. By 1909, the 14-year-old publication had a circulation of 14,000, annual advertising revenues of $100,000 a year, and a demonstrated appeal to rich sophisticates.[12] The magazine also appealed to Condé Nast. Nast, the hugely successful advertising and business manager of *Collier's* magazine, ardently believed publishing success lay in providing advertisers with a high-quality magazine delivering ads only to select readers who clearly could afford to buy what the advertisers were selling.

Nast bought *Vogue,* tightened the focus on fashion and style, changed the 64-page magazine from weekly to twice-monthly publication, and raised the price from 15¢ to 25¢ per issue. He retained Chase on the staff and kept Harrison as editor. Harrison had made at least one major and profitable contribution by publishing clothes patterns and syndicating them.

Harrison gave Chase more and more work and responsibility until she became, in effect, the managing editor. Thus, she had many dealings with Nast, who came to like and depend on her. Chase emerged as the go-between when editor Harrison and Nast stopped speaking—the result of Harrison's siding with the Turnure heirs in a losing but vexing suit against the publisher. Predictably, the conflict ended with Harrison's leaving *Vogue.*

Chase succeeded Harrison as editor in 1914, at the start of World War I. Thus began one of U.S. journalism's most famous and successful editor-publisher collaborations. Historian Frank Luther Mott pointed out that Chase, "a hard worker, intelligent, with wide interests and understanding and an able executive . . . was the ideal editor for the period of expansion on which the magazine was entering."[13] As Chase saw it, she became editor by "osmosis." She said, "I absorbed *Vogue* and *Vogue* absorbed me until, picking up knowledge as I went along, I eventually became ensconced in the post."[14]

During World War I, the French clothing industry, then the source of most high-style clothing and fashion news, shut down. That left fashion publications little to write about. Chase solved the problem by having *Vogue* organize and sponsor the nation's first fashion show with live models displaying original American designs. Called the "Fashion Fete," it brought together New York's high society with such fashion industry leaders as Bonwit Teller and B. Altman. That 1914 fete was the first of many, for it was enormously successful and immediately enhanced *Vogue*'s prestige. The magazine embarked on an era of steady circulation and advertising gains.

Chase had an eye for talent as well as fashion. She hired humorist Dorothy Parker, the renowned drama critic who captivated readers with such leads as, "The 'House Beautiful' is the play lousy." Although in Chase's 56-year reign *Vogue* was almost entirely staff-written, it nonetheless ran articles by Thomas Wolfe, William Saroyan, Bertrand Russell, Philip Wylie, Jean-Paul Sartre, Margaret Mead, and others prominent in literature, the arts, and science.

Chase presented samplings of modern art, reproducing the work of Van Gogh, Covarrubias, Grant Wood, Dali, and others. She engaged legendary photographers like Edward Steichen, Irving Penn, Cecil Beaton, and Horst Horst. With the help of art director Heyworth Campbell and, later, Mehemed Fehmy Agha and Alexander Liberman, Chase made *Vogue* a distinctive and beautiful showpiece of fashion photography. But, importantly, Chase presented fashion reporting that made her magazine the "molder of the female silhouette," as *Time* magazine put it.[15] It was mainly dedication to reporting "the mode" that caused the French government to honor her with the Legion of Honor Medal in 1936. That same year, *Vogue* absorbed the failed *Vanity Fair*,* which reemerged under its own name five decades later.

Early in her career, Chase spotted, and was instrumental in hiring, young Carmel Snow. Snow rose from caption writer to editor of the American *Vogue* after the magazine began publishing separate editions in England and subsequently in France and Germany. Snow, an exceptionally creative editor, was expected to succeed Chase as editor in chief of all *Vogue* publications. But in the Great Depression of the 1930s, when Snow perceived she was to be demoted in a cost-cutting move, she defected to *Harper's Bazaar*. Her move outraged and confounded Chase and Nast and caused Chase to postpone retirement to meet the serious competition she knew Snow would provide. In fact, Snow proceeded to make herself famous and *Harper's Bazaar* a great equal to *Vogue* in prestige, if not in circulation.

Chase commanded *Vogue* until 1952, finally relinquishing the post to Jessica Daves, who mainly pursued Chase's conservative goal of developing "the taste and manners of . . . readers." Daves was followed in 1962 by Diana Vreeland, a *Harper's Bazaar* fashion editor under Snow.

Vreeland was considered eccentric but innovative. She favored exciting, stylized photography. She gave *Vogue* new glitter, and during her eight-year tenure, she was considered the top fashion editor in the business. Her ability to spot fashion trends and style changes was considered uncanny.

Then, in 1970, *Vogue* proclaimed skirt lengths would change. The midcalf "or midi" would be "in." That was big, economically significant news in the fashion world. Buoyed by *Vogue*'s authoritative coverage, retailers crammed racks with the new-length skirts and dresses. Remarkably, though, buyers rejected the new style. *Vogue* was embarrassed. The magazine's prestige waned. Advertising revenues dipped. Retailers lost money. Vreeland lost her job.

The buyer rebellion signaled the arrival of anarchy among buyers and subsequent uncertainty in the fashion industry. It also marked the beginning of unsteadiness at *Vogue*.

To replace Vreeland, former *Vogue* art director Liberman chose Grace Mirabella, a 21-year *Vogue* veteran. Liberman was a Russian-born artist famed as a writer, photographer, and sculptor. He had become editorial director of all Condé Nast Publications (CNP) in 1962, three years after the company was sold to the Newhouse family. (In 1993, at the age of 81 and 50 years after his arrival at *Vogue*, Liberman still wielded immense power within CNP and especially at *Vogue*, flagship of CNP's 12 magazines, *Allure, Bride's,* * *Details, Glamour,* * *Gourmet,* * *GQ, House & Garden,* * *Mademoiselle,* * *Self,* * *Traveler,* and *Vanity Fair.*)

Liberman and Mirabella reorganized *Vogue*. They toned down the artwork, broadened the editorial content, and gave readers more features dealing with societal issues and culture. They eased the magazine into the era of women's liberation, and *Vogue* entered another period of prosperity. In 1987, for instance, *Vogue*'s ad revenues reached $79.5 million. Readership tripled during Mirabella's 17-year reign.

Regardless, Liberman apparently decided *Vogue* needed an editor who would reflect the "young, irreverent attitude" displayed by *Elle** magazine, an increasingly strong competitor. So, in 1988, more than three decades after she had begun work at *Vogue*, a friend—who heard the news on television—told Mirabella she had been fired, displaced by Anna Wintour.

Michael Gross reported in *New York* magazine that Wintour "took Manhattan." She ran benefits, "putting society types and columnists on her masthead, helping rewrite the social codes. Often the fizz around her was as impressive as her magazine."[16]

Wintour gave *Vogue* what media reporters called a "bouncier," "hipper" look. Fashion models were clothed in what one columnist called "combinations of couture and kitsch." *Adweek*, the trade publication, proclaimed Wintour had "brought springtime to *Vogue*"[17] Yet, she did not bring a significant rise in circulation or in ad revenues, which had begun to decline shortly after she took over.

To boost advertising in 1993, *Vogue* joined two other CNP titles and adopted use of advertising "outserts," separate magazine-like advertisements packaged and delivered in tandem with the host magazine. The ad magazine mimics the host publication, using identical typefaces, layouts, and sometimes the same models, photographers, and writers employed by the host. Critics warned that outserts blurred the distinction between the magazine and the advertisement, violating the principle that advertising and editorial matter should be entirely separate. There were predictions that *Vogue*'s use of outserts and its seeming capitulation to advertisers ultimately would affect its reputation, harming rather than helping the publication.[18]

But maybe not. *Vogue* reportedly has long thrived from maintaining close ties to its major advertisers and, despite criticism, traditionally has given them preferential editorial treatment. Moreover, in the past it has weathered every storm and sailed on as "the nation's number one fashion book."

Notes

1. Gay Talese, "The Beautiful People: Vogueland—Oshkosh It Wasn't," *Esquire*, June 1983, p. 214. The original of this reprinted article appeared in July 1961.

2. Joanne Lipman, "*Vogue* Chases Younger Audience of *Elle*, and Ads Keep Sagging," *Wall Street Journal*, July 13, 1990, p. B8.

3. Tom Mathews and Lucille Beachy, "The Battle of the Rag Mags," *Newsweek*, September 7, 1992, p. 64.

4. Marie Winn, "Liberman: Staying in Vogue," *New York Times Magazine*, May 13, 1979, p. 50.

5. Mathews and Beachy, "The Battle of the Rag Mags," p. 64.

6. Lipman, "*Vogue* Chases Younger Audience of *Elle*," p. B8.

7. Joanne Lipman, "Big 'Outsert' Really Puts Revlon in Vogue," *Wall Street Journal*, September 17, 1992, p. B12.

8. Mathews and Beachy, "The Battle of the Rag Mags," p. 64.

9. Edna Woolman Chase and Ilka Chase, *Always in Vogue* (Garden City, N.J.: Doubleday, 1954), p. 31.

10. Ibid., p. 49.

11. Ibid., p. 48.

12. Ibid., p. 68.

13. Frank L. Mott, *A History of American Magazines 1865–1885* (Cambridge: Harvard University Press, 1938), p. 760.

14. Chase and Chase, *Always in Vogue*, p. 106.

15. "A Well-Bred Magazine," *Time*, April 1, 1957, p. 64.

16. Michael Gross, "War of the Poses: *Bazaar*'s New Liz Takes on *Vogue*'s Anna," *New York*, April 27, 1992, p. 32.

17. Lipman, "*Vogue* Chases Younger Audience of *Elle*," p. B8.

18. Lipman, "Big 'Outsert' Really Puts Revlon in Vogue," p. B12.

Information Sources

BIBLIOGRAPHY:
Chase, Edna Woolman, and Ilka Chase. *Always in Vogue*. Garden City, N.Y.: Doubleday, 1954.
Gross, Michael. "War of the Poses: *Bazaar*'s New Liz Takes on *Vogue*'s Anna." *New York*, April 27, 1992, p. 32.
———. "Big 'Outsert' Really Puts Revlon in Vogue." *Wall Street Journal*, September 17, 1992, p. B12.
Lipman, Joanne. "*Vogue* Chases Younger Audience of *Elle*, and Ads Keep Sagging." *Wall Street Journal*, July 13, 1990, p. B8.
Mathews, Tom, and Lucille Beachy. "The Battle of the Rag Mags." *Newsweek*, September 7, 1992, p. 64.
Mott, Frank L. *A History of American Magazines 1865–1885*. Cambridge: Harvard University Press, 1938.
Talese, Gay. "The Beautiful People: Vogueland—Oshkosh It Wasn't." *Esquire*, June 1983, p. 214. The original of this reprinted *Esquire* article appeared in July 1961.
"A Well-Bred Magazine." *Time*, April 1, 1957, p. 64.
Winn, Marie. "Liberman: Staying in Vogue." *New York Times Magazine*, May 13, 1979, p. 50.
INDEX SOURCES: Academic, Biographical, Consumers, Magazine, Media Review Digest; Popular Magazine Review; Philanthropic Studies; Readers' Guide to Periodical Literature; Text on Microfilm.
LOCATION SOURCES: Library of Congress and other libraries.

Publication History

MAGAZINE TITLE AND TITLE CHANGES: *Vogue* (1892–1936); *Vogue, incorporating Vanity Fair* (1936–1983); *Vogue* (1983–present).
VOLUME AND ISSUE DATA: Vols. 1–(December 1892–present). Weekly (December 1892–January 29, 1910); semimonthly (February 15, 1910–1972); monthly (1973–present).
PUBLISHER AND PLACE OF PUBLICATION: Arthur Baldwin Turnure (1892–1909); Condé Nast (1909–1942); Condé Nast Publishing (owned by the Nast heirs) (1942–1963); Condé Nast Publishing (a unit of Advance Publications, Inc. owned by the Newhouse family) (1963–present). New York.
EDITORS: Josephine Redding (1892–1907); Marie Harrison 1907–1914); Edna Woolman Chase (1914–1952); Jessica Daves (1952–1962); Diana Vreeland (1963–1971); Grace Mirabella (1971–1988); Anna Wintour (1988–present).
CIRCULATION: ABC, 1993: 1,284,193 (paid, primarily single-copy sales).

August Gribbin

──── W ────

W

In 1972, few at Fairchild Publications saw much merit even in the *idea* for *W*. The whole concept seemed counter to the corporate history. Fairchild had always been a successful *specialized business* periodical publisher; it had never even issued a consumer magazine before. Moreover, advertising executives feared that this new venture could cut into the advertising revenue of *Women's Wear Daily*, Fairchild's most profitable property.[1] Besides, what did the nation need with yet another fashion magazine? *Vogue** and *Harper's Bazaar** had long dominated that publishing niche. Surely, introducing a magazine to compete in that environment was folly. John Fairchild, scion of the Fairchild family, was certain all the naysayers—including other family members—were wrong.

W was launched in 1972. Initially, it looked as if the critics were right. The periodical, a biweekly oversized tabloid, did not exactly capture enthusiasm in New York, the center of the fashion industry in the United States. Advertisers did not rush to the periodical. *W* reporters found it difficult to wrangle invitations to parties so they could cover the happenings in society. Yet, backed by the enormous financial resources of Fairchild Publications and the power of John Fairchild within the corporation and the fashion industry, the magazine survived and eventually thrived. Today, the periodical—now in a magazine format—sits in an enviable position. Its circulation is intentionally kept relatively small (by consumer standards)—between 250,000 and 275,000 of the most affluent, fashion-conscious readers, primarily women.[2] Not surprisingly, advertisers, most in the cosmetic and fashion industries, flock to the magazine. Today, *W* is seen as the chronicler of America's "social milieu" and John Fairchild's "biggest success."[3]

In 1971, when Fairchild decided to start the launch, prospects for success seemed remote. The prototype was just not "right." It featured a cartoon cover of President Richard Nixon and his wife, "looking like a couple out of a Frankenstein movie,'' Fairchild observed. The contents were not much better. A quick test confirmed that this was not going to work as a fashion publication. That was when Fairchild brought in some of the company's best people to get the publication started. He chose Michael Coady, who at the time was editor of *Women's Wear Daily* (*WWD*); fashion reporter Etta Froio; and Rudy Millendorf, one of the best art directors at Fairchild.[4] These three, along with John Fairchild, worked up the prototype for *W* that worked.

The first issue, dated April 7, 1972, featured an exclusive color sketch done by one of the hottest designers of the day, Yves St. Laurent. The writing style was clever and witty. *W* was designed to carry out Fairchild's editorial mission: ''In short, we want[ed] to produce a fashion newspaper with the speed of a newspaper, but in full color and with the smart look of a fashion magazine.'' This was a publication of fashion and ''life style, fine living, and people.''[5]

This was also probably one of the least publicized of any Fairchild launch. The first issue received no advanced publicity or advertising. The company, however, did pour money into the new publication. *W*'s format—an oversize tabloid printed on good-quality paper—was expensive to produce, as were the color reproductions in the periodical. As John Fairchild explained later, the format was important.

> Now, it's got to be big size, super big, nothing like *Vogue* or *Harper's Bazaar*, so big that everyone will see the difference. And inside we have the newest fashions in full color months before the fashion magazines can publish the same thing.[6]

In production and in staffing (Michael Coady became *W*'s first editor), everything was the best.

Only slowly did advertisers come to the new magazine. The ''big break'' for *W*, according to John Fairchild, was when Revlon, the cosmetic corporate giant, came aboard as a regular advertiser. As Fairchild explained, Charles Revson liked the size of *W*. Revson told Fairchild:

> Fairchild, that paper called *W*, I got it the other day. I like the size. I'm signing up for a full page every issue. You know why? Because it is like a billboard, a giant billboard for Revlon.[7]

Slowly, other advertisers came to the magazine. Estée Lauder, the upscale cosmetic corporation, became a regular advertiser. Soon fashion designers, drawn to the audience ''with one of the highest median incomes in the industry,''[8] were aboard.

Advertising, however, is only part of the reason for *W*'s success. Editorially, the magazine has been strong. It has never been known for investigative journalism. The periodical, however, stands as the chronicler of the rich and fashionable in American society. *W* reporters are at fashionable parties across the country, ready to cover the "news." This was difficult at first. "In the old days, it was difficult for our editors and reporters to find out what was happening on a given night in that closed-off social world," Fairchild recalled.[9] Today, however, the reporters and editors are never at a loss for invitations. The new rich as well as the old rich seem to enjoy the coverage.

Moreover, the publication also comments on the state of American society. *W* coined the term the "nouvelle society," a term, not necessarily of endearment, referring to the "new rich." Its "Tribes of New York" is still considered a classic. As *New York* magazine observed, this "anthropological classic . . . deconstructed the city's upper crust according to its various cliquish allegiances."[10]

The magazine has also thrived because it brews controversy and carries on feuds. John Fairchild claims that *W* invented the "in and out list." It is unknown if that is, indeed, the case; but surely *W* has brought the feature to a new level. As Fairchild explains, "It was not just for the hell of it [the ins and outs list] but because there is no question that people talk about the ins and outs of society, fashion, places, things, living and even of each other." The purpose, he continues, is not just to sell newspapers. "What it all comes down to is fashion. The age of plenty gives people the time, energy and money to indulge in this game of Ins and Outs."[11] But the game sometimes has been played at a price. One Swiss watch advertiser canceled his advertising when the product appeared on the "out" list. Other Swiss watch manufacturers got together and followed suit.[12]

Feuds have also fueled *W*'s success. John Fairchild, the man most closely associated with *W* and *WWD*, often uses his publications to play out squabbles with designers. While Fairchild has had his "squabbles" with the likes of Yves St. Laurent and Giorgio Armani,[13] Geoffrey Beene has "spent more time than any one of his peers in Fairchild exile."[14] He was absent from *W*'s fall publication, "The Designing Life," and casually dismissed in *W*'s giant 20th-anniversary issue thus:

> If you believe Bernadine Morris, who writes the same review of Geoffrey Beene's collection each and every season, Beene is the only American designer who "transcends fashion." He transcends customers as well, since Beene's clothes are rarely seen on any real, live women—except fashion editors, of course. And we know how much they pay.[15]

Beene, of course, has not been the only one to be criticized by *W*. The publication has often taken on the rich, the mighty, the beautiful, and the famous in its "Fashion Victim of the Month" column.[16] Some items in the "Eye" and "Uncensored" columns not only report the fashion/people news but comment upon it as well.[17] The "insider" story was further strengthened in 1991, when gossip columnist Suzy joined *W* and *WWD*.

Fashion and *W*, however, are never static. In 1993, *W* surprised its readers with a new format and a new frequency. *W* shifted from a biweekly tabloid to a 14-times-a-year (twice in October and March) oversized magazine. Fairchild explained that the move was designed to meet the needs of readers and advertisers. *W* "is a very successful magazine and we think this move will ensure an equally successful future." Surveys had shown that readers preferred a "more readable (and savable)" form than the old tabloid format.[18] The new format reduced the physical problems associated with the 20th-anniversary issue, when the large number of pages led to almost an unmanageable issue, difficult to keep together. The separate cover and the binding eliminated most of those difficulties.

The new format was greeted with enthusiasm from most readers. Most noted that the magazine format allowed them to keep the periodical, instead of just pitching it after reading.[19] The *New York Post*, the *Los Angeles Times*, *Chicago Tribune*, CNN, *USA Today*, and the *Washington Post* all had positive things to say as well.[20]

Although its format has changed, *W*'s audience has not. The publication—no matter what its format—draws to it the affluent and the urban. Slightly more than 20 percent of *W*'s subscribers are based in the fashion-conscious New York City metropolitan area. A large number of readers live in Los Angeles and San Francisco.[21] The average reader is a well-educated woman in her 40s with an average household income in excess of $100,000.[22]

The editorial content has changed little. *W* remains the "chronicler of [American] social milieu." It has to keep its editorial "edge" to compete in an increasingly crowded fashion magazine niche. *W* competes not only with the old standards of *Harper's Bazaar* and *Vogue* but with the relative newcomers *Elle*,* *Vanity Fair*,* and *Mirabella*,* all providing coverage of fashion and America's "social milieu." But *W* has held up well against the new competition. Although its circulation has been intentionally kept small, its demographics continue to be extremely attractive to advertisers, who continue to rush to the magazine.

Perhaps John Fairchild best explained the magazine's success in the publication's 20th-anniversary edition:

> After 20 years, *W* has prospered because it offers a glimpse of a special world. Many have called us a publication for the elite. Liz Smith, the sparky syndicated columnist, once wrote: "Comes the revolution, the first to go will be that group at *W*." In fact, we at *W* hope to survive the revolution and look forward with relish to reporting on it.
>
> *W* owes its life to our readers, to our advertisers, to all the fashion designers and personalities who propel our ship of style through the stormy waters of the Fashion Sea. What fun we've had chronicling these exciting times.[23]

Since *W* was launched, Fairchild has ventured into consumer magazine waters several times. None of these ventures, however, have captured the success or notoriety of *W*. The timing, the atmosphere of the country, the marketplace, and the editorial vision were ideal for the launch of *W*. Since then, the publication has adjusted to changing times—and a changing marketplace—with remarkable success. It remains to be seen if *W*—as a magazine with a new frequency cycle—can continue that track record.

Notes

1. John Fairchild, *Chic Savages* (New York: Simon and Schuster, 1989), pp. 79–81.
2. Ibid., p. 84.
3. John Taylor, "John Fairchild," *New York Magazine*, April 25, 1988, p. 82.
4. Fairchild, *Chic Savages*, p. 79.
5. Ibid., pp. 80, 82.
6. Ibid., p. 80.
7. Ibid., p. 82.
8. Ibid., p. 84.
9. Ibid.
10. Taylor, "John Fairchild," p. 82.
11. Fairchild, *Chic Savages*, p. 159.
12. Ibid., p. 160.
13. Taylor, "John Fairchild," p. 82; Andrea Gabor, "Of Power, Glory and the Rich and Famous," *U.S. News and World Report,* August 24, 1987, p. 55.
14. Gabor, "Of Power, Glory and the Rich and Famous," p. 55.
15. "The Fashion Establishment, Who Matters, from A to Z," July 20–27, 1992, p. 181.
16. See, for example, November 1993, p. 28.
17. See, for example, "Dressing for the Man," August 1993, p. 42.
18. "The New W," August 1993, p. 20.
19. "The New W," September 1993, p. 16.
20. "The Second Coming," September 1993, p. 14.
21. "W Circulation Top ADI Markets," Source: ABC Data Bank, March 19, 1990, *W* Media Kit.
22. "Demographic Profile," 1990 MRI Subscriber Study, *W* Media Kit.
23. John Fairchild, "All About W," July 20–27, 1972, p. 80.

Information Sources

BIBLIOGRAPHY:
Fairchild, John. *Chic Savages*. New York: Simon and Schuster, 1989.
Gabor, Andrea. "Of Power, Glory and the Rich and Famous." *U.S. News and World Reports*, August 24, 1987, p. 55.
Taylor, John. "John Fairchild." *New York Magazine*, April 25, 1988, pp. 80–82.
INDEX SOURCES: Access.
LOCATION SOURCES: Library of Congress and many other libraries.

Publication History

MAGAZINE TITLE AND TITLE CHANGES: *W.*
VOLUME AND ISSUE DATA: Vols. 1–(April 7, 1972–present). Biweekly (1972–1993); 14 times a year (twice in March and October) (1993–present).

PUBLISHER AND PLACE OF PUBLICATION: Fairchild Publications Inc. New York.
EDITORS: Michael Coady (1972–1993); Patrick McCarthy (1993–present).
CIRCULATION: ABC, 1993: 285,957 (paid, primarily subscriptions).

Kathleen L. Endres

WB MAGAZINE

The oldest continuously published women's sports magazine is *WB—For the Woman Who Bowls*.[1] Published by the Women's International Bowling Congress (WIBC), the largest women's sports organization in the world today, it was first started in 1936 by two male entrepreneurs from Chicago as *The Woman Bowler*.

Many of its subscribers are among the more than 2 million women that compete in officially sanctioned bowling leagues across the United States and Canada and on U.S. military bases abroad.[2] However, the popularity of women's bowling is hardly new. As rare photographs show, American women were bowling before the turn of the century, but "they did so at the risk of their reputations, most often in secluded rooms or behind curtains"[3] because early bowling alleys were most often located near pool halls and taverns.[4]

The first organized bowling leagues for "respectable" women were formed in 1907, in St. Louis, Missouri.[5] The Woman's National Bowling Association, with 40 original members, was organized in 1916, under the direction of Dennis J. Sweeney, a St. Louis bowling proprietor. A few years later a strong force of the members wanted the word "international" in the organization's name, and in 1926, the name was changed to Woman's International Bowling Congress, and the following year changed again to Women's International Bowling Congress. Ten years later a magazine targeted exclusively at women bowlers was first published, in May 1936.[6] Today, *Woman Bowler* is the oldest existing women's sports magazine and the third oldest bowling publication.[7]

According to an interview with one of the founders of the magazine, published in the 25th-anniversary edition of the magazine, it all started in the restaurant of the Harrison Hotel in Chicago. In the 1960 article, Earle Ward claims to have suggested the need for a magazine for women bowlers to John G. Hemmer, an avid bowler and billiards player, "[o]ne morning around 4 o'clock when we were having our 'nightly' cup of coffee" in the hotel's restaurant.[8] As the story goes, Hemmer, who published several magazines on bowling and billiards, listened as Ward, then employed as a publicist for Brunswick-Balke-Collender Co., said, "There were magazines for men bowlers, why not one for women?"[9] The pair discussed the idea for several weeks and decided to name their venture *The Woman Bowler*, reportedly at the suggestion of journalist Harold George of the *Chicago American*.[10]

The first 16-page issue was printed in time to be distributed by Ward and Hemmer to delegates at the 1936 convention of the WIBC in Omaha, Nebraska.

Its busy cover featured a quarter-page head-and-shoulders photograph of WIBC president Jeannette Knepprath in its center, surrounded by a red border. At the top, 13 bowling pins and a bowling ball spelled out the word woman in the magazine's title. A drawing of a bowling alley started in the lower right-hand corner and extended diagonally to the upper left-hand corner, disappearing under the photograph of Knepprath. A woman was shown bowling on the alley, and her bowling ball appeared at the top left corner of the cover, giving the appearance that it had struck the four bowling pins forming the "w" in the word "woman."[11]

In a full-page editorial on page one of the first issue, publisher Hemmer wrote:

> The birth of THE WOMAN BOWLER is not an idea of a publisher born overnight. It is the result of considerable study . . . and looked upon as a necessity in the field of women bowlers. . . . It is the first and only publication of its kind—devoted entirely to the interests of women bowlers.[12]

Annual subscription cost for *The Woman Bowler* was set at one dollar. Ward and Hemmer had hoped the WIBC delegates at the convention would adopt the magazine as their official publication. "I assure you," Ward said in an interview in 1960, "we were not swamped with the number of dollar bills we took back home to further our ambition in paying the cost of printing."[13] In fact, it was not until 1939 that delegates passed a resolution accepting the magazine as WIBC's official publication.[14]

Hemmer died in January 1937. Ward, who had left his publicity job with Brunswick to work on the magazine, continued to produce the magazine single-handedly—writing all the copy, soliciting the ads and doing the general office work—without a salary.[15] The WIBC began to donate funds to support the magazine in 1939 and, on July 1, 1945, purchased all rights to the 1,500-circulation monthly for $7,500.[16] In the agreement, Ward was retained as editor at a salary of $325 a month. He continued as editor until 1947 and continued on *The Woman Bowler* staff as an advertising representative until his death in 1962.

The first woman editor of the magazine, Georgia E. Veatch, began her duties in 1947 at the magazine's offices in Chicago. At the time of her appointment, Veatch also edited *Prep Pin Patter*, the publication of the American Junior Bowling Congress. Veatch, an avid bowler, had bachelor's degrees in physical education and education from Indiana University, as well as a master's degree in education from Loyola University.[17] During her 12 years as editor of *The Woman Bowler*, Veatch attempted to popularize bowling as both a recreation and sport among women by developing a corps of correspondents from leagues across the country. She gave the correspondents bylines and incorporated their league news, using as many photographs as she could fit into a roundup section titled, "Stars and Strikes." When the WIBC board decided to move the magazine's offices into its new headquarters building in Columbus, Ohio, Veatch declined to move and stay on as editor, although she continued to play an influential role in the WIBC organization as fifth vice president and later as first vice president. In 1974, she became the first *Woman Bowler* editor inducted into the WIBC Hall of Fame in the Meritorious Service category.[18]

A new editor, Norma Kirkendall (later, Holick) of Columbus succeeded Veatch after the move. A college graduate with some training in journalism, Kirkendall was the first nonbowler and non-board member to become editor.[19] Kirkendall served as editor from 1959 to 1962. At this point, the magazine was published ten times a year at an annual cost of $1.50.

Charles Westlake, the fourth editor of the magazine, introduced a new era for *The Woman Bowler*. Unlike his predecessors, Westlake had nearly a quarter of a century of sportswriting and publicity experience.[20] His sportswriting career started in 1939 at the *Ohio State Journal* in Columbus. After the war, he joined the sports staff at the *Columbus Citizen*, specializing in bowling and amateur sports, and then in 1959, he and four others purchased the Typographic Press in Columbus to publish the weekly *Central Ohio Bowling News*. Westlake was the first of several editors during its seven years of publishing.

Following that, he spent three seasons as publicity director for the Columbus Jets, a minor league professional baseball team, then was hired by the Ohio Trucking Association as a public information officer in 1962. However, when WIBC executive secretary Emma Phaler called Westlake's wife, Sarah, an avid bowler and friend of Phaler's, to ask what ''Charlie was doing,'' it did not take much to convince him to put his talent to work for *The Woman Bowler*.[21]

Westlake assumed editorship duties in October 1963, and the very next month he was on his way to Cuernavaca, Mexico, to cover the Fifth World Bowling Tournament. In February 1964, he unveiled ''Miss Silhouette'' as the official WIBC logo on the magazine's cover, accompanied by the slogan ''Next Time You Bowl, Bring a Friend.'' (''Miss Silhouette'' was dropped from WIBC publications in March 1969.) Also on February's cover were pictures taken by Westlake of the ''first woman bowler in space.'' According to Westlake, American Airlines wanted to demonstrate the bigness of its new cargo ship so they decided to install a bowling lane. They arranged for Silvia Wene of Philadelphia, the only woman to have rolled two sanctioned 300 games at that time, to bowl against St. Louis's Dick Weber, one of the all-time great men bowlers, on a flight from New York City to Dallas. Wene won, 146 to 144. Weber protested that the lanes were not level at 25,000 feet in the air. Westlake was on the ground at the Dallas airport, taking pictures when the big cargo plane landed.[22] In November 1966, WIBC celebrated its 50th annual convention, and Westlake edited a 72-page souvenir issue of *The Woman Bowler*. The issue featured a gold cover with a 1½" square die-cut that revealed a four-color reproduction of the WIBC flag on the inside cover.[23] WIBC membership had reached nearly 3 million, but a one-year subscription to the magazine (ten issues) cost only two dollars. In March 1968, Westlake was promoted to WIBC public relations manager, and A. W. (Augie) Karcher, who had been assistant editor under Westlake, was promoted to editor. Before joining *The Woman Bowler*, Karcher had been editor of the *Junior Bowler* in Milwaukee and had reported newspaper sports for 21 years in Iowa, Minnesota, and Wisconsin.[24] A conscientious, detail-oriented editor, Karcher used increases in the magazine's budget during his tenure to add more color and graphics throughout the magazine.[25] Karcher succeeded Westlake as WIBC public relations director, a post he held until 1986.

Helen Latham, who had worked as assistant editor of *The Woman Bowler* with Karcher and Westlake, became the third woman editor at the magazine in 1972. She was one of 16 WIBC staff members who elected to make the move from Columbus to Greendale, Wisconsin, into a new 100,000-square-foot, $3.8 million joint office building shared with the American Bowling Congress (ABC)—the rival men's organization.[26] Public relations offices for both the WIBC and the ABC were on the third floor of the building. "We had a dividing line of file cabinets and quips were constantly being thrown back and forth," Latham said.[27] Part of the rivalry stemmed from the fact that women writers were not permitted to join the male-only Bowling Writers' Association of America (BWAA). The competition for news coverage between the two organizations reached a peak in 1976, when the women formed their own organization, the National Women Bowling Writers Association. That same year, they scooped the BWAA by announcing their pick for Woman Bowler of the Year before the BWAA had finished its balloting for Bowler of the Year—male bowler, that is. Not too surprisingly, ten women, including Latham, were finally admitted to the BWAA in 1978.

During her stint as editor of *The Woman Bowler*, Latham saw her role as a writer first and as a bowler second. As she explained,

> I thought that the modern woman bowler would be more interested in what bowling meant in a woman's life than reading about the stars of the women's bowling world.[28]

In 1977, WIBC membership topped 4 million, and the magazine's circulation reached 150,000. Copies were distributed to winter league secretaries, paid subscribers, all certified bowling centers, selected bowling officials, news media, and bowling writers. A readership survey showed that *The Woman Bowler* subscribers wanted helpful tips, rule information, and league information.

Latham left the editor's post in 1979 to return to Columbus for a job in corporate public relations. Christine Igler, who had been working on the magazine as an assistant, was promoted to editor. Under her direction, the magazine combined its December/January issues and split the May/June issue so that readers would have better coverage of the annual meeting. However, after 33 years of consecutive growth, the WIBC experienced a small decline in membership during the 1979–1980 season, a precursor of a trend that would continue throughout the decade. Igler, who gave birth to a son in November 1980, was followed by Linda Krupke (Bosman), who edited the magazine for part of 1980 and 1981.[29] Cost of the 48-page magazine increased to three dollars for ten issues.

Paula McMartin took over the editor's role in 1981. She split the December/January issue into two separate issues at the start of the 1984–1985 bowling season (a season runs from August 1 through July 31) and made a number of design improvements in the magazine. The subscription rate was increased to five dollars. McMartin became WIBC public relations director in 1986, and Bill Krier was named editor to replace her. Under Krier, the magazine expanded its internal production capability with the purchase of some typesetting equipment and added a "Tip Talk" column featuring bowling advice from pros and top amateurs. With the February 1987 issue, the word "The," which had been used in the masthead with both a capital "T" and lowercase "t" over the years, no longer appeared as part of the name of the magazine.

When Krier left, Karen Sytsma, who had been hired as a staff assistant in 1986, became the magazine's 11th editor in February 1988. She introduced a "new" *Woman Bowler* in August/September 1989, with a close-up on the first redesigned cover of U.S. Olympic Festival medals from bowling's first appearance as an exhibition Olympic sport.[30] Inside, the changes included a new design, a different paper stock, more four-color photographs, and an expanded number of pages. The number of issues was reduced to eight per year; single issues were published in January, February, July, and October and combined issues in March/April, May/June, August/September, and November/December. WIBC membership dues were increased to six dollars, and individual subscriptions to the magazine also increased to six dollars. Overall, her goal was to produce a magazine of interest to its various audiences, including league secretaries, paid subscribers, top pros, top amateurs, senior bowlers, young bowlers, proprietors, auxiliary organizations, bowling writers, and association leaders.[31]

WIBC celebrated its 75th anniversary in 1991 and adopted a new slogan: "WIBC Proud of Our Past: Prepared for the Future." However, the cover of the August/September 1991 issue symbolized the tension that existed between WIBC's past and future. In fact, it generated more reader response—positive and negative—than any cover in the magazine's 55-year history. The cover featured a photograph of Flora Mitchell, who was retiring as executive secretary/treasurer of WIBC, in a golf cart with her clubs ready for a round of golf. It violated two long-standing, albeit unwritten, rules at the magazine: (1) do not devote space to any other women's sport that would compete with bowling for membership and (2) do not mention leisure activities other than bowling.[32] Sytsma explained her cover choice in a March/April 1992 editorial: "We seem to be afraid to acknowledge people have lives outside of bowling centers and bowling administration. . . . I felt comfortable and confident our readers knew that bowling was Flora's No. 1 priority for 18 years. *Woman Bowler* didn't need to show just Flora's bowling side again."[33]

Sytsma was promoted to WIBC public relations manager in February 1992 and continued as editor until October 1992, when Jeff Nowak was named the 12th editor of *Woman Bowler*. The magazine continued to be published eight times a year, featuring bowling tips from the pros, news from regional chapters, and a column on WIBC rule interpretation. Nowak, who had spent four years as an editorial assistant on the *Woman Bowler*, quickly earned recognition in *Magazine Week* for a series of issues in 1992 that profiled African American, Asian American, physically challenged, and deaf women bowlers.[34] According to Nowak, his goal was to show the range of women who bowl in WIBC leagues.

Despite such recognition and continuing editorial and design improvements, competition for advertising dollars, coupled with 14 consecutive years of WIBC membership losses, made it clear that more changes would be necessary. Although *Woman Bowler* had accepted advertising from the beginning, the magazine had primarily accepted trade advertising, steadfastly refusing "controversial" ads, for example, alcohol, tobacco, even feminine hygiene ads, for years. WIBC's policy had been to resist commercialization. However, economic realities had forced WIBC to lower its resistance beginning in the 1980s. Avon Products was granted a sponsorship role in the WIBC Queens competition in 1980, an official airline was named in 1984, an official rental car company in 1986, and a bowler's credit card was endorsed in 1987.[35]

WIBC commissioned a marketing study by the Meredith Corp. (publishers of *Better Homes and Gardens**) in 1992. As a result of the study's recommendations, a new name, new look, and new focus for the magazine were unveiled in March 1994 in a mailing to current subscribers and league secretaries. In August 1994, *Woman Bowler* officially became a 36-page quarterly titled, *WB*. Its new tag line was "*WB*—For the Woman Who Bowls." All WIBC members were eligible to receive the new *WB* by sending in a response card. The market study estimated that about 25 percent of the 2.2 million WIBC members would respond to the offer in the first year. The move was expected to increase circulation to an estimated 600,000 from its current 120,000.[36] According to Nowak:

> WIBC is the 17th largest women's association in the world, and we wanted to make the magazine a tangible benefit of WIBC membership like the Triple A or AARP do with their publications. We also want to give more voice to the typical WIBC member. We will focus on our niche—the needs of women bowlers. We will have more stories about how to bowl better, but we will also have lifestyle stories, such as fitness and time management, and maybe even some recipes. There won't be as many columns on league life, but league bowling and bowlers will be covered in feature stories.[37]

Nowak and his staff will retain editorial control over the magazine, but much of the editorial content for the new *WB* will be written outside the WIBC office, allowing the public relations staff to devote more time to marketing member services. Primary support for the redesigned *WB* is expected to come from advertising revenue, since full-page advertising rates jumped from $900 in 1993 to $12,000 in 1994. However, WIBC membership fees, which now include a free subscription to the magazine for those who want it, remained at $6 in 1994.

Other changes that loom on the horizon for the largest women's sports organization in the world may also impact the magazine. Membership distinctions between the men's and women's bowling organizations are blurring. To avoid a potential sex discrimination lawsuit, ABC took the word "male" out of its constitution in October 1993, but it is not as yet actively recruiting women to join. WIBC is examining how best to avoid a reverse discrimination lawsuit. What new inclusive membership rules might portend for the status of *WB* as the oldest continuously published women's sports magazine remains to be seen.[38]

Notes

1. Cf. *Bacon's Magazine Directory* (Chicago: Bacon's Information, 1992); *Gale Directory of Publications and Broadcast Media*, 126th ed., vol. 3 (Detroit: Gale Research, 1993); *Ulrich's International Periodicals Directory 1993–1994* (New Providence, N.J.: R. R. Bowker, 1993).

2. Bowling is not the largest participant sport for women, however. According to the National Sporting Goods Association (1993), more than 7 million women participate in softball, 7.5 million in basketball, 7.4 million in tennis, 5.6 million in golf, 26 million bicycle, 44.6 million engage in exercise walking, and close to 23 million in aerobic exercise. However, the WIBC claims to be the largest women's sports organization in the world, with more than 2.2 million members in 1994.

3. Helen Latham and Charles W. Westlake, *WIBC History, 1916–1967* (Columbus, Ohio: Woman's International Bowling Congress, 1967), p. 7.

4. Frederick W. Cozens and Florence Scovil Stumpf, *Sports in American Life* (Chicago: University of Chicago Press, 1953), p. 38.

5. Alma Nebel Spring, *History of the Women's International Bowling Congress, Inc., 1916–1942* (Milwaukee, Wis.: Women's International Bowling Congress, 1943), p. 7.

6. A. W. Karcher, *WIBC: The First 75 Years* (Greendale, Wis.: Women's International Bowling Congress, 1991), p. 98.

7. The oldest bowling magazine is *Bowler's Journal*, started in 1913 by Dave Luby, and the second oldest is *Bowling*, the publication of the American Bowling Congress; both focus on men's bowling. Charles W. Westlake interview, November 19, 1993.

8. Karcher, *WIBC: The First 75 Years*, p. 98.

9. Ibid.

10. Ibid.

11. "We've Got You Covered," August/September 1992, p. 42.

12. Latham and Westlake, *WIBC History: 1916–1967*, p. 44.

13. Karcher, *WIBC: The First 75 Years,* p. 99.

14. Ibid.

15. Latham and Westlake, *WIBC History, 1916–1967*, p. 44.

16. Karcher, *WIBC: The First 75 Years*, p. 99.

17. Masthead, April 1959.

18. Karcher, *WIBC: The First 75 Years*, p. 99.

19. Helen Latham interview, December 15, 1993.

20. Westlake interview.

21. Sarah Westlake interview, November 19, 1993.

22. C. Westlake interview.

23. Souvenir issue, November 1966.

24. Karcher, *WIBC: The First 75 Years*, p. ii.

25. C. Westlake interview.

26. Karcher, *WIBC: The First 75 Years*, p. 128.

27. Latham interview. (The public relations and editorial offices of WIBC and ABC were still on the third floor of the Greendale, Wisconsin, joint headquarters building in 1994.)

28. Latham interview.

29. Karcher, *WIBC: The First 75 Years*, p. 99.

30. Bowling does not yet have official Olympic sports status. WIBC, the American Bowling Congress, and bowling proprietors have formed an Olympic Effort Group with the goal of obtaining official recognition by the International Olympic Committee. Karen Sytsma interview, January 14, 1994.

31. Karcher, *WIBC: The First 75 Years*, p. 99.

32. Latham interview.

33. Karen L. Sytsma, "Out Front," March/April 1992, p. 4.

34. Karcher, *WIBC: The First 75 Years*, p. 99.

35. Lynne Palazzi, "Spare Me," *Magazine Week,* April 26, 1993, p. 32.

36. Jeffrey R. Nowak interview, January 11, 1994.

37. Nowak interview.

38. ABC has a comparable magazine.

Information Sources

BIBLIOGRAPHY:

Karcher, A. W. *WIBC: The First 75 Years.* Greendale, Wis.: Women's International Bowling Congress, 1991.

Latham, Helen, and Charles W. Westlake. *WIBC History: 1916–1967.* Columbus, Ohio: Women's International Bowling Congress, 1967.

Spring, Alma Nebel. *History of the Women's International Bowling Congress, Inc., 1916–1942.* Milwaukee, Wis.: Women's International Bowling Congress, 1943.

INDEX SOURCES: Sports Discus.

LOCATION SOURCES: Women's International Bowling Congress, Greendale, Wis., and other libraries.

Publication History

MAGAZINE TITLE AND TITLE CHANGES: *The Woman Bowler* (1936–1986); *Woman Bowler* (1987–1993); *WB* (1994–present).

VOLUME AND ISSUE DATA: Vols. 1–(May 1936–present). Monthly (1936–1958); 10 times a year (1959–1981); 11 times a year (1984–1989); 8 times a year (1989–1993); 4 times a year (1993–present).

PUBLISHER AND PLACE OF PUBLICATION: John G. Hemmer and Earle Ward

(1936–1939); Women's International Bowling Congress (1939–present). Chicago (1936–1939); Milwaukee (1939–1958); Columbus, Ohio (1958–1971); Greendale, Wis. (1972–present).

EDITORS: Earle Ward (1936–1947); Georgia E. Veatch (1947–1959); Norma Kirkendall (Holick) (1959–1962); Charles W. Westlake (1963–1968); A. W. Augie Karcher (1968–1972); Helen Latham (1972–1979); Christine Igler (1979–1980); Linda Krupke (Bosman) (1980–1981); Paula McMartin (1981–1986); Bill Krier (1986–1988); Karen Sytsma (1988–1992); Jeffrey R. Nowak (1992–present).

CIRCULATION: Ownership Statement, 1993: 107,274 (primarily through WIBC membership).

Pamela J. Creedon

WEIGHT WATCHERS

In the chronicles of modern American women's magazines, *Weight Watchers* occupies a special niche. The magazine, founded in 1968, promotes the Weight Watchers diet program, but, unlike trade magazines or house organs that limit their circulation to a defined group, it circulates to the general public. *Weight Watchers* magazine has always accepted advertising and sold on newsstands in an attempt to woo the health-conscious reader. Weight Watchers members, who number about 1 million worldwide, use the magazine as a tool—just one aspect of a total program to support their new eating habits and healthy way of life.[1]

Weight Watchers International (WWI), founded in 1963, cashed in on America's obsession with being thin, and more than 30 years later was a leader in the billion-dollar weight loss industry. The company's philosophy—that diet alone is ineffective without support—reinforces members' use of many diet aids, including a subscription to the monthly magazine. Indeed, the magazine promotes the goals of WWI, which has been a wholly owned subsidiary of H. J. Heinz Co. since 1978.

Like the nineteenth century's *Demorest's Illustrated Monthly** and *The Delineator,** which were published to sell dress patterns, and contemporary magazines like *Sesame Street* and *MacWorld*, which support a television show and a computer, respectively, *Weight Watchers* magazine carries an unusual mission to highlight a specific product. When *Weight Watchers* began, the owners stated that they were unique in publishing a magazine for the general public with an organization's name on its masthead.[2]

The magazine was created through the collaboration of Weight Watchers chairman Al Lippert with editor Matty Simmons, who later founded *National Lampoon* magazine and produced the National Lampoon movies. Simmons had just resigned as editor of the Diner's Club magazine, *Signature*, when he got a call in 1967 from an advertising man who suggested Simmons meet with Lippert. "I had never heard of Weight Watchers," Simmons said.[3] As a result of that meeting, the W/W Twentyfirst Corporation was founded—Simmons and a partner owned half, and Weight Watchers International owned half. The agreement called for each owner to put up $40,000 and promise to put up another $150,000 each. The magazine, however, was so successful that the owners never had to put in the additional capital.[4] With partner Leonard Mogel as publisher and Simmons as editor, they fashioned the WWI chairman's idea into "a magazine for people who weighed too much."

While a magazine that promotes a specific product has certain drawbacks—such as advertising conflicts—finding interested readers was not one of them. Indeed, one of the secrets to the magazine's success was that it culled subscribers from people who were already members of Weight Watchers. Membership lists provided direct mail access to a highly targeted audience of people who were already involved in Weight Watchers.[5] The magazine also was sold initially in about 18,000 supermarkets nationwide.[6] "We had the most incredible reaction," Simmons said. "The magazine was instantly successful." Simmons estimated that the magazine started with about 70,000 subscriptions.[7] After four issues, *Weight Watchers* had about 85,000 subscriptions and total sales of 500,000.[8] While Simmons never viewed the magazine as a way of selling the Weight Watchers program, he noted that, "of course, that was the subtle message."

Weight Watchers International, however, actually had very little to do with the magazine's editorial content, Simmons said. "They had a right to turn down advertising that conflicted with their program," he said. "But that was their only relationship."

From editorial offices in New York and with a staff of about nine people, *Weight Watchers* magazine premiered in February 1968. The 80-page issue, which sold for 50¢, introduced an editorial format that included recipes, diet advice, fashion, and beauty. Today, those topics still provide the foundation for the magazine's success.

In that first issue, the articles included a spread on Weight Watchers–approved desserts, a guide to using herbs and spices, advice on how to make your face appear slimmer, and fashions for vacation. The monthly departments included an advice column, "Ask Jean Nidetch," who was the founder of the Weight Watchers program and who had lost 70 pounds; a doctor's column that discussed the link between diabetes and obesity; and special columns "For Men Only," "For Teens Only," and "For Women Only." The featured articles that month discussed the overweight child; the story of obesity in America; a guide to nonstick cookware; a feature about men and golf; and the story of a woman who lost 150 pounds.

Weight Watchers was the right message at the right time, and it was a hit. Within a year, the magazine advertised that it had more than a million readers. Offered for $5 a year, the magazine found an enthusiastic readership. Readership has grown steadily over the years. By 1971, the magazine's readership stood at 2 million; 3 million in 1974; and 4.3 million in 1984, with a rate base of 825,000.[9] The magazine's readership peaked at about 5 million readers in the late 1980s and stood at about 4.7 million in the fall of 1993, when it cost $1.95

on newsstands or $15.97 for an annual subscription. Over the years, the company also published cookbooks that highlighted Weight Watchers recipes and, in 1991, introduced a 900 telephone line to let readers keep in touch with current events in the diet program.

Weight Watchers readers were assured that recipes featured in the magazine had been tested and approved by the Weight Watchers program and that they were "legal," a word coined by WWI to mean that a recipe was permitted on the diet program.[10] In the early days of the magazine, advertised products stated when they were approved for use on the Weight Watchers program, and the Weight Watchers seal of approval was introduced to show that advertised products were legal. *Weight Watchers* also encouraged readers to buy and save back editions and introduced a binder to hold old issues.

The magazine also has always featured articles that have no connection to weight loss or health. Mogel, the magazine's first publisher, said that articles on travel, fashion, and beauty were included because "once our readers lose their weight, they will become interested in peripheral subjects."[11] "What Do You Do If You Discover Your Child Smokes Pot?" was a feature in November 1971; the inspirational article "You've Gotta Have Hope" was featured in October 1993.

In fact, the editorial approach of the magazine has changed little. The earliest cover designs featured appetizing food, but emphasis shifted gradually to the happy (and thin) people-oriented designs of the 1990s. The magazine in 1994 also was more clearly a woman's magazine that no longer attempted to include men or teens in its editorial staples. Simmons recalled that he always viewed the magazine as a woman's magazine but that he initially wanted "to reach out" to obese men as well. "My goal was to sell magazines," he said. "We knew it was a woman's magazine, but there were men who read it. That was just part of reaching out."[12]

In 1993, 4 million of the magazine's 4.7 million readers were women. The average reader's age was 44, and her household income was $64,473. More than 63 percent of the readers were employed, 62 percent were married, and nearly 50 percent had children under age 18, while 38 percent had attended college.[13]

Simmons sold his interest in the magazine in 1970, when he was starting *National Lampoon* and needed capital.[14] The $40,000 investment had mushroomed into a sale of more than $2 million back to WWI. Twenty-First Century Publishing managed the magazine until 1975, when Family Health Magazine published it for a time under an agreement, but publication responsibilities shifted back to W/W Twentyfirst Corp., which published the magazine into the 1990s.

When Simmons left in 1975, Bernadette Carr was named editor; under her leadership, the magazine experienced its first makeover. The front covers began featuring face shots of prominent people who had lost weight. Actress Ann Margret confessed, "I Was a Blimp," and actress/singers Marie Osmond and Shirley MacLaine posed for cover photos. Typeface and graphics were modern-ized, but the content of the magazine and the regular features generally remained constant. Also in 1975, *Weight Watchers* began publishing with the subtitle, *Magazine for Attractive People*, which remained a part of the cover design until 1980. In 1976, the monthly price jumped to 75¢ for a magazine that averaged between 56 and 72 pages.

Judith Nolte took over in 1980 and introduced *The New Weight Watchers* magazine. After a few months, the magazine reverted to its old title. The typeface and cover design had changed with the change in command, but once again the editorial content remained basically stable. The magazine moved away from celebrity covers and began featuring photography of smiling (and thin) unknown models posed in the kitchen, at a desk, or in other everyday activities. Former managing editor Linda Konner served at the helm of the magazine from 1983 to 1985, when the current editor, Lee Haiken, who had been food and equipment editor, took over.

In the fall of 1993, Haiken stated that *Weight Watchers* magazine sold advertising on a rate base of 1 million. Eighty-five percent of the circulation, she said, was subscription-based. Today, the magazine runs between 60 and 80 pages and features advertising that generally supports the goals of weight loss. *Weight Watchers* magazine promotes the idea to potential advertisers that its audience is unique because it tends not to read other magazines. The national advertising rate for a four-color inside page is $29,320 for a single issue, while multiple insertions are discounted. *Weight Watchers* accepted cigarette advertising in the 1970s and early 1980s but reversed that policy after Haiken took over in 1985. It also rejected other advertising that runs counter to the WWI philosophy.

The November 1993, 66-page issue featured about 22 pages of advertisements, but six of those pages were for Weight Watchers products. Exercise machines and other diet aids figured heavily in the advertising mix.

One of the consistently most popular features has been the "success stories," monthly "before and after" articles that highlight how members of Weight Watchers and sometimes Hollywood celebrities managed to change their life through the program. From the very first issue, which featured a woman who had lost 150 pounds, to the slimming story of four fat nuns, to the father-son dieters, to Weight Watchers spokesperson Lynn Redgrave's battle against fat, the magazine monthly features inspirational success stories.

The magazine has always reflected the current thinking of the medical community and the guidelines of the U.S. government concerning how to diet. Articles emphasize the link between obesity and health problems such as heartburn, diabetes, and arthritis and comment on the latest developments in weight loss. As the Weight Watchers program expanded over the years to include an ever-increasing number of diet products and to incorporate previously forbidden foods, the magazine's recipes and advice changed, too.

In 1991, the magazine told readers it was increasing its coverage of health and nutrition information to respond to the growing interest in this area. Noting that 58 percent of *Weight Watchers* readers were very interested in health and nutrition information, the magazine stated that it was publicizing ''Weight Watchers HealthWatch 2000'' to educate the public about ways to stay healthy.

Notes

1. Membership figures, as of November 1993, from Weight Watchers International, 500 N. Broadway, Jericho, N.Y. 11753.
2. Louis Calta, ''New Magazine Aims to Help the Overweight,'' *New York Times*, January 18, 1968, p. 36.
3. Matty Simmons interview, November 1993.
4. Ibid.
5. Ibid.
6. Philip H. Dougherty, ''Advertising: Betting on the Chubby People,'' *New York Times*, May 2, 1968, p. 77.
7. Simmons interview.
8. Dougherty, ''Advertising,'' p. 77.
9. *Weight Watchers* magazine statistics from MRI.
10. ''An Important Message to All Readers of This Magazine,'' January 1969, un-numbered page.
11. Calta, ''New Magazine Aims to Help the Overweight,'' p. 36.
12. Simmons interview.
13. *Weight Watchers* reader profile for 1993 Spring, MRI.
14. Simmons interview.

Information Sources

BIBLIOGRAPHY:
Calta, Louis. ''New Magazine Aims to Help the Overweight.'' *New York Times*, January 18, 1968, p. 36.
Dougherty, Philip H. ''Advertising: Betting on the Chubby People.'' *New York Times*, May 2, 1968, p. 77.
INDEX SOURCES: Consumer Health and Nutrition Index; Magazine Index.
LOCATION SOURCES: Library of Congress and other libraries.

Publication History

MAGAZINE TITLE AND TITLE CHANGES: *Weight Watchers Magazine.*
VOLUME AND ISSUE DATA: Vols. 1–(February 1968–present). Monthly.
PUBLISHER AND PLACE OF PUBLICATION: W/W Twentyfirst Corp. New York.
EDITORS: Matty Simmons (1968–1975); Bernadette Carr (1975–1980); Judith Nolte (1980–1983); Linda Konner (1983–1985); Lee Haiken (1985–present).
CIRCULATION: ABC, 1993: 1,050,301 (paid, primarily subscriptions).

Agnes Hooper Gottlieb

WOMAN'S DAY

Woman's Day first appeared in 1937, a publication of the Great Atlantic and Pacific Tea Company (A&P). It had originated as a giveaway leaflet called *A&P*

Menus that proved so popular the store decided to expand it into a magazine. It reached 775,000 readers the first year. The publication carried a low price (2¢ by 1940, at a time when other women's journals such as *Ladies' Home Journal*,* *Woman's Home Companion*,* and *McCall's** all cost 25¢) and was sold exclusively in A&P grocery stores. The price rose throughout the 1940s, finally reaching the grand sum of 7¢ a copy in 1951. Advertising appeared from the very beginning, primarily for products handled in the A&P stores.[1]

In 1943, Mabel Hill Souvaine took over as *Woman's Day*'s editor, a position she held for 15 years. During this time she led the magazine to great success, attracting almost 5 million readers. Souvaine published a mix of homemaking tips, child-rearing advice, book reviews, and money- and time-savers, all available at a low price. The magazine expanded from its original 32 pages to well over 200 pages in these years.

Woman's Day continued to thrive and in the early 1950s was the leader among supermarket magazines in advertising revenue, taking in almost $9.4 million in 1951. That same year the publication was distributed in 4,500 A&P stores.[2] However, in the mid-1950s, 23 retail grocers and two wholesalers brought a suit against three food companies advertising in *Woman's Day*, arguing that the food companies' spending in A&P's magazine constituted a benefit to the food store chain, one not offered to these other food sellers. As the suit dragged on, some advertisers became reluctant to use the magazine; and ad revenues dropped, declining from more than $9 million in 1955 to more than $7 million in 1956 and $5.5 million in 1957. In response, the publishers began distributing *Woman's Day* outside A&P stores in 1958, placing it in thousands of drugstores, newsstands, and other grocery stores. That same year Fawcett Co., publisher of pulp magazines, purchased the title.[3]

Fawcett Co. installed a new editor, Eileen Tighe. By focusing on homemaking advice for the budget-conscious, Tighe increased circulation to almost 6.5 million by 1963. Advertising climbed to almost $14 million. Then, in 1966, Geraldine Rhoads, a former Fawcett editor, took over the magazine.

Rhoads was an experienced women's magazine staffer. She had worked on the women's magazine digest *The Woman* in the 1930s, then had moved to Fawcett publications. Rhoads had been hired to transform one of Fawcett's romance journals, *Life Story*, into a straightforward women's service journal for young married homemakers, a job she completed successfully. Rhoads had also worked at the *Ladies' Home Journal* and *McCall's* before taking over at *Woman's Day* in 1966.

Rhoads knew that changes were occurring in the lives of American women. She saw many women ready to enter the workforce as their families were growing up. Rhoads tried to reflect this new reality in *Woman's Day* by providing practical information and ways for women to use their time carefully. Rhoads also believed that "the reader is the most important person you'll ever know, and you must find ways to be indispensable to her—every single month," a necessity for this newsstand publication.[4] She defined the magazine as a trade journal for homemakers, providing useful advice for that area of her readers' lives. By the late 1970s, Rhoads had added articles on health and money management to the recipes, decorating, child advice, and fashion tips. The loud blurbs that crowded the title's cover (as they did the covers of rival *Family Circle**) told readers why they should purchase this homemaking manual. To add a spiritual element to this practical guide, the magazine published a biblical quotation on the top of the table of contents page (a practice it continues through the present).

Rhoads touched a nerve with readers, and circulation climbed from 7.2 million in 1968 to just over 8 million in 1978 (fifth in circulation of magazines overall and second only to *Family Circle* among women's titles).[5] The reliance on single-copy sales served the magazine well through the 1970s, as other magazines were hurt by rising postal rates and the costs of subscription fulfillment. By 1979, *Woman's Day* was publishing 15 issues a year, and in 1980 it topped the women's group in ad revenues.[6]

In 1977, Fawcett sold its publishing business, including *Woman's Day*, to CBS Inc. Soon the magazine was hurt by a general decline in single-copy sales occurring in the late 1970s and early 1980s. In 1982, new publisher Peter Diamandis replaced longtime editor Rhoads with Ellen Levine, formerly editor in chief of *Cosmopolitan Living* (a lifestyle magazine Levine created for Hearst Co.) and food and decorating editor for *Cosmopolitan** since 1975. Levine's mandate was to update the magazine in order to attract new purchasers while holding on to longtime readers. She planned to accomplish this by running articles on health, medical topics, and emotional issues and giving the magazine "an infusion of reality."[7] Levine succeeded in increasing advertising volume and revenues substantially for *Woman's Day*, although circulation declined through the 1980s, dropping 28 percent between 1978 and 1988.[8]

In 1987, Diamandis, along with other senior managers from CBS's magazine division and Prudential Insurance Co., purchased *Woman's Day* and the 20 other magazines in the CBS group.[9] The new business was called Diamandis Communications, Inc. However, they had barely set up shop when Hachette S.A., a French conglomerate, bought the company for $712 million as part of its plan to expand into the communications industry in the United States. Hachette had already successfully launched its fashion magazine *Elle.** *Woman's Day* was one of the chief attractions for Hachette in this 1988 acquisition.[10]

Hachette may have overpaid for the magazines. In 1989, *Woman's Day* was hurt by the aggressive entry of *First for Women,** owned by a West German publishing company, the Bauer Group, which was seeking to enter the U.S. market. *First for Women* competed by heavily discounting its initial issues and going after display space. *Woman's Day* had resisted going after subscriptions (unlike rival *Family Circle*, which began doing so in the second half of the 1980s) and so was hit especially hard by the newcomer; in the year before *First for Women*'s entry, *Woman's Day* had sold almost 98 percent of its circulation in single-copy sales.[11] *Woman's Day* was forced to begin testing subscription sales.[12] The magazine lost over 2 million in circulation between 1985 and 1989, dropping from 6,590,273 to 4,401,746.[13]

In May 1990, Diamandis Communications, Inc. (now owned by Hachette) put *Woman's Day* up for sale. However, the title was withdrawn because no buyers came near the reportedly $200 million being asked. This reflected both stagnant times in the industry and lack of confidence in the strength of *Woman's Day*'s franchise. By this time *Woman's Day* was the only "Seven-Sister" magazine to be owned alone; each of the others was owned in pairs, giving them advantages with advertisers and distributors. Some in the industry were ready to sound the death knell for *Woman's Day*.

Yet, the magazine was able to turn around. The staff put together a long-term strategy for the editorial content, including a redesign under new editor Jane Chesnutt. (Levine left in 1991 to edit *Redbook*.*) Salespeople marketed the magazine aggressively to advertisers. By 1993, the magazine led all other women's magazines in advertising pages and had increased ad revenues by 7.6 percent. Subscriptions now account for over a fourth of the magazine's sales, although it remains the leading woman's magazine in single-copy sales.[14]

Hachette Filipacchi Magazines owns *Woman's Day*, which is still edited by Jane Chesnutt. The magazine continues its tradition of serving women with advice about homemaking; today much of that counsel appears within a time-saving framework. Topics in the magazine have been expanded in response to readers' expanded lives; in addition to beauty, fashion, decorating, and food tips, an issue of *Woman's Day* can include articles on money management, finances, automobiles, and deadbeat dads. A condensed information section called "Quick" reflects understanding of women's time pressures in the 1990s.

Notes

1. Theodore Peterson, *Magazines in the Twentieth Century* (Urbana: University of Illinois Press, 1964), pp. 288–290.

2. "Food-Store Magazines Hit the Big Time," *Business Week*, February 9, 1952, pp. 108, 110.

3. Peterson, *Magazines in the Twentieth Century*, pp. 288–290.

4. Geraldine Rhoads, "How to Sell a Magazine One Issue at a Time," *SR*, September 11, 1971, p. 61.

5. Circulation figures from *100 Leading A.B.C. Magazines* (New York: Magazine Advertising Bureau of Magazine Publishers Association, 1968, 1978).

6. Cecelia Lentini, "Balancing Act in Women's Magazines," *Advertising Age*, October 19, 1981, p. S64.

7. Ira Ellenthal, "Ellen Levine: Editor in Chief of *Woman's Day*," *Folio*, April 1983, p. 70.

8. Ad volume had jumped 36 percent between 1984 and 1987, and by 1987, ad revenues had increased $4 million; see Ellen McCracken, *Decoding Women's Magazines*

(New York: St. Martin's Press, 1993), p. 285. On circulation decline, see Eric Schmuck-ler, "Sob for the Sisters," *Forbes*, April 4, 1988, p. 112.

9. Geraldine Fabrikant, "As Hard Times Hit Industry, *Woman's Day* Is Being Sold," *New York Times*, May 15, 1990, p. D1.

10. "Hachette's Blueprints for Growth," *Folio*, June 1988, pp. 23–24.

11. "Percentage of Single Copy Sales for Top 25 Consumer Magazines," *Advertising Age*, October 24, 1988, p. S34.

12. Fabrikant, "As Hard Times Hit Industry, *Woman's Day* Is Being Sold," p. D17.

13. Ira Teinowitz, " 'First' Shock Wave," *Advertising Age*, August 21, 1989, pp. 1, 66.

14. Scott Donaton, " 'Woman's Day' Now Biggest Sister," *Advertising Age*, November 8, 1993, p. 54.

Information Sources

BIBLIOGRAPHY:
Donaton, Scott. " 'Woman's Day' Now Biggest Sister." *Advertising Age*, November 8, 1993, p. 54.
Ellenthal, Ira. "Ellen Levine. Editor in Chief of *Woman's Day*." *Folio*, April 1983, pp. 68, 70.
Peterson, Theodore. *Magazines in the Twentieth Century*. Urbana: University of Illinois Press, 1964.
Rhoads, Geraldine, "How to Sell a Magazine One Issue at a Time," *SR*, September 11, 1971, pp. 61–63.
INDEX SOURCES: Access; Index to How to Do It Information; Magazine Index; MELSA Messenger.
LOCATION SOURCES: Cleveland Public Library and other (primarily community) libraries.

Publication History

MAGAZINE TITLE AND TITLE CHANGES: *Woman's Day*.
VOLUME AND ISSUE DATA: Vols. 1–(October 7, 1937–present). Seventeen times a year.
PUBLISHER AND PLACE OF PUBLICATION: Stores Publishing Co. (1937–1958); Fawcett Publishing Co. (1958–1977); CBS, Inc. (1977–1987); Diamandis Com-munications (1987); Hachette Filipacchi Magazines (1988–present). New York City.
EDITORS: Mabel Hill Souvaine (1943–1958); Eileen Tighe (1958–1966); Geraldine Rhoads (1966–1982); Ellen Levine (1982–1991); Jane Chesnutt (1991–present).
CIRCULATION: ABC, 1993: 4,858,625 (paid, primarily single-copy sales).

Mary Ellen Zuckerman

WOMAN'S HOME COMPANION

In 1990s parlance, the most widely circulated women's magazines in the United States are called the "Seven Sisters." The siblings share some enviable traits: huge circulations, long lives, and service editorial orientations.[1] This "family" once included another. The *Woman's Home Companion*, the oldest of the "sisters" and, at one time, the biggest of the "girls," died in 1957, a victim of television, decreasing advertising revenues, and a financially troubled corporate parent.

She had lived a long life. She had been born in 1873 in Cleveland with the name *The Home*. Not many took notice of S. L. and Frederick Thorpe's little creation. The local libraries did not even keep any of the first issues of the monthly. Perhaps that was to be expected. There was little evidence that this cheaply printed and cheaply produced publication would amount to much. But endure it did. In 1878, it was joined with another publication, *Little Ones at Home*, to make the *Home Companion: A Monthly for Young People*. As the title implied, the publication's focus had changed from woman's magazine to juvenile periodical. The new publication came out in monthly and semimonthly versions. Shortly after, the monthly edition was dropped; and the semimonthly continued, selling for 60¢ per year. In 1881, the magazine was sold to E. B. Harvey and Frank S. Finn. Two years later, it was sold again, this time to Mast, Crowell & Kirkpatrick of Springfield, Ohio, a company that had gotten into magazine publishing almost by happenstance.[2]

John Crowell edited the house organ of a farm implement manufacturer, Phineas Mast & Co. That publication became so popular that Mast, Crowell, and Mast's nephew, Thomas Kirkpatrick, set up a company to sell subscriptions to the house organ.[3] This corporation purchased the *Home Companion*, transformed it back into a woman's magazine, renamed the magazine the *Ladies' Home Companion* in 1886, greatly improved its editorial quality, and increased the price of subscriptions to one dollar per year. The frequency, however, remained the same; the *Ladies' Home Companion, A Practical Household Journal* came home to its readers semimonthly. Its principal competitor was a monthly called the *Ladies' Home Journal*,* which was launched the same year that Mast, Crowell & Kirkpatrick took over the struggling *Home Companion*.

That competition plagued the *Home Companion* throughout its life. It caused a name change in 1897. The *Ladies' Home Companion* became the *Woman's Home Companion* in a move to "appeal to the good sense and good taste of all readers" and to differentiate it from another publication (the *Journal*) whose "similarity [of names] is none the less annoying on that account."[4]

The confusion was natural. Not only were the names similar, but so, too, were the audiences.[5] Both offered a similar fare of editorial content: practical household advice, parenting guidance, and craft information as well as fiction. The *Ladies' Home Journal* also seemed to invite the confusion by advertising in the *Companion*.[6] These advertisements suggest that the *Companion* had a large circulation, appealing to the *Journal* and Curtis Publishing. Certainly, the *Companion*'s circulation was large. In 1895, the magazine reported it had a circulation of 177,630.[7] The magazine's circulation was increasing at such a rapid rate that the magazine had difficulty keeping track of all the new subscribers and often could not keep the guaranteed circulation for advertising up-to-date. Often, its guaranteed circulation lagged up to 10,000 subscribers behind.[8]

The year 1896 brought many changes to the *Companion*. The publishing company opened offices in New York and Chicago as well as keeping office and printing facilities in Springfield, Ohio. (By 1901, the magazine was editorially based in New York.) In addition, the magazine's frequency was cut back to monthly to enhance the literary quality of the magazine. The cost of subscribing also went down, to 50¢ a year, the same price as for the *Journal*.[9]

These moves brought no real changes to the editorial content. The magazine continued to carry material designed to help women carry out their household duties, as well as fiction as an escape from them. Some of the leading short story writers and novelists of the day contributed to the magazine: Mrs. Burton Harrison, William O. Stoddard, Bret Harte, and Mrs. Harriet Prescott Spofford. But the nonfiction really differentiated the *Companion* from its competition. The *Companion*, under editors J. F. Henderson, Arthur Vance, and Frederick L. Collins, extensively covered women's reform activities. Features told of the activities of Hull House and benevolent organizations such as the Soldier's Home Association.[10] Other features offered profiles of strong women who made a difference, practical advice for succeeding in business or going to college, and unusual adventures or travels by women.[11] The magazine even carried at least one feature written by an African American woman, Mrs. Booker T. Washington, many decades before other national women's magazines dared such coverage.[12] Departments reflected a diversity in the readership of the magazine. One covered the clubwoman; another, the working woman. Nonetheless, the editors never forgot that most of their readers were wives and mothers. The magazine's tremendously successful "Better Babies Campaign"[13] reflected the editors' commitment to decrease the rate of infant mortality.

The early editors of the *Companion* under Mast, Crowell & Kirkpatrick, which became Crowell and Kirkpatrick in 1899 and then just Crowell Publishing in 1902, seemed especially committed to social improvements. That was evident not only in the nonfiction but also in the editorials. The *Companion* editorially supported athletics and education for women ("The women who have been taught to fill only the place of the 'clinging vine' is unfitted for the new conditions of life. She is unprepared for any of the many emergencies that may burden her with responsibilities and duties requiring strength, self confidence and endurance"[14]); was against child labor (*Companion* editor Arthur Vance was a member of the national board of the Anti–Child Slavery League. The magazine published membership forms for that group and asked for contributions to be sent to needy children[15]); and was in favor of sanitary grocery stores ("[C]ockroaches and waterbugs run this way and that. The pipe is clogged up, and the water has settled in a slimy pool behind the rack." Grocers responded by calling Vance "the most scintillating ass in the United States"[16]).

If this sounds like muckraking journalism, there was much within the magazine to suggest such a conclusion. In the early twentieth century particularly, the *Companion* ran a number of articles that could easily be classified as muck-raking. The most obvious example was the campaign against child labor. Month after month, the magazine ran stories of child labor abuse in cities and in the countryside.[17] The campaign for sanitary grocery stores followed.[18] Yet, unlike many muckraking journals, the *Companion* often provided solutions. The magazine and its editor were charter members of one organization designed to rid the nation of child labor. The periodical, likewise, took in contributions to send to needy children.[19] The grocery campaign saw readers relating their own horror stories of unsanitary conditions in their neighborhood stores.[20] All the while, however, the magazine never lost sight of its other missions: to provide practical advice to women who took care of the home and to entertain them with the finest fiction of the day.

With a circulation reaching 600,000 by 1907, giving it the "largest subscription list of any ten-cent magazine,"[21] the *Companion* could afford to hire the best writers in the nation. Novelist Jack London sailed around the world as the *Companion*'s exclusive correspondent.[22] Reformer Charlotte Perkins Gilman offered essays on the role of women in society and the need for women's suffrage.[23] Henry Harrison Lewis offered a profile of Alice Roosevelt, the president's daughter, "an American Princess."[24] Journalist Rheta Childe Dorr wrote on conditions in the city.[25] The magazine could also afford to commission some of the best artists in the nation to do front covers; Howard Chandler Christy, William T. Smedley, Wallace Nutting, Bessie Pease Guttman, James Montgomery Flagg, and Harrison Fisher all did work for the *Companion*.

The rest of the century was not marked by such activism. In the first decade of the twentieth century, the *Companion* was in step with the progressive spirit and the muckraking tradition. Vance and Collins's *Companion* was a voice of reform and social change. While editor Vance was not prepared to embrace women's suffrage, he and his successor published many articles in favor of suffrage written by many of the most articulate women reformers of the day, including Jane Addams and Charlotte Perkins Gilman.[26] That type of discussion decreased considerably after 1911, when a new editor took over.

Gertrude Battles Lane, who was probably the magazine's first woman editor and who guided the magazine for the next 29 years, did not continue the muckraking spirit. She took the *Companion* to another stage of development.

By the time Lane took over, muckraking as a style of journalism had lost much of its vigor and popularity nationally. Nonetheless, the *Companion* had prospered under Vance and Collins's brand of investigative journalism. In 1911, the magazine's circulation had reached 737,764, up from 177,630 in 1895.[27] But those figures paled in comparison with the growth under Lane. By 1916, the *Companion* reached the 1 million mark; nine years later, 2 million; six years later, at the dawn of the depression, 2.5 million. The economic downturn of the 1930s could only slow the *Companion*'s growth. Circulation reached 2.9 million in April 1936. *Time* magazine noted that the *Companion* had the largest circulation of any magazine in its niche.[28]

Crowell Publishing attributed much of this success to Lane. *Time* was inclined to agree. Lane did have a flair for "editorial showmanship."[29] She sent writer Margaret Deland and the enormously popular *Companion* staffer Anna Steese Richardson to France to cover World War I; Marjorie Shuler went to Geneva to cover the International Women Suffrage Alliance after the war.[30] Lane had film star Charlie Chaplin write about his travels and engineered the first series on the "auto gypsys," "motorized vagabonds" of the United States.[31] She also started many of the innovations generally credited to the *Ladies' Home Journal*. For example, First Lady Eleanor Roosevelt wrote a column for the *Companion* soon after her husband's inauguration—and well before she began writing for the *Ladies' Home Journal*.[32] The *Companion* column, at first envisioned as a personal advice page, soon developed into an editorial page, a forum for the first lady to talk about favorite reforms.[33] It is unclear which of the two magazines first brought letters from presidents to the niche. Both offered a range of letters from presidents since Theodore Roosevelt's administration.[34]

In the end, Lane's tremendous success at the *Companion* emanated from her understanding of her audience. Perhaps, nowhere was that more apparent than in her selection of fiction. Because Lane had substantial amounts of money to spend in acquiring short stories and novels, the editor was in an enviable position. She picked wisely, and her audience seemed to approve of her selections. For example, novelists Kathleen Norris and Edna Ferber were Lane favorites. Each of these two received $85,000 for a serial.[35] That generosity was not limited to these two authors. Lane, the *Companion*, and Crowell were extremely generous when it came to the acquisition of fiction. Accordingly, many of the best fiction writers in the nation were soon contributing to the *Companion*. F. Scott Fitzgerald, A. A. Milne, Booth Tarkington, Willa Cather, Edith Wharton, and Pearl Buck all contributed to Lane's *Companion*.[36] Edna Ferber was a special favorite. Ferber's Pulitzer Prize-winning *So Big* was first published in the *Companion*. The magazine went on to serialize such Ferber works as *Showboat* and *Cimarron*.[37]

Lane was well paid for her efforts. Her $52,000 salary in 1939 was the highest paid a woman editor and probably among the highest paid to men as well.[38] Crowell's largest stockholder, Joseph P. Knapp, felt that was money well spent. As he once remarked, "Gertrude Lane is the best 'man' in the business." All of Crowell Publishing listened to her advice. She was vice president of the corporation.[39]

Although the *Companion* during this period was identified only with Lane, she alone did not put out the magazine. Lane gathered around her a talented staff of editors, most of whom were women. Among them were Anna Richardson, best known for the "Better Babies" campaign and the "Good Citizenship Bureau"; Fannie Merritt Farmer, founder of the Boston Cooking School and editor of the magazine's Cooking Department; Willa Roberts, managing editor; and 2,000 reader/editors from all parts of the United States who kept the *Companion* up-to-date throughout the year. Every year, these 2,000 women came to

New York to work for two weeks at the *Companion*'s expense.[40] Few other magazines could afford such a major expenditure.

Lane "grew" into her position as editor. Over her 29 years at the *Companion*, Lane was transformed from a timid, weak editorialist of "safe" positions to a stronger editor taking more courageous editorial stands. It was a slow transition. Prior to World War I, she took relatively "safe" stands—applauding military buildup prior to U.S. involvement in the war and urging women to conserve food during the war. (In this later stance, she had a special interest because during the war she worked for Hoover's Food Administration and put out the magazine on weekends.)[41] After the war, however, she ventured into less-charted waters. As women activists debated an equal rights amendment versus protective legislation, Lane took the more conservative road: "It is our opinion that in some cases women need more than 'equal' laws." Nonetheless, she later urged a campaign to get women elected to public office in order to repeal laws that limited females:

Only women can change these conditions, first by proving their own competence; then by electing to office women who can match the abilities of men in making and executing the laws, and finally by bringing about the hundreds of necessary changes in the laws themselves.[42]

She also defended a woman's right to work—even during the depression. "It's about time that all women got mad about this [women losing jobs because of their gender], whether or not they need or want to work themselves. People ought to get and hold a job strictly on the basis of merit."[43]

Her editorial stances prior to World War II differed greatly from her earlier comments. Prior to World War I, she applauded the idea of military buildup. Throughout the 1930s, however, the *Companion* was firmly on the side of the pacifists. She supported most disarmament plans, the World Court, and any other plan designed to keep the United States out of war. As Lane saw it, the United States could not be manipulated into war. "War is waged for the selfish ends of small groups—but sold to the people by idealistic slogans," she warned.[44] Lane did not survive to oversee the magazine's coverage of yet another war. By 1940, she was named editorial director. Longtime managing editor Willa Roberts took over as editor. Lane died in September 1941.[45] The *Companion* characterized Lane: "No feminist, she was the outstanding example of a woman executive in a large business organization."[46]

Lane had directed the *Companion* when it was the largest circulating magazine in its niche. Yet, even in her last years as editor, Lane saw the *Companion*'s growth slow and the *Ladies' Home Journal*'s growth accelerate. When Willa Roberts took over as editor, the *Companion* had slipped to number two in terms of circulation.[47] Roberts did not have much time to turn around that situation. In her brief time as editor, she carried on many of Lane's editorial policies. However, she did not carry on Lane's pacificist editorial stances. Roberts was out to rally the readers for war. The nonfiction was designed to muster support for the war effort. Features included stories on "Life in Nazified Italy" and "Occupied Greece."[48]

Roberts's editorial vision for the magazine, however, did not seem to coincide with the view of the periodical's new publisher. In 1943, Edward Anthony came on board, and Roberts resigned. William A. H. Birnie took Roberts's place. Ironically, Birnie—as editor and later as publisher—presided over the *Companion*'s precipitous competitive decline. By the mid-1950s, the magazine was having difficulty keeping up.

When Birnie took over as editor, the magazine was rushing toward the 4 million circulation mark; the magazine's circulation exceeded 3.8 million. The next few years, the magazine's circulation declined to 3.7 million and stayed there. Meanwhile, the *Ladies' Home Journal* raced forward. In 1948, the *Journal* reported a circulation of 4.6 million. The *Companion*—the magazine that for years dominated its niche or jockeyed with the *Journal* in close competition— was clearly in second place in terms of circulation. The *Companion* finally reached the magic 4 million figure in 1951; and, throughout most of the 1950s, the *Companion* retained a circulation around 4 million, even as the *Journal* hovered around 5 million. The real competition was for second place. In the early 1950s, the *Companion* had the edge; by the mid-1950s, *McCall's** was the winner.[49]

The strange thing in all this was that the *Companion* itself had not really decreased in editorial quality. The quality of the nonfiction under Birnie and the subsequent editors, Woodrow Wirsig and Theodore Strauss, had not declined. Birnie sent the well-known woman reporter Doris Fleeson to Europe to cover the war for the magazine.[50] After the war, the *Companion* dealt with topics of direct relevance to women—divorce[51] (the *Companion*'s "Marriage Clinic" column preceded the *Journal*'s "Can This Marriage Be Saved?" by eight years), abortion, breast cancer, childbirth, birth control, and dieting.[52] This harder edge, historian Theodore Peterson wrote, may have been a reason for some of the magazine's decline.[53]

Yet, the decline and fall of the *Companion*, in the end, was a business story. Throughout much of its history, the *Companion* was published by Crowell Publishing or one of its predecessors. In 1939, Crowell and Collier merged to create Crowell-Collier Publishing Co., bringing under one corporation two of the largest circulating magazines in the United States—the *Companion* and *Collier's*. The company also published the editorially fine *American Magazine* (the old *Leslie's Monthly*). In the heyday of the mass circulation magazines, Crowell-Collier did well. But the mid-1950s found the publishing company's two major properties locked in tight competitive races. As noted, the *Companion* had slipped to number three (in terms of circulation) in its niche. Things were even worse for *Collier's*. *Collier's* trailed *Life*, *Look*, and *Saturday Evening Post*. Moreover, both magazines were extraordinarily expensive to produce. In 1953, *Collier's* lost $7 million. The *Companion* was still profitable; and it, along with the company's book division, kept the publishing company afloat. Indeed, in 1953, four years before its demise, the *Companion* reported an all-time advertising high of $11,955,000. The *Companion,* however, could not sustain those figures. By 1955, advertising revenue was down slightly to $10,196,000.[54]

The year 1956 was abysmal for Crowell-Collier, *Collier's,* the *American,* and the *Companion.* In June, the company announced plans to suspend the *American,* one of the healthiest of Crowell-Collier's properties. *Collier's* and the *Companion* would split the *American*'s 2.5 million circulation. At the same time, the company announced plans to increase advertising rates for the surviving magazines.[55] That proved to be too little too late. The *Companion*'s advertising continued to decline. Crowell-Collier executives scurried around to solve the problems. Chief executive officer Paul C. Smith even proposed merging the *Companion* with *McCall's,* but nothing seemed to work.[56]

In the end, both the *Companion* and *Collier's* died. The news made the front page of the *New York Times.* Less than two weeks before Christmas 1956, Crowell-Collier announced plans to suspend both magazines, throwing 2,400 people out of work. A spokesman for the company attributed the suspensions to cash problems in meeting payrolls, paper bills, and bank loans.[57]

The *Companion* disappeared with the January 1957 issue. She was 83 at the time of her death, the first of the "sisters" to die. *Companion* obituaries emphasized business-side considerations; and most stories lacked a clear view of what this magazine had meant to three generations of women. The stories failed to mention the reform campaigns, the muckraking journalism, the advice columns, the art, the literature, the differing viewpoints—the fact that the first of the "sisters" had perished. More than 4 million women had lost a "friend," a *Companion.*

Notes

1. The "Seven Sisters" are *Ladies' Home Journal* (1883), *Good Housekeeping* (1885), *Family Circle* (1932), *Better Homes and Gardens* (1922), *McCall's* (1876), *Redbook* (1903), and *Woman's Day* (1937). These publications had circulations ranging from 3.8 million (*Redbook*) to in excess of 8 million (*Better Homes and Gardens*).

2. Frank Luther Mott, *A History of American Magazines, 1885–1905* (Cambridge: Belknap Press of Harvard University Press, 1957), pp. 763–764.

3. Theodore Peterson, *Magazines in the Twentieth Century* (Urbana: University of Illinois Press, 1956), p. 182.

4. "Under a New Name," January 1897, p. 15.

5. The *Companion* initially seemed to appeal to a primarily rural female audience. However, by the early twentieth century, the urban woman had discovered the *Companion* and became an important element of the magazine's audience.

6. See, for example, January 15, 1896, p. 13; March 1897, p. 17.

7. July 15, 1895, unnumbered page. Circulation figures for this period were not audited and were often inflated.

8. March 1, 1895, unnumbered page; "Points for Advertisers," May 1, 1895, unnumbered page.

9. January 15, 1896, unnumbered page; April 1896, p. 22.

10. Ann Stuart Wheeler, "The Wisdom of Women's Clubs," November 1896, pp. 3–4; Forrest Crissy, "The Hull House Social Settlement," October 1898, pp. 5–6.

11. Countess Magri, "The Recollections of a Midget," October 1900, pp. 1–2, 28; "Miss Marion Talbot" (dean of women's college at University of Chicago) and "Feats of Women Divers," July 1, 1895; Mary C. Stetson, "American Colleges for Women," March 1896 p. 6; Hetty Green, "The Benefits of Business Training for Women," February 1900, p. 8; Jessie Ackermann, "Wanderings through Africa," January 15, 1896 pp. 3–5; "The Heroines of the Battle of Bull Run," December 1901, pp. 11–12; "Deeds of Heroism, Patriotism and Patience of Women in the Civil and Spanish Wars," January 1902, pp. 11–12.

12. Mrs. Booker T. Washington, "The Mother's Meeting at Tuskegee," September 1899, p. 21.

13. See August 1913, pp. 3–4.

14. "Athletics for Women," January 1897, p. 15.

15. "Anti Child Labor Creed," August 1906, p. 5; "Woman's Home Companion," July 1906, p. 1.

16. "Keeping the Bins Closed," December 1907, p. 23; "Our Own Page," February 1908, p. 5.

17. Viola Roseboro and Marie Best, "A True Story of Child Slavery in Philadelphia," August 1906, pp. 3–4; John Spargo, "Child Slaves of the Slums," July 1906, pp. 3–4; A. J. McKelway, "How the Fight for Children Was Fought in Georgia," October 1906, pp. 18–19, 21.

18. See, for example, "Keeping the Bins Closed," p. 23.

19. August 1907, p. 1; October 1907, p. 42.

20. "Keeping the Bins Closed," p. 24.

21. October 1907.

22. See, for example, Jack London, "The Lepers of Molokai," January 1908, pp. 7–8.

23. Charlotte Perkins Gilman, "Good Tidings of Women—The World's Best Hope," February 1906, pp. 5, 47.

24. March 1906, pp. 6–7.

25. "A Hot Day in a Great City," August 1902, pp. 9–10.

26. "Votes for Women in 1910," January 1910, p. 3; "If I Had a Vote I Would —," October 1909, p. 5; Jane Addams, "The Working Woman and the Ballot," April 1908, p. 19; Charlotte Perkins Gilman, "Good Tiding of Women—The World's Best Hope," February 1906, pp. 5, 47.

27. July 15, 1895, unnumbered page; "*Companion* Climbs," *Time*, July 27, 1936, p. 43.

28. "*Companion* Climbs," p. 43.

29. Ibid.

30. February 1918, p. 1; August 1918, p. 2; October 1920, p. 4.

31. "*Companion* Climbs," p. 43.

32. The column debuted in the August 1933 issue under the title, "Mrs. Roosevelt's Page," p. 4. Mrs. Roosevelt's column in the *Ladies' Home Journal* was called "If You Ask Me."

33. See, for example, Eleanor Roosevelt, "Ratify the Child Labor Amendment," Sep-

tember 1933, p. 4; "Setting Our House in Order," October 1933, p. 4; "Maternal Mortality in America," June 1935, p. 4. The column ended with the July 1935 issue.

34. Theodore Roosevelt's feelings on child labor were published in the *Companion,* January 1907, p. 15, at the height of the magazine's anti–child labor editorial campaign. Subsequent presidents submitted material to the magazine on a variety of topics.

35. *"Companion* Climbs," p. 43.

36. F. Scott Fitzgerald, "The Pusher-in-the-Face," February 1925, pp. 27–28; A. A. Milne, "Mrs. Waterlow in Bed," August 1925, p. 17; Booth Tarkington, "Mrs. Bender and Napoleon," January 1928, pp. 10–11, 101; Willa Cather, "Neighbor Rosicky," February 1930, pp. 7–9, 52; Edith Wharton, "In a Day," January 1933, pp. 7–8, 46; Pearl Buck, "The Frill," March 1933, pp. 7–8, 110.

37. March 1926, p. 1; "Showboat," April 1926, pp. 7–11; "Cimarron," November 1929, pp. 7–8.

38. Kathleen McLaughlin, "Gertrude Lane as Publisher Secure in Higher Brackets," *New York Times,* February 12, 1939, p. D5.

39. Ibid.

40. *"Companion* Climbs," p. 43; *"Companion* Way," advertisement, March 1941, p. 49.

41. "Our Own Page," April 1916, p. 3; "Our Own Page," September 1917, p. 2; Sophie Kerr, "The First 75 Years," November 1948, pp. 36–38.

42. "Men and Women Shall Have Equal Rights," January 1924, p. 2; "Women in Politics and Business," April 1927, p. 2.

43. "Married Women Are Citizens, Too," February 1940, p. 1. See also, "Working Wives," October 1939, p. 1.

44. "A Task for 1929," January 1929, p. 2; "Getting Ready to Disarm," July 1931, p. 4; "The Only Way to be Neutral," January 1936, p. 4; "Why We Must Keep Out," December 1939, p. 1.

45. "Gertrude B. Lane, 1912–1941," November 1941, p. 2.

46. Ibid.

47. *N. W. Ayer & Son Directory of Newspapers and Periodicals,* (Philadelphia: N. W. Ayer & Son, 1933, 1943).

48. Martha Brown, "Life in Nazified Italy," August 1941, p. 20; Betty Wason, "I Lived in Occupied Greece," November 1941, pp. 4, 7, 8, 10.

49. *N. W. Ayer & Son Directory of Newspapers and Periodicals,* (Philadelphia: N. W. Ayer & Son, 1933, 1943, 1944, 1948, 1949, 1950, 1951, 1952, 1953, 1954, 1955, 1956, 1957).

50. Doris Fleeson, "Rendezvous with Heroes," November 1943, pp. 4, 143.

51. See, for example, April 1947, pp. 30, 68; "Survey on a national divorce law," January 1944, p. 12; Louis I. Durbin, "America's Divorce Market," July 1947, pp. 38–39; Anna W. M. Wolf, "Must Children Pay the Price of Divorce?" July 1947, pp. 40, 43. The *Woman's Home Companion* introduced a regular column called the "Marriage Clinic." This premiered eight years before the *Journal*'s better-known feature, "Can This Marriage Be Saved?"

52. Patricia Lockridge, "Abortion Is an Ugly Word," March 1947, p. 4; Mary Patrick, "The Truth about Reducing Pills," February 1947, pp. 4, 164; J. D. Ratcliff, "Breast Cancer," December 1948, pp. 32–33, 102; J. D. Ratcliff, "Birth," May 1950, pp. 38, 137–154; "Survey: What Do You Think of Birth Control?" July 1948, pp. 7–8.

53. Peterson, *Magazines in the Twentieth Century,* p. 192.

54. Paul C. Smith, *Personal File* (New York: Appleton-Century, 1964), pp. 424–425, 443.

55. "American Magazine to End, Began 80 Years Ago as *Leslie's Monthly*," *New York Times,* June 30, 1956, p. 19.

56. Smith, *Personal File*, pp. 461–462.

57. Russell Porter, "Publisher Will Suspend *Collier's* and *Woman's Home Companion*," *New York Times*, December 15, 1956, p. 1.

Information Sources

BIBLIOGRAPHY:
"American Magazine to End, Began 80 Years Ago as *Leslie's Monthly*." *New York Times*, June 30, 1956, p. 19.

"*Companion* Climbs." *Time*, July 27, 1936, p. 43.

Freeman, William M. "Advertising: *Collier's-Companion* Mystery." *New York Times*, December 23, 1956, sec. 3, p. 6.

McLaughlin, Kathleen. "Gertrude Lane as Publisher Secure in Higher Brackets." *New York Times*, February 12, 1939, p. D5.

Mott, Frank Luther. *A History of American Magazines, 1885–1905*. Cambridge: Belknap Press of Harvard University Press, 1957.

Peterson, Theodore. *Magazines in the Twentieth Century*. Urbana: University of Illinois Press, 1956.

Porter, Russell. "Publisher Will Suspend *Collier's* and *Woman's Home Companion*." *New York Times*, December 15, 1956, p. 1.

Smith, Paul C. *Personal File*. New York: Appleton-Century, 1964.

Wood, James Playsted. *Magazines in the United States: Their Social and Economic Influence*. New York: Ronald Press, 1949.

INDEX SOURCES: Readers' Guide to Periodical Literature.

LOCATION SOURCES: Library of Congress; Cleveland Public Library; and other libraries.

Publication History

MAGAZINE TITLE AND TITLE CHANGES: *The Home* (1873–1878); *Home Companion: A Monthly for Young People* (1878–1886); *Ladies' Home Companion* (1886–1897); *Woman's Home Companion* (1897–1957).

VOLUME AND ISSUE DATA: Vols. 1–83 (1873–January 1957). Monthly (1873–1878); semimonthly and monthly (?–1880); semimonthly (?–1896); monthly (1896–1957).

PUBLISHER AND PLACE OF PUBLICATION: S. L. and Frederick Thorpe (1873–1881); E. B. Harvey and Frank S. Finn (1881–1883); Mast, Crowell & Kirkpatrick (1883–1899); Crowell and Kirkpatrick (1899–1901); Crowell Publishing (1902–1939); Crowell-Collier Publishing (1939–1957). Cleveland (1873–1883); Springfield, Ohio (1883–1896); New York, Chicago, and Springfield, Ohio (1896–1901); New York (1901–1957).

EDITORS: First editors unknown. J. F. Henderson (1896–1902); Arthur Vance (1902–1907); Frederick L. Collins (1907–1911); Gertrude Battles Lane (1911–1940); Willa Roberts (1940–1943); William A. H. Birnie (1943–1952); Woodrow Wirsig (1952–1956); Theodore Strauss (1956–1957).

CIRCULATION: N. W. Ayer & Son, 1957: 4,048,111 (peak circulation, 1954: 4,441,842).

Kathleen L. Endres

WOMEN'S CIRCLE

Women's Circle, a magazine for homemakers who want to turn their hobbies into businesses,[1] was born in 1957 as a publication for pen pals. In those years, when television was only a novelty, and long-distance phone calls were reserved for emergencies, letter writing was an important form of entertainment and communication, especially among isolated homemakers. The magazine also offered poetry, household hints, and recipe sharing. Its early success helped to establish publishers Edward and Michael Kutlowski and their Tower Press, a Lynn, Massachusetts, company that had been launched in 1957 with assets of $200 and a mailing list left over from a failed book publishing venture.[2]

Women's Circle began on a shoestring; the first few issues were printed on a used press with one damaged cylinder, ensuring a certain number of fuzzy pages in each issue. Occasionally, the publication skipped an issue because the publishers lacked the funds to stockpile paper. But readers liked the concept; and, within a year, the firm had an updated press and a staff of 25 and was expanding into newsstand sales. The magazine also got a face-lift with the addition of color to the cover, although the inside pages were still printed in black and white on inexpensive newsprint, a format it retains today.

In 1959, the Kutlowskis hired their first editor, Grace Whitman, who remained for 12 years. During that time the magazine began to add human interest features about readers, especially nostalgia pieces and good-deed narratives. As interest in the domestic arts of dressmaking, knitting, and crocheting boomed in the leisure market of the 1960s, *Women's Circle* added handicrafts and simple needlework patterns. Tower Press spun off several other needlework magazines, but *Women's Circle* remained attractive to general-interest readers.[3]

When the growth of television and the women's movement raised the sophistication level of women's magazines, Tower Press hired a new editor, Marjorie Pearl, to update *Women's Circle*'s homespun look. Pearl's background was in art rather than publishing, and under her hand the magazine brightened its design and content without altering its reader-friendly tone. She upgraded handicraft designs and set higher standards for poetry acceptances. Reader interests helped to shape the editorial content; when American women began to enter the job market in growing numbers, *Women's Circle* added stories about successful home businesses, a reflection of a readership dominated by homemakers.[4]

In 1968, the Kutlowskis expanded; they built a 25,000-square-foot plant in Danvers, Massachusetts, to house a five-unit press and a workforce grown to 100. Tower Press was now publishing seven successful magazines and a half-dozen special-interest annuals, a new concept at the time. But production problems plagued the operation, deadlines were missed, and finally, in 1970, the brothers sold the facility and moved to a smaller site in Seabrook, New Hampshire. They prospered there; but Edward Kutlowski, always the firm's creative force, was not content with the status quo. He soon set up a small company of his own, House of White Birches (HWB), in order to experiment with new publications. Under the HWB imprint, he launched a series of still-successful magazines, and soon HWB absorbed Tower Press. By 1984, *Women's Circle* had about 16,000 subscribers, with a total paid circulation of 74,336. It cost $1.35 an issue, $6 a year.[5]

In 1985, the Kutlowskis retired and sold the company to Indiana publishers Carl and Arthur Muselman, who moved the HWB operation to their hometown of Berne (pop. 4,000) in the northeast corner of Indiana. *Women's Circle* editor Marjorie Pearl remained in New England. Today she edits the magazine from her home office in Lynnfield, Massachusetts, a fortuitous affirmation of the magazine's current emphasis on home-based entrepreneurship. Pearl first added features about successful home businesses in the early 1980s; reader response was so intense that by 1985, home-based businesses became the magazine's central theme. Recently, a growing reader interest in temporary employment has generated features on that topic.

Today, *Women's Circle* is a 68-page bimonthly published in alternate months, February through December. It costs $1.95 a single copy, $9.95 per year, and has a total paid circulation of about 35,850. Newsstand purchases account for about 65 percent of sales. The magazine accepts display, classified, and mail-order advertising. Classifieds occupy about five pages per issue. Most display ads are self-promotions for HWB's other magazines (currently 23 titles) or for specialties from its mail-order catalog of 2,000-plus items, such as antique postcard reproductions and pattern books.[6]

A typical issue highlights four work-at-home success stories. These cover a wide range of businesses: pet care and animal breeding, used- and rare-book selling, toy making, millinery design, freelance writing, catering and cookery instruction, and craft design and sales, among others. Stories offer information on business planning, start-up, budgeting, and marketing.

All *Women's Circle* features are written by freelance writers on speculation. Over time some regular contributors have achieved columnist status; Michigan historian Willah Weldon, who writes the column, "Circling with Willah," started as an occasional contributor in 1975. Other regular columns provide advice on health and personal problems, on fund-raising and money-saving household hints. "Collector's Corner" answers readers' questions about the value of their antiques; its author, Robert Reed, is one of the few male contributors to the magazine, which has a 99 percent female readership.[7]

Women's Circle features at least six needlework and craft ideas in each issue. Most of these are quick-and-easy projects designed to appeal to a broad range of readers, even those with only a casual interest in crafts. Projects may range from the currently trendy (plastic canvas embroidery) to the traditional (Sun-bonnet Sue, a quilt design favored by needleworkers since 1901).[8]

A strong emphasis on reader exchanges of all kinds gives *Women's Circle* an intimacy that is the key to its success in a highly competitive market. It offers strong interpersonal contact through a variety of features; the most popular is the "Friendship Exchange," a long-running column that prints reader requests for pen pals and photos of pen pal reunions. This feature, which was a hit in the magazine's earliest issues, is still so popular today that 72 percent of the respondents to a 1992 survey named it their favorite feature.[9] "Looking for Someone" publishes reader requests for information about lost relatives or friends. "Teen Scene" features young readers' requests for pen pals with similar interests (and is the only feature that accepts male pen pal requests).[10] "Twin Finder" helps to pair correspondents with the same birthdates. The "Trader's Circle" matches seekers of rare books, old craft patterns, and other esoterica with owners of same.

Letter writing may have declined in American life, but it is alive and well among *Women's Circle* subscribers. Nearly 50 percent of readers have submitted items to person-to-person columns, according to its 1992 survey. Subscribers write from all 50 states, from all the provinces of Canada, and from Europe, Asia, Africa, and Australia. Although two-thirds of her readers are homemakers, Pearl notes that television has erased old distinctions between homemakers and wage earners and between urban and rural readers. She says, "There aren't any 'country bumpkins' anymore. There may be thousands of small towns, but there is no longer a small-town mentality." She notes also that today's readers are younger than in the magazine's earlier years, and a growing number are single mothers who rely on the magazine's personal touch for support. Many are from the nurturing professions—teaching and nursing—who have retrained or up-graded their skills by returning to school. "Our readers are friendly, nurturing women with a great interest in women like themselves," Pearl says.[11] That was the magazine's rationale at birth; it remains its strength today.

Notes

1. *Consumer Magazine and Agri-Media Rates and Data*, July 1993, p. 716.
2. Marjorie Pearl, "House of White Birches; Early History," corporate report, October 19, 1990, p. 1.
3. Marjorie Pearl interview, March 23, 1993. Subscription rates and circulation figures are not available before 1985, according to editorial director Vivian Rothe.
4. Pearl interview; *Women's Circle* 1992 reader survey, p. 2. In 1992, homemakers made up 67 percent of survey respondents.
5. Pearl interview; publisher's statement, *Women's Circle*, February 1985, p. 55.
6. *Consumer Magazine and Agri-Media Rates and Data*, July 1993, p. 716; rate card, April 1, 1992; *Update,* corporate newsletter, 1992, p. 3.
7. Marjorie Pearl interview, August 18, 1993; 1992 reader survey, p. 2.
8. Vivian Rothe interview, June 30, 1993.
9. 1992 survey, p. 1.

10. Pearl interview, August 18, 1993.
11. Pearl interview, March 23, 1993.

Information Sources

BIBLIOGRAPHY:
Pearl, Marjorie. "House of White Birches; Early History," unpublished manuscript, October 19, 1990.
INDEX SOURCES: None.
LOCATION SOURCES: Library of Congress and other libraries.

Publication History

MAGAZINE TITLE AND TITLE CHANGES: *Women's Circle.*
VOLUME AND ISSUE DATA: Vols. 1–(1957–present). Bimonthly.
PUBLISHER AND PLACE OF PUBLICATION: Tower Press (1958–1985); House of White Birches (1985–present). Lynn, Mass. (1957–1968); Danvers, Mass. (1968–1970); Seabrook, N.H. (1970–1985); Berne, Ind. (1985–present).
EDITORS: Grace Whitman (1959–1971); Marjorie Pearl (1971–present).
CIRCULATION: Sworn, 1993: 49,749 (paid, about evenly divided between subscriptions and single-copy sales).

Jean E. Dye

WOMEN'S SPORTS & FITNESS

"What's in a name?"[1] Although Juliet posed this question four centuries ago to Romeo, her musing remains vital today, particularly in scholarly debates about the politics of naming. Changes in the name of a women's sports magazine, for example, have been said to symbolize the tension between strength and sexuality, between physicality and femininity, between private and commercial values. The evolution of *Women's Sports & Fitness*, once published as *womenSports* and later as *Women's Sports*, over the past three decades provides an interesting case study of how the name game is played with women's bodies.

On September 20, 1973, Billie Jean King entered the Houston Astrodome to "play" a tennis match with Bobby Riggs, the man who made "male chauvinist pig" a household phrase in America. Fifty million Americans watched the "battle of the sexes" on ABC television as King defeated Riggs in three straight games.[2]

Within three weeks after her victory over Riggs, sports columnists began to report that King and her husband, Larry, planned to start a monthly women's sports magazine called *Ms. Sports.*[3] However, *Ms.** magazine reportedly objected to the proposed name on the grounds that magazine buyers might confuse the two publications. *Ms.* at the time took advertising and had been publishing for only a little more than a year.

The magazine's name became *womenSports* just before the first direct mail piece announcing it was mailed to prospective subscribers in November 1973.[4]

The special introductory price was seven dollars for 13 issues; single copies would sell for one dollar. The tone of the piece, signed by King, outlined the magazine's direction:

> Sports are still supposed to be "a man's world." But it's not true. Between us, you and me, we can change that. It's time for young girls to grow up with their own "Michelle Mantles," their own "Bobbie Orrs," their own "Jodi Namaths" to idolize. *WomenSports* will tell the story of thousands of women atheletes [*sic*], pro, amateur and recreational who already "do their own thing" in sports.[5]

The appeal brought in 4,000 charter subscribers (a 4 percent response from 100,000 pieces) and gave the Kings the incentive they needed to seek other capital. However, investors were wary. Warner Communications turned them down, and Larry King made another 10 to 15 unsuccessful presentations to banks and investment syndicates.[6] Eventually, 13 limited partners were signed up, and the *womenSports* Publishing Company was created. Reports of the amount of capital available at the start of the venture ranged from $350,000 to $2 million.[7]

Although the Kings initially offered the editorship to a man, who turned them down, they hired a 31-year-old woman as the first editor of *womenSports* on December 3, 1973.[8] Rosalie Muller Wright left her job at *Philadelphia* magazine, described as an independent, free expression example of new journalism, to head the *womenSports* editorial staff, then in Palo Alto, California. She received a two-year contract, a $24,000 starting salary, a pension plan, and .5 percent equity in the company. Since Wright had no sportswriting experience, she hired 23-year-old Candace Lyle Hogan, who had been sports editor for about a year at the *Livermore* (California) *Independent* as her associate editor for $19,000 a year.[9] Editorial content for the magazine came from a variety of sources. Some freelance writers and newspaper sportswriters were commissioned to do articles, an internship program was established, and more than 60 women across the country contributed material as correspondents.[10]

WomenSports introduced itself to potential advertisers in January 1974.[11] Using a projected circulation base of 200,000, the full-page advertising rates for the first issue were considered fairly high—$4,500 for four-color and $3,000 for black and white—for a woman's magazine.[12] Susanne Douglas, national sales manager at *Ladies' Home Journal*,* was hired as advertising director in February and turned to her previous contacts in the industry to sell advertising space in a hurry.[13] In an interview in 1976, she recalled selling "a women's magazine focusing on sports, not a women's sports magazine" because she believed that it was necessary to overcome stereotypes held by advertising executives:[14] "[Some thought that] women in athletics were all bull dykes, they hated men, and they didn't care about hair or clothes. If they opened it up and found all volleyballs and hockey pucks, I'd never get cosmetics."[15] Pornography and offensive items, for example, a bust developer marketed by Mark Eden, were rejected. Ads that featured women in subordinate or compromising positions were also considered taboo, even if the product was acceptable.[16]

In June 1974, the first, 96-page issue of *womenSports* hit the newsstands, with Billie Jean King on its cover.[17] In fact, due to insufficient lead time and resources to build a substantial subscriber base from direct mail marketing, King's celebrity status was a major factor in the decision to go ahead with the launch of the magazine primarily through newsstand distribution. The Kings secured a contract with the Independent News, a leading national newsstand distributor, and promoted the launch in other magazines (e.g., *Ms.*, *Tennis*, *Rolling Stone*, *New Ingenue*, *Viva*, *New Times*, *Marriage and Divorce*) with trade-outs, that is, agreements to swap advertising pages.

Fourteen companies advertised in the premier issue, and Billie Jean King was pictured in six ads endorsing everything from toothpaste to tanning lotion.[18] She appeared in photographs or by name 14 times in the first issue, a fact that won her a "Thumbs Down Award" from *Advertising Age*[19] and caused critics to ask if the magazine was created solely to glorify King's achievements.[20]

From the outset, there were conflicting visions of the magazine's goals and audience. Some newsstand vendors placed the magazine with *Sports Illustrated* and *Argosy*; others placed it with *Glamour** and *Seventeen.** Larry King repeatedly said publicly that Billie Jean wanted *womenSports* to become the equivalent of a *Sports Illustrated* for women. Editor Wright reportedly did not like the comparison, in part, because timely reporting of sports events was impossible for *womenSports* due to the ten-week lead time from copy deadline to publishing. Wright said her goal was to produce a magazine for all women who chose to explore their own physical potential, not simply to report on the accomplishments of elite athletes.

Wright also made it clear that *womenSports* was "not going to be the *Ms.* of the sports world."[21] In fact, her first issue actually generated concerns about the commitment of *womenSports* to feminism. The cover photograph of Billie Jean King, for example, illustrated the tension between feminist ideals and marketing strategies—a tension that continues to generate criticism of the magazine today. The initial cover photograph, which appeared in an eight-page sneak preview insert in *Glamour* magazine, was taken at a tennis practice. It showed slightly damp, slightly disarranged hair falling onto King's forehead and a locker room–variety towel draped over her shoulders. In the studio photograph that replaced it for the premier issue, King's hair-sprayed hairdo was brushed back from her forehead, her skin showed no sign of perspiration, and her towel was of the high-quality, fluffy variety and was neatly positioned to hug her neck.[22]

WomenSports had 21,000 subscribers on board by August 1974, well ahead of projections. However, only 79,500 of the 310,000 newsstand copies of the first issue had sold.[23] By 1975, it was clear that the magazine was underfinanced, that the publisher's job required more time than either Larry or Billie Jean King was able to give, and that an intense cross-country power struggle was going on between advertising director Douglas in New York and editor Wright in San Mateo, California.[24]

Douglas claimed that the magazine was harder to sell *after* it premiered because of its harsh, militant tone.[25] She complained that stories about fashion, beauty, and travel, which would attract advertisers, were missing from the magazine. Wright argued that the magazine's role was not to reinforce beauty as something women should strive to attain.

Two early issues of the magazine sparked particular criticism from advertisers. The first was a promotion for T-shirts using the slogan, "*womenSports* has balls." Although the T-shirt sold very well, the slogan offended advertisers, antifeminists, and some feminists, who suggested that the slogan should be "*womenSports* has ovaries."[26] The second was the cover of the September 1974 issue, showing a large bowling ball looming over a college football stadium with a fuse rising out of a finger hole. Wright and her staff conceived the cover to illustrate their story on the "Revolution in Women's Sports."

On the other hand, some members of the editorial staff and some readers were offended because the magazine accepted alcohol and tobacco ads. King defended the decision in her December 1974 "Publisher's Letter" column:

[A] new magazine is a very tough business and survival economically does not allow the luxury of doing without advertising. Secondly, the cigarette and liquor industries have supported sports from the beginning and I, as a professional athlete, would be a hypocrite to accept their help in sports events and turn it down in *womenSports*.[27]

The financial situation at the magazine continued to decline. By April 1975, the number of pages was reduced to 64. The tension between the editorial and advertising departments intensified. According to Wright:

I was asked to change the whole thrust of the magazine to a lighter and fluffier product and not to take a feminist position. . . . I considered that a total sellout of the original concept of the magazine. I knew then that if I started to given [*sic*] in, to run editorials by advertisers, and publicity photographs from manufacturers, we would lose our credibility.[28]

In May 1975, after 14 issues, Wright was fired. Eight editorial and art department members quit in support. Larry King assumed the title of editor to keep the magazine afloat until a new corporate investor could be found.[29]

In January 1976, the Charter Corporation, the publisher of *Redbook*,* and *womenSports* Publishing announced a merger agreement. In it, the Kings and their limited partners were to retain editorial and publishing control, and Billie Jean was to receive a $45,000 annual salary as publisher. JoAnn Finnegan, who had been production manager at *womenSports*, served as editor during the transition. However, as soon as the magazine's editorial offices were moved to New

York, a new editor, Pamela Van Wagenen, was hired to change the magazine into a typical "woman's magazine."[30] Her last issue was November 1976. The next several issues were produced without an editor listed on the masthead.

LeAnne Schreiber, who held a Ph.D. in English literature from Harvard, was hired as editor in December 1976. Her plans for the magazine, outlined in the first issue she directed, which came out in February 1977, appeared to be in focus with the original vision of King:

> Because the basic assumption behind the magazine is profoundly feminist, there is no need to be superficially so. Our attitude toward women athletes is that they should be taken for granted, so our tone will be neither promotional nor defensive. *womenSports* will neither seek nor run scared of a "jock" image. If the term is ever applied to us, its meaning will have to be expanded to carry connotations of taste, intelligence, and sensitivity.[31]

However, circulation did not increase quickly enough to satisfy Charter Publishing, accustomed to a mass-marketed magazine like *Redbook*, not the smaller target market of a publication like *womenSports*. Publication of *womenSports* ceased in February 1978. A new magazine named *Women's Sports* started publishing about 10 months later as the official membership publication of the Women's Sports Foundation (WSF). According to Doug Latimer, the first publisher of *Women's Sports*, there was no direct financial or staff connection between *womenSports* and the new magazine.[32] He credits the idea for *Women's Sports* to Eva Auchincloss, WSF executive director.

Auchincloss, however, characterizes the relationship between the two magazines and the WSF a little differently.[33] When publication of *womenSports* was suspended, King, who was a founding member of the WSF, brought the plight of the magazine before the WSF board. According to Auchincloss, "Billie Jean King then said [to Charter], if you're going to get rid of it [*womenSports*], we want it back."[34] "We" in this case was the Women's Sports Foundation. Charter had no plans to revive the magazine and, therefore, complied willingly with King's wishes so that they did not have to make good, that is, provide substitute subscriptions, to current subscribers.

In fact, Charter "just gave it back," according to Auchincloss.[35] Immediately, Auchincloss and others at the WSF attempted to raise the money necessary for the foundation to take over publishing the magazine. Their efforts were moderately successful, but not successful enough to bail the magazine out and start anew, especially when it became clear that King was pulling out of her commitment to support the magazine under the banner of the foundation. Auchincloss was stuck, and the future of *womenSports* was in jeopardy once again.

In the summer of 1978, she approached Doug Latimer, a book and magazine publishing executive, about the need for a magazine that would give women a voice in sports.[36] Auchincloss offered him a subscriber base of all WSF members and the foundation's nonprofit mailing rate for promotions. Latimer, who had never seen an issue of *womenSports*, thought a women's sports magazine was a good idea.

> I didn't think that women were getting a fair shake in sports coverage. I thought trying to produce a magazine that would encourage women to participate in sports was a good idea. Intuitively, it sounded like an interesting publishing venture and, in my business judgment, the timing was right.[37]

Latimer and a silent partner put together "a low six figure amount" for start-up, and editorial and advertising offices for Women's Sports Publications were opened in Palo Alto, California. At the recommendation of Auchincloss, Latimer hired former *New York Times* reporter Margaret Roach as his first editor. A member of the WSF board, Roach had been at the *Times* nearly five years, the last couple as an editor in the Sports Department.[38] James D. Santy, who had experience as the vice president of advertising at *Popular Mechanics* magazine, was hired as advertising director. In January 1979, the first issue of *Women's Sports* (volume 1, number 1) was mailed to the approximately 30,000 members of the WSF.

Unlike the tensions that existed at *womenSports*, editor Roach and advertising director Santy had a great working relationship. Also, unlike *womenSports*, the magazine's advertising policy explicitly prohibited cigarette advertising. The two magazines also approached distribution differently. Newsstand distribution was curtailed, and subscribers obtained through direct marketing campaigns became the primary circulation base for *Women's Sports*. According to Latimer:

> We tried the newsstand approach but gave up on it. We found that it sold if we were placed next to *Cosmo* or *Shape*, but not if we were racked near *SI* or a bodybuilding magazine. The problem is you can't get newsstand people to put your magazine where *you* want it.[39]

Editor Roach left the magazine to return to New York in early 1980. For five months, 23-year-old Sue Hoover, who had worked on the magazine as an assistant editor beginning in late 1978, and 32-year-old, former *womenSports* accountant and *Women's Sports* assistant editor Greg Hoffman, shared editing duties. Hoover, who had a master's degree in English from Stanford, was promoted to editor in the fall of 1980 and directed the magazine for a little over a year. When she left to be with her husband in Los Angeles, senior editor Amy Rennert was promoted by Latimer to edit the magazine. Her first issue in January 1982 was the third-anniversary issue for *Women's Sports*, now boasting a national circulation that had more than doubled since start-up.

Rennert's second issue, known as the *Women's Sports* swimsuit issue, created a storm of controversy and generated a virtual gold mine of much-needed publicity. Her brother, Peter, a professional tennis player, appeared on the cover in his swimming trunks. Inside, poolside and seaside shots featured a professional male surfer, a football player, and a hockey player in bathing suits. Rennert appeared on NBC's "Today Show" and ABC "News" and was interviewed by a dozen radio talk show hosts. Newsstand copies of the issue sold out, but longtime readers threatened to cancel subscriptions.

[W]e knew we risked some female fury with "The Boys of Winter." . . . We don't all have the same sense of humor. . . . Ironically, February's cover lured thousands of women who never considered themselves "athletes" to give *Women's Sports* a closer look.[40]

In May 1984, *Women's Sports* renamed and redefined itself as *Women's Sports and Fitness*. Things began to look rosy in the mid-1980s, when the aerobics and jazzercize craze hit the country full steam. When *womenSports* hit the newsstands in 1974, Nike had just come out with its first shoe, and Reebok did not exist. A decade later, fashion, beauty, and shoe manufacturers were looking for magazines purchased by physically active women. *Women's Sports and Fitness* positioned itself to deliver that expanding niche market.

The 1984 Olympics provided the platform for a gigantic women's sports promotion in the magazine. Personal Products, manufacturers of Sure & Natural, Stayfree, and Carefree menstrual pads, bought 16 pages in each of 12 issues to preview the women's competition in each winter and summer Olympic sport. The multimillion-dollar promotion netted a revenue in the mid-six figures for *Women's Sports and Fitness.*

Rennert coedited her last issue in June 1985 with Martha Nelson, a former *Ms.* magazine editor, who would succeed her as editor. According to her final editor's column in the magazine, Rennert said she was leaving to do interviewing and write features for several magazines.[41]

In the July 1986 issue of *Women's Sports & Fitness (WS&F)*, an ampersand replaced "and" in the title. The magazine won nominations as "Most Improved Magazine" as well as the "Best Sports Magazine" for 1986 by the Western Publications Association.[42] Total circulation was up to 350,000, an increase of 50,000 over the previous year. It continued to look as if everything was coming up roses when *Sports Illustrated (SI)* contacted Latimer in late 1986 to see if the magazine was for sale. *SI* was attracted by its content and stability and its growth market in the sporting magazine industry.

When *WS&F* and *SI* reached an agreement that would provide *SI* with an option to buy the magazine, *SI* sent staff members to Palo Alto to assist with various aspects of the magazine. In early 1987, *SI* began pouring money into fancy graphics, expanded use of color, and larger runs to increase newsstand distribution. Details of a purchase contract were worked out in mid-1987. However, one week before the contract was to be signed, *SI*'s parent company, Time, Inc., announced an austerity program, and, as part of the cutbacks, Latimer was notified that *SI* would not be able to honor its purchase contract. Latimer explained what the news meant to *WS&F*:

> We had huge debts. We were operating on a scale much larger than we could afford getting ready for the sale. In essence, we were left bankrupt. We had built the circulation up to 400,000, but we had to sell post haste. We needed a buyer. It was survival.

Of the few—not very good—offers they received, according to Latimer, a decision was made to sell to Terry L. Snow, president of World Publications in Winter Park, Florida. Snow asked Latimer to stay on as a publisher's consultant for two years and continued to list Latimer as publisher in the magazine's masthead through May 1989.[43]

Snow moved the editorial offices of the magazine to Winter Park in late 1987 to share office space with his other publications, *WindRider*, *WaterSki*, and *Sport Fishing*. He announced plans to increase the size of the magazine and add several new columns. However, he also reduced the number of issues to ten in 1988 by combining the January/February and June/July issues and raised the single issue price to two dollars.[44] Snow hired Nancy Crowell, a former contributor and longtime subscriber of *WS&F*, as editor. Crowell's first issue in January 1988 observed the magazine's tenth anniversary in business. In it, she described her vision for the magazine:

> We feel it's our role to encourage *all* women to enjoy and participate in athletic activity. There are women who enjoy athletic competition. There are many women who choose not to compete, but find great satisfaction in the joy of a late afternoon run, an early morning swim, or a weekend cycling trip. And there are women who still need encouragement to take that first step. We intend to address each group.[45]

She said *WS&F* planned to expand the definition of sports to include articles on health, nutrition, and fashion. She announced the addition of a fashion section to highlight the latest trends in athletic wear since "one no longer has to wear boring gray sweats to work out."[46]

By August 1988, Crowell was replaced by Lewis Rothlein, who had been a senior editor under Crowell. Aside from the two instances in which males assumed the role of interim editor (i.e., in 1975, when Larry King's name appeared as editor while the search was on for a replacement for Rosalie Wright, and the five-month, coediting stint of Greg Hoffman with Sue Hoover in 1980), no male had ever been hired outright to edit the magazine.

Because of the editorial transition, the October/November issue was combined, and only nine issues were published in 1988. In the December 1988 issue, Rothlein addressed the numerous complaints from readers still expecting *WS&F* to be an *SI* for women:

Your letters have asked if we can fill the vacuum [lack of coverage of women's sports], and I have to say that it's tough for us to do. Because of the two- to three-month lag time between when our articles arrive and when they appear in print, event coverage, for instance, comes out stale.[47]

In 1989, the magazine promised—and delivered—ten issues again. In October, Rothlein reported the results of a readership survey. The typical *Women's Sports & Fitness* reader was a 34-year-old female who worked out four and a half times a week. Fifty percent of the readers were single and never married, 40 percent were married, 10 percent were divorced, and one out of five had children. The most popular sports and fitness activity among readers was weight training (48 percent), with running a close second (47.4 percent). According to Rothlein, "Eating Right" and "Sports Medicine" were the most popular columns in the magazine, and two-thirds of the survey respondents said sports event coverage was "just right."[48]

In January 1990, 30-year-old John Windsor, publisher of *Rocky Mountain Sports & Fitness*, bought the magazine from World Publications. He moved the magazine's editorial offices to Boulder, Colorado, where he founded *Women's Sports and Fitness*, Inc., and hired Priscilla Macy as publisher.[49] Although the January/February issue was not published because of the transition, a full eight issues were published by the end of the year. Rothlein's name appeared as editor in the March issue, along with consulting editor Jane McConnell, who assumed editor's duties in April. The magazine maintained its status as the official magazine of the Women's Sports Foundation and had its first woman editor and publisher team since the days of Billie Jean King and Rosalie Muller Wright.

Many of the new staff, from the corporation president on down the line, were serious outdoor athletes. Windsor had finished fifth in a Mountain Man Triathlon. McConnell ran the 1987 New York marathon in three hours and 44 minutes and once biked across France. Associate editor Margie McCloy completed a solo trek and rock-climbing expedition in Nepal.[50] Shorts were acceptable as office attire, and the entire staff often worked off deadline pressure with aerobics classes and once a month learned a new sport together like skate skiing.[51]

Stanford University graduate McConnell had worked at San Francisco-based *City Sports* before joining the *WS&F* staff.[52] In her first editor's column, she discussed her concept of the magazine:

[The] feeling that I'd like to carry into the magazine: [is] [t]he sense of sports as empowerment for women. I want to convey the joy and freedom of getting out on a bicycle, whether you're riding your mountain bike alone or on a trail for the first time or planning your own cycling tour through a foreign country. I'd like the magazine to truly be a celebration of women in sports.[53]

McConnell checked her vision out with readers. Formal focus groups were conducted, and reader comments were sought at women's sports events. Readers ranked sports and fitness as their second most important priority (behind family and often before work). Most readers said they considered themselves athletes but not jocks, "are inspired by women who are fit," and "consider it feminine to be into sports."[54]

The single-issue price was raised to $2.95, and a redesign—from the logo down to the text typeface—was unveiled in the November/December 1990 issue. In the new logo, the word "women's" became bolder, more assertive. With the new year, 28-year-old McConnell took over duties as both publisher and editor. Macy was reportedly "leaving for an even greater challenge: using the skills and contacts she's developed here to open doors for women internationally."[55] Marjorie McCloy was promoted to senior editor in the move.

McCloy was named editor in June 1991, so that McConnell, now publisher and editor in chief, could turn more of her attention to marketing. Another market study revealed that readers wanted more coverage of nutrition and health, more profiles of average and top women athletes, more college coverage, more extensive equipment reviews, more for the older athlete, and more "how-to" articles.[56] McConnell delivered on a number of the requests before the year was out. In September, for example, she introduced the first annual *WS&F*'s collegiate rankings.[57]

By March 1992, the staff in Boulder had grown from 8 to 30. In addition to *WS&F*, they put out two other magazines for Windsor—*Rocky Mountain Sports & Fitness* and *InLine*, described as the nation's first inline skating (i.e., roller skates on wheels) magazine.[58] Windsor rewarded the "team" with a new office building:

[W]e've been officed in the only skyscraper in Boulder (eight stories high), where we often get reprimanded for bouncing basketballs too loudly or bringing dogs or mountain bikes up the elevators. . . . we're moving into our own building and installing a climbing wall, basketball court and a small health club.[59]

WS&F won honors for its design and content in 1992.[60] It also made the consumer magazine top 20 list of circulation losers, down 31.5 percent from 240,194 in 1991 to 164,598 in 1992.[61] A marketing strategy designed by Windsor and McConnell to "weed out all but the most rugged of readers" had produced the dramatic drop in subscribers.[62] "We knew that to make this magazine profitable and targeted, we had to pare away the agency subs [subscriptions] and then build the circulation back up through a grassroots campaign."[63]

The strategy, which eventually cut the subscriber base in half, seemed to please advertisers who were looking for a magazine targeted at the serious female athlete, who was more likely to buy fairly expensive athletic equipment and apparel. In fact, ad pages were up 12 percent in 1990 and up about 25 percent in 1991 and jumped up 37 percent in 1992.[64]

In September 1993, the price of the magazine increased to $3.95, and editor McCloy's name was missing from the masthead, although she was listed as a contributing editor in October. In her October column, McConnell introduced Kathleen Gasperini, who had worked at *Rocky Mountain Sports* and *Powder* magazine.[65] Gasperini certainly fit the *WS&F* mold of the serious outdoor athlete—she once climbed Mt. Kilimanjaro and spent her honeymoon "heliskiing." A new editorial director, Mary Duffy, whose name appears directly below McConnell and above Gasperini on the masthead, also joined the staff. The former executive editor of *Fitness*, described as a *New York Times* women's magazine, Duffy works out of the company's New York office.[66] McConnell explained the new editorial arrangement to readers:

> While Kathleen can keep us on top of the trends in sports, Mary will have her finger on the pulse of the fitness scene. Kathleen personifies the outdoor lifestyle; Mary represents our urban readers who don't always have access to the mountains.[67]

In January 1994, *WS&F* produced a 20th-anniversary collector's edition, despite the fact that the anniversary issue was published as volume 16, number 1. Of course, in order to celebrate two decades of publishing in 1994, they had traced the magazine's origins to *womenSports*.

Although *WS&F* today appears to have turned a major economic corner, there is no unanimity that its evolution has resulted in a product that covers women's sports with the appropriate balance of strength and sexuality, of physicality and femininity, of private and commercial values. One extensive critical study, for example, suggested that between 1974 and 1984 the magazine directly challenged the male sports establishment editorially and featured "a clear majority of active, competitive, focused, strong sportswomen on the cover."[68] In contrast, the study argued, during the mid-1980s, the magazine shifted toward fitness consumerism with features on strong sportswomen giving way to recreational activities:

> The use of fashion models coupled with the title and logo changes substantially silenced the previous political agenda, promoted women's pursuit of personal improvement practices, and constructed women's bodies as passive, sexual objects.[69]

Another study closely examined the magazine's covers and feature stories between 1975 and 1989. It found that white females were featured in 92 percent of the articles and on 92 percent of the covers and African Americans on the other 8 percent.[70] It also reported nonathletes were more likely to be pictured on covers, and individuals in cover photos were more likely to be shown posed than in true action photos. Feature articles during the period were found to focus on sex-appropriate sports like tennis rather than aggressive team sports. The study's conclusion? "[T]his magazine's attempt to find a market may have actually reinforced several restrictive attitudes."[71]

What's in a name? If the evolution of the name and logo used by *WS&F* is examined, one thing is obvious: its emphasis on women declined as fitness increased in importance.[72] The original name and logo of *womenSports* were bold and strong, according to graphic designers.[73] It said, "We are here, so pay attention to us."[74] When *Women's Sports* emerged in 1979, it struggled with how to visually communicate the politics of the magazine with the appropriate font (i.e., typeface) and style (i.e., serif or sans serif, italic or bold), as well as the relative size of the type used to emphasize either women or sports. By 1983, the *Women's Sports* logo had appeared in at least four different ways.

When the word "Fitness" was first added in May 1984, it was 75 to 80 percent smaller than either "Women's" or "Sports," set in a different typestyle, and placed *under* the last three letters of the word "Sports." In 1985, "Fitness" gained equal status with "Women's Sports," in terms of both size and typestyle, but remained in a subordinate position. The logo changed again in 1986 when "Women's," "Sports," and "Fitness" were all the same point size and typestyle in a new three-deck head design featuring an ampersand replacing the word "and."

No one has carefully studied the content or covers of *WS&F* since Windsor and McConnell assumed control. They did, however, redesign the logo twice in their first year. In early 1990 issues, "Sports & Fitness" shared center stage—equal in size and typestyle. "Women's," however, was reduced to a smaller italic type, part of which actually rested on top of, and appeared to be supported by, the words, "Sports" and "Fitness." The new logo did not last out the year. In November, "Women's" was changed to a bold, sans serif type and clearly separated from "Sports & Fitness," which appeared in a light, classic typeface.

Although its name and logo have not changed since the end of 1990, *WS&F* will undoubtedly play the name game again in the future. Its critical role in articulating the dialectic between the historically passive feminine mystique and the emerging active female physique makes it so.

Notes

1. William Shakespeare, *The Tragedy of Romeo and Juliet*, 2, 2, 43 (New York: Harcourt, Brace and World, 1952).

2. Pete Axthelm, "The Hustler Outhustled," *Newsweek*, October 1, 1973, p. 3.

3. Janis Karen Bateman, "Billie Jean King's Publishing Adventure: A Documentary on the Evolution of *womenSports* Magazine from March 1973 through May 1975," unpublished master's thesis, University of Oregon, 1977, p. 82.

4. Bateman, "Billie Jean King's Publishing Adventure," p. 83. Names of potential subscribers for *womenSports* were obtained from the subscriber lists of *Diner's Club, Ladies' Home Journal, McCall's, Ms., New York, Psychology Today, Redbook,* and *Ski* and from several women's organizations and college physical education departments.

5. Direct mail piece for *womenSports*, December 1973, cited in ibid., p. 102.

6. Ibid., p. 86.

7. Ibid., p. 88.

8. Rosalie Wright interview, July 2, 1975, cited in ibid., p. 116.

9. Candace Hogan interview, July 2, 1975, cited in ibid., p. 121. Hogan left *womenSports* in September 1974, frustrated with her job, and Wright was not permitted to replace her.

10. Bateman, "Billie Jean King's Publishing Adventure," p. 124.

11. Ibid., p. 91.

12. In fact, fewer than 10,000 subscribers were "in hand." An eight-page sneak preview insert in *Glamour* magazine had netted 3,700 subscriptions, and the original direct mail promotion had brought in 4,000.

13. Bateman, "Billie Jean King's Publishing Adventure," p. 96.

14. Ibid., p. 98.

15. Suzanne Douglas interview, July 13, 1976, cited in Bateman, "Billie Jean King's Publishing Adventure," p. 99.

16. Ibid.

17. "Milestones in the history of *Women's Sports & Fitness*," February 1994, p. 28.

18. According to Bateman, "Billie Jean King's Publishing Adventure," p. 100, the 14 advertisers in the first issue were Clairol (three pages), Gillette, Merrill Lynch, Koret of California, Tred2, Philip Morris (Virginia Slims), Volkswagen, Colgate, Jensen-Healey, Adidas, Aztec-Tan, Ms. Sports Company (a Billie Jean King enterprise), TennisAmerica, and World Team Tennis. From June 1974 through June 1975, 71 different companies advertised in *womenSports*.

19. "Thumbsdown Awards," *Advertising Age*, December 16, 1974, p. 44. King did not appear on the cover of the magazine again until May 1977, when her return to competitive tennis after knee surgery was profiled.

20. For example, John Hall, "Ham of the Year," *Los Angeles Times*, May 23, 1974, sec. 3, p. 3.

21. John T. Parker, "Billie Jean and the *womenSports* Pitch," *Coast*, May 1974, p. 12.

22. Bateman, "Billie Jean King's Publishing Adventure," p. 132.

23. Ibid., p. 210.

24. Ibid., p. 207. The editorial offices of the magazine moved from their temporary space at the headquarters of TennisAmerica and King Enterprises in Palo Alto to San Mateo in the spring of 1974.

25. Ibid., p. 216.

26. Cheryl Bentsen, "Feminists Howl," *Los Angeles Times*, February 11, 1975, part 3, p. 4.

27. Billie Jean King. "Publisher's Letter," December 1974, p. 4. An even larger controversy arose in the March 1975 issue after a full-page, color Speedo swimsuit ad ran, featuring a blonde reclining seductively in a bikini. Douglas did not view the ad as inappropriate. Wright said that she received more than 50 letters complaining that the ad reinforced negative stereotypes of women.

28. Cheryl Bentsen, "All the King's Parsons Resign," *Los Angeles Times*, May 16, 1975, part 3, p. 12.

29. Bateman, "Billie Jean King's Publishing Adventure," p. 272.

30. Ibid., p. 273.

31. LeAnne Schreiber, "Statement of Editorial Direction," reprinted in Bateman, "Billie Jean King's Publishing Adventure," Appendix F.

32. Doug Latimer interview, January 19, 1993.

33. Eva Auchincloss interview, December 11, 1992.

34. Ibid.

35. Ibid.

36. Latimer interview.

37. Ibid.

38. At the time of Latimer's offer, Roach was participating in the eighth week of a major New York newspaper strike. Margaret Roach, "From the Editor," July 1979, p. 4.

39. Latimer interview.

40. Amy Rennert, "A Tidal-Wave Response," April 1982, p. 4.

41. Amy Rennert, "From the Editor," June 1985, p. 6.

42. Martha Nelson, "Aiming High," July 1987, p. 6.

43. Latimer interview.

44. Snow did begin to use heavier stock for the magazine's cover, but by 1989 he reduced the number of pages per issue, averaging around 70 plus cover. The price of a single issue stayed at $1 through 1978, then was increased to $1.25 in 1979, $1.50 in 1980, and $1.75 in 1986.

45. Nancy K. Crowell, "A New Age, A New Direction," January/February, 1988, p. 9.

46. Ibid.

47. Lewis Rothlein, "A Bothersome Void and a Solution," December 1988, p. 6.

48. Lewis Rothlein, "Here's Looking at You," October 1989, p. 3.

49. Susan Hovey, "Good Sports," *Folio*, June 1, 1991, p. 46.

50. Ibid.

51. Jane McConnell, "Looking Ahead," September 1990, p. 7.

52. Ibid.

53. Jane McConnell, "In Celebration of Women in Sports," April 1990, p. 6.

54. Jane McConnell, "Getting to Know You," September 1990, p. 7.

55. Jane McConnell, "Looking Ahead," January/February 1992, p. 7.

56. Jane McConnell, "Sneak Preview," November/December 1991, p. 6.

57. Jane McConnell, "The Agony & the Ecstasy," September 1992, p. 9.

58. Jane McConnell, "Team Effort," March 1992, p. 8.

59. Ibid.

60. Ibid.

61. "Circulation Losers (1993)," *Folio: Special Sourcebook* Issue 21:10 (1993), p. 163.

62. Susan Hovey, "Rate-Base Cut Gains Ad Pages for Fitness Title," *Folio*, November 1992, p. 19.

63. Ibid.

64. Ibid.

65. Jane McConnell, "New Faces," October 1993, p. 8.

66. Ibid.

67. Ibid.

68. Barbara L. Endel, "Working Out: The Dialectic of Strength and Sexuality in

Women's Sports & Fitness Magazine,'' unpublished doctoral diss., University of Iowa, 1991.

69. Ibid., p. 184.

70. Virginia M. Leath and Angela Lumpkin, ''An Analysis of Sportswomen on the Covers and in the Feature Articles of *Women's Sports and Fitness Magazine,* 1975–1989,'' *Journal of Sport and Social Issues,* December 1992, pp. 121–125.

71. Ibid.

72. Pamela J. Creedon, *Women, Media and Sport: Challenging Gender Values* (Newbury Park, Calif.: Sage, 1994), p. 124.

73. Ingrid Hubbard, personal communication, April 6, 1993; David Richter, personal communication, April 14, 1993.

74. Hubbard.

Information Sources

BIBLIOGRAPHY:

Bateman, Janis Karen. ''Billie Jean King's Publishing Adventure: A Documentary on the Evolution of *womenSports* Magazine from March 1973 through May 1975.'' Unpublished master's thesis, University of Oregon, 1977.

Bentsen, Cheryl. ''Feminists Howl.'' *Los Angeles Times,* February 11, 1975, part 3, p. 4.

Endel, Barbara L. ''Working Out: The Dialectic of Strength and Sexuality in *Women's Sports & Fitness Magazine.''* Unpublished doctoral diss., University of Iowa, 1991.

Hovey, Susan. ''Good Sports.'' *Folio,* June 1, 1991, p. 46.

Parker, John T. ''Ham of the Year.'' *Los Angeles Times,* May 23, 1974, sec. 3, p. 3.

''Thumbsdown Awards.'' *Advertising Age,* December 16, 1974, p. 44.

INDEX SOURCES: Readers' Guide to Periodical Literature; Sport Discus.

LOCATION SOURCES: Library of Congress and many university and public libraries (collections commonly incomplete).

Publication History

MAGAZINE TITLE AND TITLE CHANGES: *womenSports* (June 1974–February 1978); *Women's Sports* (January 1979–April 1984); *Women's Sports and Fitness* (May 1984–June 1986); *Women's Sports & Fitness* (July 1986–present).

VOLUME AND ISSUE DATA: Vols. 1–(January 1979–present) (*WomenSports,* vols. 1–5, 1975–1978, then suspended). Monthly (1979–1984); 11 times a year (1985); monthly (1986-1987), 8 times a year (1988); 9 times a year (1989); 8 times a year (1990–present).

PUBLISHER AND PLACE OF PUBLICATION: womenSports Publishing, Inc. (1974–1976); Charter Publishing Company (1976–1978); Women's Sports Publications, (1979–1987); World Publications, Inc. (1988–1989); Women's Sports and Fitness, Inc. (1990–present). San Mateo, Calif. (1974–1976); New York (1976–1978); Palo Alto, Calif. (1979–1987); Winter Park, Fla. (1988–1989); Boulder, Colo. (1990–present).

EDITORS: Rosalie Muller Wright (1974–1975); Larry King (1975); JoAnn Finnegan (1976); Pamela VanWagenen (1976); LeAnne Schreiber (1976–1978); Margaret Roach (1979–1980); Greg Hoffman and Sue Hoover (1980); Sue Hoover (1980–

1981); Amy Rennert (1982–1985); Martha Nelson (1985–1987); Nancy Crowell (1988); Lewis Rothlein (1988–1990); Jane McConnell (1990–1991); Marjorie McCloy (1991–1993); Kathleen Gasperini (1993–present).
CIRCULATION: ABC, 1993: 147,490 (paid, primarily subscriptions).

Pamela J. Creedon

WORKBASKET

Clara Tillotson, like a lot of people in the mid-1930s, was deeply troubled. The depression had worsened. It was becoming more and more difficult to make ends meet. Then her husband, Jack, lost his job.[1] There was nowhere to turn except to her own resources. Out of the will to survive, she launched a magazine.

She knew there were thousands of homemakers just like her, and maybe they needed instructions on how to stretch the dollar. She was convinced that women could bring a little money into the household through using their own domestic skills. Clara began selling patterns through the mail under the guise of *Aunt Martha's WORKBASKET: Home and Needlecraft for Pleasure and Profit.*[2] The name was shortened to the *Workbasket* with the February 1942 issue.[3]

Sarah Tobaben, who is currently assistant editor, said, "I'm not real sure what happened to the fictional Aunt Martha, but December of 1943 produced a Christmas Supplement that had a note to subscribers from a fictional Aunt Ellen, who has made semiregular appearance from that point."[4]

During Tillotson's time, the issues were printed on newsprint. Sometimes, the editions took a booklet form, with the gutter stapled; other times the publication took the form of a foldout.[5] The magazine often used to include foldout embroidery patterns, dress patterns, and cross-stitch iron-ons, stamped as inserts in the centerfold.

Soon the magazine became a digest published on better-quality paper. The editor had discovered that the publication had to be more durable because it was passed around in kitchens during coffee klatch and discussed over the backyard fence.[6]

Readership often extends over decades. The magazine has a perennial value to its subscribers, who tend to collect the issues and index them on their bookshelf or storage box in the same way they collect recipes and dress patterns. The collections are passed from one generation to the next. As one subscriber, Mrs. O. E. Grant of Irving, Texas, explained, "From the first day my mother-in-law let me inherit all her old *Workbasket* magazines, I fell in love with them. My subscription doesn't expire until November 1999."[7]

The editorial leadership of the *Workbasket* has passed from one woman's hands to another's. In the early 1950s, Tillotson's post passed to Mary Ida Sullivan. She held the position until 1979. Then Roma Jean Rice became the executive editor. Ida Melchisedech Olson assumed the post in November 1993.[8]

The magazine is billed as "The World's Largest Needlework and Crafts Magazine.''[9] That does not refer to its format; the periodical remains digest-sized. Readers seem to like that format. For instance, the magazine is small enough to fit in the lap of the reader while she or he is holding knitting needles and trying to figure out if the next row on the sweater is knit one, purl two or knit two, purl one.

Subscriber Y. Stewart of Bountiful, Utah, said recently that the magazine might be half of the size, but it is double the variety.[10] Today, the magazine includes crafts, recipes, gardening instruction, and hints for needlework, knitting, tatting, crocheting, stitching, cross-stitching, sewing, and crewel embroidery.

The mission of the magazine has changed as the role of women in the home has changed. The magazine's content was influenced, in turn, by the laboratory kitchen/testing procedures of the 1950s, health education issues of the 1960s, environmental issues of the 1970s, and household management paradigms of the 1980s. The contemporary reader is concerned with survival as defined by quality of life rather than saving dollars and cents to get through tough economic times. Today, according to the ''Editorial Mission Statement,'' the *Workbasket* appeals to the new ''Renaissance'' homemaker. The *Workbasket* is a women's home arts magazine ''that provides a source of inspiration, entertainment and fun.''[11]

Likewise, the advertising base has changed throughout the years. In the early years, the publication relied on classified ads only. The first display ads did not appear until 1947.[12] Since that time, the percentage of advertising space in relation to editorial matter has increased substantially with each passing decade. There are now plans to increase the number of pages to 100-plus per issue because of an expanded advertising base in the area of homegrown arts and crafts.[13]

Apparently, the volume of the advertising reflects the intense interest in cooking, crafts, gardening, and health as the new urban dweller seeks a simpler lifestyle—away from packaged recipes and craft kits. Many of the advertisements are patterns, recipes, and other paraphernalia one can order. The *Workbasket* also carries sponsored editorials and encourages negotiated, customized merchandising programs.[14]

The *Workbasket* offers advertisers an additional service to handle reader inquiries. The shopping service, called ''Information Worth Writing For,'' features an abstract on the products of a dozen advertisers. When the readers write the magazine, all their responses are collected, recorded, collated, and delivered to the advertiser every two weeks in label format.[15] An example of the shopping service is the notice carried about Schreiner's Gardens on the page titled ''Information Worth Writing For'':

Send for ''An Iris Lovers Catalog,'' 72 pages listing 450 of the newest and best bearded iris, more than 300 pictured in vivid colors. Send $3.00 (deductible from your first order).

Unfortunately, much of the advertising copy is six-point type and smaller, no doubt an outcome of the digest-sized format. Similarly, the font used for editorial copy is a relatively small nine-point serif face with extra leading. The use of small type runs counter to the fact that the readership is of an age at which eyesight diminishes, and the editorial material must be read closely in order to follow complicated instructions for knitting and crocheting. According to a reader profile generated by Mediamark Research, Inc., the average reader is 53.2 years old, and the median age is 54.4[16] The typical *Workbasket* subscriber is a mature female reader whose interest revolves around the home. The overwhelming majority of readers are grandparents; most subscribers have more than one grandchild under age 18.[17] The *Workbasket* pattern page reflects these readers' interests, including information for ordering cardigan crocheting instructions for the mature figure as well as sacque, bonnet, and bootie knitting instructions for baby.

In 1993, more than 88 percent of the readers were women, and nearly three-fourths of the subscribers were married. A minority of the subscribers represented one-member households. Nearly 80 percent were high school graduates. Less than 10 percent of the readers were college graduates.[18] As can be expected, most of the readers have blocks of time to fill at home; the subscribers are either retired or do work such as homemaking or technical, clerical, or sales.[19]

The magazine does have a male readership. Rose Bender, a subscriber from Pennsylvania, said, ''My husband loves your magazine as much as I do. Keep up the good magazine. Love it.''[20] Apparently, as the example of retired football player Roosevelt Greer doing petitpoint demonstrates, some men are—and have always been—interested in crafts. Because of increased leisure time, they now have time to pursue these kinds of creative projects. It is also becoming more popular for husband-and-wife teams to work on projects together, then sell their handcrafted products at seasonal craft and home shows.

More than 90 percent of the circulation is sold by subscription. The circulation base is 1.065 million, according to the Audit Bureau of Circulations in 1992.[21] The circulation figures further define readership: 39.2 percent of the magazine subscribers live in the suburbs, and 37.9 percent live in more rural areas. Twenty percent of the total circulation falls within the five states of Middle-Atlantic region: Ohio, Indiana, Illinois, Michigan, and Wisconsin. Other states with large numbers of subscribers are California, 72,917, and Texas, 54,876.[22]

Workbasket dominates the crafts niche. Its competitors are *Butterick Home Catalog* (circulation 308,550), *Crafts* (383,161), *Crafts N' Things* (287,828), *McCall's Needlework* (330,330), *Sew News* (233,556), and *Vogue Patterns* (219,186).[23]

Although the central focus of *Workbasket* is craft-based, the readers of the publication have at least one other interest—cats. The magazine always seems to have room for a feline. Usually, the magazine carries about six pages devoted to cats and cat products. A popular column in each issue is ''Carol's Cat Corner.'' In the column, associate publisher Carol Prebich courts avid cat lovers and includes several candid shots of readers' cats. With the "centerfolds"—snapshot-sized for the digest format—Prebich describes personal anecdotes about her favorite felines:

> Let me start by saying my pet name for the new kitten is "The Terminator." Does that tell you something? Actually, the new kitten is a delight. . . . She's a beautiful, alert, intelligent, playful, wide-eyed little bundle of white fur—and ready for the world. Not everyone is ready for her, though.[24]

The column displays a picture of "The Terminator" with her best friend, Prebich's mother, Chris Werwinski. The caption asks, "How can one tiny, innocent-looking creature possibly create so much havoc in one household?"[25] Each *Workbasket* issue also features instructions for a "Purr-Fect Project" in conjunction with "Cat Corner." This craft or needlework project always has a cat motif.

The regular features of *Workbasket* are "Centsible Crafts" (recycling items normally thrown away); "What's New" (techniques and products in needlework and crafts); "Health Tips" (health, beauty, and self-esteem); "Kid's Stuff" (projects children can complete); "Little Things" (two pages of photos and instruction for two or three small, quick, and easy craft/needlework projects), and "Fasten Off" (a short, quick, and simple project that leaves readers with a smile).

The magazine has themes, which have included "Everything Old Is New Again" (recycling items in February/March 1993), "A Madness for Music" (with a celebrity cover; one featured singer Andy Williams wearing a V-necked cardigan golf sweater in April/May 1993), "Prize-Winning Issue" (with several blue ribbon–winning projects submitted by readers for June/July 1993), and "Special Holiday Issue" (packed with holiday gift and decorating ideas in the October/November 1993 issue).

Workbasket is printed by gravure, with four colors possible, and the use of at least a 133-line screen. Bleeds are widely used because of the small format.

The magazine has always been a family-owned and -operated business. The Tillotson family ran Modern Handcraft, the publishing company that owned *Workbasket*, until September 1991. The Prebich family purchased the company and changed the name to KC Publishing. KC president and publisher is John C. Prebich; associate publisher is Carol A. Prebich; executive editor is Kay Melchisedech Olson; and assistant editor is Sarah K. Tobaben.[26] The magazine is published in Kansas City, Missouri.

Notes

1. Sarah K. Tobaben letter to author, February 5, 1993.
2. Ibid.
3. Ibid.
4. Ibid.
5. Ibid.

6. "Reader Profile," Mediamark Research, Inc., Fall 1992, insert of Advertising Promotional Packet.

7. "Why Are We the Best?" Subscribers' Statements in Promotional Packet.

8. Tobaben letter.

9. "Craft Magazine Circulation Overview," Audit Bureau of Circulations Fas-Fax, June 30, 1992.

10. "Why Are We the Best?"

11. "Editorial Mission Statement," 1993.

12. Tobaben letter.

13. "Editorial Mission Statement."

14. "Added Value" Card, in Media/Advertisers Kit, 1993.

15. Ibid.

16. "Reader Profile."

17. Ibid.

18. Ibid.

19. Ibid.

20. "Why Are We the Best?"

21. "Magazine Publisher's Statement," Audit Bureau of Circulations, for six months ending June 30, 1992.

22. "Reader Profile"; "Magazine Publisher's Statement."

23. "Magazine Publisher's Statement."

24. Carol Prebich, "Carol's Cat Corner," August–September 1992, p. 40.

25. Ibid., p. 42.

26. Tobaben letter.

Information Sources

BIBLIOGRAPHY:

Love, Barbara. "How a Digest-Size Magazine Gets Mainline Attention." *Folio*, June 1, 1993, p. 10.

INDEX SOURCES: Index to How to Do It Information; Magazine Index; Metropolitan Library Service Agency (MELSA); Magazine Article Summaries (formerly: Popular Magazine Review).

LOCATION SOURCES: Carnegie Library of Pittsburgh; Cleveland Public Library; Smithsonian Institution, and other libraries.

Publication History

MAGAZINE TITLE AND TITLE CHANGES: *Aunt Martha's Workbasket: Home and Needlecraft for Pleasure and Profit* (1935–1941); *Workbasket* (1942–present).

VOLUME AND ISSUE DATA: Vols. 1–(October 1935–present). Monthly (1935–1984); ten times a year (1985–1991); bimonthly (1991–present).

PUBLISHER AND PLACE OF PUBLICATION: Modern Handcraft Inc. (1935–1991); KC Publishing Inc. (1991–present). Kansas City, Mo.

EDITORS: Carol Tillotson; Mary Ida Sullivan (?–1979); Roma Jean Rice (1979–1992); Kay Melchisedech Olson (1992–present).

CIRCULATION: ABC, 1993: 790,228 (paid, primarily subscriptions).

Beverly S. Merrick

WORKING WOMAN

The first magazine designed specifically for women who work outside the home for a wage, *Working Woman* introduced itself in November 1976 as "the right magazine at the right time."[1] Indeed, *Working Woman* arrived on the newsstand at the height of the women's movement, when unprecedented numbers of women were participating in the paid workforce. The magazine's first editorial claimed more than half of all the wives and mothers in the United States had paying jobs, and, at the magazine's launch, its editor and copublisher, Beatrice Buckler, said, "Practically every woman who isn't working is thinking about working."[2] At the time, most women's magazines were devoted to fashion, beauty, and the interests of women as homemakers. *Working Woman* promised to be different.

> *Working Woman* is devoted completely to women in transition. The social revolution of which we are a part is creating new roles for single women, new marriage patterns, and new relationships between mothers and children, men and women. We have no traditions, no guidelines, no role models to follow. We must find them together.[3]

The magazine has not only survived but thrived, in part, because it matured with its audience as women began to take their right to a career—not just a job—for granted. More important, however, *Working Woman* has repositioned itself—moving from a magazine for all women who work, to one for well-educated, affluent, executive women with positions of power in their companies and disposable income in their bank accounts. The magazine now calls itself the largest-circulation *business* magazine in the United States.[4] Today it describes its goals quite differently than it did in 1976.

> *Working Woman* is a thought-provoking, sophisticated women's business magazine that provides strategies to enhance the achievements of successful women who are the vanguard of the business community. These independent thinkers create markets, drive markets, mold thought and set ideals for their generation.[5]

Working Woman was conceived in the mind of Beatrice Buckler while she was the executive editor and a vice president of *Family Circle** in the mid-1970s. With the help of Elizabeth Forsling Harris, who was briefly the first publisher of *Ms.** magazine,[6] she began producing a magazine that tried to be all things to all working women—from waitresses to business managers. In its first year, for example, it offered practical advice on writing résumés, asking for raises, and networking. It also offered profiles of a woman who cleaned houses for a living and another who sang in a cabaret. Waitressing was featured, as was the unfettered life of the office temporary. Husbands and boyfriends, who felt threatened by their partners' working, also got a lot of attention, as did the competing demands faced by working moms.

Like other women's magazines, it also provided makeovers, beauty tips such as how to use eye liners, recipes for "easy little dinners," tips on hobbies such as quilt making, and, of course, diets to lose those extra pounds.

Despite its promise to deliver to advertisers the much sought-after marketing target—the career-oriented women—and the fact that its early circulation of 150,000 was higher than expected,[7] the magazine did not attract much advertising in its first year. There were some ads for beauty products, liquor, and cigarettes, but not many; and there were none for the upscale items found in the magazine today. Rarely did the ads fill more than 20 percent of the magazine.

Before it was a year old, *Working Woman*'s financial backers forced Buckler to resign in a "bruising management control battle."[8] Kate Rand Lloyd, then managing editor of *Vogue*,* was brought in as editor in chief, and most of the staff was replaced. It was not enough. Within months the magazine was in the bankruptcy courts facing premature death. Then, Dale Lang, the founder of Magazine Networks Inc., stepped in and, through his newly formed company, Hal Publications, bought the magazine for $100,000 and a $300,000 promissory note.[9] He pumped in $1.5 million worth of promotion and brought its circulation up to 300,000 by the end of 1978.[10]

Lloyd stayed on as editor, and James B. Horton, a former vice president and group executive of Playboy Enterprises, was named publisher. Together they set out to reposition the magazine to appeal not to the estimated 40 million working women in the country but to the much smaller group of upwardly mobile career women earning $15,000 or more a year.[11] It was also a time when *Working Woman* began to face direct competition from other magazines vying for the attention of working women, including a new publication launched in 1978, *Working Mother*.

As it moved into the 1980s, the magazine offered advice on executive recruiting, features on successful businesswomen, and profiles of women in powerful positions outside the business world. Advice about how to ask for a raise became advice about how to turn such requests down. Beauty tips were replaced by health advice, and fashion was examined as a business. Gone were stories about working-class women and tips on needlecraft.

The new look attracted growing numbers of readers. As early as November 1980, the magazine was laying claim to the title "fastest-growing magazine" in the United States on the basis of its gains in circulation.[12] At the same time, it attracted a lot more corporate ads from companies such as Chrysler, Xerox, Hertz, investment companies, and even luxury car makers such as Cadillac and BMW. There were enough ads to fill about half the magazine, which was often more than 200 pages.

In 1983, the woman who was credited with much of *Working Woman*'s record growth in advertising revenues, Carol Anderson Taber, was promoted from advertising director to publisher, a post she still holds today. At the time she said, "Five years ago, we would have run a column on how to invest $1,000. Now, we run stories on full-scale financial planning, buying homes, making more sophisticated financial investments."[13]

The magazine's transformation was a recognition of the diverse needs and expectations of the tens of millions of working women in the United States. Lloyd said it was a mistake to try to appeal to the "typical" working woman.

> *Working Woman* learned its lesson. Like kids in a candy store, we initially had a gluttonous desire to serve our then audience of some 40 million working women. We have learned since to be happy and successful on a lean-and-mean diet. We decided, instead of trying to appeal to all the categories of working women, to go after a segment of this population— the professional, managerial, executive woman. And only a relatively few million working women share this psychological community of high ambition, high education and commitment. They're also interested in money and getting a return on their investment in themselves. . . . And as our target audience has grown—and it has, dramatically—we have consciously allowed other segments to slip away.[14]

The new direction was reflected on the magazine's cover. The logo was pinstriped for several years in the mid-1980s, and the rest of the cover sometimes resembled that of a business magazine rather than a women's publication—a signal its content was more about substance than style. Photographs of well-dressed, professional women carrying briefcases were sometimes replaced with themes stated boldly with words alone—"Women of the Corporation: The Push for the Top" in September 1983 and "How Rich Can You Get with the Money You Have" in November 1987.

In the mid-1980s a special section was added called "Enterprise." It was a digest of ideas, information, and short, inspirational stories to help women run their businesses better.

By 1984, according to the Simmons Market Research Bureau, *Working Woman* ranked first among 29 magazines in a study of the concentration of women readers in the 25–49 age group with individually earned incomes of $15,000 or more. It ranked second only to *Business Week* in a survey of women readers in the same age group who consider themselves careerists.[15]

In the 1980s, *Working Woman* faced competition from *Ms.*,* *New Woman*, *Working Mother*, and, most directly, *Savvy*. Taber said *Working Woman* distinguished itself from *Savvy* by devoting more of its editorial material—about 30 percent in total—to lifestyle-related articles (fashion, beauty, nutrition, and health) alongside its business-related articles.[16] *Savvy* claimed to target a more upscale, corporate audience than *Working Woman*, but *Working Woman* claimed its readers had a higher average income.[17] *Savvy* had slightly less than half the circulation of *Working Woman* in 1988.[18]

In 1986, Time Inc., the giant magazine publisher, bought 50 percent interest in *McCall's*,* *Working Woman*,* and *Working Mother*,*[19] in a joint venture with Dale Lang, the owner of *Working Woman*. Three years later, the New York Times Co. bought *McCall's* from the group, leaving Dale Lang with the other two magazines, both of which his company, Lang Communications, still owns.[20]

Despite the changes in ownership, the editorial and ad content of the magazine remained focused on the managerial woman. The magazine also established and maintained traditions designed to help and promote powerful women. In January, *Working Woman* publishes an annual salary survey. It tracks salaries in a broad cross-section of industries and professions, documenting where women are doing better, and where they are doing worse. In 1991, it reported that women working full-time earned a median of 70 percent of men's wages. In the first three quarters of 1992, it reported, women's wages jumped to 75 percent of men's.[21]

In 1987, under the direction of the editor, Anne Mollegen Smith, the magazine also established a Woman's Hall of Fame to honor women who "exemplify strengths different from ones women traditionally are praised for. Here, rather than beauty, motherhood or the domestic arts, we celebrate managerial mastery, financial acumen, marketing agility and commercial competence."[22] Among the first women recognized were Elizabeth Claiborne Ortenberg, the president and chief executive officer of Liz Claiborne, the first company started by a woman to crack the Fortune 500, and Billie Jean King for turning tennis into a megabuck profession for women. Each year the magazine also publishes a report on the 25 hottest careers for women.

In 1988, *Working Woman*'s publisher described the magazine's readers this way:

> *Working Woman* has the highest median personal income of any women's magazine published in the country, the highest median household income and the highest percentage of college-educated women of all the magazines measured in America. . . . What is consistent is not a demographic but a psychographic quality in the readership. They are career women. They're working because they have a career, not just a job. They're ambitious and achievement-oriented with a positive success mentality.[23]

In 1990, when Kate White took over as editor, she promised more hard business information and an expanded lifestyle features section. She described her vision of the magazine as "*Fortune* meets *Vanity Fair*."[24] She introduced new columns on management strategies and career development.

In 1991, Lynn Povich, the first woman ever appointed senior editor at *Newsweek*, took over as *Working Woman* editor in chief. The number of business columns in the magazine grew, with one called "How I Did It," a first-person account from a corporate woman about some problem she overcame or challenge she met. Another column called "Entrepreneurial Edge" focused on women-owned businesses. Under Povich's direction, the magazine also published a definitive ranking of the top 25 women business owners in the United States and a list of powerful women to watch in the 1990s.

But while strengthening the magazine's business focus, Povich has not shied away from subjects that are not directly about making and investing money. The March 1992 issue included features on women as business managers, women who go to Japan for business finishing school, and another on the seven deadly sins of management, including greed, blind ambition, and the "Mother Theresa syndrome." Sandwiched between the business stories was a face-to-face debate between Camille Paglia and Suzanne Gordon—two of the most vocal thinkers on women's issues—disagreeing about everything. A transcript of their debate was surrounded by photographs that illustrated that the discussion was animated, even hostile at times. In recent years, the magazine has also exposed the pervasiveness of sexual harassment in the Fortune 500, featured women who work in dangerous jobs, such as policewomen, and looked at the best hotels for women.

One woman who watched the evolution of the magazine from the inside for more than a decade is Kate Rand Lloyd. She took over as editor in chief just in time to watch it almost die, stayed in the job for five years, and then became an editor at large until 1992. Looking back, she said, "Moving from *Vogue* to *Working Woman* at that time was like getting off the QE2 and into a leaky rowboat. We turned it around. Now it has the largest circulation of any business magazine in the United States."[25]

In the recession of the 1990s, *Working Woman*'s circulation has stalled at 900,000[26]—the level it reached in 1988.[27] But it has continued to attract ads for such things as luxury cars, designer fashions, beauty products, office equipment, and computers. With both its advertising and editorial content it has managed to compete successfully with three other types of magazines—those aimed at working women, traditional fashion and beauty magazines, and general business publications. It has done this by finding a formula that appeals to women who earn, spend, and invest a lot of money and who spend a lot of money both on themselves and on behalf of their companies. It is a group whose rate of growth may have been slowed by the recession, but one that promises to keep expanding.

Notes

1. Beatrice Buckler, "To Our Readers," November 1976, p. 7.

2. Buckler, quoted in Philip Dougherty, "*Working Woman* to Be Published," *New York Times*, June 18, 1976, sec. 4, p. 11.

3. Buckler, "To Our Readers," p. 7.

4. Media Kit.

5. Media Kit.

6. Philip Dougherty, "Reaching Working Women," *New York Times*, November 10, 1978, sec. 4, p. 15.

7. Bob Donath, "Rebuilt *Working Woman* Set to Lure Advertisers," *Advertising Age*, June 6, 1977, p. 6.

8. Ibid.

9. Philip Dougherty, "Dale Lang Acquires Women's Magazine," *New York Times*, January 31, 1978, p. 40.

10. Dougherty, "Reaching Working Women," p. 15.

11. Stuart Emmrich, "*Working Woman* Enters 7 Sisters' Turf," *Advertising Age*, April 19, 1982, p. 24.

12. Kate Rand Lloyd, "It's Time to Celebrate," November 1980, p. 8.

13. Carol Anderson Taber, quoted in Neal Hirschfeld, "*Working Woman* Caters to the Career-Minded," *Advertising Age*, April 2, 1984, p. M22.

14. Kate Rand Lloyd, "Stereotypes Don't Pay Today," *Advertising Age*, July 26, 1982, p. M14.

15. Neal Hirschfeld, "*Working Woman* Caters to the Career-Minded," *Advertising Age*, April 2, 1984, p. M22.

16. Ibid.

17. Christopher Slaybaugh, " 'Savvy,' 'WW' Race on the Fast Track," *Advertising Age*, April 18, 1988, p. S6.

18. Ibid.

19. Geraldine Fabrikant, "Time Takes a New Approach," *New York Times*, November 21, 1986, sec. 4, p. 1.

20. Alex Jones, "Times Co. in Deal to Buy McCall's," *New York Times*, May 23, 1989, sec. 4, p. 1.

21. Lynn Povich, "Letter from the Editor," January 1993, p. 4.

22. Anne Mollegen Smith, "Editor's Note," November 1987.

23. Richard Bruner, "A Voice for Working Women," *New York Times*, October 2, 1988, sec. 12, p. 3.

24. Scott Donaton, "More Gutsy for '90s: *Working Woman* Readies Redesign," July 6, 1990, p. 37.

25. Kate Rand Lloyd, quoted in Nadine Brozan, "Lloyd Retires after 15 Years at *Working Woman*," *New York Times* July 6, 1992, p. B4.

26. Audit Bureau of Circulations for six months ending June 1992.

27. Bruner, "A Voice for Working Women," p. 3.

Information Sources

BIBLIOGRAPHY:

Brozan, Nadine. "Lloyd Retires after 15 Years at *Working Woman*." *New York Times*, July 6, 1992, p. B4.

Bruner, Richard. "A Voice for Working Women." *New York Times*, October 2, 1988, sec. 12, p. 3.

Donath, Bob. "Rebuilt *Working Woman* Set to Lure Advertisers." *Advertising Age*, June 6, 1977, p. 6.

Dougherty, Philip. "Reaching Working Women." *New York Times*, November 10, 1978, sec. 4, p. 15.

Emmrich, Stuart. "*Working Woman* Enters 7 Sisters' Turf." *Advertising Age*, April 19, 1982, p. 24.

Fabrikant, Geraldine. "Time Takes a New Approach." *New York Times*, November 21, 1986, sec. 4, p. 1.

Hirschfeld, Neal. "*Working Woman* Caters to the Career-Minded." *Advertising Age*, April 2, 1984, p. M22.

Slaybaugh, Christopher. " 'Savvy,' 'WW' Race on the Fast Track." *Advertising Age*, April 18, 1988, p. S6.

INDEX SOURCES: Business Periodicals Index; New York Times Index.

LOCATION SOURCES: Library of Congress and other libraries.

Publication History

MAGAZINE TITLE AND TITLE CHANGES: *Working Woman*.

VOLUME AND ISSUE DATA: Vols. 1–(November 1976–present). Monthly.

PUBLISHER AND PLACE OF PUBLICATION: Working Woman Inc. (1977–1983); Hal Publications (Dale Lang, owner) (1983–1986); Working Woman/McCall's group (1986–1989); Working Woman Inc. (Dale Lang, owner) (1989–present). New York.

EDITORS: Beatrice Buckler (1976–1977); Kate Rand Lloyd (1977–1983); Gay Bryant (1983–1984); Anne Mollegen Smith (1984–1989); Kate White (1990–1991); Lynn Povich (1991–present).

CIRCULATION: ABC, 1993: 859,130 (paid, primarily subscriptions).

Mary McGuire

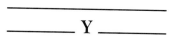

YM

YM editor Bonnie Hurowitz-Fuller would rather her version of the publication not be compared with its predecessors. It resembles not in the least the *Calling All Girls* of the 1940s and 1950s and bears only a little resemblance to the *Young Miss* it was from 1966 to 1986, when it became *YM*. In its early years, it was a publication for preteens, much of the editorial copy was comic-book style, and until 1981 it was digest-sized and printed on pulp paper. These things, as well as its name, have changed.

Born *Calling All Girls* in July 1941, the magazine became *Senior Prom* in 1949, a title that lasted until 1951. After a two-year hiatus, it merged with another Parents' Magazine publication and was *Polly Pigtails' Magazine* from 1953 to 1955. *Calling All Girls* was revived in 1955 and did not change again until 1966, when it became *Young Miss*. In 1986, the name was changed to *YM*, but because too many people were still calling it *Young Miss*, in 1989, *Young and Modern* was attached to it.[1]

The magazine, no matter the year or the name, has directed most of its attention to fashion, beauty, boys, food, and decorating, but other editorial copy has changed over the years. The April 1946 issue contains not only such stories as ''Your Pretty Easter Face'' and ''Can-Do Hair-Dos'' but also ''Your Career in Aviation.'' During the early years, the war years, the magazine mimicked society, encouraging young women to do more than housework. Stories about jobs and ways to help the country abounded. After the war, when women were sent home from the factories and back to their kitchens, those stories disappeared, and in their places were such stories as ''How to Get a Date,'' ''How to Enjoy Football,'' ''Boys Are More Romantic Than Girls'' (September 1949), ''Dressed for Pleasure'' and ''Treat Your Friends to a Buffet Party'' (April 1956). Even in November 1966, the only editorial copy that was not fashion, beauty, fiction, or humor had to do with strawberries, money, tempers, television, and parties.

Topics expanded with the influence of the women's movement and the sexual revolution in the late 1960s and early 1970s and again when drug abuse, alcoholism, and suicide became too prevalent to ignore. But even as late as 1985, former *YM* editor Phyllis Schneider is quoted as saying, "We don't have articles on birth control because it would sound as if we're condoning teenage sex."[2] Current editor Hurowitz-Fuller says *YM* will talk about any topic as long as it is of interest to young women.[3]

Changes in the magazine include changes in design and target audience as well as content. In 1981, *YM*'s owner, Gruner + Jahr USA Publishing, invested money in the publication and expanded it to full size, switched from pulp paper to coated stock, and aged it a little—for the 14- to 15-year-old girl. "If you get the older girls, you can always get the younger girls to read up," publisher Alex Mironovich says. "There's a real aspirational part of being a teenager. Our philosophy is if we can get the 19-year-old we're pretty sure we'll get the 13- or 14-year-old as well because she's going to want to read up to find out what's going on."[4]

The magazine was aged to 16 in 1986, but it was still a 12- to 14-year-old's magazine. Then, in 1989, the magazine's owners gave it a $10 million facelift and repositioned it to compete with *Seventeen*.*[5] With the August 1989 issue, the magazine was relaunched in its current format with its current focus and targeted to 16- to 19-year-olds. The gradual aging process had two purposes: to increase readership among an older group and to attract advertisers, who are more attracted to an older group.[6]

Hurowitz-Fuller, hired in January 1989, has been credited with one of the most successful magazine relaunches in history. She took the magazine from a circulation of 850,000 in 1989 to 1.5 million in August 1993. In 1992, it won the Magazine and Bookseller Hall of Fame Award for largest newsstand increase in its category. Newsstand sales now average 400,000. According to Capell's Circulation Report, *YM* ranked third in total circulation increases among all magazines for 1992.[7]

By 1993, *YM* was the fourth largest fashion and beauty magazine behind *Cosmopolitan*,* *Glamour*,* and *Seventeen*,[8] which puts it second in its category, behind *Seventeen* and ahead of *'Teen** and *Sassy*.*

Hurowitz-Fuller attributes the magazine's success to research, specifically to "getting to know the readers and getting to know what they want to read in your magazine, what they're most concerned with, most excited about, and giving them a lot of that."[9] The staff at *YM* researches everything that goes in the magazine—"Every single page, every story, every headline, every picture, every outfit is rated by the readers on a score from 'very interested' to 'did not read' and that gives us pretty clear messages," Hurowitz-Fuller says. They also have focus groups with teens several times a year and discussion groups once a month and do reader polls every couple of months.[10]

According to their research findings, personal issues are very important to today's teenage girls, so the magazine's focus is on self-discovery—helping its readers understand themselves and figure out what their talents and personality traits are and how to relate to others. The magazine offers relationship and self-discovery articles and advice columns that Hurowitz-Fuller says are extremely popular among her readers.[11] Advice columns include "Dear Katie: A Girl's Guide to Love and Life," "His Side: A Guy Answers Your Questions," and "Love Crisis: Agonizing Problems Solved by *YM*'s Editor." The most popular column is the "Say Anything," written by readers who describe in intimate detail their most embarrassing moments. The column in its current form is a recent addition, but the idea behind it is not new: *Calling All Girls* had a similar column called "Was My Face Red." A quick glance at a couple of recent issues suggests that most of the embarrassing moments have to do with unintended exposure of body parts and feminine-hygiene failure. Hurowitz-Fuller puts this column in the self-discovery category because readers not only can relate to it but can learn that embarrassing things happen to other people, too.[12]

While the magazine does contain relationship and self-discovery articles, its editorial content is more than 40 percent fashion (higher than in *Seventeen* and *Sassy*) and 13 percent beauty. Feature articles make up only 18 percent of the editorial copy.[13]

A complaint from some[14] is that *YM* spends too much time on boys—"guys," as they are known in the teen-magazine world—but Hurowitz-Fuller says, "Guys are a real obsession in the teenage years, so we do a lot on relating to guys, dating guys and how to have healthy relationships with guys. I wouldn't call us guy-obsessed, but we are relationship-focused because the girls are relationship-focused." She says this mix of self-discovery and relationships is the key to the magazine and the reason for the magazine's success. It is also what makes *YM* different from its competition. Another difference is that while *YM* covers social issues, those it covers must be directly relevant to a teenage girl's life. Teen pregnancy, alcoholism, depression, date rape, sexual harassment, abuse, and other social issues are covered from the perspective of a teen who has "experienced one of these situations and has learned from it and overcome it."[15] A story about crack addiction and homelessness was covered this way in the March 1993 issue, though it was hidden in the middle of a "special prom issue." It has also covered acquired immunodeficiency syndrome (AIDS) in this fashion, with at least two recent heartrending stories by young women with the disease.

YM will continue to evolve, according to Hurowitz-Fuller, but she does not see the basic elements of the magazine changing for a while because the teenage experience, the transformation from girl to woman, does not change. How that experience makes teenage girls feel about themselves does not change, either. Changes in the world affect them, however, and the magazine must recognize and respond to these changes, Hurowitz-Fuller says. For example, teens today are more sophisticated than they once were because so many have working mothers and, therefore, more household responsibilities.[16]

The magazine's success cannot be attributed solely to research and the editorial product; attracting readers and advertisers depends as much on using the right marketing techniques as it does on having a quality publication. Publisher Mironovich says one marketing technique used to entice older teens was public distribution on college campuses. Complimentary subscriptions were given to sororities, infirmaries, and other places where large numbers of potential readers might see the magazine. Word of mouth and the natural aging of the magazine also helped attract readers, he says. "Teenagers are very, very social. If you hit it with them, and you're doing something that works with them, then they'll pass the magazine around."[17]

Better newsstand sales did not happen through content changes alone, either. *Folio* writer Hanna Rubin credits circulation director Dennis Cohen and *YM* with the right combination of commonsense strategies. Such strategies include switching *YM* to a distributor with fewer magazines so the magazine would receive more attention, improving cover headline placement, and conducting extensive research. In the first half of 1992, newsstand sales increased 32 percent despite an increase in price from $2 to $2.25.[18] In January 1991, *YM* experimented with a winter special Issue, "Find the Real You," which was sold only on newsstands. The issue sold more than 70 percent of total copies.[19] Since then, *YM*'s 1992 winter special issue and 1993 summer special issue have given readers more opportunities to learn about themselves or perhaps more accurately, more about guys. The summer *YM* issue was "dedicated to the other topic our readers can't get enough of: guys and relationships."[20]

The changes in *YM* have attracted advertiser attention as well as reader attention. The February 1993 issue had 47 percent more ad pages than the February 1992 issue.[21] Fashion and advertising executives say of teen magazines that *YM* is the magazine to watch because its tone, while not as irreverent as *Sassy*'s, is hipper than *Seventeen*'s.[22] When Levi-Strauss decided to advertise in teen magazines, it chose *Sassy* and *YM* because "[w]e felt that *YM* and *Sassy* had captured the attention of the market we wanted to reach, even though *Seventeen* had the bigger numbers," said Art Neumann, vice president and group media director for Foote, Cone and Belding, Levi's advertising agency.[23]

Most of the advertisers in *YM* are in the beauty (21 percent), fashion (15 percent), entertainment (8 percent), and personal products (5 percent) industries, according to research by Evans et al.[24] However, of the 54 pages of advertising (45 percent of total pages) in the May 1993 issue, 56 percent were for beauty products, 20 percent for fashion, 17 percent for personal products, 6 percent for "other," and .02 percent for entertainment.

Much of the recent interest in the teen market can be attributed to two things: increased numbers in that segment of the population and the spending power of teenage girls.[25]

"Teens have to play parent more now," says Hurowitz-Fuller. "They do the shopping and they make adult purchasing decisions for the whole family. They have more money to spend because they have the family money as well as their own."[26]

She says she does not believe this interest on the part of advertisers translates into a huge increase in advertising pages in teen magazines, but she believes this will happen. "It *should* happen. These girls love to shop, and they have money to spend."[27]

Publisher Mironovich makes *YM*'s success formula seem easy: "You put out a great product, you get the reader, you get the circulation gauge, you get the advertising."[28] But circulation director Cohen is more specific: "We do our homework. We don't get caught up in hype. We go back to editorial research and give readers what they want—not what we think they should want. Now the payoffs are starting to come."[29]

Notes

1. Alex Mironovich interview, June 4, 1993.
2. Phyllis Schneider, quoted in Marie Spadoni, "Teens Targeted," *Advertising Age*, October 3, 1985, p. 50.
3. Bonnie Hurowitz-Fuller interview, June 15, 1993.
4. Mironovich interview.
5. Scott Donaton, "Teen Titles Grow Up," *Advertising Age*, June 11, 1990, p. 41.
6. Mironovich interview.
7. Media Kit.
8. "YM Up and Up," *Inside Media*, January 6, 1993, p. 8.
9. Hurowitz-Fuller interview.
10. Ibid.
11. Ibid.
12. Ibid.
13. Ellis Evans, et al. "Content Analysis of Contemporary Teen Magazines," *Youth and Society*, September 1991, pp. 99–120.
14. Gail Pool, "Magazines in Review," *Wilson Library Bulletin*, December 1990, p. 131.
15. Hurowitz-Fuller interview.
16. Ibid.
17. Mironovich interview.
18. Hanna Rubin, "Teen Idol," *Folio*, February 15, 1993, pp. 46–47, 82–83.
19. Media Kit.
20. Ibid.
21. Rubin, "Teen Idol," pp. 46–47, 82–83.
22. Maryellen Gordon, "Teen Magazines Duke It Out," *Women's Wear Daily*, January 15, 1993, p. 10.
23. Ibid.
24. Evans, et al., "Content Analysis of Contemporary Teen Magazines," pp. 99–120.
25. Gordon, "Teen Magazines Duke It Out," p. 10.
26. Hurowitz-Fuller, quoted in Gordon, "Teen Magazines Duke It Out," p. 10.
27. Hurowitz-Fuller interview.

28. Mironovich interview.
29. Rubin, "Teen Idol," pp. 46–47, 82–83.

Information Sources

BIBLIOGRAPHY:
Donaton, Scott. "Teen Titles Grow Up." *Advertising Age*, June 11, 1990, p. 41.
Gordon, Maryellen. "Teen Magazines Duke It Out." *Women's Wear Daily*, January 15, 1993, p. 10.
Pool, Gail. "Magazines in Review." *Wilson Library Bulletin*, December 1990, p. 131.
Rubin, Hanna. "Teen Idol." *Folio*, February 15, 1993, pp. 46–47, 82–83.
Spadoni, Marie. "Teens Targeted." *Advertising Age*, October 3, 1985, p. 50.
INDEX SOURCES: Children's Magazine Guide.
LOCATION SOURCES: Library of Congress; Michigan State University has many issues, particularly early issues of *Polly Pigtails* and *Calling All Girls* in its special collections; University of Central Oklahoma; Michigan State University; Radcliffe College; and other libraries.

Publication History

MAGAZINE TITLE AND TITLE CHANGES: *Calling All Girls* (1941–1949); *Senior Prom* (1949–1951); *Polly Pigtails Magazine* (1953–1955); *Calling All Girls* (1955–1966); *Young Miss* (1966–1985); *YM* (1986–1989); *YM/Young and Modern* (1989–present).

VOLUME AND ISSUE DATA: Vols. 1–(July 1941–present). Monthly.

PUBLISHER AND PLACE OF PUBLICATION: Parents' Magazine Press (1941–1949); Teen Institute, Inc., a subsidiary of Parents' Magazine (1949–1951); "21" Publishing Corporation, a subsidiary of the publishers of Parents' Magazine (1953–1962); the Better Reading Foundation (1962–1968); Parents' Magazine Press (1968–1979); Parents Magazine Enterprises, a subsidiary of Gruner + Jahr USA (1979–present). New York (1941–1951); Concord, N. H. (1953–1962); New York (1962–1968); Bergenfield, N. J. (1968–present).

EDITORS: Frances Ullman (1941–1949); Claire Glass (1947–1951); Polly Pigtails (1953–1955); Betty Sears (1953–1963); Rubie Sanders (1963–1979); Lois Cantwell (1979–1980); Suzanne Kennedy Flynn (1980–1981); Faith Garrett Vosbrinck (1981); Phyllis Schneider (1981–1986); Nancy Axelrad Comer (1986–1988); Bonnie Hurowitz-Fuller (1989–present).

CIRCULATION: ABC, 1993: 1.5 million (paid, primarily subscriptions).

Kate Peirce

Appendix: Chronology

This chronology includes only those publications profiled in this volume. For those periodicals still published today, the publisher and location are those that are current. These publications may have been started and/or owned by different publishers during their history. Readers should consult individual entries for more information. For historical magazines, the publisher cited is the one most closely associated with the periodical; the same is true for the location. In addition, in parentheses, the year of the last publication is noted. The exact issue is available in the individual entries.

1784	*Gentleman and Lady's Town and Country Magazine*, Job Weeden and William Barrett, Boston (ceased publication 1784).
1830	*Godey's Lady's Book*, Louis A. Godey, Philadelphia (ceased publication 1898).
	The National Magazine; or, Lady's Emporium, Mary Barney, Baltimore (ceased publication 1831).
1832	*The Universalist and Ladies' Repository*, The Universalist Church, Boston (ceased publication 1874).
1834	*The Ladies' Companion*, William W. Snowden, New York (ceased publication 1844).
1840	*Magnolia; or Southern Apalachian*, Philip C. Pendleton, Savannah, Georgia (ceased publication 1843).
1841	*The Ladies' Repository*, Western Book Concern of the Methodist-Episcopal Church, Cincinnati (ceased publication 1876).
1842	*Peterson's Magazine*, Charles J. Peterson, Philadelphia (ceased publication 1898).
1860	*Demorest's Monthly Magazine and Mme. Demorest's Mirror of Fashions*, William Jennings Demorest, New York (ceased publication 1899).
1862	*The Magnolia; A Southern Home Journal*, Haines & Smith, Richmond (ceased publication 1865).

1867	*Harper's Bazaar*, Hearst Corp., New York.
1873	*The Delineator*, Butterick Publishing Co., New York (ceased publication 1937).
	McCall's Magazine, Gruner + Jahr, USA, New York.
	Woman's Home Companion, Crowell-Collier Publishing, New York (ceased publication 1957).
1883	*Ladies' Home Journal*, Meredith Corp., New York.
1885	*Good Housekeeping*, Hearst Corp., New York.
1886	*Cosmopolitan*, Hearst Magazines, New York.
1892	*Vogue*, Condé Nast Publishing, New York.
1896	*House Beautiful*, Hearst Magazines, New York.
1899	*Pictorial Review*, Pictorial Review Co., New York (ceased publication 1939).
1901	*House & Garden*, Condé Nast Publishing, New York (ceased publication 1993).
1903	*Redbook*, Hearst Magazines, New York.
1913	*Southern Woman's Magazine*, Southern Woman's Magazine Co., Nashville, Tennessee (ceased publication 1918).
1919	*True Story*, Macfadden Holdings Inc., New York.
1924	*Better Homes and Gardens*, Meredith Publishing, Des Moines, Iowa.
1926	*Parents*, Gruner + Jahr, USA, New York.
1932	*Family Circle*, Gruner + Jahr, USA, New York.
1934	*Bride's & Your New Home*, Condé Nast, New York.
1935	*Mademoiselle*, Condé Nast, New York.
	Workbasket, KC Publishing Inc., Kansas City, Missouri.
1936	*WB*, Women's International Bowling Congress, Greendale, Wisconsin.
1937	*Vanidades Continental*, Editorial America, S.A., Miami, Florida.
	Woman's Day, Hachette Filipacchi Magazines, New York.
1938	*American Baby*, Cahners Publishing Co., New York.
1939	*Glamour*, Condé Nast, New York.
1941	*Gourmet*, Condé Nast, New York.
	YM, Parents Magazine Enterprises, Bergenfield, New Jersey.
1944	*Seventeen*, K III Magazines, New York.
1950	*Prevention*, Rodale Press, Emmaus, Pennsylvania.
1956	*Bon Appetit*, Condé Nast, Los Angeles.
1957	*'Teen,* Petersen Publishing Co., Los Angeles.
	Women's Circle, House of White Birches, Berne, Indiana.
1966	*Southern Living*, Southern Living Inc., Birmingham, Alabama.

1968	*Weight Watchers*, W/W Twentyfirst Corp., New York.
1969	*Health,* Family Media Inc., New York (ceased publication 1991).
	Metropolitan Home, Hachette Magazines, New York.
1970	*Essence*, Essence Communication, New York.
	New Woman, K III Magazines, New York.
1972	*Ms.*, Lang Communications Inc., New York.
	W, Fairchild Publications Inc., New York.
1973	*Playgirl*, Playgirl Inc., New York.
1974	*Women's Sports & Fitness*, Women's Sports and Fitness Inc., Boulder, Colorado.
1975	*Soap Opera Digest*, K III Magazines, New York.
1976	*Quilt World*, House of White Birches, Berne, Indiana.
	Working Woman, Working Woman Inc., New York.
1977	*Southern Accents*, Southern Accents Inc., Birmingham, Alabama.
1978	*Art & Antiques*, TransWorld Publishing Co., New York.
	Virtue, Good Family Magazines, Colorado Springs, Colorado.
1979	*Self*, Condé Nast, New York.
	Today's Christian Woman, Christianity Today Inc., Carol Stream, Illinois.
1982	*American Health,* RD Publications Inc., New York.
1983	*Barbie,* Welsh Publishing Group, New York.
	Vanity Fair, Condé Nast, New York.
1984	*Twins Magazine*, Twins Magazine Inc., Shawnee Mission, Kansas.
1985	*Elle*, Hachette Filipacchi Magazines Inc., New York.
1986	*Black Elegance*, Starlog Telecommunications Inc., New York.
1987	*Cooking Light*, Southern Progress Corp., Birmingham, Alabama.
	New York Woman, American Express Publishing Corp., New York (ceased publication 1992).
	Victoria, Hearst Magazines Inc., New York.
1988	*Golf for Women*, Meredith Corp., Lake Mary, Florida.
	Lear's, Lear Publishing Co., Inc., New York (ceased publication 1994).
	Sassy, Lang Communications, New York.
1989	*First for Women*, Heinrich Bauer Publishing, Englewood Cliffs, New Jersey.
	Mirabella, Murdoch Magazines, New York.
1991	*Ser Padres*, Gruner + Jahr USA, New York.

Bibliography

Angelo, Jean Marie. "John Mack Carter: Editor, Celebrity and Southern Gentleman." *Folio*, February 1990, p. 31.

"Biggest End." *Time Magazine*, January 30, 1939, p. 47.

Cantor, Muriel, and Elizabeth Jones. "Creating Fiction for Women." *Communication Research*, 10:1 (January 1983), pp. 111–137.

Carmody, Deirdre. "Mirabella vs. Lear's: Stylish Fight." *New York Times*, November 26, 1990, p. D8.

———. "In a Reversal, Condé Nast Closes *HG*." *New York Times*, April 21, 1993, pp. D1, D19.

Chase, Edna Woolman. *Always in Vogue*. Garden City, N.J.: Doubleday, 1954.

Creedon, Pamela J. (ed.). *Women in Mass Communication*. 2nd ed. Newbury Park, Calif.: Sage Publications, 1993.

Darnton, Nina. "*Vogue, Self, Allure*—Alex." *Newsweek*, April 8, 1991, p. 56.

Drewry, John E. (ed.). *Post Biographies of Famous Journalists*. Athens: University of Georgia Press, 1942.

Edwin T. Meredith: A Memorial Volume. Des Moines, Iowa: Meredith, 1931.

Endres, Kathleen L. "The Women's Press in the Civil War: A Portrait of Patriotism, Propaganda, and Prodding." *Civil War History* 30:1 (March 1984), pp. 31–53.

English, Mary McCabe. "How to Stay 17 and Keep Growing." *Advertising Age*, August 2, 1982, pp. M27–M28.

Entrikin, Isabelle Webb. "Sarah Josepha Hale and Godey's Lady's Book." Ph.D. diss., University of Pennsylvania, 1946.

Fannin, Rebecca. "The Growing Sisterhood." *Marketing & Media Decisions*, October 1989, p. 44.

Ferguson, Jill Hicks, Peggy J. Kreshel, and Spencer Tinkham. "In the Pages of *Ms.*: Sex Role Portrayal of Women in Advertising." *Journal of Advertising* 19:1 (1990), pp. 40–51.

Finley, Ruth E. "*The Lady of* Godey's*: Sarah Josepha Hale.*" Philadelphia: J.B. Lippincott, 1931.

Ford, James L. C. *Magazines for Millions: The Story of Specialized Publications*. Carbondale: Southern Illinois University Press, 1969.

Garnsey, Caroline. "Ladies Magazines to 1850." *Bulletin of the New York Public Library* 58:2 (February 1954), pp. 74–88.

Gerbner, George. "The Social Role of the Confession Magazine." *Social Problems* 6:1 (Summer 1958), pp. 29–40.

Harris, Dixie Dean. "And This, Dear God, Is What They Read." *Esquire*, July 1965, pp. 50–51, 105–106, 108.

History & Magazines. New York: True Story Magazines, 1941.

"The History of Playgirl." New York: Playgirl Magazine [1993].

Holme, Bryan (ed.). *The Journal of the Century*. New York: Viking Press, 1976.

Honey, Maureen. *Creating Rosie the Riveter: Class, Gender and Propaganda During World War II*. Amherst: University of Massachusetts Press, 1984.

Hovey, Brian. "Coming to America." *Folio*, May 1990, pp. 49–51.

Hoyt, Michael. "Damsels in Distress." *Columbia Journalism Review,* March/April 1990, pp. 40–41.

Janello, Amy, and Brennon Jones. *The American Magazine*. New York: Abrams, 1991.

Katz, Bill, and Linda Sternberg Katz. *Magazines for Libraries*. New Providence, N.J.: R. R. Bowker, 1992.

Kelly, R. Gordon (ed.). *Children's Periodicals of the United States*. Westport, Conn.: Greenwood, 1984.

Kessler, Lauren. "Women's Magazines' Coverage of Smoking Related Health Hazards." *Journalism Quarterly* 66:2 (Summer 1989), pp. 316–322, 445.

Kleinfeld, N. R. "A Growing Appetite for Food Magazines." *New York Times*, July 1, 1980, p. B10.

———. "Grace Mirabella, at 59, Starts Over Again." *New York Times*, April 30, 1989, sec. 3, p. 13.

"Ladies' Line Up." *Time Magazine*, February 15, 1937, p. 50

"Magazines Targeted at the New Woman." *Business Week*, February 18, 1980, p. 50

Manly, Lorne. "Women's Fitness Titles Pump Up in Shrinking Market." *Folio*, November 15, 1993, p. 22.

McCracken, Ellen. *Decoding Women's Magazines: From Mademoiselle to Ms.* Macmillan, 1993.

McMahan, Jean Marie. "*Playgirl:* New Player, Old Game." M.A. thesis, University of Oregon, 1976.

McMahon, Kathryn. "The Cosmopolitan Ideology and the Management of Desire." *Journal of Sex Research*, August 1990, pp. 381–396.

Mott, Frank Luther. *A History of American Magazines*. 5 vols. Cambridge: Harvard University Press, 1938, 1939, 1957, 1968.

Norton, Mary Beth. *Liberty's Daughters: The Revolutionary Experience of American Women, 1750–1800*. Boston: Little, Brown, 1980.

Nourie, Alan, and Barbara Nourie (eds.). *American Mass-Market Magazines*. Westport, Conn.: Greenwood, 1990.

Oberholtzer, Ellis Paxton. *The Literary History of Philadelphia*. Philadelphia: George W. Jacobs, 1906.

Peterson, Theodore. *Magazines in the Twentieth Century*. Urbana: University of Illinois Press, 1956, 1964.

Pilkington, James Penn. *The Methodist Publishing House, A History*. New York: Abingdon Press, 1968.

Powell, Joanne. "Paige Rense, Editor in Chief of *Architectural Digest, Bon Appetit & GEO.*" *Washington Journalism Review*, May 1983, pp. 36–41.

Prisco, Dorothy, "Women and Social Change as Reflected in a Major Fashion Magazine." *Journalism Quarterly* 59:1 (Spring 1982), pp. 131–134.

Reuss, Carol. *"Better Homes and Gardens* and Its Editors: An Historical Study from the Magazine Founding to 1970." Ph.D. diss., University of Iowa, 1971.

———. *"Better Homes and Gardens*: Consistent Concern Key to Long Life." *Journalism Quarterly* 51:2 (Summer 1974), pp. 292–296.

Richardson, Diana Edkins (ed.). *Vanity Fair: Photographs of an Age, 1914–1936.* New York: Clarkson Potter, 1982.

Richardson, Lyon N. *A History of Early American Magazines, 1741–1789.* New York: Octagon Books, 1966.

Richardson, Selma K. *Magazines for Children: A Guide for Parents, Teachers and Librarians.* 2d ed. Chicago: American Library Association, 1991.

Riley, Sam (ed.). *Dictionary of Literary Biography: Vol. 91, American Magazine Journalists, 1900–1960.* Detroit: Gale Research, 1990.

———. *Magazines of the American South.* Westport, Conn.: Greenwood, 1986.

Roan, Shari. "Negative Images? Twentysomethings Say Women's Magazines Can Erode Self-Esteem." *Los Angeles Times,* August 18, 1992, pp. E1, E4.

Ross, Ishbel. *Crusades and Crinolines: The Life and Times of Ellen Curtis Demorest and William Jennings Demorest.* New York: Harper and Row, 1963.

Seebohm, Caroline. *The Man Who Was Vogue: The Life and Times of Condé Nast.* New York: Viking Press, 1982.

Smith, Paul C. *Personal File.* New York: Appleton-Century, 1964.

Snow, Carmel, and Mary L. Aswell. *The World of Carmel Snow.* New York: McGraw-Hill, 1962.

Stearns, Bertha M. "Early New England Magazines for Ladies." *New England Quarterly* 2 (July 1929), pp. 420–457.

———. "Southern Magazines for Ladies (1819–1860)." *South Atlantic Quarterly 31* (January 1932), pp. 70–87.

Steinberg, Salme Harju. *Reformer in the Marketplace: Edward W. Bok and the Ladies' Home Journal.* Baton Rouge: Louisiana State University Press, 1979.

Taft, William H. *American Magazines for the 1980s.* New York: Greenwood Press, 1990.

Tassin, Algernon. *The Magazine in America.* New York: Dodd, Mead, 1916.

Tebbel, John, and Mary Ellen Zuckerman. *The Magazine in America 1741–1990.* New York: Oxford University Press, 1991.

Thom, Mary. *Letters to Ms.* New York: Henry Holt, 1987.

Wang, Caroline. "Lear's Magazine 'For the Woman Who Wasn't Born Yesterday': A Critical Review." *Gerontologist* 28:4 (April 1991), pp. 600–601.

Welter, Barbara. "The Cult of True Womanhood: 1820–1860," in Thomas R. Frazier (ed.), *The Underside of American History: Other Readings.* New York: Harcourt Brace Jovanovich, 1973, pp. 211–220.

Wood, Ann D. "The 'Scribbling Women' and Fanny Fern: Why Women Wrote." *American Quarterly* 23 (Spring 1971), pp. 3–24.

Wood, James Playsted. *Magazines in the United States: Their Social and Economic Influence.* New York: Ronald Press, 1949.

Woodward, Helen. *The Lady Persuaders.* New York: Ivan Obonlensky, 1960.

Zuckerman, Mary Ellen. *Sources in the History of Women's Magazines, 1792–1960: An Annotated Bibliography.* Westport, Conn.: Greenwood, 1991.

Index

Page numbers in **bold** refer to main entries.

About the Contributors

DAVID ABRAHAMSON is an associate professor at the Medill School of Journalism, Northwestern University, Evanston, Illinois.

JULIE L. ANDSAGER is an assistant professor in the College of Mass Communication, Middle Tennessee State University, Murfreesboro.

JENNIFER L. BAILEY is an instructor of journalism in the College of Mass Communication, Middle Tennessee State University, Murfreesboro.

KIMETRIS N. BALTRIP is a doctoral student in the College of Education, University of Akron, Ohio.

LISA BEINHOFF is a doctoral student in mass communication at the S. I. Newhouse School of Public Communications, Syracuse University, New York.

JON BEKKEN is the editor of the *Industrial Worker*, Chicago.

PAUL S. BELGRADE is an associate professor of English at Millersville University, Pennsylvania.

CARRIE BROWN is a graduate student at the University of Alabama, Tuscaloosa.

PAMELA J. CREEDON is director of the School of Journalism and Mass Communication, Kent State University, Ohio.

MARY M. CRONIN is an assistant professor in the Edward R. Murrow School of Communication, Washington State University, Pullman.

DAVID DAVIES is an assistant professor in the Department of Journalism, University of Southern Mississippi, Hattiesburg.

NORYS C. DE ABREU-GARCIA is a public relations project specialist for Tierra y Esperanza Para La Comunidad Humana Organizada (TECHO), Akron, Ohio.

JEAN E. DYE is an adjunct professor in the Communication Arts Department, University of Cincinnati, Ohio.

FREDRIC F. ENDRES is a professor in the School of Journalism and Mass Communication, Kent State University, Ohio.

KATHLEEN L. ENDRES is an associate professor in the School of Communication, University of Akron, Ohio. She is the editor of *Trade, Industrial, and Professional Periodicals of the United States* (1994).

BARBARA GASTEL is an associate professor and assistant head of the Department of Journalism, Texas A&M University, College Station.

VICTORIA GOFF is an assistant professor in the Communication and the Arts Department, University of Wisconsin, Green Bay.

AGNES HOOPER GOTTLIEB is an assistant professor and assistant chair of the Department of Communication at Seton Hall University, South Orange, New Jersey.

NORMA GREEN is a graduate program director, Journalism Department, Columbia College, Chicago.

AUGUST GRIBBIN is an assistant professor in the College of Communication, Journalism and Performing Arts at Marquette University, Milwaukee, Wisconsin.

LYNN O'NEAL HEBERLING is an instructor in the School of Communication, University of Akron, Ohio.

CAROL E. HOLSTEAD is an assistant professor in the William Allen White School of Journalism and Mass Communication, University of Kansas, Lawrence.

SAMMYE JOHNSON is a professor in the Department of Communication, Trinity University, San Antonio, Texas.

PAUL E. KOSTYU is an assistant professor in the Department of Journalism, Ohio Wesleyan University, Delaware, Ohio.

ANN E. LARABEE is an assistant professor in the Department of American Thought and Language, Michigan State University, East Lansing.

TINA LESHER is an assistant professor in the Department of Communication, William Paterson College, Wayne, New Jersey.

THOMAS N. LEWIS is a writer and editor in Cincinnati, Ohio.

PATRICIA E. LINDER is an adult education teacher for the Akron/Knight Foundation family education program, Ohio.

THERESE L. LUECK is an associate professor in the School of Communication, University of Akron, Ohio.

MARY McGUIRE is an assistant professor in the Department of Journalism and Communication, Carleton University, Ottawa, Ontario, Canada.

BEVERLY S. MERRICK is an assistant professor in the Department of Mass Communication, University of South Dakota, Vermillion.

JEAN NAGY is assistant dean of the College of Mass Communication, Middle Tennessee State University, Murfreesboro.

ANNA R. PADDON is an assistant professor in the School of Journalism, Southern Illinois University at Carbondale.

DIANA PECK is an associate professor in the Communication Department, William Paterson College, Wayne, New Jersey.

KATE PEIRCE is an associate professor in the Department of Journalism, Southwest Texas State University, San Marcos.

PATRICIA E. PRIJATEL is an associate professor in the School of Journalism and Mass Communication, Drake University, Des Moines, Iowa.

MARCIA R. PRIOR-MILLER is an associate professor in the Department of Journalism and Mass Communication, Iowa State University, Ames.

MELODY RAMSEY is a graduate assistant in the Department of Journalism and Mass Communication, Iowa State University, Ames.

JEAN MOYLE ROGERS is an instructor in the School of Communication, University of Akron, Ohio.

KELLY SAXTON is the director of Alumni Publications at the University of Alabama, Tuscaloosa.

ANN B. SCHIERHORN is an associate professor in the School of Journalism and Mass Communication, Kent State University, Ohio.

DAVID SPENCER is an associate professor in the Graduate School of Journalism, University of Western Ontario, London, Ontario, Canada.

CHERYL SLOAN WATTS is a graduate teaching assistant in the Department of Journalism, University of Alabama, Tuscaloosa.

CHARLES WHITAKER is an assistant professor in the Medill School of Journalism, Northwestern University, Evanston, Illinois.

KYU HO YOUM is an associate professor in the Walter Cronkite School of Journalism and Telecommunications, Arizona State University, Tempe.

MARY ELLEN ZUCKERMAN is an associate professor in the Jones School of Business, at the State University of New York, and editor of *Sources in the History of Women's Magazines 1792–1960* (1991).

ISBN 0-313-28631-0

9 0 0 0 0>

EAN

9 780313 286315

HARDCOVER BAR CODE